The Museum
in
America

The *Museum* in *America*

INNOVATORS AND PIONEERS

by Edward P. Alexander

ALTAMIRA
PRESS

A Division of Sage Publications, Inc.
Walnut Creek • London • New Delhi
PUBLISHED IN COOPERATION WITH
THE AMERICAN ASSOCIATION FOR STATE AND LOCAL HISTORY

For information address:

AltaMira Press
A Division of Sage Publications, Inc.
1630 North Main Street, Suite 367
Walnut Creek, CA 94596
explore@altamira.sagepub.com

Sage Publications Ltd.
6 Bonhill Street
London EC2A 4PU
United Kingdom

Sage Publications India Pvt. Ltd.
M-32 Market
Greater Kailash 1
New Delhi 110 048 India

PRINTED IN THE UNITED STATES OF AMERICA

Library of Congress Cataloging-in-Publication Data
Alexander, Edward P. (Edward Porter), 1907–
    The museum in America : innovators and pioneers / by Edward Alexander.
    p. cm.—(American Association for State and Local History Book series)
    "Published in cooperation with the American Association for State and Local History."
    Includes bibliographical references and index.
    ISBN 0-7619-8946-3 (cloth). — ISBN 0-7619-8947-1 (pbk.)
    1. Museums—United States—History. 2. Museum curators—United States—Biography. 3. Museum directors—United States—Biography. 4. Popular culture—Museums—United States—History. 5. United States—Intellectual life—History. I. American Association for State and Local History. II. Title. III. Series.
AM11.A55 1997
069'.0973—dc21
                         97-21127
                         CIP

069.0973 ALE

Cover Design: Kim Ericsson/Shooting Star Graphics

Editorial Management: Virginia Alderson Hoffman

Typesetting Services: Kim Ericsson/Shooting Star Graphics

97   98   99   00   7   6   5   4   3   2   1

Contents

Dedication

To my daughter, Mary Sheron Alexander, who helped me with part of the research, and without whose persistence and dedication this book would not have come to be published.

About the Author

Edward Porter Alexander, after receiving his PhD in American History at Columbia University in 1938, directed museums for the New York State Historical Association at Ticonderoga and Cooperstown (editing the quarterly, *New York History*) and the State Historical Society of Wisconsin (editing *The Wisconsin Magazine of History*). He then went to Colonial Williamsburg in Virginia to serve as Director of Interpretation (later Vice President). After 26 years there, he retired on a Friday and the next Monday taught his first class in Museum Studies at the University of Delaware in Newark. In six years he taught more than 300 students, most of whom work in museums in the United States and Canada. He has traveled extensively, visiting museums in such places as China, Japan, and India.

He was a founder and president of the American Association for State and Local History and president of the American Association of Museums.

Foreword

MOST AMERICANS don't go to museums, nor do most, apparently, read books. On the other hand, television and the computer supposedly claim audiences of millions. Starting some years ago, the hard—but not really verified—facts of TV viewership began to influence attendance goals for museums, which as a result made dramatic efforts to reap "popular" audiences in various ways. Vast amounts of money were expended. At the bottom end was overblown design and uselessly complicated mechanical exhibitry, while at the top was a fresh view of interpretation. By far the most enduring of these is the latter, while the former has fallen because of its prohibitive cost, invariably short life, and general impracticality. Where next? The fountains of public money have dried up. Still the museum forms a strong current in American life.

At crossroads like this, institutions look back through the clutter and review basics common to their work that will help them reconsider. This book appears at a perfect time. Edward P. Alexander finds these basics through portraits of people who shaped and, as he puts it, defined the American museum. Alexander's thirteen individuals were passionately committed to ideas, and the pursuit was pervasive in their lives. It is an amazing collection of people.

Some, like Carl Ethan Akeley (1864–1926), followed wild stars. A taxidermist, he traveled the rain forests of Africa with Theodore Roosevelt. We grimace as the baby elephant is shot by TR's son Kermit, and by the time the poor creature, stuffed and waxed with cosmetics, joins its parents and kin in the tableau "Alarm" at the American Museum of Natural History, our modern sensitivities are shaken irreparably. Yet we cannot help but admire what Alexander describes as Akeley's "youthful zest and tremendous nervous energy" and his love of what he called "Brightest Africa" that led to the creation of the distinguished African zoological halls in Chicago and New York.

Alfred Barr's (1902–1981) devotion to modern art prevails in his long shadow, New York's Museum of Modern Art. Alexander found that his work led to "a better treatment of modern art in other museums," which had long shunned it. Reuben Gold Thwaites (1853–1913) brought into flower the State Historical Society of Wisconsin, already an old institution founded in 1846. Thwaites was a newspaper editor, whom Alexander writes became "the most successful historical society director the nation had known."

William Sumner Appleton (1874–1947), a founder of the Society for the Preservation of New England Antiquities in 1910, directed it in the collection of many historic buildings and the rescue of many more from demolition. His antiquarian thirst made him collect fragments of all sorts, from wallpaper to locks, and from his efforts he spawned some of the earliest and most enduring precepts of historic preservation in this country. Frank Oppenheimer (1912–1985), founder of the Exploratorium in San Francisco, was a powerful force in popular education for the science museum.

John Kinard (1936–1989), director of the Smithsonian's Anacostia Neighborhood Museum in Washington, was a bombastic individual who opened America's eyes to the social responsibility of the museum. Katherine Coffey (1900–1972), both serving as director and taking staff functions at the Newark Museum, used all the skills of the profession to make her inner-city museum survive and flourish to the good of all in a context of racial unrest. She and Kinard believed in the power of special exhibitions to attract and educate the public, but more than that, the significance of the museum in the betterment of American life.

Edward P. Alexander's characters were all people who knew what they wanted. Most of them, as originators, mesmerized their patrons effectively, gaining solid support for their programs. But the way was sometimes blocked sufficiently to bring their creative juices to a boil. Alexander's portraits record temper explosions, resignations, rivalries; he describes men and women so determined on the paths to their objectives that most others simply stepped aside and let them go on. Few of his characters were team players, and most had little concern for what they considered extraneous details. Organizations have grown in their wakes, a dozen and more people to realize the objectives first pursued by one.

Their creative spark was not that of the artist but of the educator who would teach and, if necessary, preach. Alexander's museum masters were conveyors and interpreters of knowledge, who believed in the museum as a premier medium of communication. They saw it as more universal, more enduring in application than an ordinary schoolroom, where tensions weakened natural curiosity. "No one ever flunked a museum," writes Alexander. Among his most memorable characters, Anna Billings Gallup (1872–1956), thought museums for children should be "pure fun," and that this was the "Magic key that opens one door of knowledge after another, it is the magic wand that gives each branch of learning a potential of joy, it is the magnet that draws the crowd, the engineer that keeps them busy with efficiency of action."

Reliving these lives with Edward P. Alexander, one can but smile occasionally, thinking how the characters might have fit in to a present-day museum. Accreditation might have raised their hackles as being meddlesome. Political correctness would have offended their sense of independence. These are only surface matters. Alexander's concern is with the universals. He shows us that for all the uniqueness of their stories, we are, in our basics, the professional children of these people. They were the pioneers. All "modern" for their own time—indeed some of them radical—they were as much of their times as we may dearly hope we are of ours.

The book's one glaring omission is understandable: Alexander does not include Alexander. This great innovator in the American museum would have made the masters an even fourteen. He publishes this book at ninety years of age, yet another achievement in a long career that assumes a monumental presence in the history of historical interpretation. After five wartime years as director of the State Historical Society of Wisconsin—the most prestigous position of its kind in the nation— he resigned in 1946 to embark upon a new career as director of the division of education in restored Williamsburg in Virginia.

Colonial Williamsburg was then a restoration not twenty years old, an architecture-driven project not without its sentimental message of a Better Anglo-Saxon Past. Although academic historians remain suspicious and even dubious about historic houses and outdoor museums, their feelings on this subject a half-century ago was utter contempt. History belonged only in lectures and the written word. The source of history lay only in the written document—objects were mute and people who tried to listen to them were playing dolls.

Yet a historian of distinction had now taken up the task of interpreting Williamsburg. Deftly, with time, blazing paths where there had been no trail before, Alexander added another dimension to the physical re-creation of 18th-century life. This was history. With the charms of reenacted cooking, wood chopping, carriage-riding, and the rest, were now the challenges of ideas. What were the beliefs and philosophies generated in this colonial town? Who were the characters and how in the course of everyday life did they help forge a nation, where a ragged row of coastal colonies had been?

Alexander's move from Madison to Williamsburg can be considered one of the major events in the history of American museums. All our historic houses, capitols, courthouses, and other living museum exhibitions follow his lead and, indeed, flatter themselves sometimes that they have built even higher toward the standards he originally set.

The Museum in America: Innovators and Pioneers is yet another contribution to the field from Edward P. Alexander. Let him introduce you to people who, like himself, helped make the American museum what it is today.

WILLIAM SEALE

INTRODUCTION

Toward a Definition
of the American Museum

THE NUMBER OF MUSEUMS in the United States has grown amazingly, from a half dozen in the colonial period until now with a total exceeding eight thousand, much more numerous than any other nation. The earliest ones were chiefly collections of curiosities and oddments, often the property of one person who depended heavily on admission fees for his support. An exception to this generalization was Charles Willson Peale's Philadelphia Museum of 1786 which stressed natural history, showed more than 250 portraits and paintings, chiefly the creations of Peale and his family, and contained many historical objects. His comprehensive collection of natural science, labeled according to the Linnean nomenclature, attracted many scholars, especially from the American Philosophical Society, but Peale also provided what he called "rational amusement" with demonstrations of electrical machines and chemical experiments, organ recitals, a physiognotrace producing the visitors' silhouettes, and other participatory activities so as to instruct and often entertain as large an audience as possible from the general public.[1]

During the first half of the nineteenth century, a majority of the museums probably belonged to and were operated by very unlearned persons who installed stuffed beasts and serpents, waxwork figures, and electrical machines that gave those touching them a modest shock. These museums also presented farces, songs, dances, and similar vaudeville entertainment as a kind of cheap popular theatre. Examples of such museums were the various versions of the American Museum in New York, the Columbian Museum in Boston, and the Western Museum in Cincinnati with its hellish "Infernal Regions." On the other hand, more serious museums arose with collections that furthered the study of natural history, science and technology, history, or art such as the Academy of Natural Sciences of Philadelphia, the New-York Historical Society, or the Trumbull Gallery at Yale. They usually were governed by boards of directors or trustees and customarily had a supervisor or director who understood the subject matter that they treated. For a time museums that offered chiefly entertainment won out in the competition; their success was exemplified by Phineas T. Barnum, that master of public relations and promotion who dominated the field after acquiring New York City's American Museum in 1841. Though he did gather and display some valuable natural history collections, his emphasis was on pure entertainment. By 1870, however, his successive museums had suffered a series of disastrous fires, and he decided to leave the museum field and devote his energies to the circus.

About that time, a new day dawned with the appearance of important, first-rate institutions such as the American Museum of Natural History and the Metropolitan Museum of Art in New York, the Museum of Fine Arts in Boston, and the Art Institute of Chicago. Soon, serious museums in every field began to spring up all over the country. American museums today, however, differ greatly in size, financial resources, and functions. Some of the larger ones count their collections, yearly attendance, and budgets in the millions, have staffs reaching several thousands, and stay open long hours. Still, about three thousand of the smaller museums are directed by one person (often a volunteer), financed by tiny budgets, and are available only two or three afternoons a week.

I have already had my say in my previous book, *Museum Masters*, about a few American leaders, namely Charles Willson Peale (1741–1827) and his family in his pioneering Philadelphia Museum; George Browne Goode (1851–1896) of the Smithsonian Institution's United States National Museum; Ann Pamela Cunningham (1816–1875) of the Mount Vernon Ladies' Association; and the progressive and innovative John Cotton Dana (1856–1929) of the Newark (New Jersey) Museum. Goode, a skilled scientist himself, still asserted that public institutions like the Smithsonian "are not intended for the few but for the enlightenment and education of the masses." He emphasized the importance of meaningful exhibitions and understandable labels. Cunningham, an early force in the historic house museum field, secured and preserved George Washington's Mount Vernon plantation, to be kept always as he had known it. Dana used special exhibitions and numerous educational activities to lure all elements of the community as well as outside visitors to his museum. He sent its collections and staff members to schools, libraries, clubs, and other organizations in the area, and he devised an apprentice system to train young college graduates in museum work.

My chief purpose in the present volume is to examine carefully how several museum leaders made the education and, to a limited extent, the amusement of the general public their chief aim rather than the accumulation of objects important for the research of scholars and experts. I apply this examination to several well-known types of museums and also consider the subject of museum studies.

I begin with two natural history museum leaders. The first was Henry Fairfield Osborn (1857–1935) who in forty-two years of service made the American Museum of Natural History in New York a model of this type of museum, renowned nationally and internationally. Another master in this field was Carl Ethan Akeley (1864–1926), taxidermist in turn with the Milwaukee Public Museum, Field Museum of Natural History in Chicago, and the American Museum of Natural History. He perfected the habitat group type of exhibition used so extensively in this country and abroad to show naturally posed animals with their accessories such as rocks, soils, plants, and habitations in front of curved background paintings of actual places.

I go on to two art museum leaders. Henry Watson Kent (1866–1948) was a skilled administrator who brought the Metropolitan Museum of Art into the twentieth century with scientific methods of registration, accessioning, cataloguing, communication, and publication, and he succeeded in persuading other museums in America and Europe to use such professional methods. Alfred Hamilton Barr Jr. (1902–1981), the first director of the Museum of Modern Art, through scholarly but popular exhibitions and lucid explanations in his catalogues and books began to arouse enthusiasm for modern art among the public and to influence other museums in its favor.

In the history museum area was Reuben Gold Thwaites (1853–1913), director of the State Historical Society of Wisconsin, who made the society serve the people of that entire state and became the most successful and influential historical society director yet to appear in America. Another historical museum leader was William Sumner Appleton (1874–1947), founder and director of the Society for the Preservation of New England Antiquities, who saved more than fifty important historical and architectural buildings and sites scattered about New England.

Among four masters in specialized fields was Dr. Frank Friedman Oppenheimer (1912–1985) who founded a science and technology museum, which he christened the "Exploratorium." He devised several hundred interactive, "hands-on" exhibits that required participation from the visitors and helped them understand various scientific principles. Anna Billings Gallup (1872–1956) was curator of the Brooklyn Children's Museum, the first of that kind in the world. Her enthusiastic interpretation was known throughout this country and abroad; it helped spread children's museums worldwide. John Robert Kinard (1936–1989) operated the Anacostia Neighborhood Museum in Washington, D.C., as a combination museum, cultural arts center, meeting place for neighborhood groups, and skill training laboratory for youngsters. He expanded its functions so that it became recognized nationally and internationally for its strong civil rights advocacy and its African American history, art, and culture programs. And Katherine Coffey (1900–1972) at the Newark (New Jersey) Museum made a general museum (natural science, art, history, and technology) appeal to a whole community with many ingenious educational programs.

Botanical gardens and zoos are museums that contain living objects. Charles Sprague Sargent (1841–1927) built the Arnold Arboretum near Boston into one of the most outstanding botanical gardens in the nation and the world—a museum of living plants, a scientific station, and a popular educator. William Temple Hornaday (1854–1937) was the first director of the New York Zoological Society which operated the Bronx Park Zoo. He gathered many exotic animals and allowed them to range freely in large enclosures instead of keeping them confined in cages and small paddocks.

Finally, a museum specialist of note was Paul Joseph Sachs (1878–1961) of Harvard University and its Fogg Art Museum, who taught a museum studies course that covered all aspects of art museum work—philosophy, history, buildings, administration, collections, personalities in the art world, politics, and ethics. His students headed American art museums for a generation.

The thirteen leaders featured in this volume did much to transform the American conception of museum purpose. They believed in the collection of objects or specimens, of course, but did not consider their preservation and arrangement as important as the education of the public and service to the community. Studying and researching the objects might at times make contributions to the subject matter of natural science, art, history, or technology, but curators ought not take a supercilious view and devote themselves exclusively to the collection and its research, with their chief clientele scholars and experts. Instead, curators should work actively in the museums' educational programs;

in fact, curators, educators, designers, and administrators ought to form a team to further the educational impact of the whole museum. They should devise exhibitions and other learning activities, create lectures and demonstrations for junior, family, and senior citizen visitors; work closely with the schools to make class journeys to the museum fit in with classroom study; visit schools, libraries, clubs, and other community agencies to give advice or arrange loan exhibits or motion picture showings; and make radio and television appearances. In this way the museum would take its proper place in dispensing education of a special type for its visitors and the surrounding community.

NOTES

NOTE: Source notes and a selected bibliography are provided at the end of each chapter in this book, listing works referred to in the chapter and especially pertinent to it. Works not listed in the chapter bibliography appear with full publication data at first mention in the chapter notes and as shortened references thereafter.

1. My other writings on this section are on Peale in *Museum Masters: Their Museums and Their Influence* (Nashville: American Association for State and Local History, 1983), 41–77; "Early American Museums: From Collection of Curiosities to Popular Education," *International Journal of Museum Management and Curatorship* 6 (1987): 337–51; "The American Museum Movement Chooses Education," *Curator* 31 (March 1988): 61–80.

SELECT BIBLIOGRAPHY

Alexander, Edward P. *Museum Masters: Their Museums and Their Influence*. Nashville: American Association for State and Local History, 1983, 41–77.
_____. "Early American Museums: From Collection of Curiosities to Popular Education." *International Journal of Museum Management and Curatorship* 6 (1987): 337–51.
_____. "The American Museum Movement Chooses Education." *Curator* 31 (March 1988): 61–80.

CHAPTER 1

Henry Fairfield Osborn
Develops a Model Natural History Museum

I

HENRY FAIRFIELD OSBORN, at age thirty-four a promising young scientist, left his teaching post at Princeton University in 1891 to accept a joint appointment as professor of biology at Columbia University and curator of a new department of mammalian paleontology at the American Museum of Natural History. His post enabled the museum and university to begin to co-operate in the natural history field. Through the years, the two institutions worked together ever more closely, university professors often using the museum's collections in their research and museum curators frequently teaching at the university.[1]

The American Museum, to which Professor Osborn came, was founded in 1869 as a result of the prescience and infectious enthusiasm of Albert Smith Bickmore, who had studied at Harvard with Louis Agasiz and worked in his Museum of Comparative Zoology. Bickmore thought Cambridge too small a place for the great museum of natural history that he envisioned; he chose New York City as the ideal spot. He enlisted the aid of wealthy leaders of the metropolis, such as Theodore Roosevelt, father of the late president; Joseph H. Choate, the lawyer; Morris K. Jesup and J. Pierpont Morgan, bankers; Robert Colgate, the soap magnate; and Alexander T. Stewart, the department store entrepreneur. Afraid that Boston, Philadelphia, Washington, and Chicago were outstripping their beloved city in cultural attainments, they secured a charter from the state legislature, made Bickmore the museum's superintendent (the title used by the prestigious British Museum), and persuaded the Commissioners of Central Park, headed by the imaginative and cooperative Andrew H. Green, to allow them to house exhibits in the second and third stories of the old Arsenal Building in the park, and later to give them some eighteen acres at Central Park West and 79th Street for a permanent home.

The trustees of the American Museum and the even younger Metropolitan Museum of Art in 1871 joined to petition the state legislature to allow the city to tax itself $500,000 to pay for a building for the two museums. In support, they presented a petition signed by several thousand property owners. The movement resulted in an important compromise, in which the city agreed to own and pay for the two separate buildings that resulted, along with their maintenance and security, while the boards of trustees financed the collections, their preservation and interpretation. About one hundred municipalities through-out the country since then have adopted similar joint public and private support arrangements for their museums.

The American Museum at first put its emphasis upon public instruction rather than scientific research. It stated that the museum was "to be second to none" and "while affording amusement and instruction to the public," would "be the means of teaching our youth to appreciate the wonderful works of our Creator."[2] Bickmore was not a skillful administrator, and in 1881 he stepped down as superintendent to give courses of lectures to public school principals and teachers, and soon after to head a Department of Public Instruction. A facile and fascinating speaker, he used hand-painted stereoptican lantern slides to illustrate his lectures.

Morris K. Jesup, multimillionaire supplier of railroad equipment and a promi-nent banker, became president of the Board of Trustees in 1881 and took over the museum's administration. He came to the office almost daily and handled the smallest details. He insisted upon sound financial procedures, immaculate cleanliness and order in the building, and exhibits directed toward the general public. He asserted: "I am a plain, unscientific business man; I want the exhibits to be labelled so that I understand them, and then I feel sure that others can understand."[3] He also slowly came to appreciate the museum curators' devotion to scientific research and the need for funds to support it. He persuaded the board to back research projects and expeditions, even though many trustees continued to regard the museum as their own private property and often wished to finance exhibits that were showy and spectacular, not necessarily scientific and educational. Jesup brought Frederic Ward Putnam, director of Harvard's Peabody Museum of Archaeology and Ethnology, to the American Museum in 1894 on a part-time basis to organize a strong department of anthropology, and Putnam appointed the brilliant young Franz Boas as his assistant. Jesup also personally financed several projects that included the six-year-long Jesup North Pacific Expedition of 1897, directed by Boas. Jesup and his wife, during their lifetimes and in their wills, contributed nearly seven million dollars to the museum, mainly to the endowment fund, by far the largest gift that it had received.

Professor Osborn brought a strong scientific background and imaginative ideas about popular exhibition to the museum. President Jesup appreciated his educational and research contributions and was impressed by his willingness to handle personnel and business matters. Thus, in 1899, Jesup asked Osborn to become his administrative assistant. From that time forward, Osborn had a two-sided career at the museum as curator/scientist and administrator.

II

Henry Fairfield Osborn was born at Fairfield, Connecticut, into a wealthy, socially prominent family. His father, William Henry Osborn, was a founder and long-time president of the Illinois Central Railroad. His mother, born Virginia Reed Sturges, was firm and charitable, and young Osborn's close companion. He spent most of his boyhood in New York City, where he attended Columbia Grammar School (he later said that the discipline there was rigid) and Lyon's Collegiate Institute. His father built a summer home called Castle Rock (later Professor Osborn's favorite residence), on a hilltop overlooking the Hudson River at Garrison, New York, and added "Woodsome Lodge" as an outbuilding where his son could pursue his varied interests. At age fourteen, he published sixteen issues of *The Boys' Journal*, for which he provided most of the copy, composition, and printing. Young Theodore Roosevelt and Osborn were close friends, and their intimacy lasted into later life.

In 1873 Osborn entered Princeton University, where he studied geology with Dr. Arnold Guyot, and philosophy with the dynamic President James McCosh, a Presbyterian divine, one of the first scholars to accept the theory of evolution. He also did hard manual work in the Geology Museum, helped form a student Natural Science Association, and organized a geological camping expedition in the Catskills with two other students during the summer following their junior year. Upon graduation, the three of them made two summer treks to Colorado and Wyoming to collect fossils. In 1878–1879 Osborn studied anatomy and histology with Dr. William H. Welch at Bellevue Medical College and the College of Physicians and Surgeons. Dr. Welch thought him the best student he had ever had. The next year, he decided to go to England instead of Germany to complete his graduate laboratory work in embryology and comparative anatomy with Francis Maitland Balfour at Cambridge and Thomas Huxley in London. The Huxleys invited Osborn to their Sunday evening high teas, where Huxley complained that he was children-pecked as well as hen-pecked. Huxley introduced the awestruck young man to Charles Darwin himself, and he met many other leading scientists. He returned to Princeton to receive his Sc.D. in 1881 and begin a decade of teaching there. He tried to carry on Balfour's and Huxley's methods of informal, lively class discussion followed by closely supervised laboratory work; he urged his students not merely to memorize facts but rather to cultivate observation and creative thinking. He rose to be professor of comparative anatomy and then moved to Columbia in 1891 to teach anatomy and zoology and serve as dean of the Faculty of Pure Science. At the two universities, he taught twenty-eight classes of undergraduates and graduates; he liked to refer to them as his "biological sons," who in this country and abroad were instructing "a young army of biological grandsons."[4]

In 1880 Osborn went on a field expedition to Texas and Louisiana in search of a fossil alligator and other long-tailed amphibians. He was disappointed with his work there and decided that he lacked facility for good field exploration. He commented philosophically: "It is well to realize one's inaptitudes, so that one may better advance in the direction of which his talent does lie. *If you cannot find your research way in one direction, turn to another in which you may be successful.*"[5]

Osborn in 1881 was married to Lucretia Thatcher Perry, the daughter of General A. J. Perry. The Osborns were a charming couple, always ready to entertain their numerous friends and acquaintances; they remained unperturbed on special occasions, as when he chartered a steamboat and brought the entire meeting of the International Congress of Eugenics to "Castle Rock" for a reception. Lucretia bore five children and later wrote three books, one of them a biography of George Washington in his own words.

At Princeton, Osborn began to become a skilled paleontologist. He decided that "*the discovery of new principles is the chief end of research,*" not the routine assemblage of facts; throughout his long career, he rejoiced in making generalizations, based on exacting scientific observation and reasoning but always in language that the general public could understand. He thought that his pale-ontological observations were usually accepted but was not disturbed when they were considered controversial. He said that "*if new principles are sound they will finally gain universal acceptance; if unsound the less widely accepted they are the better.*"[6] He studied the work of Joseph Leidy, the first great American paleon-tologist, and knew intimately Edward Drinker Cope and Daniel Charles Marsh of Yale. The last two were the leading collectors of American fossils but deadly enemies. Osborn and Cope worked closely together at the Academy of Natural Sciences of Philadelphia and maintained friendly relations, though Cope could often be combative. On one occasion, he and a close friend engaged in fisticuffs, and Cope told Osborn the next day, "If you think my eye is black, you ought to see Frazer this morning."[7] In addition to studying fossils found in America, Osborn made a trip to Europe in 1886 to examine those of some tiny Mesozoic animals. He sent his graduate student, Barnum Brown, who was employed at the American Museum, to seek fossils in Como Bluff, Wyoming, thus precipitating a bitter quarrel with Professor Marsh, who accused Osborn of encroaching upon his territory. But he continued dispatching his assistants on persistent expeditions in both America and Europe and, as a result, the American Museum's holdings of vertebrate prehistoric fossils were second to none in the world.

Professor Osborn had a fresh, even radical approach for a paleontologist toward exhibition; he wished to mount the huge fossilized skeletons of the prehistoric monsters and display them to the public. He met considerable opposition from scientists, both within and outside his staff, who argued that the bones ought to be arranged in drawers and used only for study by experts. Osborn was right, of course, so far as the general public was concerned; he made "dinosaur" a household word, and the massive fossils have remained to this day the most impressive and popular of all the museum's exhibits.

After Osborn became President Jesup's assistant, it soon was clear that the aging president was slowing down. In 1901, at Osborn's suggestion, he brought Dr. Herman Carey Bumpus from Brown University and Wood's Hole Biological Laboratory to become his full-time assistant and soon made him the museum's first director; at about the same time, Osborn was elevated to the Board of Trustees and elected its second vice-president. Bumpus made great contributions to the educational program, such as sending out small collections of "nature cabinets" to the schools; they soon reached more than one million students yearly. As Jesup's health failed, he came to the museum only occasionally in his wheelchair, but it was the clever, calculating Osborn rather than Bumpus who wielded the real administrative power. Osborn turned down his election as secretary of the prestigious Smithsonian Institution in 1905, and upon Jesup's death the next year became president of the trustees, whereupon he soon retired from active teaching at Columbia.

Bumpus was jealous of Osborn's control of the museum and dared publicly to accuse him of "financial mismanagement and subtle dishonesty."[8] In 1910, the trustees investigated, found Osborn innocent of the charges, and dismissed Bumpus. Osborn then appointed Frederic A. Lucas, at that time director of the Brooklyn Museum, as director. The two men worked together somewhat more harmoniously, though Osborn continued to insist upon making the important decisions. Dr. Lucas, writing later of his fifty years as a museum man, remarked ruefully that "the director of a large museum is frequently, or largely, director in name only."[9]

III

During President Osborn's long administration of some twenty-seven years, the American Museum became recognized as a national and international institution. In the 1920s it was at its height with a growing collection nourished by about one hundred expeditions per year, excellent exhibitions that attracted heavy popular attendance, strong research and publications, and a varied educational program that reached not only the schools but family and community groups. The museum was indeed a model in the natural history field; it was ahead of its two chief American competitors—the Smithsonian Institution's National Museum of Natural History and the Field Museum of Natural History in Chicago—and competed well with the British Museum of Natural History in London.

The museum's financing was unusual and somewhat disorderly, based mainly upon gifts from the trustees and Osborn's friends. He took no salary and even contributed $40,000 to building the fossil collection. J. Pierpont Morgan's first wife was Osborn's aunt, and Morgan for a time gave $15,000 yearly to the paleontology program, a fact which Osborn kept secret. Morgan also financed the work of Charles R. Knight, the freelance painter and sculptor whom Osborn persuaded to provide striking, exciting murals and other pictures and models of prehistoric animals. Osborn obtained private funds for important expeditions, such as Carl Akeley's to obtain specimens for his planned African Hall or several trips of Martin and Osa Johnson to secure motion and still pictures of African animal life. The museum managed to support three expeditions by Roy Chapman Andrews to China, Tibet, Burma, and Outer Mongolia. The last of those tours with a fleet of automobiles and 125 camels found seventy-million-year-old dinosaur eggs, some of them with unhatched babies, in the Gobi Desert in 1943, along with other rare fossils. Osborn was overjoyed to have a prediction that he had made in 1900 fulfilled— that many prehistoric mammals would be found in Asia—and Mrs. Osborn and he hastened to visit the expedition. Osborn's keen eye even found a rare mammal tooth during the trip.

But Osborn thought that the museum's chief purpose was education, not collection. A good museum was no longer "a sanctuary or refuge, a safety deposit vault for curios"; instead it was a "progressive educational force" that "succeeds if it teaches." Before the American Association of Museums in 1917, he declared that "museum folk are educators of a special type," and he developed that idea as follows:

> We enlist in a form of education which is, in fact, most difficult, since its ideals are to present visually the laws of nature and of art in such a way as both to educate and to create a strong impression on the mind of the visitor. In other words, museum folk . . . seldom have an opportunity of speaking to their students; the expression of their thoughts and their ideals is through the exhibits which they arrange. The successful museum teacher is the one who is able to teach without speaking, as nature teaches or art teaches. He may speak only through labels on his specimens.[10]

The exhibitions at the museum were outstanding. Akeley joined its staff as taxidermist and designer in 1909 to install habitat groups, and stunning new halls of mammals opened for North America, South America, and Southern Asia. Between 1880 and 1915 the education program expanded greatly with lectures to school teachers at the museum; nature study collections and lantern slides sent to the schools; visiting school classes; special presentations for the blind; and talks by staff members at the schools. George H. Sherwood became curator of public instruction after 1906 and later was the museum's executive director. He estimated in 1926 that the education program was reaching six million persons each year. The museum also operated a trailside museum at Bear Mountain with nature trails. Osborn himself took delight in viewing the classes of school children streaming into the museum and in stopping boys and girls to ask them their impressions. He often told with much laughter of inquiring of a little red-headed fellow in the elevator, "What do you like best in the Museum?" and of his reply, in a sepulchral voice: "Fossil fishes."[11]

Osborn always encouraged his staff to do scientific investigation, and he helped establish publications to serve as outlets for research of both the staff and outside scholars. The various series included the *Bulletin* (1881–), *Memoirs* (1893–), *Anthropological Papers* (1907–), and *Novitiates* [New Acquaintances] (1921–). He began issuing the magazine *Natural History* in 1900 (at first as the *American Museum Journal*) with popular articles for the members and general public. He also contributed 7,000 volumes of his private library. Still, some biologists, especially those in genetics and physiology, considered the museum old-fashioned in its research and thought that the staff contained too many administrators and field workers without enough graduate training, and produced too few worthwhile publications.

Osborn himself set a fast pace in research and publication. During his career, he produced 940 titles with about 12,000 pages. They covered a broad field indeed—geology, paleontology, comparative anatomy, embryology, neurology, anthropology, evolution of man, biology and principles of evolution, education, conservation of forests and mammals, and biographies of men of science and letters. His two most original paleontological contributions were *The Titanotheres* [mainly fossil horses and rhinoceroses] *of Ancient Wyoming, Dakota, and Kansas*, published in two volumes by the U.S. Geological Survey in 1929, and *The Proboscides* [fossil elephants and mammoths]: *Evolution, Phylogeny, and Classification*, in two volumes which appeared after Osborn's death. His numerous more popular books included *From the Greeks to Darwin* (1894); *The Age of Mammals in Europe, Asia, and North America* (1910); *Men of the Old Stone Age: Their Environment, Life, and Art* (1915); *The Origin and Evolution of Life* (1917); *Evolution and Religion* (1923); *Impressions of Great Naturalists* (1924); *Evolution and Religion in Education* (1926); and *Creative Education in School, College, University, and Museum* (1927). A host of honors came to him from this scholarship—twelve medals, nine honorary degrees, and membership in sixty-one learned societies in fifteen countries.

All together, during Osborn's presidency, the American Museum's building area doubled, the city appropriation tripled, the endowment increased sevenfold, the scientific staff some three times, and membership more than four times. He managed to expand the physical plant so that it contained nearly twenty interconnected structures, perhaps the most important the monumental entrance building honoring Theodore Roosevelt, which the State of New York financed, with a thirty-foot-high statue in front showing Roosevelt mounted on a horse and protecting an American Indian and an African-American. One of Osborn's favorite later plans was an intermuseum promenade 160 feet wide through

Central Park to connect the American Museum and the Metropolitan Museum of Art. He considered the defeat of that project one of the greatest failures of his life.

With his broad interests, Osborn kept the museum in touch with the main movements of American life. During the First World War, he ordered all male employees to perform military and bayonet drill in the parking lot, so that they could defend the museum "against the barbarous Teutonic Horde."[12] In the 1920s, he opposed William Jennings Bryan and the crusade against teaching the theory of evolution in the Tennessee schools that resulted in the Scopes Trial. A lifelong communicant and church-goer, Osborn was startled to find himself classed publicly with Voltaire, Thomas Paine, and Robert Ingersoll as a subversive-atheist. The minister of one large New York church painted the lurid picture of obscenities in some of the plays produced in the city and of the immorality rampant there. He asked, "Who is responsible for this lewdness and this animalism?" and answered, "Henry Fairfield Osborn."[13]

Osborn was involved in a more serious dispute arising from the eugenics movement. His fellow trustee and friend, Madison Grant, in 1916 wrote *The Passing of the Great Age*, which upheld the Nordic race as superior to other Europeans, Negroes, and Orientals. He argued that the United States ought to repudiate its sentimental boast that recognized no distinction in "race, creed, or color" or else write "Finis Americae." Maudlin romanticism had made the country "an asylum of the oppressed" and was sweeping the nation toward a racial abyss.[14] Grant went on to show himself strongly anti-Semitic, anti-Negro, and a believer in sterilization of the unfit. Osborn's preface to the book praised his friend's correct scientific method and declared that the true spirit of eugenics would conserve and multiply the best spiritual, moral, intellectual, and physical forces of heredity to maintain the integrity of American institutions in the future.

When the Second International Conference of Eugenics, with Osborn as president, met at the museum in 1921, he declared that the war had "left the finest racial stocks in many countries so depleted that there is danger of their extinction" and that "our own race is threatened with submergence by the influx of other races." His address at the National Immigration Conference of 1923 continued in the same vein. He thought that the Army intelligence tests had shown that blacks had inferior minds, while "the oriental civilization, the oriental soul, is fundamentally different from the American"; and the Nordic nations were superior to Italy or the Balkans. The government ought to send skilled agents to examine those wishing to come to the United States and thus avoid the calamity of having immigrants constitute one-third the population of our insane asylums.[15]

Osborn and many of the other trustees shared the view that the American Museum ought to promote the proper education of immigrants. He wished to make it a teaching "nature institution" so as to preserve rural and old-time American virtues against immigration and urbanization. Somewhat less prejudiced than Grant, as a practical matter he added a Jewish man, Felix Warburg, to the museum board in 1910 and found him an able and devoted trustee. Osborn took a vocal part in the movement to restrict immigration, and two newspaper articles were headed: "Osborn Calls U. S. Europe's Dump" and "Lo, the Poor Nordic: Professor Osborn's Petition on the Immigration Question." He also was somewhat of an anti-feminist and insisted that women made inferior schoolteachers. After his retirement from the museum, he visited Germany in 1934 and enthusiastically praised the Nazi racial ideas. But he died the next year at his home in Garrison.

IV

Dr. Margaret Mead, for long the museum's outstanding anthropologist, made a just evaluation of Professor Osborn as president and personality. She said:

> Osborn *ran* the museum. Since then, the president has been . . . well, *normal*. The last days of Osborn were very capricious. He was powerful and capricious. Salaries were thousands of dollars apart because of his capriciousness. Osborn was a magnificent old devil. This was his dream, and he built it. He was arbitrary and opinionated. . . . he was a wealthy man, who was also a scientific explorer. . . . We would never have had the Museum without him.[16]

Dr. Sherwood, who worked under Osborn as curator and director and who sometimes was criticized as being sycophantic to him, thought that Professor Osborn's chief characteristics were breadth of vision, tenacity of purpose, fertility of mind, sympathy with youth, and eternal optimism. Perhaps he should have added something about "limitless energy."

Osborn himself insisted that a scientist could combine research investigation, teaching, and creative institutional work without doing injustice to any of them. In a scientific career, he deemed research by far the highest goal but that institutional work was justified, especially "when it is chiefly directed toward collecting materials for original research in every branch of natural history and in inspiring and training younger men in those branches."[17] In Osborn's case, creative institutional work included not only the American Museum (and for a time Columbia University), but also the New York Zoological Society which was developing the Bronx Zoo. He was a charter member there in 1895, served with Madison Grant on the executive committee, and was its hardworking president from 1909 to 1924.[18]

The American Museum of Natural History was controlled and administered by two presidents of its Board of Trustees, Jesup and Osborn, for half a century, from 1881 to 1933. They did a good job on the whole, but with power concentrated as it was, they could be arbitrary and unreasonable; that was especially true in Osborn's case. Financing was also often indefinite and uncertain when it was so dependent upon the whims of wealthy board members and their friends. Though Osborn retired during the great depression, which gravely cut back the museum's programs for a period, from that time forward, the president and the Board of Trustees usually confined themselves to raising funds and approving general policies, while the director did the everyday administration, carried out policies, handled personnel problems including appointments and dismissals, with the curators had charge of the museological functions of collection, preservation, research, exhibition, and education, and suggested policies for board consideration. The American Museum, however, recently has joined several of the larger American museums in employing as president a paid administrator, whose chief function is fundraising and other financial concerns, and placing under him the subject-matter specialist, the director. No doubt, Henry Fairfield Osborn would have approved heartily of that arrangement.

NOTES

1. This chapter is based on the following sources: American Museum of Natural History *Annual Report* 1 (1870); Roy Chapman Andrews, *On the Trail of Ancient Man: A Narrative of the Field Work of the Central Asiatic Expeditions* (New York: G. P. Putnam's Sons, 1926); William Adams Brown, *Morris Ketchum Jesup: A Character Sketch* (New York: Charles Scribner's Sons, 1910); Ralph W. Dexter, "The Role of F. W. Putnam in Developing Anthropology at the American Museum of Natural History," *Curator* 9 (1976): 303–10; Madison Grant, *The Passing of a Great Race, or the Racial Basis of European History*, 4th rev. ed. (New York: Charles Scribner's Sons, 1929); William King Gregory, "Henry Fairfield Osborn," American Philosophical Society *Proceedings* 76 (1936): 395–408; Gregory, "Henry Fairfield Osborn, 1857–1935," National Academy of Sciences *Biographical Memoirs* 19 (1938): 50–119; Gregory, "Henry Fairfield Osborn: An Appreciation," *Scientific Monthly* 41 (Dec. 1935): 567–69; Geoffrey T. Hellman, *Bankers, Bones & Beetles: The First Century of the American Museum of Natural History* (Garden City, N.Y.: Natural History Press, 1969); John Michael Kennedy, "Philanthropy and

Science in New York City: The American Museum of Natural History, 1868–1968" (New Haven: Yale University Ph.D. Dissertation, 1968); Frederic Augustus Lucas, *Fifty Years of Museum Work: Autobiography, Unpublished Papers, and Bibliography* (New York: American Museum of Natural History, 1933); *Natural History: The Journal of the American Museum of Natural History, New York* 1 (1900); Henry Fairfield Osborn, *The American Museum of Natural History: Its Origin, Its History, the Growth of Its Departments to December 31, 1909*, 2d edition (New York: Irving Press, 1911); Osborn, "Biographical Memoir of Edward Drinker Cope, 1840–1897," National Academy of Sciences *Biographical Memoirs* 13 (1930): 124–317; Osborn, *Creative Education in School, College, University, and Museum: Personal Observation and Experience of the Half-Century, 1877–1927* (New York: Charles Scribner's Sons, 1927); Osborn, *Evolution and Religion in Education: Polemics of the Fundamentalist Controversy of 1922–1928* (New York: Charles Scribner's Sons, 1928); Osborn, *Fifty-two Years of Research, Observation and Publication, 1877–1929: A Life Adventure in Breadth and Depth*, ed. by Florence Milligan (New York: Charles Scribner's Sons, 1930); Osborn, *Impressions of Great Naturalists: Darwin, Wallace, Huxley, Leidy, Cope, Balfour, Roosevelt, and Others*, 2d edition revised (New York: Charles Scribner's Sons, 1928); Osborn, "Morris K. Jesup," *Science* 27 (Feb 7, 1908): 235–36; "Henry Fairfield Osborn . . . Tributes Paid at Memorial Meetings," *Natural History Supplement* 37 (Feb. 1936): 1–14; Douglas J. Preston, *Dinosaurs in the Attic: An Excursion into the American Museum of Natural History* (New York: St. Martin's Press, 1987); Nina J. Root, "The Library of the American Museum of Natural History," *Journal of the Society for the Bibliography of Natural History* 9 (Apr. 1980): 587–91; George Gaylord Simpson, "Henry Fairfield Osborn," *Dictionary of American Biography* (New York: Charles Scribner's Sons, 1940), Supplement 1: 584–87.

2. Osborn, *American Museum of Natural History*, 11.

3. Brown, *Jesup*, 153.

4. Osborn, *Creative Education*, 4–5.

5. Gregory, "Henry Fairfield Osborn, 1857–1935," 61.

6. Osborn, *Fifty-two Years*, 63.

7. Osborn, *Impressions of Great Naturalists*, 179.

8. Hellman, *Bankers, Bones & Beetles*, 112.

9. Ibid., 152.

10. Osborn, *Creative Education*, 235, 242–46.

11. "Henry Fairfield Osborn Tributes," 5; Osborn, *Creative Education*, 22.

12. Root, "Library of the American Museum," 589.

13. "Henry Fairfield Osborn Tributes," 12–14; Osborn, *Impressions of Great Naturalists*, 163.

14. Grant, *Passing of the Great Age*, xxxiii, 263.

15. American Museum, *Annual Report*, 1921: 31–33; Henry Fairfield Osborn, "The Approach to the Immigration Problem through Science," National Immigration Conference *Proceedings* (Dec. 13–14, 1923): 3–11.

16. Hellman, *Bankers, Bones & Beetles*, 204.

17. Osborn, *Fifty-two Years*, 62.

18. William Bridges, *Gathering of Animals: An Unconventional History of the New York Zoological Society* (New York: Harper and Row, 1974).

SELECT BIBLIOGRAPHY

American Museum of Natural History. *Annual Report* 1 (1870).
Andrews, Roy Chapman. *On the Trail of Ancient Man: A Narrative of the Field Work of the*

Central Asiatic Expeditions. New York: G. P. Putnam's Sons, 1926.

Bridges, William. *Gathering of Animals: An Unconventional History of the New York Zoological Society*. New York: Harper and Row, 1974.

Brown, William Adams. *Morris Ketchum Jesup: A Character Sketch*. New York: Charles Scribner's Sons, 1910.

Dexter, Ralph W. "The Role of F. W. Putnam in Developing Anthropology at the American Museum of Natural History." *Curator* 9 (1976): 303–10.

Grant, Madison. *The Passing of a Great Race, or the Racial Basis of European History*. 4th rev. ed. New York: Charles Scribner's Sons, 1929).

Gregory, William King. "Henry Fairfield Osborn." American Philosophical Society *Proceedings* 76 (1936): 395–408.

_____. "Henry Fairfield Osborn, 1857–1935." National Academy of Sciences *Biographical Memoirs* 19 (1938): 50–119.

_____. "Henry Fairfield Osborn: An Appreciation." *Scientific Monthly* 41 (Dec. 1935): 567–69.

Hellman, Geoffrey T. *Bankers, Bones & Beetles: The First Century of the American Museum of Natural History*. Garden City, N.Y.: Natural History Press, 1969.

Kennedy, John Michael. "Philanthropy and Science in New York City: The American Museum of Natural History, 1868–1968." New Haven: Yale University Ph.D. Dissertation, 1968.

Lucas, Frederic Augustus. *Fifty Years of Museum Work: Autobiography, Unpublished Papers, and Bibliography*. New York: American Museum of Natural History, 1933.

Natural History: The Journal of the American Museum of Natural History, New York 1 (1900).

Osborn, Henry Fairfield. *The American Museum of Natural History: Its Origin, Its History, the Growth of Its Departments to December 31, 1909*. 2d edition. New York: Irving Press, 1911.

_____. "Biographical Memoir of Edward Drinker Cope, 1840–1897." National Academy of Sciences *Biographical Memoirs* 13 (1930): 124–317.

_____. *Creative Education in School, College, University, and Museum: Personal Observation and Experience of the Half-Century, 1877–1927*. New York: Charles Scribner's Sons, 1927.

_____. *Evolution and Religion in Education: Polemics of the Fundamentalist Controversy of 1922–1928*. New York: Charles Scribner's Sons, 1928.

_____. *Fifty-two Years of Research, Observation and Publication, 1877–1929: A Life Adventure in Breadth and Depth*. Edited by Florence Milligan. New York: Charles Scribner's Sons, 1930.

_____. *Impressions of Great Naturalists: Darwin, Wallace, Huxley, Leidy, Cope, Balfour, Roosevelt, and Others*. 2d edition revised. New York: Charles Scribner's Sons, 1928.

_____. "Morris K. Jesup." *Science* 27 (Feb 7, 1908): 235–36.

_____. "The Approach to the Immigration Problem through Science." National Immigration Conference *Proceedings* (Dec. 13–14, 1923): 3–11.

"Henry Fairfield Osborn ... Tributes Paid at Memorial Meetings." *Natural History Supplement* 37 (Feb. 1936): 1–14.

Preston, Douglas J. *Dinosaurs in the Attic: An Excursion into the American Museum of Natural History*. New York: St. Martin's Press, 1987.

Root, Nina J. "The Library of the American Museum of Natural History." *Journal of the Society for the Bibliography of Natural History* 9 (Apr. 1980): 587–91.

Simpson, George Gaylord. "Henry Fairfield Osborn." *Dictionary of American Biography*. New York: Charles Scribner's Sons, 1940, Supplement 1: 584–87.

CHAPTER 2

Carl Ethan Akeley
Perfects the Habitat Group Exhibition

I

WHEN CARL AKELEY as a young man in the 1870s became enamored of taxidermy, the ordinary practice of that craft was, by modern standards, extremely primitive. The hide of the animal would be steeped in a bath of salt, alum, and arsenical soap, and the dried, tanned skin then hung upside down. The carcass was stuffed with straw or rags, and the wired and wrapped leg bones inserted. The process killed pests, but shrinkage of the tanned hide could give the animal's face a comical leer, and the carcass usually was overstuffed. In any case, the animal did not look natural. Akeley asserted that taxidermy had been started by upholsterers, and he and his friend William Wheeler once burst into gales of laughter when they saw a lumpy stuffed lynx upholstered to four times its normal size and with a glass eye that peered off at an absurd angle.

Akeley soon began to try to make the animals that he worked on appear more natural. At Ward's Establishment in Rochester, New York, he used a plaster cast for a zebra's body and managed to avoid splitting the skin of its legs, but his conservative fellow taxidermists threw the experiment out on the dump. At the Milwaukee Public Museum, Akeley succeeded in mounting a muskrat colony in its proper watery element, a true habitat group that is still on display there. Later, at the Field Museum in Chicago, he achieved a modern and greatly improved taxidermy. For a time, how to substitute a light papier-maché and wirecloth manikin for a heavy cast puzzled him, but one day, on a streetcar bound for the museum, he suddenly cried out, "I've got it!" much to the amusement of the other passengers.

His final procedure called for the taxidermist to study the animal's anatomy as well as its habits in the field, and to make full photographic records of the carcass, often with a death mask of the head and casts of other portions of the body. The animal was skinned carefully; a small slit in the belly allowed the leg bones to be removed without splitting the skin of the legs; and the whole hide was scraped, fleshed, and dried. Everything was then packed in zinc-lined cases and poisoned with disulfide of carbon. In the field also, flora such as leaves, branches, mosses, and flowers were preserved in formalin or reproduced in plaster casts with color notes. Sketches were made of the area to be used as painted background.

Back in the museum workroom, Akeley fashioned a clay model that showed each muscle and tendon of the animal as well as sectional plaster molds, each lined with a thin coating of glue and muslin. When the glue had dried, papier-maché was molded in the plaster form, reinforced with wirecloth, and placed in water to melt the glue. The result was a lightweight but strong manikin. The pelt, having been treated and softened with a vegetable tanning agent, then was fitted over the manikin and shellacked to make it impervious to moisture. The bones or metal supports on the interior held the manikin in place, and the preserved animal would last indefinitely. Akeley also invented metal molds to reproduce the environmental foliage in wax.

Akeley's "enduring passion for artistic taxidermy" thus produced an authentic faunal habitat group. An artificially lighted exhibit case or diorama with a glass front showed the animal or animals with realistic anatomy and in lifelike poses. The plastic foreground of rocks, soil, plants, and accessories reconstructed the natural habitat and merged, in the rear, into a curved canvas painting of an actual scene.[1] His friend Wheeler explained Akeley's reasoning thus:

> He was thoroughly convinced that an animal is meaningless, except to a hard-shelled zoologist, unless it is presented in such a manner as to convey something of its real character, or *ethos*, which is manifested by its specific motor behavior in a specific natural environment.[2]

The director of the Milwaukee Public Museum, Henry L. Ward, asserted that Akeley was "the man of whom I can say without fear of accusation of flattery that he has done more for taxidermy in America than any other person." According to Dr. Wilfred H. Osgood, chief curator of zoology at the Field Museum, "By utilizing the methods of the sculptor, in connection with ingenious devices of his own invention, he revolutionized taxidermy and raised it to the level of a high art." And Dr. Henry Fairfield Osborn of the American Museum of Natural History said that he wished

> to express the everlasting debt which all museums in America owe to the life work of this remarkable man. We may only estimate the full measure of our debt by considering what the standards, not only of this Museum but of all museums in America, would have been without the sweep of his great achievements, which gave us a wholly new conception of the mammalian kingdom and of the close portrayal of nature in animal habitat groups.

Professor Osborn also told his staff: "This Museum has benefited throughout more than half a century by high talent among men and women in its service, but Akeley was the only genius who has been among us."[3]

Akeley's wife, Mary, was exaggerating, however, when she called his muskrats at the Milwaukee Public Museum the "first true habitat group." Several exhibitors had already produced or were producing museum groups. Charles Willson Peale, in his Philadelphia Museum in the eighteenth century, exhibited naturally posed birds and small animals with environmental features such as reproduced plants and with accurately painted backgrounds. Others exhibited less true-to-nature storytelling groups, for instance, Jules Verreaux's "Arab Courier Attacked by Lions" shown at the Paris Exposition of 1867. William Temple Hornaday in 1879, while still working at Ward's and after an expedition to India and Borneo, prepared a group of five orangutans, entitled "Battle in the Treetops," that created a sensation when shown at a meeting of the American Association for the Advancement of Science. Later, as chief taxidermist at the Smithsonian's United States National Museum, he added several outstanding groups there, employing many of the same principles that Akeley was to follow.[4]

II

Carl Ethan Akeley was born on a farm in Orleans County west of Rochester, New York, on May 20, 1864. His father, Daniel Webster Akeley, had come from Vermont, and his mother, born Julia Glidden, was a member of a somewhat aristocratic family of the Rochester area. He attended country school, did farm chores, and was an enthusiastic hunter and student of birds. At age twelve, Carl read an advertisement in the *Youth's Companion* for a book on taxidermy; it cost one dollar, but he managed to borrow a copy from an older boy. He stuffed a canary for a woman and, at age sixteen, had some business cards printed that read: "Carl E. Akeley—Artistic Taxidermy in All Its Branches." He took some lessons in painting in a nearby town and then, for some six weeks, attended Brockport Normal School during the day and, in the evening, observed an Englishman, David Bruce, painter, decorator, and amateur taxidermist, as he worked.

Bruce suggested that he go to see Professor Henry A. Ward, who ran Ward's Natural History Establishment at Rochester, collecting and selling specimens and other objects to colleges and museums and employing several taxidermists, among whom was Frederic A. Lucas, to be in turn director of the Brooklyn Museum and the American Museum of Natural History. Hornaday later described Ward as having "the nervous energy of an electric motor, the imagination and vision of Napoleon, the collecting tentacles of an octopus, and the poise of a Chesterfield."[5] Akeley walked three miles to take the train to Rochester, and then went beneath the arch made by the jaws of a sperm whale and past a big stuffed gorilla in front of the fifteen buildings of Ward's Establishment. He paced back and forth shyly and finally entered Ward's office, to be greeted with a gruff "What do you want?" Ward hired him as a student taxidermist at only $3.50 per week, though his room and board cost $4.

Akeley got to know the other taxidermists and became a close friend of William North Wheeler from Milwaukee, also aged nineteen, whom Ward had hired at $9 weekly. The two young men read the classics aloud together, took long walks, attended the Universalist Church, and went to lectures, one of them on "Which Way?" by the agnostic Robert Ingersoll, whom they found inspiring and witty. Wheeler was to meet many scientists during his long and successful career, but he later asserted that, "Of all the men I have known," Carl seemed "to have the greatest range of innate ability."[6] Akeley spent four years at Ward's, but his experimental approach to taxidermy was not always appreciated. Ward fired him after his first year, and for six months he worked in the New York taxidermy shop of John Wallace. Ward then rehired him, saying that his dismissal had been based on false reports.

Akeley decided that he would like to enter the Sheffield Scientific School at Yale, but failed the entrance examination. Wheeler, who had returned to Milwaukee to teach in the German Academy, urged him to come there and offered to tutor him. Akeley delayed leaving Ward's because "Jumbo," P. T. Barnum's famed elephant, had been killed in Canada in an encounter with a railroad locomotive, and Ward's was to treat the remains. Akeley took the leading role in preparing the huge carcass for exhibition with Barnum's circus (it later went to the Museum at Tufts University) and also in articulating the skeleton for the American Museum of Natural History.[7]

In the fall of 1886, Akeley moved to Milwaukee and set up a taxidermy shop in a barn that belonged to Wheeler's mother. He did much work for the Milwaukee Public Museum and was added to its staff, while Wheeler became the museum custodian (director) there. Akeley studied animal anatomy and experimented with producing manikins for the mounted bodies. One of the museum board members obtained a sledge from lapland, and Akeley modeled a reindeer to pull it and an authentically dressed Laplander as driver with waxen face and hands. He also did the group of orangutans from Borneo and planned a series on Wisconsin fur-bearing animals. He completed "Muskrats at Home" in 1893 and later, in his shop, prepared a horse for the Smithsonian Institution to show at the Columbian Exposition in Chicago, and a buck's head, entitled "The Challenge," that won first prize in a Sportsman's Show at New York (where, incidentally, Theodore Roosevelt was one of the judges). Akeley stayed in Milwaukee for eight years, and his friend Wheeler was the cause of his leaving. While traveling in Europe, Wheeler called on Sir William Fowler, director of the British Museum of Natural History, and told him of his friend's superior talent in taxidermy, whereupon Sir William offered Akeley a position.[8]

When Akeley left Milwaukee in 1895 on his way to London, he stopped at the Field Columbian Museum in Chicago. Dr. Daniel Giraud Elliot, the curator of zoology, offered him several taxonomic commissions, which he decided to accept, and in the next year he went to Africa with Dr. Elliot on a collecting expedition. At Chicago, Akeley perfected his procedure for producing habitat groups. He did a series on Virginia deer—life-sized dioramas showing them in spring, summer, fall, and winter. He planned several extensive habitat halls for the Field's new building, but when they failed to receive financing, he moved on in 1909 to work for the American Museum of Natural History in New York, where he remained until his death. He kept in touch with the Field Museum, however, and the two institutions often cooperated on projects.[9]

While in Chicago, Akeley was married, in 1902, to Delia J. Denning of Beaver Dam, Wisconsin. She accompanied him on two African expeditions and nursed him after an almost fatal encounter with an elephant. After World War I, the marriage deteriorated and the couple separated, Carl living in New York bachelor quarters with two companions, Vilhjamar Stefansson, the explorer, and Herbert

J. Spinden. This was probably the period that Robert Cushman Murphy recalled when coteries of writers, painters, savants, and creative men of affairs would sit late at dinner in the Century Club and get "Ake" to talk about his varied experiences.[10] In March 1923, Delia accused him of mental cruelty, and an acrimonious divorce ended the marriage. Carl was wed to Mary L. Jobe in October 1924. He was sixty years old and she, thirty-eight. Mary was an experienced mountain climber and explorer, who had made seven expeditions in the Canadian Rockies, and the Canadian Government had named a high peak there "Mount Jobe" in her honor. She also conducted Camp Mystic in Mystic, Connecticut, in summers to teach young girls physical fitness and outdoor survival skills.[11] Stefansson took her to the American Museum to meet Akeley in 1922, and she described him at work on a gorilla group as follows:

> Carl came in. He was wiping his hands on a wad of tow. His shirt sleeves were rolled above his elbows and his clothes were bespotted with plaster. Behind his flecked spectacles his eyes smiled—almost twinkled. Little did either of us dream that one day, we would be together climbing the high forested mountains of his beloved Africa.[12]

Akeley got along well with young people, and he trained several staff members to be taxidermists. Louis P. Jonas, who worked with him for three years at the American Museum, admired his "constant supply of surprising ideas" and well described him:

> The old khaki trousers he wore when he worked, the corn cob pipe he smoked but more frequently allowed to grow cold in his absorption in his task, I remember as part of his beloved personality. To me then as now it seems that the encouragement and inspiration which Akeley gave to the rising naturalists of his day were among his most valuable gifts to his fellow men—contributions which will leave a profound influence for many years to come upon those who worked with him.[13]

Akeley himself told Mary during his last African expedition: "I want twenty more good years for work. Then African Hall [his great conception for the American Museum] will be so nearly finished that the men who know my methods and have worked with me can carry it on to final completion."[14] His life was to end on that journey, but James L. Clark, Robert H. Rockwell, Richard G. Raddatz, and others completed his dream.

Akeley was also an ingenious inventor. At Chicago about 1909, the old building for the Columbian Exposition that then housed the Field Museum was losing patches of stucco. Akeley modified an air spray gun that he used in building manikins so that it could spread liquid cement and gave the building a fresh coating. His patented Cement Gun was employed on the Panama Canal and many other projects. After experiencing, on his African expedition of 1909–1910, the limitations of the motion picture camera then in use, he devised and patented the Akeley Camera, which would pan up and down, from side to side, and diagonally. It also easily made use of telescopic lens and had a faster shutter that permitted photography in poorer light. With his new camera, Akeley photographed elephants, lions, gorillas, and other African wildlife, and the team of Martin and Osa Johnson used it on their photographic explorations in Africa for the American Museum. The camera also recorded the last race of Man O'War and the Dempsey-Carpentier heavyweight fight. Robert L. Flaherty employed it for *Nanook of the North* and *Moana*, and it became the favorite of many other documentary filmmakers. The Franklin Institute of Philadelphia awarded Akeley its Scott Medal for inventing the Cement Gun and its John Price Wetherill Medal for the camera.[15]

During World War I, Akeley was a dollar-a-year man in the Engineer Corps, solving many problems. His camera photographed battlefield scenes, and the Cement Gun lined trenches and helped produce concrete boats, which, however, proved unsuccessful. He worked on large searchlights, furnishing them with a mirror system, and on an improved tank. He was constantly on call to the Shipping Board, Bureau of Standards, Ordnance Department, and National Research Council. The engineers would often remark about a problem: "Let's see what Akeley says."[16]

III

Carl Akeley was one of those fortunate broadly-based human beings whose touch of genius expressed itself in varied fields. He was equally at home in the arts of taxidermy and sculpture or the practicalities of mechanical invention. The real governing force of his life, however, became a deep, even passionate love for Africa and its wildlife. It irritated him to have it called the "Dark Continent," and he entitled his book *In Brightest Africa*. He insisted that gorillas were not the fierce, aggressive creatures they were sometimes pictured, but generally gentle and would attack humans only if defending their young. Elephants usually avoided conflicts with hunters, and the courageous lion "is a gentleman," not at all vindictive and rarely "man-eating." Akeley soon forgot the voracious mosquitoes, rampant malaria, stifling heat of the tropics, and cold, heavy rain of the mountains. He rejoiced in the Kivu area of the high Belgian Congo with its three smoking volcanic cones—Bisoke, Karisimbi, and Mikeno.

He told his wife there: "This is the Kivu at last. Here the fairies play: Isn't this forest the most beautiful, the most ancient in all the world?" He often said that he wanted "to die in the harness" and "to be buried in Africa."[17]

On Akeley's first African trip, to British Somaliland in 1896 for the Field Museum as Dr. Elliot's assistant, he was enchanted by the great herds of game that he saw. He did not kill lightly but only to secure museum specimens, to provide food for the expedition, or for bait. On that trip he obtained examples for fifteen large groups that he mounted for the museum on his return. They included the African buffalo, mountain nyala, Swayne's hartebeast, rare dibatag (Clark's gazelle), beim (small antelope), wild ass, zebra, wart hog, spotted and striped hyenas, jackal, cheetah, leopard, white-tailed gnu, quereza monkey, aardvark, black forest hog, bongo, and giant sable antelope. A dangerous high point of the tour was his hand-to-hand battle with a leopard, which, as he was hunting ostriches, sprang on him suddenly and knocked his gun to the ground after he had fired a shot that hit one paw. The beast bit him along his arm, but Akeley got his hand down its throat to keep it from biting elsewhere, partially strangled it, fell on top of it breaking several of its ribs, and finally killed it with a knife brought by one of the native bearers. Akeley's hand was mangled, his body covered with bloody scratches and bruises, upon which he poured disinfectants liberally.[18]

In 1905–1906 Akeley made his second journey, this time to British East Africa. He took a young Kikuyu lad of twelve or thirteen, Uimba Gikungu, whom he called "Bill," on the safari, and Bill served him well, usually as gun boy, on subsequent trips. Akeley was his *Bwana*, and, on the last expedition, Mary Akeley his *Memsahib*. Akeley took the white hunter, Richard J. Cunningham, with him on the first part of the tour to teach him how to hunt elephants. He then went to Uganda on his own and collected thirteen species of animals for the Field Museum's African Hall. Upon his return, he mounted the two huge elephants, "The Fighting Bulls," that still dominate the Field's entrance hall.[19]

Akeley's third African venture was for the American Museum of Natural History, in 1909–1910. He studied then mainly elephants, lions, and the lion-spearing hunts of the natives and wished to obtain elephants for an outstanding group for the museum. Theodore Roosevelt was also on safari with his son Kermit, and the two expeditions joined for a time. T. R. shot a cow elephant for Akeley's proposed group, and Kermit, a baby elephant, while Carl secured a magnificent old bull and a younger male. Upon his return to New York, he mounted an impressive group of the four, entitled "The Alarm."

James L. Clark, whom the American Museum had earlier sent to Chicago to study with him, was astonished when he joined Akeley in Africa to find him well along in treating three elephant hides. Clark commented thus: "How Akeley had done it, I cannot guess, but by dint of working all night himself and by working the natives as well, he had managed to get the skins of three of those huge beasts before we arrived."[20] Such bursts of energy were typical of Akeley, and he frequently labored all night in the field or later at the museum when mounting specimens.

On that expedition, Akeley was attacked and almost killed by a raging bull elephant when his gun jammed. He had the presence of mind to grasp the two tusks and swing between them, but the beast mashed his chest with its trunk and pushed the tusks into the ground, intent upon crushing him to death. Fortunately, the tusks struck a stone or other impediment, and the elephant left him for dead in order to attack some of the bearers. Akeley was unconscious for about six hours; the natives thought he had expired and superstitiously refused to touch him. They did send word to the camp, and Delia Akeley pressed through the night to reach him. He had suffered a broken nose, his cheek cut open to the teeth, one eye closed, his forehead bleeding, and several ribs cracked and protruding into the lungs. He spent several months recovering, and some of his friends thought that he was slowed down permanently by the attack. One positive result of the incident was that, upon his return home while still recuperating, he began to plan a great African Hall for the American Museum.[21]

Akeley's fourth tour to Africa, in 1921–1922, went to the high gorilla country of the Belgian Congo. Mr. and Mrs. Herbert E. Bradley of Chicago accompanied him along with their five-year-old daughter, Alice, a governess, and a woman secretary. Akeley took the women and the child along to show that Africa, with its gorillas, was a relatively safe place. He was intent upon obtaining a mountain gorilla group for his African Hall. Bradley shot a huge male, known as the "Giant of Karisimbi," and Akeley secured a younger male, a female, and her four-year-old son. The male he shot came crashing down a steep incline but was stopped by a tree, and Akeley skinned it in that precarious position. The female took a similar fall into a deep abyss, where he had difficulty in securing the hide. Mrs. Bradley was worried about his health and wrote:

We reached the camp and found Mr. Akeley looking as if years instead of days had intervened. He was very worn; he had done the work of ten men under particularly trying conditions; he had started with a fever, had been infected with jiggers . . .; he had killed his gorillas in most inaccessible places where his natives had balked at following; he had skinned and skeletonized and dissected without rest, and now energy and appetite had deserted him. We felt troubled when we saw him, but a good dinner . . . began to make him feel better.[22]

Akeley was transported by the beauty of the volcanic Kivu region and vowed to return to gather proper surface and plant accessories and to bring along an artist to paint the awe-inspiring scene for background. Upon his return to the museum, he mounted the four gorillas in a naturally posed group with the old bull thumping its chest.[23]

During the next few years, Akeley completed drawings and blueprints for his African Hall and made a scale model. The main room was to be 152 feet long, 60 feet wide, and 30 feet high. On a platform in the center would stand the great elephant group, "The Alarm," flanked by black rhinoceroses at one end, and white rhinos at the other. By this time Akeley had become a skillful sculptor. He planned to install life-sized bronzes that showed three Nandi natives hunting lions while armed only with spears. In one sculpture, two of the natives had thrown their spears, wounding one of the lions, while the third hunter stood ready to meet their onset. Another bronze had the lion and lioness charging, and the third portrayed the hunters chanting a requiem over the dead beasts. Stanley Field, president of the Field Museum, was so impressed by the sculptures that he agreed to pay for two bronze copies of each plaster original, one set to be exhibited in each of the two African Halls. At the other end of the American Museum's installation, one would see other Akeley bronzes—of a combat between a lion and buffalo; "At Bay," showing an elephant caught in a trap; and "Jungle Football," with four baby elephants playing with a dirt ball, a fragment of a sun-baked ant hill.

The hall was to be dimly illuminated but with two levels of forty well-lighted habitat groups in hermetically sealed alleyways behind glass so as to provide uniform temperature and humidity. Four larger corner groups on the first floor showed a dozen species on the equatorial river Tana; a plains group with baboons, zebras, and elands; a Congo forest with gorillas, okapi, and chimpanzees; and a desert water hole with a sixteen-foot-high reticulated giraffe drinking while surrounded by other animals. Below the second level, a bronze bas-relief in twenty-four panels portrayed African natives in their villages with their domestic animals or on the hunt.

President Osborn of the American Museum was enthusiastic about Akeley's plan for the new hall, and agreed to ask the City of New York to finance a new wing to contain the African Hall; he urged Akeley to secure funding for another tour to obtain animals. In 1925, Daniel E. Pomeroy, a wealthy friend of Carl's from New York, took him to meet George Eastman, the Kodak photographic entrepreneur, who also was a big game hunter. Akeley described his project to Eastman with unrestrained enthusiasm and at once, undiplomatically, asked him for a million dollars. The outcome was that Eastman put up $100,000 for four habitat groups, Pomeroy $25,000 for one, and his friend, Colonel Daniel B. Wentz of Philadelphia, $25,000 for another. The three men were to go on safari in Africa with Akeley to secure animals for their groups; unfortunately, Colonel Wentz died before he could leave, but his contribution remained. The American Museum also sent two preparators—Robert H. Rockwell and Richard C. Raddatz—and two artists to paint background scenes—Arthur A. Janson and William R. Leigh.[24]

Carl and Mary (it was her first journey to Africa) left in January 1926 for London, where they completed gathering supplies. They then stopped in Brussels to meet King Albert. Carl had suggested in 1922 that the king set aside an area ten miles square in the Kivu region as a sanctuary for mountain gorillas and other wildlife, and the king had established Parc National Albert in 1925. He now asked Carl to survey the plot during the expedition, and he agreed to have Dr. Jean M. Derscheid, the Belgian zoologist, go along.

The Akeleys went on by way of Genoa, the Suez Canal, and Mombasa to Nairobi in Kenya. There they soon met Eastman and Pomeroy as well as Martin and Osa Johnson, who were photographing African animals. When the Akeleys in three lorries and a Chevrolet car began to gather specimens, Carl was depressed to see that wildlife was disappearing under the onslaughts of farmers, ivory poachers, and greedy big game hunters. The Akeleys met an old Boer farmer, who emphatically wished to see the "vermin zebra" exterminated. After hunting buffalo fruitlessly in the Tana River region, Carl said: "I have not appreciated the absolute necessity of carrying on the African Hall . . . as I do now after this painful revelation. *The old conditions, the story of which we want to tell, are now gone and in another decade the men who knew them will be gone.*"[25]

The expedition had some lighter moments, as in May on Carl's birthday, when Mary arranged a surprise party with a wonderful cake, a bouquet of wildflowers gathered by Leigh, clever place cards drawn by Jansson, and special drinks concocted by Raddatz.[26] There were also some solid successes. Mary Akeley was a good executive (she called herself a "proper safari manager and general factotum") and soon took over the difficult task of dealing with the native bearers. Carl shot a magnificent reticulated giraffe bull and a female, and in Tanganika they saw a total of 146 lions, of which Carl obtained excellent motion pictures. Bill, the gun boy, sighted a fine black-maned lion that *Memsahib* shot. But by August, Carl was running a high fever, apparently typhoid, and was alarmingly weak. Mary had him loaded into a lorry and sat beside him as they set out over 300 miles of rough country for Nairobi. After treatment at the hospital there, Carl reluctantly spent three weeks in the Kenya Nursing Home.

On October 14, despite Mary's protests, he insisted that he had recovered, and they started for the Kivu. Carl still was far from well but always outdistanced Mary on the trail; he told her what his secret was: "There is only one way to get through. I just put my head down and go." On October 18, they celebrated their second wedding anniversary. The native porters sang to them and received the customary *baksheesh*, or gratuity. The expedition reached the Kivu in November, but Carl frequently had to be carried in a hammock, with Mary walking beside him. By November 13, he was spending the day in bed, and on November 17, he died, perhaps from pneumonia, dysentery, typhoid, or exhaustion. He was buried on Mount Mikeno in a grave cut eight feet into the soft lava rock; a concrete slab covered the coffin of native mahogany, bearing the simple inscription: "Carl Akeley/November 17, 1926."

Rockwell, the preparator, and Leigh, the artist, later wrote books that described the expedition. Both men were enchanted by the African countryside and awed by Akeley's personality and his driving determination. Rockwell said that "Carl saw as his great mission in life the preservation for posterity of a monumental and lifelike record of the fauna of this great bright continent. To the best of my ability I dedicated myself to the same ideals that had fired this creative genius."[27] Leigh thought that he "was in the company of a great— a tremendous temperament . . . a great soul—a blazer of new trails." He added: "Such a spirit as Akeley's does not often appear in this world. He had the rare quality—seldom understood or appreciated because it is so unusual—of complete devotion to art. It was his God."[28] Both men observed that he did not get along with Eastman, who refused to give him an additional $500,000 for his project. Rockwell described personalities well. He found Pomeroy a jovial, happy companion in contrast to the somber, cold, and dour Eastman, and he thought "feminine little Osa [Johnson], a courageous daredevil if I ever saw one."[29] Akeley gave Rockwell much responsibility and had him shoot specimens in addition to gathering plants and other environmental material for the habitat groups.

Mary Akeley was determined that the expedition should be completed, and she assumed its leadership. She later wrote: "We had to keep faith with him who had such faith in us. There was nothing else to do." She located the spot that Carl had chosen as background for his gorilla group (he had thought it the "most glorious scene in Africa") and set Leigh to making sketches, while Raddatz and she photographed the rocks, trees, and foliage of the site and took samples in formalin or plaster casts that would enable the preparators to create an accurate foreground. In April 1927, the Akeley-Eastman-Pomeroy Expedition reached the United States, sixteen months after it had departed.[30]

The Akeley African Halls at the American Museum and the Field Museum, both of them conceived and partially mounted by Carl Akeley, were dedicated in 1927, but the New York one was not opened in largely completed form until 1938. Mary Akeley did much to keep her husband's memory alive. She was an accomplished writer, capturing the African scene much more vividly than Carl. She produced seven good books on Africa, between 1929 and 1951, mainly on Akeley's work, using Carl's journals and her own daily diary as a basis. Delia Akeley threatened to sue Mary for libel because, in telling of Carl's deadly encounter with the bull elephant, she had credited the courageous dash through the night to reach him to Bill, the gun boy, instead of Delia. The first Mrs. Akeley made an African expedition of her own in 1925 and wrote a book about it, and an earlier work of hers was devoted to J.T., Jr., a pet monkey that Carl and Delia had acquired on one trip. Both wives thus took advantage of their African experiences to claim a share in Akeley's fame.

Mary Akeley continued to take a deep interest in the Parc National Albert in the Belgian Congo. King Albert formally inaugurated it in 1929 with an enlarged area of 500,000 acres. An American Committee for the park was formed with President Osborn a member and Mary Akeley as secretary. The king bestowed upon her the Cross of the Knights of the Order of the Crown of Belgium. She took two more African trips, one to South Africa to inspect wild animal sanctuaries and another to the Congo, during which she revisited Carl's grave.[31]

Carl Akeley's contributions to museums were outstanding. He perfected the habitat group that showed animals and their environment accurately, effectively, and hopefully permanently. Careful study of animal anatomy and *ethos*, of the rocks, soil, and plants of the habitat, and of scenic backgrounds would guarantee the naturalness and liveliness of the exhibit. Attention to the use of lasting materials in the whole display, safe lighting, and nonfluctuating temperature and humidity would insure a high degree of permanence. Good natural history museums in America and throughout the world adopted Carl Akeley's version of the habitat group.

But Akeley had come to have a higher personal aim. His youthful zest and tremendous nervous energy, tempered with kindliness and blessed with a whimsical sense of humor, found a passionate outlet. As his friend Pomeroy put it: "Akeley lived for Africa. He knew the primitive Africa and he saw it being destroyed. Then to preserve and portray Africa for posterity became the single purpose of his life. He dedicated his life to the task of bringing Africa to America."[32] And as one surveys the two African memorial halls, in Chicago and New York, one must conclude that he succeeded brilliantly.

NOTES

1. Carl E. Akeley, *In Brightest Africa*, memorial edition (Garden City, N.Y.: Garden City Publishing Co., 1932), 4–5; Mary Jobe Akeley, *Carl Akeley's Africa: The Account of the Akeley-Eastman-Pomeroy African Hall Expedition of the American Museum of Natural History* (New York: Dodd, Mead & Co., 1929), 300–08; Mary Akeley, *The Wilderness Lives Again: Carl Akeley and the Great Adventure* (New York: Dodd, Mead & Co., 1940), 14–19, 196–99, 223–24; "Akeley's African Hall," *Mentor* 13 (Jan. 1926): 1–52; "Akeley Memorial Number," *Natural History* 27 (1927): 133–60; Nancy Oestrich Lurie, *A Special Style: The Milwaukee Public Museum* (Milwaukee: Milwaukee Public Museum, 1983), 14–20; Robert Cushman Murphy, "Carl Ethan Akeley, 1864–1926," *Curator* 7 (Dec. 1964): 307–20; Douglas J. Preston, *Dinosaurs in the Attic: An Excursion into the American Museum of Natural History* (New York: St. Martin's Press, 1986), 78–93; Mary L. Jobe Akeley Papers, American Museum of Natural History, 6 boxes.
2. Mary Akeley, *Wilderness Lives Again*, 35.
3. Ibid., 76, 361–62; Murphy, "Carl Ethan Akeley," 307.
4. Mary Akeley, *Wilderness Lives Again*, 30–32; Edward P. Alexander, *Museum Masters: Their Museums and Their Influence* (Nashville: American Association for State and Local History, 1983), 43–77; William Temple Hornaday, *Taxidermy and Ecological Collecting: A Complete Handbook* (New York: Charles Scribner's Sons, 1891), 99–178, 218–304. The "Arab Courier Attacked by Lions" is illustrated in *Curator* 6 (1963): 178.
5. Sally Gregory Kohlstadt, "Henry A. Ward: The Merchant Naturalist and American Museum Development," *Journal of the Society for the Bibliography of Natural History* 9 (Apr. 1980): 651.
6. Mary Akeley, *Wilderness Lives Again*, 20–21; William Morton Wheeler, "Carl Akeley's Early Boyhood and Environment," *Natural History* 27 (1927): 135.
7. Carl Akeley, *Brightest Africa*, 1–8; Mary Akeley, *Wilderness Lives Again*, 4–12, 39–101; "Carl Ethan Akeley," *Dictionary of American Biography*, 1: 132–33.
8. Carl Akeley, *Brightest Africa*, 8–10; Mary Akeley, *Wilderness Lives Again*, 22–39; Lurie, *Milwaukee Public Museum*, 14–20.
9. Carl Akeley, *Brightest Africa*, 10–19; Mary Akeley, *Wilderness Lives Again*, 12–26, 202–07; Chesly Manly, *One Billion Years on Our Doorstep;...Six Articles on the Chicago Museum of Natural History* (Chicago: Chicago Museum of Natural History, 1959), 55–64.
10. Murphy, "Akeley," p. 308.

11. New York *Times*, Oct. 21, 1923; New York *World*, Oct. 19, 1924; New York *Herald*, Oct. 19, 1924; New York *Herald Tribune*, Apr. 15, 1927; Lewis E. Akeley to Roy Chapman Andrews, Dec. 12, 1936, all in Mary L. Jobe Akeley Papers.

12. Mary Akeley, *Wilderness Lives Again*, 189–201; Preston, *Dinosaurs in the Attic*, 86–88; "Mary Jobe Akeley," *Geographical Journal* 12 (Dec. 1966): 597–598; *Notable American Women: The Modern Period* (Cambridge, Mass.: Harvard University Press, 1980), 8—10.

13. Mary Akeley, *Wilderness Lives Again*, 215, 362–63.

14. Ibid., 220. See also 378–85.

15. Carl Akeley, *Brightest Africa*, 164–68; Mary Akeley, *Wilderness Lives Again*, 114–16, 141–43; F. Trubee Davidson, "Akeley, the Inventor," *Natural History* 27 (1927): 124–29; Clyde Fisher, "Carl Akeley and His Work," *Scientific Monthly* 24 (Feb. 1927): 109–11.

16. Carl Akeley, *Brightest Africa*, 168–72; Mary Akeley, *Wilderness Lives Again*, 210–12.

17. Mary Akeley, *Carl Akeley's Africa*, 189–90.

18. Carl Akeley, *Brightest Africa*, 63–67, 97–103, 114–38; Mary Akeley, *Wilderness Lives Again*, 39–59; Mary Akeley, *Carl Akeley's Africa*, 1–4; Carl Akeley and Mary L. Jobe Akeley, *Adventures in the African Jungle* (New York: Dodd, Mead & Company, 1930), 68—95; Carl and Mary Akeley, *Lions, Gorillas, and Their Neighbors* (New York: Dodd, Mead & Company, 1933), 217–36.

19. Carl Akeley, *Brightest Africa*, 131–33; Mary Akeley, *Wilderness Lives Again*, 78–101; Carl and Mary Akeley, *Adventures in the African Jungle*, 25–46; Manly, *One Billion Years*, 55–64.

20. Mary Akeley, *Wilderness Lives Again*, 105.

21. Carl Akeley, "Elephants," *World's Work* 41 (Nov. 1920): 77–92; Mary Akeley, *Wilderness Lives Again*, 103–07, 119–26, 135–37; Carl and Mary Akeley, *Adventures in the African Jungle*, 1–24, 180–94.

22. Mary Akeley, *Wilderness Lives Again*, 181.

23. Carl Akeley, *Brightest Africa*, 188–210, 221–24, 229–32; Carl and Mary Akeley, *Lions, Gorillas and Their Neighbors*, 124–48; Mary Hastings Bradley, "In Africa with Akeley," *Natural History* 27 (1927): 161–73.

24. Carl Akeley, *Brightest Africa*, 251–67; Akeley, "African Hall: A Monument to Primitive Africa," *Mentor* 13 (Jan. 1926): 10–22; Mary Akeley, *Wilderness Lives Again*, 208–12, 223–43, 378–85.

25. Mary Akeley, *Wilderness Lives Again*, 290.

26. Robert E. Rockwell, *My Way of Becoming a Hunter* (New York: W. W. Norton & Co., 1955), 216–18.

27. Ibid., 216.

28. William R. Leigh, *Frontiers of Enchantment: An Artist's Adventures in Africa* (New York: Simon and Schuster, 1938), 6, 252.

29. Rockwell, *Becoming a Hunter*, 208–09, 232.

30. Mary Akeley, *Wilderness Lives Again*, 244–314, 322–23, 340–41.

31. Ibid., 342–58, 378–85; Mary Akeley, *Carl Akeley's Africa*, 247–58; Manly, *One Billion Years*, 55–64; "Akeley Memorial African Hall," 1–89; Carl Akeley, "African Hall" and "Have a Heart: A Statement and Plea for Fair Game Sport in Africa," *Mentor* 13 (Jan. 1926): 10–22, 47–50; Baron de Cartier de Marchienne, "Akeley, the Conservationist," *Natural History* 27 (1927): 115–17; Fisher, "Akeley and His Work," 117; "Mary Jobe Akeley," *Geographical Journal* 112 (Dec. 1966): 597–98; Delia J. Akeley's books are *"J.T., Jr.," the Biography of an African Monkey* (New York: Macmillan Company, 1928) and *Jungle Portraits with Original Photographs* (New York: Macmillan Company, 1930). See also her "She Feels Safer in the Jungle!" Kansas City *Journal-Post*, July 15, 1928, in Mary Jobe Akeley Papers. Mary Akeley's

books, in addition to those cited above, are *Restless Jungle: With Many Illustrations* (New York: R. N. McBride and Company, 1936); *Rumble of a Distant Drum: A True Story of the African Hinterland* (London: George C. Harrap & Co., 1948); and *Congo Men: Historical Background and Scientific Aspects of the Great Game Sanctuaries of the Belgian Congo* (London: Victor Gallancz, 1951).

32. Mary Akeley, *Wilderness Lives Again*, 223–24.

SELECT BIBLIOGRAPHY

Akeley, Carl E. "African Hall: A Monument to Primitive Africa." *Mentor* 13 (Jan. 1926): 10–22.

_____. "Elephants." *World's Work* 41 (Nov. 1920): 77–92.

_____. "Have a Heart: A Statement and Plea for Fair Game Sport in Africa." *Mentor* 13 (Jan. 1926): 47–50.

_____. *In Brightest Africa.* Memorial edition. Garden City, N.Y.: Garden City Publishing Co., 1932.

Akeley, Carl and Mary L. Jobe. *Adventures in the African Jungle.* New York: Dodd, Mead & Company, 1930.

_____. *Lions, Gorillas, and Their Neighbors.* New York: Dodd, Mead & Company, 1933.

Akeley, Delia J. *"J.T., Jr.," the Biography of an African Monkey.* New York: Macmillan Company, 1928.

_____. *Jungle Portraits with Original Photographs.* New York: Macmillan Company, 1930.

Akeley, Mary Jobe. *Carl Akeley's Africa: The Account of the Akeley-Eastman-Pomeroy African Hall Expedition of the American Museum of Natural History.* New York: Dodd, Mead & Co., 1929.

_____. *Congo Men: Historical Background and Scientific Aspects of the Great Game Sanctuaries of the Belgian Congo.* London: Victor Gallancz, 1951.

_____. *Restless Jungle: With Many Illustrations.* New York: R. N. McBride and Company, 1936.

_____. *Rumble of a Distant Drum: A True Story of the African Hinterland.* London: George C. Harrap & Co., 1948.

_____. *The Wilderness Lives Again: Carl Akeley and the Great Adventure.* New York: Dodd, Mead & Co., 1940.

"Akeley Memorial Number." *Natural History* 27 (1927): 133–60.

"Akeley's African Hall." *Mentor* 13 (Jan. 1926): 1–52.

Alexander, Edward P. *Museum Masters: Their Museums and Their Influence.* Nashville: American Association for State and Local History, 1983.

Bradley, Mary Hastings. "In Africa with Akeley." *Natural History* 27 (1927): 161–73.

"Carl Ethan Akeley." *Dictionary of American Biography*, 1: 132–33.

Davidson, F. Trubee. "Akeley, the Inventor." *Natural History* 27 (1927): 124–29.

de Marchienne, Baron de Cartier. "Akeley, the Conservationist." *Natural History* 27 (1927): 115–17.

Fisher, Clyde. "Carl Akeley and His Work." *Scientific Monthly* 24 (Feb. 1927): 109–11.

Hornaday, William Temple. *Taxidermy and Ecological Collecting: A Complete Handbook.* New York: Charles Scribner's Sons, 1891.

Kohlstadt, Sally Gregory. "Henry A. Ward: The Merchant Naturalist and American Museum Development." *Journal of the Society for the Bibliography of Natural History* 9 (Apr. 1980): 651.

Leigh, William R. *Frontiers of Enchantment: An Artist's Adventures in Africa.* New York: Simon and Schuster, 1938.

Lurie, Nancy Oestrich. *A Special Style: The Milwaukee Public Museum*. Milwaukee: Milwaukee Public Museum, 1983.

Manly, Chesly. *One Billion Years on Our Doorstep;...Six Articles on the Chicago Museum of Natural History*. Chicago: Chicago Museum of Natural History, 1959.

"Mary Jobe Akeley." *Geographical Journal* 12 (Dec. 1966): 597–598.

Mary L. Jobe Akeley Papers. American Museum of Natural History. 6 boxes.

Murphy, Robert Cushman. "Carl Ethan Akeley, 1864–1926." *Curator* 7 (Dec. 1964): 307–20.

Notable American Women: The Modern Period. Cambridge, Mass.: Harvard University Press, 1980.

Preston, Douglas J. *Dinosaurs in the Attic: An Excursion into the American Museum of Natural History*. New York: St. Martin's Press, 1986.

Rockwell, Robert E. *My Way of Becoming a Hunter*. New York: W. W. Norton & Co., 1955.

Wheeler, William Morton. "Carl Akeley's Early Boyhood and Environment." *Natural History* 27 (1927): 135.

CHAPTER 3

Henry Watson Kent
Standardizes Functions
of the Art Museum

I

H ENRY WATSON KENT became the paid assistant secretary of the Metropolitan Museum of Art in 1905. He was recruited by Robert W. de Forest, sometimes referred to as New York's first citizen, who was serving as trustee and secretary of the museum during a period of reorganization. "General" Luigi di Cesnola (1832–1904) was a previous trustee and secretary, and then its first salaried director from 1879 until his death. He was a master of self-promotion (for example, he used the title of general when he had been only a colonel in the Civil War), and he unsuccessfully schemed to sell the museum two collections of Phoenician, Greek, Assyrian, and Egyptian artifacts that he had excavated while serving as United States Consul in Cyprus. Cesnola was hard working and spent long hours in the museum, but he ruled his small staff in autocratic and volatile fashion. He was accused of indiscriminately placing heads, arms, legs, and other features on the statues in the Cypriote Collection, and he resisted opening the museum on Sunday afternoons, though the trustees finally reluctantly did so in 1891. The younger trustees disliked the way Cesnola tactlessly antagonized trustees, staff, and the public and made a determined effort to dismiss him in 1895, but he managed to weather the storm.[1]

The founders of the Metropolitan in its charter of 1870 agreed to conduct a museum and library of art, to encourage and develop the study of fine arts and the application of arts to manufactures and practical life, and to furnish popular instruction and recreation. Though the trustees gave some lip service to having the museum serve the community, no great effort was made in the educational area, aside from offering some elementary art courses to students for a time and providing occasional special exhibitions and lectures.

The reorganization of the museum after Cesnola's death greatly expanded its scope and operations. J. Pierpont Morgan soon became president of the trustees; not only was he a world-class financier but the greatest art collector of his day. He persuaded wealthy friends to join him as trustees and, when an annual deficit occurred, would go around the board room table, his intense black eyes commanding gifts. He secured as the new director Sir Caspar Purdon Clarke, head of the South Kensington (Victoria and Albert) Museum in London. Edward Robinson, director of the Museum of Fine Arts in Boston, became assistant director. Sir Caspar was largely a figurehead and Robinson, the museum's chief executive, became director in 1910. But the everyday administration was in the hands of Kent, strongly backed by de Forest, who succeeded Morgan as president. Kent lived near the de Forests, and he would stop often for a working breakfast on his way to the museum.

Kent was appalled by the lack of system that he found. Cesnola had tried to make all the decisions himself. There was only one typewriter and one telephone (in the library), no information desk, little communication with the staff, and animosity among the three curators that occasionally led to fisticuffs. Kent set up normal business procedures and regarded himself as "the *entrepreneur* between the initiators of all action, the trustees, and their employees."[2] He instituted scientific methods of registration, accessioning, cataloguing, communication, and publication. De Forest and he were determined to make the museum an educational institution. Kent, long a close friend of John Cotton Dana, director of the Newark (New Jersey) Museum, said that their friendship "was also an education for me in public relationships, of which he was a master."[3] The two men vied to see which one could do the most to make his museum serve its community. Dana in 1920 needled Kent, saying that the Metropolitan's attendance was just under one million yearly, the same as the Newark library and museum in "a God-forsaken town in the estimation of many, in a still more God-forsaken state, in the estimation of others; and a very unimportant museum therein."[4]

In the curatorial field, Kent made many contributions, especially in the collection of American antiques that resulted in the American Wing. Meanwhile, Morgan and de Forest backed Egyptian expeditions and obtained other outstanding collections that began to make the Metropolitan a museum of national and even international importance. It started gradually to abandon many of the materials in the Cypriote Collection and in its comprehensive holdings of plaster casts.

All in all, Kent was the "dean" of American museum education for many years. He lived up to his motto of "art for the people's sake . . . for the enjoyment, for the study, and for the profit of the people." And Calvin Tomkins probably is right in considering him "without doubt, the greatest museum man of his generation."[5]

II

Henry Watson Kent was born on September 28, 1866, at Boston, the son of Robert Restieaux and Eliza (Watson) Kent and a descendant of sturdy New England Puritan families. He attended Boston Latin School for a time and then, from 1881, the Free Academy of Norwich, Connecticut. He and his sister roomed there with the Rev. Charles T. Weitzel, and Kent studied German with him. He worked at the Boston Public Library during the summer of 1884 and, that fall, embraced the "profession of Librarianship" by entering the experimental library science course at Columbia College, taught by Melvil Dewey, whose students served as interns in the Columbia Library and became thoroughly familiar with innovative library procedures that included decimal classification. Kent pointed out later that Dewey's library students were trained first of all as public servants, while museum curators and directors of that day had no such background and thus "few of them seem to have imbibed the notion of the importance of that relationship."[6] Ill health caused Kent to drop out of the program and go to Florida in 1886, but he returned two years later, to work in the card catalogue section of the library. Professor William R. Ware, who headed the department of architecture at Columbia, then made a crucial suggestion, that Kent ought to try museum work. His opportunity came in 1888 when he was offered the position of librarian at the Peck Library of the Norwich (Connecticut) Free Academy and curator of the newly established Slater Memorial Museum there. Both institutions occupied the impressive Slater Memorial Building, which contained academy classrooms and an auditorium that provided the community with an atheneum and lyceum for lectures, music, and small study groups.

Edward Robinson, at that time the learned curator of classical collections at the Museum of Fine Arts, was brought in to select, purchase, and arrange in chronological order 124 plaster casts of Greek sculpture and architecture and 103 of Italian, some of them on revolving pedestals. They comprised the main collection of the museum, though in addition there were electrotypes of Greek coins, small Renaissance plaster reproductions, and numerous photographs of paintings and European architecture. According to a speaker at the opening ceremonies, the museum had "a collection unsurpassed, perhaps unequaled, by any that is owned by any college in the land."[7] One of Kent's first tasks was securing a plasterer to install fig leaves in the right places on the casts before the opening of the museum.

During his twelve years at the Norwich library and museum, Kent carried on a vigorous and varied program. He arranged twenty-seven special exhibitions in order to secure repeat visitation from the community and to attract viewers from many states and several foreign countries. Among the subjects treated were Barbizon paintings; rugs, tapestries, embroideries, and brocades; portraits of men and women of early Norwich; local silversmiths; Norwich publications; children's books; and fine bindings. Yearly attendance at the museum during the period reached as high as 12,000.

The academy established an Art School, Normal School, and manual training department, all of which worked closely with the museum. The art classes stressed design and its application to industries; some academy graduates became designers in the textile and jewelry factories that were so numerous in the region. Kent taught various academy and Art School classes, often in the museum galleries, on history of art, history of sculpture, and Greek sculptures. He had for long been enthusiastic about fine printing and bookbinding, and he persuaded the academy to secure a small press and establish a course in printing that sometimes provided labels and did other small jobs for the museum. On one occasion, he helped the students stage seven tableaux from the *Iliad*, making their own costumes and constructing a Greek chair.

Kent arranged several public school class visits, not a usual museum activity in that day. First graders made sketches of the casts and toured the museum; one time, "an almost terrified hush" took place when a small black boy, wide-eyed, pointed at a huge centaur and whispered: "There is God!"[8] Pupils from more advanced grades made visits, and a Saturday morning art class included sketching and stories about the casts. Nor did Kent neglect the Peck Library. He built it up to contain 12,000 volumes and 65 periodicals and newspapers, with author and title catalogue. The students used it constantly, and the public was invited to do so every afternoon. It was one of the largest school collections in the country and, in the field of art, ranked with college libraries.

Meanwhile, Kent was studying early American history, architecture, and arts and crafts, so respected in the community, and meeting prominent early collectors of decorative arts. Among them were H. Eugene Bolles and Dwight Blaney of Boston, George S. Palmer of New London, and Harry Harkness Flagler of New York. They were collecting paintings, furniture, silver, textiles, and other examples of Americana at a time when the art museums of the country were devoted almost exclusively to European and Near Eastern art from ancient times to the nineteenth century. In 1883, Kent made an extensive, eight-month European tour, visiting museums from Turkey, Greece, and Italy to Germany and Britain, taking notes accompanied by sketches of administration, services to the public, catalogues, exhibit displays, publications, and such practical matters as chairs, benches, pedestals, and bulletin boards. He was impressed by the historical period rooms he saw in Zurich, Nuremberg, and Munich, which sought to give visitors a journey through history, and by Director Wilhelm Bode's period rooms and other innovations in Berlin.

At home, Kent was in demand to advise museums on collecting and installing casts—at the Rhode Island School of Design; the Metropolitan Museum, which sent its special committee on casts to Norwich and had Kent arrange its exhibition; the Buffalo Fine Arts Academy; the City Library Association in Springfield, Massachusetts, where he began his friendship with John Cotton Dana; and, somewhat later, the Carnegie Institute in Pittsburgh.

At that time, art historians were convinced that original ancient sculptures were no longer obtainable and that American museums ought to form comprehensive cast collections for the sake of art students, aspiring artists, and the many high school and college pupils studying Greek and Latin. Thus, Pierre Le Brun, the architect assembling casts for the Metropolitan, expressed the common wisdom when he wrote in 1885:

> Collections of casts are springing up in all the older communities, and they have a completeness and a unity not found possible in museums of originals. Such collections must undoubtedly be the main dependence of our American fine-art institutions. . . . We cannot hope to stock them adequately with antiquities. Chances of acquiring valuable collections of originals are rare and will become rarer.[9]

Such predictions underestimated the efforts of archaeological expeditions, the expansion of museum collections to include Oriental, European, and even American decorative arts, and the tremendous increase of American wealth that allowed collectors and museums to take advantage of revolutionary changes in Europe which released treasures thought to be permanently fixed there.

Kent was a well-organized administrator who gave meticulous attention to detail and the completion of projects. Those qualities impressed de Forest, and led to Kent eventually being hired by the Metropolitan. His personality is fascinating to examine: a bachelor, he was later renowned for his icy reserve and rigid self-control, but he had a multitude of good friends in the Norwich community as well as among collectors of Americana throughout the region and the bibliophiles who cherished fine printing and the arts of book production. He got along well with the students in his classes, especially the young women, and he later hired several of them at the Metropolitan.

In 1900, Kent left Norwich to become assistant librarian of the Grolier Club in New York. That organization had been formed in 1884 to promote the arts involved in the production of books and to advance the use of good paper, typography, presswork, illustrations, and binding. Its founders were either students of fine printing or practitioners of the printing trades. They admired French progress in that field and named their club after Grolier, the French sixteenth-century bibliophile. They were also wealthy and maintained a comfortable clubhouse, where they accumulated a superb library, held well-attended stereoptican lectures and special exhibitions, and issued handsomely crafted publications.

Kent admitted that he had moved to the Grolier "with the hope that I might go on to the Metropolitan Museum,"[10] but he delighted in bibliographical work and in 1903 became librarian of the club. He formed close friendships with the great bookmen of the day, such as Robert Hoe, manufacturer of rotary printing presses; William Loring Andrews, collector of New York historical prints; and Samuel P. Avery, successful art dealer and philanthropist. Kent also became acquainted with the leading typographers and printers, including the veteran Theodore L. Devine, Daniel Berkeley Updike, Bruce Rogers, and Carl P. Rollins, as well as the engravers Rudolph Ruzica and August Jaccaci; afterwards, he used such talent in issuing Metropolitan publications.

Kent enjoyed living in New York, and he joined the Century Club and, for a time, the Players Club. He was never happier than he was at the Grolier, and he maintained his enthusiasm for the printing arts for the remainder of his life. He served as president of the Grolier Club for six years and of the American Institute of Graphic Arts for three years. The institute gave him its gold medal in 1930 "in appreciation of a career of notable influence in the field of graphic arts" and "the deepest influence on typography."[11] The Pierpont Morgan Library in 1938 arranged a special exhibition of printing done at the Metropolitan under Kent's supervision and praised him for "raising the standard of institutional printing to that of one of the Fine Arts."[12] The extent of his interest and influence is glimpsed in the bibliography of his publications prepared by Lois Leighton Comings for his autobiography, *What I Am Pleased to Call My Education*; of a total of 185 entries, some 75 are devoted to the art of bookmaking.

III

As assistant secretary of the Metropolitan, Kent took the minutes of the trustee meetings, and his attendance there kept him fully informed of policies and let the trustees know him well and appreciate his services. As soon as he arrived at the museum, he began to devise businesslike systems for handling its usual activities. Not only was his own position added to the staff, but also those of a registrar and a photographer. If an object was offered by gift or bequest and was accepted by the trustees after favorable recommendations by the director, the curator concerned, and the trustee committee, Kent notified the director with copies to the curator and registrar, who already had received the object. The number placed in the accession book and on the object itself included the year and the numeral indicating its order in the annual accessions. A catalogue card was then prepared with the photograph of the object reproduced on the back. Secretary, registrar, photographer, curator, and sales department all saw the card, added information and made what entries they needed from it. Purchases were treated somewhat similarly, though the price was included in the record. Kent in 1911 gave a full account of the system to the annual meeting of the American Association of Museums in Boston and urged his listeners to use such an arrangement in their museums and let him have any suggestions for improvement.[13]

Kent established an information desk at the entrance to the museum. It answered members' and visitors' questions and sold post cards, photographs, slides, and museum publications. He edited the museum *Bulletin*, which began publication late in 1905; it carried articles on acquisitions and art history matters by the curators and full accounts of educational activities so as to keep members, staff, and other museums informed. It began as a quarterly but was so popular that, within a year, it changed to a bimonthly and then a monthly, ultimately attaining a circulation of 16,000. Kent also secured a small press to print labels, announcements, menus, and the like. He arranged for the *Bulletin* and other larger printing jobs, including books, to be done by good designers and printers so that, beginning in 1921, the museum usually had one or more titles listed in the *Fifty Best Books of the Year* chosen by the American Institute of Graphic Arts. The Morgan Library's special show of Metropolitan publications said that Kent had "added to his other duties the fostering of the Museum Press . . . with such enthusiasm and genuine love for beautiful printing that it has become an artistic asset to the Museum."[14]

A reading of the *Bulletin* during Kent's administration shows that he gave attention to the smallest details. Among many possible examples of his care, a "rolling-chair" was offered for those who could not walk, and later on, someone could be hired to push it for fifty cents an hour. Alterations were made to improve the electric wiring, and rest rooms were rejuvenated. Changes were frequently noted for the museum's restaurant, and it finally was turned into a cafeteria. Chairs were provided in the galleries to decrease visitors' "museum fatigue." Of great importance, a Metropolitan Museum Employees Association was begun, and years later it staged a minstrel show for de Forest's eightieth birthday, while several special exhibitions were held of the art work of the employees. Kent looked after such details as part of the duties of his entrepreneurship.[15]

Even more significant, however, were Kent's efforts, always backed by de Forest, to provide a strong educational program. First of all, he analyzed the museum's audience and classified it as follows:

1. The idle and curious, who came on holidays with their friends to see what it was all about.
2. The people who came with a desire to learn.
3. The real students of art and archaeology, who knew what they wanted and how to study.
4. The teachers and pupils of the public schools, who came because the School Board told them to do so.
5. The practical people, manufacturers and designers, who employed the arts of design as part of their business.
6. The artist who wanted to widen his knowledge, and the copyist.
7. Museum members who paid for their privileges or inherited them.[16]

Kent at once began to improve facilities for handling visitors in accord with his analysis. In the school field, for example, the friendly Sir Caspar spoke to high school teachers of English one Saturday on how the museum could help their students, and a similar session was held for teachers of economics and history. A classroom accommodating 250–300 with stereoptican equipment, blackboard, and easels was set aside for teacher and student groups, who were admitted free of charge while ordinary visitors usually paid. A new lecture hall with improved acoustics would hold 400 listeners. In 1908, Kent added an expert guide to the staff, who took school classes studying chiefly art, history, dressmaking, or applied design about the collection. School classes were free, but individuals were charged 25 cents. Kent thus was following the example of the Museum of Fine Arts in Boston, which a year earlier had established its office of "docent." As attendance increased, a second guide was added who also visited the schools. The class tours elicited favorable comments from the students, such as: "How soon may we come again?" and "I was here yesterday, and I saw the armor myself, and now I am bringing my mother to see it."[17] Kent also began to send slides, mounted photographs, textiles, casts, and other objects to the schools for classroom use and to lend such materials at the Information Desk to libraries, hospitals, and other community centers at a modest charge. The city superintendent of schools cooperated by assigning Dr. James P. Haney, supervisor of art in the high schools, to work with the museum.

Kent inaugurated a broad-based lecture program designed to appeal to all the different audiences. It reached members; members' children; the general public with art history sessions every Saturday and more popular talks on Sunday; public school teachers and pupils; students in the New York art schools; and aspiring designers along with department store buyers and salespeople. Story hours were held for children every Saturday morning, as well as special classes for the disabled. The speakers came from the staff—for example, Director Robinson with six lectures on Greek art and Albert Lythgoe and Herbert Winlock on Egyptian excavations—or were visiting authorities from home or abroad. The teachers heard educational leaders, such as Dr. G. Stanley Hall, president of Clark University, or Professor Frank Jewett Mather of Princeton, and they also learned what other museums were doing in the field from Louise Connolly of Dana's Newark Museum or the charismatic Anna Billings Gallup, curator of the Brooklyn Children's Museum. New York University, Columbia Teachers College, and City College offered lecture courses at the museum, for which tuition was charged. In 1918, musical concerts, with David Mannes as conductor, were held on certain Saturday evenings and became most popular; they were financed by private contributions, often by John D. Rockefeller, Jr.[18]

Kent was especially interested in using the museum, in accord with its charter, to assist industrial design. Not only were lectures provided for designers, furniture makers, interior decorators, weavers, other craftspeople, and department store supervisors and sales clerks, but a series of industrial exhibitions was begun. Its thirteenth edition, held in 1934, drew 139,296 visitors in 63 days, record attendance for a show of that length. Kent also experimented with lending museum materials widely, at first with traveling exhibitions in the country east of the Mississippi through the American Federation of Arts. Then, in 1935, after a branch museum he planned failed to receive financing, he sent circulating exhibits on Chinese and Japanese art, European armor, and ancient Egypt to community groups in the city. He was hoping to develop a chain of branch exhibit centers, and by 1938 there were seven collections on tour, serviced by Works Progress Administration workers, in one college, four high schools, one branch library, one museum, and one "Y" branch, that reached a total of 474,912 viewers. These community exhibits, a conscious effort to meet demands for the decentralization of the museum's collection, now included motion pictures, many of them made by the museum, and it also added radio broadcasts to its extension activities.[19]

The expansion of the education program enhanced Kent's position at the Metropolitan. In 1907 he was appointed supervisor of museum instruction and six years later, upon de Forest's accession to presidency of the trustees, Kent became secretary. He also headed the department of industrial relations. He received assistance with his heavy load when Richard F. Bach, formerly of the Columbia School of Architecture, came in 1918 to work with trade journals, manufacturers, and designers, and when Huger Elliott, former principal of the Pennsylvania Museum's School of Industrial Art, arrived in 1925 to handle museum instruction. Kent also appointed George Lauder Greenway to be assistant secretary.[20]

Kent's skillful and energetic administration changed the whole concept of the purposes of the Metropolitan Museum. When he began work, it was a traditional art museum of that day devoted to the collection, conservation, and research of art objects, but de Forest and he made its first aim to provide visual instruction. As Bach expressed it, the Metropolitan became a museum of service, a museum of daily use, a museum to aid industry, and a museum that was an instrument of education. The New York *Times* declared that the museum's annual report of 1923

> makes it clear that this Museum is not a mere repository for things gathered out of the past from many civilizations, but that it is a live educational force. It is not a place alone of conserving and recording; it is an institution for teaching

through its collections the love of [art] . . . The diffusion of art in its highest forms will not only be helpful to the students and artisans of every branch of industry, but will "tend directly to humanize, to educate and refine a practical and laborious people."[21]

Kent was determined that the new concept of the museum should be understood nationally and internationally. As early as 1908, he organized a session at the London meeting of the Third International Art Congress on museums and the schools. Roger Fry of London, Alfred Litchtark of Hamburg, and others spoke. Viscount Sudeley, a member of the British House of Lords, was so impressed that he secured an act of Parliament appointing guide lecturers for London museums with special emphasis on teachers and school pupils. Kent attended sessions of the Museums Association of Great Britain and sent Elliott and Bach to other meetings, such as that of the Sixth International Congress on Art Education held in Prague. Kent also took a leading part in the formation of the American Association of Museums in 1906 and regularly attended its annual meetings. In the *Bulletin*, he followed the activities of American and European museums and the annual meetings and special seminars of their professional organizations. He was determined to see that a skilled museum profession should develop both in America and abroad.[22]

Kent often left the collections and research upon them to the director and curators, but he was the chief force in persuading the Metropolitan to gather and exhibit American paintings and decorative arts in period room settings. While at Norwich, he had come to appreciate Americana and to know its chief collectors. In 1909 when the Hudson-Fulton Celebration was held in New York, the Metropolitan decided to offer a special exhibition of Dutch old master paintings by Rembrandt, Hals, Vermeer, and others as well as some decorative arts. Kent pointed out that the show ought to include Americana for the Fulton part of the celebration. Edward Robinson, soon to become the director, opposed the idea because he shared the common opinion of art historians of the day that European or ancient art was far superior to that of America. Robinson consulted his former co-workers and friends at the Museum of Fine Arts, who supported his opinion. Kent, however, convinced de Forest, chairman of the commemoration committee, of the soundness of his concept and assured him that such an exhibition would attract popular enthusiasm and attendance. The result was that the museum borrowed American paintings, furniture, silver, and other art objects of the period 1625–1825 from the leading collectors of the day. The materials, arranged along the walls in the museum galleries, constituted the first exhibition of American antiques to be held in the city. It aroused great public excitement in the forty-one days it was shown and attracted greater attendance than did the Dutch masterpieces.

During the exhibition, H. Eugene Bolles told Kent that he would like to sell his collection then on display. Kent at once went into action. He invited Mr. and Mrs. de Forest and R. T. Haines Halsey to be his guests on a trip to New England. They talked with George Francis Dow, curator of the Society for the Preservation of New England Antiquities in Boston, and visited the three pioneer American period rooms that he had done in 1907 while curator at the Essex Institute in Salem. They saw other such installations at Danvers, Topsfield, Beverly, and Boston. When they returned home, Mrs. Russell Sage (de Forest was her lawyer) agreed to purchase the Bolles Collection for the museum, which also began to acquire such rooms with their interior architecture intact. Mr. Halsey, an experienced collector who had become a museum trustee and chairman of the committee on American decorative arts, took the lead in assembling those materials.

In 1922, Mr. and Mrs. de Forest (her father had been the first president of the museum) announced that they were financing entirely, at no cost to the city, a new wing to house the American rooms. They purchased the 1822–1824 facade of the old United States Assay Office (originally the United States Branch Bank) on Wall Street and gave it to the museum to serve as an entryway for the new wing. Kent pored over the plans, using Swiss and German museums as precedents. In 1924 the American Wing was opened with about a dozen eighteenth- and early nineteenth-century original rooms and two reproduced seventeenth-century ones from Massachusetts. Halsey, who worked harmoniously with Kent and de Forest, was the chief designer and curator of the project. The American Wing was an immediate hit with the public and had great influence on the dozens of historic houses being opened as museums, on many art museums, and later upon Colonial Williamsburg and the Henry Francis du Pont Winterthur Museum.[23]

Kent backed George Gray Barnard and his medieval cloister collection and rejoiced when John D. Rockefeller, Jr., financed its purchase for the Metropolitan. It opened in 1938 as The Cloisters in the elevated Fort Tryon Park site overlooking the Hudson. Kent also played an important role as consultant for the Cleveland Museum of Art, opened in 1916, helping design its building and plan its collection. He took a more cautious stance when it came to contemporary art at the Metropolitan; his warning was that "to buy the modern in haste is to repent at leisure."[24] Kent's later years at the Metropolitan were a period for receiving honors. The Architectural League of New York awarded him its Michael Friedman medal for "his service in the cause of industrial art." He was a leader in the Walpole Society of connoisseurs that he helped start in 1909, and he was elected a vice-president of the American Association of Museums. Hamilton College and Brown University gave him honorary degrees. He was sounded out for the directorships of art museums in Boston, Philadelphia, Buffalo, Indianapolis, and Cleveland, and for the librarianship of Williams College.[25]

But along with the honors went some disappointments. Kent's always carefully maintained reserve and his cultivated British accent brought some accusations that he was a frightful snob, and his young women assistants who called themselves his "willing slaves" could also be a source of ridicule. Kent in the beginning welcomed William M. Ivins, the museum's first curator of prints, for the two men shared a common interest in fine printing, but they came to quarrel loudly and bitterly. Kent's letter of introduction for one of his young women going abroad to study museum methods in London, Vienna, Berlin, and Paris stated that she "will occupy herself with the process of reproduction in those cities." The letter filled Ivins with malicious glee. More seriously, he once accused Kent of pushing him out of a taxi and causing him to fall on the curb. Kent also had to put up with Alan Priest, curator of Eastern art and a confirmed practical joker. Learning of the ship on which Kent was returning from Europe, he wrote the immigration officials that a notorious narcotics smuggler was aboard and gave them an exact description of Kent with his white hair and thin mustache. Kent had to undergo a searching examination from head to toe.[26]

Affairs took an unpleasant turn for Kent when Francis Henry Taylor became director of the Metropolitan in 1940. He had had a brilliant administration at the Worcester Art Museum with fascinating special exhibitions that attracted much interest from professionals as well as the public. Taylor, however, was a very different person from the seventy-four-year-old Kent—outgoing, impetuous, and given to telling humorous stories, many of them indelicate. He also had positive ideas about museum administration and considered Kent's methods old-fashioned and somewhat precious. He appointed Laurence S. Harrison his business administrator and had him report on each of the museum's departments. Kent demanded to see the reports on his sections, but Harrison said that only Taylor could approve that action. Kent went to see Taylor but submitted his resignation a few days later, to take effect at year's end. The Board of Trustees accepted the resignation with reluctance, made Kent secretary emeritus, praised his "unselfish, devoted, and untiring energy and intelligent and constructive foresight," and continued to call on him occasionally for advice. Though he undoubtedly felt that he had been treated shabbily after his thirty-five years of service, Kent maintained his reserve and did not complain in his autobiography. He died from a heart attack on August 28, 1948, in the summer hotel he regularly frequented.[27]

Kent was a most distinguished museum man for his day. He did much to make the premier aim of the American museum educational, but he did not neglect its collection, preservation, and research functions. In fact, he could be proud of his business-like organizational improvements that were so badly needed when he began work. And he did much to add professional standards to museum undertakings, not only in his own institution but also nationally and internationally. The museum world that he left in 1940 was a very different and much improved place from that of fifty years earlier, and he had played a responsible and valiant part in the change. To the end, his great ideal had been that "most austere of all mental qualities, a sense of style" based upon "attainment and restraint."[28]

NOTES

1. The chief sources on Kent and the Metropolitan Museum are Nathaniel Burt, *Palaces for the People: A Social History of American Art Museums* (Boston: Little, Brown, 1977); Stephen Mark Dobbs, "Dana and Kent and Early Museum Education," *Museum News* 50 (October 1971): 38–41; Howard Hibbard, *The Metropolitan Museum of Art* (New York: Harper & Row, 1980); Winifred E. Howe, *A History of the Metropolitan Museum of Art*, 2 vols. (New York: Metropolitan Museum of Art, 1913, 1946); Henry Watson Kent, *What I Am Pleased to Call My Education*, edited by Lois Leighton Comings (New York: Grolier Club, 1949); Henry Watson Kent and Florence N. Levy, *Catalogue of an Exhibition of American Paintings, Furniture, Silver, and Other Objects of Art, 1625–1825* (New York: Metropolitan Museum of Art, 1909); Leo Lerman, *The Museum: One Hundred Years of the Metropolitan Museum of Art* (New York: Viking Press, 1969); Calvin Tomkins, *Merchants and Masterpieces: The Story of the Metropolitan Museum of Art* (New York: E. P. Dutton, 1970). For Cesnola, see also Elizabeth McFadden, *The Glitter and the Gold: A Spirited Account of the Metropolitan Museum of Art's First Director, the Audacious and High-Handed Luigi Palma di Cesnola* (New York: Dial Press, 1971).

2. Tomkins, *Merchants and Masterpieces*, 116.

3. Kent, *My Education*, 102. See also Edward P. Alexander, "John Cotton Dana and the Newark Museum: The Museum of Community Service," in *Museum Masters: Their Museums and Their Influence* (Nashville, Tennessee: American Association for State and Local History, 1983), 377–411.

4. Dobbs, "Dana and Kent," 40.

5. Ibid., 39–40; Tomkins, *Merchants and Masterpieces*, 115.

6. Kent, *My Education*, 17.

7. Ibid., 49.

8. Ibid., 63.

9. Ibid., 108–09.

10. Ibid., 114. See also Brander Matthews, "The Grolier Club," *Century* 39 (Nov. 1889): 86–97.

11. Kent, *My Education*, 132–33.

12. Ibid., 152.

13. Metropolitan Museum *Bulletin* 2 (1907): 54–57; 6 (1911): 169–70; Kent, *My Education*, 141–43.

14. Metropolitan Museum *Bulletin* 33 (1938): 265–67.

15. Metropolitan Museum *Bulletin* 2 (1907): 85; 3 (1908): 233; 4 (1909): 85–86, 140; 5 (1910): 100; 7 (1912): 198–99; 10 (1915): 34; 13 (1918): 227–28; 17 (1922): 221; 20 (1925): 111; 23 (1928): 166; 30 (1935): 254; 38 (1939): 25–26.

16. Kent, *My Education*, 144–45.

17. Metropolitan Museum *Bulletin* 6 (1911): 63–64. See also 2 (1907): 85; 3 (1908): 46–47, 180; 5 (1910): 63–64, 201–07; 6 (1911): 148, 176; 7 (1912): 158–61; 8 (1913 supplement, Sept.): 6; 9 (1914): 223; 12 (1917): 205–06; 21 (1926): 202–17; Kent, *My Education*, 146–47.

18. Metropolitan Museum *Bulletin* 3 (1908): 46–47; 4 (1909): 230–31; 5 (1910): 63–64; 6 (1911): 63–64, 240; 7 (1912): 20–21, 158–61; 8 (1913): 110–11, 252, supplement (Sept.), 6–11; 9 (1914): 132, 190–94; 10 (1915): 112, 128–29, 241–42; 11 (1916): 182–204; 13 (1918): 52, 290; 15 (1920): 169; 16 (1921): 39; 17 (1922): 86; Kent, *My Education*, 147–49.

19. Metropolitan Museum *Bulletin* 4 (1909): 231; 6 (1911): 158; 9 (1914): 132; 10 (1915): 33; 11 (1916): 111, 189; 12 (1917): 93–94, 121; 13 (1918): 205–06, 290; 18 (1923): 311–12; 21 (1926): 20, 202–17; 22 (1927): 61; 23 (1928): 59; 24 (1929): 96–97, 158–67; 28 (1933): 183–84; 29 (1934): 186, 162, 182–84; 30 (1935): 18, 92–93; 31 (1936): 148–49; 33 (1938): 249–52; 35 (1940): 74–76; Howe, *Metropolitan Museum History*, 2: 203–05; Kent, *My Education*, 153–58.

20. Metropolitan Museum *Bulletin* 3 (1908): 46–47; 13 (1918): 288; 20 (1925): 137; 27 (1932): 147; Kent, *My Education*, 135, 156–57; Howe, *Metropolitan Museum History*, 2: 22, 69, 177.

21. Metropolitan Museum *Bulletin* 19 (1924): 91–92. See also 22 (1927): 238.

22. Kent, *My Education*, 145–46; Metropolitan Museum *Bulletin* 22 (1927): 224–25; 31 (1936): 149.

23. Metropolitan Museum *Bulletin* 4 (1909): 75–76, 181–83, 189, 196–97, 219–20, 230–31; 5 (1910): 5–16, 60; 17 (1922, part II): 1–23; 19 (1924): 251–65; Kent, *My Education*, 83–84, 160–64; Kent and Levy, *Catalogue of an Exhibition*; Howe, *Metropolitan Museum History*, 2: 22, 35–38; Wendy Kaplan, "R. T. H. Halsey: An Ideology of Collecting American Decorative Arts," *Winterthur Portfolio* 17 (Spring 1987): 43–53; Tomkins, *Merchants and Masterpieces*, 195–204.

24. Metropolitan Museum *Bulletin* 20 (1925): 166–77; 21 (1926): 114–20; 30 (1935): 98–100; Kent, *My Education*, 164–65; Tomkins, *Merchants and Masterpieces*, 249–50.

25. Metropolitan Museum *Bulletin* 20 (1925): 189; 27 (1932): 262; 29 (1934): 183–84; 31 (1936): 149; Kent, *My Education*, 161–62, 165–66.

26. Tomkins, *Merchants and Masterpieces*, 212–13, 241–42, 279.

27. Ibid., 266–76.

28. Kent, *My Education*, 167–68.

SELECT BIBLIOGRAPHY

Alexander, Edward P. "John Cotton Dana and the Newark Museum: The Museum of Community Service." In *Museum Masters: Their Museums and Their Influence*. Nashville, Tennessee: American Association for State and Local History, 1983.

Burt, Nathaniel. *Palaces for the People: A Social History of American Art Museums*. Boston: Little, Brown, 1977.

Dobbs, Stephen Mark. "Dana and Kent and Early Museum Education." *Museum News* 50 (October 1971): 38–41.

Hibbard, Howard. *The Metropolitan Museum of Art*. New York: Harper & Row, 1980.

Howe, Winifred E. *A History of the Metropolitan Museum of Art*. 2 vols. New York: Metropolitan Museum of Art, 1913, 1946.

Kaplan, Wendy. "R. T. H. Halsey: An Ideology of Collecting American Decorative Arts." *Winterthur Portfolio* 17 (Spring 1987): 43–53.

Kent, Henry Watson. *What I Am Pleased to Call My Education*. Edited by Lois Leighton Comings. New York: Grolier Club, 1949.

Kent, Henry Watson, and Florence N. Levy. *Catalogue of an Exhibition of American Paintings, Furniture, Silver, and Other Objects of Art, 1625–1825*. New York: Metropolitan Museum of Art, 1909.

Lerman, Leo. *The Museum: One Hundred Years of the Metropolitan Museum of Art*. New York: Viking Press, 1969.

Matthews, Brander. "The Grolier Club." *Century* 39 (Nov. 1889): 86–97.

McFadden, Elizabeth. *The Glitter and the Gold: A Spirited Account of the Metropolitan Museum of Art's First Director, the Audacious and High-Handed Luigi Palma di Cesnola*. New York: Dial Press, 1971.

Metropolitan Museum *Bulletin*. Vols. 2–38 (1907–1939).

Tomkins, Calvin. *Merchants and Masterpieces: The Story of the Metropolitan Museum of Art*. New York: E. P. Dutton, 1970).

CHAPTER 4

Alfred Hamilton Barr Jr.
Brings Modern Art to the Museum

I

A NEW MUSEUM OPENED in New York on the afternoon of November 7, 1929. Six small galleries on the twelfth floor of the Hecksher Building on Fifth Avenue and 57th Street contained a special loan exhibition entitled *Cezanne, Gauguin, Seurat, and van Gogh* to introduce the Museum of Modern Art. The first afternoon was reserved for invited guests, but, next day, the general public came flooding in. Such openings of the museum's special exhibitions from the beginning were considered chic social events, and many of those attending were dressed to the nines. The times were not auspicious for the new venture, for the precipitous and alarming collapse of the stock market in the previous month had signaled the start of the worst economic depression of the twentieth century. But the museum founders and the participating public were unaware that industrial and social blight would encompass the whole globe and, ten years later, merge into catastrophic world war.

The founders of the new museum were three women, familiarly known as "The Ladies." All three were wealthy collectors of art produced from the latter part of the nineteenth century to their own day. Miss Lillie (often called "Lizzie") P. Bliss, whose father was a rich textile merchant and manufacturer, attended the famed Armory Show of 1913 devoted to advanced European art of the time. Its most shocking single piece was Marcel Duchamps's *Nude Descending a Staircase*. Miss Lillie admired Arthur B. Davies, the romantic artist who was the chief organizer of the show and, under his guidance, purchased five of the paintings—two Redons, two Degases, and a Renoir. She went on to obtain other works by these artists and by Cezanne, Seurat, Matisse, Picasso, and Toulouse-Latrec, more than one hundred examples in all. Miss Lillie was shy and retiring but may be considered the intellectual leader of the founding trio.

The second lady was Abby Aldrich (Mrs. John D., Jr.) Rockefeller, daughter of a powerful United States senator, sister of a leading banker, and wife of the wealthiest philanthropist in the country. She had collected the productions of modern American and European artists for many years and, since her husband had more conventional tastes, she made her purchases with her "Aldrich" money and had a private gallery upstairs in their home for her own and her children's enlightenment and pleasure. Mrs. Rockefeller was the trio's most capable organizer, a skillful problem solver full of energy, and a calm, warm person who communicated well with others. The third lady was Mary Quinn (Mrs. Cornelius J.) Sullivan. She had taught art for many years and, at age forty, had married a successful lawyer. Lillie Bliss and she were close friends, who helped Davies finance the Armory Show and listened to his pleas for the establishment of a museum to promote the new art. As a person, Mary Quinn was the most enthusiastic of the founders, described by another of her friends as a "whizbang" and "sparkplug."[1]

Lillie Bliss and Abby Rockefeller were vacationing in Egypt during the winter of 1928 and talked about founding the new museum; when Mrs. Rockefeller returned from Europe later that spring on the same ship with Mrs. Sullivan, they exchanged views on the subject. Back home, the three continued their discussions, and, late in May, Mrs. Rockefeller invited A. Conger Goodyear to luncheon with them. A colonel in the first World War, he had business interests in Buffalo. The Ladies were attracted by his enthusiasm for modern art, of which he had an extensive collection. He had served as trustee of the Albright Gallery in Buffalo and briefly as president until the trustees voted him off the board when he purchased a Picasso for the gallery. In the middle of the lunch, Mrs. Rockefeller, speaking for the Ladies, asked Goodyear to become chairman of a committee to organize "a new gallery or museum in New York that would exhibit works of art of the modern school."[2] Goodyear asked for a week to think over the proposal but called the next day to accept.

The new chairman added three members to the committee—Frank Crowninshield, the editor of *Vanity Fair*, a collector of modern paintings and sculpture, and an experienced publicist; Professor Paul J. Sachs, teacher of the well-known "museum course" at Harvard, curator of the Fogg Museum there, and a leading collector of drawings; and Josephine Boardman (Mrs. Winthrop

Murray) Crane, widow of an executive of the Crane Paper Company; he had been governor of Massachusetts and a United States senator. The committee decided upon "The Museum of Modern Art" as a name and petitioned the Regents of the University of the State of New York for a charter. They stated that the purposes of the new institution were "establishing and maintaining in the City of New York, a museum of modern art, encouraging and developing the study of modern arts and the application of said arts to manufacture and practical life, and furnishing popular instruction." The Regents granted a provisional charter on September 19. With the Board of Trustees official, it added several new members, all leading collectors of modern art—Stephen C. Clark, Samuel A. Lewisohn, Chester Dale, Duncan Phillips of Washington, and three others. Of these, only Clark and Lewisohn took prominent parts in the new museum. The trustees raised $115,000 for each of the first two years and rented space in the Hecksher Building at $12,000 per annum.[3]

The next important step was the appointment of a director. Professor Sachs, who was well acquainted with the art museum field and had trained many of its personnel, recommended Alfred Hamilton Barr Jr., twenty-seven years old and teaching art history at Wellesley College. After he had visited Mrs. Rockefeller twice at her summer home in Seal Harbor, he was appointed director in 1929, with a salary of $10,000 plus $2,500 for travel, and made a member of the board. His friend Jere Abbott became associate director, and there were three other paid staff members and one volunteer.

Goodyear went abroad to try to borrow works for a French exhibition, but he, Crowninshield, Sachs, and Barr had wished to open the museum with the work of modern American artists. The Ladies, however, insisted adamantly upon a French show. Its thirty-five Cezannes, twenty-six Gauguins, seventeen Seurats, and twenty-seven van Goghs attracted long waiting lines and overburdened the Hecksher elevators. When the exhibition closed a month later, some 47,000 persons had seen it. The newspapers and art critics found it superb. And Barr was responsible, not only for its attractive arrangement, but for the handsome catalogue that contained pictures and descriptions of each work as well as his perceptive and thoughtful Foreword.

II

Alfred Hamilton Barr Jr. was born in Detroit on January 28, 1902, the son of Barr, Sr., and Annie Elizabeth (Wilson) Barr. The father, a Presbyterian minister, was a graduate of Princeton and its Theological Seminary, and the mother had attended Vassar for two years. The home's emphasis on serious intellectual achievement had much to do with the son's scholarly thoughtfulness and zeal. The family moved in 1911 to Baltimore, where Alfred attended the Boys' Latin School. He collected tin soldiers (with his friends refighting the battles of Gettysburg and Waterloo), played chess, and engaged enthusiastically in birdwatching. He edited the *Inkwell*, the school paper, and was graduated *cum laude* in 1918 as the Head Boy who delivered the class valedictory. That fall he entered Princeton with a four-year scholarship and, the next year, decided to major in art, largely because of a class he took in medieval art with Professor Charles Rufus Morey that included architecture, sculpture, painting, the minor arts, and crafts. He then had "Modern Painting" with Professor Frank Jewett Mather and upheld Matisse's worth in arguments with his teacher. Barr graduated a Phi Beta Kappa with high honors in 1922 and attended graduate school there the next year, receiving his M.A.

In 1923 Barr began teaching art history at Vassar and, in the next spring, staged an *Exhibition of Modern European Art* there with sixty-one items borrowed from New York dealers. He spent the summer in Europe and, in the fall, entered Harvard Graduate School as fellow and teaching assistant. He took courses with Professor Sachs on drawings of the old masters and on engraving and etching. In the spring of 1925 he passed his oral examination for the doctorate, and Professor Sachs wrote Professor Morey at Princeton to congratulate him "on the perfectly splendid student you have developed" in Barr. In the examination, Sachs thought "that he acquitted himself better than any candidate during the time I have been here" and "that he had thought deeply and ranged widely over the whole field" of art history.[4]

That fall, Barr returned to Princeton for a year as preceptor in art and archaeology, and in 1926 he became associate professor of art history at Wellesley, living in Cambridge and attending Professor Sachs's "museum course." He also organized an exhibition on modern art for the Fogg Museum. In the spring of 1927, Barr taught with missionary zeal the first undergraduate course in modern art offered in this country; it included architecture, graphic design, photography, music, the theatre, motion pictures, decorative arts, and crafts. He devised an unusual entrance examination for the course and referred to its seven young women students as his "children." He put on an *Exhibition of Progressive Modern Painting from Corot to Daumier to Post-Cubism* at Wellesley's Farnsworth Museum with thirty-five pictures.

In the fall of 1927, Barr set out for a year in Europe, for which Professor Sachs arranged a grant, with his friend Jere Abbott. They visited London, Holland, and Germany, where they spent four days at the Bauhaus in Dessau and were impressed by the way it interrelated painting, graphic arts, architecture, crafts, typography, theatre, cinema, photography, and industrial design. They went on to Russia (Moscow, Leningrad, and Novgorod), Warsaw, Vienna, and Paris, visiting museums and closely inspecting architecture everywhere. Upon his return, he taught another year at Wellesley and, in the spring, received a prestigious Carnegie fellowship to the Institute of Fine Arts at New York University but, before he could begin work there, accepted the directorship of the Modern Museum.[5]

Barr obviously had learned much about modern art during his university and teaching experience. (He went on to receive his doctorate from Harvard years later with his book on Picasso serving as his dissertation.) He had visited museums here and abroad and knew how to borrow art works for exhibition, install them tellingly, and write convincing catalogues about them. As a person, he was low-keyed and somewhat shy, but his knowledge was great, his enthusiasm unlimited, and his approach to modern art almost religious in its crusading intensity.

Professor Agnes Ringe, who taught art at Vassar, brought her associate and friend, Margaret Scolari, to see the museum's opening exhibition and introduced her to Barr. She was a native of Italy; her father Virgilio was an antiques dealer in Rome, and her mother, born Mary Fitzmaurice, was Irish. "Marga," as Barr soon called here, was fluent in most European languages and was teaching Italian at Vassar. She also was a knowledgeable art historian. Marga and Alfred were married in May 1930, at first by a New York justice of the peace and then in Paris at the American Church so as to satisfy his mother. Marga was of the greatest help to Barr, who was not adept at foreign languages. She acted as interpreter with European artists, collectors, museum directors and curators, and dealers; her study of art and her sociability also helped make her an invaluable member of the Barr team. In addition she handled the practical concerns of the household and shared the economic burden, teaching art at the Spence School for thirty-seven years beginning in 1943. The Barrs had one child, Victoria, but neither of them attained much intimacy with her. Barr dedicated his book on Picasso to Marga, and, in acknowledging her enormous help with research and translation for his volume on Matisse, he wryly concluded: "In fact, without her, the author might not have survived his book."[6]

III

Special exhibitions were from the first the main concern of the Modern Museum, and the trustees and small staff worked furiously to stage two of them in the last two months of 1929 and six more the following year. Alfred and Marga began to go to Europe in the summer to secure art for future shows. The second exhibition on *Paintings by Nineteen Living Americans* attracted only about half the attendance of the opening one and received much adverse criticism from the art establishment, including, of course, the artists not invited to exhibit. The next show on *Painting in Paris from American Collections* with Picasso and Matisse as the stars more than regained public popularity, but *Forty-six Painters and Sculptors Under Thirty-five Years of Age* and *Painting and Sculpture by Living Americans* again secured fewer viewers and aroused considerable hostile comment. Still, everyone could agree that the museum was presenting exciting, even when controversial, exhibitions. Barr's mixture of scholarship and showmanship was making a large audience aware of the new art.

But the museum wished to be more than a gallery for special exhibitions. The Founders' Manifesto had promised a series of shows of the modern work of American and European artists for the first two years but also stated their intention "to establish a permanent public Museum which will acquire, from time to time, collections of the best modern works of art."[7] Much discussion took place among trustees and staff as to whether they should pass on to other more historically oriented museums, such as the Metropolitan, works that time showed to have permanent worth, just as the Luxembourg Gallery did in Paris for the Louvre. The idea of such an established relationship was dropped for the moment, but Goodyear talked of the collection as a kind of river with new works coming in now and then, and others going on elsewhere, while Barr defined the ideal permanent collection as a torpedo with its nose "the ever advancing present, its tail the ever receding past." He said later:

> The Museum is aware that it may often guess wrong in its acquisitions. When it acquires a dozen recent paintings it will be lucky in ten years if three will still seem worth looking at, and if in twenty years one should survive. For the future the important problem is to acquire this one; the other nine will be forgiven . . . and forgotten. But meanwhile we live in the present, and for the present these other nine will seem just as necessary and useful, serving their purpose by inclusion in exhibitions so long as their artistic lives shall last. Sooner or later, time will eliminate them.[8]

The permanent collection at first was tiny—five paintings and eight sculptures—and Barr's proposal to show it in a separate room was voted down. In 1931, however, Lillie Bliss died and left the museum most of her splendid collection. One condition of the bequest required that, within three years, the museum raise an endowment large enough to assure its continuation. The executors of the will at first placed that goal at $1 million, but later, in view of the raging economic depression, reduced it to $600,000, and the trustees succeeded in raising it.[9]

In 1932 the Rockefellers gave the former home of John D., Sr., on 53rd Street to the museum, and it moved there from its crowded quarters in the Hecksher Building. By then, Barr had worked himself to the edge of a nervous breakdown; assisted by his small staff, he had organized sixteen exhibitions and issued sixteen catalogues, carefully planned, enticingly written, and beautifully illustrated. The trustees wisely granted him a year off with half pay, and the Barrs spent the time in Europe, visiting artists, collectors, and museums, and still making arrangements for future shows. He was shocked to learn how Hitler, who had just come to power in Germany, was destroying modern art, and he wrote a series of articles entitled "Hitler and the Nine Muses" expressing his alarm but could find publication for only one of them, in Lincoln Kirstein's small *Hound & Horn* magazine at Harvard.[10]

A van Gogh exhibition in 1935 attracted nearly 125,000 viewers who, at 25 cents a head (the first time the museum charged admission), brought in more than $20,000. The police had to be called to keep the long waiting lines in order. Department stores sold color transparencies and ladies' dresses in van Gogh colors. The exhibition went on a triumphal tour to the Pacific coast and back; it reached a total of nearly 900,000 persons.[11]

Often, the shows stirred controversy, especially two in 1936 on *Cubism and Abstract Art* and *Fantastic Art, Dada, and Surrealism*. The latter contained Meret Oppenheim's *The Fur-lined Teacup*, complete with fur-lined saucer and teaspoon, and Duchamp's *Why Not Sneeze* with a small cage filled with sugar lumps and a thermometer. Barr's preface in the catalogue for the second exhibition explained that "Surrealism as an art movement is a serious affair and for many it is a philosophy, a way of life, a cause to which some of the most brilliant painters and poets of our age are giving themselves with consuming devotion." But the newspapers and the general public had a humorous field day. The show was to travel, and Goodyear and some other trustees tried to get Barr to eliminate what they considered ridiculous objects, but he refused to do so, and the museum's policy of not interfering with the decisions of a director of any exhibition was upheld, no matter how reluctantly.[12]

In 1938, after six years of negotiation by Goodyear, the museum sent *Three Centuries of American Art* to be exhibited at the Louvre's Jeu de Paume in Paris. In addition to the customary works of art selected mainly by Goodyear, the show contained exhibits of architecture, motion pictures, and photography. The French critics were "absolutely vicious" in judging both the historical and modern paintings and sculpture but found the architecture stimulating and praised Barr's catalogue. The movie showings (five times daily) frequently generated long lines and were recognized as a peculiarly American form of art. Unfortunately, though, attendance at the main exhibition was meager.[13]

As early as 1929, Barr had proposed to the trustees the extension of the museum's activities to cover architecture, industrial design, photography, stage settings, decorative arts, and motion pictures. He had taught his undergraduate class at Wellesley modern art based on that broad definition, and on his European trips had admired the way the Bauhaus was furthering that conception. The trustees postponed the plan, but in 1932 Barr began to implement it. With his friends Philip Johnson and Henry-Russell Hitchcock, he presented the *Modern Architecture: International Exhibition* that featured what Barr called the "International Style." They had been working on the show for two years, and it contained the designs of more than fifty modern architects including Wright, Gropius, Le Corbusier, Oud, and Mies van der Rohe; the new functionalism was emphasized with many models and photographs. It was the museum's first traveling exhibit and circulated among eleven other museums and a department store. As a result, Barr succeeded in establishing a new Department of Architecture with Philip Johnson as its unpaid director.[14]

Other parts of the broader art plan appeared through the years, the organization of new departments usually following important special exhibitions. *Motion Pictures, 1914–1934* resulted in the Film Library, which soon was showing old movies in the auditorium. Several smaller photographic shows and then *Photography, 1839–1937* preceded the organization of the Department of Photography. Philip Johnson's exhibition on *Machine Art* in 1934 and a series on industrial design that began with *Useful Household Objects Under $5* led to the Department of Industrial Art in 1940.[15]

In 1935 the museum established a Department of Circulating Exhibits with Elodie Courter, a Wellesley graduate, at its head. It sent out shows, the contents approved by Barr himself, chiefly to colleges, universities, libraries, museums, and department stores throughout the country. In its first six years, nearly one hundred exhibitions were displayed more than one thousand times in 222 cities of the United States, Canada, and Hawaii. Thus, thousands of persons, many of them enthusiastic college students, learned of the attractions of modern art. The museum also developed many educational activities for the schools, though Barr was not too interested personally in that area. But Victor d'Amico, a wonderfully warm art educator, joined the staff in 1937. He sent exhibits and slides to the New York high schools, conducted tours for their students at the museum, set up a Young People's Gallery with Saturday classes, and helped organize a National Committee on Art Education that improved the teaching of art in many schools of the region.[16]

The museum moved into greatly enlarged quarters in 1939. The old Rockefeller house was torn down, and a sleek, modern, functional building took its place. It had six floors with auditorium and lounge in the basement; three stories with movable partitions and flexible lighting for exhibits; two floors for Library, Film Library, and offices; and a penthouse Members' Lounge with a terrace. A Sculpture Garden visible from the building was situated in the rear. Philip L. Goodwin, a board member, had been the chief architect, but his traditionalism had been modified by his assistant, the young Edward Durrell Stone, a convinced modernist. Barr, then in Paris, had tentatively promised to employ Mies van der Rohe, but Goodyear and Nelson A. Rockefeller had chosen an American architect instead. Barr resigned from the building committee in protest, though his ideas continued to be transmnitted through staff members. He was largely responsible for the use of a new translucent material (Thermolux) on the entrance side of the museum and for the natural lighting employed throughout. The building committee and architects had opposed these features, and it was necessary later to build a false wall because the Thermolux let in too much light.[17]

At a trustee dinner two days before the opening of the new building, a changing of the guard took place. Goodyear (probably reluctantly) and Mrs. Rockefeller resigned as president and vice-president, and Stephen Clark became chairman with Nelson Rockefeller as president. Professor Sachs, who had been Barr's strongest backer on the board, urged the trustees in the next decade to devote more energy and funds to films, architecture, photographs, the Library, and a choice permanent collection. He warned against "*the danger of timidity*" and insisted that the museum "must continue to take risks" and "continue to be a pioneer . . . bold and uncompromising." Goodyear, who had often been Barr's chief opponent on policy matters, said at the dinner:

The pituitary gland, you know, has a very profound influence in the growth of the body. The skeleton cannot prosper without it, and when its activity is diminished, this leads to obesity and mental defects. Our pituitary gland is Alfred Barr. . . . It is useless for me to attempt to tell you what Alfred has done for us. I need only say, look about you.[18]

The change in the board leadership was the beginning of serious trouble for Barr. The trustees had always taken a greater share in the museum's administration than he would have preferred. When young Edward M. M. Warburg was appointed to the board in 1932, he argued unsuccessfully that the director ought to be given a free hand with exhibitions and other administrative matters; he thought that "Mrs. Rockefeller, Goodyear, Sam Lewisohn, and some of the others were frustrated museum directors."[19] Nelson Rockefeller, as the new president, brought some efficiency experts to analyze the staff and whether expenditures could be reduced. As a result, two upper staff members were dismissed, and another one resigned. All this was done without consulting Barr, who was then in Paris. Rockefeller went to Washington in 1940 as coordinator of the Office of Inter-American Affairs, and John Hay Whitney, who replaced him, joined the Air Force in 1942. Stephen Clark then became both chairman and president.[20]

Mr. Clark was a quiet, somewhat shy man who did not communicate well nor understand Barr. As a collector and connoisseur, he found Barr's taste erratic and sometimes frivolous, as when he exhibited Joe Milone's fantastically tinsel-bedecked shoeshine stand. Clark also was a good businessman, much concerned about the museum's finances and convinced that Barr was a careless administrator. Barr, on his part, could be uncommunicative and difficult. Goodyear referred to his fine Italian hand, and some critics called him a Svengali or Tallyrand in his relations with the trustees, but the fact is that he was often unperceptive and untactful. Despite Clark's worries about finances, Barr asked for raises for his staff and even sought a salary of $15,000 for himself. (He withdrew that request after Clark's shocked terse response.) The confrontation between the two men came to a head on October 16, 1943, when Clark wrote Barr that "in these difficult times the relatively unimportant work you are doing does not justify a salary of $12,000 a year." He ought to give his time to writing books and "assume the position of Advisory Director at a salary of $6,000 a year."[21] The letter was written with the approval of the more active and influential trustees. Mrs. Rockefeller tried to soften the blow somewhat by pointing out how important it was to the cause of modern art for Barr to write definitive books on the subject. But he was denied an office in the museum and apparently was expected to do his writing mainly at home. Barr simply refused to leave and fitted out a small cubicle for himself in the Library. He wrote his mentor Sachs that he was "still pretty damn sore" about the demotion and asked: "Were all the planning and all the exhibitions, and all the paintings I have bought and the standards I have fought for—was it someone else?"[22]

Most of the staff continued to consult Barr as if he were still director. By the time of the annual meeting in 1946, Clark had softened his animosity considerably. He reported that freeing Barr from administrative routine had had good results, as the trustees had hoped. He had organized a fine exhibition of the collection of paintings and sculpture; his book on Picasso was about to appear; he was to deliver the Mary Flexner lectures at Bryn Mawr; and he was providing the editorial supervision of the Penguin series on American artists. All in all, Clark said, Barr was continuing to contribute "more than anyone to the strict maintenance of the Museum's integrity and artistic standards."[23] In June 1946, Clark retired as chairman and president, to be succeeded by John Hay Whitney and Nelson Rockefeller.

Barr was a talented writer with a facility for clothing his innovative ideas in clear, easily understood language. His catalogues of the museum's exhibitions, which brilliantly explained aspects of modern art, were eagerly sought after by art museums, both here and abroad, so that they soon went out of print. But for Barr, always the perfectionist, writing was extremely difficult. He was never satisfied but insisted on many versions; he indulged in much procrastination and often missed deadlines. He failed to produce an authoritative, comprehensive book on modern art, its history and meaning, though he did write an excellent forty-eight page booklet, issued in 1943 and entitled *What Is Modern Painting?* It seductively broke down the barriers between modern art and the ordinary person, was lauded by scholars, and became a best seller with the public. After many struggles, he managed to produce two full-length and definitive master-pieces—*Picasso: Fifty Years of His Art* in 1946 and *Matisse: His Art and His Public* in 1951.[24]

Barr's position began to improve markedly with the coming of René d'Harnoncourt to the staff in 1944, at first with the peculiar title of vice-president in charge of foreign activities and director of the Department of Manual Industry. A former Austrian count, he was an authority on Mexican and American Indian art and unusually skilled in museum installation. More important, he was a "gentle giant" (six feet seven and 230 pounds) who understood people and knew how to obtain harmony in an institution. His social rank impressed the trustees, and he came to be cherished by the staff. He appreciated Barr's great ability and insisted that he be a member of his five-man Coordinating Committee that had the direction of the museum from 1946 until d'Harnoncourt was promoted to the directorship three years later.[25]

A woman trustee in the inner circle described what was happening thus:

> No one else could have become director and at the same time kept Alfred, who is really the backbone of the Museum, happy and functioning. René set out to reinstate Alfred, and built the whole thing around him. René can cope with Alfred, and he can hold a group of prima donnas together. Specialists, such as museum curators, are perfectionists, you know, and they get into a state of nerves. It's hard for them to meet a deadline. They're dedicated people, but they're edgy, and René gives them a sense of excitement and drama that enhances their feeling for their work.

And Barr himself had this to say:

> René is a man I have enormous affection for. And appreciation. This place is a madhouse, because of the pressures, the number of people who want to get into the act, and a temperamental board of trustees and staff. He holds it together. . . . I think he's the most patient man I've ever known—Lincolnian really—and I'm an authority on testing patience, since I'm chronically irritable and tend to need people to complain to.[26]

IV

At d'Harnoncourt's firm suggestion, Barr was made director of collections in 1947, and he continued at that post until his retirement twenty years later. His major contributions were in the paintings and sculpture department, and he passed judgment on every item added to those collections. But, of course, he had much influence in other areas, especially architecture, industrial design, photography, and films. Though Barr still sometimes felt bitter about his demotion, his new position took advantage of his main talents as idea man, inspirational innovator, and maintainer of quality standards, while relieving him from the administrative minutiae that he handled less well.

The museum collection had first become important with Lillie Bliss's bequest and then expanded with Mrs. Rockefeller's substantial gifts of paintings, drawings, and sculpture and of the museum's first sizeable purchase fund of more than $30,000. Another generous donor was Mrs. Simon Guggenheim, who in 1937 of her own volition came to see Barr and began to finance specific purchases for him, such as Picasso's *Mirror*, *Three Musicians*, and *She-goat* bronze, Rousseau's *Sleeping Gypsy*, and Chagall's *I and the Village*. Altogether, she furnished more than two million dollars for such acquisitions. The trustees and many other collectors contributed more and more modern masterpieces. Barr and others on the staff were always glad to advise and help serious collectors, many of whom gratefully remembered the museum with gifts or bequests.[27]

The question of passing along works of art to other museums concerned the museum for many years. In 1934, President Goodyear and William Sloan Coffin, president of the Metropolitan Museum of Art, entered into a series of negotiations. Coffin suggested that the Metropolitan's Hearn Fund, of about $15,000 yearly for the purchase of paintings by living American artists, be administered by a committee of the two institutions. Any paintings acquired should be shown at the Modern for ten years or more and then, if the Metropolitan wished, pass on to it. The trustees of the Modern approved the suggested arrangement, but Coffin died before his trustees could discuss the matter, and it was dropped.[28]

In 1944 the museum, under Stephen Clark's administration and partly for financial reasons, decided to sell at public auction some of its holdings considered less permanent. The funds received were to be used to purchase twentieth-century art, chiefly by living artists, and no work by a living North or South American artist was included in the sale. In all, 108 items were disposed of, though 63 of them were contributed by the trustees from their own collections. The museum discards included four Cezanne oils and watercolors, two Seurat drawings, and one Matisse. The museum received only a disappointing $55,189 from the sale.[29]

When Henry Francis Taylor became director of the Metropolitan in 1940, he began to hold conversations with both the Modern and the Whitney Museum in an effort to harmonize their collecting and exhibition practices. Taylor was a much different personality from Barr, his humor and expressions of opinion often bawdy, as when he referred to the Modern as "the whorehouse on Fifty-third Street" or to "those pansies" who worked there. He, however, left the negotiations with the other museums to his president, Roland L. Redmond, who was an accomplished lawyer; Stephen Clark and Nelson Rockefeller were also trustees of both the Modern and the Metropolitan. Redmond worked closely with Barr and with Juliana Force of the Whitney to secure the *Three Museum Agreement of 1947*. Under it, the Metropolitan was to concentrate on classic art; the Whitney, on American art; and the Modern, on both American and foreign modern art. The three were to exchange items from their holdings for special exhibitions. The Modern sold the Metropolitan twenty-six works of art for $191,000, and the Metropolitan sent the Modern on extended loan Maillol's *Chained Action* sculpture and Picasso's *Portrait of Gertrude Stein*. But the agreement, which was to last for five years, was an uneasy one. The Whitney had talked of building next to the Metropolitan but, when disputes arose, dropped out of the arrangement after a year. The Modern decided not to renew the pact in 1952, chiefly because it had become convinced that important donors might not wish to leave their cherished masterpieces to a museum that might pass them along. The next year, President John Hay Whitney announced the important change in policy that abandoned the transferral of collections to other institutions. It promised to keep on view in the museum's own galleries masterpieces of the modern movement, though works judged not to have that quality would still be sold or traded. The failure of the *Three Museum Agreement* probably did not harm the cause of modern art, for the Metropolitan began to build on its own collection in that field and the two other museums continued their vigorous efforts.[30]

When Barr retired in 1967 after thirty-eight years of service, the Board of Trustees appointed him its counselor, and he continued to advise occasionally on various matters. Numerous honors came to him, and his recommendations were often sought on important decisions in the art museum field. Unfortunately, however, his memory, which had always been so remarkable and served him so well, began to fail, and he came to suffer the ravages of Alzheimer's disease. Despite Marga's constant devoted care and her frantic attempts to find some medical cure, he was forced to spend his last six years in a convalescent home, where he died on August 15, 1981.

Barr's career had indeed been a remarkable one. In 1929 modern art had been looked down upon in the United States by the art world and most artists as well as by the general public. Many had agreed with Dean Inge, who thought "the revolting productions of the modernist school" resembled "now the work of a very unpleasant child, now the first efforts of an African savage, and now the delirious hallucinations of an incurable lunatic."[31] But Barr's exhibitions of the French Impressionists and post-Impressionists together with the clear, reasonable explanations of his catalogues attracted public interest and aroused enthusiasm. Similarly, American nineteenth-century artists like Homer, Ryder, Eakins, Whistler, and George Caleb Bingham were, in general, well received. The backing of the museum that such shows produced stood it in good stead when more radical works were exhibited, such as cubism, abstract art, fantastic art, and surrealism. Barr had done much to alter the whole art field. When he retired, *Newsweek* commented: "In the old days, a museum was a stately cenotaph for defunct genius, full of the hush and odor of sanctity. Barr changed all that and literally seduced the public off the street with showmanship and genius." Professor Sachs said that the museum had become "a telling instrument in the field of general education" and had "liberalized the policies of every one of our leading museums . . . even the most complacent." And Hilton Kramer wrote in 1987 that Barr gave the art museum a new role. No longer was it to be regarded as a refuge from the conflicts and controversies of contemporary life. Henceforth it would take up its mission at the very crossroads where tradition and innovation meet, and act as a guide to the present as well as the past.[32]

The success of the Modern also led to better treatment of modern art in other museums. In New York, the Whitney Museum of American Art (1930) and the Solomon R. Guggenheim Museum (1937) appeared on the scene with strong commitment to the modern movement, and the Metropolitan in 1949 set up its own Department of Contemporary (now Twentieth Century) Art. Elsewhere in the United States, other museums friendly to the modern approach were strengthened, such as the Art Institute of Chicago, Albright-Knox Gallery of Buffalo, Phillips Gallery in Washington, and Boston's Institute of Contemporary Art. The international influence of the Modern Museum was also great. American travelers sometimes were surprised to find that many Europeans regarded it as the premier museum in the new world. The museum's International Council reinforced that impression by sending exhibitions to Asia, Africa, Australia, Latin America, and Europe, and lending art works to American ambassadors. All these developments made Barr one of the most influential museum masters yet to flourish in this country.

NOTES

1. The most readily available sources on the museum and Barr are: Alfred H. Barr Jr., *Defining Modern Art: Selected Writings of Alfred H. Barr Jr.*, edited by Irving Sandler and Amy Newman (New York: Abrams, 1986); Barr, *Painting and Sculpture in the Museum of Modern Art, 1929–1967* (New York: MOMA, 1977); Margaret Scolari Barr, "Our Campaigns," *New Criterion* (Summer 1987): 23–74; *Contemporary Authors: A Bibliographical Guide to Current Authors and Their Work*, edited by Clara D. Kinsman (Detroit: Gale Research Company, 1975), vols. 49–52: 47–48; Emily Genauer, "The Fur-lined Museum," *Harper's Magazine* 189 (July 1944): 129–38; A. Conger Goodyear, *The Museum of Modern Art: The First Ten Years* (New York: MOMA, 1943); Geoffrey T. Hellman, "Imperturbable Noble: René d'Harnoncourt," *New*

Yorker 36 (May 7, 1960): 49–112; Hellman, "Profile of a Museum," *Art in America* 40 (Feb. 1964): 27–64; Hilton Kramer, "Alfred Barr at MOMA: An Introduction," *New Criterion* (Summer 1987): i–iii; Russell Lynes, *Good Old Modern: The Museum of Modern Art* (New York: Atheneum, 1973); Dwight Macdonald, "Profiles: Action on West Fifty-Third Street," *New Yorker* 29 (Dec. 12, 1953): 49–82; *New Yorker* 29 (Dec. 19, 1953): 35–72; Alice Goldfarb Marquis, *Alfred H. Barr Jr.: Missionary for the Modern* (Chicago: Contemporary Books, 1989); Museum of Modern Art *Bulletin* 1–30 (1933–1962); Museum of Modern Art, *The Lillie B. Bliss Collection, 1934* (New York: MOMA, 1934); Museum of Modern Art, *The Museum of Modern Art, New York: The History and the Collection* (New York: Abrams, 1984); Rona Roob, "1936: The Museum Selects an Architect," *Archives of American Art Journal* 23, No. 1 (1983): 22–30; Roob, "Alfred H. Barr Jr.: A Chronicle of the Years 1902–1929," *New Criterion* (Summer 1987): 1–19; John Russell, "Visionary Curator, Cautionary Tale," New York *Times*, July 26, 1989.

2. Lynes, *Good Old Modern*, 9.

3. Goodyear, *First Ten Years*, 12, 16.

4. Lynes, *Good Old Modern*, 20; Marquis, *Barr*, chap. 2.

5. Marquis, *Barr*, 2–3, chap. 3; Roob, "Barr, 1902–1929," 1–19.

6. Margaret Barr, "Our Campaigns," 24; "Margaret Scolari Barr," New York *Times*, Dec. 31, 1987; Marquis, *Barr*, 71–76, 161–62, 269–70; Roob, "Barr, 1902–1929," 19.

7. Goodyear, *First Ten Years*, 15, 84.

8. Hellman, "Profile of a Museum," 27; Marquis, *Barr*, 116–17.

9. Barr, *Modern Museum Painting and Sculpture*, xi; Goodyear, *First Ten Years*, 82; Marquis, *Barr*, 115–16.

10. *Magazine of Art* (Oct. 1945): 212–22; Marquis, *Barr*, 102–09.

11. Goodyear, *First Ten Years*, 54–57; Lynes, *Good Old Modern*, 132–36; Marquis, *Barr*, 131–35.

12. Goodyear, *First Ten Years*, 57–59, 62–64 (quotation on p. 63); Lynes, *Good Old Modern*, 137–46; Marquis, *Barr*, 149–61.

13. Goodyear, *First Ten Years*, 73–82; Lynes, *Good Old Modern*, 183–85; Marquis, *Barr*, 161–67.

14. Margaret Barr, "Our Campaigns," 28; Goodyear, *First Ten Years*, 137–39; Lynes, *Good Old Modern*, 285; Marquis, *Barr*, 85–87.

15. Lynes, *Good Old Modern*, 180–81, 318.

16. Goodyear, *First Ten Years*, 93; Lynes, *Good Old Modern*, 117–20, 260–61; Marquis, *Barr*, 122–23, 161.

17. Goodyear, *First Ten Years*, 125–32; Lynes, *Good Old Modern*, 171, 193–95, 355; Marquis, *Barr*, 167–70; Museum of Modern Art, *History and Collection*, 19; Roob, "Museum Selects an Architect," 22–30.

18. Goodyear, *First Ten Years*, 96; Lynes, *Good Old Modern* 199–203 (quotations on pp. 200–01); Marquis, *Barr*, 171–73.

19. Lynes, *Good Old Modern*, 153.

20. Margaret Barr, "Our Campaigns," 54–56, 60, 64; Genauer, "Fur-lined Museum," 132; Lynes, *Good Old Modern*, 213–14, 222, 224.

21. Margaret Barr, "Our Campaigns," 68; see also 67–73; Lynes, *Good Old Modern*, 240–43; Marquis, *Barr*, 200–10.

22. Lynes, *Good Old Modern*, 246–47.

23. Marquis, *Barr*, 211–12; Museum of Modern Art *Bulletin* 13 (Feb. 1946): 4, 20.

24. Marquis, *Barr*, 91–92, 215–18, 265–67; *Matisse: His Art and His Public* (New York: MOMA, 1951); *Picasso: Fifty Years of His Art* (New York: MOMA, 1946); *What Is Modern Painting?*

(New York: MOMA, 1943).

25. Lynes, *Good Old Modern*, 265–71; Marquis, *Barr*, 284–86, 345; Museum of Modern Art *Bulletin* 15, No. 4 (1948): 25.

26. The quotations are in Hellman, "René d'Harnoncourt," 27, 50, 52.

27. Lynes, *Good Old Modern*, 295–96; Marquis, *Barr*, 11, 117–18.

28. Goodyear, *First Ten Years*, 39–40.

29. Margaret Barr, "Our Campaigns," 73; Lynes, *Good Old Modern*, 295–97; Marquis, *Barr*, 223–24.

30. Lynes, *Good Old Modern*, 250, 287–91; Marquis, *Barr*, 245–47; Museum of Modern Art *Bulletin* 15 (Fall 1947): 20; Calvin Tomkins, *Merchants and Masterpieces: The Story of the Metropolitan Museum of Art* (New York: E. P. Dutton, 1970), 304–10.

31. Goodyear, *The First Ten Years*, 26; Marquis, *Barr*, 347, 355–56.

32. The quotations are in Lynes, *Good Old Modern*, 352, 405.

SELECT BIBLIOGRAPHY

Barr, Alfred H., Jr. *Defining Modern Art: Selected Writings of Alfred H. Barr Jr.* Edited by Irving Sandler and Amy Newman. New York: Abrams, 1986.

———. *Painting and Sculpture in the Museum of Modern Art, 1929–1967.* New York: MOMA, 1977.

Barr, Margaret Scolari. "Our Campaigns." *New Criterion* (Summer 1987): 23–74.

Contemporary Authors: A Bibliographical Guide to Current Authors and Their Work. Edited by Clara D. Kinsman. Detroit: Gale Research Company, 1975. Vols. 49–52.

Genauer, Emily. "The Fur-lined Museum." *Harper's Magazine* 189 (July 1944): 129–38.

Goodyear, A. Conger. *The Museum of Modern Art: The First Ten Years.* New York: MOMA, 1943.

Hellman, Geoffrey T. "Imperturbable Noble: René d'Harnoncourt." *New Yorker* 36 (May 7, 1960): 49–112.

———. "Profile of a Museum." *Art in America* 40 (Feb. 1964): 27–64.

Kramer, Hilton. "Alfred Barr at MOMA: An Introduction." *New Criterion* (Summer 1987): i–iii.

Lynes, Russell. *Good Old Modern: The Museum of Modern Art.* New York: Atheneum, 1973.

Macdonald, Dwight. "Profiles: Action on West Fifty-Third Street." *New Yorker* 29 (Dec. 12, 1953): 49–82; and 29 (Dec. 19, 1953): 35–72.

Marquis, Alice Goldfarb. *Alfred H. Barr Jr.: Missionary for the Modern.* Chicago: Contemporary Books, 1989.

Museum of Modern Art *Bulletin* 1–30 (1933–1962).

———. *The Lillie B. Bliss Collection, 1934.* New York: MOMA, 1934.

———. *Matisse: His Art and His Public.* New York: MOMA, 1951.

———. *The Museum of Modern Art, New York: The History and the Collection.* New York: Abrams, 1984.

———. *Picasso: Fifty Years of His Art.* New York: MOMA, 1946.

———. *What Is Modern Painting?* New York: MOMA, 1943.

Roob, Rona. "1936: The Museum Selects an Architect." *Archives of American Art Journal* 23, No. 1 (1983): 22–30.

———. "Alfred H. Barr Jr.: A Chronicle of the Years 1902–1929." *New Criterion* (Summer 1987): 1–19.

Russell, John. "Visionary Curator, Cautionary Tale." *New York Times*, July 26, 1989.

Tomkins, Calvin. *Merchants and Masterpieces: The Story of the Metropolitan Museum of Art.* New York: E. P. Dutton, 1970.

CHAPTER 5

Reuben Gold Thwaites
Makes a Historical Society
Reach the People of a State

I

A MERICAN HISTORICAL SOCIETIES appeared soon after the end of the Revolution and the adoption of the Constitution. They aimed to collect the books, newspapers, manuscripts, and objects, at first both of natural science and history, that would keep the American experience alive and through meetings and publications disseminate that history throughout the country and even abroad. The earliest organizations were the Massachusetts Historical Society (1791) in Boston, the New-York Historical Society (1804), and the American Antiquarian Society (1812) in Worcester, Massachusetts. By the time of the Centennial Exposition at Philadelphia in 1876, there were more than seventy societies, extending from Texas through every state to the Atlantic.[1]

Nearly all the historical societies were independent, private membership bodies governed by a Board of Trustees and Executive Committee and receiving their financial support from membership dues and donations. The Massachusetts and Antiquarian ones were unusual in that their members were elected because of their scholarly contributions or publications. The three pioneer organizations placed chief emphasis upon building research libraries, but all of them in the beginning gathered museum materials. Massachusetts sought "specimens of natural and artificial curiosities, and a selection of every thing which can improve and promote the historical knowledge of our country, either in a physical or political view."[2] The New York Society's constitution stated that its object "shall be to discover, procure, and preserve whatever may relate to the natural, civil, literary, and ecclesiastical history of the United States in general, and of this State in particular," and it promised to collect not only library materials but "specimens of the various productions of the American Continent and of the adjacent Islands, and such animal, vegetable, and mineral objects . . . deemed worthy of preservation."[3] The American Antiquarian Society wished "to preserve such relics of American Antiquity as are portable, as well as to collect and preserve those of other parts of the Globe" and "specimens, with written accounts respecting them, of fossils, handicrafts of the Aborigines,&c."[4] For a time it collected actively, especially in the fields of American Indian archaeology and antiquities.

Only the New York Society continued for long to amass museum materials. Massachusetts soon gave away everything except portraits and some valuable New England historical artifacts. The Antiquarian Society agreed with its librarian Christopher Columbus Baldwin that "a library should contain nothing but books, coins, statuary, and pictures" and that it was "absurd to pile up old bureaus and chests, and stuff them with old coats and hats and high-heeled shoes."[5] By 1854 it was bestowing its natural history and anthropological collections upon other institutions. New York from the start secured American portraits and paintings, decorative arts, and other historical objects but often ventured into wider fields. It accepted Plains Indian and pre-Columbian artifacts from Central and South America; Luman Reed's extensive collection of paintings, many of them European; James Lenox's thirteen huge marble Nineveh sculptures; Dr. Henry Abbott's Egyptian collection (then the best in the country with 1,100 pieces including three large mummified bulls); and the 438 canvases of Thomas Jefferson Bryan's "Gallery of Christian Art." Not until the present century did the society begin to get rid of its extraneous holdings. Most of the other Eastern societies concentrated upon collecting libraries, publishing articles and books on state and local history, and holding meetings with lectures and special events. Through the years, however, many of them acquired historic houses, often as headquarters, gathered decorative art objects with which to furnish them, and sometimes were given comprehensive regional museum collections.

Wisconsin formed a private state historical society in 1846, two years before reaching statehood. For a time, it seemed likely to adopt the Eastern independent type of organization, and a strong faction tried to make it into a private club, the membership confined to those with a scholarly interest, or even to follow the Massachusetts and American Antiquarian restrictive models. But the arrival in Madison of Lyman Copeland Draper (1815–1891), the driving collector of manuscripts, newspapers, books, interviews, and other materials of the trans-Allegheny frontier, changed all that. He succeeded in obtaining a charter and constitution for the State Historical Society of Wisconsin in 1854 that called for a broad amateur membership statewide; but though anyone could join by paying dues of a dollar per year, the number of members remained small. Draper was the society's corresponding secretary, and with great ingenuity, tireless energy, and contagious enthusiasm, he used all kinds of promotional devices including honorary memberships and national and foreign exchanges to build an important historical research library, portrait gallery, and small cabinet of museum objects. The State Legislature in 1854 granted the society $500 with which to purchase books and other materials and, the next year, doubled that amount with $500 for Draper's salary. Wisconsin was the first state to make regular annual appropriations for its historical society and has continued that practice ever since.

Draper's main interest was the society's library, but in the museum field, he did build a creditable portrait gallery. He sent many American artists handsomely engraved certificates making them honorary members and requesting examples of their work. Robert M. Sully, of Richmond, Virginia, for example, contributed a copy of his portrait of Black Hawk, the Sauk chief; paintings of Black Hawk's son and of the glowering Winnebago medicine man, the Prophet; and a fanciful likeness of Pocahontas with flowers in her hair and pearls at her ears. Draper persuaded Sully to depart for Wisconsin to become the society's artist in residence, but on the way, in Buffalo, New York, the artist died during a drunken spree. Draper then secured Samuel M. Brookes and Thomas H. Stevenson, English born but living in Milwaukee, as official artists. He induced many governors and other political, industrial, and cultural leaders to present their likenesses and managed to finance portraits of several Indian chiefs. In 1886 the gallery contained 135 paintings, mainly portraits but some representations of Wisconsin towns, canals, and battlefields of the Black Hawk War. They constituted a documentary view of early Wisconsin and, on the practical side, were useful in securing legislative support from the leaders whose portraits graced the gallery. Other museum materials were less significant but included coins, medals, Indian antiquities (especially the Perkins Collection of rare copper implements), objects of pioneer life, and Civil War military equipment.

Draper thus was a great success as a historical society organizer and promoter. He built one of the leading historical libraries of the nation; obtained a small but influential statewide membership; and secured continuing appropriations from the state. Before he retired at the end of 1886 after thirty-three years of service, he cannily chose as his successor Reuben Gold Thwaites, a Madison newspaper editor, who was to become the most successful historical society director that the nation had known.[6]

II

Reuben Gold Thwaites was born May 15, 1853, at Dorchester, Massachusetts, the son of George and Sarah (Bibbs) Thwaites, natives of Yorkshire, England, who had come to Massachusetts three years earlier. Reuben attended common school in Dorchester but at age thirteen moved with his parents to a farm in Omro near Oshkosh, Wisconsin. After working as a farmhand and going to public school, he taught elementary classes and systematically instructed himself in collegiate subjects. He also began to write for newspapers in the area and, as a staff member of the Oshkosh *Times*, in 1872 reported on the Democratic presidential convention in Baltimore. He became "a fire-eating Granger" and backed Joseph H. Osborn, his brother-in-law, who headed the Wisconsin State Grange from his farm near Oshkosh. Thwaites also began to become acquainted with the Indian tribes of Wisconsin and in 1876 wrote a piece for the *Times* on "Oshkosh, the last of the Menominee Sachems."

In 1874–1875 the young journalist became a special student at Yale University, taking post-graduate work in English literature, economic history, and international law. He admired greatly one of his instructors, William Graham Sumner. In 1876 Thwaites moved to Madison as city editor (later managing editor) of the Republican *Wisconsin State Journal* under the editorship of General David Atwood. As a reporter of legislative proceedings and political conventions he was well acquainted with the public men of the state. He supplied Eastern newspapers with Wisconsin news and later covered state legislative affairs for the Chicago *Tribune*. He made many friends and led an active social life. He became an early member of the exclusive Madison Literary Club and wrote an account of its first decade. He was an adjutant's clerk in the Lake City Guard, which he accompanied to Eau Claire in 1881 when Governor William E. Smith ordered it to help suppress the riotous conduct of mill hands and rivermen striking against the twelve-hour day.

In 1882 Thwaites was married to Jessie Inwood Turvill, also the scion of English immigrants. They had one son, Frederick, in 1883; he later taught geology at the University of Wisconsin and for a time was curator of its Geological Museum. The Thwaites' summer home, Turvillwood, was situated on Lake Monona, and Mrs. Thwaites was a cordial hostess who entertained their frequent visitors, including many Indians. She was a devoted botanist and gardener; later she and the son often accompanied Thwaites on his travels.

In 1884–1885, Thwaites visited New Mexico and Colorado and considered establishing a newspaper in that area. He suggested to his friend Frederick Jackson Turner, then a budding historian at the university, that he join him in the venture. But his career goal changed when Lyman Draper persuaded him to become assistant corresponding secretary of the State Historical Society, and in January 1887 he succeeded Draper as secretary (later superintendent).[7]

During his newspaper days, Thwaites had become a fluent writer and editor. He knew how to present the gist of complex matters and situations in clear, easily read prose and, faced with constant deadlines, to prepare articles and stories rapidly. He was punctilious about grammar and syntax, as Louise Kellogg said later: "never too busy to discuss the value of placing a comma correctly."[8] He also understood people and their motives and feelings. All those qualities made him an effective administrator and leader, so that he gave promise of taking the State Historical Society far in his quest to reach all the people of Wisconsin.

III

When Lyman Draper retired, the Historical Society was housed in crowded, non-fireproof rooms in the State Capitol on Capitol Square. Its library of 118,666 titles contained mainly books on American history, bound newspapers, American patent reports, genealogy and heraldry, Shakespearian literature, and maps and atlases. It was adding about 2,500 titles yearly. The most numerous manuscript collection, which concerned the trans-Allegheny frontier, was Draper's personal property, available to researchers only with his permission. Draper also edited ten volumes of *Collections* of documents, articles, and interviews on Wisconsin history.

The society was financed by a combination of public and private money. Its General Fund of $5,000 yearly was appropriated by the State Legislature, which in addition paid the salaries of Draper and two assistants as well as expenses for printing, postage, express, and some binding and book purchasing. The private Binding Fund, accumulated from annual and life membership dues and sales of duplicates, came to about $17,000.[9]

"Energy, thy name is Thwaites," wrote Lucien S. Hanks, longtime curator and then-treasurer of the society; and the new corresponding secretary justified the description as he applied modern business practices throughout the society and proved himself a superb administrator. Thwaites added library materials systematically and paid close attention to exchanges with other institutions both in this country and abroad. He began a card catalogue of books and secured a better arrangement for newspapers. He sought Wisconsin manu-scripts zealously, a field in which Draper had taken little interest, and visited historic spots around the state each year, obtaining Wisconsin materials and interviewing Indians, early traders, and settlers. He persuaded the Wisconsin Press Association to ask its members to send the society early imprints, examples of job printing, and newspapers. He encouraged Professor Turner to bring his advanced history class to a comfortable seminar room in the library; he also published in the *Proceedings* articles by graduate students. He cooperated with the university in collecting materials on foreign nationalities in the state, a process that he aided with personal visitation. Wisconsin, he thought, had a greater variety of those groups than any other American state—Germans, Scandinavians (Norwegians, Swedes, Finns, and Icelanders), Irish, British, Canadians, Bohemians, Dutch, French, Poles, and Belgians. He had the library collect Wisconsin authors and American labor history, the latter with the aid of Professor Richard T. Ely. By the end of Thwaite's administration, the library had tripled in size.[10]

Thwaites succeeded in gathering with great care a cadre of intelligent, capable, and industrious younger women to help him conduct the activities of the society. He often made their positions more exciting by involving them in editorial work for its publications. Thus the brilliant Annie Amelia Nunns, who began work in the library in 1899, was soon toiling long hours, often at night, on the seventy-three volumes of the *Jesuit Relations* and the thirty-two volumes of *Early Western Travels*; she became Thwaites's executive secretary and, upon his death, served as assistant superintendent under his three successors until she died in 1942. Mary S. Foster and Iva A. Welsh started work in the library in 1897 and retired forty-seven years later as, respectively, chief of the Reference Division and head cataloguer. Dr. Louise Phelps Kellogg began helping Thwaites as editor in 1902, was promoted to senior research assistant, and answered hundreds of questions yearly about society materials and Draper manuscripts as well as writing more than a dozen important books and countless articles on early Wisconsin and Midwest history. Her notable research achievements were recognized when she became the first woman to serve as president of the Mississippi Valley Historical Association and the first woman to receive an honorary doctorate from the University of Wisconsin. Thwaites's command of historical knowledge, good nature, and sense of humor caused such women to become devoted to him, and in fact made it difficult for his first two successors to elicit the same kind of loyalty.[11]

The art gallery and museum were starved for funds, most of which went to the library, and had to depend upon donations from members and patrons. The gallery continued to concentrate on Wisconsin, but the museum remained more eclectic. Since the university had natural history and geological collections, Thwaites thought that the society should confine its holdings to ethnology, archaeology, and history. But its accessions included a yucca plant from California, Chinese chopsticks, a horseshoe from Antwerp, a Filipino insurgent's uniform, a piece of the scaffold from which John Brown was hanged as well as a pair of iron firedogs from his birthplace, and other objects from Italy, Japan, Korea, and Mexico. Thwaites brought back from his travels in Britain bricks, flints, and pottery from the Roman remains of Verulamium near Silchester and a blackthorn shillelah and piece of the "Blarney stone" from Cork. Such widely gathered artifacts could possibly occasionally be justified in that the museum was serving university students. At the same time, valuable Wisconsin materials were accumulated, such as the silver ostensorium presented to the St. Francis Xavier Mission in De Pere in 1696 by Nicholas Perrot, the French commander in the West (deposited in the museum by Catholic Church authorities), Winnebago and Chippewa wigwams, a Winnebago dugout canoe, and a stove from the first state capitol. The society also was most proud to possess Daniel Boone's powder horn. And the museum was popular, attracting legislators, university faculty and students, numerous public school classes, and visitors seeing the sights of the capital city; they soon totaled 60,000 yearly.[12]

Thwaites's first great triumph was the obtaining of a new building for the society on the university campus, a splendid structure that still serves it well. Draper had tried without success to secure $50,000 for a new headquarters in 1881, and the legislature had killed a later attempt to erect such a building as a Civil War memorial. President Thomas C. Chamberlain of the university and Thwaites began discussing a joint structure in 1890; the latter was delighted because he thought that a building on the campus would portray "the Society as an educational institution," draw readers to the library, and attract more museum visitors when "placed near the collections in Science Hall." The society's

Board of Curators endorsed the idea unanimously, "provided the title of the site shall rest in the name of the Society as the trustee of the state." To help secure legislative backing, Thwaites obtained impressive testimonials to the great worth of the Historical Society's work from twenty-eight leading library and historical authorities throughout the country, including Woodrow Wilson and Theodore Roosevelt. The legislative act of 1895 provided that the university furnish the site, to which the society would hold title. The Building Commission spent more than a month visiting libraries in Washington, Philadelphia, Princeton, New York, Brooklyn, Newark, N. J., Southport, New Haven, Providence, Boston, Cambridge, Albany, Buffalo, Pittsburgh, and Allegheny, Pennsylvania. In October 1900 the completed, highly fire-resistant building was dedicated with speeches by Governor Edward Scofield, President Charles Kendall Adams of the university, and Secretary Thwaites. (The society was fortunate to have moved when it did, for the state capitol burned in 1904.)[13]

Though Thwaites considered the library more important than the museum, he recognized the latter's value as he wrote in 1891:

> To the world, the library is by far the most valuable; it is a great workshop for scholars, and they are the core of civilization; abroad, the society's library and its original investigations have alone given it prestige. The society, however, can do excellent missionary work among the masses, by making its museum more attractive, and by having especial regard to its possibilities as a factor in public education.[14]

And in 1903 he admitted: "[The museum] is the department of our work which chiefly appeals to the general public. Its importance as a factor in popular education is not to be over-estimated."[15]

The new building contained the society library in one wing and that of the university in the other. The art gallery and museum were on the top, fourth floor, illuminated from above by skylights. Separate halls contained ethnology, war history, framed photographs and engravings, bric-a-brac, and curiosities, while paintings were hung on the walls with sculptures below. The museum had only one attendant, the faithful Ceylon C. Lincoln who had been the society's janitor at the capitol. A northwest wing had been postponed by the state, and the society soon was telling the legislature how badly it needed more space. The state had to increase the society appropriation because of the added expense of the new building, even though the university paid half of the cost of public utilities, cleaning, and policing. The society's General Fund was raised to $15,000, and a separate state fund of $5,000 was added for library acquisitions.

Thwaites continued to have a difficult time with finances because the new appropriations did not quite meet the expenses incurred by moving into the new building. Beginning in 1907, however, the legislature added another $5,000 to the General Fund and from that time onward made other increases so that the society was less hard-pressed. By 1913 it was receiving $70,948 in state funds, and the private endowment had grown to $73,638. Upon Draper's death in 1891, his will left his manuscripts, books, homestead, and other property to the society. After the homestead was sold, the Draper Fund exceeded $11,000 and was used to bind the Draper manuscripts and for other expenses and publications about that collection.[16]

The library still received the lion's share of the funding, while the museum remained largely dependent upon gifts for accessions and special activities. It did, however, make some progress. President Robert L. McCormick donated two large, carefully researched paintings by Edwin Willard Deming of New York, portraying *Jean Nicolet's Landing in Wisconsin*, 1634, and *Braddock's Defeat*, 1775. Miss Ellen A. Stone of Lexington, Massachusetts, bestowed nearly two hundred colonial kitchen implements that had belonged to her great-grandfather, and Thwaites visited several extant colonial kitchens in the Boston area and chose one as a model for the society's reproduction. It proved so successful that he contemplated adding a log cabin of pioneer days. Dr. and Mrs. Charles Kendall Adams made a magnificent gift of books, pictures, and museum objects, and Mrs. Adams's personal jewels were sold to set up the Mary M. Adams Art Fund. But the museum collections remained general with separate rooms for Piranesi etchings and Arundel prints, a large display of Pueblo pottery from Arizona and New Mexico, a Japanese flute, and Eskimo artifacts. The museum walls were improved by installing planking covered with cloth. The Madison Art Association staged three special exhibitions in the museum during 1902–1903 with appropriate lectures and continued such offerings each year. Some of them displayed George Washington materials, Oriental handicrafts, European pottery, and Philippine weapons.[17]

The museum took an important step forward in 1908 with the appointment of Charles E. Brown as its chief. As secretary of the Wisconsin Archaeological Society and editor of its quarterly journal, he was to give one-third of his time to that society and two-thirds to the Historical Society. He at once began classifying and rearranging the collections, added Chippewa and other Indian materials, wrote an educational leaflet on the museum and a teachers' guide, and continued his energetic efforts to preserve and mark Indian mounds around the state. "Charlie" Brown got along well with people and was a popular speaker who enjoyed traveling. He turned over all the natural history specimens to the university and began to present many small special exhibits. Separate cases and screens were devoted to Wisconsin settlement, education, agriculture, religion, lumbering, mining, manufactures, commerce, and medicine. In 1911 the chief special exhibitions dealt with Increase A. Lapham, Wisconsin pioneer scientist; the tercentenary of the King James Bible; powder horns including, of course, Daniel Boone's; and Zionist colonies in Palestine. The next year, fifteen exhibitions lasted from one to three weeks; same of them concerned the centenary of Charles Dickens; Indian obsidian implements; and old-style valentines. The controversial Kensington Runestone, said to have been left in Minnesota in 1362 by traveling Norsemen, was shown for a single day. Educational programs with public school and university classes increased in number, as did special events such as an elaborate and picturesque Indian harvest dance with fifty university students and summer school pilgrimages around Lake Mendota inspecting Indian mounds.[18]

Thwaites and the society officers congratulated themselves on their wisdom in placing the museum in charge of such a competent expert, and in 1909 the society asked the legislature for a special annual appropriation of $3,500 to be used for better administration and growth of the museum. The request received considerable public backing and, two years later, an annual grant of $2,000 was approved with one of $1,500 for the Archaeological Society. The private Antiquarian Fund also was amended so that it could be used "in the general administration of the museum." A card catalogue of 9,000 entries covered museum objects. Some of the exhibitions were on fans, postage stamps, agriculture and horticulture, the centennial of Commodore Perry's victory on Lake Erie, and Japanese block prints.[19]

All the varied activity led to increased museum accessions (as many as 4,000 yearly) and to much larger attendance that reached 100,000 per annum. In 1911 the legislature agreed to an appropriation of $162,000 in three annual installments, with which to complete the northwest wing of the building; it, of course, would expand the museum on the fourth floor, but that project was not finished until the year after Thwaites's death. On October 22, 1913, the day before the annual meeting was to convene, Thwaites died suddenly. He had made his customary preparations for the meeting including his detailed Executive Committee report. The shocked board met only for a brief business session and adjourned until December 19 when a memorial service was held in the Assembly

Hall of the Capitol with Governor Francis F. McGovern presiding and Frederick Jackson Turner delivering his *Memorial Address*.[20]

IV

Thwaites made many other innovative advances in the society's work. While they did not involve the museum directly, they caused more Wisconsin citizens as well as some national and international historical leaders to become aware of the society, its collections and progress. A Wisconsin archives act of 1907 began to bring state records to the society. Thwaites also backed historic preservation and recommended restoring the territorial capital at Belmont and marking historical spots throughout the state, a project that the Federated Women's Clubs were promoting. He instituted one of the most comprehensive publication programs yet undertaken by an American historical society. In trying to make the annual meetings of the society more stimulating, Thwaites experimented with a peripatetic two-day field convention at Green Bay in 1899, and later in Milwaukee and again in Green Bay. He secured a new law that encouraged the formation of local historical societies auxiliary to the State Society, the first two at Green Bay and Ripon and soon a total of fifteen in the state. He issued *Bulletins of Information* to encourage and instruct the local societies and museums, and they frequently invited Thwaites or Charlie Brown to speak at their meetings. Thwaites's philosophy of having the society serve the whole state fitted well with the Wisconsin Idea developed by the university, which held that it owed a duty to the state and that its faculty should provide support and impartial advice in solving state problems. His philosophy was compatible, too, with the Progressive Movement sweeping the country and blossoming in the state under the vigorous leadership of Robert M. La Follette.[21]

Not only did Thwaites travel extensively through the state collecting manuscripts, museum objects, and other materials and interviewing Indians and old timers. He made several lengthy canoe voyages in the region, once with his wife and ten-year-old son down the Monongahela to Pittsburgh and along the Ohio to Cairo, Illinois, on the Mississippi. He made two trips with his wife to England and Europe, visiting libraries and museums, improving the society's exchange arrangements, and arranging for the copying of Wisconsin materials in the archives in London and Paris. He later went to the Rocky Mountains to retrace part of the route of Lewis and Clark and to Berkeley, where he advised the University of California to acquire the Bancroft Library. Thwaites customarily attended the annual meetings held about the country by the American Library Association, of which he was president in 1899, and by the American Association of Museums, in which he took a leading part.[22]

Professor Turner and Thwaites worked closely together to advance the interests of both the society and the university. Turner continued to hold his advanced seminar at the society, of which he was an active board member, serving on important committees, often as chairman—Advisory, Library, Printing and Publication, among others. In 1893 the American Historical Association held its annual meeting in Chicago at the Art Institute as part of the Columbian Exposition. Both Thwaites and Turner read papers at one session, Thwaites on "Early Lead Mining in Illinois and Wisconsin" and Turner on "The Significance of the Frontier in American History," a seminal presentation famed in the annals of American historiography and still very much alive today.[23]

Professor Turner properly summed up Thwaites's services to the historical society world:

> What would the Historical Society be today but for the services of that skilled business administrator, that assiduous collector, that scientific editor: And not only the Wisconsin society, but many others . . . have been to school to him and carried his methods . . . to other states. . . . To a degree that can hardly be recognised, he has changed the conception of the [western] historical society.[24]

Thwaites and the Wisconsin example indeed encouraged many other states to form similar historical agencies and conduct broad-gauged programs—for instance, Iowa, Minnesota, Indiana, Kansas, and Ohio. They also participated in the national Conference of Historical Societies, in the formation of which Thwaites took a leading part in 1904. It met at the American Historical Association's annual winter meeting each year and in 1940 became the independent and influential American Association for State and Local History. The state societies also helped found the Mississippi Valley Historical Association (today the Organization of American Historians) in 1907, of which Thwaites became president five years later.[25]

One informal glance at Thwaites remains to be mentioned. When Dr. Milo M. Quaife succeeded him as superintendent in 1914, he had an amusing conversation with Bennie Butts, born a slave but whom Thwaites had hired years before as a messenger and now, an aged man, was in charge of a society washroom. "Doctor," he said, meaning Thwaites, "on his arrival in the library, always exchanged his shoes for a pair of slippers which he wore during the day," Bennie meanwhile cleaning and polishing the shoes. Quaife was too young and brash to agree to continue the practice, but it is pleasant to think of Thwaites energetically padding about his appointed rounds in his slippers.[26]

NOTES

1. For the independent historical societies, see Stephen T. Riley, *The Massachusetts Historical Society, 1791-1959* (Boston, The Society, 1959); R. W. G. Vail, *Knickerbocker Birthday: A Sesqui-Centennial History of the New-York Historical Society, 1804–1954* (New York: The Society, 1954); Cliffold K. Shipton, "The American Antiquarian Society," *William and Mary Quarterly* 2 (1945): 164–172; Shipton, "The Museum of the American Antiquarian Society," in Whitfield J. Bell and others, *A Cabinet of Curiosities: Five Episodes in the Evolution of American Museums* (Charlottesville: University Press of Virginia, 1967), 35–48; Julian P. Boyd, "State and Local Historical Societies in the United States," *American Historical Review* 40 (Oct. 1934): 10–37; Leslie W. Dunlap, *American Historical Societies, 1790–1860* (Philadelphia: Porcupine Press, 1974); Walter Muir Whitehill, *Independent Historical Societies: An Enquiry into Their Research and Publication Functions and Their Financial Future* (Boston: Boston Athenaeum, 1962).

2. Whitehill, *Independent Historical Societies*, 8.

3. Vail, *Knickerbocker Birthday*, 31, 33.

4. Shipton, "Museum of the American Antiquarian Society," 36; Whitehill, *Independent Historical Societies*, 68.

5. Shipton, "Museum of the American Antiquarian Society," 40–41.

6. The two chief works on Draper and Thwaites are William B. Hesseltine, *Pioneer's Mission: The Story of Lyman Copeland Draper* (Madison: State Historical Society of Wisconsin, 1954); Clifford L. Lord and Carl Ubbelhode, *Clio's Servant: A History of the State Historical Society of Wisconsin* (Madison: The Society, 1967). They are especially valuable because they use manuscript sources found at the Society. See also Edward P. Alexander, "An Art Gallery in Frontier Wisconsin," *Wisconsin Magazine of History* 29 (Mar. 1946): 281–300.

7. For Thwaites, see Hesseltine, *Pioneer's Mission*; Charles F. Lamb, "Sawdust Campaign," *Wisconsin Magazine of History* 22 (Sep. 1938): 12; Clifford L. Lord, *Keepers of the Past* (Chapel Hill: University of North Carolina Press, 1965), pp. 53–66; Lord, "Reuben Gold Thwaites," *Wisconsin Magazine of History* 47 (Autumn 1963): 3–11; Lord and Ubbelhode, *Clio's Servant*; Robert McCluggage, "Joseph H. Osborn, Grange Leader," *Wisconsin Magazine of History* 35 (Spring 1952): 12; Frederick Jackson Turner, *Reuben Gold Thwaites: A Memorial Address* (Madison: State Historical Society, 1914).

8. David Kinnett, "Miss Kellogg's Quiet Passion," *Wisconsin Magazine of History* 62 (Summer 1979): 277.

9. State Historical Society of Wisconsin, *Proceedings, 1887–1913*, 28 vols., cover Thwaites's administration. For Draper, see *Proceedings, 1887*: 10–13; *1902*: 10; State Historical Society of Wisconsin, *Collections, 1885–1888*, 10 vols.

10. *Proceedings, 1889*: 13–24, 26–28, 40, 47; *1890*: 50, 57–63; *1891 (Dec.)*: 70–71; *1893*: 34; *1894*: 33, 34; Lord and Ubbelhode, *Clio's Servant*, 84–100.

11. "Annie Amelia Nunns, 1868–1942," *Wisconsin Magazine of History* 25 (Mar. 1942): 261–63; "Louise Phelps Kellogg, 1862–1942," *Wisconsin Magazine of History* 26 (Sep. 1942): 6–7; "Mr. Brown, Miss Foster, Miss Welsh," *Wisconsin Magazine of History* 28 (Dec. 1944): 132–34; Kinnett, "Miss Kellogg's Quiet Passion," 267–99; Lord and Ubbelhode, *Clio's Servant*, 85–86.

12. *Proceedings, 1889*: 40–47; *1890*: 56–57; *1891 (Jan.)*: 52, 61–63, 68–70; *1892*: 68–72; *1895*: 49, *1897*: 43, *1898*: 31; *1900*: 77–78; *1903*: 72–75; *1904*: 88–91.

13. *Proceedings, 1889*: 48–50; *1894*: 73–84; *1895*: 54–60; *1896*: 29; *1897*: 7–11, 47, 50; *1898*: 7–10; *1899*: 24–25; *1900*: 32–34; Vernon Carstensen, "Adventure in Cooperation," *Wisconsin Magazine of History* 34 (Winter 1950): 95–99; Lord and Ubbelhode, *Clio's Servant*, 101–10, 122–26; Reuben Gold Thwaites, ed., *Exercises at the Dedication of Its New Building, October 19, 1900* ... (Madison: Democrat Printing Co., 1901); Jackson E. Towne, "President Adams and the University Library," *Wisconsin Magazine of History* 35 (Summer 1952): 257–61.

14. *Proceedings, 1891 (Dec.)*: 66.

15. *Proceedings, 1903*: 34.

16. *Proceedings, 1891 (Dec.)*: 31–37; *1893*: 35–36; *1896*: 19, 40–42; *1900*: 9–12, 29; *1901*: 18, 30–31; *1902*: 24–29; *1907*: 22–24; *1913*: 23–28; Lord and Ubbelhode, *Clio's Servant*, 178–179, 190–192.

17. *Proceedings, 1901*: 13, 18, 27–29, 89–90; *1903*: 35–36; *1904*: 37–40, 89–91; *1905*: 43–47; *1906*: 54–56; *1907*: 51–52; Lord and Ubbelhode, *Clio's Servant*, 179–180.

18. *Proceedings, 1908*: 41, 48–53; *1909*: 34–36; *1910*: 30–32; *1911*: 30–33; *1912*: 31–37; *1913*: 36–41; Lord and Ubbelhode, *Clio's Servant*, 181–187.

19. *Proceedings, 1909*: 34–36; *1910*: 30–33; *1911*: 13, 23; *1912*: 36; *1913*: 36–41.

20. *Proceedings, 1911*: 3–14, 42–43; *1913*: 11–12; *1914*: 45–46; Lord and Ubbelhode, *Clio's Servant*, 146–147, 197–198.

21. *Proceedings, 1899*: 5, 44, 52, 103–108; *1900*: 16, 26–27; *1901*: 20–21, 96; *1907*: 38–39, 102; Lord and Ubbelhode, *Clio's Servant*, 140, 142–145, 152–154, 167, 172–178.

22. *Proceedings, 1891 (Jan.)*: 32–33; *1897*: 46–47; Lord and Ubbelhode, *Clio's Servant*, 164; Reuben Gold Thwaites, *Historic Waterways: Six Hundred Miles of Canoeing down the Rock, Fox, and Wisconsin Rivers* (Chicago: A. C. McClurg, 1888); Thwaites, *Our Cycling Tour in England: From Canterbury to Dartmoor Forest, and Back by Way of Bath, Oxford and the Thames Valley* (Chicago: A. C.McClurg, 1892); Thwaites, *Afloat on the Ohio: An Historical Pilgrimage of a Thousand Miles in a Skiff, from Redstone to Cairo* (Chicago: May and Williams, 1897); Thwaites, *A Brief History of Rocky Mountain Exploration, with Especial Reference to the Expedition of Lewis and Clark* (New York: D. Appleton and Company, 1904); Thwaites, *The Bancroft Library: A Report Submitted to the President and Regents of the University of California* . . . (Berkeley: University of California, 1905).

23. *Proceedings, 1890*: 4; *1893*: 79–112; Ray Allen Billington, *Frederick Jackson Turner: Historian, Scholar, Teacher* (New York: Oxford University Press, 1973), 126–27.

24. Billington, *The Genesis of the Frontier Thesis: A Study in Historical Creativity* (San Marino, Cal.: Huntington Library, 1971), 214; Lord and Ubbelhode, *Clio's Servant*, 194–95.

25. *American Historical Review* 10 (Apr. 1903): 493–94; 11 (Apr. 1906): 502–05; Lord and Ubbelhode, *Clio's Servant*, 156–67.

26. Milo M. Quaife, "Some Memories of Forty Years," *Wisconsin Magazine of History* 38 (Summer 1955): 252.

SELECT BIBLIOGRAPHY

Alexander, Edward P. "An Art Gallery in Frontier Wisconsin." *Wisconsin Magazine of History* 29 (Mar. 1946): 281–300.

American Historical Review 10 (Apr. 1903) and 11 (Apr. 1906).

"Annie Amelia Nunns, 1868–1942." *Wisconsin Magazine of History* 25 (Mar. 1942): 261–63.

Billington, Ray Allen. *Frederick Jackson Turner: Historian, Scholar, Teacher.* New York: Oxford University Press, 1973.

_____. *The Genesis of the Frontier Thesis: A Study in Historical Creativity.* San Marino, Cal.: Huntington Library, 1971.

Boyd, Julian P. "State and Local Historical Societies in the United States." *American Historical Review* 40 (Oct. 1934): 10–37.

Carstensen, Vernon. "Adventure in Cooperation." *Wisconsin Magazine of History* 34 (Winter 1950): 95–99.

Dunlap, Leslie W. *American Historical Societies, 1790–1860.* Philadelphia: Porcupine Press, 1974.

Hesseltine, William B. *Pioneer's Mission: The Story of Lyman Copeland Draper.* Madison: State Historical Society of Wisconsin, 1954.

Kinnett, David. "Miss Kellogg's Quiet Passion." *Wisconsin Magazine of History* 62 (Summer 1979): 277.

Lamb, Charles F. "Sawdust Campaign." *Wisconsin Magazine of History* 22 (Sep. 1938): 12.

Lord, Clifford L. *Keepers of the Past.* Chapel Hill: University of North Carolina Press, 1965.

_____. "Reuben Gold Thwaites." *Wisconsin Magazine of History* 47 (Autumn 1963): 3–11.

Lord, Clifford L., and Carl Ubbelhode. *Clio's Servant: A History of the State Historical Society of Wisconsin.* Madison: The Society, 1967.

"Louise Phelps Kellogg, 1862–1942." *Wisconsin Magazine of History* 26 (Sep. 1942): 6–7.

McCluggage, Robert. "Joseph H. Osborn, Grange Leader." *Wisconsin Magazine of History* 35 (Spring 1952): 12.

"Mr. Brown, Miss Foster, Miss Welsh." *Wisconsin Magazine of History* 28 (Dec. 1944): 132–34.

Quaife, Milo M. "Some Memories of Forty Years." *Wisconsin Magazine of History* 38 (Summer 1955): 252.

Riley, Stephen T. *The Massachusetts Historical Society, 1791–1959.* Boston, The Society, 1959.

Shipton, Cliffold K. "The American Antiquarian Society." *William and Mary Quarterly* 2 (1945): 164–172.

_____. "The Museum of the American Antiquarian Society." In Whitfield J. Bell and others. *A Cabinet of Curiosities: Five Episodes in the Evolution of American Museums.* Charlottesville: University Press of Virginia, 1967.

State Historical Society of Wisconsin. *Proceedings.* 28 vols. (1887–1913).

Thwaites, Reuben Gold, ed. *Exercises at the Dedication of Its New Building, October 19, 1900* . . . Madison: Democrat Printing Co., 1901.

Thwaites, Reuben Gold. *A Brief History of Rocky Mountain Exploration, with Especial Reference to the Expedition of Lewis and Clark.* New York: D. Appleton and Company, 1904.

_____. *Afloat on the Ohio: An Historical Pilgrimage of a Thousand Miles in a Skiff, from Redstone to Cairo.* Chicago: May and Williams, 1897.

_____. *The Bancroft Library: A Report Submitted to the President and Regents of the University of California* . . . Berkeley: University of California, 1905).

_____. *Historic Waterways: Six Hundred Miles of Canoeing down the Rock, Fox, and Wisconsin Rivers.* Chicago: A. C. McClurg, 1888.

_____. *Our Cycling Tour in England: From Canterbury to Dartmoor Forest, and Back by Way of Bath, Oxford and the Thames Valley.* Chicago: A. C. McClurg, 1892.

Towne, Jackson E. "President Adams and the University Library." *Wisconsin Magazine of History* 35 (Summer 1952): 257–61.

Turner, Frederick Jackson. *Reuben Gold Thwaites: A Memorial Address.* Madison: State Historical Society, 1914.

Vail, R. W. G. *Knickerbocker Birthday: A Sesqui-Centennial History of the New-York Historical Society, 1804–1954.* New York: The Society, 1954.

Whitehill, Walter Muir. *Independent Historical Societies: An Enquiry into Their Research and Publication Functions and Their Financial Future.* Boston: Boston Athenaeum, 1962.

CHAPTER 6

William Sumner Appleton
Preserves Important Sites
Throughout New England

I

S UMNER APPLETON WAS IN A discouraged mood during the early years of the twentieth century. Though he had enjoyed a Harvard education and European travel and led a full social life with deep interest in the arts, the theatre, music, and athletics, he was lonely and often depressed. He missed his three sisters who had married, and his real estate business venture had been unsuccessful. He had few financial worries since his father, upon his death in 1903, had left him a comfortable trust fund. But futility and diletantish lack of purpose characterized his life at the time.

Sumner had known Old World buildings and museums of distinction when, at age thirteen, he spent a year in Europe with his family and then, after graduation from Harvard in 1896, made the Grand Tour with a favorite tutor. His wide American travels included the Columbian Exposition of 1893 in Chicago, the mining camps of Nevada, San Francisco recovering from its earthquake, the charming town of Annapolis with its impressive ancient buildings, and photographing tours to record many of New England's surviving landmarks.

Sumner Appleton finally discovered a consuming purpose for his life when, in 1905 at age thirty-one, he served as secretary for the committee that succeeded in saving and restoring Boston's Paul Revere House. He then began to see the need for preserving from destruction the seventeenth-, eighteenth-, and early nineteenth-century buildings of historical and architectural distinction, not only of Boston but of all New England.[1]

At the end of 1909 and early the next year, Appleton met with Charles Knowles Bolton, an acknowledged cultural leader of Boston, and persuaded him to become president of a new historical preservation organization. On April 2, 1910, Appleton, Bolton, and sixteen carefully chosen men and women, first citizens of the community, incorporated the Society for the Preservation of New England Antiquities (SPNEA). Sumner, as corresponding secretary, was in the beginning the entire staff (he served for thirty-seven years without taking any salary and while making almost daily gifts of objects and funds to the society) in a small, crowded office in one half of a room. He at once began editing a *Bulletin* (it was later renamed *Old-Time New England*) to keep society members and other interested readers informed of the programs of historic preservation, not only in New England but in the whole country and abroad.

The first issue of the *Bulletin* (May 1910) contained Appleton's definition of the society's purpose, which ran:

> Our New England antiquities are fast disappearing because no society has made their preservation its exclusive object. That is the reason for the formation of this Society. . . . The situation requires aggressive action by a large and strong society, which shall cover the whole field and act instantly whenever needed to lead to the preservation of noteworthy buildings and historic sites. That is exactly what this Society has been formed to do.

The new organization would welcome members of other societies and those by residence, birth, or in any other way connected with New England and would seek to save blockhouses and garrison houses, early settlers' homes, seventeenth-century residences with their overhanging second stories, Georgian mansions, post-Revolutionary townhouses, taverns, structures with literary associations, battlefields, and old trails. And a new note was sounded: buildings "which are architecturally beautiful and unique" were as important as those of special historical interest. "It is proposed to preserve the most interesting of these buildings by obtaining control of them through gift, purchase, or otherwise, and then to restore them, and finally to let them to tenants under wise restrictions, unless local conditions suggest some other treatment." Society members would be permitted to visit the buildings at specified times. The society would also establish a museum, in which to keep parts of destroyed old buildings, decorative art objects, and all kinds of historical materials that would show the cultural development of New England just as the Germanic Museum in Nuremberg and the National Museum at Munich were doing in Bavaria. Associate members of the society would pay dues of $2; active members, $5; and life members, $50. The endowment fund from life memberships would be used to purchase old houses. Thus, Appleton hoped "that the antiquities handed down from our ancestors shall be passed on unimpaired to our descendants."[2]

Historic preservation had begun in this country about 1850 with the purchase of the Jonathan Hasbrouck House, Washington's headquarters at Newburgh, New York, by the State of New York, and the rescue of Washington's plantation of Mount Vernon on the Potomac River by Ann Pamela Cunningham and the Mount Vernon Ladies' Association of the Union. Perhaps twenty or thirty other historic house museums had opened since then, and the appearance and rapid use of the automobile soon would activate many others. Alice Winchester was right, however, when she wrote of the society: "But it was new to organize such work on a broad basis, covering so large an area as the whole of New England, and it was new to direct its efforts to preservation not only of early buildings but of all that represented the past life of the area."[3]

Sumner Appleton's thirty-seven annual reports as corresponding secretary (he later added "and Real Estate Manager" to his title) were published in the Bulletin and Old-Time New England. He was always frank about the society's financial affairs; he listed its numerous needs and calculated the endowments necessary to meet them in the hope that members and other readers would supply gifts and bequests. He had thought optimistically that annual dues and the life membership endowment fund, plus local contributions, would permit the society to purchase two old buildings yearly and meet the cost of their repair and restoration. Obtaining 2,000 members who would pay dues of about $6,000 would provide maintenance funds, helped by operating most of the buildings as residences, some as museums with entrance fees, and a few as tearooms, antique shops, community centers, or some other kind of adaptive use. Those kinds of operations would allow most of the buildings to remain on the tax roll.[4]

After five years, however, the society had fewer than 1,500 members and only $8,450 in the life membership fund. Though it was helping community organizations such as historical societies, museums, family associations, and interested individuals so as to save at least one or two properties each year, it owned only three buildings, two of them heavily mortgaged. It had but two employees (Appleton and his capable secretary, Miss E. Florence Addison), who occupied two rooms in the fireproof building of the New England Historic

Genealogical Society, though Appleton felt that he needed two rooms for the museum collection, two for loan exhibitions, one for the library, and two for offices. In 1918, he reported that "the work of owning and maintaining a number of widely scattered old houses, and keeping them all as nearly as practicable in their original condition, is an experiment in this country. We have no sign posts to guide us and from the beginning have had to feel our way along." He had changed from thinking that his first duty was to repair and restore a building. Instead, he gave precedence to securing an endowment of at least $5,000 for each house so as to cover its ordinary upkeep.[5]

Appleton was much concerned also with the society's museum and library functions. Its museum should preserve not only architectural fragments and wallpapers but also furnishings, textiles, clothing, tools, dolls, toys, and other objects to show the area's cultural development. It should conduct frequent loan exhibitions; some of the early ones included a colonial parlor with furniture and furnishings; samplers; needlework; pictures; mourning jewelry; silhouettes; wax portraits and miniatures; and heraldry. So far as the library went, he thought only a few reference books were needed, but that photographs of New England buildings and social life, postcards, negatives, sketches, measured drawings, plans, and other visual materials should be collected aggressively. Appleton persuaded young Thomas T. Waterman, a rising architect, to visit houses with him and make measured drawings for the society's collection. (By the time of Appleton's death, the society's graphic holdings contained more than 600,000 items). Both museum and library required more space, while the former needed display cases and the latter, filing cabinets. The two operations were staffed by volunteers but obviously soon ought to have paid professional help.[6]

Appleton without success tried to promote an outdoor or open-air museum for New England. He admired the pioneer efforts in that field: Skansen at Stockholm, the Sandvig Collection at Lillehammer in Norway, and other European attempts with proper interior furnishings, suitable landscaping, and costumed interpreters and craft demonstrators. In his 1919 report, he outlined his plan thus:

> This would mean a group of six tiny villages covering New England's history up to date, each village with its meeting house situated on the village green or facing the village square and surrounded by the typical buildings of its period. . . . Probably few of these buildings would be of the first rank, for all such our Society must aim to keep on the original sites, but there are a host of lesser buildings of minor importance, still worth preserving, which would serve for the purpose of

the outdoor museum. . . . Sooner or later such a museum will surely be started somewhere in New England and it would be pleasant indeed if it could be done under the auspices of our Society.

In his last annual report of 1946-1947, Appleton advocated also importing buildings from England to portray a village from which New England ones were derived.[7]

By its tenth anniversary in 1919, the society was well on its way. It owned seven historic buildings, including the Harrison Gray Otis House (1795) in Boston, which had become its headquarters. A distinct step forward took place when George Francis Dow joined the staff that year, to remain until his death in 1936. An indefatigable researcher and learned local historian, he supervised the museum, edited the magazine, and served as a font of historical knowledge. He was a pioneer in the preservation movement who, as curator and secretary of the Essex Institute at Salem, in 1907 had installed three period rooms of 1750–1800 based on careful research and then had enlarged the Institute's backyard to receive one of Salem's oldest buildings, the John Ward House (1684), as a kind of miniature outdoor museum. He also had restored the Parson Capen House (1683) for the Topsfield Historical Society and later would reconstruct two seventeenth-century rooms for the American Wing of the Metropolitan Museum of Art.[8]

To sum up, in ten years Appleton had made the society the strongest historic preservation organization in the whole country, and, with its new headquarters and the resourceful Dow on its staff, it was ready to expand its influence.

II

William Sumner Appleton, Jr., was born at Boston on May 29, 1874, at the house his grandfather Nathan Appleton had built on Beacon Street. Nathan was a successful textile merchant and cotton manufacturer who left his son, William Sumner Appleton, Sr., comfortably fixed; he attended Harvard (A.B., A.M., and LL.B.), studying history and art. He was married to his cousin, Edith Stuart Appleton. The younger Sumner attended Miss Garland's School in Boston, St. Paul's in Concord, New Hampshire, and Hopkinson's School in Boston. His health was frail, and he was in a wheelchair recovering from diphtheria when he took his examination for Harvard. There, he studied French, history, fine arts, Latin, philosophy, economics, government, and English. He also attended the Saturday Evening Dancing Class, and he had a bet with a friend that made each of them pay five cents every time they used a swear word, though they made an exception for "To Hell with Yale." Sumner was an editor of the student magazine, the *Advocate*, but he suffered from weak eyes so that someone had to read to him to prepare for examinations. After graduation, he remained a staunch Harvard supporter, belonged to the Harvard clubs of Boston and New York, and always bought season tickets to the football games.

Upon his return from a Grand Tour of Europe, Sumner entered the real estate business in 1898 with Lombard Wilson but withdrew after three years when he almost suffered a nervous breakdown. While he was recovering, he spent summers at Moon Island on Squam Lake near Holderness, Hew Hampshire, where he played tennis, went canoeing, and swam at the beach. At home, he often invited young ladies to accompany him to cotillions, billiards, plays, or concerts (they referred to him as "Uncle Sumner"). He went calling on Sunday afternoons in frock coat and silk topper with cane. But he followed the example of his two Uncle Appletons and never married.

In 1905 Sumner Appleton met with a committee to save the Boston State House from damage by a subway and then began work with the Paul Revere Association. In 1906–1907 he took graduate courses at Harvard in botany, mining and metallurgy, and architecture. He began to visit Massachusetts historic sites systematically—at Salem, Newbury, Bedford, and Lexington. Then, starting work with the Preservation Society, he continued on that course for thirty-seven years until his death at Lawrence, Massachusetts, after a short illness on November 24, 1947.[9]

Everyone who knew Sumner Appleton agreed that he was modest, earnest, enthusiastic, democratic, wise, and patient. Edward J. Hipkiss, curator at the Museum of Fine Arts, declared: "To such a man wordy appraisal of his aims or his successes is pleasing, but he is a bit shy and puzzled about what others write or what they say in speeches. He gives his all in doing." Charles Knowles Bolton, who worked with him at the society for twenty-two years, recalled: "In all these years he has never lost his temper, but often when I, as President, said or did something which did not meet with his approval, a look of pain came over his face that only a Rembrandt or Franz Hals could have caught." His daily work routine was unconventional, and he sometimes became so absorbed in a problem that he lost track of time and might call a staff member or trustee in the middle of the night. Charles Messer Stow, the antiques editor of the New York *Sun*, knew Sumner well; he thought that "his greatness did not come from doing spectacular things blatantly. It came from doing quietly and modestly things of supreme importance to future generations." Stow joked that "he sometimes was dubbed parsimonious and many a bout with a disgruntled cab driver followed a nickel tip." His selfless but driving force for the Society for the Preservation of New England Antiquities was also well described as "by birth, instinct, preference and profession a New Englander."[12]

III

Sumner Appleton's highest aim was that the society acquire and preserve buildings of great historical and architectural importance. The first step in the process was to be sure that a building was authentic. He used local historians and antiquarians to do thorough research on the building's history, often publishing their work in the *Bulletin* or *Old-Time New England*. He himself usually did the architectural research. He traveled constantly through New England examining structures that might be worth saving. He learned to strip sample sections of exteriors and interiors to discover what changes had taken place through the years, to remove wallpaper and interpret stenciling, and to scrape coats of paint so as to find the original colors. "Photograph, measure, and record" was a primary rule. He believed in preferably doing no restoration work or as little as absolutely necessary and in making sure that what was done was carefully marked and recorded. He described himself as "the most conservative restorer . . . and a building is in safe hands when I have charge of it." He also turned for advice to skilled antiquarian architects like Norman Morrison Isham or Joseph Everett Chandler. In 1940, Charles Knowles Bolton summed it up: "In all these thirty years Mr. Appleton has acquired enormous knowledge of building construction details." And any structure the society took had to meet his high standards.[13]

Once the society secured ownership of a building and repaired and restored it enough to insure its continuation, the next step was to discover some practical use that would contribute toward its maintenance. One device was to rent a building such as the Swett-Isley House (1670) in Newbury, the society's first acquisition (all houses cited here are in Massachusetts unless otherwise indicated), in this case for use as a tearoom. The second acquisition, the Samuel Fowler House (1810) in Danvers, would eventually revert to the society after the "life right" of a tenant expired, and for a time it served as the society's secondary museum. The third property, the Cooper-Frost-Austin House (1657) at Cambridge, was leased out at $50 a month for a tearoom and antique shop. The Quincy Memorial (1804) in Litchfield, Connecticut, and Bleakhouse (about

1796) in Peterborough, New Hampshire, are additional examples of the frequently used life-right arrangement. Another commonly employed approach, as at the Short House (1733) in Newbury, had a custodian with or without family in residence who collected an admission fee from all visitors except society members. The Sarah Orne Jewett Memorial (1774) at South Berwick, Maine, was operated as a museum in remembrance of that author; its adjoining Dr. Theodore Eastman Memorial (1851) served as a community center. The society not only used the Harrison Gray Otis House (1795) as its headquarters but also Elias Haskett Derby's Barn (1798) at Watertown for storage. The Spaulding Grist Mill (about 1840) and a Cooperage Shop (about 1825) at Townsend were both gifts of the Spaulding Fiber Company. The Peabody Family Burying Ground and Elias Smith Burying Ground (both 1775) at Middletown were maintained by a $10,000 endowment from the George August Peabody Estate.[14]

As Charles Hosmer has shown so well, Appleton could be tenacious as well as resourceful in saving a property. The Abraham Browne House (about 1663) in Watertown was in a ruinous state in 1915 and about to be torn down. Appleton failed to interest in its preservation Browne descendants, the Watertown Historical Society, a New York architect, or even his own trustees, who voted against allowing a special drive for $10,000 in its behalf. He then bought the house himself for $4,000 down. Finally, a small group of members raised money for its purchase and restoration, and the trustees accepted it in 1922. Appleton wrote his sister later that the Browne House

> is my own personal monument and the fact that it is now standing at all is simply because I got mad and decided that it shouldn't be pulled down, but I would hate to tell you how many thousands I had to risk paying myself had my efforts failed. At one time it seemed as though I would have to sell everything I owned.[15]

These examples indicate the wide variety of properties the society obtained and some of the ingenious ways of helping support them that Appleton developed. At the time of his death, the society owned fifty-six houses, about one-third of which were of the seventeenth century. Most of them were situated in Massachusetts, though Maine, New Hampshire, and Connecticut each had three, and Rhode Island, two. There was none in Vermont. Of the fifty-six properties, fifteen had come as gifts, twelve as bequests, four by ordinary purchase, and four by means of special drives.[16]

Appleton was nearly always willing to help other organizations secure historic properties when that appeared to be the preferable arrangement. Despite his reluctance to entrust a property to the Federal Government, he had the society in 1936 transfer its Richard Derby House (1762) at Salem to the National Park Service to become part of the Salem Maritime National Historic Site. The Laws House (about 1803) at Sharon, New Hampshire, was turned over to the Sharon Art Center. Appleton objected strongly in 1919 when the Metropolitan Museum of Art purchased and planned to move the Wentworth-Gardner House (1760) in whole or in part from Portsmouth, New Hampshire, to be incorporated into its American Wing. The museum heeded his protest and agreed to sell the property to the society, which administered it for about eight years but failed to raise the necessary payment and in 1940 permitted it and its neighboring Tobias Lear House (about 1740) to go to a local Portsmouth organization. Another example of cooperation occurred in 1935 when Appleton took a leading part in the five-day whirlwind drive that resulted in the acquisition of the Christopher Gore House (1805) in Waltham for $75,000; the society began by pledging $5,000, while the Massachusetts Society of Colonial Dames, the Trustees of Public Reservations, and the Massachusetts Society of Architects also made large contributions to the down payment. Appleton spoke frequently and enthusiastically before local groups and persuaded many community organizations to save houses; the society sometimes contributed funds in effecting such arrangements. Municipalities also occasionally helped, as when the mayor of Newport, Rhode Island, in 1916 arranged to preserve the Old Brick Market (1762).[17]

The society gave advice to preservation projects in many other places, such as Charleston, Baltimore, Philadelphia, Savannah, and several in Canada. Though it decided not to contribute when a New Jersey organization requested financial help, it publicized the matter in the hope that New Jersey might form its own preservation society. Appleton also recommended aid for many worthy projects including Mount Vernon and Westover in Virginia, the Brewton-Pringle House in Charleston, and Governor Keith's Graeme Park in Montgomery County, Pennsylvania.[18]

The venerable English Society for the Preservation of Public Buildings asked the SPNEA for funding help in 1924, a request refused on principle, though worthwhile British projects were described in *Old-Time New England* in the hope that they might attract gifts from individuals. The magazine regularly carried news of the British National Trust for Places of Historic Interest or Natural Beauty (1896), and the society was proud that that organization had been patterned after the Trustees of Public Reservations in Massachusetts (1891). The activities of other British organizations—for instance, the Society for the Preservation of

Commons, Footpaths, and Open Spaces—and appeals of churches for help with their repair and restoration were also publicized. During the First World War, the society, concerned about the possible destruction of European landmarks, sent resolutions to President Wilson urging him to seek their preservation and to offer safekeeping in this country of moveable art objects. It also approved the protest of the Society for the Preservation of Ancient Buildings against moving distinguished English houses such as Warwick Priory and Agecroft to America.[19]

Appleton favored making preservation assistance available throughout the nation. He would retain the front-line work of the patriotic-ancestral and local historical societies, but in 1919 proposed having four large regional organizations take the leadership—his own society, of course, along with the Association for the Preservation of Virginia Antiquities, the American Scenic and Historic Preservation Society of New York, and the Archaeological Institute of America. They should build up endowments that would enable them to purchase valuable architectural and historical properties and then deed them to local agencies, which would manage them. By 1926 he was urging the Archaeological Institute to adopt a different plan, which he described as follows:

> What is needed in this country is a fund of say five million dollars in the hands of a board of trustees having power to distribute its income up and down the whole country wherever most needed in order to preserve what is best. Probably the most efficacious way of using this would be to pay for the endowment of a property, provided local interest attended to the purchase. The endowment is generally the most expensive and difficult part of the undertaking and its application to the house could always be made dependent on its purchase within a certain definite time and its proper use by some local body.[20]

Appleton's national plans did not succeed. Probably no private organization could have carried them out on such a scale. Even the National Trust for Historic Preservation, chartered at Washington in 1949, for long had little success in securing properties of its own or subsidizing those of local agencies. The Historic Sites Act of 1935 did give the National Park Service authority to receive and maintain important historic structures and sites, and the expansion of the Federal Government's role since then has resulted in a stronger national system of historic preservation.

By far the greatest problem of the society was financial. At first, Appleton thought that a large membership would provide the necessary funds. By 1929, with constant appeals and energetic solicitation, 3,000 members had been obtained;

they brought in about $10,000 annually. The deepening economic depression, however, soon cut the membership in half. As early as 1913, the trustees had decided that special contributions above dues could be called for, and as many as three drives were held annually for carefully described projects. Often they sought only four or five thousand dollars, but larger sums were sometimes needed, as for the purchase of the Otis House headquarters ($22,725). In the late 1930s during the depression, such special drives were undersubscribed several times. After Helen F. Kimball gave $1,500 for an Emergency Fund in 1913 and Helen Collamore's bequest of $5,000 followed three years later for the upkeep of the society's real estate, gifts and bequests increased steadily. Minor sources of income included admission fees at the buildings and advertising (which had to have an antiquarian tone) in *Old-Time New England*. Appleton really made remarkable progress in obtaining funds in many ingenious ways. When he died in 1947, the society's real estate holdings were valued at $857,700 and its endowment at $507,800.[21]

Another pressing need of the society was space for its rapidly growing museum and library collections. Ten years after the society acquired the Otis House, the City of Boston decided to widen the street on which it faced. The society then bought four adjoining lots behind it and moved the Otis House forty feet back and thirty-five feet upward so as to occupy two of them. Two buildings on the other lots were joined to form a fireproof museum, library, and office complex. The society then began to create period rooms in the Otis House as well as holding special loan exhibitions there and in its other building. In 1932 furniture and other Washingtoniana were shown to commemorate the 200th anniversary of that hero's birth, and in the next year drawings and photographs of Colonial Williamsburg in Virginia. Appleton commented that "the group restoration of Williamsburg is so closely along the same lines of what we are doing in scattered units that the results are of greater interest to us, perhaps, than to any other single group in the country."[22]

The society enjoyed observing two important anniversaries. At its twenty-fifth in 1935, seven of the dozen survivors of the eighteen incorporators reenacted the first meeting of April 16, 1910, the ladies in the group donning costumes of that day. "The participants entered into the spirit of the occasion," the report of the meeting recorded, "with much zeal to the great entertainment of an audience that filled to overflowing the entire hall in the basement of Otis House." President William Crowninshield Endicott, an incorporator and treasurer for the first twenty years, said that "William Sumner Appleton is 'it,' to use a slang expression. His dream has been realized. Had it not been for him and his enthusiasm the Society would not have the standing that it has today."[23]

The thirtieth anniversary in 1940 was planned as a tribute to Appleton. Only four of the surviving seven incorporators could be present. Charles Knowles Bolton traced the society's history and Appleton's leading part in it and then moved that the room in which they were meeting at Otis House henceforth be known as Appleton Hall and that a committee be appointed to install a suitable tablet "memorializing Mr. Appleton's monumental service to the Society." The motion, of course, passed unanimously, and Appleton Hall later was elegantly furnished.[24]

Appleton provided wisely for the continuation of his efforts for the society. Bertram K. Little of Boston, who possessed great business ability, deep historical knowledge of New England, and, with his wife, Nina Fletcher Little, lively interest in collecting its surviving cultural objects, in 1932 became Appleton's chief assistant and virtual associate director as well as trustee and recording secretary. His fifteen years of experience in that role coupled with his sound scholarship allowed him to take over smoothly as director and corresponding secretary upon Appleton's death. For another twenty-three years, with devoted service he energetical carried the society's work to higher levels with many useful innovations.[25]

Sumner Appleton was a key figure in American historic preservation. He developed sound principles that have been accepted as standards in that field. He preached the preservation gospel up and down the land and even abroad— in visits to old buildings, speeches to preservation groups, trenchant articles in *Old-Time New England*, and a voluminous correspondence. He always stood ready to take architects, property owners, or publicists with him to visit historical and architectural treasures in order to make his points amid the three-dimensional evidence. And Appleton's services were well recognized. The Trustees of Public Reservations in 1944 gave him an award for Distinguished Service for Conservation with a handsome silver tray. In 1946 the American Scenic and Historic Preservation Society of New York bestowed upon him its George McAneny Medal in a moving ceremony. Later, the magazine *Antiques* devoted an entire issue to the society with real appreciation of Appleton's imaginative innovations and energetic efforts. As his friend Charles Messer Stowe told him: "You have met success and frustration with even hand, but victory for preservation has been so often on your side that historians of the nation revere you." And Charles Hosmer was right in regarding him as "the first full-time preservationist in twentieth-century America."[26]

NOTES

1. The chief sources for this chapter are: "Special Issue: Society for the Preservation of New England Antiquities," *Antiques Magazine* 97 (May 1960), with articles by Alice Winchester, 464–65, Bertram K. Little, 466–68, and Abbott Lowell Cummings and Helen Comstock, 469–75; two superb treatments by Charles Hosmer, Jr.: *Presence of the Past: A History of the Preservation Movement in the United States Before Williamsburg* (New York: G. P. Putnam's Sons, 1965); *Preservation Comes of Age: From Williamsburg to the National Trust, 1926–1949*, 2 vols. (Charlottesville. Va.: University Press of Virginia, 1981); Bertram K. Little, "William Sumner Appleton," in Clifford L. Lord, *Keepers of the Past* (Chapel Hill: University of North Carolina Press, 1965), 215–22. Massachusetts Historical Society *Proceedings* 69 (Oct. 1947–May 1950) 70–80; *Old-Time New England* 30 (Apr. 1940): 106–110; 38 (Apr. 1948): 70–80; and Katherine H. Rich, "Beacon," *Old-Time New England* 66 (Jan.–June 1976): 42–60. Appleton's own sparse account is in *Who Was Who in America, 1945–1950* (Chicago: A. N. Marquis, 1950), 2: 29.

2. Society for the Preservation of New England Antiquities *Bulletin* 1 (May 1910): 4–7. See also Hosmer, *Presence of the Past*, 12, 238–44; Little in *Keepers of the Past*, 216–18.

3. Edward P. Alexander, *Museum Masters: Their Museums and Their Influence* (Nashville, Tenn.: American Association for State and Local History, 1983), 177–204; Hosmer, *Presence of the Past*, 35–37, 41–62; Winchester, "Special Issue: SPNEA," 466.

4. SPNEA *Bulletin* 3 (July 1912): 12–21.

5. Hosmer, *Presence of the Past*, 241, 242; Hosmer, *Preservation Comes of Age*, 1: 138–39; SPNEA *Bulletin* 6 (Apr. 1915): 18–22; 9 (Nov. 1918): 24–25.

6. William Sumner Appleton, "Destruction and Preservation of Old Buildings in New England," *Art and Archaeology* 8 (May–June 1919): 177–79; Cummings and Comstock, "Special Issue: SPNEA," 469–75; Hosmer, *Presence of the Past*, 241; Campbell Kaynor, "Thomas Tileston Waterman: Student of America's Colonial Architecture," *Winterthur Portfolio* 20 (Summer/Autumn 1985): 105–06; Little, "Special Issue: SPNEA," 422–25; SPNEA *Bulletin* 3 (Aug. 1913): 14; 6 (Apr. 1915): 18–22.

7. Laurence Vail Coleman, *Historic House Museums: With a Directory* (Washington, D.C.: American Association of Museums, 1933), 105, 133, 135; Hosmer, *Presence of the Past*, 246, 255–56; Hosmer, *Preservation Comes of Age*, 1: 161, 167–68; *Old-Time New England* 22 (July 1933): 3–13, 38 (Oct. 1947): 50; SPNEA *Bulletin* 10 (Oct. 1919): 23–24.

8. Coleman, *Historic House Museums*, 134; Hosmer, *Presence of the Past*, 213, 216, 250–51; Hosmer, *Preservation Comes of Age*, 1: 136; *Old-Time New England* 11 (July 1920): 40; (Apr. 1921): 187, SPNEA *Bulletin* 9 (Nov. 1918): 6–16; (Feb. 1919): 1–3.

9. Little, "Appleton," in Lord, *Keepers of the Past*, 215–222.

10. *Old-Time New England* 34 (Jan. 1944): 53.

11. *Old-Time New England* 30 (Apr. 1940): 107–10.

12. Hosmer, *Presence of the Past*, 257; *Old-Time New England* 38 (Apr. 1948): 75–77.

13. Hosmer, *Preservation Comes of Age*, 1: 133; Little, in *Keepers of the Past*, 220 and "Special Issue: SPNEA," 469; *Old-Time New England* 30 (Apr. 1940): 107–10; SPNEA *Bulletin* 3 (July 1912): 14–15; (Feb. 1913): 12–18, 20–24.

14. SPNEA *Bulletin* 2 (Aug. 1911): 9–13; (Mar. 1912), 1–9; 3 (July 1912): 1–7; 9 (Nov. 1918): 6–16; *Old-Time New England* 12 (Apr. 1922): 163–66; 19 (July 1928): ix; 22 (July 1931): 47–48; (Apr. 1932): 192; 24 (July 1933): 17–25; 28 (July 1937): 25–26; Hosmer, *Presence of the Past*, 241–42, 246–50.

15. Hosmer, *Presence of the Past*, 246–50; *Old-Time New England* 13 (Apr. 1923): 181–82.

16. Little, "Special Issue: SPNEA," 466; *Old-Time New England* 32 (July 1941): 11–12; (Apr. 1942): 115; 33 (Apr. 1943): 44; 39 (Oct. 1948): 52–60.

17. Hosmer, *Presence of the Past*, 222–31; Hosmer, *Preservation Comes of Age*, 1: 143, 147–50, 201–06; *Old-Time New England* 27 (July 1936): 25; 28 (July 1937): 25–26; (Apr. 1938): 133–34, 146–47; 30 (July 1939): 34; (Apr. 1940): 137; 40 (Apr. 1950): 219–26; SPNEA *Bulletin* 6 (Jan. 1916): 2–11.

18. Appleton, "Old Buildings in New England," 179–81, 183; Hosmer, *Presence of the Past*, 252–55; *Old-Time New England* 11 (Apr. 1921): 182; 12 (Apr. 1922): 181–82; 24 (July 1933): 30–31.

19. Hosmer, *Presence of the Past*, 255–56; Little, in *Keepers Of the Past*, 220; *Old-Time New England* 15 (Oct. 1924): 91–92; 16 (Apr. 1926): 173–74; 18 (July 1927): 48; (Jan. 1928): 141–43; 21 (Oct. 1930): 85–87; SPNEA *Bulletin* 5 (Dec. 1914): 19.

20. Edward P. Alexander, "Sixty Years of Historic Preservation: The Society for the Preservation of New England Antiquities," *Old-Time New England* 61 (Summer 1970): 14–19; Appleton, "Old Buildings of New England," 179–83; Hosmer, *Presence of the Past*, 273–97.

21. Hosmer, *Presence of the Past*, 244–45; *Old-Time New England* 12 (Apr. 1922): 187; 15 (July 1924): 44–45; 27 (July 1937): 25–26; 28 (Apr. 1938): 153; 29 (Apr. 1929): 149; 39 (July 1948): 28; SPNEA *Bulletin* 3 (Feb. 1913): 11; 4 (Aug. 1913): 15; 7 (Dec. 1916): 2; 8 (Mar. 1917): 1–16; 9 (Nov. 1918): 25.

22. Hosmer, *Presence of the Past*, 251; *Old-Time New England* 17 (Oct. 1926): 90–96; 18 (Oct. 1927): 95–96; 22 (Apr. 1932): 152–61; 23 (Jan. 1933): 127; 24 (July 1933): 30–31; 27 (Apr. 1937): 155–57.

23. *Old-Time New England* 26 (July 1935): 32–33.

24. *Old-Time New England* 30 (Apr. 1940): 107–10.

25. Hosmer, *Presence of the Past*, 257; Hosmer, *Preservation Comes of Age*, 1: 179–82; *Old-Time New England* 23 (July 1932): iii; 39 (July 1948): 12–14; (Oct. 1948): 52–60; 61 (July–Sep. 1970); 14–25.

26. Hosmer, *Preservation Comes of Age*, 1: 133; *Old-Time New England* 34 (June 1944): 49–53; 38 (Apr. 1948): 73–77; "Special Issue: SPNEA," 464–502.

SELECT BIBLIOGRAPHY

Alexander, Edward P. *Museum Masters: Their Museums and Their Influence.* Nashville, Tenn.: American Association for State and Local History, 1983.

Appleton, William Sumner. "Destruction and Preservation of Old Buildings in New England." *Art and Archaeology* 8 (May–June 1919): 177–79.

Coleman, Laurence Vail. *Historic House Museums: With a Directory.* Washington, D.C.: American Association of Museums, 1933.

Hosmer, Charles, Jr. *Presence of the Past: A History of the Preservation Movement in the United States Before Williamsburg.* New York: G. P. Putnam's Sons, 1965.

_____. *Preservation Comes of Age: From Williamsburg to the National Trust, 1926–1949.* 2 vols. Charlottesville. Va.: University Press of Virginia, 1981.

Kaynor, Campbell. "Thomas Tileston Waterman: Student of America's Colonial Architecture." *Winterthur Portfolio* 20 (Summer/Autumn 1985): 105–06.

Little, Bertram K. "William Sumner Appleton." In Clifford L. Lord. *Keepers of the Past.* Chapel Hill: University of North Carolina Press, 1965.

Massachusetts Historical Society *Proceedings* 69 (Oct. 1947–May 1950).

Old-Time New England. Vols. 11–66 (1920–1976).

Rich, Katherine H. "Beacon." *Old-Time New England* 66 (Jan.–June 1976): 42–60.

"Special Issue: Society for the Preservation of New England Antiquities." *Antiques Magazine* 97 (May 1960).

SPNEA *Bulletin.* Vols. 1–10 (1910–1919).

CHAPTER 7

Frank Friedman Oppenheimer
Uses Visitors as Part of Museum Experiments

I

WHILE HE WAS TEACHING PHYSICS at the University of Colorado in Boulder beginning in 1950, Frank Oppenheimer began to conceive a new kind of museum of science and technology. He and his associate, Malcom Correll, assembled in a large attic space a "Library of Experiments," which they used in enthusiastic and exciting teaching and then left in the hallways for their undergraduate students to operate, study, and enjoy. The library eventually contained some eighty experiments, all of them requiring hands-on participation from their viewers, not the mere pushing of buttons or turning of switches but instead the activation of the experiment, the involvement of the participant's sensory perception—sight, hearing, smell, or touch—and varied efforts to find the limitations of the experience. The students used the exhibits in their own individual ways, often with what Oppenheimer called "playfulness." "Turn the dials, manipulate, change the controls, do it yourself" were the phrases associated with the participatory exhibits, and their users often remarked, "How nice to be in a museum where touching is encouraged."[1]

In 1965 Oppenheimer received a Guggenheim fellowship that allowed him to spend the next year at University College in London, during which he visited the leading European museums of science and technology. In London the Science Museum at South Kensington impressed him with its hands-on experiments, its Children's Room, and the traveling shows of interactive exhibits it sent about

Britain. In Paris he admired the college students who acted as demonstrators at the Palais de la Découverte. And the Deutsches Museum in Munich, undoubtedly then the best museum of science and industry in the world, elicited his praise for its numerous experiments, for letting technicians and craftsmen work visibly among its exhibits, and for its training programs for schoolteachers during summers and school terms, even though he criticized what he considered the museum's rigid overcom-partmentalization of physics. Oppenheimer was an avid visitor of museums throughout his life and always ready later to apply useful practices that he observed to his own operation. Thus he mentioned receiving help with his project from the Corcoran Gallery, National Gallery, and the Smithsonian's National Museum of Natural History in Washington, the Franklin Institution in Philadelphia, Ontario Science Center in Toronto, Chicago Museum of Science and Industry, State Art Museum in Copenhagen, a small historic house in Vermont, and the Steinhart Aquarium in San Francisco.[2]

Oppenheimer took a leave of absence from the University of Colorado in 1969 in order to set up a museum of hands-on exhibits at the old Palace of Fine Arts (which he renamed the Palace of Arts and Science) in San Francisco; it opened its doors to the public that September. The Palace, with a cavernous hall of 86,000 square feet—1,000 feet long, 40 feet high, and 120 feet wide— had been built for the Panama-Pacific Exhibition of 1915 that honored the completion of the Panama Canal. A semicircular classical beaux-arts building with pink Corinthian columns, it was designed by Bernard Ralph Maybeck and was adjacent to the City Marina on a tree-lined approach to Golden Gate Bridge. Since that exhibition had closed, at various times the palace had housed eighteen tennis courts, an Army motor pool, two fire departments, a warehouse for overseas shipments, and a storage depot for telephone directories. The city now paid for its extensive renovation and rented it to the museum for one dollar per year. Oppenheimer disliked the word "museum" because he thought it had a passive connotation for many people, and he thus coined the name "Exploratorium." The Corcoran Gallery helped him obtain the show, "Cybernetic Serendipity," which the British Institute of Contemporary Arts in London had prepared, for the opening, for which he also secured a model from the Stanford Linear Acceleration Center. But the heart of the new Exploratorium consisted of interactive, dynamic, and entertaining experiments (which soon numbered 300) scattered about the huge space and before long attracting 300,000 visitors yearly.[3]

II

The Exploratorium's main purpose was not the collection of objects but instead the teaching of the principles of science and technology by means of interactive, hands-on experiments, similar to those Oppenheimer had developed at the University of Colorado. The "Enchanted Tree" at rest was plain looking, but a sound-sensitive microcomputer caused it to light up in varied colors whenever anyone clapped, whistled, or shouted before it. That experiment showed how sound energy was converted into electric energy and then into light energy. The "Distorted Room" appeared rectangular at first glance but had a slanting floor; a person moving across it, viewed from a slit on one side, appeared to change from a giant into a dwarf. Thus the visitor learned something about visual perception and perspective. One of the most popular demonstrations was the dissection of a cow's eye with a sharp razor. Visitors at first were repelled by the experiment but then awed when the demonstator extracted the clear round transparent lens and passed it around to be looked through. A "Catenary Arch" could be built with a set of wooden blocks in the same shape in reverse of a suspended chain. If one clapped hands in front of the "Echo Tube," the sound came back like a ricocheting bullet; and "Everyone Is You and Me" made the viewer's and a companion's faces merge into a single joint image. The "Shadow Box" had strobe lights that caused a phosphorescent rear screen to retain momentarily shadow images in sharp relief when children leaped, danced, and somersaulted in front of it; and a walk-in "Kaleidoscope" transformed the reflections of three youngsters into a crowd of images. A "Pedal Generator" required fast pedaling to keep three electric lights bright; the "Momentum Machine" whirled one about dizzily; and the "Vidium" (oscilloscope) produced colors and patterns when a visitor spoke or sang into a microphone. Then there were lasers, stroboscopes, holography, computer poetry, space craft models, a large gyroscope, and a cathode ray tube. These were only samples of the hundreds of experiments that kept children as young as three or four as well as adults engrossed and amused. Each exhibit had two cards beside it; one described the scientific phenomenon, and the other told how to bring the experiment to life.[4]

Oppenheimer since childhood had been interested in art and art museums. He came to believe that both art and science were needed to describe and understand the world of nature. Thus he defined the Exploratorium as a museum of science, art, and human perception and enlisted artists on his staff as well as scientists. In 1973 he obtained grants to finance a year-long artist-in-residence program, and it became a permanent educational feature of the museum. Several spectacular exhibits were created by various artists. The "Sun Painting" by Robert Miller consisted of a revolving mirror that directed sunlight from a hole in the roof onto a series of prisms and mirrors which broke it into a mixture of subtle hues and nuances of pure color. The "Tactile Dome" developed by August Coppola became a favorite exhibit. It was a geodesic dome thirty feet in diameter, totally dark on the inside; a visitor climbed, crawled, and slid on the stomach along walls, floors, and ceilings while experiencing hot and cold temperatures, rough and smooth surfaces, tight and open spaces, rope networks, close-fitting tubes, and the textures of corduroy, fur, vinyl, and birdseeds. An "Aeolian Harp" by Douglas Hollis was placed on the roof over an entrance to the museum; it was activated by the wind and produced different sounds from soft humming to complex harmonics caused by the wind's turbulence. Thus Oppenheimer acquired interactive exhibits for understandings of both art and science.[5]

The new museum was governed by the Palace of Arts and Science Foundation of twenty-three members, with eight scientists (three of them Nobel laureates) and the remainder leaders from business, labor, civic life, and the arts. Its president was the head of the Homestead Mining Company; the two vice-presidents were connected with the University of California; the treasurer had retired from the Owens Illinois Glass Company; and the secretary was secretary-treasurer of the International Longshoremen's and Warehousemen's Union. The finances came from federal, state, county, city, private foundation, corporate, and individual grants, as well as from some 260 members. At first, both admission and parking were free of charge, but one could make a donation by dropping a coin in a box, thus activating a sound and light display, so pleasing that many viewers dropped another coin in order to see it again. The Exploratorium was open from 1 to 5 p.m., Wednesdays through Fridays, 7 to 9:30 p.m. on Wednesday evenings, and from noon to 5 p.m. on weekends. Mornings were reserved for school children who constituted the predominant audience during the week, while adults formed the majority on weekends. A 1978 survey found that 26,000 came in scheduled school groups from kindergarten through college, with more than 50 percent of them from grades 5–6. In the yearly total of 300,000 visitors, 50 percent were over 21 years of age; 25 percent were under 10; 30 percent came from San Francisco, with 40 percent from other parts of the Bay Area and 30 percent from outside the region.[6]

The experiments at the Exploratorium usually were built in its carpentry, machine, and electronic shops, and the artists, technicians, and craftsmen working in them were visible to the public at one end of the great hall. Ideas for new exhibits were always welcomed, and industries, federal agencies, artists and scientists from throughout the country, and visiting students made suggestions. The exhibits had a home-made look and were done rather crudely when they were first placed on the floor. The public's reaction to them was closely observed, and then they were revised in more permanent form. They might be tested again and, if necessary retested until they satisfied the staff.[7]

The Exploratorium had no regular guards or guides but instead "Explainers" in distinctive red jackets. They were patterned after the demonstrators of the Palais de la Découverte, but most of them were high school students paid $2.25 per hour. Ten of them worked full time (twenty hours) during the week, and another ten part-time for eight hours per day on weekends. They consisted of an equal number of young men and young women, and more than half of them were orientals, blacks, or Hispanics. Applicants were interviewed by the museum staff, chosen because of their ability to communicate, trained in an eight-hour orientation session, and then kept up to snuff with two half-hour lectures on weekends. The explainers kept an eye on the exhibits so that the museum experienced no vandalism. They roamed about the floor answering questions from the visitors and assisting them with the experiments. Another half-dozen high school students were hired each summer to help construct and repair exhibits.[8]

Oppenheimer started a School in the Exploratorium (SITE) for upper grade and junior high teachers of the San Francisco and Marin County public schools. It was modeled on the Deutsches Museum's schools for teachers and aimed to acquaint them with scientific phenomena and to stimulate their perceptual awareness. In the school year 1974/1975, 600 of them attended all-day sessions once a week for five weeks or eight weekly two-hour periods. They used hands-on methods; for example, in studying vision, they used the cow's eye dissection and experimented with lenses, prisms, magnifying glasses, light angles, and filters. Oppenheimer had artists speak to them and even a poet who discussed the musical textures of words. After the course, they could use a lending library of props and portable exhibits in their classrooms and encourage students to invent their own experiments. The parents of students often became enthusiastic about the course, and in one instance they raised money to permit another class to participate in the program.[9]

A Medical Technology Series in 1979 attracted attendance of 50,000 in six months. The program was planned with local physicians and medical researchers and used volunteer health technicians to help the participants interact with the equipment. Monthly programs were devoted to "Speech and Hearing," "Vision," "The Heart-Lungs," "Movement and the Body," "Imaging the Body: From X-Rays to Ultrasound," and "The Technology of Treatment: Cancer Therapy." Those attending could lie on the X-ray table and watch their own EKGs. In the appropriate months they could take hearing tests, preschool and adult vision tests, lung volume and stress tests, and foot examinations. Equipment was demonstrated and explained by medical researchers, and volunteer health professionals encouraged visitor interaction, answered questions, and analyzed the devices. Questionnaires at the end of the course showed that the participants had come out of general curiosity or because they or a relative were ill, and their reactions were generally most enthusiastic. The Exploratorium encouraged other museums to offer similar courses.[10]

A Dissemination Program supported by the Kellogg Foundation for five years provided internships of two to five weeks to 125 museum professionals (81 from the United States and 44 from other countries) to enable them to study the Exploratorium exhibits and adapt them for their own museums. A Conference on Science and the Media attracted representatives from television, newspapers, magazines, book publishing, and libraries, as well as scientists from museums and universities. Another Conference on the Elements of Coed Design was equally successful. The Exploratorium issued three *Cookbooks* that explained in detail the preparation and duplication of 201 exhibits; thus it shared its expertise with science centers and other types of museums. Many academic faculty members attended such activities and returned to their campuses and communities to institute Exploratorium practices.[11]

All in all, Oppenheimer succeeded in starting a new kind of museum that continued to make innovations and soon built up an enthusiastic following; it became known nationally and internationally as the progressive and trail-breaking leader of the science and technology museum field.

III

Frank Friedman Oppenheimer was born in New York City on August 14, 1912, the son of Julius and Ella (Friedman) Oppenheimer. As he grew up there, he made frequent visits to the American Museum of Natural History, the Metropolitan Museum of Art, and later the Museum of Modern Art. He attended Johns Hopkins University at Baltimore, where he received a B.S. in 1933. He then began research on particles in the Cavendish Laboratory at Cambridge University in England and also visited the Institute di Arceti in Italy. He returned to the United States to continue nuclear studies at the California Institute of Technology in Pasadena and received his Ph.D. there in 1939. He was a research associate at Stanford for two years and then began work with Ernest O. Lawrence at the Radiation Laboratory of the University of California at Berkeley on the electromagnetic separation of uranium isotopes. He moved on to the Los Alamos, New Mexico, Weapons Laboratory late in 1943; his older brother Robert, another atomic physicist, was in charge there. As part of the Manhattan Project, Frank supervised the instrumentation of the first successful nuclear explosion at the Trinity test site. He often said jokingly that he was "the uncle of the atomic bomb."[12]

Oppenheimer was married to Jacquenette Yvonne ("Jackie") Quant in 1936. They both were dismayed by the economic depression of the 1930s and were seeking "an answer to the problems of unemployment and want in the wealthiest and most productive country in the world." Thus they joined the Communist Party in 1937 but became disillusioned and left it three and one-half years later. Their strong social conscience remained, however, and Frank in 1945 became a leader in the Association of Los Alamos Scientists (ALAS) formed "to promote the attainment and use of scientific and technological advances in the best interests of humanity." It later became the National Federation of American Scientists. They feared for the future of the world in face of the enormous destructive force of nuclear weaponry and attempted to institute some kind of civilian or international control. Though they failed, Oppenheimer never stopped trying. In 1965 he wrote a guest editorial in the *Saturday Review* commenting on the book entitled *Brighter Than a Thousand Suns* and arguing that nuclear weapons made future wars inconceivable, that the armament race was unconscionable, and that an immediate solution must be found to allow the settlement of world problems without resort to war.[13]

In 1947 Oppenheimer left the Manhattan Project to become assistant professor of physics at the University of Minnesota. There he did landmark research on cosmic rays, chasing hydrogen balloons across the Minnesota countryside and later through the Caribbean. The balloons ascended some twenty miles and enabled him to become a co-discoverer of the heavy nuclei component of cosmic rays. In 1949, however, his career in physics was cut short when he was called before the Un-American Activities Committee of the United States House of Representatives. He admitted there his former membership in the Communist Party and talked freely about his actions, but he courageously refused to identify other party members (many of them his friends) "because that might be used to impugn the loyalty of others, whom I know nothing against." His work at the Oak Ridge and Los Alamos laboratories counted in his favor, for General Leslie R. Groves, the head of those operations, had written a letter of praise for his efforts, and the committee did not hold him in contempt. But he was forced to resign his post at Minnesota, and no other university or institute dared hire him. He attended the Denver International Cosmic Ray Symposium at Idaho Springs in the same year, and his paper there "received one of the few spontaneous bursts of applause." Frank's brother Robert in 1954 was declared a security risk by the Atomic Energy Commission because of his attempts to control atomic weaponry, though he remained director of the Institute for Advanced Study at Princeton with the full backing of its trustees.[14]

Oppenheimer decided in 1949 to move with his wife and two children (Judi, 9, and Mike, 6) to a cattle ranch of 380 acres situated near Pagosa Springs, high in the Blanco Basin of Colorado. A good craftsman (carpenter, plumber, and mechanic), he became a successful rancher. He also was elected to head the local Cattle Ranchers' Association. He remarked that he "never had the slightest trouble from anyone about the Communist thing." In 1957 Oppenheimer began to teach science to a class in the county elementary school at Pagosa Springs. He was an innovative teacher who "really cared about getting his students excited" over learning; he even conducted some classes in a local junkyard. Robert H. Johnson, the Jefferson County superintendent of schools, was impressed by his work and asked him to teach a special physics class made up of twenty-six top ranking seniors from the eight high schools of the county. Again he enjoyed great success and went on to administer a University of Colorado summer institute for teachers of physics. Though he kept serving as a consultant to the county schools, he soon moved in 1959 to Boulder (his daughter Judi was entering her sophomore year there), where he became professor of physics at the university and developed the library of experiments which was the predecessor of the Exploratorium. He became more and more interested in education and in 1969 began giving his chief attention to his new conception of a museum.[15]

Thus after brilliant careers as an atomic and cosmic rays researcher and as an outstanding teacher of science from elementary and high school through college and university, he devoted the remaining seventeen years of his life to a new kind of teaching museum. His wife Jackie was a full partner in that activity and became head of the museum's graphic department, where she excelled in making the language of science intelligible to the general public. And Oppenheimer's original contributions in his varied fields brought him considerable fame. In 1973 he delivered the Robert A. Millikan lectures before the American Association of Physics Teachers; in 1979 he received the Kirkwood Award for Distinguished Service from the California Institute of Technology and soon similar honors from the University of Colorado and the American Association of Museums. He was also the subject of a Nova television program sponsored by the Smithsonian Institution. He died at his home in Sausalito, California, on February 3, 1985. But his Exploratorium continues to keep alive his fresh and forceful ideas about education and museums.[16]

IV

Frank Oppenheimer was not only a keen observer but a deep thinker, ever probing below the surface of phenomena trying to discover their true meaning. It is thus rewarding to examine his speeches and writings in sequence in order to understand the development of his ideas. That process also allows one better to define the Exploratorium which is indeed the culmination of a long intellectual search. Oppenheimer first came to the attention of the museum world when he attended the Smithsonian Institution's Conference on Museums and Education held in 1966 at the University of Vermont in Burlington. In a formal address on science and technology museums, he asserted that they made people aware of the wholeness of our culture and that science and technology were as important components of that culture as art and history. Though such science museums were expensive and had no sure recipe for success to follow (the Deutsches Museum, however, was a good model), a medium-sized city of 100,000 or more could develop one by accumulating a core of demonstration apparatus, models, and reproductions of significant experiments. The Science Museum in Paris, the University of Colorado's demonstration laboratory, and the London Science Museum's traveling exhibits were all worth examination. Science museums appealed to passive visitors or wanderers as well as to school classes with docents, to children and adults, and to community educational programs and correspondence school courses. Local industries could help set up exhibitions and encourage their personnel to use them. Perhaps Americans, surrounded by so much science and technology on all sides, needed fewer such museums, but they were especially important for developing countries which ought to support strongly the acquisition of laboratory equipment and the institution of teacher training courses.[17]

In the discussion period at the conference, Oppenheimer held the audience spellbound with a remarkable extemporaneous passage. Though he said that he was a non-museum person, he considered museums terribly important because they filled holes in one's experience and provided synthesis for objects of great variety. Both art and science made one aware of one's surroundings and changed "the way one looks at oneself and the rest of the world." Both of them were concerned increasingly with the inaccessible and trying to find new techniques to reach it.[18]

Dr. Albert Eide Parr, the former director of the American Museum of Natural History who had retired to become a senior scientist there and was speaking and writing many articles on the significance of museums, was attending the conference and was deeply impressed by Oppenheimer's remarks. The two men had much in common. Oppenheimer as a boy of four or five had learned to ride a bicycle, though his legs were too short to reach the pedals all the way round. He then was delighted to teach the other children of the neighborhood to ride. Parr had grown up in Norway and, as a boy of the same age, had taken a trip across the bay to buy fish for his family. He remembered how much he had learned in wandering about the stores, civic buildings, fire station, and museum that he passed and from the adult conversations that he overheard on the way. He regretted that many of the homes of children were in the suburbs far removed from city centers and that the automobile had made such treks too dangerous for children to walk there. Parr thought that Oppenheimer's vision of the museum offered some substitute for learning through experience; he visited him when he was setting up the Exploratorium and, from his own broad background, helped make it a powerful teaching force.[19]

Parr encouraged Oppenheimer to explain his ideas for the Exploratorium that he was about to open, and he did so in a 1968 article in the American Museum of Natural History's professional museum magazine, *Curator*. First of all, people needed to understand the science and technology so important in their world. While books, magazine articles, television, motion pictures, and general science courses in the schools offered some help, they lacked props, that is, apparatus that people could handle; trying to explore science and technology without props was like telling a person how to swim without going near the water. Oppenheimer then outlined a possible form for an exploratorium or science center in five main sections. The first would deal with hearing: musical instruments; everyday sounds and noises; the physics of sound—vibration, oscillation, resonance, interference, and reflection; the physiology of the ear; and industrial techniques such as speakers, microphones, acoustics, hearing aids, telephone, radio, and sonar. Next would come vision with the physics of light; the eye; pigment manufacturing; television; photography; infrared and ultraviolet lighting; and lasers. The third section on taste and smell would consider food; perfume; the chemistry involved; and food and cosmetic industries. The fourth would examine clothing and housing; perceptions of hot, cold, and roughness; the physics of heat; and fibers and building materials. And last would come control of the body in dancing, athletics, and bicycle riding; muscles and nerves; and semicircular canals.

Such a museum could start by saving and using science fair exhibits; securing apparatus shown in educational television science programs; placing in a central location laboratory equipment developed by schools and colleges; and obtaining objects from industry and scientific organizations. He summed up the objective of such a museum as follows:

> A museum should not be a substitute for a school or classroom but it should be a place where people come both to teach and to learn. Visitors should be able to find it refreshing and stimulating. Above all it should be honest and then convey the understanding that science and technology have a role which is deeply rooted in human values and aspirations.[20]

For the remainder of his Exploratorium career, Oppenheimer expanded his ideas on museums and museum education. He used many different approaches in defining the Exploratorium. Once he said: "I intended a kind of woods of natural phenomena that were organized and selected in some way so that people could take many constructive paths. This is not a museum, it's a curriculum."[21] He insisted that "the whole point of education is to transmit culture, and museums can play an increasingly important role in the process. It is a mistake to think that preserving culture is distinct from transmitting it through education."[22] And the Exploratorium never needed an education director; the entire museum was devoted to education. One commentator found Oppenheimer "a gentle yet forceful man with a mission: to make the understanding and appreciation of science a source of enrichment in people's lives."[23]

The methods used by the Exploratorium are best described by the experiments and the way they worked. Still, some generalizations are possible. Oppenheimer thought that exhibit materials

> should give the viewer the opportunity to explore and manipulate them. Individual exhibits . . . must be of value at a variety of levels which range from rela-

tively superficial sightseeing through to a broad and deep understanding. The exhibit must provide a multiplicity of interacting threads and pathways which visitors can select.[24]

Nor was sightseeing or one-shot wandering about the exhibits bad; one must remember that sightseeing provided exceptional stimulation and insights for a Marco Polo or a Darwin. Again, Oppenheimer stated that "only a limited amount of understanding comes from watching something behave; one must also watch what happens as one varies the parameters that alter the behavior." Even more important was "the flexibility that allows exhibits to be used for play." Many times he emphasized that playfulness should be encouraged, and he pointed out how much both animals and children learned through play.[25]

Oppenheimer was especially interested in the contrasting educational practices of schools and museums. He thought that too much was expected of the schools and listed ten things that they were supposed to accomplish: make learning appear worthwhile; teach skills; cultivate values; transmit culture; produce creative individuals; develop physical and mental fitness through athletics; make the most of both gifted and challenged students; keep young people off the streets and out of their parents' hair; eliminate prejudice; and certify students for employment or further education.[26] Good teachers must set up environments and situations conducive to learning and help get students unstuck when they could not understand something. But most classroom programs were two-dimensional and used lectures, blackboards, television programs, and motion pictures. Museums, on the other hand, provided "a reversible, deflectable, three-dimensional form of education." Visiting students were free from learning tensions; no one ever flunked a museum, and one museum was not a prerequisite for another. But museums often had not understood their educational purpose; their exhibits had not paid attention to touch or kinasthesia; and the public had regarded them as merely a leisure-time activity. The Exploratorium's rationale, however, was "developing a core of participating exhibits and demonstrations that elucidate the mechanisms of human sensory perception involved in sight, hearing, touch, etc." It was "to provide a learning environment outside the classroom situation where individuals may develop an understanding of human sensory perception." And it was most important that the museum and academic worlds work together toward that end.[27]

Thus Oppenheimer contributed to the museum education field. His participatory Exploratorium was soundly established and bringing new liveliness and zest into science centers and even to their art and history cousins. Some of his ideas were too advanced for the present time. For example, he thought that cities ought to establish Museum Districts just as they had School Districts. He also suggested Library Districts, Recreation and Park Districts, and Educational Television Districts. But he was always hopeful that "if people spend a little more of their lives in a museum, it will change what happens in the classroom."[28]

Frank Oppenheimer's Exploratorium has continued influential. Dr. Robert L. White, formerly professor of electrical engineering at Stanford University, succeeded him as director and still considered the Exploratorium's mission "to make the world around us understandable and fun." Its exhibits soon numbered 750, and its annual attendance grew to 500,000. Its sway has been worldwide, and similar science exhibits and museums are now found in New York, Paris, Hong Kong, Oklahoma City, Helsinki, Atlanta, Beijing, San Diego, Stockholm, Milwaukee, Barcelona, Ann Arbor, Osaka, Phoenix, Toronto, Singapore, and elsewhere.

The exhibit growth and storage needs of the original Exploratorium in San Francisco, however, demanded much new space; the floor area was doubled and a separate 750-car parking garage erected. Also, a sounder financial underpinning evolved. Oppenheimer had had to depend mainly on sporadic government and foundation grants and earned income, but later substantial yearly coporate and individual support was obtained to provide steadier funding. And a less personal, more conventional management organization and style was adopted. But Oppenheimer's inspired vision and innovative practices were still in use, and they continued to produce valuable changes, not only in the science field but in the whole museum world.[29]

NOTES

1. An excellent full treatment of the museum subject is Hilde Hein, *The Exploratorium: The Museum as Laboratory* (Washington, D.C.: Smithsonian Institution Press, 1990). Other sources for this chapter are American Association of Museums, *Museums for a New Century* (Washington, D.C.: AAM, 1984); K. C. Cole, "The Art of Discovery in San Francisco—Exploratorium," *Saturday Review* 55 (Oct. 14, 1972): 40–43; Victor J. Danilov, "The Exploratorium of San Francisco Twenty Years Later," *Museum* 163 (1989): 155–59; Judy Diamond, Terry Vergason, and Gaile Ramey, "Exploratorium's Medical Technology Series," *Curator* 22 (Dec. 1979): 281–98; Kenneth W. Ford, "The Robert A. Millikan Award, 1973," *American Journal of Physics* 41 (Dec. 1973): 1309–10; Marvin Grosswirth, "San Francisco's Exploratorium Makes You Part of the Action: Its Exhibits Give New Meaning to the Concept of the Hands-on Visitor," *Science Digest* 7 (June 1980): 60–64; Sherwood Davidson Kohn, "It's OK to Touch at the New-Style Hands-on Exhibits," *Smithsonian* 9 (Sept. 1978): 78–83; Eric Larrabee, ed., *Museums and Education* (Washington, D.C.: Smithsonian Institution Press, 1968); Mary Ellen Munley, *Catalysts for Change: The Kellogg Projects in Museum Education*

(Washington, D.C.: Kellogg Projects, 1986), 7–20; Barbara Y. Newsom and Adele Z. Silver, eds., *The Art Museum as Educator* (Berkeley: University of California Press, 1978), 299–305, 440–42, 697–98; Frank Oppenheimer, "Aesthetics and the 'Right Answer'," *Humanist* 39 (Mar./Apr. 1979): 18–26; Oppenheimer, "The Exploratorium: A Playful Museum Combines Perception and Art in Science Education," *American Journal of Physics* 40 (July 1972): 978–84; Oppenheimer, "A Rationale for a Science Museum," *Curator* 11 (Sept. 1968): 206–09; Oppenheimer, "Schools Are Not for Sightseeing" and "Some Special Features of the Exploratorium," in Katherine J. Goldman, ed., *Opportunities for Extending Museum Contributions to Pre-College Science Education* (Washington, D.C.: Smithsonian Institution, 1970), 7–11, 115–18; Oppenheimer, "A Study of Perception as a Part of Teaching Physics," *American Journal of Physics* 42 (July 1974): 531–37; Oppenheimer, "Teaching and Learning," *American Journal of Physics* 41 (Dec. 1973): 1310–13; Paul Preuss et al, "Education with an Edge: An Introduction to the Educational Programs at the Exploratorium," *Physics Teacher* 21 (Nov. 1983): 514–19; Al Richmond, "Doctor Oppenheimer's Exploratorium," *Nation* 211 (July 6, 1970): 6–9; Evelyn Shaw, "The Exploratorium," *Curator* 15 (1972): 39–52; Kenneth Starr and Oppenheimer, "Exploratorium and Culture: Oppenheimer Receives Distinguished Service Award," *Museum News* 61 (Nov./Dec. 1982): 36–45.

2. Hein, *Exploratorium*, 4–5; Oppenheimer, "Schools Are Not for Sightseeing," 7–11; Starr and Oppenheimer, "Exploratorium and Culture," 43–45.

3. Hein, *Exploratorium*, 1, 32–39; Newsom and Silver, eds., *Art Museum as Educator*, 697–98; Oppenheimer, "Aesthetics and the 'Right Answer'," 22; Oppenheimer, "Exploratorium: Playful Museum," 978–84; Richmond, "Doctor Oppenheimer's Exploratorium," 6–9; Shaw, "Exploratorium," 39–40.

4. Hein, *Exploratorium*, 71–123, illustrations after 146, 147–70. See also Cole, "Art of Discovery," 40–43; Grosswirth, "San Francisco's Exploratorium," 61; "How Do Lasers Work? What Is Eye Logic? Exploratorium," *Sunset* 154 (Feb. 1974): 40; Munley, *Catalysts for Change*, 10; Newsom and Silver, eds., *Art Museum as Educator*, 299–300; Oppenheimer, "Aesthetics and the 'Right Answer'," 24–26; Preuss et al, "Education with an Edge," 518; Shaw, "Exploratorium," 46, 48–49.

5. Hein, *Exploratorium*, 147–70.

6. Grosswirth, "San Francisco's Exploratorium," 63; Hein, *Exploratorium*, 20–21; Newsom and Silver, eds., *Art Musewn as Educator*, 697–98; Richmond, "Doctor Oppenheimer's Exploratorium," 6–9; "San Francisco Museum Stresses Involvement," *Physics Today* 24 (June 1971): 62.

7. Hein, *Exploratorium*, 45–70; Oppenheimer, "Exploratorium: Playful Museum," 978–79; Shaw, "Exploratorium," 48.

8. Hein, *Exploratorium*, 135–39; Newsom and Silver, eds., *Art Museum as Educator*, 440–42.

9. Hein, *Exploratorium*, 129–35; Newsom and Silver, eds., *Art Museum as Educator*, 299–305; Preuss et al, "Education with an Edge," 518.

10. Diamond et al, "Exploratorium's Medical Technology Series," 281–98.

11. American Association of Museums, *Museums for a New Century*, 94; Raymond Bruman, *Exploratorium Cookbook I* (San Francisco: Exploratorium, 1975); Ron Hipschmann, *Exploratorium Cookbook II, III* (San Francisco: Exploratorium, 1981, 1987); Danilov, "Exploratorium Twenty Years Later," 158; Hein, *Exploratorium*, 187–88, 210–11; Munley, *Catalysts for Change*, 7–20.

12. Ford, "Millikan Lecture Award," 1309–10; Grosswirth, "San Francisco's Exploratorium," 60; David Hawkins, "Frank Oppenheimer (obituary)," *Physics Today* 38 (Nov. 1985): 122; Hein, *Exploratorium*, 7; *Who Was Who in America* (Chicago: A. N. Marquis Company, 1985), 8 (1982–1985): 308.

13. Hein, *Exploratorium*, 9, 11; "An Ex-Red Oppenheimer," *Newsweek* 33 (June 27, 1949): 25–26; Frank Oppenheimer, "The Mathematics of Destruction," *Saturday Review* 48 (Jan. 16. 1965): 20; Alice Kimball Smith, *A Peril and a Hope: The Scientists' Movement in America, 1945–47* (Chicago: University of Chicago Press, 1965), 115.

14. "Condon and Oppenheimer at International Cosmic Ray Meeting," *Science News Letter* 56 (July 9, 1949): 21; "Ex-Red Oppenheimer," 25–26; Ford, "Millikan Lecture Award," 1309–10; Hawkins, "Frank Oppenheimer," 122–24; Hein, *Exploratorium*, 11; "Investigation of the Brothers," *Time* 53 (June 27, 1949): 14–15.

15. Ford, "Millikan Lecture Award," 1309–10; Hawkins, "Frank Oppenheimer," 122–24; Hein, *Exploratorium*, 11–14; "Return from Exile," *Newsweek* 54 (Sept. 14, 1959): 72.

16. Ford, "Millikan Lecture Award," 1309–10; Hein, *Exploratorium*, 62–63; Oppenheimer, "Study of Perception," 531–37; Starr and Oppenheimer, "Exploratorium and Culture," 36–45.

17. Labaree, ed., *Museums and Education*, 167–68.

18. Ibid., 207, 213–16.

19. Oppenheimer, "Teaching and Learning," 1312; A. E. Parr, "The Child in the City: Urbanity and the Urban Scene," *Landscape* 16 (Spring 1967); Starr and Oppenheimer, "Exploratorium and Culture," 40–41.

20. Oppenheimer, "Rationale for Science Museum," 206–09.

21. Kohn, "It's OK to Touch," 81.

22. Grosswirth, "San Francisco's Exploratorium," 61; American Association of Museums, *Museums for a New Century*, 57.

23. Ford, "Millikan Lecture Award," 1309; Starr and Oppenheimer, "Exploratorium and Culture," 38.

24. Shaw, "Exploratorium," 42–43.

25. Newsom and Silver, eds., *Art Museum as Educator*, 268–69, 300; Oppenheimer, "Aesthetics and the 'Right Answer'," 25; Oppenheimer, "Exploratorium: A Playful Museum," 979–83; Oppenheimer, "Schools Are Not for Sightseeing," 9.

26. Frank Oppenheimer, "The Exploratorium and Other Ways of Teaching Physics," *Physics Today* 28 (Sep. 1975): 9.

27. Newsom and Silver, eds., *Art Museum as Educator*, 698; Oppenheimer, "Some Special Features of the Exploratorium," 115; Oppenheimer, "Schools Are Not for Sightseeing," 7–11; Oppenheimer, "Teaching and Learning," 1311; Starr and Oppenheimer, "Exploratorium and Culture," 45.

28. Newsom and Silver, eds., *Art Museum as Educator*, 304; Oppenheimer, "Exploratorium and Other Ways of Teaching Physics," 11.

29. Danilov, "Exploratorium Twenty Years Later," 158–59.

SELECT BIBLIOGRAPHY

American Association of Museums. *Museums for a New Century*. Washington, D.C.: AAM, 1984.

American Women: The Official Who's Who among the Women of the Nation. Los Angeles: Richard Blank, 1935.

Bruman, Raymond. *Exploratorium Cookbook I*. San Francisco: Exploratorium, 1975.

Cole, K. C. "The Art of Discovery in San Francisco—Exploratorium." *Saturday Review* 55 (Oct. 14, 1972): 40–43.

"Condon and Oppenheimer at International Cosmic Ray Meeting." *Science News Letter* 56 (July 9, 1949): 21.

Danilov, Victor J. "The Exploratorium of San Francisco Twenty Years Later." *Museum* 163 (1989): 155–59.

Diamond, Judy, Terry Vergason, and Gaile Ramey. "Exploratorium's Medical Technology Series." *Curator* 22 (Dec. 1979): 281–98.

Ford, Kenneth W. "The Robert A. Millikan Award, 1973." *American Journal of Physics* 41 (Dec. 1973): 1309–10.

Grosswirth, Marvin. "San Francisco's Exploratorium Makes You Part of the Action: Its Exhibits Give New Meaning to the Concept of the Hands-on Visitor." *Science Digest* 7 (June 1980): 60–64.

Hein, Hilde. *The Exploratorium: The Museum as Laboratory*. Washington, D.C.: Smithsonian Institution Press, 1990.

Hipschmann, Ron. *Exploratorium Cookbook II, III*. San Francisco: Exploratorium, 1981, 1987.

"How Do Lasers Work? What Is Eye Logic? Exploratorium." *Sunset* 154 (Feb. 1974): 40.

"Investigation of the Brothers." *Time* 53 (June 27, 1949): 14–15.

Kohn, Sherwood Davidson. "It's OK to Touch at the New-Style Hands-on Exhibits." *Smithsonian* 9 (Sept. 1978): 78–83.

Larrabee, Eric, ed. *Museums and Education*. Washington, D.C.: Smithsonian Institution Press, 1968.

Munley, Mary Ellen. *Catalysts for Change: The Kellogg Projects in Museum Education*. Washington, D.C.: Kellogg Projects, 1986.

Newsom, Barbara Y., and Adele Z. Silver, eds. *The Art Museum as Educator*. Berkeley: University of California Press, 1978.

Oppenheimer, Frank. "Aesthetics and the 'Right Answer'." *Humanist* 39 (Mar./Apr. 1979): 18–26.

_____. "The Exploratorium and Other Ways of Teaching Physics." *Physics Today* 28 (Sep. 1975): 9.

_____. "The Exploratorium: A Playful Museum Combines Perception and Art in Science Education." *American Journal of Physics* 40 (July 1972): 978–84.

_____. "The Mathematics of Destruction." *Saturday Review* 48 (Jan. 16. 1965): 20.

_____. "A Rationale for a Science Museum." *Curator* 11 (Sept. 1968): 206–09.

_____. "Schools Are Not for Sightseeing" and "Some Special Features of the Exploratorium." In *Opportunities for Extending Museum Contributions to Pre-College Science Education*. Edited by Katherine J. Goldman. Washington, D.C.: Smithsonian Institution, 1970.

_____. "A Study of Perception as a Part of Teaching Physics." *American Journal of Physics* 42 (July 1974): 531–37.

_____. "Teaching and Learning." *American Journal of Physics* 41 (Dec. 1973): 1310–13.

Parr, A. E. "The Child in the City: Urbanity and the Urban Scene." *Landscape* 16 (Spring 1967).

Preuss, Paul, et al. "Education with an Edge: An Introduction to the Educational Programs at the Exploratorium." *Physics Teacher* 21 (Nov. 1983): 514–519.

"Return from Exile." *Newsweek* 54 (Sept. 14, 1959): 72.

Richmond, Al. "Doctor Oppenheimer's Exploratorium." *Nation* 211 (July 6, 1970): 6–9.

"San Francisco Museum Stresses Involvement." *Physics Today* 24 (June 1971): 62.

Shaw, Evelyn. "The Exploratorium." *Curator* 15 (1972): 39–52.

Smith, Alice Kimball. *A Peril and a Hope: The Scientists' Movement in America, 1945–47*. Chicago: University of Chicago Press, 1965.

Starr, Kenneth, and Frank Oppenheimer. "Exploratorium and Culture: Oppenheimer Receives Distinguished Service Award." *Museum News* 61 (Nov./Dec. 1982): 36–45.

CHAPTER 8

Anna Billings Gallup
Popularizes the First Children's Museum

I

IN 1899 PROFESSOR WILLIAM HENRY GOODYEAR, curator of fine arts for the Brooklyn Institute of Arts and Sciences, returned from a European trip during which he had been greatly impressed by the natural history exhibits which were attracting many young people at the Manchester Museum in England. He suggested to Franklin William Hooper, director of the institute, that they set up a children's museum for natural history in the old Adams House, which the institute formerly had used for a warehouse, in beautiful little Bedford (today Brower) Park. Hooper liked the idea, and the city leased them the old building at a nominal rental; it was remodeled, redecorated, and provided with electric lights. On December 16, 1899, the Brooklyn Children's Museum opened its doors, the first children's museum in this country and in the world.

The new museum planned to treat every branch of natural history, attempt to "delight and instruct the children who visit it," and "stimulate their powers of observation and reflection." It hoped to be a "wonder house for children" and would aim

> through its collections, library, curator, and assistants . . . to bring the child or young person, whether attending school or not, into direct relation with the most important subjects that appeal to the interest of their daily life, in their school work, in their reading, in their games and rambles in the fields, and in the industries which are carried on about them.

The museum at first had only two exhibit rooms, but they soon expanded to six on the first floor. The Model Room contained charts, colored cartoons, and natural history specimens purchased from Émile Deyrolle of Paris for about $92; along with such unusual items as a papier maché silkworm (five feet long) and a snail (three and a half feet) that could be taken apart. The Animal Room had models of a mastodon as well as some of today's creatures; the Botanical Room featured forty-two giant dissectible flowers; and in the Anatomical Room were enlarged models of the human heart and human ear that also could be separated into sections. A Lecture Room with forty seats and lantern slide projector was presided over by the first curator, Dr. Richard Ellsworth Call, a trained and enthusiastic science teacher who arranged and labeled the exhibits and conducted the lectures. On the second floor of the building was a library, at first containing only 300 volumes on natural history, and the curator's office; and in a tower on the roof were meteorological instruments.[1]

II

The Children's Museum began to expand as an educational instutution when Anna Billings Gallup joined the staff in May 1902 as assistant curator. She had been born on November 9, 1872, in Ledyard, Connecticut, the daughter of Christopher M. and Hannah Eliza (Lamb) Gallup, and took pride in being a maternal descendant of Elder William Brewster of the Plymouth Colony. After attending public school in Ledyard and the Norwich Free Academy, she enrolled in 1889 in the Connecticut State Normal School at New Britain, from which she was graduated four years later. She then taught biology for four years at the Hampton (Virginia) Normal and Agricultural Institute. She stopped teaching to enter the Massachusetts Institute of Technology, from which she received a Sc.B. degree in 1901. She then instructed in biology for another year at the Rhode Island State Normal School in Providence before coming to the Children's Museum. She was thirty years old, an imaginative, energetic, and persuasive science teacher.[2] Carolyn Spencer has given the following description of her:

> Behind all this activity stands a tall, dark-eyed, pleasant-faced woman, with a soft musical voice and a ready smile. Ever ready to give a helping hand to a boy or girl, to encourage, to cheer, and to stimulate interest, Miss Anna Billings Gallup is the guiding star of the Brooklyn Children's Museum.[3]

She at once began to give half-hour illustrated talks to children from second grade through grammar school on botanical subjects, such as "Little Fall Wanderers" (maple seeds and the like). But she soon started to learn how to use museum objects for instruction. She devised short labels in simple language and large, readable type and saw that the table desk museum cases were cut down to the right height for youngsters, with labels on hinged boards that hung from the cases so that the children could lift them to easy reading distance. She made a bird calendar, listing under each month birds to be found in the neighboring Prospect Park, and also did labels for plants and trees there. She mounted and labeled pressed plants for a herbarium, conducted meetings of the Nature Study and Humboldt clubs, and led walks in the parks. She liked to take her charges through the museum rooms, unlocking cases as they went along so that the children could handle objects and pet live animals.

Gallup said later that the museum was "in the van of progressive education" and

> in a word, the Children's Museum *way of learning things* is pure fun. This *way* is the magic key that opens one door of knowledge after another, it is the magic wand that gives each branch of learning a potential of joy, it is the magnet that draws the crowd, the engineer that keeps them busy with efficiency of action.[4]

The following summer, Gallup spent her vacation studying and collecting in the Marine Biological Laboratory in Bermuda as a member of a New York and Harvard University group, bringing back corals, lizards, sponges, fishes, mollusks, seaweeds, and a Great Surinam Toad. Her talks then concerned not only zoology but sounds, high and low tones, musical instruments, the human voice and ear, the barometer, air pressure, and frictional electricity. In 1904 she was promoted to curator, and Mary Day Lee, trained in physics and chemistry, became assistant curator. She guided some of the boys who were experimenting with astronomy and wireless telegraphy, and took a share in the lecture program. Agnes E. Bowen soon held a similar position for history.

The museum collection was expanding to include arts, technology, geography, and history. In 1903 Gallup had toured Europe for four months, visiting many museums; Dr. F. A. Brower, a curator of the British Museum and member of the editorial staff of the British Museums Association's *Museums Journal*, helped her plan the trip.[5] Upon her return, she added talks on the Alps, Russia, Italy, Holland, London, and Paris. The next year, she saw to it that her sixth graders studied the Andes, the Amazon, Argentina, Chile, Japan, China, and Korea, while the seventh graders considered San Francisco, Chicago, New Orleans, and Boston, and those in the eighth grade, pyramids, temples, statues, and sphynxes. Meanwhile, the younger students heard about warblers, hummingbirds, Baltimore orioles, and scarlet tanagers, or ants, hornets, spiders, and butterflies. She also gave practical talks such as "The Care of Aquariums" and called in a scientist to explain "How to Collect and Preserve Insects." She presented seasonal lectures that included "How Christmas Began and Is Celebrated in Other Lands," "Thanksgiving in the Colonies," and discussions of Lincoln and Washington on national holidays.

Gallup took great interest in the live animal collection. The toad was joined by "Bunny," which wandered in of its own accord; "Fluff," a tame owl; "King Cole," a crow; "General and Mrs. Green," frogs; "Petie" and "Dickie," two white rats; "Plato," a spider monkey from South America that observed its first anniversary at the museum with a feast of peanut brittle and malaga grapes; and numerous snakes and insects, as well as fish in the museum aquarium. Bees were kept in an observation hive and a colony of ants in a glass case. One boy had formed an astronomical group that used two telescopes on the roof. Some fifteen other boys built a wireless telegraph station to communicate with their homes and other operators within a hundred-mile radius, and eventually with Paris and Honolulu. Austin M. Curtis and Lloyd Espinchied were leaders of that group. The boys also replaced fuses, repaired apparatus, and installed a telephone system for the museum.

III

Classroom teachers found that some of their pupils had begun to take deep interest in studying science and asked them where they had acquired their developing knowledge. One nine-year old answered quickly: "In the Children's Museum and I expect to become a great scientist."[6] The teachers started bringing their classes from kindergarten through high school to the museum; in 1906, for example, there were 561 class visits from 125 schools, and 17,351 students came to lectures. For 1910 the total yearly attendance was 187,612.

The museum furnished a docent, a young college graduate, to welcome all young visitors; find out the child's chief interest, whether birds, insects, minerals, or geography; and serve as guide with informal questions and oral tests as they proceeded. The docent sometimes used competitive museum games, distributing cards of graded questions to be answered by closely inspecting objects and their labels and doing research in the library; the youngster answering the most questions correctly in some twenty minutes would be declared the winner. Jigsaw puzzles were also at hand to be assembled. Eventually, the Brooklyn Board of Education assigned four regular teachers for full-time service at the museum. On weekends and holidays, students often spent the day there, eating lunch in the park nearby. Gallup was especially proud of the museum's after-school activities. They included a laboratory with minerals and experiments in physics and chemistry. In the "busy bee room," the younger children studied specimens under magnifying glasses and microscopes. Eight subject matter courses lasted several weeks and led to credits and engraved silver medals. The students pressed and labeled plants for their herbariums, classified minerals, and mounted insects. The after-school scholars formed ten clubs that dealt with bees, carpentry, crafts, junior and senior sciences, the LDH Guild (literature, dramatics, history), microscopes, photography, Pick and Hammer (woodworking tools), and stamps. There was a popular Children's Museum League, where the youngsters held discussions and gave lectures on nature subjects; they paid ten cents for a button and life membership. The museum also served as headquarters for Girl Scout and Boy Scout nature programs.[7] Gallup thought that after-school work

> attracts children to active pastime of the highest educational value. It challenges their minds with real things, subjects of beauty and great interest. . . . But best of all it develops the child's latent powers, gives him experiences that cause him to respect his own work, offers him standards of values and enters him into a consciousness of the worth of his own efforts.[8]

Several of the students who came to the museum regularly in later life showed good results from their devotion. One, after graduating from a university, saved the wheat crop of Indiana from a plague. Another became professor of plant breeding at Cornell University. Three of those who worked on the telegraph secured positions as operators an oceangoing steamships that journeyed to the South, Puerto Rico, and Europe. Of these, Austin Curtis secured a permanent position in South America, gathered an impressive collection of butterflies and moths in Brazil and Argentina, which he presented to the museum, and sent it the spider monkey "Plato" from Colombia, while Lloyd Espenschied was a prominent researcher for radio systems, and his son, Lloyd, Jr., came to the museum frequently.[9]

Gallup was actually the executive head of the museum from the time she became curator, though it was under the supervision of the Brooklyn Institute of Arts and Sciences and its director. After about twenty-two years of service, she seems to have become curator-in-chief at her own suggestion. The story goes that one of her budget requests had been turned down by a city board, and to soften the blow, those in charge said that she might have the one thing she wanted most, whereupon she chose the title, curator-in-chief. It remained in use at the museum for more than forty years but was finally changed to director when the Children's Museum became independent and had its own board, long after Gallup's retirement.[10]

Through the years the museum was always expanding its facilities and activities. The lecture room was enlarged to 100 seats and received improved slide and motion picture projectors. Educational films were shown daily except on the crowded Sundays and holidays. The library occupied several rooms and contained 8,000 volumes. The astronomy section added a planetarium to its telescopes on the roof. Disabled children were welcomed and taken on "please touch" tours. The history rooms procured models such as Henry Hudson's "Half Moon" and Robert Fulton's "Clermont," as well as dioramas of political and military historical events, doll houses, and dolls dressed in the costumes of many nations. A journal was started and enlarged to include news of the Brooklyn Institute; it went to the schools, libraries, and museums of the city. A loan collection of some 5,000 items with stuffed birds, butterflies, minerals, costumed dolls, and 30,000 mounted pictures was distributed by its own truck to schools, libraries, churches, clubs, and other community groups. Individual children could take home for study birds, insects, and many specimens carefully mounted in boxes. By 1929 the loan service was making one million contacts each year. Prize contests on birds, trees, history, minerals, and aquatic life were held; in 1917 they attracted entries from eighty children in thirty schools. A year later, the museum began participating in an Americanization program that helped immigrant families become American citizens.[11]

IV

Gallup did her part in arousing interest and sometimes obtaining financial support for the museum. She spoke to mothers' clubs in Brooklyn; the New York State Science Teachers meeting at Cornell University; the Alumni Association of M.I.T. at Boston; 1,000 public school teachers, principals, and superintendents at five Teachers' Institutes; the State Library Association; and scores of other groups. She worried about funds for the museum, for the city paid only salaries and limited running expenses. She pointed out again and again the need for a larger lecture room; though its capacity had been expanded it was still much too small. In 1919 she gave her talk on Lincoln six times to a total of 721 children, while Lee repeated hers on Washington seven times to 973 students. The children endured long waiting lines and often could not get into the lecture room. One principal called to complain that twenty of his students had to miss a presentation. Gallup was disappointed several times, as in 1915 when the city failed to provide a new fireproof building with an auditorium to seat at least 500.[12]

Gallup made a great step forward in 1916 when she enlisted Helen Butterfield (Mrs. John J.) Schoonhoven in forming the Women's Auxiliary of the Children's Museum. Schoonhoven asserted then: "Our quest is for an intelligent understanding of a great objective, and a constant adherence to an enduring idea in education." The auxiliary gave tea parties for teachers and principals; sponsored an annual bridge tournament that included such luminaries as Edna St. Vincent Millay and Hendrik van Loon; and raised money in other ingenious ways. It brought many new programs into action. Schoonhoven built a strong organization of 2,500 able and active women—headed by Ida Willets (Mrs. I. Sherwood) Coffin as president—and a strong, forceful Executive Board. Membership, social aid and Americanization committees and a thriving speakers' bureau were soon consolidated into an Education Committee of fifteen members. The auxiliary persuaded women's clubs, civic groups, school executives and teachers, and many individual donors to finance its activities. In 1917 various community women's clubs began purchasing ten models or dioramas created by Dwight Franklin for the geography room. They included Eskimos harpooning a whale; Lapps encamped beside their reindeer herd; penguins, seals, and gulls in the desolate, frigid Antarctic; an aboriginal Australian kangaroo hunt; Carib Indians stalking monkeys in Brazil; Bedouins with their camels at an oasis in the Sahara; and Masai attacking a lion invader of their village in British East Africa. Later, twenty-five dioramas added to the world history room included several models of the pursuits of primitive man, Phoenician traders, Marco Polo, the Magna Carta, Prince Henry the Navigator, Columbus, Gutenberg, George Washington, and the Wright Brothers operating their flying machine at Kitty Hawk. The public schoolteachers of New York City raised money for another group of thirty diaramas, many of them chosen by Professor Dixon Ryan Fox of the History Department of Columbia University; they soon began appearing in the American history room.[13]

The auxiliary gave the museum $10,000 in 1920 for a Franklin W. Hooper Loan Collection Fund to honor his role in founding the first children's museum, and on that occasion Gallup spoke of the museum "as an open door for children to a knowledge of the wonderful things of the world." Other contributions helped finance a part-time science curator, numerous summer field trips (as many as thirty-six one year), the film library, and a car to transport museum lecturers to the schools, as well as helping build an endowment fund, which in 1930 reached $12,000.[14]

One of the most important services of the auxiliary was persuading the city to spend nearly $500,000 to purchase a neighboring lot and modernize its Victorian house so as to help the museum meet its pressing space needs. The new building contained the enlarged library, a more spacious auditorium, the loan collection, and rooms for general community meetings and for the Boy Scouts. An auxiliary member soon contributed $8,000 for an elevator to serve the three-story structure.[15]

On June 4, 1929, the Women's Auxiliary carried out a notable observance of its annual Children's Day. Eleanor (Mrs. Franklin D.) Roosevelt, then the First Lady of the State of New York, met with some 500 children in Bedford Park, they carrying balloons in various bright colors inscribed, "Visit the Brooklyn Children's Museum." She then spoke to the auxiliary members in the newly acquired neighboring building and expressed her deep admiration of the museum's work. It was one of the auxiliary's red-letter days.[16]

In her thirty-five years of service, Gallup made the Brooklyn Children's Museum into a potent educational force. She successfully opposed a plan to move the museum to the Brooklyn Institute's main building, insisting that the children must feel their institution belonged only to them. She summed up her conviction on this point thus:

> A museum can do the greatest good and furnish the most effective help to the boys and girls who love it as an institution, who take pride in its work for them and with them, and who delight in their association with it. To inspire children with this love and pride in the institution, they must feel that it is created, and now exists for them, and that in all of its plans it puts the child first. The child must feel that the whole plant is for him, that the best is offered to him because of faith in his power to use it, that he has access to all departments, and that he is always a welcome visitor, and never an intruder.[17]

In another place she said: "Knowledge itself all children love. It is the labor of organizing knowledge that they find distasteful. Inject happiness into the process of learning and you turn the child's work into educational play." And Gallup had a basic principle on how to arrange effective exhibits and activities.

It was simply: "Follow the child around." Thus she insisted that, at the museum, "No new program was accepted until the children had pronounced it full of promise." This emphasis caused one youngster to advise an adult friend: "Perhaps if you have a child with you, you can get into the lecture room."[18]

Gallup, always a magnetic speaker, passionately promoted children's museums and outlined "How Any Town Can Get One." Educators in a community first should secure trustees and a salary for a carefully chosen director and find an unused suitable space in the town. Children then would pour in, be delighted, bring their parents, and obtain the support and pride of the grown-up community. The success of the Brooklyn institution caused several other museums to begin working with children—the Children's Room at the Smithsonian Institution, the American Museum of Natural History, the National Museum of Wales in Cardiff, and others in St. Johnsbury (Vermont), Stepney Borough in London, Milwaukee, Charleston, San Francisco, Cleveland, Berlin, Australia, and New Zealand. Other such American museums (twenty-two of them by the 1930s) sprang up in Boston, Detroit, Indianapolis (now the largest in the world), Fort Worth, Corpus Christi, Little Rock, Jacksonville, Portland (Oregon), Seattle, and Troy in Rensselaer County, New York. Much later, in the 1980s, an Association of Youth Museums was organized, which soon had more than 200 members.[19]

By the time Gallup retired in 1937, the Children's Museum's yearly attendance had reached 600,000. She was known throughout the nation and abroad. A charter member present at the formation of the American Association of Museums in 1906, she regularly attended and often spoke at its annual meetings. In 1937 she persuaded that body to establish a Children's Museum Section; often Schoonhoven and a delegation of auxiliary members accompanied Gallup to its meetings. As early as 1909, the Hudson-Fulton Celebration had given her an award, and in 1930 the National Institute of Social Sciences presented its gold medal in recognition of "her distinguished service to humanity as curator-in-chief for more than a quarter century." The British *Museums Journal*, which always followed her career closely, recorded her deeply felt thanks to the institute, especially for its "public recognition of a life-giving idea" and her hope that it would "send Children's Museum service to higher levels and extend it to widening circles of children." The *Journal* commented that "our readers will rejoice in this honor bestowed on one who has been an inspiration and example to the whole museum world."[20]

Museum workers from all over America came to see Gallup and the Children's Museum, many of them hoping to establish one of their own. Museum studies courses also visited; Laura M. Bragg of the Charleston Museum brought the class she was teaching at Columbia University, and the apprentices from the Newark Museum's training program came twice. Museum people of foreign countries corresponded and often appeared at the museum from Brazil, Colombia, India, Australia, New Zealand, and elsewhere.[21] In 1955, the year before her death, she received the William Hornaday Memorial award for service and leadership in the junior museum field. That same year, she was invited to attend the Indianapolis Children's Museum's thirtieth birthday party. She did not feel up to making the journey but sent her regrets, saying: "I am glad our children's museums are creeping up into big money. It took many years for human thought to realize what we were talking about when we wanted for the country a new kind of museum."[22]

The Brooklyn Children's Museum has continued along the path that Gallup outlined and still provides vigorous leadership in its field. In 1969 its two old Victorian mansions could no longer meet city housing standards and had to be razed. The museum moved to a new location temporarily in a former poolhall and automobile showroom in Crown Heights and became known as "MUSE." Its varied and exciting programs continued to attract enthusiastic youngsters for twelve hours a day. In 1976 under Lloyd Hezekiah, a Trinidad-born but Brooklyn-educated director, the Children's Museum left MUSE, which continued as a neighborhood African-American museum, and returned to its former site in Bedford Park but to a new, innovative $3.5-million building. The structure lies forty feet underground with the entrance at the top through a former subway kiosk. A "people tube" runs 180 feet through the hill with a flowing stream in the center. Its auditorium seats 250. Major exhibits have concerned *The Mystery of Things,* their shape, form, color, and material; *Night Journeys,* an exploration of sleep and dreams; *Animals Eat,* which examines their food chain and environmental habitat; *The Boneyard,* containing human and animal skeletons; *Under Your Feet,* on geology and animal and insect life underground; and *Collection Connections in the Children's Resource Library.* The last exhibit allows children to conduct individual investigations using not only reading, audio-visual materials, and computers, but also object study boxes that include coins and butterflies, or deal with such topics as Plains Indians, Africa, and Jewish traditions.[23] Anna Billings Gallup surely would have rejoiced to see her dream of a new building so ingeniously carried out and put to such imaginative uses.

NOTES

1. The direct quotations are found in "The Children's Museum of the Brooklyn Institute," *Scientific American* 82 (May 12, 1900): 296–97. Other accounts of the museum are Peter Farb, "An Island of Nature," *National Parent-Teacher* 54 (Apr. 1960): 10–12; Anna Billings Gallup, "A Children's Museum and How Any Town Can Get One," National Education Association *Addresses and Proceedings* 64 (1926): 951–53; Gallup, Address Before the Congressional Club, Washington, D.C., Feb. 7, 1930; Gallup, Radio Broadcast on Children's Museums, Education and Fun, Brooklyn Children's Museum, Oct. 20, 1937 (transcript); Gallup, "A Museum for Children," National Institute of Social Sciences *Journal* 3 (1917): 107–09; William Henry Goodyear to Franklin W. Hooper, Jan. 17, 1899, Brooklyn Children's Museum MSS.; Herbert and Marjorie Katz, *Museums U.S.A.: A History and Guide* (Garden City, N.Y.: Doubleday, 1963), 209–12; Philip Mershon, *The Brooklyn Children's Museum: The Story of a Pioneer* (Brooklyn: Brooklyn Children's Museum, 1959); Gabrielle V. Pohle, "The Children's Museum as Collector," *Museum News* 85 (Nov./Dec. 1979): 32–37; Smithsonian Institution, *Women's Changing Roles in Museums: Conference Proceedings* (Washington: Smithsonian Institution, 1986), especially Melinda Young Frye, "Women Pioneers in the Public Museum Movement," 11–17, and Jean M. Weber, "Images of Women in Museums," 20–26.

2. *American Women: The Official Who's Who among the Women of the Nation* (Los Angeles: Richard Blank, 1935), 1; Mershon, *Children's Museum*, 4; *Who Was Who in America* (Chicago: A. N. Marquis, 1935), 3: 310; *Who's Who in America* (Chicago, A. N. Marquis, 1940), 1: 21; *Who's Who in the East* (Washington: Mayflower, 1930), 797–98; Barbara Fletcher Zucker, *Children's Museums, Zoos, and Discovery Rooms: An International Reference Guide* (New York: Greenwood, 1987), 153–56.

3. Carolyn Spencer, "Miss Gallup, Curator of Children's Museum, Introduces Youngsters to Wonders of Nature," unidentified, undated newspaper clipping, Brooklyn Children's Museum Scrapbook.

4. Gallup, Radio Broadcast, 1937, p. 1.

5. The periodical reports of the Children's Museum during Miss Gallup's service are found in *Children's Museum Bulletin* 1–18 (Oct. 1902–Mar. 1904); *Children's Museum News* 1–8 (Apr. 1904–Mar. 1905); *Museum News* (Apr. 1905–May 1913); *Children's Museum News*, vols. 1– 24 (Oct. 1913–May 1937). This footnote covers *Children's Museum News* 12 (Oct. 1924): 136.

6. Gallup, Radio Broadcast, 1937, p. 1; *Children's Museum News* 10 (Feb. 1923): 37.

7. "A Children's Museum," *Scientific American* 112 (Mar. 13, 1915): 250; Laurence Vail Coleman, *The Museum In America: A Critical Study*, 3 vols. (Washington: American Association of Museums, 1939), 2: 253; Miriam S. Draper, "The Children's Museum in Brooklyn," *Library Journal* 35 (Apr. 1910): 154; Anna Billings Gallup, "The Children's Museum as Educator," *Popular Science Monthly* 72 (Apr. 1908): 371–79; Gallup, Congressional Club, 1930, pp. 3, 6; Gallup, "A Museum for Children," 109; Catharine Kneeland, "Museum for Children," *Hygeia* 17 (Aug. 1939): 743; Mershon, *Children's Museum*, 3, 8; *Museums Journal* 30 (Aug. 1930): 65; (June 1931): 291; Sydney Reid, "Children's Wonder House," *Independent* 72 (Jan. 4, 1912): 30–36.

8. Brooklyn Institute *Museum News* 3 (Oct. 1907): 13; 5 (Jan. 1910): 55–57; (May 1910): 119; Anna B. Gallup, "Brooklyn Children's Museum," *School and Society* 32 (Dec. 27, 1930): 865–66.

9. *Children's Museum News* 10 (Feb. 1923): 37; 12 (Oct. 1924): 121; Draper, "Children's Museum," 153–54; Gallup, "A Children's Musuem," 952–53; Gallup, "Children's Museum as Educator," 371–79.

10. Mershon, *Children's Museum*, 4, 9.

11. Brooklyn Institute *Museum News* 2 (Feb. 1907): 84–85; 3 (Feb. 1908): 88; 4 (Feb. 1917): 102–03; 5 (Oct. 1917); 6 (Jan. 1918): 30; 7 (Feb. 1920): 25–29; *Children's Museum News* 10 (Feb. 1923): 37; 12 (Oct. 1924): 121; Rose Mary Daly, "Films for Fledglings," *Saturday Review of Literature* 32 (Nov. 19, 1949): 58; Draper, "Children's Museum," 153–54; Gallup, Congressional Club, 1930, p. 5; Gallup, "Brooklyn Children's Museum," 865–66; Katz and Katz, *Museums U.S.A.*, 210–11; Mershon, *Children's Museum*, 4, 9–10; "Museums and Visual Instruction: World History Series of Models," *Elementary School Journal* 30 (June 1930): 722; Zucker, *Children's Museums*, 151–56.

12. Auxiliary of Brooklyn Children's Museum, *25th Anniversary* (Brooklyn, 1941), 16 pp.; "Brooklyn Children's Museum Proposed New Building," *School and Society* 41 (Feb. 16, 1935): 226; Brooklyn Institute *Museum News* 3 (Feb. 1908): 89; 4 (Oct. 1916): 71; (Dec. 1916): 88; 5 (Feb./Mar. 1918): 36–38; 7 (Feb. 1920): 18–20; Draper, "Children's Museum," 153; Anna B. Gallup, "The Work of the Children's Museum," American Association of Museums *Proceedings* 1 (1907): 144–47; Gallup, Congressional Club, 1930, p. 5; Mershon, *Children's Museum*, 7–8; "Museums and Visual Instruction," 722; *Museums Journal* 14 (May 1915): 357–58; New York *Times*, Dec. 4, 1939, 201; Reid, "Children's Museum House," 35–36.

13. *Children's Museum News* 11 (Mar. 1924): 100; 14 (Oct./Dec. 1928): 66–68; 18 (Oct. 1930): 6; 20 (Jan. 1933): 29, (Mar. 1933): 36; 21 (Apr. 1934): 11, 24; 22 (Mar. 1935): 1–7.

14. *Children's Museum News* 7 (Feb. 1920): 18–20; 18 (Feb. 1931): 38.

15. Brooklyn Children's Museum, *The Geographical Models* (Brooklyn, 1917), 16 pp.; Children's Museum Auxiliary, *25th Anniversary*, 16 pp.; *Children's Museum News* 11 (Feb./Mar. 1924): 98; 12 (Oct. 1924): 124–25; (Oct./Dec. 1928): 70; 18 (Nov. 1930): 12; Mershon, *Children's Museum*, p. 10.

16. *Children's Museum News* 17 (Oct. 1929): 77.

17. Gallup, "A Children's Museum," p. 951.

18. Anna Billings Gallup, "Memories and Satisfactions," *Children's Museum News* 27 (Dec. 1939/Jan. 1940); Eleanor M. Moore, *Youth in Museums* (Philadelphia, University of Pennsylvania Press, 1941), 8, 51–54, 56.

19. Draper, "Children's Museum," 150; Gallup, "A Children's Museum," 953; Gallup, "Children's Museum as Educator," 379; "Growth of Children's Museums," *Hobbies* 53 (Mar. 1948): 26; Sherwood Davidson Kohn, "It's OK to Touch at the New-Style Hands-on Exhibits," *Smithsonian* 9 (Sep. 1978): 81–83; Kneeland, "Museums for Children," 743; Nancy Kriplen, *Keep an Eye on That Mummy: A History of the Children's Museum of Indianapolis* (Indianapolis: The Museum, 1982); Pohle, "Children's Museum as Collector," 32–37; Reid, "The Children's Wonder House," 36; "Youth Museums Number," *History News* 44 (Nov./Dec. 1989).

20. Children's Museum News 10 (May 1923): 61–63; 12 (Oct. 1924): 121; 13 (Oct. 1925), 294; 14 (Oct. 1926): 4; 16 (Oct. 1930); 18 (Apr. 1931): 54; 24 (May 1937); Frye, "Women Pioneers," 13–15; Mershon, *Children's Museum*, 10; *Museums Journal* 30 (July 1930): 25; *Who Was Who*, 3: 310.

21. *Children's Museum News* 7 (Oct. 1919): 6, (Nov. 1919): 12; 10 (Nov./Dec. 1922): 16, (Feb. 1923): 37; 13 (Mar./Apr. 1926): 229; 14 (Oct. 1926): 4, (Feb./Mar. 1927): 36.

22. Gallup, "Children's Museums," 951–53; Kriplen, *Keep an Eye on That Mummy*, 94.

23. Ellen Perry Berkeley, "MUSE: Bedford-Lincoln Neighborhood Museum, Brooklyn," *Architectural Forum* 129 (Sep. 1968); Kohn, "It's OK to Touch," 81–83; Pohle, "Children's Museum as Collector," 32–37; Zucker, *Children's Museums*, 152–53. Ms. Nancy Paine, the Children's Museum's Curator of Collections, kindly has supplied the up-to-date information in addition to reading and making helpful suggestions on this chapter.

SELECT BIBLIOGRAPHY

Auxiliary of Brooklyn Children's Museum. *25th Anniversary*. Brooklyn, 1941.

Berkeley, Ellen Perry. "MUSE: Bedford-Lincoln Neighborhood Museum, Brooklyn." *Architectural Forum* 129 (Sep. 1968).

Brooklyn Children's Museum. *The Geographical Models*. Brooklyn, 1917.

"Brooklyn Children's Museum Proposed New Building." *School and Society* 41 (Feb. 16, 1935): 226.

"A Children's Museum." *Scientific American* 112 (Mar. 13, 1915): 250.

Children's Museum Bulletin. Vols. 1–18 (Oct. 1902–Mar. 1904).

Children's Museum News. Vols. 1–24 (Oct. 1913–May 1937).

"The Children's Museum of the Brooklyn Institute." *Scientific American* 82 (May 12, 1900): 296–97.

Coleman, Laurence Vail. *The Museum In America: A Critical Study*. 3 vols. Washington: American Association of Museums, 1939.

Daly, Rose Mary. "Films for Fledglings." *Saturday Review of Literature* 32 (Nov. 19, 1949): 58.

Draper, Miriam S. "The Children's Museum in Brooklyn." *Library Journal* 35 (Apr. 1910): 154.

Farb, Peter. "An Island of Nature." *National Parent-Teacher* 54 (Apr. 1960): 10–12.

Gallup, Anna Billings. "A Children's Museum and How Any Town Can Get One." National Education Association *Addresses and Proceedings* 64 (1926): 951–53.

_____. Address Before the Congressional Club, Washington, D.C., Feb. 7, 1930.

_____. "Brooklyn Children's Museum." *School and Society* 32 (Dec. 27, 1930): 865–66.

_____. "The Children's Museum as Educator." *Popular Science Monthly* 72 (Apr. 1908): 371–79.

_____. "A Museum for Children." National Institute of Social Sciences *Journal* 3 (1917): 107–09.

_____. Radio Broadcast on Children's Museums, Education and Fun, Brooklyn Children's Museum, Oct. 20, 1937 (transcript).

_____. "The Work of the Children's Museum." American Association of Museums *Proceedings* 1 (1907): 144–47.

Goodyear, William Henry, to Franklin W. Hooper, Jan. 17, 1899. Brooklyn Children's Museum MSS.

"Growth of Children's Museums." *Hobbies* 53 (Mar. 1948): 26.

Katz, Herbert and Marjorie. *Museums U.S.A.: A History and Guide*. Garden City, N.Y.: Doubleday, 1963.

Kneeland, Catharine. "Museum for Children." *Hygeia* 17 (Aug. 1939): 743.

Kohn, Sherwood Davidson. "It's OK to Touch at the New-Style Hands-on Exhibits." *Smithsonian* 9 (Sep. 1978): 81–83.

Kriplen, Nancy. *Keep an Eye on That Mummy: A History of the Children's Museum of Indianapolis*. Indianapolis: The Museum, 1982.

Mershon, Philip. *The Brooklyn Children's Museum: The Story of a Pioneer*. Brooklyn: Brooklyn Children's Museum, 1959.

Moore, Eleanor M. *Youth in Museums*. Philadelphia, University of Pennsylvania Press, 1941.

"Museums and Visual Instruction: World History Series of Models." *Elementary School Journal* 30 (June 1930): 722.

Pohle, Gabrielle V. "The Children's Museum as Collector." *Museum News* 85 (Nov./Dec. 1979): 32–37.

Reid, Sydney. "Children's Wonder House." *Independent* 72 (Jan. 4, 1912): 30–36.

Smithsonian Institution. *Women's Changing Roles in Museums: Conference Proceedings*. Washington: Smithsonian Institution, 1986.

Zucker, Barbara Fletcher. *Children's Museums, Zoos, and Discovery Rooms: An International Reference Guide*. New York: Greenwood, 1987.

CHAPTER 9

John Robert Kinard
Expands the Neighborhood Museum

I

"THIS PLACE," SAID JOHN R. KINARD, the director of the Anacostia Neighborhood Museum in Washington, D.C., "has brought people who wouldn't otherwise be caught dead in a museum." Its exhibitions often might be based on "requests found in the suggestion box, giving local residents a real feeling of 'this is our place'." At the museum, neighbors could "meet to discuss local problems and try to find ways of improving them," and its exhibits and programs expressed every aspect of the Anacostia experience—psychological, spiritual, social, and political. Thus such a museum could meet the practical needs of its community, while attracting a significant number of neighborhood people at all levels.[1] And finally, Kinard asserted, such a museum should concern the common people:

> Our country and its museums have scandalously never told us the truth about Western society. Because presentations were written about the middle-class white Americans by middle-class white Americans who study and write about what interests them, their presentations on our society represent the life of celebration, of achievement and conquest. This is not of interest to most Americans, for our lives are lived striving to achieve self-identity, and to make something out of everyday life.[2]

The Anacostia Neighborhood Museum was the result of a dream of Dr. S. Dillon Ripley, the always innovative secretary of the Smithsonian Institution. In

1966 he began considering the establishment of an experimental community "storefront" or neighborhood museum as a branch of the Smithsonian. A group of citizens known as the Greater Anacostia Peoples, Inc., in a predominantly black area of Washington east of the Anacostia River with a population of some 257,000, persuaded the Smithsonian to establish the branch in Anacostia. More than ninety local citizens met as a Neighborhood Advisory Committee, and the Smithsonian sent Charles Blitzer, then director of its office of Education and Training, and Mrs. Caryl Marsh, a consultant to the city's Recreation and Parks Department who had worked on neighborhood social problems, to help them as well as technicians to convert the run-down, abandoned Carver movie theatre on a main street, Nichols (now Martin Luther King, Jr.) Avenue, into a museum. A committee consisting of Stanley J. Anderson, Almore M. Dale, Mrs. Marian Conover Hope, and Alton Jones were leaders in the movement.[3]

Mrs. Hope, seeking a director for the new museum, had John R. Kinard, a friend of her son's, go to see Blitzer, who was impressed by that vigorous and decisive thirty-year-old black community worker. Blitzer sent him to Dillon Ripley who surprised him with the greeting, "Thanks for taking the job." Kinard knew nothing about museums, but he later recalled: "I thought what the hell. Everybody ought to take a leap once in their lives—just jump and not know where they'll land."[4]

On September 15, 1967, the Anacostia Neighborhood Museum staged a gala opening attended by about four thousand community citizens and residents of the entire metropolitan area, featuring an 84-piece band, two jazz combos, and an enthusiastic block party with energetic youngsters and adults serving refreshments. Exhibits borrowed from the Smithsonian's National Museum of Natural History, National Museum of American History, and National Zoo included an 1895 store of early Anacostia with a post office; metal toys, butter churn, ice cream maker, coffee grinder, and water pump; as well as live monkeys, a large green parrot, other birds, and a black snake. A group of young local artists known as the Trail Blazers painted a mural of primitive life in Africa on a nearby fence, and the lot across from the museum contained a dinosaur, Uncle Beasley, on which children delighted to climb. A projector with slides was available in the museum, and show boxes of small natural history exhibits with bird and animal skins, shells, and fossils could be examined. The community accepted the new institution as its own and maintained it carefully. No unpleasantness took place there during the Washington race riots of that period, and no losses occurred from vandalism. The museum was estimated to cost $125,000–150,000 per year, covered at first by Smithsonian private funds and foundation grants. When that figure proved too small, the local community raised $7,000 to match a grant, with indivudual contributions ranging from five cents to one dollar. A local businessman also provided a bus to take children downtown to the Smithsonian for Saturday morning classes.

II

John Robert Edward Kinard was born in Washington on November 22, 1936, the son of Robert Francis and Jessie Beulah (Covington) Kinard. After graduation from Springarn High School in 1955 and a year and a half at Howard University, he went to Salisbury, North Carolina, studying history and graduating there with a B.A. degree from Livingstone College in 1960 and a Bachelor of Divinity degree from Hood Theological Seminary in 1963. While in college, he spent one summer in Tanzania with Operation Crossroads Africa helping build a dining room and dormitory for students. Upon the urging of Dr. James Robinson, founder of Crossroads, Kinard returned to Africa as a paid staff member with American and Canadian volunteers, working with local students in Tanzania, Kenya, and Zanzibar on self-help programs, and he was made coordinator of all Crossroads projects from Cairo to Zimbabwe. In 1964 he came back to Washington, serving as a counselor of the Neighborhood Youth Corps, organizer with the Southeast Neighborhood House, and analyst of social programs in counties on the Eastern Shore of Maryland.

On November 14, 1964, Kinard was married to Marjorie Anne Williams, who had been a classmate at Livingstone, and the couple went on to have three daughters—Sarah, Joy, and Hope. In 1966 he became assistant pastor of the John Wesley African Methodist Episcopal Zion Church in northwest Washington. He served on many local educational and cultural boards and committees that included the Washington Performing Arts Society and the Corcoran Museum of Art. The *Washington Magazine* in 1974 selected him as a "Washingtonian of the Year."[5] Tragically, John R. Kinard died at age fifty-two on August 5, 1989, after a lengthy illness of myelofibrosis, a disease of the bone marrow. As Dr. Robert McC. Adams, then the Smithsonian head, put it, Kinard was "the founding director and guiding light of the Anacostia Neighborhood Museum . . . one is tempted to say *his* museum" for twenty-two years. And, according to the British expert Kenneth Hudson, he "developed the Anacostia Museum into one of the small number of museums of influence in the world."[6]

III

The chief teaching device of the Anacostia Neighborhood Museum was the special exhibition. An early one prepared in conjunction with the Museum's Youth Advisory Council of about twenty teenagers and with the assistance of Smithsonian curators and exhibition experts was devoted to *This Thing Called Jazz*; it was accompanied by lectures and discussions, jazz performances, and gospel singing. Another show on *Frederick Douglass, the Sage of Anacostia, 1817?–1895* portrayed that pioneer black leader and his world; it was sent about the United States by the Smithsonian Institution Traveling Exhibit Service (SITES). The Junior League of Washington gave the museum a grant that established a Mobile Division with a bright blue van, serviced by an educator, which carried somewhat abbreviated exhibitions, speakers, learning kits, and books to schools, libraries, playgrounds, churches, hospitals, and other community organizations. Outstanding shows treated *Black Patriots of the American Revolution* with 7,000 booklets on the subject sent to the schools; *Toward Freedom: The Civil Rights Movement since 1954*; and the fascinating *Lorton Reformatory: Beyond Time*, presented with the active involvement of inmates at that correctional institution and including an original play and concerts by its band and gospel choir. Perhaps most sensational of all was *The Rat: Man's Invited Affliction* with live rats running about in one showcase and much advice to the viewers on how to rid their homes of that pest. The exhibition traveled on to the Buffalo Science Museum, where it was equally successful. These are a few examples of the more than thirty-five major exhibitions presented in the first eight years of the museum's existence.[7]

The displays continued throughout Kinard's administration. Some later ones included *Blacks in the Westward Movement* (five copies distributed in thirty states by SITES); *Black Women: Achievement Against the Odds*; *The Anacostia Story: 1608–1930*; *Out of Africa: From West African Kingdoms to Colonization*; *Portraits in Black: Outstanding Negroes of American Origin*; *The Renaissance: Black Arts of the 20s*; *Black Wings: The American Black in Aviation* (borrowed from the Smithsonian's Air and Space Museum and redesigned); *The Real McCoy: Afro-American Invention and Innovation, 1619–1930*; and *Climbing Jacob's Ladder: The Rise of the Black Church in Eastern American Cities, 1740–1877*.[8]

These exhibitions attracted heavy attendance from the Washington area; visitors also came from all over the country and from abroad to see them and to consult with Kinard. Numerous smaller educational programs made the museum a bustling community center, for Kinard regarded his charge as a combination museum, cultural arts center, meeting place for neighborhood groups, and skill training center for youngsters. Education chief Zora B. Martin, later Zora Martin-Felton, worked with Kinard and the museum from its beginning; she conceived and developed a successful grant proposal for the Mobile Division and conceptualized and served as curator for the rat exhibit. She early recruited a black Santa Claus at Christmastime and with a community committee developed a kit for the African-American Kwanzaa Celebration. An Annual Festival of the Arts in Anacostia produced skits, plays, concerts, and dance programs. Other yearly exhibits displayed paintings and sculptures by the District of Columbia Art Association or featured student art shows.

A local opinion poll showed that citizens thought the neighborhood's chief problems were crime, drugs, housing, unemployment, and education, and the museum staged exhibits and programs focusing on those issues. Do-it-yourself corners were set up for the plastic arts and other crafts. An exhibit design and production laboratory sought to train Anacostia young people for museum work; in 1976 it accepted 10 trainees, chosen from 100 applicants. A Children's Room in the exhibit area provided an opportunity to develop experimental programs and offered demonstrations in making soap, butter, ice cream, taffy, and candles. Puppet theaters accompanied some exhibitions. The community helped send three Youth Advisory Council members to Africa and others to Puerto Rico, the Bahamas, and Haiti.[9]

The last exhibition in the renovated movie theater took place in 1985–1986, and early the next year the museum moved to Fort Stanton Park, where the Design and Production Department had had quarters since 1976. The new site also contained an exhibition hall, multipurpose room, and office space, while the wooded park outside had picnic tables and benches. At the age of twenty, the Anacostia Neighborhood Museum changed its name and became simply the Anacostia Museum. It had evolved from a strictly local institution to a museum recognized nationally and internationally for its treatment of African-American history, art, and culture as well as for its strong civil rights advocacy. It continued to attract heavy community participation with Lunch Bag Forums of lectures, concerts, and dramatic presentations, as well as a popular Family Day. Special events also helped interpret its exhibitions; for example, a four-day workshop instructed teachers on the history of the black church, and a seminar on "Conservation for the Lay Person" drew church historians, archivists, and others. A computerized inventory of the permanent collections was also completed.[10]

IV

Kinard's experience at Anacostia gave him many definite ideas about museums. First of all, he was sure that the old kind of museum with its emphasis on collection, conservation, research, and even interpretation and display was not enough. Instead, a museum always should stress social change and public service; its exhibits and educational programs ought to enable a community better to understand and work toward solving its current problems. A museum must not be a place for the entombment of relics, but rather, as Neil Harris had said, should be devoted to "reaching a large lay audience, capturing its attention, increasing its knowledge, and shaping its sense of possibility."[11] In a speech to the International Council of Museums (ICOM), Kinard stated that a museum should deal with "the everyday life of everyday men and women," instead of with "the rich and princely playthings and the best of the past."[12]

He was never satisfied with the accomplishments of the Anacostia Museum; so much remained to be done. Museums ought to understand the needs, problems, and inspirations of those who did not visit them. Kinard told the Museum Educators of the American Association of Museums (AAM) in 1977:

> We have left undone the greatest portion of our public responsibility, and that is to evaluate ourselves against those who don't visit museums. For that testimony—provocative, sobering and critical—may be what we need to make our finest contribution to the times of which we are a part, and the future.[13]

This point of view was emphasized in the museum's "Revised Mission Statement" of 1981 which ran:

> The Anacostia Neighborhood Museum should continue to be a neighborhood institution which, while it may focus especially upon the history and culture of Anacostia as a local community and collect objects related to that focus, shall above all be a center for experimentation in the ways museums can reach and involve segments of the population they are not reaching.[14]

Kinard was somewhat unhappy about part of this statement which had emanated from a committee Secretary Ripley had appointed to study the museum. He felt that the wording tended to limit the museum too much to the neighborhood when, in actuality, it was already reaching a national and international audience with its emphasis on the African-American heritage and the whole field of civil rights. Different exhibitions were devoted to those subjects throughout the years, such as *This is Africa*; *Africa: Three Out of Many:—Ethiopia, Ghana, Nigeria*; and others. Such programs had made the museum evolve from a strictly local institution, and they were often dramatized by participatory special events; for example, *An Afternoon of Ghanaian Culture* included drumming, dancing, a fashion display of African clothing, and an "African Food Fair", as well as the usual lectures, films, and teacher seminars.[15]

Kinard showed his unwavering faith in the broader aspects of the museum's work in his Foreword to Louise Daniel Hutchinson's *Out of Africa: From West African Kingdoms to Colonization* (1979):

> For out of Africa and cascading down the corridors of time have come earthshaking ideas, beautiful things, resources, riches, and people. Collectively, they have made wealthy all nations of the earth, for centuries past, and until this very day. If in fact the protest marches, freedom rides, sit-ins, kneel-ins, and pray-ins of the 1960s are to be more than a shallow victory, the black American must understand his history and heritage if he is to reshape his future. . . . As Arthur Schomburg has noted: "For the African American, a group tradition must provide compensation for prejudice. History must store what slavery took away. For it is the special damage of slavery that the present generation must repair."[16]

Kinard's fertile ideas, charismatic personality, and hard, slogging work were much appreciated by his associates. Zora Martin-Felton, who had worked so closely with him since the opening of the museum, said that "John did whatever he had to at the museum, from creating exhibitions to running the vacuum cleaner. He has touched all our lives in a profound manner."[17] Adolphus Ealey, curator of the Barnett-Aden Gallery, thanked Kinard for his concern and assistance with an exhibition on that art museum and described him as "this friend and man of all seasons."[18] Louise Hutchinson, who wrote a history of Anacostia, admired "the constant support and encouragement of one man who continues to open doors and provide opportunities for the growth and development of his staff."[19] And Ralph Burgand, director of New York State and Community Relations, at a Seminar on Neighborhood Museums concluded:

> I think our problem is to create more John Kinards, someone who understands that there are voices in the community. . . . John, if you went from door to door, which is the last thing, somebody would speak to you before they would speak to me.[20]

Kinard had great influence on the American museum movement. He attended and spoke frequently at the national meetings of the AAM and served as its vice-president in 1981–1982. He was a member of the board of the AAM's North-eastern Museums Conference (today the Mid-Atlantic Association of Museums). He took a leading part in forming the African American Museums Association in Detroit in 1978 and was its treasurer in 1982–1983. He visited numerous museums and museum conferences throughout the country, always impressive with his outgoing personality and moving oratory. As a result, museum leaders from all over the land came to him for advice and inspiration.[21] "John Kinard was among those who changed the face of American museums," said Tom Freudenheim, the Smithsonian assistant secretary for museums. "He not only directed a creative and dynamic program . . . but . . . the Anacostia Museum served as a model for a growing number of African American museums around the country—indeed for other ethnically oriented museums as well." Leonard Jeffries of the Black Studies Department of the City College of New York described Kinard "as a teacher, preacher, and soldier in the war against racism."[22]

Kinard was also well known internationally. In 1971 he spoke at the regular triennial meeting of ICOM in Paris and later attended a conference sponsored by the Ditchley Foundation in England. He met ICOM's venerable, highly respected secretary, Georges Henri Rivière, and the two became fast friends. Rivière came from France to Washington to explore a neighborhood museum first hand, and both men were interested in the new ecomuseums that tried to bring museums and their communities together to solve local problems. The movement began in Canada in the 1970s and soon spread through France, Mexico, Spain, and Portugal. Kinard wrote another important article for ICOM in 1985 on "The Neighborhood Museum as a Catalyst for Change."[23] He was called upon to address many museum meetings in Europe, Africa, and the Caribbean. A fascinating instance was his speech on "Museums as Instruments for Social Change" at the annual conference of the Southern African Museums Association at Pietermaritzburg, South Africa, in 1987, at which he dared to criticize openly the racism which white South Africans were displaying. After his talk, a white national administrator declared it "one of the most stringent and worst attacks on white South Africans that he had ever heard." Whereupon, some seventy (one-third) of the delegates walked out of the conference to show their disapproval of the administrator's harangue and their support of Kinard. John later joked about the incident that he had been "the fox let into the chicken coop."[24]

In July 1989 during Kinard's final illness when he was in great pain and had lost 60 pounds, he gave an interview to a Washington *Post* reporter. The resulting article was entitled "Lion of the Anacostia Museum: Director John

Kinard and His Lifetime Mission of Conscience," in which he showed himself indignant with the Smithsonian and with Ripley's successor as secretary, Robert McC. Adams, because they were not providing the Anacostia Museum with enough resources to carry out his program and to obtain an adequate, much larger headquarters at Poplar Point on the bank of the Anacostia River. Kinard also backed the erection of a new comprehensive National Museum of African American History on the Washington Mall. He bluntly blamed the neglect of these projects upon "racism" and called Secretary Adams a "closet racist" who mistreated and slighted blacks. Adams responded that the Smithsonian was making progress achieving changes in these areas but admitted that "John had a point of view that needs to be expressed within the institution" and that he as secretary had "certainly never tried to get him to tone down." Former Secretary Ripley wrote ruefully: "Here was a man who needed every ounce of support and encouragement which we could give; I am only sorry that such support and encouragement could not be more bountiful."

Kinard on his part said that "Adams will tolerate views that he doesn't like or agree with, without being punitive—at least in my regard. . . . But that doesn't mean that anything gets done." He was also disturbed by Adams's costly plan to move the main part of the Museum of the American Indian from New York to a Washington site near the Mall.

Kinard ended his interview with the Washington *Post* as follows:

> I wasn't chosen for this position. I didn't seek it out. The job found me . . . I believe it's the will of God that I'm here. I'm a servant, and I follow. So when I shuffle off this mortal coil, if it can be said of me that "he was a good servant," that will be enough. I just play my role, and when I'm gone, somebody else will come along and pick up where I leave off. Just to be a good servant is all I aspire to.[25]

In that July also, a young woman from the Smithsonian called on Kinard to interview him for an oral history. She intended to have several more sessions with him, but he died before they could be held.[26]

Finally, though I know it is somewhat risky to do so, I'd like to end on a personal note. I had met John Kinard at various AAM functions and in about 1970 I invited him to come to Colonial Williamsburg and bring with him Zora Martin and several other key staff members to discuss with our principal directors how we were treating the subjects of blacks and slavery in eighteenth-century Williamsburg. I was dissatisfied with out interpretation of those topics, especially

since blacks constituted more than 50 percent of Williamsburg's colonial population. Well, John and his group were shocked by our neglect and told us so
frankly. Zora in 1971 wrote a highly critical account of what they saw. Great
numbers of black school children were visiting us, but she thought the introductory
film, of which we were so proud, showed only "happy, well-fed, well-clothed
blacks working in the fields or around the large plantation house" but "nothing
to indicate that they were dissatisfied with their status." Most black employees
visible about the project worked at manual labor, often as waiters, waitresses,
busboys, or gardeners; there were no black docents or interpreters. And the white
hostesses who took visitors about made small mention of slavery or blacks. Zora
concluded: "A visit to Williamsburg reinforces the antiquated belief of minimal
black participation and smiling faces."[27]

When I retired at Colonial Williamsburg in 1972, I came to the University
of Delaware to teach in a Museum Studies program. During some six years I
had an enrollment of about 360, chiefly graduate students, and I invited John
to come each year to speak to my classes on "Neighborhood Museums." I was
always amused that, though he devoted a moderate amount of time to museums,
his chief interest obviously was the civil rights movement; still, I thought it well
for the students to hear that subject discussed from an African-American view-
point. Sometimes John brought along an associate, and on one occasion a young
black student about to graduate from high school, and the class engaged in some
spirited discussions.[28]

The best single word to describe John Kinard is "charismatic," and his wide
knowledge, boundless energy, good humor, and imaginative speaking made him
a great hit. It was a real disaster for the museum world that he had to die so young.

NOTES

1. "Museums: Opening Eyes in the Ghettos," *Time* (June 21, 1968): 78; *Anacostia Neighborhood
Museum, Smithsonian Institution, Sept. 15, 1972 [Fifth Anniversary]* (Washington: Smithsonian
Institution, 1972), 1–2; John Kinard in *Smithsonian Year: Annual Report of the Smithsonian
Institution, 1969*: 565. I am most grateful to Zora Martin-Felton and Gail S. Lowe of the
Anacostia Museum and my daughter, Mary Sheron Alexander, for reading this chapter and
making helpful suggestions for its improvement. I also had insightful interviews with Charles
Blitzer and Stephen E. Weil.

2. John Kinard, "The Visitor Versus the Museum," in *The Visitor and the Museum*, edited by
Linda Draper (Seattle: Museum Educators of the American Association of Museums, 1977), 4.

3. *Smithsonian Year, 1969*: 6–12; *1988*: 6–11; *Anacostia Neighborhood Museum, Smithsonian
Institution, 1966–1967* (Washington: Smithsonian Institution, 1977), ii, 1–3; John R. Kinard
and Esther Nighbert, "The Anacostia Museum," International Council of Museums, *Museum*

24, no. 2 (1972): 108; Caryl Marsh, "A Neighborhood Museum that Works," *Museum News* 47 (Oct. 1968): 14–16; Zora Martin-Felton and Gail S. Lowe, *A Different Drummer: John Kinard and the Anacostia Museum, 1967–1989* (Washington: Anacostia Museum, 1989), 17–19.

4. Martin-Felton and Lowe, *Different Drummer*, 20–21; Washington *Post* (July 19, 1989): D10.

5. *Anacostia Neighborhood Museum [Fifth Anniversary]*, 9, 43; *John R. E. Kinard, 1936–1989: A Memorial Tribute* (Washington: Smithsonian Institution, National Museum of Natural History, 1989), 4 pp.; John R. Kinard, "The Neighborhood Museum as a Catalyst for Social Change," *Museum* 148 (1985): 217; "John R. Kinard" (obituary), New York *Times* (Aug. 7, 1989)II: 6; Martin-Felton and Lowe, *Different Drummer*, 1–4, 7–12, 21–22, 26–27, 28–30, 69–70; *Museums: Their New Audience: A Report to the Department of Housing and Urban Development* (Washington: American Association of Museums, 1972), 111; "Oral History Project: Interview with John R. Kinard, Director, Anacostia Museum, July, 1989" (Archives and Special Collections of the Smithsonian Institution), 41 pp.; "Tribute for John Kinard," *The Torch, Smithsonian Institution Monthly Newspaper* 89 (Sept. 9, 1989): 8; Michael Welzenbach, "Lion of the Anacostia Museum: Director John Kinard and His Lifetime Mission of Conscience," Washington *Post* (July 19, 1989): D1, D10–11; *Who's Who in the South and Southwest, 1973–1974* (Chicago: Marquis Who's Who, 1974), 403.

6. *Smithsonian Year, 1989*: 31, 101; Kenneth Hudson, *Museums of Influence* (Cambridge: Cambridge University Press, 1987), 170–81; Martin-Felton and Lowe, *Different Drummer*, 51–56, 59.

7. *Smithsonian Year, 1969*: 565–67; *1970*: 108–09; *1971*: 103–04; *1972*: 19, 119; *1973*: 14, 158–60; *1974*: 219–21; *1975*: 251–55; Kinard and Nighbert, "Anacostia Neighborhood Museum," 102–09; Marsh, "Neighborhood Museum," 14–15; Martin-Felton and Lowe, *Different Drummer*, 23–28.

8. *Smithsonian Year, 1975*: 251–53; *1976*: 248–50; *1977*: 160–69; *1978*: 210–13; *1979*: 268–70; *1980*: 265–66; *1981*: 251–53; *1982*: 270–72; *1984*: 179–80; *1985*: 102; *1986*: 20; *1987*: 102; *1988*: 98; *1989*: 100–02; Martin-Felton and Lowe, *Different Drummer*, 27–28, 36–38.

9. *Smithsonian Year, 1969*: 565–67; *1972*: 19; *1973*: 158–60; *1979*: 268–70; *1980*: 265–66; *The Torch* 80: 8; Martin-Felton and Lowe, *Different Drummer*, 23–24, 56–57.

10. *Smithsonian Year, 1985*: 27; *1986*: 20; *1987*: 102; *1988*: 98; Martin-Felton and Lowe, *Different Drummer*, 32–33, 37.

11. Kinard, "Neighborhood Museum as Catalyst," 217–21; Neil Harris, "Museums, Merchandizing, and Popular Taste: The Struggle for Influence," in *Material Culture and the Study of American Life*, edited by Ian M. O. Quimby (New York: W. W. Norton, 1976), 142.

12. John Kinard, "To Meet the Needs of Today's Audience," *Museum News* 50 (May 1972): 15–16.

13. Kinard, "Visitor Versus Museum," 44.

14. *Smithsonian Year, 1981*: 283.

15. *Smithsonian Year, 1987*: 102; Martin-Felton and Lowe, *Different Drummer*, 33.

16. Louise Daniel Hutchinson, *Out of Africa: From West African Kingdoms to Colonization* (Washington: Smithsonian Institution Press, 1979), 11–12.

17. *The Torch* 80: 8.

18. Anacostia Neighborhood Museum, *The Barnett-Aden Collection* (Washington: Smithsonian Institution Press, 1979), 13.

19. Louise Daniel Hutchinson, *The Anacostia Story* (Washington: Smithsonian Institution Press, 1977), xv.

20. Emily Denis Harvey and Bernard Friedberg, eds., *A Museum for the People: A Report of Proceedings at the Seminar on Neighborhood Museums, Held November 21, 22, 23, 1968* (New York: Arno Press, 1971), 31.

21. *The Torch* 89: 8.

22. Ibid.: 1, 8; Martin-Felton and Lowe, *Different Drummer*, 41–50.

23. Kinard, "Neighborhood Museum as Catalyst," 217–23; Kinard, "To Meet the Needs of Today's Audience," 15–16.

24. *The Torch* 89: 1; Martin-Felton and Lowe, *Different Drummer*, 12–14; the fox and chicken coop remark was made to my daughter, Mary Sheron Alexander.

25. Washington *Post* (July 19, 1989): D1, D10–11.

26. See note 5 above for this oral history.

27. Zora Martin, "Colonial Williamsburg—A Black Perspective," in *Museum Education Anthology* (Washington: Museum Education Roundtable, 1984), 83–85. In 1983 she returned to Colonial Williamsburg and reported racial interpretation considerably improved. Zora Martin-Felton, "And Afterward, 1983," in *Museum Education Anthology*, 85–86.

28. Martin-Felton and Lowe, *Different Drummer*, 72–74.

SELECT BIBLIOGRAPHY

Anacostia Neighborhood Museum. *The Barnett-Aden Collection*. Washington: Smithsonian Institution Press, 1979.

Anacostia Neighborhood Museum, Smithsonian Institution, 1966–1967. Washington: Smithsonian Institution, 1977.

Anacostia Neighborhood Museum, Smithsonian Institution, Sept. 15, 1972 [Fifth Anniversary]. Washington: Smithsonian Institution, 1972.

Harris, Neil. "Museums, Merchandizing, and Popular Taste: The Struggle for Influence." In *Material Culture and the Study of American Life*. Edited by Ian M. O. Quimby. New York: W. W. Norton, 1976.

Harvey, Emily Denis, and Bernard Friedberg, eds. *A Museum for the People: A Report of Proceedings at the Seminar on Neighborhood Museums, Held November 21, 22, 23, 1968*. New York: Arno Press, 1971.

Hudson, Kenneth. *Museums of Influence*. Cambridge: Cambridge University Press, 1987.

Hutchinson, Louise Daniel. *The Anacostia Story*. Washington: Smithsonian Institution Press, 1977.

_____. *Out of Africa: From West African Kingdoms to Colonization*. Washington: Smithsonian Institution Press, 1979.

John R. E. Kinard, 1936–1989: A Memorial Tribute. Washington: Smithsonian Institution, National Museum of Natural History, 1989.

Kinard, John R. "The Neighborhood Museum as a Catalyst for Social Change," *Museum* 148 (1985): 217.

_____. "To Meet the Needs of Today's Audience." *Museum News* 50 (May 1972): 15–16.

_____. "The Visitor Versus the Museum." In *The Visitor and the Museum*. Edited by Linda Draper. Seattle: Museum Educators of the American Association of Museums, 1977.

Kinard, John R., and Esther Nighbert. "The Anacostia Museum." International Council of Museums, *Museum* 24, no. 2 (1972): 108.

Marsh, Caryl. "A Neighborhood Museum that Works." *Museum News* 47 (Oct. 1968): 14–16.

Martin, Zora. "Colonial Williamsburg—A Black Perspective." In *Museum Education Anthology*. Washington: Museum Education Roundtable, 1984.

Martin-Felton, Zora, and Gail S. Lowe. *A Different Drummer: John Kinard and the Anacostia Museum, 1967–1989*. Washington: Anacostia Museum, 1989.

"Museums: Opening Eyes in the Ghettos." *Time* (June 21, 1968): 78.

Museums: Their New Audience: A Report to the Department of Housing and Urban Development. Washington: American Association of Museums, 1972.

"Oral History Project: Interview with John R. Kinard, Director, Anacostia Museum, July, 1989." Archives and Special Collections of the Smithsonian Institution.

"Tribute for John Kinard." *The Torch, Smithsonian Institution Monthly Newspaper* 89 (Sept. 9, 1989): 8.

Welzenbach, Michael. "Lion of the Anacostia Museum: Director John Kinard and His Lifetime Mission of Conscience." Washington *Post* (July 19, 1989).

CHAPTER 10

Katherine Coffey
Attracts the Community
into a General Museum

I

KATHERINE COFFEY, AGED TWENTY-FIVE, left her position as executive secretary of the Alumnae Association of Barnard College in 1925 to become staff assistant at the Newark Museum in New Jersey. In her new post she had the opportunity to work closely with John Cotton Dana, the museum's founder and one of the most progressive and innovative museum directors in the country. She began to help him plan the construction of the new building that Louis Bamberger, charter trustee and officer who owned Newark's leading department store, was giving to the museum. Dana appreciated "the reliable skill of Coffey" and found her both capable and easy to work with. As soon as the handsome new headquarters with its large, walled garden at the rear was opened in March 1926, Coffey assumed many tasks in the design and installation of special exhibits of art, history, and natural science, as well as the conduct of other educational activities; they attracted families throughout the city—blue collar workers and their employers, those with immigrant backgrounds, and the well-to-do. Coffey also directed the museum's new pioneering training program, which taught about nine young college graduates yearly and had them work as apprentices in the various departments of the museum.[1]

Coffey found the Newark Museum an exciting place in which to work. Dana had been trained in the law and took delight in argumentation and controversy. He recruited several capable women to help him with the museum. Beatrice

Winser, his assistant librarian and museum director, was a strong and skilled administrator who looked after the everyday affairs, assisted by Margaret Gates and Alice W. Kendall. Louisa Connolly, an experienced educator, visited sixty-five museums around the country to report on their educational programs and advise the Newark Museum in that field; she also taught in the Training Program. Thus Coffey was fortunate to work with an energetic boss who stirred her imagination and stimulated her to put forth her utmost effort and, at the same time, to become a member of a talented team that cooperatively carried out sound programs.[2]

II

Katherine Coffey was born in New York City, May 15, 1900, the daughter of John J. and Mary (Wallace) Coffey. She attended Barnard College at Columbia University and was graduated with an A.B. degree in 1922. (She received an M.A. in 1953 from Rutgers University and honorary doctorates later from Rutgers and Seton Hall.) As an undergraduate, she took an active part in college life, was chairman of the Freshman Greek Games Committee, president of the Sophomore Class, and vice-president of the Undergraduate Association. She then served in 1923–1924 in the responsible position of executive secretary with the alumnae association.

At the Newark Museum, upon Dana's death in 1929, Beatrice Winser was made librarian and museum director in his place, and two years later, Coffey was promoted to curator in charge of exhibitions, educational programs, and museum training. She received a fellowship from the Oberlander Trust of the Carl Schurz Foundation in 1936 and visited Europe to study museums there. Later, during World War II, she did canteen work overseas with the Eighty-sixth Division of Engineers. When Winser stepped down in 1947, Alice Kendall succeeded her with Coffey as assistant director, and upon Kendall's retirement two years later, Coffey became director, remaining in that post until her retirement in 1968. Coffey did much extra-curricular museum work during her directorship. She was a member of the Council of the American Association of Museums, 1953–1956, and president of the Northeast Museums Conference (today the Mid-Atlantic Association of Museums) for two years. She was the organizer and first chairman of the Museum Council of New Jersey and an elected member of the Association of Art Museum Directors. She belonged to an important AAM committee that persuaded the Smithsonian to take over the museum of the Cooper Union in New York as the Cooper-Hewitt National Museum of Design.[3]

Six months before her retirement, Samuel C. Miller, formerly assistant director of the Albright-Knox Gallery in Buffalo, had become her understudy, and he succeeded to the directorship. She was then elected a trustee of the museum, and the Katherine Coffey Endowment Fund of $100,000 was established in her honor. She lived in New York City during her retirement but remained active as a consultant of the New Jersey Historical Society and was a member of the new Accreditation Commission of the American Association of Museums. She died suddenly on April 4, 1972.[4]

III

To understand Coffey's contributions to the Newark Museum, we need to examine the three fields in which she took major responsibility—special exhibitions, educational activities, and museum training. The museum offered a total of some 150 major exhibitions during her service between 1926 and 1968, an average of about three and a half yearly. In addition, there were many smaller shows. While she had the leading role in staging the exhibitions, the curators, who numbered between six and seven, usually wrote the catalogues, for which, aided by assistants, they did much of the research. William H. Gertz, Jr., curator of painting and sculpture, was the author of many of them.[5]

The museum was much interested in promoting the cause of contemporary art. Some of the chief exhibitions during Coffey's time treated *Paintings and Sculptures by Living Artists* (1926); *Modern American Watercolors* (1930, 1948); *Color Photography* (1940); *Contemporary American Negro Art* (1944) with the work of thirty leading painters and sculptors; *Contemporary Prints* (1946); *Changing Tastes in Painting and Sculpture, 1795–1946*; and *Abstract Art from 1910 to Today* (1956).

The museum paid much attention to New Jersey artists. A show of their work was held every three years from 1952 through 1968. Other displays introduced some comparatively unknown state artists in *Native Talent* (1948); examined *Modern Architecture in New Jersey* (1955); and exhibited 110 works from a staff-compiled list of over 1,000 *Early New Jersey Artists, 1783–1920* (1957). An elaborate celebration of New Jersey's three centuries (1966) comprised eight exhibitions.

The museum was proud when it persuaded Holger Cahill to organize the first exhibition in the country of *American Primitive Painting* (1930), which was circulated to museums in Chicago, Toledo, and Rochester, New York. The next year, the museum presented the pioneer show of *American Folk Sculpture* with ship figureheads, cigar store Indians, weathervanes, and bird and animal carvings.

Dana began the practice of exhibiting the products of New Jersey industries in an effort to persuade their managers, workers, and the whole community to take pride in their achievements as well as to attract them to the museum. Shows in that area during Coffey's day included *Nothing Takes the Place of Leather* (1926); *Jewelry Made in Newark* (1929); *Aviation: A Newark Industry* (1932), featuring the Newark Airport; *Modern Miracles: Chemistry Changes the World* (1934), stressing the fact that New Jersey ranked second in the United States in chemical industries; *War and Peace: The Industrial Front in the Newark Area* (1945), in which fifty-six firms participated; and *Newark in World Trade* (1949).

The museum appealed to consumers as well as to local firms by pointing out that low-priced goods could be well designed. *Inexpensive Articles of Good Design* (1928, 1929) contained objects that cost between ten and fifty cents procured from local five-and-ten-cent and department stores. *Christmas Gift Suggestions of Good Design* (1950) showed goods valued from ten cents to ten dollars; that exhibit was often repeated and after 1956 contained works for sale by New Jersey artists and craftsmen.

The museum did many exhibitions of art from all over the world. Its own collection of Tibetan art is one of the best in the country and was displayed in *Tibetan Life and Culture* (1949). *Primitive African Art* (1928) was followed much later by *Art in the Life of Africa* (1954), which examined the tribal concept of art as religion. Two shows treated *Art in Judaism* (1957) and *Art in Buddhism* (1958). *Japanese Prints and Their Influence* (1953) was followed by *Arts of Japan* (1954), while *Islands of the Pacific* (1939) concerned Oceania, as did *Arts of the South Sea Islands* (1967). *Theatres of War* (1943) used the museum's ethnological and oriental collections to picture the Pacific areas in which American troops were fighting. Focusing on India and Iran were *20th Century Indian Art* (1956) and *Paintings of Persia and Mughal India*. *Three Southern Neighbors—Ecuador, Peru, Bolivia* (1941) was a Latin American "good neighbor" exhibition. And several shows covered British, Italian, and Spanish art.

The museum's science collections were used in *The Geology of New Jersey* (1951); *The Physical Sciences* (1960) on the mysteries of light, electricity, magnetism, and sound with visitor-operated, "hands-on" displays; and *The Natural Sciences* (1968) showing New Jersey birds, fossils, and minerals. The museum emphasized the advance of technology with *From Shank's Mare to 16 Cylinders*

(1930) on the rise of the automobile; *Atomic Energy* (1948); *Approaching Mars* (1956); and *Satellite Science* (1958).

The special exhibitions were by far the most popular attractions of the museum. They drew heavy attendance, not only new visitors especially interested in the fields covered but a steady, large number of repeat visitors. The shows utilized the museum's growing collections, in addition to borrowing occasionally from other museums.

Coffey, both as staff member and then director, had much to do with the development of the museum's other educational activities.[6] The exhibitions were always accompanied by programs of lectures, demonstrations, discussions or workshops that attracted much community participation. Special tours were instituted for the blind that allowed them to handle ceramics and baskets. The opening of the new building resulted in the establishment of a Department of Education that worked more intimately with the schools in tailoring museum class visits to the schools' curriculums. The museum also dispatched exhibits to the schools, and its Lending Department grew to contain 10,000 objects. Staff members also went to the schools, clubs, and other community organizations to lecture or participate in varied activities. The museum's Reference Library was open to both the public and the staff, and it exchanged publications with other institutions throughout the country. Teachers came to the museum to take credit courses in using museum objects offered by the local State Teachers' College with the backing of the Newark Board of Education.

The museum had early organized a Junior Museum with its own exhibits and classes in drawing, painting, modeling, and crafts, and a Museum Club with a life membership charge of a mere ten cents that encouraged youngsters to collect stamps, coins, natural history specimens, and other objects. Those activities led to much after-school and weekend student participation. A Junior Museum Council, made up of representatives from the numerous junior clubs, staged an annual pageant, which was eventually replaced by an exhibition of its year's work.

The economic depression of the 1930s reduced the city appropriation for the museum markedly, but the staff kept its regular activities afloat and began to offer adults, many of them unemployed, Sunday afternoon classes in sketching, modeling, and nature study. Staff members volunteered to supervise the program without pay, and visiting lecturers frequently participated. Those classes developed into the Newark Nature Club, the Newark Science Workshop, and the Arts Workshop for Adults with courses in weaving, painting, ceramics, sculpture, and the like. In 1933, too, the museum began to present concerts, given monthly from November through March.

In 1953, a new Spitz Planetarium, the gift of Mr. and Mrs. Leonard Dreyfus, opened with regular astronomical shows; the couple gave $50,000 for its upkeep and in 1960 added an Optical Observatory. In 1977 the museum acquired the John H. Ballantine House next door and added a four-story extension in the rear, into which moved the Junior Museum, Lending Department, Arts Workshop for Adults, and Reference Library. The house itself later was restored with period rooms furnished with New Jersey decorative arts. Two other additions were the old Newark Schoolhouse of 1784, properly furnished and in 1939 placed in the museum's spacious garden, and the Newark Fire Museum, installed in 1967 in the former Ballantine Carriage House and also moved to the garden.

Members who joined the museum—numbering 2,173 by 1969— received many privileges, including lectures, special events, film showings, and family trips. A monthly *News Notes* was mailed to them as well as a quarterly entitled *The Museum*, which contained articles on the collections and local history. In 1950 a Members' Room was opened, and they were invited to borrow paintings and prints for their homes and offices. The whole community was encouraged to use the study collections and consultation service; and circulating exhibits of paintings and prints went to educational institutions.

In listing the museum's activities in her 1959 report, Coffey pointed out:

> We are fortunate that the direction given the Museum by its founders allows for
> flexibility that makes it possible for us to meet the demands of changing times,
> and the needs of the community. The Museum is not static in its collections,
> programs or activities; only in the integrity does it remain unchanged.[7]

The changing times to which Coffey referred were illustrated in the makeup of Newark's population. When the museum was founded in 1909, Newark contained about twenty European nationalities including German, Irish, Italian, Russian, Polish, Lithuanian, and Hungarian, but few blacks (only about 2.8 percent of the population). During the First World War, blacks began to migrate to the city despite the fact that only menial jobs were open to them, and after the Second World War, they moved from the South in droves so that by the time Coffey retired, they constituted nearly 60 percent of the population. White flight to the suburbs that included many of the upward-bound European nationalities was helping make Newark a black city. The blacks suffered shameful segregation, lived in appalling slums, and were subject to much crime, venereal disease, tuberculosis, infant mortality, lead poisoning, and drug abuse. One of every four was on some type of government relief, and unemployment for young men, aged sixteen to twenty-five, reached 40 percent.

In July 1967 after the police killed a black man engaged in a crime, black discontent erupted into five days of rioting, and downtown stores and other places were looted and burned. The Governor ordered in the State Police and the National Guard, and order was restored with the use of truncheons and guns; it was found that twenty-three blacks had died in the melee. But the museum, despite its location in the central city, was untouched during the disturbances. In attempting to serve the whole community, it had welcomed many black visitors. It had held four important exhibitions on black culture, one of which displayed the work of thirty black painters and sculptors, while the other three treated African art as part of the black heritage.[8]

The next crucial test of the museum came in February 1969, just after Coffey's retirement, when the Newark City Council voted unanimously to discontinue on April 1 the appropriations for both the Public Library (about $12 million) and the museum (nearly $800,000). The action took place during the museum's African Festival which included an ambitious exhibition of *African Art* and smaller shows on *Photos of People of Africa* and on prints, paintings, and collages by local artists who called themselves "Black Motion." The festival included motion pictures, a fashion show, and music, dancing, and drumming; it attracted members of both the black and white communities as well as United Nations representatives of African countries, many of them in their native costumes.

When an all-day hearing was held on the plan to stop the appropriations, more than 400 citizens from all parts of the community jammed the council chamber to oppose the motion. The Council of Racial Equality (CORE), National Association for the Advancement of Colored People (NAACP), Urban Coalition of Newark, New Jersey Library Association, university and college spokespersons, and many others strongly, sometimes passionately, supported the museum and library, and demonstrators journeyed to the state capital at Trenton to implore Governor Richard J. Hughes and the State Legislature to increase the state appropriation. (The council's real motive for dropping the appropriations was based on the hope of obtaining greater state and county support.) As a result of the continuing agitation, the City Council rescinded the February vote, the state increased its museum support to about one-third of the total, and one county appropriated $50,000. Since that time, the museum has continued to offer its community-supported programs, and the blacks who succeeded in electing Kenneth

Gibson, a black engineer, mayor in 1970 and taking over the city government, have steadily supported the museum.[9]

IV

On February 5, 1925, Dana had announced that the museum would offer a "School for Museum Workers," beginning that fall. It would last for nine months, enroll not more than twelve college graduates, and be devoted to the management of museums. Formal teaching would take place for about ten hours each week, but the students also would do actual work in the different museum departments and act as interpreters or docents for its special exhibitions. The program was successful from the start, and nine bright young women were graduated in the spring, all but one of them going to work in museums.

Coffey, as supervisor of the training course, did a great deal of work selecting the students, supervising their programs, and helping them find jobs. The students considered her exacting but fair.[10] In the second year, another nine pupils were graduated, all but one taking museum positions. In the fifth year, eight of fifty applicants were accepted; they came from seven states and six colleges. By 1942, when the course was interrupted because of the war, 108 young women and men had been trained, and most of them were working in museums in the United States or Canada. In 1961 Coffey announced that the program would resume.[11]

The Newark Museum training course was one of the two most important ones in the country at that time; the other one, taught by Paul Joseph Sachs at Harvard's Fogg Art Museum, was devoted to art museums. Museum studies courses soon began to multiply elsewhere, but Henry Watson Kent, secretary of the Metropolitan Museum of Art and Dana's close friend, thought that many of them made the mistake of trying to give instruction in art history or other subject matter. He insisted that a good course in museum studies should teach museum management or economy and leave subject instruction to colleges and universities. And Newark followed that practical principle.[12]

Coffey made a clear statement of her museum philosophy when she wrote an article in *Museum News* during a controversial discussion of the place of research, education, and public service in museum work.[13] She began by praising the late George Brown Goode of the Smithsonian's United States National Museum, who defined a museum as "an institution for the preservation of those objects which best illustrate the phenomena of nature and the works of man, the utilization of these for the increase of knowledge and for the culture and enlightenment of the people."[14] She also approved his quotation from Sir Henry Cole, the founder of what became the Victoria and Albert Museum in London, which ran:

> If you wish your schools of science and art to be effective, your health, the air, your food to be wholesome, your life to be long, your manufactures to improve, your trade to increase and your people to be civilized, you must have museums of science and art to illustrate the principles of life, health, nature, art, and beauty.[15]

Coffey insisted not only that a museum's purpose was to collect and preserve objects but that its chief functions were research, exhibition, and education. Museums founded around great collections of science and art, usually in large cities, had a dual responsibility for both sound subject matter research and the enlightenment of the swarms of visitors they attracted. Smaller museums could do less subject matter research but devote themselves mainly to education and public service; even then, however, they needed to do sound educational research. University museums had to have less concern for education of the general public, while for the scholars and students that they served, subject-matter research was all important.

Coffey concluded that the purpose of each individual museum ought to be abundantly clear to both its trustees and staff, and that the professionalization of the museum staff was highly desirable. Curators should be interested not only in their collections and connoisseurship but also in education, and educators ought to understand the subject matter so important to the curators. The director should be a well-trained professional who comprehended the overall purpose and functions of the museum and knew how to inspire both curators and educators to work together harmoniously for the common good of the museum. Striving vigorously to carry out these ideals enabled Coffey to insure that the Newark Museum remain a powerful community source of education and culture.

Katherine Coffey served the Newark Museum for some forty-three years, nearly twenty of them as director. One of the few women museum heads in the country, she was well known and highly respected for work in her own museum and for her outside activities. The Mid-Atlantic Association of Museums, which she had served so well as president, in 1972 established the prestigious Katherine Coffey Award, given annually to a man or woman "for distinguished accomplishment in the museum profession." Thus her name and contributions are preserved justly in the annals of American museum history.

NOTES

1. For Coffey, see Katherine Coffey, "Operation of the Individual Museum," *Museum News* 40 (Oct. 1961): 26–29; *Museologist*, 125 (Oct. 1972); *Museum News* 50 (June 1972): 60; Newark Museum *News Notes* (May 1972): 1–2; *Who's Who in America* (Chicago: A. N. Marquis, 1956) 28 (1954–1955): 513. The direct quotation is in Frank Kingdon, *John Cotton Dana: A Life* (Newark, N.J.: Public Library and Museum, 1940), 161–62.

2. Kingdon, *Dana*, 161–62.

3. *Museum News* 40 (Oct. 1961): 16; 42 (Jan. 1964): 37–38; 44 (Nov. 1965): 6; 47 (Sept. 1968): 6; 50 (June 1977): 60.

4. *Museum News* 47 (Sept. 1968): 6; (May 1969): 27.

5. This section on exhibitions is based on *A Survey: 50 Years of the Newark Museum* (Newark, N.J.: Newark Museum Association, 1959); *The Newark Museum, Collections and Exhibitions, 1959–1968: Survey 60* (Newark, N.J.: Newark Museum, 1969); *Art Digest* 18 (Apr. 15, 1944): 20; *Museum News* 38 (1960–1961) and 47 (1967–1968) with frequent mentions and especially 38 (Feb. 1960): 4; 42 (Mar. 1964): 37, 44. For Gertz, see *A Survey: 50 Years*, 29–32; *Museum News* 45 (Sept. 1966): 49.

6. The educational activities are described in Katherine Coffey, "Service," *A Survey: 50 Years*, 23–25; *The Newark Museum: A Chronicle of the Founding Years, 1909–1934* (Newark, N.J.: Newark Museum Association, 1934), 14–15, 20, 26, 31–34, 36–38; Newark Museum, *A Museum in Action: Presenting the Museum's Activities* (Newark, N.J.: Newark Museum, 1944); *Museum News* 42 (Mar. 1964): 37.

7. *A Survey: 50 Years*, 25.

8. Daniel Gaby, "Newark: The Promise of Survival," *Nation* 219 (Dec. 14, 1974): 619–22; Tom Hayden, *Rebellion in Newark: Official Violence and Ghetto Response* (New York: Vintage Books, 1967); Kenneth T. and Barbara B. Jackson, "The Black Experience in Newark: The Growth of the Ghetto, 1870–1970," in *New Jersey since 1960: New Findings and Interpretations*, edited by William C. Wright (Trenton: New Jersey Historical Commission, 1972), 36–56; Ron Perambo, *No Cause for Indictment: An Autopsy of Newark* (New York: Holt, Rinehart and Winston, 1972); Clement A. Price, "The Beleagured City as Promised Land: Blacks in Newark, 1917–1947," in *Urban New Jersey since 1970*, edited by William C. Wright (Trenton: New Jersey Historical Commission, 1975), 10–45; Ralph Whitehead, "Behind the Violence in Newark: Anatomy of a Riot," *Commonwealth* 86 (Aug. 11, 1967): 492–94.

9. Samuel C. Miller, "An African Festival at the Newark Museum," *Museum News* 47 (May 1969): 25–27; "Crisis in Newark," *Library Journal* 94 (Mar. 15, 1969): 1081; "Newark City Council Votes to Drop Library," *Library Journal* 94 (Mar. 15, 1969): 1083; "Newark City Council Rescinds Library Budget Slash," *Library Journal* 94 (Apr. 1, 1969): 1403–04; Russell Lynes, "After Hours: How to Make Politics from Art and Vice Versa," *Harper's Magazine* 239 (Aug. 1969): 21–24; *Museum News* 47 (Apr. 1969): 3; "Victory from the Jaws of Defeat: A Tribute to the Newark Public Library," *Wilson Library Bulletin* 45 (Apr. 1969): 740–47.

10. Session on "The Legacy of John Cotton Dana," at which Elizabeth Dusenberry, a former Newark museum apprentice, spoke. Mid-Atlantic Association of Museums *1990 Annual Meeting* (Oct. 31, 1990), 18.

11. *American Museum of Art* 20 (Dec. 1929): 710; 21 (Dec. 1930): 726–29; *Museum News* 39 (June 1961): 7; (Oct. 1961): 4; Newark Museum, *A Museum* 1 (May 1925): 42–43; (Sept.-Dec. 1925): 67; 2 (Jan. 1927): 117.

12. Henry Watson Kent, *What I Am Pleased to Call My Education* (New York: Grolier Club, 1949): 165–66.

13. *Museum News* 40 (Oct. 1961): 26–29. See also 42 (Jan. 1964): 37–38; 44 (Nov. 1965): 6; 46 (Oct. 1967): 42.

14. *Museum News* 40 (Oct. 1961): 27.

15. Ibid.: 26.

SELECT BIBLIOGRAPHY

A Survey: 50 Years of the Newark Museum. Newark, N.J.: Newark Museum Association, 1959.

"Crisis in Newark." *Library Journal* 94 (Mar. 15, 1969): 1081.

Kingdon, Frank. *John Cotton Dana: A Life.* Newark, N.J.: Public Library and Museum, 1940.

Gaby, Daniel. "Newark: The Promise of Survival." *Nation* 219 (Dec. 14, 1974): 619–22.

Hayden, Tom. *Rebellion in Newark: Official Violence and Ghetto Response.* New York: Vintage Books, 1967.

Jackson, Kenneth T. and Barbara B. "The Black Experience in Newark: The Growth of the Ghetto, 1870–1970." In *New Jersey since 1960: New Findings and Interpretations.* Edited by William C. Wright. Trenton: New Jersey Historical Commission, 1972.

Kent, Henry Watson. *What I Am Pleased to Call My Education.* New York: Grolier Club, 1949.

Lynes, Russell. "After Hours: How to Make Politics from Art and Vice Versa." *Harper's Magazine* 239 (Aug. 1969): 21–24.

Museum News. Vols. 38–47 (1960–1969).

"Newark City Council Votes to Drop Library." *Library Journal* 94 (Mar. 15, 1969): 1083.

The Newark Museum: A Chronicle of the Founding Years, 1909–1934. Newark, N.J.: Newark Museum Association, 1934.

Newark Museum. *A Museum in Action: Presenting the Museum's Activities.* Newark, N.J.: Newark Museum, 1944.

The Newark Museum, Collections and Exhibitions, 1959–1968: Survey 60. Newark, N.J.: Newark Museum, 1969.

Perambo, Ron. *No Cause for Indictment: An Autopsy of Newark.* New York: Holt, Rinehart and Winston, 1972.

Price, Clement A. "The Beleagured City as Promised Land: Blacks in Newark, 1917–1947." In *Urban New Jersey since 1970.* Edited by William C. Wright. Trenton: New Jersey Historical Commission, 1975.

"Victory from the Jaws of Defeat: A Tribute to the Newark Public Library." *Wilson Library Bulletin* 45 (Apr. 1969): 740–47.

Whitehead, Ralph. "Behind the Violence in Newark: Anatomy of a Riot." *Commonwealth* 86 (Aug. 11, 1967): 492–94.

CHAPTER 11

Charles Sprague Sargent
Plants an Outstanding Botanical Garden

I

J AMES ARNOLD, A PROSPEROUS BUSINESSMAN of New Bedford, Massachusetts, had a charming English-style garden on his eleven-acre estate and took great interest in horticulture. When he died in 1863, he left part of his residuary holding to three trustees to be applied "for the promotion of agricultural and horticultural improvements, or other Philosophical or Philanthropic purposes."[1] George B. Emerson, the leading trustee, was a part-time botanist who wrote the book, *Trees and Shrubs Growing Naturally in the Forests of Massachusetts* (1846), and in 1872 he persuaded his fellow trustees to bestow the bequest on Harvard University to establish an Arnold Arboretum. Harvard decided to set aside 137 acres of its land in Jamaica Plain west of Boston and six miles from the university. The Arnold bequest came to about $50,000 but at first yielded only $3,000 yearly. According to the agreement of the trustees and the university, the arboretum was to contain "as far as practicable, all the trees, shrubs, and herbaceous plants, either indigenous or exotic, which can be raised in the open air" at Jamaica Plain.[2] Charles Sprague Sargent was made director of the Harvard Botanic Garden, professor of horticulture, and director of the new arboretum.[3]

Born in Boston, April 5, 1841, Sargent was the son of Ignatius and Henrietta (Gray) Sargent. Ignatius was a wealthy East India merchant, banker, and financier; both he and his wife were descended in prominent families and were members of the city's top social elite. Ignatius in 1845 purchased "Holm Lea" ("Inland

Island Pasture"), a 130-acre estate in Brookline, and developed there an outstand-ing garden. Young Charles was sent to Epes Sargent Dixwell's School for boys and in 1858 entered Harvard. He took Latin, Greek, French, Spanish, Italian, chemistry, astronomy, physics, metaphysics, and four courses of rhetoric (in which he failed to learn to speak in public). He had no work in botany. He was a wretched student and for a time appeared likely to be expelled for lack of application, but he managed to graduate in 1862, standing eighty-eighth in a class of ninety.

Soon after graduation, he enlisted in the Union Army as a first lieutenant assigned to the Second Louisiana Infantry. As aide-de-camp to General Nathaniel P. Banks in New Orleans, he took part in the Teche and Louisiana Red River campaigns, the siege of Port Hudson, and the capture of Mobile. He rose to be a brevet major, praised for his "faithful and meritorious service" against Mobile, and was honorably discharged in 1865. He then spent three years traveling in Europe. Upon his return, he apparently could not decide upon a career but settled for the time being upon managing the Holm Lea estate. There, however, he began to be interested in botany and horticulture and was meticulous in calling plants by their Latin names.

Why Sargent was appointed to his three positions at Harvard remains somewhat of a mystery. He had been a poor student and had only limited experience, though he did belong to Boston's upper class. He was liked by Francis Parkman, the historian, a neighbor deeply interested in horticulture who had served as pro-fessor of that subject for a year at Harvard. He may have nominated Sargent as his successor.[4]

Soon after that, Sargent made a promising marriage to Mary Allen Robeson, a dozen years younger than he, whose father owned prosperous cotton mills. Sargent himself could often be dour, uncommunicative, and unsociable, while Mary was always cheerful and outgoing. She had considerable artistic talent and later did watercolor illustrations for Sargent's Collection of Woods. She com-municated well with their two sons and three daughters and shielded them from their father's sometimes petulant corrections.

In 1874 the Sargents made a combined business and honeymoon trip to Europe. He was much impressed by the Royal Botanic Garden at Edinburgh and thought it even surpassed the one at Kew. He got along well with Sir Joseph Hooker, Kew's director, and with his son-in-law and eventual successor, William Thiselton-Dyer, who was about his age. He also visited Alphonse de Candolle, the Swiss botanist, at Geneva and Joseph Decaisne at the Jardin des Plants in

Paris. Sargent always made it a point to meet the leading botanists and horticulturists of the world and to keep in touch with them.

Sargent maintained a close relationship with Professor Asa Gray of Harvard, who practically tutored him in the science of botany. He made many improvements in the Botanic Garden and stocked its nursery with plants that he planned to use in the arboretum. In 1877 the university dropped him as professor of horticulture before he did any teaching there, and soon he gave up direction of the Botanic Garden and concentrated all his efforts on the arboretum. As he wrote on its fiftieth anniversary:

> He found himself with a worn-out farm partly covered with natural plantations of native trees nearly ruined by excessive pasturage, to be developed with less than three thousand dollars a year available for the purpose. He was without equipment or the support and encouragement of the general public which knew nothing about an Arboretum and what it was expected to accomplish.[5]

Sargent then made a move that greatly improved the arboretum's chances for success. Frederick Law Olmsted, the landscape architect, conceived the idea of a continuous park system for Boston that would run from the city center for some seven miles. The arboretum lay in the path of that development, and he asked Sargent to join him in making it part of the park system. It would be open for recreation to city citizens, and in return Boston would pay for laying out roadways and footpaths, maintaining and policing them, and furnishing a water supply. Sargent backed the plan enthusiastically and enlisted Asa Gray to help persuade a reluctant President Charles Eliot of Harvard to adopt it. When the City Council voted against the development, Sargent cannily devised a petition in its favor, for which he secured the signatures of 1,305 of the most influential taxpayers. The council changed its mind, and in 1882 Harvard transferred 120 acres of arboretum land to the city, which purchased another 45 acres for the tract, the whole of which was leased to the university for 1,000 years, renewable for the same period, at one dollar per year.

Sargent at once began to develop his project with great energy. He planned for the arboretum to fulfill four functions—as a museum of living plants, a scientific station, school of forestry and arboriculture (which did not develop), and popular educator. He had surveyed the property and found only 123 species of woody plants. He quietly dropped the provision of the 1872 agreement that called for herbaceous plants. He set out new trees in groups to show their natural sequence, usually with a dozen specimens for each species. By the time the arboretum reached its fifteenth anniversary, he had planted 120,000 trees and shrubs. Sargent was a shrewd judge in choosing assistants, and he scored a real hit when he hired as superintendent Jackson Dawson, who took charge of the nursery and proved a marvelous propagator, serving faithfully until his death in 1916.

In order to make the arboretum a scientific center, Sargent began to accumulate a herbarium and wrote his close friend, Dr. George Engelmann, the German-trained physician and botanist, who was helping Henry Shaw develop the Missouri Botanical Garden in St. Louis, that he proposed to confine the herbarium "(for many years at any rate) to trees & shrubs of 1st North America and the whole temperate zone."[6] He also began to gather a library of important and often rare books. Both herbarium and library were his personal property, which he kept in a room at Holm Lea until 1890, when he gave them—by then 1,000 herbarium specimens and 6,000 volumes—to the arboretum. They were to be housed in a new administrative building that had been donated by Horatio Hollis Hunnewell. The new facility welcomed botanists, landscape designers, park superintendents, nurserymen, and students, providing them with a commodious room where they could spread out specimens and books. Sargent himself, always ready to discuss their problems and advise them, and Charles Edward Faxon, a scholarly naturalist, had their offices in the new building. Faxon was the curator and an accomplished botanical artist who provided drawings for Sargent's various books; he served until his death in 1918.

In the educational field, the arboretum made steady progress. In 1886 Sargent added a young Canadian botanist, John George Jack, as his third principal assistant, who lectured on arboriculture and instituted field classes. His knowledgeable and enthusiastic teaching with walks through the arboretum was an instant success. Sargent also started a weekly magazine, *Garden and Forest*, in 1888 with himself as "conductor" and William Augustus Stiles, a skilled journalist, as editor. The conductor contributed frequent short notices on "New or Little Known Plants," usually with engravings or photographs, "Notes on American Trees," "Notes on Forest Fauna of Japan," book reviews, and unsigned editorials that supported his numerous forestry interests. The magazine was published in New York City without arboretum sponsorship but was a strong supporter of its program; unfortunately, it lost money steadily (much of it Sargent's) and was abandoned after ten years.

Sargent's biggest problem with the arboretum was financial. The endowment at most brought in only about $8,000 yearly, and expenditures often were double that. Sargent contributed much money himself (estimated at about $250,000 throughout his lifetime) and frequently called upon his friends for funds. When he faced a shortage, he would give a dinner party at which he outlined the problem and the amount he was giving; his guests would then agree to contribute. He readily admitted that his assistants were badly underpaid, but although they grumbled, they remained loyal.

The arboretum under Sargent was a one-man institution. In the office he worked long hours and on weekends and holidays. He took care of a mountain of correspondence. While his assistants admired "the Professor" and his single-minded devotion, he was sometimes gruff and despotic, a true czar though often a wise one. He admired and trusted his staff but did not regard them as social equals or invite them to Holm Lea for dinner.

II

While the arboretum was getting underway, Sargent began to examine the forests of North America, and he became a leader in the movement to preserve them. His first publication, *A Few Suggestions on Tree Planting*, appeared in 1875, and the Massachusetts Society for Promoting Agriculture, of which he was a trustee, reprinted 10,000 copies for public distribution. The society elected him president and soon began to make annual contributions of at least $2,500 to the arboretum.

Asa Gray suggested Sargent to the United States Department of the Interior to report on the forests for the Census of 1880, and he agreed to undertake that large and difficult mission. He enlisted botanists to examine the trees in defined regions and persuaded the government to publish his preliminary *Catalogue of the Forest Trees of North America* to guide them. In the summer of 1880 he journeyed west with his friends Engelmann and Charles C. Perry to "examine the trees in the mountainous regions of Utah, Washington, Oregon, British Columbia, California, and Arizona. Engelmann was then seventy years old, rheumatic, and overweight; Perry reported that he was "quite lively but does not enjoy the push and hurry of Sargent," and Engelmann wrote Gray of "the terrible strain Sargent's restlessness and energy put us under. . . . he rarely took or allowed more than '5 minutes' for anything. . . . Well, with all that, we had a glorious time."[7] Sargent's resulting *Report on the Forests of North America (Exclusive of Mexico)* made him known throughout the country. The 612-page volume was an extensive examination of 412 species of trees, the properties of their wood, and their uses. The problem of forest fires was considered, and he urged that the Federal Government investigate the effect of forests upon rivers. The *Report* was by far the best treatment that had appeared, and retained its usefulness for many years.

Sargent had a reactionary and distrustful attitude toward government and its part in American affairs. As he wrote his friend Thiselton-Dyer in 1898:

> If I lived in England I should be a jingo. It is the business of England to civilize the world and boss the inferior races. We are not equipped for that sort of work . . . and the curse of universal suffrage is always with us—a perfect millstone around America's neck—a splendid thing in theory and for small communities where everybody is more or less educated and honest. It is a grievous failure, however, in our big cities, and it will prevent our ever having a public service which will enable us to compete with the rest of the world in the government of colonies. Americans are capable of doing a lot of good work; it is done, however, by corporations and individuals quite outside the government. There is no better proof of the correctness of this statement than the quality of the scientific work done by Government as compared with that produced by the Universities. . . . We are going to have serious trouble sometime in this country. Lots of people are going to be killed and a lot of wealth wasted. If this results in the end in restricted suffrage the sacrifice won't be too great.[8]

Sargent obviously was a nineteenth-century Victorian, comfortable in his wealth, absorbed in a successful scientific career, and certain that responsible individualism was far superior to any possible governmental supervision in the hands of mere politicians. Descended from English stock in the colonial period, he was suspicious of increasing immigration from all over Europe, contemptuous of "inferior races," and fearful of "universal suffrage."

As soon as Sargent had dispatched his census report to Washington in 1883, he left for Montana as a member of the Northern Transcontinental Survey, a project sponsored by railroad interests. The expedition made its way across the Rockies, through northern Washington, and over the Cascades to Portland. When the railroad backers lost interest, no publication of its findings appeared, but Sargent wrote an article in the *Nation* which made the first suggestion of what is now Glacier National Park. He emphasized the breathtaking beauty of the area and argued that a forest preserve there would protect the three great rivers of the continent—the Missouri, Columbia, and Saskatchewan.[9] Eventually, the park was established in 1910.

In 1883 Morris K. Jesup, president of the American Museum of Natural History, persuaded Sargent to head a commission to investigate what New York State should do about an Adirondack Forest Reserve. The state already owned about 40,000 acres there and was adding private land forfeited for nonpayment of taxes. The commission's report of 1885, much of it Sargent's work, stressed the value of the forest and warned against the great numbers of fires and the lax lumbering practices. It rejected state control but favored a three-man, unpaid, nonpolitical commission to manage the forest and enforce fire protection and good lumbering on both state-owned and private tracts. The residents of the area, lumber interests, and railroads transporting timber successfully opposed the report and obtained a compromise with five well-paid, political commissioners and weak restrictions on fires and lumbering. Sargent was disgusted and even more convinced that government action in such areas was only too often fruitless.

Meanwhile, President Jesup had conceived adding a new Collection of North American Woods at the American Museum, and he asked Sargent to gather it. Jesup at first impressed Sargent as a fine businessman and able administrator, "one of the very few Americans who wants to make the best use of his money & spend it for something better than nice houses and bad pictures."[10] Sargent saw to securing some 106 specimens of trees. He had whole tree trunks six feet tall properly cut and polished to show vertical, horizontal, and diagonal sections; they were illustrated by life-size watercolors of their foliage, flowers, and fruit, ultimately painted by Mary Sargent. All of the rapidly mounting bills were paid by Jesup. During the fifteen years the two men worked together, frequent quarrels took place, Sargent insisting upon a full and meticulous scientific collection and Jesup trying to reduce the heavy costs. The Jesup collection opened in 1885 amid plaudits from the press but never had much popular appeal. One consolation for Sargent was that he acquired a collection of smaller specimens of the woods for his museum at the arboretum.

Sargent then decided to write a sylva of North American forests as an expansion of his census report, for he thought the nation badly needed a scientific description of its trees. He had gathered seeds or plants of many of them on his trips to the Northwest, and he began systematically to visit the West Indies, North Carolina, Florida, Louisiana, Alabama, and Texas, securing specimens and making notes. Sometimes he took Faxon along to provide sketches; on other tours his wife accompanied him. He also explored trees in northeastern Mexico, as well as in England, France, Italy, and Germany. In 1891 the first volume of the *Silva* appeared, dedicated to "Asa Gray, Friend and Master." The finished work ran to fourteen volumes with 585 specimens and 740 plates. In the preface, Sargent wrote:

> To be really understood, trees must be studied in the forest; and therefore . . . I
> have examined the trees of America growing in their native homes from Canada

to the banks of the Rio Crande and the mountains of Arizona, and from British
Columbia to the islands of southern Florida. I have watched many of them in the
gardens of this country and those of Europe, and there are hardly a dozen . . .
I have not seen in a living state.[11]

The reviewers were enthusiastic about the book. Nathaniel L. Britton predicted that it would "rank with the works of science and art that are recognized
the world over." John Muir, the naturalist, then becoming a close friend of Sargent,
wrote a flowery review in the *Atlantic Monthly*, which said: "Though accustomed
to read the trees themselves, not written descriptions of them, I have read it
through twice as if it were a novel, and wished that it were longer."[12]

In 1894 the Secretary of the Interior asked the National Academy of Sciences
to devise a "rational forest policy for the forest lands of the United States."[13]
Sargent was appointed chairman of the investigatory commission along with three
other academy members. He got Gifford Pinchot, a non-academy man, added
to the commission, a move which he later regretted. The group followed the
northern Rockies along the Canadian border and then through Washington,
Oregon, California, and Arizona to Colorado. Early in 1897 their preliminary
report urged President Cleveland to proclaim thirteen new forest reserves of more
than 21 million acres. Cleveland was about to retire from the presidency, but
he dared to issue the proclamation. The Western states and Congress objected
strenuously and brought pressure on incoming President McKinley to rescind
the proclamation, but Sargent secured an interview and finally convinced him
to let it stand. The commission's final report called for good methods of forest
management and protection and for the use of federal troops until a trained
forest corps could be created. It also proposed parks for Mount Ranier and the
Grand Canyon. Congress refused to pass any of the proposed legislation. To make
things worse, Pinchot, though he had signed the report, a few days later got
the Secretary of the Interior to allow him to prepare "what was described as
a practical plan for the national domain."[14] Sargent was outraged by what he
considered Pinchot's betrayal. He gave up further efforts to obtain a rational forest
policy and devoted his energies to improving the arboretum and to scientific
writings about forests and trees.

III

In developing the arboretum's living collection, Sargent at first gave attention
only to American plants. But soon he decided that, in accord with the agreement

of the trustees and Harvard, the arboretum ought to contain all the trees and shrubs, either indigenous or exotic, which could be raised in the New England climate. William S. Clark, former president of the Massachusetts College of Agriculture, sent him seeds from Japan, and Dr. Emil Bretschneider of St. Petersburg, many of north China trees. In 1892 Sargent decided to go himself to Japan. Professor Gray had early noticed "the extraordinary similarity between the Floras of Eastern North America and Japan."[15] Sargent and his young nephew, Philip Codman, who was studying landscape architecture with Olmsted, spent ten weeks on Hokkaido and Nippon, the two principal Japanese islands. They visited forests, gardens, and nurseries; made a valuable acquaintance in professor Kingo Miyabe, a botanist in the college of Sapporo, and scaled Mount Hakkoda with young James Herbert Veitch, nephew of the head of a prominent English nursery firm.

Sargent returned to the arboretum with about 200 varieties of plants and 1,225 herbarium specimens. He wrote an account of the trip in an attractive, informal style for *Garden and Forest* and then issued it in book form.[16] He stressed Japan's need for flood control and building materials and pointed out that timber to China and Australia and staves to California would be valuable exports. The living collection of the arboretum gained greatly from Sargent's trip, raising many new species, to name a few: *Acer nicoense*, Japanese barberry, *Magnolia selicifolia*, and the Kaemfer azaleas. Sargent returned to Japan in 1903 during a six-month round-the-world journey with his son Robeson, who had studied landscape design, and his old friend John Muir. They went to England, through Europe to St. Petersburg, Moscow, the Crimea, across Siberia by rail, Manchuria, Peking, Korea, Japan, Shanghai (from which Muir set off on his own), Singapore, Java, and home.

During this same period of time, Sargent also wished China more thoroughly explored for the arboretum. He kept in touch with the Veitches in England, who selected a young botanist, Ernest Henry (later nicknamed "Chinese") Wilson, for their plant hunter. He had been well trained in nurseries and studied botany in university classes. In 1899 he set out for China by way of Boston, where in five days he met Professor Sargent, who became a hero in his eyes, and visited the arboretum and Holm Lea with its garden. Wilson got on well with the Chinese and, despite the unsettled conditions of the Boxer Rebellion, reached the Ich'ang area in central China. He stayed there until 1902, secured plentiful seeds of the Dove Tree (*Davidia*) which the Veitches had hoped he would find, and returned to London with hundreds of other seeds and nearly 2,600 kinds of herbarium specimens. He made a second tour in 1903 with instructions to bring back the Yellow Poppywort and went much farther west, using Loshan near Tibet as a base. He made many perilous journeys, found plentiful seeds of the Poppywort and of 2,000 other species, and collected 5,000 herbarium specimens.

In 1905-1906 Sargent spent six months, accompanied by Robeson, in western South America—Ecuador, Peru, and Chile. They returned via England, where they persuaded Wilson to go to China for the arboretum at greatly increased pay. He spent 1907 in central and western China, sending the arboretum 2,262 packages of seeds, 1,473 varieties of living plants, 2,500 species of herbarium specimens, and 720 photographic plates. He returned to Boston in 1909 but departed again the next year. He had sent Sargent 1,285 packets of seeds when a landslide on the main road left him with a badly broken leg; he could not get back to Boston until the spring of 1911. Unsettled conditions prevented his return to China, but he took two successful tours of Japan, coming back with fifty species of the spectacular Khrume azalea. He also visited Korea and Formosa, and then in 1920 went to Australia, New Zealand, India, Kenya, Rhodesia, and South Africa. As a result of seven Chinese journeys, Wilson introduced more than 1,000 new species in England and the United States, and "succeeded in collecting and introducing a greater number of plants than any other collector."[17]

Sargent also sent out several other plant explorers to China. One of the most capable was the experienced Austrian botanist and collector, Joseph Francis Charles Rock, an authority on Hawaiian flora who could speak Chinese. He left in 1924 to explore the mountain ranges of northwestern China and southern Tibet. He found few trees there but secured seeds and cuttings of hardier forms of species that would do well in New England. But he did not return to Boston until after Sargent's death.

IV

In examining the first fifty years of the arboretum in 1922, Sargent thought that it had become the greatest existing collection of hardy trees and shrubs, many of them new plants obtained through explorations. Much still needed to be done, of course, assembling information about trees in many parts of the world and examining tropical forests which were disappearing at an alarming rate. The expanded living plant collection was a major factor in increasing the arboretum's worth as a scientific institution. Sargent considered the herbarium the largest and most important in the world; its specimens numbered about

200,000. The library contained more than 37,000 books and 8,400 pamphlets and was perhaps unsurpassed in its field. These resources attracted more and more scholars and serious students who received a warm welcome and friendly assistance. In looking ahead, Sargent called for a department to study diseases in trees, another to examine dangerous insects and their control, and a third for breeding new species of plants.

In the educational area, the arboretum sought to teach both scholars and the general public. In 1911 Sargent began publishing a *Bulletin of Popular Information* (the name later changed to *Arnoldia*) with short articles on plants in bloom and other current news, and in 1919 he founded a scientific quarterly, *Journal of the Arnold Arboretum*, which also served as an outlet for staff research. Though Sargent was the nominal editor, Alfred Rehder did most of the actual work. A German immigrant, he had begun as a day laborer in 1898, but Sargent had put him in charge of the *Bradley Bibliography*, a guide to the woody plants of the world. An accomplished and tireless scholar, he wrote more than a thousand articles during his service; upon Faxan's death, he also became curator.

Sargent himself continued to produce publications, two of the most important: *Manual of the Trees of North America* and *Trees and Shrubs of New or Little Known Ligneous Plants*. He had an amusing experience with the Mount Vernon Ladies' Association of the Union. At the invitation of its regent, he visited Mount Vernon in 1901 in order to consider making its trees conform to those known to George Washington. He generously waived any fee, but when he demanded a free hand in the project, the headstrong Ladies refused his services. A new regent in 1914 persuaded him to try again and worked with him to defeat quarrelsome Ladies' committees from time to time. He made a plan, based on the Washington Diary, showing where each tree should stand and greatly improved the historical authenticity of the Mount Vernon grounds. In this case as in his previous experiences with the Federal and New York State governments, he could not understand why an expert should be called in and then have his advice ignored.

Sargent had much influence in the botanical scientific field through his voluminous correspondence and his generosity in sending out seeds, plants, and advice. How the process worked is well shown by the 328 letters he wrote between 1914 and his death in 1927 to personnel of the Rochester (New York) Park System. He enlisted their close collaboration, requested information on various plants, kept them informed of Chinese Wilson's explorations, sent numerous seeds and plants, and advised them on their trips around the country. Yet he insisted that the arboretum must also help the ordinary gardener and plant lover to learn more about trees and shrubs and their uses. For popular enlightenment, he depended heavily upon the plantings themselves. Their year-round changes not only brought out-of-town visitors but thousands of Boston citizens who came to regard the arboretum as a great civic attraction.

The greatest need of the arboretum, thought Sargent in 1922, was more endowment. It had increased, through his efforts, from $103,848 to $808,176, with an extra construction fund of $129,257 immediately available for improvements. (The endowment finally did exceed one million in 1926). In summarizing what had happened in the first fifty years, Sargent concluded:

> The Arnold Arboretum is . . . a station for the study of trees as individuals in their scientific relations, economic properties and cultural requirements and possibilities. . . . It has been managed not merely as a New England museum but as a national and international institution working to increase knowledge of trees in all parts of the world and as anxious to help a student in Tasmania or New Caledonia as in Massachusetts. An institution with such ambitions must be equipped to answer any questions about any trees growing in any part of the world which may be addressed to it. During the first fifty years of the Arnold Arboretum only the foundations of such an establishment have been laid.[18]

Sargent's last years were not too happy. In 1918 Robeson, his son and close companion, died suddenly, and two years later, Mary Sargent also passed away, at age sixty-six. The next seven years were lonely ones for him, though except for persistent gout, he enjoyed remarkably good health. The last two of his fifty-five years at the arboretum, he came to the office for shorter periods and had to be driven around the grounds in a small automobile. Finally, on March 22, 1927, he died peacefully. He left the arboretum $30,000, two-thirds for the library and the other third to be invested to grow for 100 years. Then, of the new total, all could be used for running expenses except $10,000 which was to increase for another 100 years.

Sargent's career was indeed a remarkable one. By persistent hard work, careful planning and a pervasive sense of order, good administration and sound judgment of personnel, and cooperation with the botanical gardens and leading scientists in the field, he acquired the botanical and horticultural knowledge that he needed. And his willingness to share know-how as well as seeds and plants with others did much to establish his leadership.

The arboretum has continued since as a leading botanical garden of the nation and the world, and the new emphasis mankind is placing on population and environmental puoblems makes it ever more valuable. Though enlarged in scope since Sargent's day, the Arnold Arboretum still maintains the high standards and aspirations that he gave it.

NOTES

1. Quoted in Stephane Barry Sutton, *Charles Sprague Sargent and the Arnold Arboretum* (Cambridge, Mass.: Harvard University Press, 1970), 30. We are fortunate to have this well-researched and insightful biography.

2. Charles S. Sargent, "The First Fifty Years of the Arnold Arboretum," *Journal of the Arnold Arboretum* 3 (Jan. 1922): 127–71.

3. Other chief works on Sargent and the Arboretum are: Arnold Arboretum, *Bulletin of Popular Information* (May 2, 1911–Dec. 13, 1940), 8 vols.; Arnold Arboretum, *Journal of the Arnold Arboretum* 1 (July 1919); W. T. Councilman, "Charles Sprague Sargent, 1841–1927," in M. A. De Wolfe Howe, ed., *Later Years of the Saturday Club, 1870–1920* (Freeport, N.Y.: Books for Libraries Press, 1968; first published, 1927), 286–94; A. DesCares, *A Treatise on Pruning Forest and Ornamental Trees*, introduction by Charles S. Sargent, 3d ed. (Boston: A. Williams, 1881); Frances Duncan, "Professor Charles Sprague Sargent and the Arnold Arboretum," *Critic* 47 (Aug. 1905): 115–19; *Garden and Forest: A Journal of Horticulture, Landscape Art and Forestry* (Feb. 9, 1888–Dec. 29, 1897), 10 vols; Richard A. Howard, "The Arnold Arboretum at the Century Mark," *Longwood Program Seminars* 3 (Dec. 1971): 33–35; Alfred Rehder, *The Bradley Bibliography: A Guide to the Literature of Woody Plants of the World* (Cambridge, Mass.: Riverside Press, 1911–1918), 5 vols.; Charles Sprague Sargent, *Excerpts: Letters of, to Rochester Park Personnel* (Rochester, N.Y.: Rochester Chapbooks, 1961); Sargent, *Forest Flora of Japan: Notes on* (Boston: Houghton, Mifflin, 1894); Sargent, *Manual of the Trees of North America (Exclusive of Mexico)* 2d ed. enlarged (Boston: Houghton, Mifflin, 1933; first ed., 1905); Sargent, ed., *Plantae Wilsonianae: ... Woody Plants Collected in Western China for the Arnold Arboretum ... 1907, 1908, and 1910 by E. H. Wilson* (Cambridge, Mass.: Harvard University Press, 1913–1917), 3 vols.; Sargent, *Report on the Forests of North America (Exclusive of Mexico)* (Washington, D.C.: Government Printing Office, 1884); Sargent, ed., *Scientific Papers of Asa Gray* (Boston: Houghton, Mifflin, 1889), 2 vols.; Sargent, *The Silva of North America: ... Trees Which Grow Naturally in North America Exclusive of Mexico* (Boston: Houghton, Mifflin, 1891–1902), 14 vols.; Sargent, ed., *Trees and Shrubs of New or Little Known Ligneous Plants* (Boston: Houghton, Mifflin, 1905, 1913), 2 vols.; Sargent, *The Trees of Mount Vernon*, rev. ed. (Mount Vernon: Ladies' Association, 1926); Sargent, *The Woods of the United States: ... Their Structure, Qualities, and Uses* (New York: D. Appleton, 1885); Stephane Barry Sutton, *The Arnold Arboretum: The First Century* (Jamaica Plain: Arnold Arboretum, 1971); Elswyth Thane, *Mount Vernon: The Legacy* (Philadelphia: J. B. Lippincott, 1967); E. H. Wilson, *America's Greatest Garden: The Arnold Arboretum* (Boston: Stratford, 1925); Wilson, *A Naturalist in Western China*, introduction by Charles Sprague Sargent (New York: Doubleday, Page, 1913), 2 vols.; Donald Wyman, *The Arnold Arboretum Garden Book* (New York: D. Van Nostrand, 1954).

4. Sutton, *Sargent*, 28–29.

5. Sargent, "First Fifty Years," 132.

6. Quoted in Sutton, *Sargent*, 64.

7. Quoted in Sutton, *Sargent*, 87–88.

8. Quoted in Sutton, *Sargent*, 192–93.

9. *Nation* 37 (Sept. 6, 1883): 201.

10. Quoted in Sutton, *Sargent*, 106.

11. Sargent, *Silva*, 1: v.

12. *Garden and Forest* 3 (Dec. 3, 1890); John Muir, *Atlantic Monthly* 92 (July 1903): 9–10.

13. Quoted in Sutton, *Sargent*, 159.

14. Quoted in Sutton, *Sargent*, 167.

15. C. S. Sargent, "Asa Gray," *Garden and Forest* 1 (Feb. 29, 1888): 1.

16. Sargent, *Forest Flora of Japan*.

17. Alfred Rehder, "Ernest Henry Wilson," *Journal of the Arnold Arboretum* 2 (Oct. 1920): 185.

18. Sargent, "First Fifty Years," 168–69.

SELECT BIBLIOGRAPHY

Arnold Arboretum. *Bulletin of Popular Information*. May 2, 1911–Dec. 13, 1940. 8 vols.

Arnold Arboretum. *Journal of the Arnold Arboretum*. Vol. 1 (July 1919).

Councilman, W. T. "Charles Sprague Sargent, 1841–1927." In *Later Years of the Saturday Club, 1870–1920*. Edited by M. A. De Wolfe Howe. Freeport, N.Y.: Books for Libraries Press, 1968. First published, 1927.

DesCares, A. *A Treatise on Pruning Forest and Ornamental Trees*. Introduction by Charles S. Sargent. 3d ed. Boston: A. Williams, 1881.

Duncan, Frances. "Professor Charles Sprague Sargent and the Arnold Arboretum." *Critic* 47 (Aug. 1905): 115–19.

Garden and Forest: A Journal of Horticulture, Landscape Art and Forestry. Feb. 9, 1888–Dec. 29, 1897). 10 vols.

Howard, Richard A. "The Arnold Arboretum at the Century Mark." *Longwood Program Seminars* 3 (Dec. 1971): 33–35.

Rehder, Alfred. *The Bradley Bibliography: A Guide to the Literature of Woody Plants of the World*. Cambridge, Mass.: Riverside Press, 1911–1918. 5 vols.

_____. "Ernest Henry Wilson." *Journal of the Arnold Arboretum* 2 (Oct. 1920): 185.

Sargent, Charles Sprague. *Excerpts: Letters of, to Rochester Park Personnel*. Rochester, N.Y.: Rochester Chapbooks, 1961.

_____. "The First Fifty Years of the Arnold Arboretum." *Journal of the Arnold Arboretum* 3 (Jan. 1922): 127–71.

_____. *Forest Flora of Japan: Notes on*. Boston: Houghton, Mifflin, 1894.

_____. *Manual of the Trees of North America (Exclusive of Mexico)*. 2d ed. enlarged. Boston: Houghton, Mifflin, 1933. First ed., 1905.

_____. *Report on the Forests of North America (Exclusive of Mexico)*. Washington, D.C.: Government Printing Office, 1884.

_____. *The Silva of North America: ... Trees Which Grow Naturally in North America Exclusive of Mexico*. Boston: Houghton, Mifflin, 1891–1902. 14 vols.

_____. *The Trees of Mount Vernon*. Rev. ed. Mount Vernon: Ladies' Association, 1926.

_____. *The Woods of the United States: ... Their Structure, Qualities, and Uses*. New York: D. Appleton, 1885.

_____. ed. *Plantae Wilsonianae: ... Woody Plants Collected in Western China for the Arnold Arboretum ... 1907, 1908, and 1910 by E. H. Wilson*. Cambridge, Mass.: Harvard University Press, 1913–1917. 3 vols.

_____. ed. *Scientific Papers of Asa Gray*. Boston: Houghton, Mifflin, 1889. 2 vols.

_____. ed. *Trees and Shrubs of New or Little Known Ligneous Plants*. Boston: Houghton, Mifflin, 1905, 1913. 2 vols.

Sutton, Stephane Barry. *The Arnold Arboretum: The First Century*. Jamaica Plain: Arnold Arboretum, 1971.

_____. *Charles Sprague Sargent and the Arnold Arboretum*. Cambridge, Mass.: Harvard University Press, 1970.

Thane, Elswyth. *Mount Vernon: The Legacy*. Philadelphia: J. B. Lippincott, 1967.

Wilson, E. H. *America's Greatest Garden: The Arnold Arboretum*. Boston: Stratford, 1925.

_____. *A Naturalist in Western China*. Introduction by Charles Sprague Sargent. New York: Doubleday, Page, 1913. 2 vols.

Wyman, Donald. *The Arnold Arboretum Garden Book*. New York: D. Van Nostrand, 1954

CHAPTER 12

William Temple Hornaday
Founds a Varied and Popular Zoo

I

WILLIAM TEMPLE HORNADAY was born on a farm near Plainfield, Indiana, on December 1, 1854, the son of William and Martha (Varner) Hornaday; the family later moved to Iowa. As a boy, Hornaday spent time between Indiana where he was familiar with turtles, yellow perch, croppies, squirrels, and little green herons and Iowa with its prairie chickens, quail, ground squirrels, and pocket gophers. His brother Calvin taught him to hunt, but he later maintained, perhaps in exaggeration because of his support for the conservation of wildlife, that he had shot only one gray squirrel, one blue jay, one little green heron, two prairie chickens, and one woodpecker in order to examine how they were made. Modern guns, he said, made killing game for sport too easy, and he later did so only to obtain scientific specimens.

By the time he was fourteen, both his parents were dead; he attended public school in Knoxville, Iowa, and then in 1870 went to Oskaloosa College for one year. There he received a sound grounding in English that later helped him fluently write many books and articles. He also was entranced to watch a professor skin and mount a crow. As a boy, he had seen two beautifully mounted ducks in Ambrose Ballweg's game store in Indianapolis, but could not find out how the taxidermy was done. In 1871 Hornaday entered Iowa State College at Ames. He studied botany, zoology, museums and museology, paleontology, anthropology, and geology. President Walsh saw him mount a great white heron successfully, relying upon his memory of the crow and with an Audubon engraving of a heron as a guide. The president hired him for work in the college museum at nine cents per hour. By the end of his second year, he was resolved to pursue museology, especially taxidermy, as a career, rather than to engage in business and making money.[1]

He decided, however, that instead of finishing his last two years of college, he would go to Professor Henry A. Ward's world-famous Natural Science Establishment in Rochester, New York, and become an apprentice taxidermist. Ward hired him at six dollars per week. The young man was thrilled to see the work of experienced taxidermists such as Frederic S. Webster, an expert at mounting birds, and John Martens, who had come from Hamburg bringing along iron squares to which leg irons of mounted carcasses could be attached; and he made several close friends, among them Frederic A. Lucas, who would become director of the American Museum of Natural History. Some of the good-natured apprentices posed partially nude for Hornaday when he was working on an orangutan group, and he occasioned amusement among his friends when he sent home from South America a capybara with two pairs of left legs, fore and aft.

In 1874 Professor Ward sent Hornaday out as a collector for a six-year period, at first to Florida, Cuba, Barbados, Trinidad, Venezuela, and British Guiana, and then to India, Ceylon, the Malay Peninsula, and Borneo. The professor accompanied him part way on the India trip, and they collected natural history specimens while visiting museums and art galleries in Liverpool, London, Paris, and a half dozen Italian cities. In the Far East, Hornaday hunted widely and got along well with the natives, whom he paid to collect for him; he preserved all specimens with care and returned with the richest zoological collection yet made by one man—a huge mass of skins, skeletons, and skulls of mammals, birds, reptiles, fishes, crustaceans, starfishes, corals, and a few insects. He described his travels so vividly in a book, *Two Years in the Jungle* (1885), that it ran through a dozen printings.[2]

When Hornaday got back from the East Indies, he was married, on September 11, 1879, to Josephine (jokingly called "Empress Josephine") Chamberlain of Battle Creek, Michigan. He dedicated the jungle book "To My Good Wife Josephine whose presence both when seen and unseen has ever been the sunshine of my life." The union lasted until his death; they had one daughter who provided them with three grandchildren. Hornaday took great pride in being a devoted family man.[3]

In 1880 the young naturalist worked on a pioneering habitat group of orangutans that he had collected in Borneo and which his fellow taxidermists helped model. It was called "A Fight in the Tree-Tops" and attracted much attention when shown at a meeting of the American Association for the Advancement of Science in Saratoga. He and some seven others formed the Society of American Taxidermists, which soon held competitive exhibitions at Rochester, Boston, and New York. At the last one (1883), Hornaday's "Coming to the Point," a grouping with a hunting dog and six partridges, won a special medal, and the elephant "Mungo" that he had modeled with a manikin process he had invented received a silver medal as "best piece in the entire Exhibition."[4]

In 1882 Hornaday became chief taxidermist at the Smithsonian Institution's United States National Museum, where he worked harmoniously and happily with George Brown Goode, the museum's director, and Spencer Fullerton Baird, secretary of the Smithsonian. He made many advances in the science of taxidermy, one of the most important being the use of clay as a filling material on the outside of a manikin, which made it possible to affix the hide with all the proper curvatures and indentations of the living animal. The manikin itself consisted of a wooden center board with wires running to the legs, the whole covered with excelsior tied with cords and surmounted by clay. Those developments made it possible to produce a convincing replica of the animal in a lifelike pose. He believed that taxidermists ought to receive credit on museum labels for their work, and Brown Goode adopted that rule for the National Museum.[5]

Hornaday did much to develop the concept of habitat groups, so popular today in natural history museums. About 1886 he completed a small group of three coyotes in a natural setting, an exhibit widely studied and much admired. He made a three-month hunting trip that fall and winter to the Big Dry badlands of Montana to secure specimens of American bison; his buffalo group exhibit included buffalo grass and other authentic accessories. Morris K. Jesup, president of the American Museum of Natural History, came down to inspect the coyote and buffalo groups with enthusiasm.[6]

Hornaday also had the idea of enlarging the small number of live animals kept in a paddock beside the Smithsonian building into a genuine zoological park. In 1888 Congress appropriated $200,000 for a Rock Creek Park site of 168 acres, and the National Zoological Park was soon formed, to be operated by the Smithsonian with Hornaday as designer and director. He wished to attract the general public rather than only professional zoologists and collectors, and he insisted upon letting the animals roam freely in the park's large ranges. He secured a woven wire fence that would contain the beasts but allow the public to view them. But alas! Hornaday did not get along with Baird's successor as

Smithsonian secretary, Samuel P. Langley, who, according to Brown Goode, "wished him to subordinate himself more than he was willing." And so, Hornaday resigned in 1890 because of "great Langley disillusionment" and "the death of my plans for a really great Zoological Park." He supposedly left zoology and taxidermy forever and moved to Buffalo to become secretary of the Union Land Exchange, a large real estate business.[7]

In saying goodbye, Hornaday made another contribution to zoological science when he wrote *Taxidermy and Zoological Collecting* (1891), "a complete handbook for the amateur taxidermist, collector, geologist, museum-builder, sportsman, and traveller." Its 362 pages described, with admirable clarity and sometimes eloquence, hunting and collection, the selection and study of specimens, treatment of skins in the field, and the whole mounting process in the laboratory. Dedicated to G. Brown Goode, "whose liberal policy has done so much for American taxidermy," the book became the acknowledged classic on the subject and had seventeen printings by 1909.

II

The New York Zoological Society was formed in 1895 as a result of a movement led by Madison Grant, a young lawyer, who was determined to protect American big-game animals from senseless slaughter and possible extermination. The Boone and Crockett Club, an organization of wealthy, concerned sportsmen with Theodore Roosevelt as president, hoped that a zoological garden might be established in one of the parks acquired by New York City in 1888. The cause received a great boost when Henry Fairfield Osborn of the American Museum of Natural History walked into Grant's office and volunteered his help. The society's executive committee adopted the "new Principle" that the larger wild animals "should be shown not in paddocks but in the free range of large enclosures, in which the forests, rocks, and natural features of the landscape will give the people an impression of the life habits and other native surroundings of these different types." As soon as the State Legislature and the city agreed upon the creation of the society, the appointment of an executive director became all important. Hornaday's work with the National Zoological Park was well known, and after a thorough investigation by Osborn and a search committee, he was appointed and took office in April 1896.[8]

The society now had three energetic, strong-willed, and driving men sharing its direction: Professor Osborn as chairman of the executive committee, Madison

Grant as its secretary, and Hornaday. Their opinions clashed violently now and then. Osborn and Grant stood behind Hornaday in his quarrels with the public and appreciated his aggressive actions in behalf of wildlife conservation, but he was always vocal and would throw an occasional tantrum. Grant found him difficult and soon made any complaints he had to Osborn who then, with a combination of tact and firmness, persuaded Hornaday to do as they thought best. Grant once wrote Osborn: "The best way is to let Mr. Hornaday speak his mind, and then we can meet privately and decide what we are going to do."[9]

The new director's first important action was to visit the different New York parks to choose the one most suitable for a zoological garden. When he spent a day in the southern section of Bronx Park (the northern part had been given to the Botanical Garden), he was astonished and enchanted to find an unbroken wilderness with virgin woods, spacious meadows separated by rocky ridges, and abundant ponds, bogs, and streams on the 264-acre tract. He at once enthusiastically recommended that site over Van Cortlandt Park, which a committee of experts previously had suggested. The executive committee ratified his choice and sent him off to Europe with a purse of $13,000 with which to buy animals. In two months he visited fifteen zoos in England, Belgium, Holland, Germany, and France, noting carfully their management, means of support, buildings, methods of exhibition, pleasure grounds and restaurants, and maps and plans. He was much encouraged when some of the European directors told him: "With such ground, and the money New York will give you, you can do anything you choose."[10]

During the next year the city agreed that the society should raise $250,000 over a three-year period for animals and buildings, the latter to belong to the city. It would provide roads, grading, fences, and water, as well as police protection. Admission was to be free of charge for five days each week. Most important, the society should choose and direct all personnel and have entire management of the garden's affairs. Through the years, the arrangement became similar to that worked out for several New York museums with buildings, maintenance, and protection furnished by the city and the collection, museum, and educational programs provided and managed by the private board of trustees.[11]

Hornaday made a plan for the garden that was examined critically but only slightly modified by several experts and the executive committee. It called for a Baird Court bordered by a Lion House (patterned after London's), Elephant House (after Antwerp's), Antelope House (after Frankfurt's), and Reptile House (after London's but with improvements). Hornaday was proud that Our Bird House, Monkey House, sub-tropical House, Winter House for Birds, Administration Building, Bear Dens, Wolf and Fox Dens, Alligators' Pool, Burrowing Rodents' Quarters, Squirrel installations, Beaver Pond and Aquatic Rodents' Ponds, all are features absolutely new, both in design and general arrangement. There also was a Flying Cage for Birds 150 feet long, 75 wide, and 50 high that contained living trees and a flowing stream.[12]

The next problems were to secure a capable staff and animals. Hornaday enlisted three talented young men to serve as assistant curators and take much of the responsibility for hiring keepers, caring for animals, and handling the everyday administration. J. Alden Loring was in charge of animals; he had worked eight years for the Biological Survey as a field naturalist and two years as an animal keeper in London's zoo. Raymond Lee Ditmars took over the reptiles; he had been an assistant at the American Museum of Natural History and a reporter for the New York *Times*; he gave his own collection of forty specimens of reptiles to the society. Charles William Beebe, a graduate student of Professor Osborn's known for his restless energy and interest in birds, supervised the birds. Hornaday appointed his nephew, H. Raymond Mitchell, who was a clerk, cashier, and agent of the Santa Fe Railway, as the garden's chief clerk (later manager) to handle financial matters, and added other important specialists—veterinarian, photographer, and cook to prepare the animals' food.[13]

Hornaday was a czar who ruled his staff with an iron hand, supervised closely, and was quick to reprimand shortcomings. Still, he stood behind decisions of the principal staff members, tried to pay them adequately (though their salaries were much lower than for comparable work in commerce and industry), and took an interest in their personal affairs. He occasionally had difficulties with Grant and Osborn about personnel. A few months after Loring's appointment, Grant became dissatisfied with "the very careless way" in which he handled the animals. In November 1900, while Hornaday was on an animal-buying trip in the West, Grant, with Osborn's concurrence, suspended Loring. When the director heard about it, he wrote Osborn a blistering letter about "the new kind of madness" that caused the two executive committee members to interfere with his administration "without any sort of warning to me." The decision, however, was not reversed, and Beebe took charge of the animals as well as the birds. Modern museum professionals must sympathize with Hornaday and conclude that Grant and Osborn, despite their zeal for the society, went too far in their almost daily attention to administrative matters properly left to a director.[14]

In May 1899 Hornaday began to stock the garden with animals, obtained either by gift or purchase. The first two accessions were white-tailed prairie dogs.

Birds and smaller animals arrived in great numbers, and rarer acquisitions included a giant anteater from Venezuela, three gray wolves, four California sea lions, nine American elk, six pronghorn antelopes, three young orangutans (which Mrs. Hornaday took home to care for), a Bengal tiger, two polar bears, and two huge reticulated pythons (twenty-six and twenty-two feet long). Hornaday was especially interested in American bison and began to assemble a sizeable herd, which ranged in a twenty-acre enclosure.

Hornaday did not succeed in raising a herd of pronghorns, moose, caribou, or mule deer and concluded that it was exceedingly difficult to acclimatize those animals on the Atlantic Coast. Though a fine beaver pond was scooped out in a natural bog between two ridges, that exhibit was not popular because beavers are nocturnal animals seldom visible during daytime visiting hours. Animal escapes always attracted much public attention. A young female wolf terrified the neighborhood for five days; a policeman fired at her but missed, and she ran into a cellar where she was recaptured. Sea lions escaped from their pool, and one of them spent three weeks in the Bronx River before being retaken. Hornaday himself helped subdue a Borneo sun bear but was bitten in the hand; unfortunately, the bear died from exhaustion.[15]

The opening day ceremonies for the Zoological Park on November 8, 1899, attracted a crowd of about two thousand, led by city officials, representatives from other museums and institutions of higher learning, and wealthy donors intent upon seeing what their money had bought. Professor Osborn, as chief speaker, pointed out that the park was projected on a larger scale than ever attempted by the small, confined gardens of Europe.[16] Hornaday himself did not speak, but he must have been elated to see his dearest charge progressing so well. His fertile ideas and abundant energy were paying off. His demanding but imaginative administration; his personal handling of a mountain of correspondence; and his hard-hitting interviews, letters to press and public, and magazine articles were keeping the park in the news, usually in a favorable light. He was determined to accumulate and disseminate animal lore for millions. The park, though open to experts and collectors, would stress popular zoology in writing, photography, editing, printing, lecturing, and broadcasting. In an article he wrote after his retirement, he said that a director could make or break such an institution. His greatest worry was the death of his animals, his chief delight receiving wonderful new arrivals; the highest praise he could receive was: "Your animals are looking fine."[17]

III

Hornaday was always a positive person, often dogmatic, aggressive, and belligerent. He believed in putting everything in writing—orders to all members of his varied staff and answers to correspondents, newspaper notices, and comments that in any way concerned the park or himself. He insisted that his curators leave all public correspondence to him and often wrote or dictated his way through an enormous pile of letters and memorandums. He also sent off a stream of letters to the editor and magazine articles, to say nothing of writing some twenty long and detailed books. His fierce energy kept him working, usually twelve or more hours a day at the office or at home on weekends and holidays. In his quarrels with Osborn and Grant, Hornaday might lose on some issues, but he frequently won because he was on the spot, decisive, and prompt to take action. So far as the curators and other staff members went, he supervised closely; in 1923 they begged to have half days off on Saturday, but he reluctantly but firmly refused because of the cost. He also was adamant about newspaper interviews or articles that the curators might originate. Their names were not to appear blatantly, but all credit must be given to the society and perhaps to its director.

Hornaday's tiffs with the newspapers and their reporters were frequent. He wished them to remember to use "New York Zoological Society" or "Park," never that despicable term, "Bronx Zoo." He also decried amusing but silly stories about his animals that reporters might dream up, and he reminded them often that truth frequently is stranger than fiction. The public also had to conduct itself in seemly fashion at the park. First of all, no photographs were allowed; that prohibition led to many quarrels, but he insisted that the society had photographs for sale and was entitled to that income. Then he had trouble with the park's neighbors; packs of dogs managed to enter the garden and attack deer, and certain vagrants drifted in to shoot songbirds. Finally, a Rubbish War erupted as visitors carelessly dropped paper containers and other trash along park pathways. Hornaday designed a three-foot-high trash basket in the shape of a tree stump and distributed 200 of them about the park. He had to put up with a good deal of silliness from the public. Some said that the giraffes were suffering from tonsilitis, and the Tonsilene Company sent a bottle of its product to help them. A great Smells Battle took place when a well-meaning correspondent maintained that he could cure the peculiar musky odor secreted by civet cats in the Small Animal House. But in any case the public was deeply interested in the park and its animals.[18]

The beasts themselves frequently furnished controversy. In 1904 "Gunda," the elephant from India, began to become unruly, especially during recurring periods of sexual excitement or musth. He knocked down one keeper and nearly killed another. He was whipped on the trunk and then had his feet chained to the floor of the cage. The public protested to the newspapers that the keepers were treating him cruelly. Hornaday explained why such measures were necessary, but the protests continued. When Gunda's behavior became worse, he had to be shot. "Khartoum," a huge elephant from the Blue Nile, took delight in breaking every zoo fence and door until Hornaday had 4,567 needle-pointed spikes installed in strategic spots. Was Hornaday's treatment of elephants and other animals too violent? Perhaps so, by modern standards, but in those days it was agreed that animals must always obey their keepers.[19]

In 1906 an unusual incident took place. An African Pygmy from the Congo, named Ota Benga, was exhibited (Hornaday preferred the word "employed") playing with his own chimpanzee and other apes in a cage. The practice continued for less than a week, because black ministers insisted that it was a flagrant case of race bigotry. Ota Benga moved to the Colored Orphan Asylum, then to several other places, and finally committed suicide. When David Garnett's novel entitled *A Man in the Zoo* (1924) caused a New Yorker to volunteer to put himself on exhibition, Hornaday refused, saying that the book aroused "Bitter Reflections" of his "first offense in the display of Man as a Primate."[20]

In 1918–1920 the Zoological Society was investigated by the Tammany administration under Mayor John F. Hyland and his commissioner of accounts, David Hirshfield. They objected to the society's keeping the income from restaurant, animal rides, photographs, and the like, while other city parks let such concessions to the highest bidder who turned over profits to the city. They argued that the city ought to assume the operation of the park and run it under the rules of the Municipal Civil Service Commission. The society cited its legal grant of 1897 and pointed out that it had donated more than $700,000 to the park, had seen that city monies were spent with honesty and care, and so far had instructed and entertained nearly 25 million visitors. The Hirshfield Report asserted that "Hornaday rules the Zoo and the City's park lands like an autocrat—a monarch in his own principality—and looks down with disgust upon common people." One witness said of the employees: "Everybody trembles when they see him." But the New York newspapers that had fought with Hornaday so often stood up for him and the society. They asked scornfully: "Shall we Hylandize the Zoo?" and characterized the report as an obvious attempted power grab.

The whole investigation was often painful, but the Zoological Park and its director emerged stronger than ever in the loyalty and affection of most New Yorkers.[21]

Throughout the years the park and society maintained that they were operating the greatest zoo in the world. Hornaday moved steadily to secure the buildings to complete his original plan, and he added many new features. In 1900 the park pioneered in hiring a veterinarian to look after its animals and soon added Dr. W. Reid Blair, trained in that science at McGill, who later became assistant director and succeeded Hornaday when he retired. The society took over the Aquarium in Castle Garden at the Battery and appointed its director upon Hornaday's recommendation. He also gave artists, sculptors, zoologists, and students special privileges in the park, and Ernest Thompson Seton, Carl Rungius from Germany, Charles P. Knight, and others painted murals and made sculptures for the various buildings. For a time the park had an art gallery financed by park members. Grant and Hornaday also enthusiastically created an old-fashioned "National Collection of Heads and Horns," raised $10,000 for it, and contributed their own considerable holdings of such trophies. But neither the art gallery nor the heads and horns attracted the public, and they were eventually dropped.[22]

In the research field, Hornaday founded *Zoologica: Scientific Papers of the New York Zoological Society* in 1907. William Beebe was its chief contributor; a skilled and prolific researcher and writer, he produced impressive scientific articles and volumes. In 1919 he partially cut his ties with the park, became honorary curator of birds, and began to spend most of his time at his Tropical Research Station in British Guiana. Lee Saunders Crandall, Beebe's assistant, was his successor; he had begun as an unpaid student keeper in 1908 and went on to serve the society for sixty-one fruitful years.[23]

The Zoological Society made considerable educational progress. Ditmars, the former reporter on the New York *Times*, provided his friends of the press with many striking, yet authentic, stories about the zoo and its animals. He also proved expert at producing motion pictures; his forty-three reels of the "Living Natural History" series were shown in the park and at theatres and schools throughout the country. Hornaday in 1925 allowed himself and the staff to make weekly broadcasts for the Radio Corporation of America, and some of the curators continued to appear occasionally. But a curator of educational activities was not added to the staff until 1939 under Dr. Blair's administration.[24]

The entry of the United States into the First World War sent Hornaday into a frenzy of patriotic activity. He tried to cut down the food rations of the animals, but when they lost weight, he had to give up that move, though he added economical cornbread to their diet. Half of the Lion House was turned over to the Red Cross. He formed Company A of the Zoological Park Guards, uniformed and equipped with rifles; they drilled frequently and conducted armed patrols from sunset to sunrise. Hornaday participated in seven defense organizations and wrote pamphlets such as "A Searchlight on Germany" (50,000 copies and reprinted in 13 newspapers) and "Awake! America." He urged zoos not to patronize German dealers and wished to cut off the society's subscriptions to German books and periodicals (President Grant refused to do so). When the war ended, the park sent 329 mammals, birds, reptiles, and amphibians to restock the Antwerp Zoo.[25]

In his 1920 Annual Report, Hornaday put down his basic philosophy for zoological gardens, as follows:

> The first, the last and the greatest business of every zoological park is to collect and exhibit fine and rare animals. Next comes the duty of enabling the greatest possible number of people to see them with comfort and satisfaction. In comparison with these objects, all others are of secondary or tertiary or quaternary importance. The breeding of wild animals is extremely interesting, and the systematic study of them is fascinating, but both these ends must be subordinated to the main objects.[26]

Without any doubt, Hornaday attained his chief objectives. On the outbreak of war in 1914, the park contained 4,729 specimens of 1,290 species, and by the time of his retirement in 1926, annual attendance had reached 2.5 million. But as Kenneth J. Polakowski has pointed out recently:

> Many zoos at this time [about 1985] began to move away from the traditional goals of providing recreation and entertainment while amassing large varieties and numbers of species. The quality of a zoo is no longer measured by the number of species it contains, but rather by the quality of its exhibits, its educational programs, its propagation results, and its research and conservation activities.[27]

Thus Hornaday did not value the various zoo functions as zoo leaders do today. Of course, the depletion of wild animals in what were once primitive areas of the earth has greatly increased since his day, and the modern zoo has become a center for the conservation and propagation of endangered species.

Nor did Hornaday adopt the latest methods of exhibition of wild animals. Carl Hagenbeck's private zoo at Stelligen in Hamburg in 1907 largely did away with bars and cages; it used moats to keep predators and prey apart as well as animals and the public. Hornaday praised Hagenbeck for having "the temerity to build . . . a private zoological garden so spectacular and attractive" and considered him the greatest zoological park creator in the world. Later, in 1919, Hornaday's intense anti-German feelings may have influenced the advice he gave the director of the St. Louis Zoo against building moated and barless bear pits. Hornaday said that when he was erecting his own bear dens in 1899, Hagenbeck had strongly urged his methods, but Hornaday had rejected them because of the great disadvantage of "having our bears separated from our visitors by a distance of sixty or seventy feet"; he preferred using the woven wire fence. (St. Louis went ahead to build moated dens with realistic concrete rockwork.) He also successfully opposed Dr. Blair's desire to experiment with moats. Since then, however, Blair's successors have used them extensively, as in the "African Plains" exhibits with its "Lion Island," or in "Tropical Asia."[28]

It is not too harsh a judgment to say that in Hornaday's later years, the Zoological Park was beginning to fall behind the more progressive zoos of the world. Fortunately, its new president Fairfield Osborn and several later innovative directors brought it back to its former eminence. It is now generally agreed that the Bronx Zoo, the San Diego Zoo and Wild Animal Park, and the National Zoo at Washington are the three great American leaders.[29]

IV

Hornaday early decided that a most important part of his duties at the Zoological Society was the conservation of American wildlife. In 1905 he became chief executive of the American Bison Society and helped set up buffalo herds in Oklahoma, Montana, and South Dakota. He opposed sportsmen, boys, market hunters, plumage gatherers, and egg collectors who were slaughtering birds and animals. He did much to secure state and national laws and international treaties to protect animals threatened with extinction and tried unsuccessfully to obtain a federal law to establish game preserves in national forests. He wrote two books on *Our Vanishing Wild Life* (1913) and *Thirty Years War for Wild Life* (1931) in his best battling, no-holds-barred style. After his retirement, he devoted most of his time to various conservation projects.[30]

The magazine *Outdoor Life* in 1930 summed it up well:

> In the long and often weary annals of conservation progress, no man has been less bowed beneath reverses or less satisfied with success than Dr. Hornaday. Determined and intransigent, it was never his policy to go around or under an

opponent; smashing straight through his opposition, he has left a long trail of personal enemies in his wake—but has never looked back. Sold out by game-hogs in high places, rebuffed by organizations purporting to have conservation purpose, deserted even by high-principled and well-intentioned leaders who felt him too radical and truculent for his time, much of Dr. Hornaday's far-seeing effort has been single-handed. In his day of triumph, let his indomitable persistence be remembered.[31]

Thus in the sixty-four years of his active career from apprenticeship until his death in retirement, Hornaday had made countless contributions to zoology in America and the world—improving the theory and practice of taxidermy, developing a great zoological garden, and conserving wildlife threatened with extinction. Many honors came to him—gold medals, honorary degrees, and honorific membership in zoo and conservation organizations around the world. A 10,000-foot peak in Yellowstone Park was named "Mount Hornaday." And Iowa State College, proud that as a student there he had found his calling, placed a large boulder in front of the College Library with a bronze plaque that justly commemorated "his contributions to zoology and conservation which have been of immeasurable benefit to America."[32]

NOTES

1. For Hornaday's early life, see William T. Hornaday, "My Fifty-Four Years of Animal Life: Personal Reflections of a Big Game Hunter and Naturalist," *Mentor* 17 (May 1929): 3–5; Hornaday, *Camp-Fires on Desert and Lava* (Tucson: University of Arizona Press, 1983; original edition, 1908), xxiii–xxiv; Hornaday, *Taxidermy and Zoological Collecting* (New York: Charles Scribner's Sons, 1891), 62–64; "William Temple Hornaday," *Who Was Who in America* (Chicago: A. N. Marquis Company, 1942), 1 (1897–1942): 588; "Dr. Hornaday" (obituary), *Commonwealth* 25 (Mar. 19, 1937): 583; Fairfield Osborn, "William Temple Hornaday" (obituary), *Science* 85 (Mar. 7, 1937): 445–46; Edward A. Preble, "William Temple Hornaday: An Appreciation" (obituary), *Nature Magazine* 29 (May 1937): 303–04; William Bridges, *Gathering of Animals: An Unconventional History of the New York Zoological Society* (New York: Harper & Row, 1974), 20–24.

2. William T. Hornaday, "Masterpieces of American Bird Taxidermy," *Scribner's Magazine* 78 (Sept. 1925): 262–63; Hornaday, *Two Years in the Jungle: The Experiences of a Hunter and Naturalist in India, Ceylon, the Malay Peninsula, and Borneo* (New York: Charles Scribner's Sons, 1885); Hornaday, "My Fifty- Four Years," 5–6; Hornaday, *Desert and Lava*, xxiii–xxiv; Hornaday, *Taxidermy and Zoological Collecting*, 10, 52, 135, 175, 195–96, 221–24, 272; Osborn, "Hornaday," 445; Preble, "Hornaday," 303; Bridges, *Gathering of Animals*, 21.

3. Hornaday, "My Fifty-Four Years," 7; Hornaday, *Two Years in the Jungle*, iii; *Who Was Who*, 1: 588; Preble, "Hornaday," 304.

4. William T. Hornaday, "Masterpieces of American Taxidermy," *Scribner's Magazine* 72 (July 1927): 6; Hornaday, *Taxidermy and Zoological Collecting*, 221–22, 230–33.

5. Hornaday, "Masterpieces of American Bird Taxidermy," 272; Hornaday, *Taxidermy and Zoological Collecting*, 112–13, 127, 130–31, 140–42, 163, 174, 211, 213–14; Bridges, *Gathering of Animals*, 22.

6. Hornaday, "Masterpieces of American Bird Taxidermy," 265–66; Hornaday, "Masterpieces of American Taxidermy," 8–9; Hornaday, *Taxidermy and Zoological Collecting*, 233–35, 245–46.

7. Bridges, *Gathering of Animals*, 17, 20, 24, 55–56; Hornaday, "My Fifty-Four Years," 7; William T. Hornaday, *Thirty Years War for Wild Life: Gains and Losses in a Thankless Task* (New York: Arno and the New York Times, 1970; original edition, 1931), 167–68; Osborn, "Hornaday," 445–46.

8. Quotation in Bridges, *Gathering of Animals*, 16. See also, 1–30.

9. Ibid., 43–44, 64–68, 79–82, 300; "Dr. Hornaday's Retirement as Director of the New York Zoological Park," *Scientific Monthly* 23 (July 1926): 88–93.

10. Bridges, *Gathering of Animals*, 40 (quotation); see also, 29–40, 130–31; William T. Hornaday, "The New York Zoological Park," *Century Magazine* 39 (Nov. 1900): 85–102.

11. Bridges, *Gathering of Animals*, 36–37; William T. Hornaday, "The New York Plan for Zoological Parks," *Scribner's Magazine* 46 (Nov. 1909): 590–605.

12. Bridges, *Gathering of Animals*, 40–42, 46–50, 86, 118.

13. Ibid., 57–64, 76–77; Raymond L. Ditmars, *The Making of a Scientist* (New York: Macmillan, 1937), 11–48; Robert Henry Welker, *Natural Man: The Life of William Beebe* (Bloomington: Indiana University Press, 1975).

14. Bridges, *Gathering of Animals*, 64–67.

15. Ibid., 68–76, 82–84; William T. Hornaday, "Behind the Scenes in a Great Zoo," *Mentor* 15 (Aug. 1927): 3–4.

16. Bridges, *Gathering of Animals*, 89–98.

17. Hornaday, "Behind the Scenes," 8.

18. Bridges, *Gathering of Animals*, 172–91, 362–63, 406; Hornaday, "Behind the Scenes," 9–10.

19. Bridges, *Gathering of Animals*, 231–32, 247–56; Hornaday, "Behind the Scenes," 5.

20. Bridges, *Gathering of Animals*, 223–30, 388.

21. Ibid., 338–45.

22. Ibid., 141–64, 306–13, 329–33, 337–38; Hornaday, "My Fifty-Four Years," 9; William T. Hornaday, "Wild Animal Models at the Zoo: How New York Painters and Sculptors Work from Nature in Their Representations of Wild Life," *Scientific Monthly* 122 (Feb. 7, 1920): 134.

23. Bridges, *Gathering of Animals*, 290–305, 388–97; Lee Saunders Crandall, *The Management of Wild Animals in Captivity* (Chicago: University of Chicago Press, 1964); Crandall in collaboration with Bridges, *A Zoo Man's Notebook* (Chicago: University of Chicago Press, 1966), 1–5.

24. Bridges, *Gathering of Animals*, 402–05, 417, 425; Ditmars, *Confessions of a Scientist*, 221–41.

25. Bridges, *Gathering of Animals*, 364, 369–79.

26. Ibid., 414.

27. Ibid., 362; Kenneth J. Polakowski, *Zoo Design: The Reality of Wild Illusions* (Ann Arbor: University of Michigan School of Natural Resources, 1987), 5, 21–22.

28. Bridges, *Gathering of Animals*, 377, 387–88, 411–13; Polakowski, *Zoo Design*, 8, 82–83.

29. A good description of the later Bronx Zoo is Bernard Livingston, *Zoo Animals: People, Places* (New York: Arbor House, 1974), 263–79.

30. Bridges, *Gathering of Animals*, 204–06, 257–73, 276–78; William T. Hornaday, *Camp-fires in the Canadian Rockies* (New York: Charles Scribner's Sons, 1906), 7–8, 213–64; Hornaday,

"My Fifty-Four Years," 9; William Temple Hornaday, *Our Vanishing Wild Life: Its Extermination and Protection* (New York: New York Zoological Society, 1913), x, 208–397; Hornaday, *Thirty Years War*, 150–56, 168–70, 179–81, 199–206, 223–30.

31. Hornaday, *Thirty Years War*, iv.

32. Bridges, *Gathering of Animals*, 409–10, 440; "Dr. Hornaday," *Commonwealth* 25 (Mar. 19, 1937): 583; Hornaday, "Behind the Scenes," 5; "Hornaday—Conservationist," *Nature Magazine* 21 (May 1933): 256; "Dr. Hornaday's Retirement," 88–93; Osborn, "Hornaday," 445–46; Preble, "Hornaday," 303–04.

SELECT BIBLIOGRAPHY

Bridges, William. *Gathering of Animals: An Unconventional History of the New York Zoological Society*. New York: Harper & Row, 1974.

Crandall, Lee Saunders. *The Management of Wild Animals in Captivity*. Chicago: University of Chicago Press, 1964.

Crandall, Lee Saunders, with William Bridges. *A Zoo Man's Notebook*. Chicago: University of Chicago Press, 1966.

Ditmars, Raymond L. *The Making of a Scientist*. New York: Macmillan, 1937.

"Dr. Hornaday's Retirement as Director of the New York Zoological Park." *Scientific Monthly* 23 (July 1926): 88–93.

"Hornaday—Conservationist." *Nature Magazine* 21 (May 1933): 256.

Hornaday, William T. "Behind the Scenes in a Great Zoo." *Mentor* 15 (Aug. 1927): 3–4.

_____. *Camp-fires in the Canadian Rockies*. New York: Charles Scribner's Sons, 1906.

_____. *Camp-Fires on Desert and Lava*. Tucson: University of Arizona Press, 1983 (original edition, 1908).

_____. "Masterpieces of American Bird Taxidermy." *Scribner's Magazine* 78 (Sept. 1925): 262–63.

_____. "Masterpieces of American Taxidermy." *Scribner's Magazine* 72 (July 1927): 6.

_____. "My Fifty-Four Years of Animal Life: Personal Reflections of a Big Game Hunter and Naturalist." *Mentor* 17 (May 1929): 3–5.

_____. "The New York Plan for Zoological Parks." *Scribner's Magazine* 46 (Nov. 1909): 590–605.

_____. "The New York Zoological Park." *Century Magazine* 39 (Nov. 1900): 85–02.

_____. *Our Vanishing Wild Life: Its Extermination and Protection*. New York: New York Zoological Society, 1913.

_____. *Taxidermy and Zoological Collecting*. New York: Charles Scribner's Sons, 1891.

_____. *Thirty Years War for Wild Life: Gains and Losses in a Thankless Task*. New York: Arno and the New York Times, 1970 (original edition, 1931).

_____. *Two Years in the Jungle: The Experiences of a Hunter and Naturalist in India, Ceylon, the Malay Peninsula, and Borneo*. New York: Charles Scribner's Sons, 1885.

_____. "Wild Animal Models at the Zoo: How New York Painters and Sculptors Work from Nature in Their Representations of Wild Life." *Scientific Monthly* 122 (Feb. 7, 1920): 134.

Livingston, Bernard. *Zoo Animals: People, Places*. New York: Arbor House, 1974.

Polakowski, Kenneth J. *Zoo Design: The Reality of Wild Illusions*. Ann Arbor: University of Michigan School of Natural Resources, 1987.

Welker, Robert Henry. *Natural Man: The Life of William Beebe*. Bloomington: Indiana University Press, 1975.

"William Temple Hornaday." *Who Was Who in America*. Chicago: A. N. Marquis Company, 1942. Vol. 1 (1897–1942): 588.

CHAPTER 13

Paul Joseph Sachs
Teaches a Pioneering Course in Museum Studies

I

P AUL J. SACHS WAS one of the greatest teachers of museum studies who has yet appeared in America. For nearly a quarter century, starting about 1921, his museum course at Harvard University and its Fogg Art Museum trained graduate students who became curators and directors in the leading art museums of the country. "Uncle Paul," as he was affectionately but surreptitiously called by the students, was an unusual personality, only five feet, two inches tall, always immaculately dressed with a pearl stick pin in his tie, a passionate and prescient collector of master prints and drawings, famed gourmet, and possessed of a volcanic temper. But his deep love for art, enthusiastic spirit, and generosity brought him friends throughout the cultural world and among his students as he placed them in promising positions and continued carefully to follow their careers. An observer at the exhibition that honored his seventieth birthday described him as follows: "His closely cropped white hair makes a handsome contrast with emphatically black Groucho Marx-like eyebrows and a neatly trimmed bushy gray mustache; behind rimless eyeglasses dart snappingly alert eyes—eyes that have especially looked lovingly at art."[1]

Professor Sachs had a few pioneering predecessors in the field of museum studies. Mrs. Sarah Yorke Stevenson, assistant curator of the Pennsylvania Museum (now the Philadelphia Museum of Art), in 1908 began to help young men and women with at least a high school diploma prepare for work in art museums.

She gave lectures on museum techniques, demanded critical reports of visits to all the Philadelphia museums, and had the students perform practical tasks in her own institution. The course soon expanded to two years, with one year devoted to art history, and continued until Mrs. Stevenson's death in 1921.

Professor Homer K. Dill, director of the Museum of Natural History at the State University of Iowa in Iowa City, in 1908 experimented with a class in museum studies; within three years it had developed into a four-year program with the degree given in natural science but a minor concentration in museum work that included taxidermy, exhibit techniques, freehand drawing, and modeling. That course had no difficulty in placing its graduates and still continues today.

Miss Myrtilla Avery at the Farnsworth Museum in Wellesley College began to train young women to be art museum assistants in 1910 in her "Museum and Art Library Methods" course. The students were to acquire educational, library, clerical, and exhibition skills. Upon graduation, however, they experienced difficulty in obtaining museum employment. The course was dropped and reinstated several times, and last offered in 1941.

Another museum studies course of much importance, roughly contemporary with that of Sachs, was begun at Newark, New Jersey, in 1925 by John Cotton Dana, the director of both the public library and museum there. The program, supervised directly by his assistant, Katherine Coffey, involved apprenticeship; it accepted students with a college degree and paid them a monthly stipend. For one academic year they listened to lectures on phases of museum work and actually assisted in the various departments of the museum. The two weeks between semesters were devoted to visiting other museums. At first, all the apprentices were women, but men later participated. By 1942, 108 young women and men had been graduated, and most of them were working in museums in the United States and Canada.

In general, however, most museum trustees and directors agreed with Frederic A. Lucas, chief of the Brooklyn Museum, who insisted in 1910 that curators were "born and not made," could not be produced by training courses alone, and were "the result of the combination of natural ability and circumstances." For the most part, museum directors and curators continued to be turned out in subject-matter courses (preferably in graduate school), and they learned the nuts-and-bolts side of museum work on their first job.[2]

Professor Sachs demanded that his students add to their year-long graduate museum course subject-matter competence in art history with a thorough knowledge of museum history, functions, and ethics. He offered "Museum Work and Museum

Problems" weekly during the academic year, often at his home, Shady Hill. The course treated the history and philosophy of art museums, their organization and management, their buildings, and the functions of collection, installation, conservation and storage, recordkeeping, educational policies, and museum ethics. Sessions were supposed to last three hours, but Sachs's enthusiasm, ingenious approaches, and encouragement of lively student discussion often prolonged the meetings for another hour or so. Directors and curators from the Fogg and other leading museums in this country and abroad occasionally came to lecture and lead the discussion, and during university winter and spring vacations, Sachs took the students to visit museums (preferably behind the scenes), private collectors, dealers, and auction halls. The students were responsible yearly for two major exhibitions at the Fogg, for which they did the research, installation, labels, and catalogues. Each student was required to spend $50 on an object for his collection; Sachs told Agnes Mongan, his research assistant, "that when it hit your own pocketbook, you'd consider things you wouldn't think of with someone else's money."[3] They were also to visit a gallery and write an essay explaining which of its two or three paintings they would wish to obtain for their own museum. All in all, the course was stimulating, demanding, and mind stretching, indeed memorable.[4]

II

Paul Joseph Sachs was born in New York City on November 27, 1878, the eldest of three sons of Samuel and Louisa (Goldman) Sachs. His father was a partner in the international banking firm of Goldman Sachs Company, and his mother, the niece of another partner, Henry Goldman. Paul, at age eight, began to attend the Sachs School conducted by his Uncle Julius; he later described the school as "a second home, a Paradise."[5] In 1894 his father took him to Europe, where he visited the great museums. The next year, he took the entrance examination for Harvard, passing in German, French, and history but failing Latin, Greek, algebra, geometry, and physics. In 1896 he succeeded in conquering the tests and entered Harvard, where he studied French, other modern languages, philosophy, and especially the fine arts which captured his ardent attention. His professors included Charles Herbert Moore, an accomplished artist, and Martin Mower, who "more than any one man, taught me to see."[6] He shyly attended a reception given by the venerable Charles Eliot Norton, the first teacher of art in an American university, at his home, Shady Hill, which Sachs was later to occupy.

When Sachs was graduated in 1900, Professor Moore offered him an assistantship, but it paid only $750 and his father refused to supplement that meager sum. As a consequence, the young man joined the Goldman Sachs firm and was sent to Boston. His first notable success there was selling some railroad bonds, the commission for which he spent chiefly on a portrait painted by his mentor, Professor Moore. The next year, he was transferred to New York and in 1904 made a partner. He also was married then to Meta Pollack, who joined him in exploring museums and visiting print dealers. She was an outgoing, friendly person who made their guests feel at home—a splendid contrast to his sometimes shy and reticent manner.

Sachs had collected stamps as a boy, and his bedroom walls were covered with reproduced wood engravings clipped from magazines and auction catalogues. During college he had begun to buy prints and drawings; he used the $700 accumulated from his grandfather's $25 annual birthday gifts to buy etchings by Dürer, Cranach, Rembrandt, and Claúde . Alfred Barr later recalled that Sachs once told the class of his triumph in outbidding the British Museum, Berlin, and Dresden at the Earl of Pembroke's sale for Antonio del Pollaiuolo's drawing, *Fighting Nudes*. On another occasion, he was chagrined to find that he had bought a forgery of Dürer's *The Riders of the Four Horses of the Apocalypse* but kept it for use later to help train his students to detect frauds.[7]

Edward Waldo Forbes had become director of the Fogg Museum at Harvard in 1909.[8] He was a wealthy collector who presented a somewhat rumpled appearance and dreamy expression but was determined to make the Fogg the best university art museum in the country. He proved to be tenacious and ingenious as well as an excellent money raiser. The Fogg that he took over was a discouraging place—"a building," he said, "with a lecture hall in which you could not hear, a gallery in which you could not see, working rooms in which you could not work, and a roof that leaked like a sieve."[9] Forbes persuaded Sachs to join the museum's visiting committee in 1911, and he soon became its chairman. The two men, so different in personality, got along well together, and Forbes was soon urging Sachs to become his assistant director. When the Harvard Board made that appointment in December 1914, Sachs resigned his partnership at Goldman Sachs, spent several months in Italy and the United States studying other museums, and then moved Meta and their three small daughters to Shady Hill in Cambridge. Sachs later praised Forbes and asserted that "it is to him that I owe the best years of my life which have been spent in the service of the University."[10]

III

Paul Sachs's second career developed in three main directions: teaching, museum administration, and collecting. Soon after his arrival at Harvard, he was asked to give a paper before the Archaeological Institute of America; he was somewhat apprehensive about undertaking it, but, upon Meta's urging, agreed to do so. As a result, some of his listeners invited him to join the Wellesley College faculty as an instructor in art, and he lectured there in 1916–1917. After service as captain and then major in the Red Cross during the First World War (he was too short to be accepted in the regular armed services), he was made an assistant professor of fine arts at Harvard. At his courses in French art and in drawings and prints, he strode back and forth in front of the class, consulted copious notes, and used slides and a pointer. If an assistant showed the wrong slide, a violent eruption might occur, and at the end of the session, a broken pointer might be found on the floor. But his teaching proved exciting to the students because of his contagious enthusiasm and his ability to make them see and appreciate the quality of art objects.

Sachs moved steadily up the academic ladder as associate professor, professor, and department chairman. Special honors came to him for his teaching; in 1929 he gave the Lowell Lectures at Harvard; in 1932–1933 he was exchange professor at the Sorbonne in Paris, with side appearances in Berlin and Bonn; and in 1942 Harvard gave him an honorary doctorate as a "lover of the fine arts, who deserted a business career to become an accomplished teacher."[11] After he retired from the Fogg in 1945, he continued teaching at Harvard for three more years.

In museum administration, Sachs was most competent. His business experience had trained him in advance planning, and he was always well organized, prompt, energetic, and decisive. The Fogg Museum ran smoothly and efficiently under the joint command of Forbes and Sachs. They devoted themselves and their fortunes to the museum but did not duplicate each other in teaching students. Forbes trained them in art conservation, and Sachs prepared them for curatorship. Both men did well in raising funds, and, beginning in 1923, they headed a campaign that secured ten million dollars for Harvard, two million of which went for the new Fogg building opened in 1927 and its endowment. President Lowell called Forbes and Sachs "those exuberant mendicants, the Siamese twins."[12] They both were generous in giving the museum many outstanding works of art, and they left a distinguished building, a superb collection, a library rich in books, slides, and photographs, and a reputation for scholarly activity enhanced by their own efforts and those of their staff and students.

Sachs's success as a museum administrator brought him many extracurricular duties. He was one of the seven founders of the Museum of Modern Art in New York in 1939. Its director, Alfred H. Barr Jr., and curator of graphic arts, William S. Lieberman, had been his students, and its print and drawing galleries were named for Sachs. He served on the Administrative Board of Dumbarton Oaks for nearly twenty-five years and on the Editorial Board of the *Art Bulletin* for more than twenty. And scores of university presidents and deans as well as museum trustees and directors from here and abroad came to secure his advice. He was a trustee of the Museum of Fine Arts, Boston; Cincinnati Museum; and of Smith, Wellesley, and Radcliffe colleges. He also worked with various health groups and with the National Urban League. The Metropolitan Museum of Art tried to procure him as head of its new print department with the likelihood of his succeeding to the directorship, but he suggested his close friend, William M. Ivins, Jr., who accepted the appointment. Sachs continued to be seriously considered for that and other museums' directorships, but he chose to remain at Harvard.

As a collector, Sachs had a passionate love for quality in art objects. He thought that his keen eye and understanding of quality had been developed under the tutelage of Carl Dreyfus of the Louvre and the French painter, Leon Bonnat, whom he visited often. A young student, he said, could profit greatly from "contact with an older, more experienced and enthusiastic collector."[13] When he came to work at Harvard and the Fogg, Sachs already had an excellent collection of prints and drawings. He believed that he did not have enough money to collect master paintings and sculptures but that master prints and drawings were abundantly available and reasonable in price. He began to circulate his collection among his students. He discovered, however, that he had many duplicates of prints in the Fogg and Boston's Museum of Fine Arts. He therefore decided to concentrate upon collecting drawings and began to sell his prints and use the proceeds for more drawings. At the time, there were few American collectors in that field, and Sachs became a great connoisseur and leader; in fact, no one did more to make master drawings appreciated and cherished. Through the years, Sachs was most generous in giving prints and drawings to the Fogg and early decided that it was to receive his whole collection. Yet he insisted that no credit be given him for loans and gifts on either labels or in catalogues. (He took a similar attitude in giving anonymously many fellowships to students for study or travel.) He also collected books, many of them outstanding rarities, and gave them to the Fogg or Harvard; when he moved from Shady Hill, 4,000 volumes went to the university. So modest had he been that when the catalogue of the Memorial Exhibition honoring him was published, even his closest friends were astonished to learn the range of his collection and the magnitude of his gifts to the Fogg. Altogether, the checklist of his contributions contained more than 2,690 art objects, and that did not include textiles and furniture.[14]

Sachs retired from the associate directorship of the Fogg (he and Forbes left at the same time) in 1945. A great celebration and exhibition was held three years later on his seventieth birthday. Soon after that, Meta and he moved from Shady Hill to a comfortable apartment overlooking the Charles River. But he continued collecting to the last. For a time, another print connoisseur, W. G. Russell Allen, and Sachs often sought art works together. Allen was six feet, four inches tall, and, as Agnes Mongan says, they made a "picturesque pair" as they visited museums, called on dealers, and attended auctions.[15] Sachs's students continued to visit him at the apartment, bringing news of the latest doings in the art and museum worlds. Meta Sachs died at age eighty-one in 1961, and Sachs himself, in his library surrounded by books, prints, drawings, and other art objects, peacefully expired on the morning of February 17, 1965, at the age of eighty-two.

IV

Sachs experimented in 1921 with a museum course, which he permanently established two years later and continued teaching through the 1944–1945 academic year. He may have decided to offer it because of a conversation he had during a train ride with Henry Watson Kent, secretary of the Metropolitan Museum. The course covered all aspects of museum work as well as personalities in the art field, but also placed strong emphasis on art history and art objects. He told Agnes Mongan, a favorite collaborator of his: "First use your eye and your sensitivity, then the book learning."[16] The class was small, usually two dozen or fewer, and often met at Shady Hill, the students occupying comfortable chairs in front of Professor Sach's desk. After each class, an assistant distributed detailed mimeographed notes covering the lecture, discussion, and any announcements.

At the opening session of the course, Sachs sketched the basic requirements. Each student should develop a specialty but be acquainted with the whole field of art history, including its bibliography. He should know everything going on at the Fogg Museum and make personal contacts with many dealers. He should cultivate visual memory, master the long reading lists, make the issues of *Art News* a virtual textbook, and form the habit of taking notes. And Sachs later stressed the need for good organization in student papers and sorrowfully noted lapses in their use of English. He was generous in allowing students to use his library at Shady Hill.

Sachs gave his students a heavy load of assignments. They must make written reports on their reading of books and periodicals, on histories of great museums, visits to museums, and conversations with dealers. They needed to prepare book reviews suitable for the *Saturday Review* or an article for *The Arts* on an art object of special interest to them. The Fogg offered a multitude of projects—drawing an architectural plan; cataloguing a photograph; deciding whether art books should be checked out from Harvard or the Fogg; moving, rearranging, and labeling exhibit cases; commenting on flooring, chairs, and lighting; and scores of other tasks, both theoretical and practical. At the end of the course, when the students made suggestions for its improvement, they wished fewer written reports. Sachs pointed out, in reply, that he did not require examinations in the course and said that he deliberately overloaded them because museum workers needed to become accustomed to being overloaded.

Sachs shared his own museum problems with the students. He would bring in his correspondence for two or three days and ask how it should be answered. He would get the students to write a presentation to a granting agency for a new building for the Museum of Modern Art, and after it had been fully discussed in class, present it to the Museum's Executive Committee, on which he was serving. He would request volunteers to investigate an actual museum problem, write out a solution, talk it over with the class, and then go to discuss the result with the institution's board. Sachs also showed the class hundreds of slides of art objects, demanding their identification and provenance. He gave personal thumbnail sketches of numerous collectors, dealers, and other personalities in the art field. At the end of the course, he asked the students to list the most significant events of the past year in the art world in America and abroad. All of these various approaches captured intense student attention and made them feel part of the museum community that they were planning to enter.[17]

The ideal graduate of the course, Sachs thought, should be a scholar connoisseur, able both to recognize and appreciate the quality of art objects and to conduct accurate research on their physical characteristics and historical provenance. He considered that his own strengths lay in teaching and administration but that he was inadequate in the field of historical research. He admired greatly Agnes Mongan, who often acted as co-author with him, and praised "her unflagging zeal and her special capacity for research."[18] As John Walker, one of his students, put it: "He was someone who could really make you want to be a collector. None of the rest could. They could teach you the history of art, but Paul was the one that made us all want to be collectors."[19] He thought that visual memory was all-important for art museum professionals, and he would ask the students to memorize all the objects on exhibition at the Fogg. And Sachs might pick at random any of scores of art objects in his living room at Shady Hill and demand that the students identify them and their place in history.

Many leaders of the art world visited Sachs, such as Dr. Adolf Goldschmidt of the University of Berlin, Professor A. M. Hind of the British Museum, and W. G. Constable of London's National Gallery. They would participate in the classroom teaching. Later on, he invited some of his successful students to return in that role. Sachs was also a famed gourmet, who once said more or less jokingly: "Anyone who professes an interest in the fine arts and is indifferent to the joys of the palate is suspect with me."[20] Meta and Paul's dinner parties at Shady Hill were renowned, and students were invited now and then to share in the delicious food and stimulating conversation. After Stravinsky had dined there on one occasion, he composed a piece in honor of the evening. Other cultural celebrities who came included Courtauld, Kenneth Clark, Erwin Panofsky, and Sigfried Giedion.

Sachs gave up his winter and spring vacations in order to take the students on tours of museums, private collections, dealers, and auction houses. They would visit outstanding collectors such as the Robert Lehmans, Grenville Winthrop, Lord Duveen, the Stephen Clarks, the Philip Lehmans, the Sam Levinsons, the John D. Rockefellers Jr., Joseph Widener, the Carroll Tysons, and Henry McIlhenny.

The students took their exhibitions at the Fogg most seriously and organized themselves so as to get the most from them. Thus in 1944 the team that produced *Blake to Beardsley: A Century of English Illustration* had William S. Lieberman as director, Richard McLanathan, secretary, and Felice Stampfle, catalogue supervisor. Sachs demanded that such projects be clearly defined and closely supervised; he distrusted the internships provided by many institutions that allowed a student to float about a large museum "as a kind of spare part."[21]

Sachs believed that any museum director must have training in curatorship, that "he should enter upon his directorial duties only through the curatorial portal." He had no confidence in the bright young man who became director of a small museum and then gradually assumed much larger responsibilities without a thorough knowledge of art history, a trained eye, and a real understanding of art objects. "If such a man ends with a staff of competent curators, he does not know what their work is or why they do it," said Sachs. On the other hand, he thought his students should "look upon the educational department of a museum as intimately related to, and a part of their official work as future curators." They must not retreat into esoteric scholarship or superciliously look down their noses at museum educators, public relations personnel, or even directors. They always should hold high the torch of quality and remember that "museums exist, not so much to amuse as to educate the public, to give it some sense of excellence."[22]

Sachs summed up his philosophy with consideration for the broader purposes of museums as follows:

> While yielding to no one on the importance of forming usable collections of quality and bringing to bear upon their interpretation the highest curatorial and scholarly standards, one should never forget that in America at least, the museum is a social instrument highly useful in any scheme of general education. . . . The primary need of our museums is guidance through the scholar's approach. . . . I find it unreasonable to fear that with scholars in control of museums, the vital need for sound popular education in the humanities and in social studies would be put in jeopardy.[23]

In another place, he advised against any dilution of museum quality when he wrote:

> Let us be ever watchful to resist pressure to vulgarize and cheapen our work through the mistaken idea that in such fashion a broad public may be reached effectively. That is an especially tempting error because of the intense competition for public attention in America. In the end a lowering of tone and standards must lead to mediocrity.[24]

Sachs was not always close to his students during their stay, and John Walker complained that he "could never remember who I was, a disheartening experience for a student who had come to Harvard especially to sit at his feet."[25] Yet when Lincoln Kirstein, Edward M. M. Warburg, and Walker formed the Society of Contemporary Art at Harvard, Sachs joined Forbes in helping them raise funds and had the Fogg staff pack and ship their exhibits. He also served on their board with Miss Lizzie Bliss, Frank Crowninshield, Mrs. John D. Rockefeller Jr., and Conger Goodyear, all of whom were important in founding the Museum of Modern Art. Sachs's action was generous and even courageous, for Boston patrons and the Museum of Fine Arts showed real animosity toward modern art and for Picasso, Matisse, Mogliani, Braque, et al. Sachs was interested chiefly in European art of an earlier period but was broad-minded enough to back his students in offering more contemporary artists.

Sachs set a demanding standard for the students so far as their museum careers were concerned. They must work in behalf of their institutions all the time and with all their heart Agnes Mongan, with an A.B. from Bryn Mawr and M.A. from Smith, had returned from a year abroad when Sachs hired her as research assistant at the Fogg in 1928. He told her then: "I shall *never* ask you what hours you are keeping or how you are spending your time. I shall assume that as long as you work for us, wherever you are and whatever you are doing, you are working for the good of the Fogg Museum."[26] She afterwards realized that he was following the same rule for himself at both Harvard and the Fogg.

Sachs was especially helpful to his students when they began to go abroad or to apply for jobs. On one occasion, he wrote 103 letters and 107 cards of introduction for a student traveling to Europe. He served as a one-man placement agency and frequently mentioned job openings to his classes; for example, Edith Standen in 1928 noted five vacancies that he had listed—museums at St. Louis, Cincinnati, and Seattle and teaching positions at Amherst College and Pittsburgh University. Sachs wrote by hand long, carefully crafted letters on the students' behalf and sometimes even accompanied an applicant to meet a Board of Trustees. He also advised and supported former students when they ran into difficulties on the job. He suggested Alfred Barr for the directorship of the Museum of Modern Art, stood by him when he encountered trouble with his board, and helped him retain an influential place on the staff. Perry Rathbone corresponded frequently with Sachs as he made his way upward as director of the Detroit Institute of Art, St. Louis Art Museum, and then Museum of Fine Arts in Boston.

Sachs's students came to hold top curatorial and directorial spots in the art museum world. Among them were James J. Rorimer and Edith A. Standen at the Metropolitan Museum; John Walker at the National Gallery; Barr and Lieberman at the Museum of Modern Art; Perry Rathbone; John Coolidge at the Fogg; Jean S. Boggs at the National Gallery of Canada; Richard Howard at the Birmingham Museum of Art; Thomas Howe at the California Palace of the Legion of Honor; Otto Wittmann at the Toledo Museum of Art; Gordon Washburn at the Albright-Knox Art Gallery; Henry Trubner at the Seattle Art Museum; A. Everett Austin at the Wadsworth Atheneium; Charles C. Cunningham and John M. Maxon at the Art Institute of Chicago; Felice Stamfle at the Pierpont Morgan Library; Leslie Cheek Jr. at the Virginia Museum of Fine Arts; Richard McLanathan at the American Association of Museums; and Samuel Sachs II (Paul's grandnephew) at the Minneapolis Institute of Art. As Leslie Cheek pointed out, the former students constituted a network of art museum professionals who kept in touch with one another.[27]

Paul Sachs could indeed be proud of his museum course. He had trained several scores of young men and women who became the leaders in the American and Canadian art museum field for a generation. He had insisted that they know art history and understand art objects, but also had actually experienced the nitty-gritty, practical side of museum work. By his own example, he made them see the satisfaction and even the joy of working in the new profession, and he set sensible but lofty standards for teachers who were to follow him in the American museum studies field.

NOTES

1. "Paul Joseph Sachs" (New York *Times* obituary, Feb. 19, 1965), 35.

2. Karen Cushman, "Museum Studies: The Beginnings, 1900–1926," *Museum Studies Journal* 1 (Spring 1984): 8–16; Melinda Young Fry, "Women Pioneers in the Public Museum Movement," in Smithsonian Institution, *Women's Changing Roles in Museums: Feb./April Proceedings* (Washington: Smithsonian, 1986), 11–17; Jane R. Glaser, "Museum Studies in the United States: Coming a Long Way in a Long Time," *Museum* 156 (1987): 268–74. For John Cotton Dana, see Edward P. Alexander, *Museum Masters: Their Museums and Their Influence* (Nashville: American Association for State and Local History, 1983), 377–411.

3. Ada V. Ciniglio, "Pioneers in American Museums: Paul J. Sachs," *Museum News* 55 (Sept./Oct. 1976): 70.

4. The chief works describing Sachs and his career are: Edward P. Alexander, "A Handhold on the Curatorial Ladder," *Museum News* 52 (May 1974): 23–25; Ciniglio, "Paul J. Sachs," 48–51, 68–71; Cushman, "Museum Studies," 12–13; Agnes Mongan, *Memorial Exhibition: Works of Art from the Collection of Paul J. Sachs, 1878–1965* (Cambridge, Mass.: Harvard University, Fogg Art Museum, 1965), 7–13; Mongan, "Paul Joseph Sachs (1878–1965)," *Art Journal* 25 (Fall 1965): 50–52; New York *Times*, Feb. 13, 1965; Paul J. Sachs, *Modern Prints & Drawings: A Guide to a Better Understanding of Modern Draughtsmanship* (New York: Alfred A. Knopf, 1954); Sachs, Museum Course, Typescript Copy of Notes (1930), 243 leaves; Sachs, "Preparation for Art Museum Work," *Museum News* 24 (Sept. 1, 1946): 6–8.

5. Ciniglio, "Paul J. Sachs," 49.

6. Ibid., 50.

7. Ibid.

8. Harvard University, William Hayes Fogg Art Museum, *Edward Waldo Forbes: Yankee Visionary* (Cambridge, Mass.: Harvard University, 1971).

9. Ibid., vii.

10. Agnes Mongan and Paul J. Sachs, *Drawings in the Fogg Museum of Art: A Critical Catalogue*, 3 vols. (Cambridge, Mass.: Harvard University Press, 1940), 1: xii.

11. Ciniglio, "Paul J. Sachs," 69.

12. New York *Times*, Feb. 19, 1965.

13. Mongan and Sachs, *Drawings in the Fogg Museum*, 1: viii-xii.

14. Mongan, *Memorial Exhibition*, 199–214.

15. Ibid., 7–13.

16. Ciniglio, "Paul J. Sachs," 69.

17. This analysis of the class is based upon Sachs, Museum Course Typescript, 1930.

18. Mongan and Sachs, *Drawings in the Fogg Museum*, 1: xii.

19. Ciniglio, "Paul J. Sachs," 69.

20. New York *Times*, Feb. 19, 1965.

21. Sachs, "Preparation for Art Museum Work," 6–8.

22. Ibid.

23. Ciniglio, "Paul J. Sachs," 71.

24. New York *Times*, Feb. 19, 1965.

25. John Walker, *Self-Portrait with Donors: Confessions of an Art Collector* (Boston: Little, Brown, 1974), 24–25; Ciniglio, "Paul J. Sachs," 70–71.

26. Mongan, *Memorial Exhibition*, 13.

27. Park Rouse, *Living by Design: Leslie Cheek and the Arts, a Photobiography* (Williamsburg, Va.: Society of the Alumni of William and Mary College, 1985), 46.

SELECT BIBLIOGRAPHY

Edward P. Alexander. "A Handhold on the Curatorial Ladder," *Museum News* 52 (May 1974): 23–25.

_____. *Museum Masters: Their Museums and Their Influence*. Nashville: American Association for State and Local History, 1983.

Ciniglio, Ada V. "Pioneers in American Museums: Paul J. Sachs." *Museum News* 55 (Sept./Oct. 1976): 70.

Cushman, Karen. "Museum Studies: The Beginnings, 1900–1926." *Museum Studies Journal* 1 (Spring 1984): 8–16.

Fry, Melinda Young. "Women Pioneers in the Public Museum Movement." In Smithsonian Institution. *Women's Changing Roles in Museums: Feb./April Proceedings*. Washington: Smithsonian, 1986.

Glaser, Jane R. "Museum Studies in the United States: Coming a Long Way in a Long Time." *Museum* 156 (1987): 268–74.

Harvard University, William Hayes Fogg Art Museum. *Edward Waldo Forbes: Yankee Visionary*. Cambridge, Mass.: Harvard University, 1971.

Mongan, Agnes. *Memorial Exhibition: Works of Art from the Collection of Paul J. Sachs, 1878–1965*. Cambridge, Mass.: Harvard University, Fogg Art Museum, 1965.

_____. "Paul Joseph Sachs (1878–1965)." *Art Journal* 25 (Fall 1965): 50–52.

Mongan, Agnes, and Paul J. Sachs. *Drawings in the Fogg Museum of Art: A Critical Catalogue*. 3 vols. Cambridge, Mass.: Harvard University Press, 1940.

Rouse, Park. *Living by Design: Leslie Cheek and the Arts, a Photobiography*. Williamsburg, Va.: Society of the Alumni of William and Mary College, 1985.

Sachs, Paul J. *Modern Prints & Drawings: A Guide to a Better Understanding of Modern Draughtsmanship*. New York: Alfred A. Knopf, 1954.

_____. Museum Course, Typescript Copy of Notes (1930).

_____. "Preparation for Art Museum Work." *Museum News* 24 (Sept. 1, 1946): 6–8.

Walker, John. *Self-Portrait with Donors: Confessions of an Art Collector*. Boston: Little, Brown, 1974.

A BRIEF EPILOGUE:

The American Museum Progresses

IN LOOKING TO THE FUTURE, the American museum should stress several principles. First of all, each individual museum ought to define clearly its mission and see that its board, director, and staff fully understand it. Then the function of each of these components should be carefully defined and differentiated: the board to provide financing, appoint the director, and approve all general policies; the director to choose his staff and control the day-to-day administration; and the staff to see to the functions of collection, preservation, research, exhibition, and education. The staff also must strive for high professionalism both in its training and in keeping in touch with the latest activities of regional, national, and international museum organizations. The museum should play a far-reaching role in its community and make public service a key goal of its educational programs.

If considerable success can be attained in following these principles, the future of American museums will be assured.

Index

JOSEPH BANKS AND THE BRITISH MUSEUM: THE WORLD OF COLLECTING, 1770–1830

To the trustees, officers and benefactors of the
British Museum, 1770–1830

JOSEPH BANKS AND THE BRITISH MUSEUM:
THE WORLD OF COLLECTING, 1770–1830

BY

Neil Chambers

LONDON
PICKERING & CHATTO
2007

Published by Pickering & Chatto (Publishers) Limited
21 Bloomsbury Way, London WC1A 2TH
2252 Ridge Road, Brookfield, Vermont 05036-9704, USA
www.pickeringchatto.com

BRITISH LIBRARY CATALOGUING IN PUBLICATION DATA

Chambers, Neil
  Joseph Banks and the British Museum: the world of collecting, 1770–1830
  1. Banks, Joseph, Sir, 1743–1820 2. British Museum – History 3. Collectors
  and collecting - Great Britain – History – 18th century 4. Collectors and collecting
  – Great Britain – History – 19th century
  I. Title
  069.5'0941'09033

ISBN-10: 1-85196-858-X
ISBN-13: 978-1-85196-858-9

This publication is printed on acid-free paper that conforms to the American
National Standard for the Permanence of Paper for Printed Library Materials

Typeset by P&C

Printed in the United Kingdom at
the University Press, Cambridge

CONTENTS

ACKNOWLEDGMENTS

I would like to thank Dr D. King-Hele FRS, Professor J. Gascoigne, Dr K. Stimson, Dr P. Carr, Ms J. Kapusta and Dr L. Glyn for their helpful comments and suggestions on drafts of this work, first circulated in 2002.

LIST OF ILLUSTRATIONS

The interior of the main library room at Soho Square overlooking Dean Street. Sepia wash drawing, c. 1828, by Francis Boott. Reproduced by permission of the Natural History Museum, London.

The study at Soho Square. Sepia wash drawing, c. 1828, by Francis Boott. Reproduced by permission of the Natural History Museum, London.

PREFACE

The 250th anniversary of the British Museum provides an opportunity to reconsider the early growth of the Museum's collections. Founded in 1753 on major collections made by Sir Hans Sloane,[1] the development of the British Museum through to the first third of the nineteenth century may deserve particular attention. This period has sometimes been unfavourably contrasted with a later time of reform during which the collections were housed in a new building, were increased in size and scope and were placed under the supervision of more and better-trained staff. Indeed, according to this view, the nineteenth century saw the introduction of a variety of improvements, all of which led gradually to more modern ways of managing London's major collections. Compared to the undeniable progress apparent in the nineteenth century, the conduct of trustees and officers in the generation immediately after Sloane's has been regarded as somewhat inadequate, and the condition of certain collections has been questioned too.

Such an interpretation provides a convenient way of thinking about the British Museum as an institution, and of presenting its history in stages that fit (or do not fit) into modern preconceptions about museums, their function and meaning. Yet early efforts may still be worthy of reassessment. Indeed, it might be useful to regard the achievements of the initial phase as making possible, rather than making necessary, the changes that came afterwards, some of which were anticipated in the decades before 1830 anyway. Such an approach helps because it requires consideration of how the early trustees and Museum officers viewed the progress that they made with the collections and in managing the Museum as a whole. It relies on a closer examination of their priorities, and of the ways in which they accumulated and distributed objects. This emphasis on the aims, and even on the limitations that shaped the Museum's collections in the beginning, broadens our sense of the Museum's historical development, and it is this that enables us to see later advances in terms of significant contributions made from 1770 to 1830.

In the years 1770 to 1830 the British Museum grew from being the first national museum to be established, one based on a small number of large collections formerly in private hands, into an international repository that was truly global in scope. The growth of the Museum, and the ways in which it altered in structure and adapted to the demands placed on it, provided the basis for future progress, the problems and failings that were encountered themselves often suggesting ways forward. The ensuing pages concentrate on this transition and its importance, taking the career of one of the Museum's more eminent trustees and benefactors as the main subject for reconsideration. They are intended to provide some new insights for those interested in the expansion and adjustment of the Museum to the world of collecting that opened up during his long and eventful career.

The general approach adopted here is that used during the preparation of a short account of the career of a late trustee and benefactor of the British Museum, Sir Joseph Banks (1743–1820). This account was read at a conference held at the Museum to commemorate its 250th anniversary, 'Enlightening the British: Knowledge, Discovery and the Museum in the 18th Century', 4–5 April 2002. The account came in a session entitled 'Trade and Empire', which determined its basic themes, and was called 'Joseph Banks, the British Museum and Collections in the Age of Empire'. The present volume enlarges on the themes of the conference account, adding to the description given there of the nature and extent of Banks's contribution to the early history of the Museum.[2]

At the same time, it refers to the overall state of the Museum, to the different (and sometimes differing) attitudes of those employed in managing the collections and to the way in which the Museum was itself just one among a number of different London-based institutions concerned with collecting. These aspects provide the context for discussing Banks, showing how his conduct both as a trustee and benefactor was itself shaped by the enormous growth in the quantity of material arriving in the capital. However, the heavy emphasis on Banks is not intended to imply that he deserves any more attention than other trustees or the Museum officers of his day. A general reappraisal of the Museum from 1770 to 1830 would certainly reveal more about its workings than one limited to Banks alone. Nevertheless, the period dealt with in this book spans the time when Banks's influence was most keenly felt. His character and outlook make him a useful figure on which to concentrate at a critical period in the history of the British Museum, and indeed of collecting generally.

FOREWORD

The reputation of the great national museums of the United Kingdom is based on the size and importance of their collections. This is especially true of natural history, and the great British expeditions of the eighteenth century formed the early bases of the wonderful collections now held by the Natural History Museum, London. Of course, the Natural History Museum was not itself a legal entity until the British Museum Act of 1963 formally separated it from the British Museum, even though the natural history collections had been moved to Alfred Waterhouse's wonderful building in South Kensington on its completion in 1881. Joseph Banks's important contribution to the national natural history collection predates these two events, but his legacy remains an important part of the Museum's historical collections.

Banks was born to a landed family, and throughout his life used his wealth to pursue a passion for natural history, particularly botany, that had fired his imagination as a schoolboy on finding his mother's copy of Gerard's *Herbal*. At Eton College and Oxford University he developed his interest outside of the established curriculum, using his wealth to pay for his own tutor and to employ others to help him collect plants. This ability and determination to pursue his own interests was perhaps Banks's defining characteristic.

The second half of the eighteenth century was an important period in the history of natural history. The work of Carl Linnaeus, some thirty-six years senior to Banks, had brought taxonomy and systematics to the fore in laying down the foundations of modern nomenclature. This work clearly inspired Banks, whose first major endeavour after leaving Oxford was a trip to Labrador and Newfoundland. His resulting descriptions of the plants and animals of these locations, using the Linnean system of classification, helped establish his reputation, and he became a Fellow of the Royal Society that same year, 1766.

Banks gained a place on the scientific expedition mounted under James Cook by the Royal Navy. This was Cook's first voyage of discovery to the South Pacific, launched on HMS *Endeavour*, which left Britain in 1768. Typical of the man, Banks insisted on equipping the natural history components of the expedition at his own expense. As is well known, the expedition further enhanced

Banks's own reputation, and it included such notable events as the naming of the common garden plant *bougainvillea* (after Cook's French counterpart, Louis-Antoine de Bougainville) in Brazil, observing the transit of Venus in Tahiti and mapping some of the east coast of Australia after the historic landfall in Botany Bay. More specifically, the scientific achievements of the expedition, in recording new species and the collection of specimens brought back to Great Britain in 1771, was unparalleled. This may well have been the greatest of all voyages of discovery. Although Banks planned to go on Cook's second expedition that left the following year, difficulties regarding accommodation for Banks and his assistants resulted in their not going. Instead, Banks planned and executed a scientific expedition to Iceland.

Throughout his life Banks contributed actively to scientific communication at home and abroad. In common with many leading scientists of the time, Banks was a prominent member of a number of important learned societies, and he was very active in shaping the relations that existed between them. Banks became President of the Royal Society in 1778 at the astonishingly young, by modern standards, age of thirty-five, a position he held until his death in 1820. Nobody before or since has served a presidency of such length. Indeed, such was the esteem in which Banks was held that when he tendered his resignation on the grounds of incapacity through ill health, the council of the Society requested he withdraw it and continue. This he did, dying a short while later.

Private as opposed to public collections were the order of the day in the eighteenth century, but Sir Hans Sloane set something of a precedent by allowing the state to purchase his collections after his death, at significantly less than their true value, but at the then still remarkable cost of £20,000. These collections formed the basis of the British Museum, opened in Bloomsbury in 1759. So significant were Banks's own collections that from the time of his moving his London home to Soho Square in 1777, a visit there was regarded as of no less importance to natural historians than to the British Museum itself. Banks also contributed massively to the development of living collections and, through his role as adviser to George III, he made the Royal Botanic Gardens at Kew a leading institution in the field of economic botany and a centre for the scientific study of plants, including species introduced from overseas.

Dr Michael Dixon
Director of the Natural History Museum, London

INTRODUCTION

No attempt has been made in this work to enter into the historiography surrounding Banks, or the reasons for the uneven treatment he has received from different writers. It should be noted, however, that views about Banks's relationship with and contribution to the British Museum are mixed. Banks has recently been described as 'tyrannical' and a 'Dictator'.[1] Even those mindful of the debt owed him by London's societies and museums have tended to be critical in their assessments. For example, the great bequest to the Museum of his entire herbarium and library, both exceptional in their content and organization, has been characterized as one way in which Banks hindered rather than helped the Museum and botany, presumably by not completing and transferring everything before he died.[2] The flow of donations Banks conveyed to the Museum, and his own specialization in botany, will therefore be things to investigate a little further here, as will the coordinated ways in which he worked with staff and visitors at the Museum, using his own assistants and collections to support both. An outline of some of the activities Banks engaged in as a trustee will also be attempted in order to give an impression of how he dealt with officers and collections during his long tenure, and to try to discover whether his involvement can really be construed merely as detrimental and interfering.

At variance with the view of Banks as powerful and arbitrary is another contrasting interpretation. Some have described his contribution at the British Museum as insignificant during the period of his trusteeship. They have wondered 'how it was that a man of such ability and character, who was a leading influence in the scientific world of his time, should not have had a greater impact on an institution that, under Charles Morton, had lost its sense of purpose and direction'. Morton, a physician, was Principal Librarian in charge of the Museum from 1776 to 1799. His administration was apathetic, and probably did impede the Museum, and to this historians have been able to add further reasons why Banks's commanding influence was not more prominently felt. They argue that Banks was unable to exert as much influence at the Museum as elsewhere because he was 'one of a group of trustees subject to a group of official trustees presided over by three Principal Trustees with an archbishop as spokesman'.[3] This is certainly true. The Museum's senior hierarchy was indeed cumbersome, and like any cumbersome hierarchy this must

1

have acted as a check on independent and purposeful action. Worse, as a trustee with scientific interests Banks became increasingly isolated as more politicians and peers joined the board. During his time at the Museum there was a marked decline in the number of trustees who were also Fellows of the Royal Society with authentic claims to scientific knowledge. For someone of Banks's interests and position, this presented yet another and a potentially more serious difficulty.

The Royal Society was incorporated by charter in 1662, and was the capital's major philosophical society. Banks was its President from 1778 to 1820, the longest anyone has served in this capacity, but during his presidency the influence of scientific Fellows at the Museum seemingly waned. This should have diminished Banks's power, adding force to the argument that he was in no position to make a difference at the Museum, but that, in fact, is not entirely the case, for a number of Fellows were still to be found there in these years. However, they tended to be Museum officers rather than trustees, so that in some fields science continued to be well represented. Banks could and did work closely with these officers, and the ways in which he did so are important in understanding how he operated at the Museum. Additionally, Banks tried hard to work with the new trustees, and found clever ways of doing so, especially when the support of Parliament or government was needed. Reference will therefore be made in the following account to some of Banks's political connections, but these were not central to his Museum career, and it is clear that the influence he possessed at a very senior level at Bloomsbury was ultimately limited.

For instance, in 1804 a Welsh friend, John Lloyd, asked Banks to gain him a place as a trustee. Banks was clear about two things. Firstly, he had no authority at the Museum to arrange such an appointment. Secondly, he was loath to try if the person concerned rarely visited London: 'I sincerely wish it may be in my power to Promote your wish of being a Trustee of the Museum tho it will be better for my poor Conscience if it Turns out as it has hitherto done that I have no influence at all for in Truth I Shall not be able to Palliate to myself the impropriety of Choosing a man destind to Reside ten meetings in Wales for Every one he will [be] Able to Attend in London.'[4] Banks took the responsibility of being a trustee seriously. He did not regard the position as an empty honour, fit only for sharing among those seeking advancement or status. As a trustee his attendance at general and standing committees shows a diligence that deserves some credit, and if the ties of friendship and of class mattered at all to Banks, it tended to be where they could assist the Museum.[5] Using these, and the political connections that existed, Banks worked to promote the Museum's interests where he could.

More importantly, Banks often acted in less conspicuous ways at the Museum, ways which have not as a consequence been so well recognized. Since Banks could not take overall decisions on his own authority, he worked closely with Museum officers on certain collections, and he channelled a vast array of material to Bloomsbury. These became effective alternatives to being in charge. A multitude of smaller tasks still allowed him to coordinate affairs, and perhaps even extended his influence more subtly. The current study explores these types of activity, and an important aspect will therefore be the relationship Banks had with some of the Museum officers, and, no less significant, the use they made of direct access to him. In some notable cases he sat side by side with officers working through specimens, while officers could and did enlist his aid in pressing for the purchase of or reorganization of collections. Banks seems to have had more impact at this lower level, and this was due as much to the help he gave as it was to his social and scientific standing.

Although the Museum's officers were frequently Fellows of the Royal Society, unlike many of the trustees, this was not the only reason why Banks had such productive relations with a number of them. It appears that it was his willingness to support their work and careers, especially in natural history, that really gave him a claim to their confidence. It has frequently been asserted that as President Banks dominated the Royal Society, but insofar as this is true it does not seem to have impinged on the Museum's administration.[6] Indeed, Banks understood the importance of making basic distinctions between the different bodies with which he was associated, not least in the way he distributed collections among them. He always responded warmly to drive and determination in others, highly valuing these qualities. He was also reasonably fair in his dealings, and consulted the officers to obtain information and opinions whenever this was necessary.

This was increasingly how the trustees as a whole conducted business, especially once Joseph Planta became Principal Librarian in 1799. Planta was very capable, and was a Secretary at the Royal Society from 1776 to 1804. Not long after his appointment the written reports that officers submitted to the trustees started to be retained,[7] and committees were regularly set up to implement changes arising from successive reviews of the Museum. These procedures were important, and will be described in order to show how the Museum was managed, and how trustees like Banks could work effectively with officers, even when, as with Planta, the relationship was occasionally a little uneasy. The way the Museum was run after Charles Morton provides evidence not only of the organizational pressures felt after 1800, but also of the gradual progress that was made in coping with these pressures.

By the turn of the century an important moment in the Museum's development had been reached. More private collections were being purchased by or donated to the Museum as a public body. This happened in fields where the Museum exceeded what private individuals and societies could sustain, or where there was a deficiency at Bloomsbury that needed to be rectified by particular acquisitions. From 1800 onwards the Museum grew rapidly, but the growth was predominantly of classical and ancient remains, which started to eclipse natural products. This caused internal pressures with which officers were forced to contend, and it also meant that the Museum's structure had to be altered to accommodate the greater range of collections that it held. The main change was to establish specialist departments separately responsible for antiquities and for natural history. In this way basic distinctions were made between different types of material. Later on this process led to the creation of distinct museums devoted to man-made and to natural products, and some of the collections at Bloomsbury were moved to other locations in the capital.

Such distinctions were not confined to Bloomsbury. Since at least the 1790s Banks's own collecting had concentrated on botany, books and certain natural history manuscripts and illustrations. In other words, he specialized too, but as a private individual. He therefore decided to donate important ethnographic and zoological collections to the British Museum, wishing to see them join other similar collections rather than keep what he would not fully develop himself. This does not mean that everything Banks gave away went to the British Museum. In some cases Banks thought other collectors, like the anatomist and surgeon John Hunter, deserved some of his zoological specimens. Gifts like these were made to those with a specialist interest of their own, in this case because Hunter had created an eminent private collection with many anatomical and zoological specimens in it. Furthermore, Banks occasionally preferred institutions like the Company (later and hereafter the Royal College) of Surgeons over the British Museum. This happened when he thought they might do a better job of storing and using the collections that they received, which again reflects his concern that material he gave away should be of use to research collections of real value.

The relationship between public and private collections was by no means a simple one. Specimens frequently moved from one collection to another, and sometimes onwards again to other collections. John Hunter's museum, for example, was purchased by the nation following Hunter's death, and entrusted to the Royal College of Surgeons. At the College it was placed under the supervision of a board of trustees, and, perhaps unsurprisingly, Banks became one of these trustees. He therefore ended up overseeing specimens that he had already given away once: a pattern that repeated itself in the years leading to 1820. Other patterns emerged, and at a general level these concerned the growing size and reputation of certain institutions, each of which performed particular functions in an extended collecting network. Banks was linked to a number of these institutions, and his efforts at this level appear to have been directed towards ensuring that, when they became available, collections of different kinds were appropriately placed.

As with the Royal College of Surgeons, a choice had to be made between bodies like the British Museum, the gardens at Kew and the Royal Society in order to determine which was most suitable to receive material. These choices shaped collecting and collections in the capital, and so they will be discussed in what follows. They also helped to define relationships between the institutions and individuals organizing knowledge in London, here collectively called London Learned Society, determining how this varied group operated as part of a network stretching well beyond the metropolitan centre. This network grew apace during Banks's lifetime, and as it did the quantity and diversity of material arriving in London from around the world necessitated greater strategic coordination. Institutions had to work in ways that supported one another by developing particular strengths and capabilities, and so there was a tendency to concentrate material in designated repositories. Such a tendency prefigured the increase in the nineteenth century of specialist museums and libraries, but it required additional administrative skill to be maintained. No less vital was the global vision necessary to make the most of the new and distant opportunities to collect that proliferated in this period. Banks's efforts show an awareness of this, and so his strategic manipulation of this wider network will be described in the ensuing account, as will the ways in which London Learned Society operated and changed as that network expanded.

It should be noted that Banks did not sell his collections, or profit from them financially. Instead, he frequently made gifts that enhanced his standing among collectors, gained him positions of seniority in institutions or which furthered learning itself. In return he obtained material for his personal collections, initially through his own travels, and later by exchange or purchase. In these ways Banks's influence over collecting and collections became pervasive. In the present work the emphasis is on what happened to collections accumulating in and around London, and how individuals like Banks tried to coordinate their growth and use. This became more necessary as the costs and technical requirements of maintaining large collections increased. The museum builders of Banks's day were engaged in an enormous task, and their ambitious efforts to order and present knowledge often strained late eighteenth-century resources and skills, not least at a place like the British Museum, where the widest range of material was kept.

In his early career, then, we see Banks as an explorer gathering rich collections, a number of which he gave to the Museum. We see that he made distinctions between different institutions, and this is apparent in the way that he distributed collections. Later in life Banks maintained a remarkable flow of gifts to the British Museum, many coming from colonial contacts as well as from some of the most intrepid naturalists and travellers of the day. He also became a sturdy member of various Museum committees, particularly as the Museum started to adapt to the demands being placed on it in the first decades of the nineteenth century. These were crucial years of financial struggle at Bloomsbury. Space, staff and equipment were frequently in short supply, and managing growing collections in these circumstances presented some serious challenges. Trustees and staff were compelled to take difficult decisions on how best to cope, and some of the more controversial occasions when this was necessary will be described later in this volume. These demonstrate not only the attitudes and practical considerations of those responsible for the collections, but also the pressures that they faced.

In all of this, Banks was one of the trustees whose pragmatism and commitment to Museum affairs did not diminish. He was willing to persevere, and while it cannot be said that he was correct in every decision he took, it still seems worthwhile to examine what he and others did – and why – in order to comprehend

Portrait of Sir Joseph Banks, painted shortly after the return of HMS *Endeavour*, 1771, by Benjamin West. Reproduced courtesy of Lincolnshire County Council, the Collection, Art and Archaeology in Lincolnshire.

When asked whether he would tour the continent, Banks reputedly said: 'Every blockhead does that. My Grand Tour shall be around the world'. For collectors with broad enough horizons and broad enough purses a world of exploration lay beyond the confines of Europe's capitals, courts and ancient sites.

1 BANKS AS AN EARLY TRAVELLER AND COLLECTOR, AND THE BRITISH MUSEUM

Rich new opportunities to collect became available with the overseas activity that gathered pace from the 1760s onwards.[1] Indeed, travel and collecting, particularly in natural history and ethnography, changed and grew on a global scale during the lifetime of Joseph Banks, a process he did much to encourage. In this period the quantity and scope of material returning to Europe's museums from distant lands increased enormously, and this had important consequences for repositories, some of which struggled simply to keep pace. Many private individuals sought objects, and some mounted exhibitions for money, creating realistic habitat groups and employing advanced preservation techniques. The two most eminent exponents of this type of museum in Banks's day were Sir Ashton Lever and later William Bullock.[2] Commercial ventures like theirs differed from the collections Banks kept, being more varied in content, whereas Banks's were used in specialist research rather than in public displays for financial profit. All, however, drew on the results of exploration, as did the British Museum. The British Museum was one place to which more and more objects and specimens were sent from the world's growing empires, yet even its capacity to cope was limited. By Banks's death in 1820 Montagu House had been outgrown by its collections, and there were plans to reconstruct the Museum buildings. So it was to the first wing of Robert Smirke's new building that Banks's great herbarium and natural history library were taken after being transferred to the Museum in 1827 in accordance with his will. There they joined 'natural and artificial' products[3] brought or given to the Museum by Banks over more than fifty years, many of which he had obtained not only from within the boundaries of empire but beyond them.

Banks's bequest was the last important service he rendered the Museum, and with it the majority of his private collections had finally passed into public ownership. The move had been anticipated by his conduct regarding collections throughout London, and by the way in which he managed his own from an early stage. For from 1778, the year he was elected President of the Royal Society and thereby became an ex-officio trustee, Banks started to divide his collections along lines that indicate generally to us today how he regarded and ordered not only them, but many others belonging to the bodies with which he was most closely associated. The pattern of what Banks gave to the British Museum, what he held back, and what he sent elsewhere shows that he thought collections should be shared among persons and institutions that were capable of housing and using them. In effect, Banks assessed and distributed the imperial influx, a function he performed no less assiduously than that of dispatching collectors or marshalling contacts abroad in the first place. This function became more important as the quantities of incoming material grew, and Banks tended to favour the British Museum as the repository holding the widest range of material, particularly when considering where to send his own collections.

From his central position Banks was able to organize more than the natural history collections with which he is usually associated. For example, he assisted the British Museum in the acquisition of books and papers, a review of David Garrick's collection of Elizabethan and Jacobean plays being among the first tasks he undertook as a trustee in 1779. He even conveyed a number of classical antiquities to the Museum, these mainly being donations from the Society of Dilettanti, but he also ensured that antiquities Horatio Nelson captured from a French ship in the Mediterranean in 1803 came to the attention of government. Banks's involvement with collections across the capital, and his connections with various societies, strengthened his reputation as someone able to handle all manner of objects, whether natural or artificial. However, it was Banks's early experiences that set the basic pattern of his later career as a collector, and established his special place in the interrelated fields of travel, natural history and ethnography.

Banks started to gather plants from abroad and to encounter native peoples on a trip to Newfoundland and Labrador in 1766,[4] but it was his exploits as a wealthy young civilian naturalist on the voyage of HMS *Endeavour* that gave him Europe-wide fame, and brought him to royal notice. This classic mission, launched in 1768 under Lieutenant James Cook, sailed to the Society Islands in the Pacific to observe the transit of Venus across the face of the sun. Observing the transit would enable the sun's parallax to be determined, from which the distance of the earth from the sun could be calculated, this now being used as a basic astronomical unit of distance.[5] The voyage also yielded accurate charts, such as those of the islands of New Zealand, and of the east coast of Australia, which Cook claimed for the Crown on Possession Island on 22 August 1770.[6] Along with detailed written accounts of the lands and cultures encountered, the voyage found no evidence for the existence of 'Terra Australis Incognita', a theoretical southern continent that some geographers believed lay in higher latitudes. Moreover, valuable experience had been gained, not least by Banks, who later became an authority on such voyages.

Banks led a party of collectors and illustrators on the *Endeavour* voyage, and was accompanied by a close friend, Daniel Solander.[7] Solander, a former pupil of the great Swedish naturalist, Carl Linnaeus,[8] gained leave from employment as an Assistant Librarian at the British Museum to go with Banks. Together the two men described the plants and animals that were collected, using the taxonomic system devised by Linnaeus, which allowed naturalists to classify natural products in a systematic way and with greater ease. Overall, the mission set a pattern for those that followed, and heralded not only a dramatic increase in the quantity of Pacific collections returning to Europe for analysis, but also the rapid growth of European control and organization of the distant lands being described. An important London base for exploration and natural history was quickly established when *Endeavour* returned. On getting back in July 1771, Banks disembarked his collections, which were sent to his home at 14 New Burlington Street. This done, number 14 became, in effect, an early 'Museum of the South Seas', anticipating the opening of similar displays at the British Museum. It provided a previously unavailable centre for those seeking knowledge of the places visited by Cook and Banks, and Banks had help arranging his collections from a young Edward Jenner, who went on to become famous as a surgeon and pioneer of smallpox vaccination.

Reactions were marked. The Reverend William Sheffield, Keeper of the Ashmolean Museum,[9] felt 'utmost astonishment' at what he saw on a visit in 1772, and could 'scarce credit my senses'. In the first of three rooms in which the Banks collections were arranged, Sheffield met with the 'Armoury', which contained all 'the warlike instruments, mechanical instruments and utensils of every kind, made use of by the Indians in the South Seas from Terra del Fuego to the Indian Ocean'.[10] The second held 'the different habits and ornaments of the several Indian nations', with a collection of insects, and 'the bread and other fruits preserved in spirits'. Here, too, was the great herbarium. The third and final room contained a very large collection of mammals, birds, fish and reptiles in spirits. This was also where the paintings and drawings of plants and some animals were located, these having been mostly completed by Sydney Parkinson, the gifted artist Banks took on the voyage as one of his party.

Apart from the ethnographic items, which were indeed a considerable achievement, the single sample of flora at New Burlington Street was not surpassed by any other brought to Europe until the next century.[11] Recent estimates suggest that the voyage yielded over 30,000 plant specimens, comprising more than 3,600 species, of which some 1,400 were new to science. From the animal kingdom as a whole more than 1,000 species may have been collected, of which some of the insects and molluscs have survived, but few other specimens remain.[12] Moreover, Sheffield thought Solander's descriptions of the plants and animals that were collected 'fit to be put to the press'.[13] This was not done, but the engravings of new plant species that Banks commissioned were eventually published in the twentieth century.[14]

Sheffield's admiring wonder is understandable, and was evidently shared by George III, who by 1773 was being advised by Banks on the development of the Royal Gardens at Kew, themselves incorporated into Banks's schemes to increase and exploit plant discoveries from overseas.[15] Some of the plants Sheffield singled out for special comment might therefore have been discussed with the King before Sheffield's account. New Zealand flax (*Phormium tenax* Forst.) had practical benefits for a maritime power seeking supplies of cordage and cloth, and Sheffield enthused: 'this will perhaps be the most useful discovery they made in the whole voyage'. It is possible he caught this idea from Banks and exaggerated it, for in his own assessment of the collections Banks concluded: 'Out of these, some considerable oeconomical purposes may be answerd, particularly with the fine Dyes of the Otaheitians, & the Plant of which the new Zelanders make their Cloth ...'.[16]

Alongside scientific aims, then, the potential 'oeconomical purposes' of any natural or artificial product were a high priority, and they gained in importance for entrepreneurs and naval commanders entering the Pacific in the years following the 1760s. Sheffield's mention of the famous breadfruit (*Artocarpus altilis* Parkinson) reminds us why, and of how Banks fostered an inter-tropical network of botanic gardens that exchanged plants and seeds of economic use and scientific interest. It was to the gardens at Kew, a central 'clearing house' in Banks's extended plant network, that the ill-starred William Bligh returned years later, having successfully completed his second attempt to transplant breadfruit from the Pacific to plantations in the West Indies.[17] As the boundaries of the empire broadened so too did those of collecting, one activity providing the other with the knowledge and resources necessary for growth.

Such were the interrelated scientific and imperial issues beginning to emerge at New Burlington Street, which by 1777 was too small to contain Banks's steadily growing library and other collections. Not everything in the 'immense magazine of curiosities' Sheffield described (sometimes a little inaccurately) fell within Banks's core interests of botany and bibliography. When in 1777 Banks moved into 32 Soho Square, a property he retained for the remainder of his life, and as he obtained the overarching positions in London Learned Society that he also held to the end – at the Royal Society, the British Museum and Kew – the time had come to decide where to place his major collections. Apart from the gifts he invariably made to friends, Banks appears to have reasoned that anything not strictly to do with his herbarium and library might be offered to one of the institutions with which he was connected. Thus, he gave his ethnographic collections *en masse* to the British Museum, which was rapidly becoming more of a centre for such material than Soho Square.

2 ETHNOGRAPHY

Banks's treatment of ethnographic collections shows that he perceived the British Museum to be an appropriate place to send material that lay outside his main concerns, rather than to retain it, thereby assembling the range of natural and artificial curiosities for which showmen like Lever and Bullock were renowned. In terms of donations of ethnographic collections from the Pacific, Banks was certainly following a precedent set by the Admiralty regarding Samuel Wallis's and George Carteret's collections, which were sent to the Museum in February 1770. Wallis led an epic mission into the Pacific in 1766 to look for 'Terra Australis Incognita', a non-existent theoretical southern continent, and on his way he discovered and named King George the Third's Island (Tahiti, called Otaheite by its inhabitants). Returning to England in 1768, it was Wallis who recommended this island as the place to observe the transit of Venus, a task which James Cook was chosen to undertake.

In February 1770, Admiralty Secretary Philip Stephens, a supporter of Banks's efforts to gain Solander a place on the *Endeavour* along with all the equipment Banks also required, informed the Museum trustees of the 'offer of several Curiosities from the late discovered Islands' in the Pacific.[1] This gift probably formed an early nucleus for the South Sea Room, started at the request of the Admiralty in 1775 to receive further gifts from Cook's voyages. The Sloane and some other manuscript collections were moved to make way for this new material,[2] and the cost of the work was £122 11s. 8d.[3] As a guide, then, but not necessarily an invariable rule, from at least 1770 onwards collections acquired by the Admiralty on missions launched under the Royal Navy were regarded as belonging to the nation, and so might be sent to the country's main Museum.

Exploration and Trade: 1768–95

In keeping with this, but as a private individual, Banks braved indignation from foreign savants when he offered the British Museum his entire collection of ethnographic artefacts. Writing in 1782 to Jan Ingenhousz, the Dutch plant physiologist, he defended his decision saying: 'I am sorry that Mr. Jacquin is so angrey that I have not yet fulfilld my Promise of sending him arms & curiosities

11

from the South Sea the reason I have not yet done it is that in order to give preference to the British Museum who engagd to fit up a room for the sole purpose
of receiving such things I long ago sent all mine down there consisting of several
Cart Loads'.[4] Banks was culpable here for not cataloguing the objects before-
hand, but it seems they were not dealt with rapidly on receipt, and in any case he
expected that 'the major part of my things will be Sent me back again'.

The donations referred to were probably those made first by Banks himself in
October 1778 in a timely personal gesture just before standing successfully for
election as President of the Royal Society. Then, in November 1780, he also led
officers and men from Cook's final voyage in the donation of a 'very large Collection of Artificial Curiosities Utencils, dresses &c from the South-Sea Islands, the
West Coast of North America and Kamschatka lately visited by His Majesty's
Ships the Resolution & the Discovery ...'.[5] On this occasion Banks was given
'particular Acknowledgements ... for his considerable and repeated liberalities to
the Museum', and Solander, with assistance from two circumnavigators, gunner
William Peckover and carpenter James Cleveley, was instructed to arrange and
label everything.[6] The South Sea Room was suitably organized to accommodate
the new material, and open by August 1781.[7]

A clear pattern was emerging in which Banks directed the 'artificial products' obtained from voyages of discovery generally towards the British Museum,
while he tended to distribute the 'natural' collections of living plants and seeds
to Kew Gardens, making a similar basic distinction between the two types as was
applied at Soho Square. There, too, natural history and especially botany prevailed, while ethnographic material first visited the British Museum. The natural
and the artificial were being separated out by Banks, who increasingly concentrated on botany, so that in due course he also sent the Museum specimens he
obtained from other branches of natural history, especially those relating to
zoology. Thus, the Museum was the recipient of enormous quantities of material
through Banks, who was able to operate this trans-institutional regime because
he was a senior figure in a number of prominent London bodies.

Indeed, Banks was President when in 1781 the Royal Society finally conceded
that it was in no position to maintain its Repository.[8] Banks oversaw the transferral to the British Museum of this valuable collection,[9] parts of which survive
today in institutions like the Natural History Museum, London. For example,
in the Museum's Botany Department there is a collection of 3,750 dried plant
specimens, which the Society had received from Chelsea Physic Garden and
passed on to the Museum in 1781.[10] One of many options for historic collections like the Royal Society's was therefore to pass into public possession, while
individuals could specialize, as Banks was doing.[11] And if the Royal Society had
relinquished its Repository, strong in natural history, at least that collection had
not passed beyond the control of the President, who was also a Museum trustee.

Banks's influence over the routes by which collections reached London, and how they circulated once there, was fast becoming an important shaping factor in the distribution and development of collections across the capital.

In ethnography this meant that some sea captains saw Banks as the obvious person to allocate their collections. One, George Dixon, a veteran of Cook's last voyage, approached Banks in this capacity in 1789. He had been dispatched by a syndicate of London merchants, who had formed the King George's Sound Company, to open up a trade in otter furs between the north-west coast of America and the markets of China and Japan. Accompanied by Nathaniel Portlock in the *King George*, Dixon sailed in the *Queen Charlotte*, returning with more by way of cartographic and ethnographic results than profits from otter pelts. He named an island in the Dixon Entrance to Hecate Sound after Banks and, with Nathaniel Portlock, he published a two-volume account of the voyage, dedicating his volume to Banks.[12] It was a compliment returned, for Banks had given advice on the mission, and he had named Dixon's boat the *Queen Charlotte*.

What is more, Dixon gave Banks 'Various Articles from the N:W: Coast of America', which are listed in the Museum's minutes since it was Banks who presented them in May 1789. These included mineral substances, eating implements, beads and other ornaments, tobacco leaves and a native game:[13]

> Various Articles from the N:W: Coast of America brought by Capt. Dixon, and presented by Sr. Joseph Banks, viz
> An Ornament worn by the women, on the under Lip.
> A large Ladle made of horn, probably of the American Buffaloe
> A Messing Bowl, or Porringer, in the form of an human Figure.
> Stones impregnated with Pyrites, and fibres of Plants, used as flint, steel and Tinder.
> A Stone of green Granite.
> A Paper of Tobacco, such as the natives Chew.
> A Piece of rock Crystal, and some Beads.
> Thirty four small Cylinders of Wood, variously marked, used in playing at a Game.

Here was a sample of crafts and manufactures, and of the materials employed in them, all of which drew the attention of those wishing to learn more about foreign cultures as subjects of study in their own right. Additionally, the donation contained items of interest to those seeking knowledge of natural resources, of native techniques developed for their use and of trading opportunities. As a whole, Dixon's mission shows the extent to which Banks was regarded by some navigators as an authority to consult on private as well as public enterprises, not only as to how they might be mounted, but also as to the disposal of their physical collections at the end. In 1780 another Cook veteran, James King, had declared: '... I look up to you as the common Centre of we discoverers'.[14] This comment was made in connection with the publication of the account of Cook's voyages, which Banks helped to manage, but it was an epitaph that might have served just as well for Banks at the British Museum during this period.

For his part, Banks saw that he could match his position as advisor to business and government on exploration with that of being a trustee at the British Museum and unofficial director of Kew, one role supporting another. An example of how this worked, though still very much one embroiled in the same commercial and political rivalries that Dixon sailed into, was that of Archibald Menzies, a Scottish surgeon and botanist.[15] Banks first gained Menzies a position under James Colnett on the *Prince of Wales*,[16] a ship accompanied by the *Princess Royal* under Charles Duncan in another vain attempt to seek a trade in furs. Menzies was away with Colnett from 1786 to July 1789, when the *Prince of Wales* anchored in the Thames, and Banks received a box of dried plants collected by the diligent Scot.[17] Menzies was allowed free access to Banks's library and herbarium to sort his collections, 32 Soho Square being by now a powerful auxiliary to both Bloomsbury and Kew.[18] He kept a set of plant specimens for himself, but he also ensured that specimens were sent to the botanic gardens at Edinburgh and at Kew. This was all in keeping with organized attempts to enhance these gardens with material from voyages of discovery and trade.

An altogether more significant international event provided the occasion of Menzies's next mission, which was on HMS *Discovery*, under George Vancouver, from 1791 to 1795. This was to seal the Convention with Spain of 28 October 1789, and thereby to conclude the Nootka Sound crisis. This confrontation, resulting from British commercial and strategic activity in the preceding years, effectively ended wide-scale priority claims by the Spanish in the Pacific[19] – although French ambitions remained. Banks obtained Menzies an appointment on the *Discovery*.[20] He helped to draft the scientific instructions,[21] themselves perhaps the most comprehensive statement of the methods employed on such missions from 1768 to 1820. Banks also defended Menzies's conduct following serious disagreements with Vancouver on the way back.[22]

We see a familiar set of priorities in Banks's organization of the materials brought back by Menzies. Banks had already dispatched the plants and seeds to Kew before the Home Secretary, William Henry Cavendish Bentinck, Duke of Portland, had even consulted the King as to where everything should go. Many of the living plants had been lost due to the arguments with Vancouver, and Banks was concerned that what remained should survive. Portland wrote merely to confirm that Banks's decision was approved, leaving it to him to decide what additional seeds should go to the Royal Gardens.[23] The herbarium specimens were taken to Soho Square, where they could be sorted. Menzies undertook this work with the help of Banks and more so that of Banks's librarian, Jonas

Dryander, and his assistant, Samuel Toerner. Together, they prepared sets of duplicates to be given to patrons and friends, one set of which Banks received.

The artificial curiosities, meanwhile, were for the British Museum, where Banks presented them a week after hearing from Portland of the King's wishes.[24] They had been held at Soho Square, but Banks seems to have learned from earlier experiences of sending such collections to be sifted at the Museum. Before releasing everything he had a list made by his amanuensis, William Cartlich, of 112 ethnographic items. These came from Otaheite (Tahiti), the Sandwich Islands (Hawaii), Nootka, Cross Island, New Georgia Islands, Port Trinidad, Cook Inlet and the north-west coast of America. The list commenced with an important piece, which was a 'complete Mourning Dress' from Tahiti. However, the publication of Menzies's experiences was never completed, somewhat to Banks's annoyance, for he blamed Vancouver for the loss of many live plants between St Helena and England on the return journey.[25] This was ironic, because, like Menzies, Banks published little of his collections, much to the subsequent frustration of taxonomists.

Nonetheless, the flow of ethnography continued wherever seamen plied their trade for such items, or wherever settlers came to stay. Banks often admired the skill of native workmanship. He was fascinated by local customs, and he tirelessly sought any information people possessed about their own environment. Banks also remained a generous patron of those seeking ethnographic material. Indeed, he was apt to give away objects quite freely, and what was not taken by the British Museum from his own collection was instead divided among members of his coterie. This group included men like Lord Sandwich, who gave a large collection of Cook ethnography to Trinity College, Cambridge, where it created considerable interest among visitors to the Wren Library.[26] Other recipients of gifts from Banks were Sir William Hamilton, Charles Francis Greville, Johan Alströmer, Johann Fabricius[27] and Johann Friedrich Blumenbach, the anthropologist at Göttingen University. In a similar gesture to that of Lord Sandwich, Banks gave a number of important objects to Christ Church, Oxford, his former university college.[28] Oxford was another destination favoured by donors of Pacific material, Johann Reinhold Forster and Johann Georg Adam Forster, the father-and-son team that took Banks's place on the second Cook mission, having sent gifts there in 1776. It is clear, too, that great collectors of exotica like Sir Ashton Lever and William Bullock obtained Banks material.[29] Even the angry naturalist, Nicolaus Joseph Jacquin, might eventually have been spared something more than the shells and rather laboured excuses that Banks sent in August 1785.[30]

Later Status and Organization: 1808–18

By June 1808 the South Sea Room[31] was being reorganized to display objects from the increasing coastlines and continents that had been visited. At this time Charles Konig, Assistant Keeper in the Department of Natural History and Modern Curiosities, reported gifts from Banks of cloth and matting from Madagascar. These were probably intended to coincide with the changes in the South Sea Room, and it was Konig who moved in a quantity of 'artificial curiosities' that had been languishing in the basement, including many from the north-west coast of America that Banks had previously presented.[32] Everything was set out in a geographical arrangement[33] intended to 'illustrate particular Customs of different Nations; their Religion, their Government, their Commerce, Manufactures or Trades'.[34] As such, the displays were intended to provide a 'window' on the world for visitors, but, with stated aims like these, many who climbed to Room 1 on the Upper Floor might have caught reflections of the links and preoccupations of competing empires in the cabinets that they saw. The cases covered Europe, Asia, Africa, South America, the east and west coasts of North America, Tahiti, the Sandwich Islands and Marquesas, the Friendly Islands (Tonga), and New Zealand, with various small articles being placed on a separate table.[35]

It is worth noting in both the minutes and the published Museum *Synopsis* for 1808, as well as in other sources like officers' reports, a certain indifference of tone to the so-called 'Modern Artificial Curiosities'. According to the *Synopsis*, such material comprised mostly unlisted 'donations'. Since these donations were not 'strictly of a scientific nature' some might 'be set aside, to make room for others of more intrinsic value', while the majority was stored 'in a less conspicuous part of the house' – a euphemism for anything consigned to the basement.[36] Damp and cluttered, the basement was a thorny issue, and the fact that so much ethnography ended up there provides evidence of the lower status accorded such collections. In the summer of 1815, when a move to the old Bird Room was being contemplated for the modern artificial curiosities, Planta was requested to go through everything to decide what was worth keeping on public view, and to 'report upon the best mode of disposing by sale or otherwise of the rest'.[37] The language used on such occasions is indicative of the attitude of Planta to ethnography, and more so that of Konig. When sorting through the basement, Konig reported 'throwing out the vilest trash which was kept there under the name of Artificial Curiosities ...'.[38] Yet the attitude of Museum officers was not shared by the public, which was fascinated by such material and eagerly came to see it. Indeed, Museum displays of ethnography remained popular, and in their own way foreshadowed much greater Victorian exhibitions in the middle of the century, not least the Great Exhibition of 1851.

The flow of such 'curiosities' continued until the last years of Banks's life. In 1818 yet another attempt to search for the Northwest Passage was launched, with ships being sent northwards in pairs under John Ross and William Edward Parry, and under David Buchan and John Franklin. Afterwards, ethnographic and natural history collections from the missions were given by the Admiralty to the British Museum, some being passed on by Banks.[39] By this time the British Museum was regarded by many sailors and travellers as a suitable destination for the 'curiosities' they obtained. Thus, as the oceans and their related cultures were explored, the British Museum benefited from the perception that it was a fitting repository for such material. Impetus for this view had clearly been provided by the Museum's own reputation, by Admiralty procedures and by the independent acts of explorers and trustees like Banks, who privately maintained a supply of objects, like the excavated stone tools from Guadeloupe that he gave in 1816. These were an archaeological addition typical of the range of his interests.[40] So was his gesture in passing on seven species of birds from the west coast of Greenland with some shells that William Edward Parry gave him in 1818.[41] Giving such material to Banks had come to mean that it was almost certain to find its way to the British Museum.

Conclusion

Despite the lower scientific status accorded ethnography at this stage, its presence at the Museum was dramatically increased by gifts made by explorers like Banks. Banks offered large portions of the ethnographic collections he made on HMS *Endeavour* to the British Museum, and he also gave away most of what he received from subsequent Cook missions. He seems to have encouraged a number of sailors during this period to do the same. The Museum *Synopsis* for 1808 was the first general guide to be printed for use by the public. Promoting the idea of the British Museum as a repository of exploration it describes how the collections grew, acknowledging the central role Banks played in channelling material to its different departments: 'To this list [of benefactors] must be added the name of the Right Hon. Sir Joseph Banks, Bart. K.B., who, after his return from his circumnavigation, deposited at different times in the Museum numerous collections of natural and artificial curiosities from the newly discovered islands in the South Seas, which, with considerable additions since made by the Admiralty, Capt. Cook, and other officers who have since performed similar distant and perilous voyages, forms now one of the most conspicuous parts of the Museum'.[42]

After the *Endeavour* voyage the flow of ethnographic material to the Museum increased considerably, and the rate of increase became even more rapid from 1800 onwards. As a generation of seamen extended knowledge of the oceans in the wake of James Cook, and as national rivalries developed in the 1780s, especially between Britain and Spain on the north-west coast of America, with Arthur Phillip sailing for the east coast of Australia on 13 May 1787, Banks took whatever opportunities arose to increase understanding of the geography, natural history and societies that were being discovered. Of course, this could all be exploited for commercial and strategic gain, but it also yielded collections that Banks circulated among the major institutions and scholars with whom he was linked, especially the British Museum. Such generosity greatly encouraged interest in and study of ethnography across Britain and Europe.

In 1790, along with other ethnographic items from Menzies's voyage with Colnett and Duncan, Banks presented to the British Museum 'a Garment made of the bark of the Cupressus Thyoides, a fishing line made of a kind of Fucus, and four specimens of bark & flax'.[43] The distinction between the 'natural' and the 'artificial' is a little blurred here. Natural products could be put to commercial and maritime uses, such as in man-made cordage or cloth, and these concerns were certainly interwoven with those of discovery in the infant study of ethnography. Yet the early ethnographic collections also represent a moment when not just one form of civilization was changed, but when most forms were changed. The growth of European voyaging around the globe during Banks's lifetime led to increased encounters between previously separate peoples. Inevitably, each collected from and traded with the other, and as contacts developed all were co-modified.

Collections from voyages of discovery. 'No. 77 A quantity of small sinew fishing lines'. Reproduced by permission of the British Museum.

3 NATURAL HISTORY AND ZOOLOGY

The history of the dispersal of Banks's zoological specimens from the Cook voyages is as complex as that of the ethnographic objects, and for similar reasons. Since Banks did not amass major private collections in branches of natural history other than botany, when the time came he looked to donate large portions of Pacific material elsewhere. This entailed channelling quantities of material to the British Museum, so that in the 'Book of Presents', 1756–1823, there is a preponderance of animals, birds, fish, insects, rocks and minerals from Banks but scant mention of any plants from him. In addition to making these donations, Banks maintained especially close working relationships with some Museum officers. One of Banks's main Museum contacts was Charles Konig, who tended to concentrate on earth sciences, but Banks also had contacts with other Museum officers like Edward Whitaker Gray, George Shaw, the youthful John Edward Gray and the talented William Elford Leach, the latter being a particularly generous benefactor of the Museum, like Banks.[1] These officers were primarily concerned with natural history, and were therefore the ones who received Banks's gifts on behalf of the Museum, and who most regularly sought his advice and support regarding Museum business.

We see in Banks's relationship with these officers something resembling that which existed with their maritime and Admiralty counterparts. Some were picked for their posts by Banks, and in one or two cases strong attachments formed, leading to sustained mutual assistance, and even interdependence. Banks's first and formative contact of this kind at the Museum was with Daniel Solander, who was employed in 1763 at a salary of £100 to make a 'Catalogue of the Collections of Natural History in the Museum'.[2] Solander introduced the ideas of his master, the great Swedish naturalist Carl Linnaeus, to the organization of the Museum collections, and he went on to assist with those of Banks.[3] Linnaeus's ideas were not substantially modified or superseded in the Museum until the days of Leach's generation, which preferred more natural systems later developed in France.

Banks's early gifts of birds and animals indicate the widening range of his contacts abroad, as distinct from the gifts he made of material that he obtained directly through his own exploration. This extended range is another and an important element in the pattern of what he gave. For example, in the 'Book of Presents' under Banks's name we find stuffed birds from Senegal, and then a tiger cat; from South Carolina Banks gave a collection of fish, and in 1784 he passed on a collection of forty-nine bird skins from Brazil, Bombay and China, these last possibly coming from William Pigou and John Duncan, both attached to the East India Company at Canton.[4] Banks might well have been prompted to give the birds by Edward Whitaker Gray, who went on to become a rather lax Keeper of the Department of Natural and Artificial Curiosities. Gray had recently been working in the Bird Room,[5] where Banks's birds were mounted for display at a cost of 3s. 6d. each.[6] What is apparent is that Banks was not restricted to the limits of his own collecting activities, but was able to rely on his reputation in other countries, and on the letters and collectors he sent to increase his global reach.

He was therefore an important link to wider networks supplying London Learned Society with specimens. Indeed, in volume 1 of the Museum's 'Book of Presents' we find that Banks is the most prolific individual donor, with more separate entries than anyone else. These, however, do not include much by way of botany. Instead, zoology, mineralogy, books and manuscripts are most common, with the plants Banks received being retained, exchanged or shared with Kew. With time Banks could draw on colonial possessions, including those established in New South Wales.[7] In April 1790 he gave 'three Birds, the Skin of an Animal, and the Tail of a Sting Ray, from New South Wales', probably sent by Arthur Phillip, the first Governor from 1788 to 1792.[8] Banks's range of contacts was growing with his status,[9] and as the range of empire itself increased so too did the diversity of natural and artificial products arriving at the British Museum through him. He was an especially fruitful source of material from the Pacific.

As with the artificial curiosities forwarded to the Museum by Banks, an arrangement was reached whereby he advised on the best place for natural history collections to go. Precedent in such cases was to send them to the British Museum or to Kew, although plenty of material circulated more widely than that. The impact of this increased circulation, and of the greater quantity of material arriving at the Museum, needs to be appreciated. The basement of the Museum has been mentioned in this regard, and it will be necessary later on to enquire into the difficulties encountered as the Museum collections grew. Before that we must consider why and how a number of collections in London shifted from private to public ownership during Banks's time as a Museum trustee. Both as a trustee and as a collector Banks encouraged this trend through the planned way in which he helped manage the overall distribution of collections in the capital, including his own.

Fom Private to Public: The Transferral of Some Major Collections,
1771–1805

Banks tended not to retain permanently collections that lay outside his core interests of botany and bibliography. This made practical sense in that he could concentrate on developing prominent collections in his chosen core areas, while donating material to collectors or institutions specializing in other fields. Thus in 1792 he made major donations of zoological specimens to the British Museum, and to the celebrated Scottish surgeon and antomist, John Hunter. Banks's gift to the Museum was among the larger and more important South Sea zoological collections that had been donated by a private individual up to that date. It included material from the *Endeavour* mission and from Cook's 'subsequent Voyages'. Banks, like the Museum, had benefited from a series of gifts made by the naturalists and crew members on Cook's second voyage, 1772–5. Indeed, when Cook's ships arrived back in late July 1775 there was something of a sale of curiosities, and this helped to disperse material almost immediately. For example, the London dealer George Humphrey obtained many shells that he sold to the Duchess of Portland and to the Literary and Philosophical Society of Danzig, among others. Demand was high both in London and throughout Europe for objects from these voyages. As more ships returned in the years after Cook, Pacific collections were distributed among a mix of naturalists, curio hunters and brokers, who sold and exchanged shells, skins, plants and artefacts with particular eagerness.

For Banks, material was forthcoming from Johann Reinhold Forster and Johann Georg Adam Forster, the father-and-son team that took his place on the second mission, from Cook himself, and from other officers and sailors. Cook's collections went directly to Solander's apartments at the British Museum. Four casks of these were for Banks, and they contained birds and fish, with a box of plants from the Cape of Good Hope also destined for Cook's erstwhile travelling companion.[10] In August the elder Forster delivered a listed collection of birds, fish and other animals to Bloomsbury,[11] and in September he offered duplicate specimens of insects to Banks and to the British Museum.[12] From what Solander understood, the Forster collections were to be divided between the British Museum, the Royal Society, Banks, Marmaduke Tunstall and Sir Ashton Lever.[13] This was a typical group of institutions and individuals variously interested in South Sea articles. The last of them, Lever, was in essence a virtuoso, justly famed for his heterogeneous exhibitions of natural and artificial products.[14] Originally based at Alkrington Hall, Manchester, Lever called his collections the Holophusicon (or Holophusikon) to signify that they embraced all of nature. He charged an admission fee to those wishing to see his collections, which from 1775 were located at Leicester Square, in a former royal residence no less.

Banks could add to the proceeds of the second Cook voyage all the plants, seeds and insects gathered by David Nelson on the third, 1776–80. Nelson was Banks's personal collector at a rate of £35 a year.[15] Additionally, the dying Charles Clerke, who commanded HMS *Discovery*, bequeathed his collections to Banks in a warm final letter.[16] In doing so, he passed on 'the best collection of all kinds of matter ... that have fallen in our way in the course of the voyage'. There is no mention in Clerke's letter of any other claim on this material, although one appears to have been made by Lever. It seems, too, that Banks received most of the birds from this mission, and part of the collections of the late naval surgeon, William Anderson.[17] Seamen like John Marra, gunner's mate on the *Resolution*, volunteered shells and other objects to Banks.[18] Lever, the ornithologist John Latham and the voracious naturalist and travel writer Thomas Pennant all expressed an interest in treasures of these kinds.

Banks would have kept the plant collections, but many of the animals were given away. As explained, in January 1792 Museum officers were invited to Soho Square to take away every specimen not already represented at the British Museum, thanks being given to 'Sir Joseph Banks, for his very valuable Donation'.[19] Banks's tendency was to favour the British Museum in such important matters. The Museum was given first refusal of his ethnographic collections and, besides plants, the Museum was given the choice of his natural history collections as well. The 1792 gift was a valuable accession, and included many specimens preserved in spirit. As on other occasions naturalists across Europe were disappointed in their requests for specimens of this quality, for Banks was firm that the British Museum ought to have what it wanted before anyone else. Writing to Johann Friedrich Blumenbach in Göttingen the next year, Banks explained: 'I have some time ago presented to the British Museum the whole of the Collections made by me in the South Sea that were Preservd in Spiritu vini, among them was one species only of Turtle that has not been as far as I know describd it is a water animal & very small I caught it when at Batavia during a Flood in the River there which overflowd a small Field near the house I inhabited, I have no drawing of it or I would with Pleasure Communicate it to Mr Schopf of Anspac to whom I beg you to give my best Compliments'.[20]

It was the remodelling in 1791 of the library at the rear of his Soho premises, made necessary as Banks's herbarium and library grew, that probably prompted the gift of zoology to the British Museum. Something like architectural alterations, here supplied by George Dance Junior, could explain the decision to relinquish large collections, although the choice of to whom would not have been taken lightly. Increasingly, the British Museum was seen as an institution both worthy and capable of housing major collections that private owners were not prepared or able to keep, and this despite the limited space and staff Montagu House had to cope with it all. Another example of this tendency was the transferral to Bloomsbury of the Royal Society's Repository in 1781. This coincided with the Society's move to new apartments at Somerset House, which had been designed by Sir William Chambers, but which had insufficient room for the Society's Repository. Seeking another place for their eminent collection, the Royal Society looked to a public establishment instead.

As President of the Royal Society, Banks was well placed to assist with the arrangements, since he was a trustee of the Museum too. In February he announced to the other trustees, many of whom were still Fellows, that the Society's Repository was ready for transfer.[21] Daniel Solander had assisted in maintaining the Repository at the Society, and he also knew the British Museum collections well. Ideally suited for the task, he was instructed to move everything and then sort it all once at the Museum.[22] However, he had all too short a time in which to do this, for the next year he died of a brain haemorrhage after collapsing at Banks's Soho home.[23] The loss of such a capable naturalist was a profound blow both to Banks and to the Museum. Nevertheless, with Banks as a major collector, as President of the Royal Society and as an active trustee it is clear that the British Museum was being given a high priority in the choice of the most valuable collections available in London. It is also clear that strategic links between key bodies in the capital were being carefully maintained both through the collections themselves and through the staff at each. After Solander's death the Reverend Paul Henry Maty was appointed Under-Librarian in the Department of Natural and Artificial Productions. Maty was Principal Secretary of the Royal Society from 1778 to 1784, and although he clashed with Banks and resigned the Secretaryship, there remained nonetheless a significant number of Society Fellows among the Museum's officers.[24] Whatever the eventual composition of the trustees, this network of Fellows in the Museum's departments and at other related institutions in London only served to increase Banks's general influence and with it his ability to coordinate collections.[25]

In due course other Banks collections made their circuitous ways to the British Museum. Many were acquired in the nineteenth century when the Museum was fully established in its leading London role as the premier public body responsible for collections. Some came as parts of larger donations and purchases, gradually filtering through the network of organizations Banks had known to the central repository of the British Museum. Even some of the material Banks gave to Hunter reached Bloomsbury, arriving in 1845 through a donation from the Royal College of Surgeons. Banks's original 1792 specimens were kept separate in Hunter's museum, being called the 'New Holland Division'. Hunter died in 1793 and in 1796 Banks was asked to report to government on Hunter's collections, which Banks did, emphasizing their relevance to medical science and anatomy.[26] The collections were purchased by the nation for £15,000, and in 1800 they became the basis of the museum of the Royal College of Surgeons. When the

College donated 348 specimens to the British Museum in 1845, some came from the 'New Holland Division', and a small number were registered as having once belonged to Banks.[27] That they were eventually lodged at the Museum was, perhaps, a fitting end for such material.

Similarly, in 1815 Banks presented a collection of shells, insects and crustaceans to the Linnean Society. When, like the Royal Society before it, the Linnean Society could no longer maintain a museum, Banks's material was part of a donation of insects and shells that it gave to the British Museum. Made in 1863, this donation now provides an important source of type specimens, the insects having been worked on in the early 1770s by Johann Fabricius, the Danish entomologist.[28] The Linnean Society donation was preceded in 1855 by the collections of the Zoological Society of London, sold to the Museum for £500. Much later, in 1911, the Geological Society gave its extensive collections to what was by then the Department of Mineralogy at the Natural History Museum, London. In making these transferrals each of the societies followed the early example set by the Royal Society. When London's societies gave up their collections in this way, it was generally because they saw national institutions as a more fitting location for such material. It was not just the societies concerned with science that thought like this either, for those that dealt primarily with antiquities, such as the Society of Dilettanti, were also benefactors of the British Museum.

Gradually, then, significant private collections came to the British Museum through purchase or donation. The trend was a widespread one, and throughout this study examples will be provided of how it accelerated steadily as the nineteenth century progressed. Yet, as with Banks's ethnographic collections, the transferral of his zoological and other materials from private to public possession did not mean that the collections themselves received better treatment than Banks had bestowed on them. Nor did it mean that they remained intact. The development of collections up to and including this period was not one leading invariably from mixed 'cabinets of curiosities' to highly organized and documented collections. Nevertheless, Banks is still a good example of someone who specialized to advantage. Likewise, at the British Museum, departments were slowly created to concentrate on the separate disciplines emerging in natural history and antiquities, and, as they were, greater order was imposed on the collections. At the same time, fewer and fewer private collectors were able to match the Museum's scope and variety. The costs alone of doing so were prohibitive.

In his later years, Banks continued to receive and to circulate material, not necessarily as the result of his own travels, but through the exertions of other travellers who visited the capital or corresponded from across Britain, Europe and the world. He was also in contact with explorers sent from London on various missions abroad. He did not, however, try to form an extensive private cabinet from many fields, as had been done by others in the past. Instead, his role was more that

of a private person at the heart of a network of organizations and individuals centred on the capital. In some ways it could be said that he was at the heart of what
became a learned empire, one based on increased travel and communication.
From this central position Banks was able to contribute in significant ways to the
growth and distribution of many collections accumulating in London, including
those at the British Museum.

Banks as a Museum 'Agent' in the Market for Natural History: 1782–1810

In December 1782 Edward Whitaker Gray[29] commented on recommended
changes to the Department of Natural and Artificial Productions.[30] A naturalist and physician, Gray was Keeper of the Department from 1787 to 1806,
and he was also a Secretary of the Royal Society from 1797 to 1804. Banks
and his friend and early patron, William Watson (an original trustee, and yet
another Fellow of 1741), were asked to inspect the Department in response to
the recommendations. Thus began Banks's supervisory involvement in natural history at the Museum. During his long career one thing would become
increasingly obvious to officers and trustees alike. The basement, to which
much of the Royal Society's Repository had been consigned, was a muddle in
which many objects had deteriorated to an extent that no eighteenth-century
conservation technique could possibly remedy. As the collections at the British
Museum grew, and as they were catalogued, so the overall strain on space and
staff also grew. The situation was severe with regard to the condition of the
basement, which worsened steadily under successive Keepers, each of whom
failed to confront the problem. In particular, the storage and preservation of
skins, stuffed animals, specimens in spirit and large skeletons all seem to have
posed greater problems than material in the earth sciences or botany. Since
the Museum would not be rebuilt for another forty or so years some drastic
measures were eventually taken, but Gray was hardly the man to initiate them.
Content with his basic duties, like others he avoided the basement, and following the inspection by Banks and Watson turned his attention to alterations in
the Bird Room.[31]

These alterations were completed in January 1784, when Gray examined
birds that had been purchased, producing an estimate for having them stuffed
and placed in the collection.[32] In July he was ordered to make a proposal for cleaning, classifying and labelling the contents of the Insect Room. Importantly, Gray
was also instructed to look for duplicates of animals and birds in the Department,
and to report on their condition for sale.[33] Along with gifts and exchanges, sales
and auctions were very much a feature of the natural history 'market' in most
countries, and a shaping factor in the historical growth of museums across the

The British Museum in Montague House, 1780, guarded by the York Regiment during the Gordon Riots, drawing by Paul Sandby. Reproduced by permission of the British Museum.

globe in the eighteenth and nineteenth centuries.[34] London's museums were no exception. In particular, the capital's commercial museum collections were built up and disposed of through sales, but the British Museum was also active in the marketplace. It sometimes used sales and exchanges of duplicates to free space and to raise funds, these funds invariably being spent on new specimens or to make essential repairs. Such sales are one reason why scholars interested in the history of collections and naturalists using them for the purposes of classification now struggle to locate and identify early material that was dispersed or reorganized many years ago.

That said, the market for natural history was not always a profitable one, and the Museum tended to rely no less on exchanges and donations to obtain specimens than it did on paying for them. In response to the enquiry about selling duplicates, Gray thought that there were 'few or no purchasers of subjects of natural history'.[35] The market for coins and antiquities seems to have been generally more lucrative than that for animal and bird specimens, although shells, rocks and minerals were popular. With little chance of generating enough income to obtain more specimens through sales, it was important to have a trustee like Banks. Banks was keenly aware of what was available in London, and he was able to obtain numerous exotic items that might not otherwise have reached Bloomsbury. Perhaps stimulated by the recent work on ornithology, in August 1784 he gave a collection of dried bird skins from Brazil, Bombay and China. As suggested above, some of these were probably sent by William Pigou and John Duncan, both of whom recognized Banks as someone not only interested in such material, but also well placed to assess and distribute it.

This was significant, because from 1771 onwards London became ever more of a global centre for exploration and trade, and the routes by which specimens circulated and were acquired widened considerably, especially throughout the Pacific. As they did, Banks's standing as a person able to operate and to an extent control such routes was enhanced. All manner of items started to flood in, and from a variety of sources. In 1790 the Privy Council's Committee for Trade and Plantations gave the British Museum 'various specimens of Birds, Fish, Reptiles & Fossils'.[36] Banks became a member of this Committee in 1797, thereby further developing his personal network. From another contact in Britain's expanding commercial empire came 'A fish of a new Genus, and two horns of the same, one of which had been taken out of the bottom of the Asia East India Man'. The latter were gifts presented by Banks in 1790, at the same time that he gave 'three Birds, the Skin of an Animal, and the Tail of a Sting Ray, from New South Wales', which have also been mentioned above. Such quantity and scope soon became almost more than the Museum could contain. Thus, we find Gray being repeatedly requested to inspect his Department for duplicates, and to pay particular attention to the basement, something he chose to avoid tackling.[37]

For his part, Banks continued to supply valuable specimens. Indeed, among the Museum's trustees and donors he was remarkable for the varied extent of the material he tirelessly channelled to Bloomsbury. It is Banks's range that is perhaps the most impressive aspect, stretching, as it did, from the Far East to the West Indies, and from the South Seas to the orchards of England. Following what he had already given, Banks passed to the Museum 'an Antelope from Sumatra, & an Otter', a 'Male & female of a Curious Species of Bird from Sumatra', 'Part of a Jaw-bone, similar to those found on the banks of the Ohio, brought from St Domingo, where it was taken as plunder ... [and] A branch of a Crab Tree diseased in a singular manner'.[38] Little lay beyond his notice, and among the donations made there was plenty that was genuinely new to science. With the turn of the century, and after years of experience in dealing with a variety of material beyond the reach of almost any other person in Britain, Banks took an unusual step. He proposed a direct system of exchange between himself and the Museum, which by law was only allowed to dispose of duplicates.[39] The trustees agreed, perhaps seeing in Banks an exceptional opportunity to increase the Museum's collections.

Banks thereby became almost a Museum 'agent', not merely donating items, but obtaining them from and for the Museum. The strict conditions imposed by the trustees on this arrangement were 'that all such articles as Sir Joseph shall deposit in the British Museum, shall be considered as a part of the Collection, and actually the property of the Trustees, from the time they are delivered to the Officers of the House; and that the Trustees shall have full power, at all times, to reject every application from Sir Joseph Banks for duplicates in exchange for them, which they may think unreasonable'.[40] Immediately following this resolution Banks accelerated the rate, quantity and rarity of his donations. Indeed, at the very meeting where his proposal had been approved, 9 April 1802, he deposited geese from Botany Bay and a collection of Japanese minerals and fossils sent to him by a merchant called Isaac Titsingh.[41] These were followed in May by bird skins from Botany Bay, and in June by minerals from New South Wales, a pair of paddles from Western Port, and the head of an 'Argus Pheasant from Sumatra'.[42] The pheasant came from John Macdonald, a military engineer formerly stationed at Fort Marlborough, Bengkulu, while the increase of material from Australia at the turn of the century coincided with the arrival in New South Wales of the new Governor, Philip Gidley King, and the return to Britain of his predecessor, John Hunter. Other sources in Australia included the botanist Robert Brown, who sent back seeds for Kew, and men like Lieutenant James Grant, who had been exploring through Bass Strait to Western Port in the autumn of 1801, carrying with him on the *Lady Nelson* a young naturalist by the name of George Caley. Caley was Banks's paid collector in the colony from 1800 to 1810, and he was yet another source of news, seeds and specimens.[43] The scope and quantity of Banks's donations in these years show that by the turn of the century collecting was being conducted on a truly global scale.

What his donations also reveal is that, alongside the navigators and settlers mentioned here, Banks exploited other networks on behalf of the British Museum. Perhaps the most significant of these networks was formed by scientific colleagues and the numerous societies comprising the grand eighteenth-century Republic of Letters. The Republic provided Banks with access to traditional links extending throughout the philosophical community in Britain and Europe generally, enabling him to supplement contacts elsewhere with information, advice and research on collections, much of it of an advanced kind. For example, in March 1803, not long after Banks had reached his agreement with the Museum regarding exchange material, he presented specimens of a meteorite fall at Siena,[44] about which he had corresponded with Giovanni Fabbroni and William Batt, both of whom were useful contacts in Italy.[45] The fall at Siena in June 1794 has special significance because historians now regard it as marking the beginning of what has become the modern science of meteoritics. Analysis in the eighteenth century of this and other falls convinced philosophers that falling stones did indeed come from the heavens, an advance on previous thinking, and Banks encouraged investigation of the subject through the donations that he made.[46] Since the entire meteorite collection of the Museum comprised only seven meteorites, the Siena specimen was an important contribution. It was one Banks added to with others like the Benares and Wold Cottage stones. These joined fragments of Otumpa, a large iron meteorite found in Argentina, which was presented by the Royal Society in 1788.[47] Furthermore, in 1803 Jean Baptiste Biot sent specimens from the L'Aigle fall through Banks.[48] In this way, the Museum's early meteorite collection was gradually enlarged, and with it understanding of astronomy.

Of particular significance in this respect was a comparative study of a number of falls made by the chemist Edward Charles Howard from about 1800 to 1802. Banks supported Howard, who thought the falls reported around the world were related, and could be explained by material originating in space. One view gaining wider acceptance was that meteorite stones and irons came from volcanoes on the moon. This was incorrect, but it allowed that their origins were extraterrestrial, which had previously been disputed.[49] Banks's own feeling was that a new scientific field might be opening up, and he was eager to see it grow. To assist he ensured that increases in the Museum's meteorite collection were linked to active study in what was a puzzling area for astronomers of the day. Consequently, Howard had access to Museum and other meteorite specimens around London to support his work, but Howard was not the only chemist to benefit from Banks's intervention at the Museum. Banks's 'exchange account' operated in useful ways for a number of chemists seeking rock and mineral collections to investigate. Among them was Charles Hatchett, who carried out scientific tests on mineral samples obtained through the Banks account. Further tests performed on specimens from the Museum collections included those of William Hyde Wollaston, the inventor in 1809 of the reflecting goniometer. In March 1809 and again in November 1815 he conducted experiments on material obtained through Banks.[50] Thus, the Museum continued to profit generally from Banks's connections in what it received, as did those conducting research using its collections.

Wider exchanges between institutions were another way in which links within the Republic of Letters were developed to benefit the British Museum. Accordingly, in November 1803 an important collection of fossilized and recent bones was given to the Museum by the Emperor of Russia. This donation was organized by Banks, and sent to Britain by the President of the St Petersburg Academy, Nicolas Novossiltzoff.[51] Following everything else Banks had directed to the Museum in the last year or so, this latest collection must have amply satisfied the trustees' expectations of their agreement. No other single individual matches Banks in these years for the range of gifts presented. He, more than anyone else, seems to have been able to tap the manifold routes through which natural history flowed into, out of and around Britain. The exotic array of material conveyed to the Museum by Banks continued, and it must have been an interesting moment for trustees when he announced at meetings some new present, or for officers when one was delivered at the doors of the Museum. In the years that followed, the trustees and officers were regaled with the skin of a white kangaroo from Van Diemen's Land (Tasmania), minerals found in Surrey and a large Oyster shell from the Ganges. Banks added to these an ember goose from Lincolnshire, a new species of goose from Port Dalrymple with a mammal, and then some 'Native Minium'.[52] It was a remarkable contribution resulting from Banks's no less remarkable command of collecting networks. In return he used his 'exchange account' only occasionally, and then mostly for the benefit of others wishing to conduct research or to increase their museums.[53] Similarly, his own collections were also made available to others, but Banks did not treat his agreement with the Museum as a means of enlarging his own herbarium or library. Indeed, the reverse was ultimately the case.

Besides the specimens that circulated among the collectors and dealers of London, there was also a steady flow of naturalists arriving in the capital to consult its major collections. These visitors proved to be useful sources for acquiring all manner of news and material, and in their minds, Banks's centre first at New Burlington Street, and then from 1777 at Soho Square, served as a powerful auxiliary to the British Museum. One such visitor was Pieter Camper, a Dutch anatomist, who visited London in 1785. Camper was a follower of the great French naturalist, Georges Louis Leclerc, Comte de Buffon, and a critic of Carl Linnaeus's taxonomic system. Camper worked at Soho Square, and he also spent a good deal of time at the British Museum, especially in its basement, where some of the osteological collections were stored. Banks assisted with arrangements for Camper's work in London, and on returning to his estates in Holland in 1786, Camper wrote to thank Banks:

> No where there is to be found a house, a library, a company as that of Sir Josephs! No where a man of that taste, of that politeness to Foreigners, and of that public Spirit, which distinguishes you above all I met with in my travels, tho' pretty frequent to the most capital towns of the Continent ... As often as I look over the manifold obser-vations, and drawings I had the opportunity to collect in London, especially in the Museum Britt: I acknowledge the excellency of your Country, and the liberal way of thinking of the learned that adorn it. They kindle afresh that Enthusiasm, which is so necessary to the progress of all arts and sciences, and which I have not yet intirely lost tho' an ould man![54]

Camper had every reason to feel enthusiastic, for he had proposed an exchange of duplicate horns, bones and teeth with the British Museum. Gray was instructed to sort out the required duplicates, and, this done, in December 1785 the trustees decided to accept Camper's offer.[55] In return Camper added to his letter thanking Banks a 'List of the Petrifactions from St. Peters Mount at Maestricht, to be sent in exchange to the Brittish Museum', consignments of which followed in March 1786.[56]

Research conducted in London in this way served only to strengthen Banks's networks, and to further enable him to obtain information and material from abroad. Another visiting naturalist was Olof Swartz, a Swedish pupil of Linnaeus, and a botanist of whom Banks thought a great deal. In 1787 Swartz came to London from the West Indies with plant collections he wanted to study and to publish. With Banks's help he gained access to Sloane's herbarium at the British Museum,[57] and was, like Camper, welcomed at Soho Square. Numerous natural-ists benefited from using Soho Square and Bloomsbury in conjunction like this, gaining no less from Banks's rich herbarium and his specialist library than they did from the national collections themselves. In 1788 Swartz forwarded to Banks fifty copies of the results of his work, first published in *Nova Genera et Species Plantarum, seu prodromus*.[58] These copies were for Banks's own library, and for sale and circulation in Britain, including to the British Museum. Such were the polite gestures by which scientific relations were maintained, and knowledge and collections enlarged. Both as a trustee and as President of the Royal Society Banks displayed a marked willingness to extend hospitality to foreign naturalists like Camper and Swartz, and to make a range of facilities available to them. This had the effect of encouraging the exchange of ideas, specimens and publications on a greater scale.

In December 1787 Banks donated seeds to the Museum,[59] perhaps for its garden, and in November 1788 Camper sent engraved heads of the Asiatic and African rhinoceroses.[60] By way of return Camper obtained from the Museum 'the

Jaw of the Animal incognitum, from the Ohio'.[61] Later on Banks repaid Swartz's gift with a copy of a volume that he had produced, *Icones selectae Plantarum quas in Japonia*.[62] This comprised a selection of engraved Japanese plants that Banks published from original illustrations by Engelbert Kaempfer, a German traveller who had visited Japan from 1690 to 1692. The Kaempfer plant illustrations Banks used were held in the Sloane collections at the British Museum, collections Swartz had been able to study because of Banks's help. Banks explained to a book dealer at Tübingen that his book was not for sale, but 'was publishd for the Sake of my friends as a present for those who were so good as to assist me in Forming my Library ...'.[63] It could not have been more appropriately bestowed on anyone else than Swartz, for Swartz had recommended Samuel Toerner, an MA from Uppsala University, to assist Jonas Dryander in Banks's library from 1792 to 1797.[64] The Swedish contribution to the growth and cataloguing of Banks's library was indeed substantial, as it was to the organization of Banks's herbarium and the development of the collections at the British Museum.

During Banks's life his personal Soho collections were used to support those of the Museum, the two complementing one another. That Banks specialized, as he had a right to do with his own herbarium and library, was sensible, but he ensured that both were made available to those employed at and visiting the Museum. Joint research was produced as a result of this coordinated approach, which in practice does not seem to have been at all prejudicial to the Museum, and which culminated in Banks's final collections going to Bloomsbury in 1827. During his lifetime Banks also channelled an impressive array of material to the Museum, much of it derived from networks extending globally from London. These are some of the characteristic ways in which research was assisted by Banks, and collecting promoted by his activities. It should be remembered, too, that of the many applications to Banks concerning access to the British Museum's collections, a considerable number were to do with antiquities and the Museum's library. They came not just from scholars in Britain, but from foreign visitors as well, and Banks was just as eager to help with these as with applications related to natural history. His reputation for organizing collecting in the capital was well known across Europe and beyond, as was his willingness to help intellectuals visiting London Learned Society.

Reorganization and the Basement: 1805–10

The compilation of general histories through a single comprehensive collection of natural or artificial objects became increasingly impracticable for private individuals and groups. As described, this appears to have been recognized at the Royal Society, which relinquished its Repository in 1781. Even large public institutions like the British Museum found it harder and harder to accommodate and preserve all they received. Indeed, in this period attempts at the Museum to find space for and to organize just the natural history collections demonstrate the difficulties a national body confronted, with Museum officers still struggling to complete a survey of British natural history at the end of Banks's life. Added to this was the difficulty of accommodating vast new collections of antiquities, and impressive libraries, all of which started to arrive with greater frequency from the turn of the century.

Banks's personal example certainly corroborates the view that specialist collections were a useful alternative to retaining everything natural and artificial a major collector might obtain. In many ways he anticipated a time when specialist departments and institutions would be established to handle different types of material, and in this section we consider how these started to emerge in response to the nineteenth-century influx. We also see how Banks tried to assign material to those places where it could best be stored and used, a principle he followed when dealing with collections throughout the London area. This did not mean that it was always possible for collections to remain intact. As with the history of Banks's own collections up to the twentieth century, the separation, exchange and circulation of material was an important element in the way most collections shifted and were treated prior to a place finally being found for them. No less important were the demands on staff, their need for more and better equipment and the necessity of room to house everything. At the Museum limitations in all of these areas were felt acutely from the turn of the century, and the conditions in which some collections were kept proved less than ideal. In such circumstances some were simply refused as too expensive or large to cope with. Others, such as those held in the basement of the Museum, were sent elsewhere, a controversial decision that requires examination in terms of how the collections were being distributed in the capital. These are therefore some of the central factors affecting natural history at the Museum, and collecting generally, especially from 1800 onwards.

In June 1805 a review of the Museum was initiated partly in response to the growing pressures. It was a wide-ranging review, and involved 'what is wanting to be done in each department of the Museum (reports concerning which, were this day delivered in)'. In keeping with what was by then a regular Museum procedure, the matter was referred to a committee, which consisted on this occasion 'of the Speaker of the House of Commons, Sir Joseph Banks and Mr. Sloane'.[65] Having taken these steps, at a general meeting held on 13 July orders were issued to every department, and preparations for the Annual Visitation were directed to be made in Natural History. These preparations entailed the cleaning and cataloguing of specimens, and inscriptions being placed in the different rooms.[66] Each was a welcome improvement, but more important changes than this had become necessary. As a result, in the reports and meetings that followed, the Museum's overall structure was changed to reflect disciplinary divisions increasingly apparent due to the greater size and complexity of the collections.[67] In effect, these changes ushered in recognizably modern forms of organization to the Museum and its collections, with the consequence that the Museum became much less like the mixed cabinets of the past. From this time onwards specialist departments were created to manage the collections, separating them out, and sorting and cataloguing them with gradually increasing coverage and competence.

The reviews directly affected Edward Whitaker Gray because the natural history collections were found to be in generally poor condition, and, following his death late in December 1806, fundamental restructuring was implemented. The main change came in February 1807 when the antiquities were split from natural history, thereby separating the 'natural' from the 'artificial', and ordering knowledge in a more modern way, although the ethnographic material remained within the new Department of Natural History and Modern Curiosities. Taylor Combe was put in charge of the Department of Antiquities and Coins, while George Shaw became responsible for Natural History and Modern Curiosities. We see in this change a process that led ultimately to the development of a new Natural History Museum at Kensington later in the nineteenth century, one founded on collections from Sloane and Banks, but distinct from the antiquities left at Bloomsbury. Banks had been ordering and distributing his own collections along systematic lines from an early date, and was fully aware of the need to discriminate between different types of material. In this sense he may be regarded as part of a trend in public and private collecting that became more powerful with time, and which had taken firm root at the British Museum by 1807.

Gray's death provided a natural break with the past, and at an important moment in the history of the Museum new staff were needed to fill posts in major new departments. Banks had helped gain Combe his appointment at the Museum in 1803, and in July 1806 Banks was also asked to look at home and abroad for a naturalist to join the Museum staff, probably in anticipation of the impending changes.[68] He settled on Charles Konig, with whom he had a close working relationship. Konig was a German naturalist who had been employed as an assistant in Banks's library and herbarium from 1801 to 1807. Initially interested in botany, Konig later turned to mineralogy, and was made Keeper of Natural History and Modern Curiosities in 1813, also becoming Foreign Secretary at the Royal Society in 1830.[69] Konig's assistant in 1814 was the talented William Elford Leach, like Banks a particularly generous benefactor of the Museum.

These additions strengthened the staff responsible for natural history at the Museum, but there was still a great deal for each of them to do. Faced with so much, some officers tended to concentrate on one area rather than try to cover everything. Leach, for example, favoured zoology and entomology, while Konig came to prefer earth sciences. Konig's single-minded devotion to the earth sciences would itself have implications for other collections at the Museum in due course, but, on starting at the Museum his botanical expertise was the obvious thing on which to draw. Among the first tasks considered for him was to look at cataloguing the plants and seeds 'scientifically', and to prepare a catalogue of all the books in Natural History. Konig's supervision was given to Banks,[70] and the catalogue of books to emulate was that of Banks's own library, as completed by Jonas Dryander.[71] These things show how strong the linkage between Bloomsbury and Soho Square was, with staff being supplied to the Museum by Banks, and the catalogue of his library providing a model for those being developed at the Museum. They also show that the year 1807 saw some evidence of renewed vigour in the work and organization of the Museum.

In March 1807, Shaw, an outgoing personality and a truly prolific publisher on natural history (invariably using the Linnaean system), suggested that a general catalogue of the animal kingdom was needed. He wanted it to start with 'the Linnæan Mammalia, & proceed thro' the remaining branches, some of which having been already prepared by Dr. Solander, Dr. Gray, etc.'. Shaw's was an ambitious plan, and he referred to the basement, where he thought there were many things worth cleaning and displaying. For the time being, however, he wanted to continue sorting the shells he was working on, and to commence selecting material for the general catalogue of the animals in the Museum.[72] It was the beginning of a contentious and difficult series of events, for Shaw was soon complaining quite bitterly about the dispersal of collections, and especially about the state of the basement, arguing that it was not possible to catalogue in the 'lower rooms'.

So decayed was much of the material there that William Clift of the Royal College of Surgeons was in the habit of calling at the Museum to obtain specimens for lecture material. News of the situation must have filtered back to the College through Clift and others. Naturalists on the continent were certainly aware of it. Pieter Camper wrote to Banks as early as June 1786 to say that the osteological collection in the basement was 'most shamefully neglected, and of a great value to my opinion'. In 1787 Camper went further when he advocated a clear-out of the basement, with 'what is Superfluous' being disposed of, and the rest being restored and reorganized.[73] Camper's was a drastic suggestion, but it was obvious that something needed to be done after years of neglect extending back well before Banks's time. Importantly, the need to act was at long last gaining support among a number of Museum officers who had become exasperated at the state of the basement.[74]

Shaw was not the only one with harsh things to say on the subject.[75] In May 1808 he and Joseph Planta inspected the area together, and they had many cabinets removed, much decayed 'rubbish' destroyed and quantities of duplicates set aside. This was an important step in the direction Camper had previously indicated, and as a result of what he saw, Planta requested that a standing committee be set up to give instructions about the 'very miscellaneous Accumulation' in the basement.[76] His comments were part of a report he made on the subject, dated 14 May 1808. The trustees responded immediately, and at a meeting on the day that Planta's report was read, Banks was appointed to lead a standing committee tasked with reviewing the articles Planta suggested should be brought up for display. The committee was also instructed to transfer all duplicates from every department into the basement and to ventilate and dry the basement rooms.[77]

It was a broad remit designed to address issues both Planta and Shaw had raised, but, due to fits of gout 'which seizd me a few days only after I receivd the commands of the Trustees,'[78] and a visit to his country estates, Banks was unable to report until the next year.[79] Banks saw this as an opportunity to remove material from the basement that might be of use elsewhere, but which was currently being neglected. This was consistent with his view regarding collections generally, and he also wanted to free much-needed space in which to store books and other material. He drafted his report early in February 1809, sending it to be checked by Charles Abbot, another Museum trustee and Speaker of the House of Commons. Abbot made some minor alterations to the report, and returned it to Banks that month, having approved of it. Banks then made a final draft, dated 11 March 1809.[80]

The sequence of events here is significant because in his report Banks advised separating the 'most interesting Articles' in the basement from the 'rubbish & lumber'. These were words used by all the officers to describe decayed material found in the basement, and Banks thought that such material should be left behind for sorting and disposal later. Of much more importance in his view were other collections languishing at that time in the damp. He listed these in his report, and they included some impressive scientific material, namely: the osteological collection; 'Monsters preservd in Spirits'; calculi (human and other animals); anatomical paintings, preparations and injections (probably from the Royal Society originally); mummies from Egypt and Teneriffe; birds and other animals in spirits; and a large collection of horns of various animals. This list appears to have been based on an undated report by Shaw, written about June 1808, in which Shaw stated that these items should be sold.[81] Although not the same in every detail, the two lists strongly resemble one another. Taking due notice of Shaw's earlier advice, then, and checking with other trustees, Banks produced his report after more than one attack of gout, and having been out of London for a while.[82]

Making one remarkable reference to the sensibilities of pregnant women, who he thought might be upset by the 'Monsters preservd in Spirits', attributing 'to them the blemishes & misconformations of their future of[f]spring', Banks argued that if the osteological and anatomical collections were not on display, and perhaps never could be displayed, they ought to be put to use in active study and analysis. A more suitable place than the basement of the British Museum was,

Banks suggested, alongside the 'Anatomical & Physiological Collections' of the late John Hunter, recently purchased by the nation, and housed at the Royal College of Surgeons. When he could, Banks tended to favour the College with such material, possibly because he knew what might happen to it at the Museum. The horns, however, were an exception since these were used to distinguish species. Banks thought they should be placed on show, as they once had been. Otherwise, the material Shaw had identified, and Banks had outlined, ought to be used in conjunction with the Hunterian collections, a slightly more convenient arrangement for Clift, who had been carrying off what he could anyway.[83]

The main emphasis in Banks's report fell on the public duty of the trustees, and the limited extent to which these collections were being utilized in the basement:

> it is submitted that it is almost a duty incumbent on the Trustees of the
> British Museum, who are in fact the Trustees of the Public, to transfer these
> things from an Establishment on which they are an evident burthen, to one
> where they will be of eminent utility, in promoting the best purposes for
> which it was originally endowd, that of furnishing Public Lectures for the
> advancement of Medical knowledge ...

Banks added that experimental learning would be encouraged by this transfer through the dissection of specimens, through demonstrations using them and through the chemical tests that could be performed on things like the calculi. The transfer of collections to enhance public benefits was a powerful argument, and one, no doubt, that had motivated the Royal Society when it finally gave up its Repository.

The weaknesses in Banks's position were just as apparent, despite his closing remark: 'I trust little if any thing of argument can be adducd on the opposite side ...'. They lay in the Museum's comprehensive approach to collections, which, while it caused inevitable problems of management, also meant that greater coverage was achieved at Bloomsbury than elsewhere. This had implications for those seeking large samples of material for comparison. If collections were broken up, these would be impossible to find. The depth and scope of the material at the British Museum was one of the significant advantages it offered, and the notion that such collections should be assessed only by their value as gallery material did not sufficiently address the issue of coverage.

Moreover, in response to Banks's recommendations Joseph Planta cogently and correctly argued that the removal of the osteological collections would be an especial loss for naturalists needing to study skeletons at the Museum.[84] His comments on the animals in spirit were equally convincing, drawing attention to their value to naturalists, and stressing their fate if used for things like public dissections. Another consideration was that the historical integrity of collections would be violated if they were broken up. Banks must have been aware of all these things.

However, he evidently felt that the lack of use of the collections was an overriding concern likely to jeopardize the material itself if it continued to rot in the dampness of the basement, or, worse, if it was consigned to the pyres successive officers lit in the Museum garden for objects that had deteriorated beyond repair.[85]

The basic thrust of Banks's argument was that the impressive size and quality of the Museum's collections would be easier to maintain if everything was thoroughly sorted. There was no suggestion that the collections should be wantonly dismantled simply to move them somewhere worse than the basement. It was more that leaving the basement in its current state was unacceptable, and however hard the choices before the trustees and officers, something now had to be done. Taking action raised the awkward question of what to do with collections that could not easily be placed on display, but which were valuable for research. There was nowhere else on site to put them, yet all were being neglected in the basement. Furthermore, a number of these collections were bulky or damaged, and some were both, so that the need for a final decision was pressing. In fact, the basement presented a series of genuinely difficult problems to solve, and was not dealt with lightly.[86]

At a general meeting on 15 April 1809 discussion took place 'so far as relates to the referring to the Consideration of Sir Joseph Banks, the Report of Dr. Shaw, respecting the Articles in the Basement Story; and the Minutes of the meeting on the 11th of March last, when the Report of Sir Joseph Banks was read ...'.[87] Banks's report was tabled, and then the trustees, among whom were Banks and Abbot, accompanied Planta and the staff of the Natural History Department to the basement and to Rooms 9, 10 and 12 upstairs, where the natural history collections were also deposited. For some of the trustees a visit to the basement might well have been an unusual occurrence, but not for Banks. With them went Everard Home, a close friend and personal physician to Banks. Home was a trustee and professor at the Royal College of Surgeons, and he stated that the material in the basement that Shaw had identified and Banks had then surveyed ought to join the Hunterian collections. According to the minutes, this included: the osteological collection; the monsters in spirits; the anatomical paintings; the preparations and injections; '& finally all the Articles of the above description in the several Rooms so visited'. An order was given by the meeting for a valuation of this material to be made, and the officers were also asked to respond to Banks's report, which they did, making pertinent comments and observations.[88]

After this the way was open for the transfer to take place. At a general meeting in April, the officers' reports having been read, a unanimous decision was taken to pass to the Royal College of Surgeons 'The whole of the Osteological Collection The Monsters in Spirits The Anatomical Preparations, Injections & Paintings The Stuffed Quadrupeds, & other Animals & Articles of Natural History of Animals at present deposited in the Basement Story ... And in the Rooms above ... all the

Calculi, Human & Brute, & all Duplicates of Natural History [that] are unfit to be preserved in this Museum'.[89] This represented more than Banks had stipulated, being an enormous amount in all. The horn collection stayed on Banks's recommendation, one that all the officers endorsed. This was to be mounted in the galleries for the public. In May Mr Lochee, of the valuers King and Lochee, set the price of the basement collections intended for transfer at £180. The material was then purchased by the Royal College of Surgeons for its museum, to which Clift carried everything in wooden boxes.[90]

Thus the basement was cleared of its more important collections, most leaving the Museum for another public institution, one with a specialist interest in them. By November 1809 the majority had been moved to the Royal College of Surgeons, and Shaw was eager to know whether he could dispose of what he termed 'worthless' shells and insects that were left behind.[91] What remained in the basement was used to supplement other Museum collections, or exchanged or given away. The remainder suffered the fate reserved for so-called lumber and would have been destroyed. Shaw had suspended work on the ornithological collection while the basement required attention, but he now resumed cataloguing the birds, using the Linnaean system that he employed without deviation.[92] As he did so, he selected duplicates to be sent to the Royal College of Surgeons, and he also made a point of reporting that he was happy with the state of the Department.[93] Whatever else Shaw achieved, this was an assessment somewhat at variance with the actual condition of the collections at the end of his tenure in 1813. In fact, Shaw did little more than his predecessor had to care for the physical state of the collections.

Other officers joined Shaw in the task of assessing the remnants in the basement. Konig applied his botanical knowledge in sifting through the vegetable products left there. Finding a number of things that might be preserved, he awaited Banks's opinion on them.[94] In February 1810 Banks was formally asked by the other trustees to inspect the seeds and fruits Konig had identified, and to give instructions on where to place them.[95] In this way Banks continued to assist the officers in the hard and dirty work of sorting through the basement, where little if anything might otherwise have been done. The mutual reliance that grew out of such involvement is particularly apparent in the relationship between Konig and Banks, with Konig seeking Banks's 'Judgement & Assistance' in the examination of dried plants on the tables in Rooms 9 and 10.[96] Besides donations, Banks was willing to give considerable time and energy to Museum activities. This led to a degree of dependence on him among some officers. His fellow trustees also seemed willing to ask him to tackle projects in the Museum that they did not feel sufficiently qualified or perhaps inclined to attempt themselves. As a result, Banks was still being called to the basement during the summer months of 1810 to see what the Museum officers were doing there.

In July Planta reported that he had made a 'considerable clearance of the unimportant contents of the Base Story' with help from Shaw, Combe, Konig and Banks. He said that 'all the Articles decidedly useless, & for which no price cou[l]d be expected, had been destroyed; but much that is of little value had been retained, on which it was meant to bestow further examination'.[97] In October Planta referred to removing what he called 'lumber' from the basement, and selling several old glass cases.[98] As these things disappeared the issue of the basement clearance was finally drawing to a close, although ill-feeling lingered between officers at both of the institutions involved. Some felt that certain collections should not have been transferred, while others complained that what they had received was not of a good enough quality. It seems unlikely in these circumstances that there was ever going to be an easy way to please everybody, especially when dealing with such a long-standing and difficult problem. It is equally unlikely that Banks was happy with the way the basement had been neglected. The care with which he looked after his own library and herbarium provides a stark contrast to the basement situation that he confronted in 1808.

Banks's judgment was by no means infallible, as the basement episode shows, but his assistance was unflagging. Having been asked to look into the basement, he was determined to see the job finished according to the best decisions he was able to make in consultation with Museum staff and other trustees. One way of coping with such a large problem was to assign the collections to another public institution with specialist interests and capabilities. While we see Banks gradually divesting himself of his own collections, and assisting in the transferral of those of private societies and individuals to the British Museum, we can also see that material was sometimes channelled away from Bloomsbury. As one instance of this, Banks and some of the Museum officers appear to have thought that certain basement collections would be better stored and used at the Royal College of Surgeons. It would not be until the Keepership of John Edward Gray that the Museum's osteological collections started to be rebuilt with the acquisition of Brian Hodgson's collection of skins and bones, and the opening in 1848 of a vault, once again in the basement, for osteology.

The basement episode illustrates the network of organizations and individuals controlling London's collections during this period, and how they sought to distribute those collections among bodies that might make best use of them. It also illustrates how hard it sometimes was to make decisions about where to allocate material when there was no convenient specialist institution dedicated to natural history. When the British Museum started to struggle with such collections, many of which were difficult to preserve, the options available for relocating them were limited, even in a city like London. London Learned Society eventually adapted to cope with this, and signs of that may perhaps be discerned in the basement episode, for later in the nineteenth century new museums, libraries and other repositories were built to help deal with precisely the problems that Banks's generation faced. This did not necessarily mean that collections from the previous century remained intact, and separating major collections into specialist institutions continued to raise questions of the kind discussed here.

It was this process that eventually sundered the working partnership of Banks's natural history library and herbarium in the 1880s, a very bad decade for the unity of his greatest collections. In this decade Banks's herbarium was moved to Kensington to become part of the new Natural History Museum situated there, while his library was kept at Bloomsbury, a division Banks certainly never intended when he bequeathed both of these collections to the nation. Additionally, major private sales of his surviving papers started to take place, thereby dispersing his correspondence and memoranda. The increased concentration of collections in public hands meant that some were reorganized or relocated to suit prevailing ideas and the priorities of the institutions that took possession of them. Those collections that that did not come to rest in public institutions, because they were refused by or removed from them, were often sold off.[99] The fate of Banks's various papers, which never found a single permanent home, are perhaps the most obvious example of this.

So there were paths out of public ownership for material, some of which was originally donated to the British Museum by private individuals and societies. Such paths led to other public bodies or back to private hands through things like sales and exchanges, and some of Banks's own gifts to the Museum were undoubtedly disposed of in these ways. At the British Museum considerations of space, funds, technical capabilities and staffing are essential to understanding how the natural history collections developed, not just in Banks's day, but well into the nineteenth century. Throughout the nineteenth century debates took place regarding which collections could be accommodated at Bloomsbury, and whether moving some away was a wise course. One proposal was to make further transfers to the Royal College of Surgeons, but this was not done.

As a result, the zoological and other natural collections stayed at Bloomsbury, and continued to grow. As they increased, especially with the addition of the collections of the Zoological Society of London, the reputation of the Museum for the conduct of science was enhanced. Housing the collections remained a problem, but a major release of material on the scale described above did not take place again until the removal of all the natural history collections to the new specialist museum constructed at Kensington. When it was finally completed, this museum was intended to avoid confusion and conflict with other Bloomsbury collections by drawing a firm line between the management of material from separate disciplines. It meant that from 1883 onwards the British Museum no longer contained a major type of founding collection, one for which it had originally been renowned. Instead, from this time onwards its fame rested more on antiquities, and on its library and other man-made products gathered from around the world.

Coordinating Zoology: Some Acquisitions, 1810–16

Well before Planta's clearance, in March probably, Shaw had almost finished his catalogue of ornithology, and had commenced 'the Linnæan *Amphibia*, a clan in which the Museum is particularly rich'.[100] In May of 1811 he finished this, and proposed continuing with the 'fishes'.[101] Whereas Shaw had struggled with such work before, he now seemed able to make more rapid progress. In his final years at the Museum, then, Shaw at least had the satisfaction of being able to cover ever more of the specimens and collections he anticipated cataloguing in March 1807. Thus, by May 1812 he had finished his catalogue of fish, and wanted to move on to the molluscs, and after that the crustaceans and insects.[102] By February 1813 he reached the molluscs, when the arrival of interesting Brazilian insects distracted him. He wanted to investigate these immediately for any new species.[103] In April he thought of arranging an exhibition of insects for visitors, 'which is to be considered as rather popular than strictly scientific'.[104] But this was something he never completed, as later in 1813 he died, and in September Charles Konig was made Under-Librarian in the Department of Natural History.[105] Konig's appointment was a significant one. He was committed to the Museum, and built up its mineralogical collections in particular, remaining an officer until he died in 1851.

Another important appointment came in 1814 when William Elford Leach was made Konig's assistant. During his seven years at the Museum, Leach worked hard to improve the collections, especially those in entomology. In doing so he combined with Banks to organize the purchase of more collections, and he also used sales and exchanges to increase the Museum's holdings. Leach was a man of independent wealth like Banks, and he was no less devoted to the Museum. From the start he set about a variety of tasks with characteristic energy (agile and slight, Leach would leap two or three steps at a time when climbing the Grand Staircase of Montagu House, and was apparently able to vault a stuffed zebra in the upper gallery). As other officers did, Leach sought to establish an exchange network with a number of museums, referring in one of his first reports to contacts with the museum at Turin.[106] In April he was occupied sorting the animals without vertebrae. When organizing collections, Leach rejected the Linnaean system in favour of the natural one used by Georges Cuvier and other French philosophers, most of whom he met and knew. This was an advance on previous thinking, and made Leach a leader among Museum naturalists breaking with Linnean nomenclature. He was also interested in molluscs, and in a busy first year wanted to incorporate quantities of Museum material into the Cracherode collection to make that collection more complete. This done, he planned to 'adopt it for the use of Conchological Students'.[107] In July he set about reducing the insects into genera, requesting cabinets to display them.[108] He could report, too, that recently-purchased birds were on show.

Thus, Leach covered a full range of Museum work in his duties, and if he did not always get along with other officers, notably Planta and Konig, both of whose orders he was apt to ignore, his contribution seems to have been understood and valued by trustees like Banks. Indeed, there are a number of examples of Leach working with Banks to enlarge the natural history collections, just as there are for Konig and Banks. Both Leach and Konig were willing to coordinate agreed opinions with Banks on the value of possible purchases and the organization of natural history in the Museum, opinions which the other trustees then found hard to refuse. In February 1815, for example, Leach suggested purchasing collections belonging to Mr Wilkin (probably Simon Wilkin (1790–1862), a collector and publisher). Leach reported that Wilkin had 'resolved to dispose of his collection containing the fourteen hundred insects collected in New Holland, Brasil and North America, for the sum of 100£, and as I am extremely anxious to increase and to render respectable the collection of the Museum, in this as in all other departments, I have taken the liberty of entreating you to offer this cabinet to the Trustees at their next general meeting ...'.[109]

This, written to Banks on 9 February, shows how Leach sought to expand the Museum collections. He was not afraid of pushing Banks in such matters either. On the day of the trustees' general meeting, 11 February, Leach wrote again to emphasize that Wilkin's collection 'contains two thousand four hundred insects, (inste[a]d of the number mistated in my last note) that is nearly 1,000 more than I mentioned'.[110] Characteristic in his generosity, Leach promised that 'Should the trustees purchase Mr Wilkin's cabinet, I will in addition to the collection of neu-ropterous insects & British fishes, give to the Museum three drawers of rare foreign insects (which I purchased at a time when I intended to form a collection of exotic insects for myself) amongst which are a fine specimen of Scarabæus longinanus of which species five specimens only are known ...'. Banks responded positively to these urgings, and ensured that the purchase was approved, with thanks being given to Leach by the trustees.[111] The working arrangement between Leach and Banks proved effective, and it operated for the remaining years of Banks's life.

In 1815, while Konig was occupied with the purchase of Baron Von Moll's collections,[112] Leach was concentrating on crustaceans and preparing to move the birds from their room.[113] In due course the old Bird Room would receive British zoology,[114] and the growth of this collection was to be a theme in the relationship between Leach and Banks. A related theme arose from the grow-ing awareness that a preoccupation with foreign flora and fauna had tended to distort collecting, and consequently British natural history had been somewhat neglected. Thus, while Banks maintained a characteristically broad range of donations, it appears that there were concerted efforts to sharpen the focus of collecting at Bloomsbury. These efforts were part of a Museum-wide approach to collecting that gained impetus in the last ten years of Banks's life, with more than one department being involved. In Natural History there was an attempt to create a more comprehensive British zoological collection, and to form a British mineralogy and also a geological collection. Similarly, from 1811 to 1812 Joseph Planta initiated plans 'to compleat the Collection of Printed Books in the Library respecting the British Islands, & the several Possessions of the British Empire'.[115] Such an approach seems to have been founded on the hope that by concentrating like this achievable improvements would be made, and that those referring to the Museum would find adequate collections for the country of which it was the main repository.

A collection became available in February 1816 that helped to further such aims. This belonged to George Montagu, an ex-army captain from the American colonies and a capable naturalist, who made good progress in the scientific study of British fauna, especially in Devon. His work and collections showed his range, including ornithology, molluscs, crustaceans, fish, sponges and sea anemones.[116] At a meeting on 10 February the trustees were told that 'the Collection of British Zoology made by the late Colonel Montagu of Knowle in Devonshire, valued at £1200, will be an useful addition to the Museum'.[117] The trustees were also told that 'Dr. Leach ... has a Collection of British Crustacea, Shells, and Insects, tending to render the first-mentioned Collection still more complete than it is at present, valued at £600, which he would be ready to give to the Museum in the event of the former Collection being purchased ...'. By attaching his own gift Leach was again trying to encourage the Museum to acquire a collection, and the trustees decided to refer the purchase to Banks and to the Treasury.[118]

Banks was sympathetic to Leach's plans, and reported to the trustees that Montagu's collection was the 'most extensive of British Zoology offered to Sale'. He evidently felt that this was an opportunity to develop the Museum's collections in an area where they needed to be more comprehensive. This was consistent with emerging Museum policy at this time, but it also seems to have been a view Banks himself held. According to a rough note by Henry Ellis, Secretary of the Museum from 1814 to 1828, Banks thought that 'the British Museum should possess as complete a Collection as possible of the Zoology of the British Isles, tho' he [Banks] does not admit the expediency of forming a complete or even an Extensive Collection of Exotic Zoology'.[119] Such was Ellis's version of the views and language expressed by Banks. However, his note certainly reinforces the sense of a contemporary feeling that Britain's zoology had been neglected. Indeed, notwithstanding the many foreign specimens Banks donated, he had previously suggested that this was the case, so that we may understand Ellis's note as high-lighting a long-standing problem that Banks and others sought to address.

Some years before, in 1788, Banks wrote about this bias towards collecting specimens from outside Britain. He mentioned it in a letter to Robert Ferryman, a clergyman living near Bath.[120] In his letter Banks commented that 'as far as my knowledge of the world will enable me to judge the Science of Zoology is not at present sufficiently in vogue to allow any professor of it whose scene of action is no larger than the British Islands to deserve for his Labors such support ...'[121] It was a discouraging view, and if the situation had not improved significantly since 1788, increased emphasis at the Museum on acquiring British specimens and collections was one way of compensating. This did not, of course, preclude accepting foreign material. The balance of Museum collecting was being adjusted, but foreign zoology could not be altogether shunned without risking deficiencies in important areas. This seems to have been generally understood, for even as the Montagu purchase was being considered, Museum officers continued to promote a full range of collections through donations and exchanges.

In fact, what Banks and Leach were doing was to make the strongest case they could at a senior level for purchasing Montagu's collection. The appeal of concentrating on Britain's zoology as a means of achieving worthwhile results in a specific area was being emphasized to trustees who might not have shared Banks's and Leach's passion for natural history. Banks was certainly pushing the other trustees into a purchase by stressing its necessity, with, it appears, Leach's full knowledge and support. Indeed, early in March Leach went to see Banks at Soho Square, writing subsequently to the Speaker about this, restating that Banks advised the purchase of Montagu's collection.[122] In his June report, offering specimens from his own cabinet, Leach hoped to create 'the most complete assemblage of the animals of Great Britain that has hitherto been made ....'[123] Encouraged by such a prospect, the purchase was authorized by the trustees, 'Sir Joseph Banks having signified his opinion that the price is reasonable and the acquisition valuable to the Museum'.[124] The sum, paid in instalments over three years, was £1,100.

It was Leach who suggested exhibiting British zoology in the old Bird Room,[125] and a further twist in negotiations was the offer made by James Francis Stephens, a Victualling Officer at the Admiralty, and a keen entomologist. Following the incorporation of Montagu's collections, Stephens wanted to give specimens from his own extensive cabinet that were not in the Museum.[126] The trustees decided to write to the Admiralty to gain Stephens leave during August so that he could go through his material, and this was granted.[127] Thus, we can see that British zoology at the Museum was considerably strengthened in 1816.[128] By November Leach wanted to undertake an extended tour of Britain looking for 'peculiar Species of Zoology', paying special attention to the coasts. This was 'for the purpose of collecting them for the Museum', because, he added pointedly, 'the

Trustees have resolved to confine their attention to British Zoology ...'[129] Leach's request was granted, and at their meeting the trustees also gave him permission to exchange insects 'at present wanting in the Museum Collection'. However, the trustees laid down strict conditions about the period of any tour and how to make up time afterwards. This, and the tone they adopted towards him, might well have provoked Leach to exceed the duration allowed by three months, which did not endear him to Planta or Konig. When Planta wrote asking Leach to return, Leach simply requested another three weeks off. When he did eventually get back to the Museum in early 1817, Leach resumed work sorting through the zoological collections, while the old Bird Room was being readied for the British zoology to which he had contributed so much.[130]

Final Years: 1816–20

Overall, the policy remained to increase collections based on the best quality material available through purchase, exchange or donation. This was pursued under financial limits that sometimes meant when one collection was bought another could not be afforded. Despite this, by the end of Banks's life some officers reported that certain natural history collections were unrivalled in their scope and standard in Britain. If the Museum was able to stand comparison with its European counterparts in natural history, then these were the areas in which its main strengths lay. The role of Leach, a man who never had to worry about his income, and who was sometimes not overly concerned about his attendance either, was an important factor in this.

Donations continued to arrive, and, as if to prove that items from abroad were still readily accepted by the Museum, in 1817 Banks presented 'two Varieties of the British ringed Snake; two Nests of the Edible Swallow of Java ... a Lemur from Madagascar ... and a horned Chameleon ...'[131] He was enriching the Museum in much the way he had always done.[132] His working relationship with Leach was still functioning too, with both men cooperating when the late John Francillon's collections were offered for sale in April 1817. These included insect specimens and drawings of the insects and birds of Georgia. On inspecting the Francillon collections Leach reported seeing '22242 specimens, 10832 species of insects and 5037 figures exhibiting the changes of the insects of Georgia together with figures of 266 species of American birds and above 1,000 figures of insects and birds on single sheets of paper', the whole being offered at a price of £1,400. He predicted that if the Museum bought the collections parts of its own holdings would be the finest in Britain, and by exchanging duplicates they could become the finest in the world.[133]

The Francillon collections were auctioned in three parts, in May and July 1817, and then in June 1818, the latter two sales being predominantly of British and then foreign insects. In the first week of July 1817 Leach presented to the Museum 600 species of insects gathered from Falais, and, in addition to that, 800 species of Brazilian insects collected by the naturalist William Swainson were also donated. At the same time Leach wanted the trustees to acquire the Francillon drawings, and any insects that might be sold at a moderate price.[134] However, late in July Leach's hopes were disappointed. The Treasury responded that in the 'present Circumstances of the Country', Francillon's collections could not be afforded.[135] So, as work on the collections progressed this year, Leach identified a number of zoological duplicates as a potential source of funding to purchase some of the Francillon insects. He thought that £100 might be raised by auctioning this Museum material, of which he wanted to spend no more than £70.[136] Purchases were duly made at the final Francillon auction in June 1818, especially of the three orders of Hymenoptera, Neuroptera and Diptera. This was done on Banks's authority and after obtaining his advice. Leach contented himself with the thought that the new material rendered 'that part of the collection of the Museum the most perfect in the world'.[137] The outlay of a mere £40 was covered by the Museum.[138]

Once again, Leach had found in Banks a useful trustee for furthering his plans, but the formidable financial constraints that prevented the Museum from buying even the most highly recommended collections should be noted. Failure to enter the market for collections at this time was mostly due to poor economic conditions quite beyond the control of any single trustee. The European economy was depressed following the Napoleonic wars, and this affected spending by the British government, a circumstance that in turn curtailed the activities of the Museum. That the refusal of some purchases caused bitterness cannot be denied, but such acrimony, like most personal rivalries and differences, counted far less than the real restrictions by which trustees and officers were circumscribed.

The year 1818 was notable because interest in the possibility of a Northwest Passage was once again stirring. Two missions were dispatched in search of this elusive sea route, which generations of explorers hoped would lead from the Atlantic to the North Pacific. For years governments, the Admiralty, merchants and the Royal Society had periodically revived the idea of discovering a northern link between the two oceans, and the 1818 missions were launched following reports that Arctic ice was retreating and a path might at last have opened up. The missions, each comprising two ships, departed in spring at the suggestion of Banks as President of the Royal Society. One mission was to Baffin Bay, under Captain John Ross in HMS *Isabella* and Lieutenant William Edward Parry in HMS *Alexander*. The other was to the north of Greenland and Spitzbergen, under Captain David Buchan in HMS *Dorothea* and Lieutenant John Franklin in HMS *Trent*. Both carried many instruments for experiments, and personnel to conduct them, but neither revealed a great deal about the geography of the regions visited. Despite brave efforts to reach higher latitudes, ice forced Franklin back, 80° 34′ being the farthest north he travelled. Meanwhile, Ross penetrated to 75° in Baffin Bay, where ice was also found. He wrongly concluded that there was no outlet through Lancaster Sound, and so returned to England. All four ships were back at Deptford by late November 1818.

Although the primary aims of the missions were not achieved, particularly since Lancaster Sound had eluded Ross, they yielded other results in the form of collections that were made. As was customary with such voyages, material from the collections was destined for the British Museum. Thus, on 14 November the trustees were informed that Buchan had written on behalf of the Lords of the Admiralty to present a 'List of Specimens of Natural History'.[139] The letter and accompanying list still exist. They detail a number of starfish brought up from depth, and other marine fauna, as well as rocks collected on Spitzbergen, and 'Coral Rock' gathered at sea from a depth of 220 fathoms. Under 'Miscellaneous' Buchan listed the remains of a male polar bear and 'a large Male Walrus', with other walrus parts. Man-made items were listed too. These included four decorated metal buttons from 'Coffins' found under a 'heap of Stones'. The buttons were located among a number of graves on an island in Fair Haven, and were uncovered on 4 July. Minerals, shells, horns from reindeer and an arctic fox in his winter fur also appear.[140]

Leach was ordered to have the birds that Buchan presented stuffed and put on display, exhibitions of birds always being popular with the public.[141] On 12 December Leach reported on these, and on other gifts from Ross, plus some from the astronomer and future President of the Royal Society Edward Sabine, who also travelled north on the missions.[142] Leach could report, as well, that Banks had donated a new species of goat from the Himalayan Mountains. Later in December yet more material arrived. Ross gave 'an immense Polar Bear, a bearded Seal, a variety of Greenland Dog, and twenty one Skins of Birds', while Sabine presented '35 Species of Marine Animals, consisting of Fishes, Mollusca, Vermes, Medusa, and intestinal Worms, from Baffin's Bay'.[143] Such were the gifts from the missions of which Ross called Banks 'the father', and in their range they reflect collections that had been arriving at the Museum from other voyages during more than fifty years of global exploration.[144] In the same month Konig reported on the minerals that were donated. Most of the fragments brought back were of a 'primitive formation, such as granite, mica slate, primitive hornblende-rock &c'. More had been sent than was required by the Museum, and he proposed forwarding duplicates to 'the Revd Mr Buckland, Prof of Geology in the University of Oxford'.[145]

Conclusion

In April 1817 Banks announced to the trustees that he had received letters from William John Burchell, then living in Fulham, but formerly resident at the Cape of Good Hope, and a great explorer and naturalist. Burchell wished to donate a collection of animals 'of the Antelope and Giraffe kind', on condition that he reserved the right to describe them himself.[146] This was approved, although late in 1819 and early in 1820 Burchell complained that his collection had not been stuffed and mounted.[147] The trustees therefore decided to look into the state of preservation of specimens in the Natural History Department. Thus, Banks was appointed to the last standing committee in which he would participate, to examine the state of specimens 'still remaining unpreserved; and to give such directions as may be necessary for the preservation of the same and for the setting up of such parts of the Collection as they may think require it …'.[148]

However, it was all rather late in the day for Banks, who died in June 1820. As we have seen, he had willingly assisted the Museum's officers in coordinated attempts to develop parts of zoology and entomology, which were not, it must be admitted, his principal interests in natural history. Despite these efforts the concentrated attention that zoology in particular required would have to wait for later generations. Nevertheless, it still seems reasonable to conclude that, along with everything else, Banks had done a considerable amount to help as a trustee, especially in terms of the donations he made and purchases that he supported. Similarly, Leach had tried to improve the collections and to care for them, but by 1822 he was also gone, having resigned due to ill health. This was an especial loss for zoology and entomology at the Museum, because Leach was a man of initiative and energy, who did a great deal to modernize the approach to science at Bloomsbury. Not since Daniel Solander had quite such a talented naturalist been responsible for the collections. At one point he may even have been Banks's choice to take charge of the Natural History department, but neither man lived to see this happen. In 1821 control was given instead to John George Children, whose background was not in natural history.[149] That the exertions of Banks and Leach had limited overall impact may partly be due to the difficult financial circumstances the Museum operated under, and these have already been referred to, but a lack of staff of Leach's calibre in the years that followed was also a factor.

Both Banks and Leach continued their efforts for as long as they could. In 1819 Leach was at work on foreign and British corals and shells, and in July he reported that he had presented to the Museum corallines collected in various parts of the world, including some found by Banks with Cook.[150] The last twelve months had been good for the Museum in Leach's view. He wrote that 'the Museum has been very considerably enriched, by specimens of Birds and Quadrupeds presented by the Admiralty, by Sir J. Banks, and the Hudson's Bay Company, Mr Bowdich and by the contribution of various individuals', himself included.[151] In the same report, one written in May, he offered an important collection of classified coral-lines for £20. These came from the collection of Louis Dufresne, who worked at the Muséum National d'Histoire Naturelle, and Leach, with his usual enthusiasm, commented that they were 'almost indispensable to the Museum'. Leach main-tained his pace into 1820, when he was working not only on shells, but on birds as well. In May Leach requested bottles and spirit to better preserve 'a vast number of very rare animals in Spirit, which have been presented by Sir J. Banks; Major Smith and Dr Meryon; as well as those lately received from Mr Redman ...'.[152]

Banks's final lifetime donation had not yet arrived. That came in June, when Leach recorded a gift of fifty rare kinds of birds from Ceylon (Sri Lanka), probably sent to Banks by Alexander Moon, superintendent of the Royal Botanic Garden at Colombo.[153] Banks thereby presented items of current interest to Leach's work at the Museum, a fitting gesture at the end. By this time, though, it was necessary to rebuild the Museum to accommodate natural history and the many antiquities acquired in the last twenty years. All collections had grown considerably since 1800. In zoology, the British side had been refined and enlarged somewhat, and its foreign counterpart had increased as exploration of the globe continued. How-ever, we must note that in the years immediately after Leach and Banks there was probably less progress made at the Museum in zoology than in other branches of natural history.

Later on, nineteenth-century standards and organization were gradually introduced, and zoology caught up with other disciplines, such as those in the earth sciences. Thus, a more even balance was achieved in the treatment of natural history at the Museum, for which John Edward Gray deserves particular credit. Gray, who joined the Museum in the early 1820s in a junior position, became Keeper of the Zoological Branch in 1840, and it was he who made the zoological collections truly world class.[154] The great nephew of Edward Whitaker Gray, as a young man John was introduced to Banks by Leach, meeting many of the leading naturalists of the day at Soho Square. Few places could have provided a better start in London Learned Society than Banks's house, with its natural history col-lections and the stream of travellers, officials and philosophers who visited there. So far as Banks is concerned, we should regard him primarily as a great donor of material in natural history, and as someone who sought to obtain specimens for the Museum from numerous sources around the world. In these respects his con-tribution was similar to that made in ethnography. We might also notice in Banks a trustee who worked with Museum officers when asked to do so, and who actively supported their careers and plans to develop the collections. His involvement at this level reveals much about the efforts, techniques and limitations of collecting in this period, a period, nonetheless, of considerable change and growth.

4 INVESTIGATING NATURAL HISTORY: EXPANDING LIMITS AFTER 1800

The phase of commerce and exploration that yielded so little by way of knowledge of the Northwest Passage, or gains in fur trading, strengthened science and opened more of the seas and oceans. It coincided, as well, with a decade of relative peace. This lasted from the Treaty of Versailles in September 1783 to the declaration of war on England by revolutionary France in February 1793. With war voyages of discovery into the Pacific virtually ceased, and they resumed again only at the turn of the century. Then came a famous mission assisted by Banks, that of HMS *Investigator*, the Napoleonic Wars interrupting further similar missions until after 1815. The *Investigator* mission will be the subject of the next sections, and with it some of the political and scientific priorities that determined the course of exploration in this period. These show how Banks maintained relations with the Admiralty, and how the Royal Navy was incorporated into the Banksian network as a useful means of supplying London Learned Society with additional collections and information.

The final seafaring ventures that Banks participated in were to the Arctic North, where, as we have seen, ships went to search for a northern route to the Pacific in 1818. At about the same time, 1817 to 1820, Lieutenant Phillip Parker King sailed southwards in the cutter *Mermaid*. He surveyed the north-west coast of Australia, thereby completing the remaining gaps in earlier charts made by Matthew Flinders from 1802 to 1803. King's work showed what had already been established in arms and exploration, which was that Australia was now a British possession, something a French mission in the *Uranie*, under Louis de Freycinet, could do little to alter. King also carried with him another Kew collector under Banks's supervision, the capable Allan Cunningham. Cunningham dispatched the last plants from Australia that Banks would ever see.

Arrangements for Public Collections on Voyages of Discovery:
HMS Investigator, 1801–5

At the turn of the century it was still not clear whether Australia was a single landmass, and if not what divided it. Determining this would affect any claim to the continent as a whole, and establish what navigable routes to the interior might exist. Banks had been suggesting an equipped mission to open up the country since at least 1798,[1] and with the rising menace of Napoleon, French and British strategies in exploration were once again directed to the southern oceans.[2] Thus, when Banks provided passports for a French voyage to these waters, he also warned the First Lord of the Admiralty of a possible 'Political manoeuvre'.[3] So it was that the *Investigator* was hastily dispatched under Matthew Flinders partly as a British response to the launch from Le Havre on 19 October 1800 of the French vessels the *Géographe* and the *Naturaliste* under Nicolas Thomas Baudin.[4] The names of the French and indeed the British ships disguised with a fine Enlightenment veneer some of the real motives for their departure.

Nevertheless, in its scientific essentials the *Investigator* was following an established programme as defined by the example set on *Endeavour* and maintained by Banks. It deserves special mention here, for from the beginning the collections made were to be passed on to the British Museum after being assessed at Soho Square. Indeed, the small scientific party that Banks assembled signed an explicit agreement at Soho Square about the public ownership of these materials, and this detailed the terms under which the collections were to be used and distributed.[5] The party consisted of Robert Brown, an outstanding naturalist; Ferdinand Bauer and William Westall, two artists; Peter Good, a gardener, and John Allen, a miner from Derbyshire. Management of this group was delegated by the Admiralty to Banks, who also put forward Matthew Flinders as mission commander.[6] Flinders was an excellent choice. Brave and diligent, he was an experienced navigator who had previously corresponded with Banks about Australian exploration, and who went on to perform his arduous task with great determination.[7] By the time of the *Investigator* voyage, Banks's grasp of arrangements qualified him to take complete charge in the eyes of Admiralty officials like Evan Nepean. Writing as Secretary of the Admiralty, Nepean confirmed that 'Any proposal you make will be approved. The whole is left entirely to your decision.'[8] This freedom to organize missions allowed Banks to staff and equip them in ways that might not otherwise have been possible, and to extend the range of collecting in the Pacific.

The *Investigator* voyage is one of the most remarkable on record. Having recently married Ann Chappelle on 17 April 1801, Flinders departed Spithead in command of HMS *Investigator* on 18 July. He called at the Cape of Good

Hope before crossing the Indian Ocean, reaching Cape Leeuwin at the south-west edge of Australia on 6 December. Flinders spent nearly a month at nearby King George's Sound before surveying the Great Australian Bight. Working eastwards, Flinders lost seven crew when the longboat they were in failed to return from a trip to the mainland to find water. Cape Catastrophe is so named because of this sad event. Flinders then explored Spencer Gulf, surveying Port Lincoln, which was named in honour of his home county. Kangaroo Island was also charted, as was Yorke Peninsula and the Gulf of St Vincent. It was hoped during this stage that a strait leading northwards into the continent might be dis-covered, but instead on 8 April 1802 Flinders met Baudin sailing in the opposite direction. Cordial exchanges were made, and having breakfasted together the commanders carried on, the place of their meeting being named Encounter Bay. Flinders was an excellent navigator and produced reliable charts of the entire coast, later correcting Baudin's claim that much of the land west of Encounter Bay was discovered by the French and not earlier Dutch explorers.

Having sailed through Bass Strait, Flinders visited King Island, located between Australia and present-day Tasmania, this area proving exceptionally rich in plant and animal life. Then he visited Port Philip (Melbourne) before arriving at Port Jackson on 9 May. From here Flinders sent many specimen cases back to Britain, and left numbers of living plants with Philip Gidley King, the Governor of New South Wales. Flinders next followed in the wake of *Endeavour*, travelling up the east coast of Australia in company with the tender *Lady Nelson*. He explored Hervey and Keppel bays, and a group of small islands near the lat-ter. By mid-August he had reached the Great Barrier Reef, which he described, noting in particular its formation from coral. He also recognized and took into account the effect of a ship's iron fittings on its compass bearings. Flinders sailed on northwards some 500 miles before he passed through the Great Barrier Reef to open sea, reaching Cape York Peninsula and sailing through Torres Strait, between Australia and New Guinea. *Lady Nelson* had previously turned back owing to damage to her sliding keel and other technical difficulties, but Flinders carried on. He explored the Gulf of Carpentaria from November 1802 to March 1803, but the *Investigator*'s timbers were found to be in poor condition. Flinders sailed to the Dutch settlement at Timor, but, with no other ship available, he decided to sail westward and back round the south of Australia, becoming the first person to circumnavigate the continent. Port Jackson was reached again on 9 June 1803, after which Flinders sailed for home as a passenger in the storeship HMS *Porpoise*, only to be shipwrecked on a reef, now known as Wreck Reef. Flinders navigated the ship's cutter back to Sydney, rowing some 700 miles in two weeks, and arranged the rescue of the marooned crew.

Meanwhile, Brown and Bauer had continued their collecting, and so it was not until November 1805 that most of the scientific party were back in London with their collections following an epic mission disrupted primarily by the rotten state of some of the timber in the *Investigator*, the shipwreck of the vessel Flinders took for the return trip to England and his subsequent detention in Mauritius. On sailing into Port Louis in the schooner *Cumberland*, which Governor King had supplied for the journey home, Flinders found that the Peace of Amiens had collapsed, and that Britain and France were once more at war. From December 1803 to June 1810 he was confined on the island by its governor, a suspicious man who did not trust Flinders's passports, nor the largely rhetorical claim that science was neutral in this period. This was a tragedy for a bright, young officer. Following his eventual release and return to Britain, Flinders survived just long enough to see his account of the mission in print, dying on 19 July 1814, the day after *A Voyage to Terra Australis* was published.[9] He was only forty years old. Alongside the ordeals Flinders endured, and the collections the naturalists made, the circumnavigation of Australia must be ranked as one of the great historic feats of the mission he led, and he has also been credited with naming the continent of Australia.

At Soho Square, Banks supervised the disposal of the collections according to the contract drawn up at the beginning. Despite what had been lost on Wreck Reef in August 1803, Banks could report to the Admiralty that the packages of seeds sent back periodically by Brown were already growing at Kew, where they provided 'the newest ornaments of that extensive and possibly unparaleled collection'.[10] Banks concluded that the Admiralty would order the remaining collections to be deposited 'in the national repository of the British Museum', and he advised sending there a number of bird skins, about 150 in all, some animals that were damaged on the voyage, a case of insects and three boxes of minerals. The rest of the collections were to stay at Soho Square, where, on Banks's advice, Brown and Bauer were paid by the government to work on them. This extended employment followed the precedent set by the draughtsmen for Cook's second and third voyages, and did not depart significantly from the pattern of work emerging since Cook's first voyage, nor from known Admiralty procedures. The botanical material amounted to 3,600 plant species, and there were some 2,000 drawings by Bauer to assess as well. Banks estimated that three years would be required to organize the plants systematically, and to complete the most 'interesting part only of the immense collection of scetches'.

In the event, the problems of dealing with so many new species led Brown to use the system of the leading French botanist, Antoine Laurent de Jussieu, and to adapt it to his own needs. This, and the sheer quantity of plants to deal with, meant a delay until 1810 when Brown produced a short yet deeply influential volume called *Prodromus Florae Novae Hollandiae et Insulae Van-Diemen*.[11] Although it was not followed by a major publication based on the mission collections as a whole, Brown's *Prodromus* is recognized as one of the great early works in global taxonomy for botany. Meanwhile, Bauer prepared some of the finest botanical illustrations and engravings yet made, a number of which he published in three small fascicles of his own, *Illustrationes Florae Novae Hollandiae*.[12] The publications arising from the *Investigator* voyage were not great in number, and the mission itself certainly had limitations, yet scientifically important collections had been made, Flinders had accurately charted much of the coast of Australia, and the mission's impact was to be a lasting one, widely felt in Australia and the Pacific.

Resources and the Earth: Some Historical Points, 1798–1805

For all its problems, the *Investigator* mission paid greater attention to the earth than preceding British missions, and certainly more than Menzies was able to do with Vancouver. Of course, the number of naturalists who sailed in French missions exceeded those sent by the British. Strict economy was a consistent feature of British exploration, and something Banks complained about on more than one memorable occasion, his withdrawal from Cook's second circumnavigation being perhaps the most famous example of his disapproval at arrangements for a voyage. The restrictions placed on collecting rocks and minerals during the *Investigator* mission, ones Banks warned Brown about,[13] were determined only in part by Banks's own emphasis on botany. There were obvious limits to what was physically possible for a small team on a ship like *Investigator*.

Nevertheless, with some difficulty Banks found a miner near his estate at Overton, in Derbyshire. Holding out the prospect that precious metals might be found during the mission, Banks wrote to his steward at Overton, William Milnes, admonishing him that 'if the real advantage of the engagement was known abundance of your people would be desirous of engaging in it, and if I get one from Cornwall, which I must do if I fail in Derbyshire, it will be severely reported hereafter. I myself, you know, made a much more dangerous voyage when I was young.'[14] Derbyshire pride was at stake, but there was not much time to plan the voyage, and Banks was willing to cast around the country for volunteers as part of the hurried arrangements that were made. During the mission he expected mineral specimens to be gathered from the surface, or from the vicinity of exposed strata,[15] but he did not exclude the possibility of some excavation at places where *Investigator* stopped long enough, and crew and timber could be spared from her. There is, however, almost a sense of unreality in the suggestions he made for sinking shafts into the earth when time, manpower and timber permitted. In fact, these were severely lacking at crucial stages during the voyage, and a note of caution in Banks's advice might well reflect a realistic sense of what was possible on such a mission. This does not mean that Banks had no interest in the soils and rocks of Australia. He had long desired to establish the possible uses of any resources there, and to understand more of the continent's geography and geology. Indeed, some of the earliest samples of any soil or mineral sent back to Britain from Australia came to Banks from Arthur Phillip, predating the *Investigator* altogether. These show some of the ways in which Australian geology started to attract attention before 1800.

As soon as the samples arrived back in Britain, Banks started to distribute them to individuals wanting to learn more about the characteristics and possible uses of Australia's minerals. Scientific analysis was necessary for this, and it was deemed especially important to establish whether any minerals valuable to industry existed there. For example, in 1790 Josiah Wedgwood conducted experimental tests on a black and white mineral specimen from Sydney.[16] This was done at Banks's request, and he provided the sample Wedgwood used. Wedgwood published a paper in the Royal Society's *Philosophical Transactions* describing the results of his tests. He did not come to any firm conclusion about the mineral specimen, except that a black component in it did not appear to be what he termed 'molybdaena', but a rather pure kind of 'black-lead'. He also made and distributed commemorative medallions using clay from New South Wales that Banks had supplied, these being the earliest example in Britain of a manufactured article being produced using such material from Australia. In his paper, Wedgwood described the clay as 'an excellent material for pottery', and ventured the idea that it 'may certainly be made the basis of a valuable manufacture for our infant colony there'.[17]

Others on the continent of Europe also received Australian mineral samples from Banks, including Johann Friedrich Blumenbach, whose studies ranged beyond anthropology to include botany and mineralogy. Blumenbach's analysis largely supported Wedgwood's findings: 'I sacrificed a part of the Sand you were so kind to favour me with, even before I receiv'd Mr Wedgwood's account, to some small experiments, who as I now see agreed in general perfectly with his analysis. Only the black shining parts which I compared with our Saxonian Molybdæna seem'd to me rather of this Kind than of black lead.'[18] Later, Charles Hatchett tested specimens of the same sample of earth, named Sydneia, but could not reproduce Wedgwood's results. Instead, Hachett found his specimen to be a mixture of the oxides of silicon, iron and aluminium, together with graphite.[19] It is apparent, then, that in the years prior to the *Investigator* information about minerals from abroad, including those from Australia, was being circulated among commercial and scientific figures in Banks's network. This helped to stimulate interest in exploration generally, and suggested particular possibilities with regard to Australia.

That Banks's network stretched back to the Australian colonies themselves should come as no surprise. Banks was a useful route for news and specimens from the Pacific region as a whole. His contacts there were strong and long-standing, and all the governors of New South Wales from Phillip onwards corresponded with him about iron, coal, copper and other ores and minerals.[20] Phillip's earliest dispatches from Sydney to Banks are replete with reference to all manner of natural resources, to the aboriginal people, to the land itself and to the progress of the colony. This followed the well-established tradition of travellers and explorers reporting a broad range of phenomena, and, of course, it related to wider imperial concerns manifested with the First Fleet. Moreover, exploration of Australia's rocks and minerals was not confined to sea-going expeditions. As Banks and many others knew very well, boring for deeper samples could be done more easily by settlers, starting with the areas surrounding their colonies, rather than by assigning such heavy work to voyagers coming from Britain. Consequently, in 1799 boring rods were made in London by Mr Wapshot, who was appointed for the job by Banks. These were loaded on a whaler sailing out with the new Governor, Philip Gidley King, because their 'weight is so considerable'.[21] The aim was to try for coal.[22] By 1801 some were even proposing iron works in New South Wales to make the colony less dependent on the mother country, and possibly a source for her growing trade and industry, as Wedgwood had earlier suggested.[23] This was one practical way of uncovering and utilizing the geology that perforce *Investigator* ignored, and should be regarded as such in discussions of the exploration then being pursued.

The search for ways of determining what mineral riches lay beneath the earth was becoming ever more important. No less important was the desire to understand the earth's structure and the forces that had shaped it. Central collections were created at the British Museum to meet these requirements, some of which were intended to show the geology of whole areas. Collections from abroad could be fitted into such schemes, and Banks ensured the transfer of those from the *Investigator* for this reason. The historic value of the mineral collections that returned from that mission, small in size though these were, should not be underestimated. They provide the earliest extant collections from Australia still at the Natural History Museum, London. Coming from the second, northern leg of the voyage around the continent, lasting from July 1802 to June 1803, the material is 'reasonably representative' of the rocks encountered. For all its limitations, and there is no doubt that in the earth sciences this mission was limited, it achieved notable results, and probably could have delivered little more given the disasters that took place.[24]

Conclusion

It may have been just as well that *Investigator* was not encumbered with more equipment given the way she struggled. For his part, Banks ensured that a sample of minerals from the British Museum was supplied to Brown before his departure in order to help with work on the mission.[25] This was no sign of neglect, and the fate of these minerals only reinforces our awareness of the difficult circumstances everyone laboured under, the Museum material probably being lost on Wreck Reef, along with the specimens collected by Brown in Southern Australia, and part of what Flinders collected too.

Back in Britain it was Banks who reminded the Admiralty in 1811 that the surviving earth collection from the *Investigator* should go to the British Museum, the Lords of the Admiralty asking him to undertake 'the trouble of giving the necessary directions for depositing the specimens'.[26] This was in fulfillment of the agreement signed at Soho Square that such collections were public property. Banks's letter to the Admiralty outlines his view of the collection's importance, and its place among the Museum's other mineral collections, then being reorganized. Referring to the fact that the Admiralty had not given directions about 'a Considerable number of Specimens of the Rocks & Stratified Stones of Australia ...', Banks pointed out that:

> These Specimens tho not beautifull or at all amusing to a Common Observer are interesting in a high degree to those persons who Study Geology a Science which at present makes rapid advances towards perfection as Likely to prove highly beneficial to the public by giving to the Posessors of Land/*ed Property*/ the means of Obtaining Cheap & accurate information relative to the /Situation of the/ articles of value whatever they may be that Lie under the Surface of their Estates
>
> The Trustees of the British Museum have given orders to have a Geological / *Collection*/ Series arrangd Separately from their Mineralogical Collection in order to promote & Encourage the improvement of this new and interesting branch of Knowledge allow me therefore to Request you to /*move*/ Submit to their Lordships the matters above Stated in order that they may Consider whether it will be a Proper measure that the Geological Collections Made in the voyage of the investigator be placd in the British Museum to make a Part of Collections now forming by the officers of the dept of natural history /there/ for the benefit of the Public who have free admission /*to Study*/ to /*inspect*/ visit the apartments and view the Collections deposited in them.[27]

As with other similar missions, those who participated in this one were allowed to keep material that was not wanted by the authorities. This was not precluded by the agreement signed at Soho Square before the *Investigator* departed. In due course, Brown presented the Museum with some of his private collections from the mission,[28] and his herbarium was incorporated in the Museum collections after he died. Apart from the 1811 transfer to the British

Museum, other material went to the Geological Society of London, and in 1911 its collection also moved to the Natural History Museum. Various specimens in Brown's personal collection of Australian rocks and fossils, made once the mission had broken up and Flinders had departed for England, were given away to friends and some may well have been sold on the London market too.

Charles Konig, from a drawing by Eden Upton Eddis, 1831, *Bulletin of the British Museum (Natural History) Historical Series* (1969). Reproduced by permission of the Natural History Museum, London.

Konig was questioned in 1835 by the Select Committee appointed to inspect the Museum's affairs:

Question: You are occasionally called in by the Trustees? Do you stand the whole time? Konig: We never sit down; it is not etiquette.

(*Parliamentary Papers*, 1835, pp. 2589–630)

5 EARTH SCIENCES

Banks did not collect minerals himself, but this did not mean that he was not concerned with earth sciences in this period, nor uninvolved with the development and use of such collections at the British Museum. Indeed, his refusal to accommodate minerals and other substances was a positive gain for the Museum. Drawing on his international connections, and his estate at Overton in Derbyshire, where mining offered profits to a landowner interested in structural geology, Banks maintained a steady supply of specimens to Bloomsbury.[1] Addressing Banks as 'a Man who for the space of half a Century has shewn himself the most zealous Cultivator and Promoter of the Sciences', one Danish correspondent offered 'a small Set of Norwegian and Swedish Minerals', hoping they would find a place in 'Your Mineral Cabinet'. Banks politely declined the offer, explaining that 'I have Sir no collections of minerals myself'. Instead, he forwarded this gift to the Museum, where 'the Public Treasuries of Science [are] preserved ... for the honor of the Countrey & the use of Students'.[2] Likewise, when Sir William Hamilton sent Banks samples from Etna, Banks responded: 'I should thank you more for Collections of dried Plants made by Graefer than for Collections of the Produce of Etna which you Know is not exactly in my way it will do however for the British Museum where I will place it ...'.[3] The British Museum, then, is an important place to look for evidence of Banks's involvement with the earth sciences.

Presents 'through the medium of Sir Jos. Banks': 1800–15

Much of the material Banks sent to the British Museum eventually came under the supervision of the Assistant Keeper in the Natural History Department, Charles Konig. Konig, a German naturalist, had been employed from 1801 to 1807 as an assistant to Jonas Dryander, Banks's Soho Square librarian and curator. Alongside specimens and visiting scholars, staff also made their way to the British Museum via Banks's nearby home. Konig spent his time increasing the Museum's collections, and arranging and recording them, and during a long career he concentrated more and more on the mineral and fossil collections. Konig and Banks worked closely together. Indeed, one of the most frequently repeated phrases in Konig's reports up to 1820 was 'through the medium of Sir Jos. Banks', so that the Museum's 'Book of Presents' shows at least as much given by Banks to mineralogy as to zoology, some of it coming from New World territories then being explored.

In December 1809 Konig could report the arrival of minerals from New Holland (Australia), 'a continent as yet very little known with regard to its mineral productions', to be followed in February of the next year with 'crystallized White Topaz from New South Wales & another Article belonging to the secondary Fossils', all from Banks.[4] The number and variety of Banks's gifts from 1810 to 1815 is remarkable. Banks was the chief individual donor of rocks and minerals in this period, through a series of separate gifts supplying specimens from the Pacific, the West Indies, North and South America, Russia and Ireland, as well as internally from Britain. It is in the British Museum, as at his Derbyshire estates, that we find Banks most active in the early earth sciences. The extent of his involvement is apparent in the table 'Book of Presents: Donations from Banks 1767–1820' (see following page). This shows the pattern of Banks's donations through the years, and especially how prolific he was in fields other than botany prior to 1820. It shows, too, that Banks increased the number of gifts he made in all fields during the last years of his life.

Other records provide further evidence of Banks's commitment to the mineral collections. A survey of a number of his donations to do with the earth sciences from 1810 to 1815 supports the view that he gave large quantities of rocks, minerals and fossils. This material came from a range of global sources well beyond the reach of most other collectors in London. During these five years at standing committees alone Banks presented:

BM CE 3/9 2476 [26 volcanic specimens mostly from Guadeloupe – 8/12/1810], 2492 [ores from India – 6/4/1811], 2499 [New Holland (Australian) minerals, from exploration – 8/6/1811], 2512 [specimen of an 'Alluvial Mass' from Brazil in which diamonds were reputedly found – 11/1/1812], 2533; BM CE 5/2 481 ['Native Magnesia, Green Tourmaline and Crystallized Mica' – 14/11/1812, from Professor Bruce, a useful North American contact]; BM CE 3/9 2538 [Banks conveyed a 'Slab of Tourmaline' from New South Wales on behalf of William Bligh, whom Banks selected and approached to be governor in 1805 – 9/1/1813], 2540 [grains of 'gold' from Wicklow in Ireland – 13/2/1813], 2549 [volcanic substance erupted on the Pacific island of Bourbon in September of 1812 – 12/6/1813], 2557 [volcanic substances erupted in the West Indies – 13/11/1813], 2559 [more volcanic substance erupted in the West Indies, on Barbados and St Vincent – 11/12/1813], 2563 [from the Geological Society, via Banks, some minerals from Ireland – 6/1/1814], 2566 ['Gold' and rocks from Wicklow in Ireland, through Banks, and donated by the Royal Society – 12/2/1814], 2575 [new mineral from Siberia – 1/6/1814], 2582 [meteorite stone from Moravia, conveyed by Banks on behalf of the Imperial Museum of Vienna, and an iron meteorite sent by Professor Bruce of New York – 12/11/1814], 2589 [collection of volcanic specimens from Guadeloupe – 14/1/1815].[5]

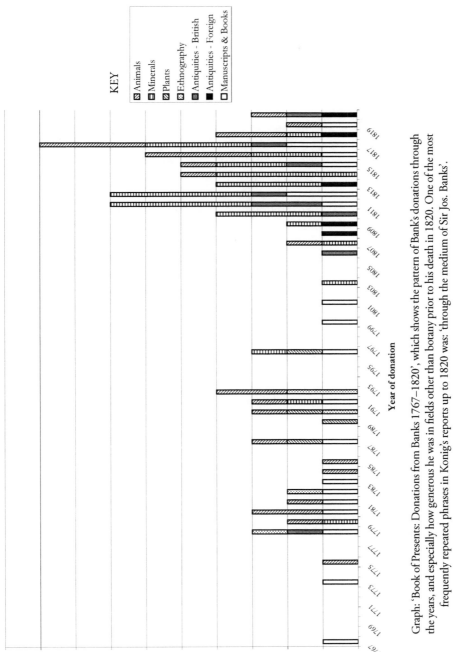

Graph: 'Book of Presents: Donations from Banks 1767–1820', which shows the pattern of Bank's donations through the years, and especially how generous he was in fields other than botany prior to his death in 1820. One of the most frequently repeated phrases in König's reports up to 1820 was: 'through the medium of Sir Jos. Banks'.

Banks's international contacts in the earth sciences remained strong and productive. He is hard to match in the early nineteenth century as a donor of minerals, and his generosity coincided with a period of growth at the Museum in this branch of natural history, and an increase in its wider study and national importance. According to the officers' reports, in January 1811 he gave silver ore from Buenos Ayres, and British specimens as well.[6] Then in March there is mention of a collection of South American minerals that Konig had been working on, sent to Banks by the traveller and naturalist, Baron Friedrich von Humboldt, and given by Banks to the Museum.[7] Another gift referred to in the officers' reports is native silver from Peru.[8] Here, it was the wealth of South America that attracted attention, but specimens from Sweden, Australia or his own country estates were no less attractive to Banks.

Indeed, Konig's grateful reports for the entire period make frequent and detailed mention of the material listed above, and much more. They show that Banks's range was his strength, and this in turn helped to make him a significant figure in the promotion of earth science at the British Museum in the early nineteenth century. Overall, his contribution was threefold. Firstly, he assisted with missions abroad, and ensured that collections of rocks and minerals returned to the British Museum in much the way they did in other branches of natural history. Secondly, he was one of the major donors of material at the Museum throughout this period, employing a wide network of contacts to supply material. Thirdly, and importantly, in Konig he found for the Museum a man who made it his particular business to organize and increase the mineral and related collections. This last development was perhaps the greatest of Banks's contributions to earth science at the Museum.

Growth and Consolidation: 1799–1810

The early years of the nineteenth century saw concentrated work on the rocks and minerals at the Museum, with more time, space and money being devoted to combining and increasing these collections. As more material arrived, the tendency was to reorganize existing Museum collections to accommodate it. At the turn of the century the main Museum collections included Sir Hans Sloane's minerals and fossils, amounting to nearly 10,000 catalogued specimens. Added to this impressive if somewhat mixed collection was another that belonged to the Reverend Clayton Mordaunt Cracherode, and this was catalogued according to the system of Carl Linnaeus. Cracherode, a trustee who died in 1799, was a generous benefactor, who also gave the Museum important collections of books, drawings, prints, coins, gems and shells.[9] Unfortunately, the Sloane collection was dispersed in sales starting during the Keepership of Edward Whitaker Gray. In 1803 some 2,000 duplicates identified by Gray were auctioned for £258 13s.

8*d.*, and a further 1,700 were sold in 1816 for £210, with a number being thrown away because they were deemed to be of no scientific value.[10] The Sloane and Cracherode collections were united in the Mineral Room with a third major collection, that of Charles Hatchett, and it was here in May 1807 that Konig started his work at the Museum. He came, therefore, to a consolidated Museum collection that had been prepared recently by both Gray and Charles Hatchett.

Konig had access to a supportive trustee who knew the Museum's holdings reasonably well, for it was Banks who suggested and then oversaw the purchase in 1799 of Charles Hatchett's valuable mineral collection.[11] Banks was on the standing committee that recommended the purchase for £700, the other committee members being Charles Francis Greville and Philip Rashleigh. This group reported that the Hatchett collection contained 7,000 specimens, and they categorized these under a series of headings.[12] Referring to the Museum collections as a whole, the committee also observed that there was a need for a good set of British minerals from places like 'Derbyshire, Cornwall or the Lead hills', and that a 'systematic Collection of Minerals is much wanted' for research purposes. They thought, too, that an arrangement of duplicate minerals from Cornwall and Derbyshire should be exhibited for the public.[13] In short, the arrival of Hatchett's collection prompted a more general review of the composition and state of the existing Museum earth collections.

The committee's 1799 report was therefore an important one. It laid clear emphasis on mining and manufacturing interests, as well as on the expectation of visitors that there should be a comprehensive collection of good British specimens at the Museum. These were some of the issues gradually taken up with Konig's introduction, but initially Banks and the others thought that Hatchett should organize his own collection. This was a good choice, since while doing so he identified a new element that he named columbium, now known as niobium, atomic number 41. Besides suggestions as to the disposal of duplicates through sale, exchange or, if they were deemed worthless, by destruction, a small collection from abroad received particular comment. This was the one made by Archibald Menzies on the north-west coast of America in accordance with Banks's instructions. The committee advised that it be kept separate, since it 'supplies a kind of mineralogical history of an extensive Coast very little known'.[14]

Working with Konig from May 1807 onwards, Banks saw some of the aims in the 1799 report achieved, and rooms provided to hold the resulting collections. These grew enormously, and by 1811 the ageing floors of the Museum were being strengthened to support them. Careful organization was necessary to increase collections on this scale, and Konig was the man to ensure this was imposed. Conscientious, even compulsive, Konig liked to arrange the minerals himself, personally handling some 12,000 specimens, all of which he individually labelled. He was therefore temperamentally well suited to his first major task in mineralogy, that of sorting and cataloguing the Sloane and Hatchett collections. For this Konig used 'the new emendated System of Werner', based on the ideas of Abraham Gottlob Werner, an influential mineralogist and geologist, who taught at the Freiberg Academy.[15] Konig later modified Werner's system, preferring a 'natural order founded on external characters; not, however, without consulting the chemical composition of the substances as far as convenience would admit of'.[16] He also increased the limited Museum equipment, in January 1809 ordering 'an Aerometer an Electrometer, & a Goniometer'.[17] Although he was not a great figure in science, Konig had quickly established a reputation at the Museum for thoroughness and efficiency.

By November 1809 Konig had finished his catalogue, reporting that the Geological Collection was on public display.[18] With his catalogue undergoing its final revision, Konig was 'ready to receive the orders of the Rt Hble Sir Joseph Banks on the subject of the several partial collections of Minerals in the Museum, and respecting the mode in which they are to be catalogued'.[19] The earth collections were being brought firmly under control, and while Konig toiled away at his catalogues and refined his working methods, Banks continued to scour the globe for rocks and minerals, donating in June 'fine specimens of Indian Corundum or Diamond Spar, and a rare specimen of the Iron Ore from the East Indies, yielding that superior kind of steel known by the name of Wootz'.[20] The latter substance came from India, and Banks distributed it, as he did material from other parts of the world, to be experimented on by industrialists and a number of Fellows of the Royal Society. Konig's reports up to 1820 are studded with gifts like this, and they show how closely Banks and Konig cooperated. If Banks's opinion counted, Konig must have been glad when in 1809 his former employer approved the Geological Catalogue that had been started, and also the Catalogue of Secondary Fossils, and that of the Principal Minerals. Banks must have been glad too at the way Konig had taken to curatorial work at the Museum.

Apart from Banks's regular donations, the year 1809 saw further increases in the collections. It also saw a tightening of the bonds that operated at Bloomsbury in the promotion of natural history. When Charles Francis Greville died in April, the fate of his mineral collection drew Konig and Banks together in a joint attempt to ensure its purchase. Greville, one of Banks's close friends, possessed a collection of international repute, but made no provision for its future. Seeing an important opportunity, Konig immediately corresponded with Banks and Joseph Planta about it. He wanted the Museum to acquire the Greville collection, and argued for 'forming a systematic, and economical collection, and a collection for indigenous Minerals'.[21] Before being presented to the trustees as a whole these plans were discussed with Banks and Charles Abbott, another influential trustee and Speaker of the House of Commons. Like Leach, Konig prepared the way for such changes by enlisting Banks's support. He could rely on this since the plans he proposed were traceable, in part, to those first outlined in 1799.

A keen French mineralogist in exile in Britain, the Comte de Bournon, had catalogued and managed the Greville collection prior to its transfer, but Konig had little sympathy with the ideas of the Frenchman, and so Bournon was not invited to help at the Museum.[22] Instead, Konig took charge of the incoming material. Following its purchase in May 1810 for £13,727, and its lodgment at the Museum in June,[23] he reported on the size of the Greville collection as being 14,800 specimens. He also commented tellingly on how matters were conducted in order to obtain the collection, explaining that 'on the repeated applications of Mr. Konig to the Rt. Honble the Speaker and Sir Joseph Banks, a negotiation was entered upon with the executors which terminated in a valuation that exceeded the most sanguine expectation'. More than once in these years Banks joined with the Speaker of the House of Commons when the purchase of a large collection was being organized. It was a useful combination that helped to manage the complicated business of obtaining support from Parliament for public expenditure on Museum collections. Konig's advice in this same report was to consolidate the Greville with the other major collections, aiming at 'collections as complete as possible'.[24] His satisfaction at having secured such an acquisition was obvious, and with collections in the earth sciences growing more rapidly than those in any other branch of natural history, it is perhaps unsurprising that Konig turned increasingly to this field.

Organization, Major Donations and Purchases: 1810–20

In these ways, then, the Museum collections were growing in size, their arrangement and cataloguing being undertaken by Konig, with Banks supervising and supporting from time to time. Having requested that the mineral collections be moved to the Saloon, to be exhibited in the manner of the Cracherode collection,[25] Konig started to place them there in 1812. This was the year before he was promoted to Under-Librarian in charge of the Natural History Department.[26] Needless to say, Banks was on the standing committee that approved the change to the Saloon, and further that the old Mineralogy Room be used for a geological collection. Not only was Banks accessible to officers like Konig, his involvement in various committees allowed him to assist effectively in furthering their plans. Thus, when the library and minerals of Baron Von Moll were offered for sale in Munich,[27] Konig and Henry Hervey Baber were dispatched to view them. The standing committee convened to organize this trip met at 32 Soho Square on 14 February 1815, and it was from there that the instructions for Baber and Konig were issued.[28] Such purchases were, of course, what Banks and

Konig wished to see, but they came at a price because other desirable collections could not be afforded.

For example, those of the Marquis de Drée were declined because, as Banks explained to Sir Charles Blagden, 'we have Sent Baber & Konig To Treat for the Purchase of Baron Molls Library at Munich which if Purchasd will Exhaust our Present Funds'.[29] The money needed to buy de Drée's collections was spent instead on those of Von Moll, and to afford these it was necessary to sell the remaining stock in the Edwards Fund, stock that the Museum had relied on for library purchases for a number of years. It should be stressed that difficult decisions like this became more common as financial restrictions increased in the post-war years after 1815. Indeed, the progress of the Museum during Banks's lifetime should be seen against a background of persistent war and tension that hindered (and on some occasions helped) what was achieved. Lack of funds was one of the main historical reasons why large collections were not bought more frequently, and why portions might be acquired at auction rather than taking everything that had been initially offered. There were limits to what the Museum could spend in the international market for collections, and concessions sometimes had to be made.

Konig referred to the possible purchase of de Drée's collections in later reports,[30] but the tone of these reports indicates that he knew he should concentrate his arguments on the Von Moll sale if anything substantial was to be gained. He proposed, too, that the old Mineral Room be used for the geological collection.[31] Konig appears to have wanted the growing earth collections to be displayed in a series of connected rooms at the top of the main staircase, which would have been an impressive array. His ambition was growing with the collections, and with persuasive force he advocated their continued expansion. With all the arrangements in the Saloon completed, and despite several donations 'principally from the Rt Hble Sir Joseph Banks', he still felt that there was not enough geological material for 'a systematic arrangement on a scale proportionate to that of the other collections'. Konig argued that geology was a rising discipline, 'now so universally followed', and that therefore more attention needed to be paid to it at the Museum. He knew, too, that it was a discipline Banks did much to patronize, and Konig's arguments were also designed to appeal to trustees like Banks, who wished to see the Museum collections developed in an area of such importance to science and industry. Here was another reason for Konig and Baber to go to Germany to obtain collections from the Von Moll sale.

Making this trip took Konig back to the country of his birth, and provided an excellent opportunity to renew acquaintances and to make further contacts through which to obtain specimens. Konig envisaged expanding his connections, and with them the exchange networks available to the Museum. Such connections would operate in a similar way to those maintained by Banks and

Museum officers like Leach. All three men were active members of the Republic of Letters, cultivating especially productive networks of natural history. As Konig described it, in a report prior to the trip, 'the exchange of duplicates for other specimens that may be offered, is a usual and convenient mode of completing collections ...'. In this way he hoped to obtain 'objects of Mineralogy, Botany, Zoology &c', in particular suggesting a 'correspondence' with the Duke of Saxe-Weimer, who had visited the British Museum, and with the Society of Jena.[32] These were issues to be discussed at the preparatory meeting at Soho Square on 14 February, just four days after Konig's report. The details having been settled, Konig and Baber departed with authority to purchase the Von Moll collections if they thought them worth acquiring, which they did.

The trip was therefore a successful one, and Konig reported on the new collections on his return from Munich. He said that the minerals were in nine cases, of about 4 by 1½ feet, some containing specimens 'of great scarcity & beauty ... especially from Salzburg and Tyrol; and a considerable number of others which may be advantageously exchanged or sold'. There was also a small collection of dried plants, which Konig thought would 'form a good basis for a general herbarium'.[33] Along with Von Moll's library, these collections were a considerable accession. In 1816 another valuable acquisition was made when the mineral collection of Count Beroldingen was purchased for £1,000. Konig had inspected it 'at the desire of the Rt Hble Sir Joseph Banks', and then recommended the purchase. Beroldingen's collection consisted of 12,000 specimens, 'being formed with a view to illustrate the collector's own ideas developed in his mineralogical & geological writings'.[34] The progress made in the previous twenty years was such that in May Konig could report that the consolidated mineralogical collections were 'in such a state of order and systematic arrangement as to be supposed more extensively useful to the Student than any other Public assemblage of this kind ...' Always busy, Konig had by that time commenced sorting the 'Secondary fossils'.[35]

The mineral displays were a popular attraction at the Museum, but increases in the mineral collections were so great that the floors of the Saloon needed to be strengthened. In November 1816 Konig therefore asked for this to be done, cast-iron pillars being used. It was not the first time that such action was necessary, and the iron pillars stood as evidence of the strain being placed on old buildings housing enormous collections.[36] Konig, however, sought yet more material. Pursuing a theme, he wanted the empty Room 1 on the upper floor in which to assemble a collection of British specimens, since 'Nothing is more frequently enquired after, by native as well as by foreign visitors than a collection of British Minerals'.[37] This was significant. The British Museum could not be seen to be deficient in an area of such scientific and national importance. The costs of starting the collection could, Konig thought, be covered by a recent sale of duplicate minerals that raised £210, with extra specimens being acquired by exchange. Thus, a collection of British Minerals was established, and with it the collections as a whole were approaching the size, coverage and organization anticipated from as early as 1799.

By March 1817 Konig had nearly finished work on the British Minerals, now to be placed in Room 10, this being considered by the surveyor as the only one capable of supporting such a weight.[38] Yet still Konig wanted to increase his rapidly growing mineral empire. Building on what he ascertained on his trip to Munich, Konig now looked to expand the European networks of donation, exchange and sale that he advocated so enthusiastically throughout his career.[39] Thus, in January 1817 he was given permission to exchange Museum duplicates, all of which were to be carefully recorded under Banks's watchful eye.[40] In an extensive report of July 1818, Konig detailed the personal contacts he had in mind for exchanging specimens at Pisa, Florence, Siena, Piacenza and Asti, and he also suggested using the 'curators of many other Museums on the continent'.[41] It was a plan that showed only too clearly the extent of his own ambitions for the Museum's rock and mineral collections. Meanwhile, donations from abroad continued to arrive.

In April 1817 Banks presented two large lumps of metallic iron from Australia, and two more pieces of the Indian steel called wootz. These were yet more arrivals from distant parts of the world, and ones of potential interest to Britain's rising manufacturing industries, which Banks always tried to encourage.[42] As suggested, the applicability of mineral collections to the interests of landowners and industrialists was a matter of increasing importance. So far as the Museum and Banks are concerned, we can see how Banks's own work with pioneers in practical geology influenced the organization of collections at Bloomsbury. It is therefore to the last years of Banks's life that we now turn in order to understand how geological surveys of Britain extended knowledge of the earth and revealed more about the ways collections made from it could be used to interpret the earth's structure and composition.

Banks's own estate concerns in Derbyshire, near Ashover, involved lead mining, which by 1808 had all but ceased on the veins found there. Despite this, his interest in the study of geology did not wane. Indeed, it became more evident in the last decade of his life. Significantly, this period coincided with Konig's development of geological and British mineral collections at the Museum, and, of course, the gathering pace of industrial revolution. It was from his Derbyshire residence at Overton Hall that Banks started to organize the geological transects and surveys made by John Farey. These revealed the strata, minerals and soils of the area. Farey, a surveyor and geologist, dedicated to Banks a geological transect that crossed the Banks country properties. This transect extended from near Matlock to Overton Hall, through Ashover, eastwards across England, past the main Banks estates around Revesby Abbey in Lincolnshire, and thence to Trusthorpe on the east coast. Farey finished this work in 1808, and followed it with two volumes in 1811 and 1813 under the title *General View of the Agriculture and Minerals of Derbyshire*, the first of which contained mostly geology.[43]

These were developments in British geology of considerable importance to landowners and to the discipline itself, as Banks indicated to Barthélemy Faujas de St Fond in February 1811: 'Geology becomes more & more in Fashion I hope we Shall before long advance Somewhat the Limits of that Science We have now Some Practical men well versd in Stratification who undertake to Examine the Subterraneous Geography of Gentlemens Estates in order to discover the Fossils likely to be usefull for Manure for Fuel as Grind Stones Mill Stones &c & Employment begins to be given to these people The Consequence must be a Rapid improvement if the Laborers in this great work Can find means as I think they will of being Paid for the Skill'.[44] The phrasing and ideas here echo those Banks used when writing to the Admiralty at almost exactly this time about the collections from the *Investigator*. They show the ways in which Banks promoted geological exploration at home and abroad, and that to do this he stressed the close relation of geological understanding both to the landowning interest and to the rising industrial class.

At home Banks was in contact with a number of the most influential manufacturers of his day, and his acquaintance with some of them was long and warm. Among these were men like Matthew Boulton and James Watt. Banks actively promoted the Soho works at Birmingham, as a privy councillor seeking commissions from government for Boulton to produce new coinage. Josiah Wedgwood was another friend, who, as we have seen, showed a scientific interest in minerals sent back to Britain from Australia. Boulton, Watt and Wedgwood all became Fellows of the Royal Society in the mid-1780s, and thereby strengthened the Society's early links with some of the intellectual and industrial leaders of the Midlands. In various ways, all of these figures sought to draw on the deepening knowledge of geology and to encourage its growth. In order to further promote this growth the Museum report of 1799 that Banks helped to write had indicated some ways in which the collections at Bloomsbury might be extended to cover more of Britain's minerals. Areas like Derbyshire (with its deposits of lead, fluorite and barytes) and Cornwall (with deposits of tin, copper, zinc, lead, iron, and some silver) were suggested as particular places on which to concentrate.

This need to improve knowledge of Britain's mineral deposits and geology is increasingly apparent in Konig's reports in the years following 1810. Thus, when Konig stressed the need to understand British geology better, it was partly for the benefit of landowners and manufacturers of the kind referred to here. These concerns, and a genuine desire to further knowledge for its own sake, were no less evident in Banks's patronage of the pioneering geologist, William Smith, whose principles had inspired Farey. Smith, regarded as the father of British geology, dedicated a landmark geological map to Banks, who led subscriptions to Smith's work with £50, and who displayed his maps at Soho Square. The map that Smith dedicated to Banks was the first countrywide geological map ever produced. It was beautifully illustrated and grandly entitled *Delineation of the Strata of England and Wales with part of Scotland; exhibiting the Collieries and Mines; the Marshes and Fen Lands originally Overflowed by the Sea; and the Varieties of Soil according to the Variations in the Sub Strata; illustrated by the Most Descriptive Names.*[45]

Unfortunately, Smith ran into debt, and following publication of this great work on 1 August 1815 he wanted to sell his geological collection. This comprised numerous rock specimens and the fossils peculiar to each, arranged in the order that they lay in the earth. Smith had discovered that a bed of rock at any level in the succession could be distinguished by its characteristic fossil remains, and the geology of an area thereby determined. His collection was bought for the nation in June 1816, and it laid the foundation of stratigraphy and palaeontology at the British Museum, and hence later at the Natural History Museum, London. However, the price Smith obtained from government for his collection was not as high as he had hoped. After the sale, haggling involving Smith, Konig, Planta and certain government officials over the purchase and organization of the collection led to lengthy delays in it being incorporated and displayed.[46] Nevertheless, the growth of the earth collections continued, with men like Banks making regular donations, and Konig driving development forward.

Infirmity had begun to limit Banks's activities, and the Museum was soon to start reconstruction, but Banks remained enthusiastic about Smith's work. He tried to impress Konig with the importance of Smith's collection. Indeed, it was Banks who urged Konig to recommend its purchase in August 1815,[47] and Konig's subsequent reports show that Banks persisted in his support for Smith. In July 1816 Konig reported that the Smith collection was of 'Organic remains intended to illustrate the Geology of England', and that Smith was willing to arrange it for the Museum 'in the succession of the Strata in which those fossils are found'.[48] Having availed himself of 'Sir Joseph's superior insight into these matters', Konig reported on the Smith fossils in greater detail. He explained that they 'are indicative of the presence of the strata in which they are respectively found; and therefore highly interesting to those persons who wish to become acquainted with the geological nature of their estates in order to derive profit from the quality of the undersoil as well as from the fertility of the surface'. The significance of collections like Smith's was partly their 'utility',[49] in this case to those seeking to enhance yields from their estates, and to supply industry through improved scientific knowledge of geology. It was a theme Banks had been pursuing for some time prior to 1816.

While he still could, then, Banks impressed his views on Konig. Mining and industry must therefore be counted among the obvious concerns that Konig had in mind when he sought to establish a collection of British Minerals, one also intended for the use of numerous visitors to the Museum from home and abroad. As a trustee and landowner Banks's main contribution to these developments was the interlinked support and encouragement he offered, support and encouragement to which Konig, Smith and Farey could attest only too well. When promoting such individuals, Banks sought not only to raise economic activity in Britain, but to advance the science of geology and to supplement and perfect the mineral and rock collections at the British Museum. These collections increased during Konig's career, becoming the most extensive in Britain. This was achieved by concentrating on them in a determined way, something Konig seems to have been only too happy to do.

Conclusion

By May 1818 Room 10 was almost ready to be opened to display the British Minerals,[50] and Konig was looking to increase the geological collection as a whole.[51] In 1819 he was occupied with fossils, which he thought might be displayed in Room 8, if the zoological collections there were moved. Konig wanted to replace these with 'the whole of the splendid collection of Secondary Fossils'. Parts of zoology would therefore end up in the basement, but, Konig enthused, 'the succession of the mineralogical collections (from the Saloon to the Room for British Minerals) would be no longer interrupted, and the landing place of the staircase would be cleared of the Quadrupeds which now disfigure it'.[52] Judging from the *Synopsis* for 1820, this was one alteration that could not be allowed. Some sort of balance was needed in the overall treatment of natural history at the Museum, and zoology could not be relegated in this way.[53] Even so, it was not until 1840, when John Edward Gray became Keeper of what was by then the Zoological Branch, that zoology received the full attention it required. Energetic and extremely capable, Gray took Konig's position as the leading scientific figure among the staff at the Museum until the days of Richard Owen, whose dominating influence overshadowed the end of Gray's distinguished career. As Superintendent of the Natural History Department, it was Owen who oversaw the move of the natural history collections to a new museum. This was opened at Kensington in 1881 following sharp differences concerning the need for relocation and the problems of splitting natural history from the library and other collections at Bloomsbury.

As with the ethnographic collections, zoology never held quite the same fascination for Konig that the earth sciences did. Konig found himself increasingly superseded by the thinking and approach of a new generation of naturalists emerging at the Museum during his later years. Nevertheless, it is apparent that Banks and Konig formed a useful working partnership, and that during his lifetime Banks favoured the Museum with material he did not collect, especially in the earth sciences. Once again, we see Banks as a private individual specializing in botany and books while handing on material he did not want to more appropriate collections. The extent and value of Banks's lifetime donations was considerable, as was his steady participation in Museum committees, and the labours he sometimes undertook alongside officers working on the collections. It is also important to note that Museum officers like Konig reported considerable improvement in the size and organization of some collections in this period, and tried to encourage their display and use for research purposes. These were positive developments, particularly in the earth sciences, which Konig tended to favour. However, with so much to care for at the British Museum, concentrating on some collections, when others needed just as much attention, clearly had disadvantages as well as advantages.

6 LIBRARIES AND ANTIQUITIES

Although Banks never went on the traditional Grand Tour, he did handle classical Greek and Roman objects in London collections. He knew great connoisseurs such as William Hamilton, Richard Payne Knight and Charles Townley, and participated in plans to construct buildings at the British Museum to house some of their collections. He examined these collections, thought about their accommodation and display, and negotiated their transfer to the British Museum. Sometimes he was even asked to keep important pieces at his own house in Soho Square prior to their removal to Bloomsbury. Moreover, Banks was also able to make donations of antiquities, such as in November 1809 when he presented bas-reliefs of Jupiter and Ceres that he had received.[1] Banks therefore participated in the enormous increase of mainly classical antiquities at the Museum after 1800, and did what he could to help in the considerable task of coping with everything as the Museum buildings were all but overwhelmed.

These were exceptional years for the Museum. Significant private collections of antiquities were purchased in the first third of the nineteenth century, and at its beginning the defeat of Napoleon's invasion of Egypt brought valuable collections that the French surrendered at Alexandria. Alongside these, major libraries were acquired from private collectors, usually by purchase, and some truly eminent libraries arrived at the Museum in the years leading up to and following Banks's death. Banks's own natural history library was received in 1827, this and his herbarium being the two greatest single gifts he made to the Museum. By the time that Smirke's new building was underway most of the major collectors and connoisseurs that Banks knew had also died, but as a group they had provided material for the national collections on a scale to match any later generation of individuals pursuing private interests at their own expense.

As a donor Banks's main contribution was to natural history and the libraries, and during his life he maintained a series of useful contacts for the Museum through which various items were obtained. As a trustee he diligently attended committees and meetings, and was involved in restructuring the Museum's organization to cope with the specimens, books and antiquities that arrived. To these activities may be added his protracted concern with antiquities of most kinds. This might not have been on quite the scale of his other engagements, but Banks was nonetheless a useful source of material for the Museum. He was an active travelling antiquary in his early years, conducting a number of excavations in Britain, while later on he participated more in the organization of antiquities located at the Museum or circulating elsewhere in London. As in botany, we see in this pattern how Banks started his career with fieldwork and collecting, and ended it primarily as a patron and administrator.

The last years of Banks's career saw problems over the acquisition of some of the larger collections arriving from the Mediterranean and North Africa. These problems raise general issues in terms of the Museum and collecting in this period. The obligations of the Museum, the expectations of collectors, the market prices available for collections and the funds government might provide for them to be purchased, transferred and housed all led to controversial differences. These issues will need to be considered in later sections, but, to begin with, it is to Banks's field and library work that we turn in an effort to understand how he made an impact in London and at the British Museum in the years leading to the 1790s.

British Traveller and Digger: 1767–80

Apart from Banks's other concerns at the British Museum, mainly to do with natural history and ethnography, another important theme emerges. This relates Banks's own interests in antiquities and bibliography to the organization and growth of collections in these fields at the Museum. Banks did not retain antiquities, and the pattern of his donations and of his involvement with their organization at the British Museum and elsewhere is an interesting study. As in other disciplines, he tended to give away material he did not collect, and therefore favoured the Museum with a range of antiquities that he obtained. Another destination for gifts was the Society of Antiquaries, to which he was elected a Fellow on 27 February 1766, some two months before being elected a Fellow of the Royal Society. Just over a year after entering the Antiquaries, at the anniversary meeting of 1767, Banks was elected to the Society's council.[2] He was elected again in subsequent years, sitting more regularly as a council member later in life.

Banks's election to the Society of Dilettanti came in 1774, several years after his elections to the Antiquaries and the Royal Society. It followed the *Endeavour* voyage, when he was still a popular bachelor living freely in London. At the Dilettanti he joined a select group, one of whom was his old patron at the Admiralty, Lord Sandwich. Others in this set included William Hamilton, Thomas Dundas, Kenneth Mackenzie and Constantine John Phipps, the last having accompanied Banks to Newfoundland and Labrador in 1766. The Dilettanti taste was for classical antiquities and lively conviviality, and Banks partook heartily of both. However, by 1778 this lifestyle was changing as he started to contemplate marriage, and began to assume more formal duties in London societies. Shouldering more of the responsibility for managing the societies of which he was a member enhanced Banks's overall standing among them. In February 1778 he became Very High Steward of the Society of Dilettanti, in March he was made Secretary, and by April he was Treasurer.[3] The Royal Society was the oldest and most powerful of the London societies, and being its President provided Banks with a large portion of the influence he subsequently deployed so effectively in the cause of exploration. Thus, when, in November 1778, he was elected President of the Royal Society for the first time, Banks's rise to the top of London Learned Society was all but complete. Marriage to a rich co-heiress in March 1779 put the seal of respectability on Banks's status as a leading figure in London's scientific and social circles.

Later on Banks helped to coordinate certain collections of antiquities between the Antiquaries, the Dilettanti and the British Museum in much the way he did, albeit on a far grander scale, for ethnography and natural history. He was able to do this because of the links that existed between these bodies and because of his own standing in each of them. Joint membership of the capital's societies was typical of the connections to which an educated man might aspire in Georgian London, and through them Banks was able to increase considerably the level of control he exerted. Yet Banks's early interests extended beyond the London world of neo-classical fashion and learning to the study of British remains, especially of a prehistoric kind. Before settling down to married life, and the regular pattern of meetings and committee work that London Learned Society demanded, Banks undertook a youthful period of fieldwork in Britain. Alongside his other achievements, this activity was sure to have gained the notice and approval of antiquaries in the metropolis, for it combined the two traditional field pursuits of antiquities and natural history. Both were important to Banks's development, with his work as a travelling antiquary having rather more to recommend it than previously thought, his barrow digging proving especially interesting. Fortunately, Banks left records of some of the sites he examined, and these show how he worked and gained in understanding as a barrow digger through to the 1780s.

In the records Banks left there is little evidence that he speculated on the general pattern and history that burial mounds and other monuments might collectively reveal, but he does appear to have been reasonably systematic in his approach to excavation itself. Tracing some of Banks's digs enables us to see his basic approach, and to assess his initial commitment to antiquarian studies with which, in their various forms, he never really lost touch. Of course, Banks made no claim to be an expert in these studies. Indeed, the conventional view is that this was a time when antiquarian research slumbered, and that in the middle and late eighteenth century barrow study lay fallow.[4] If evidence to the contrary exists, then some of it might be discerned in the intelligent amateur fieldwork being conducted by and with the help of figures like Banks. But it needs to be remembered that for some in his day the recording and collection of objects from the field, whether natural or artificial, was redolent of the all too often indiscrimate approach of the virtuosi of the seventeenth century. Antiquaries were frequently the object of derision or contempt, not least from those attached to the traditions of classical written history, or who simply could not see the point of collecting relics and assorted fragments for no obvious reason. What also needs to be remembered about the context in which Banks worked is that understanding of prehistory was severely restricted. Bishop Ussher had dated the creation to 4004 BC, and chronology of this kind hampered consideration of extreme antiquity. When they were understood as such, archaeological discoveries were largely described as Druidical (Celtic), Roman, Saxon or Danish. More often, artefacts like flint arrowheads and stone axes were thought to be elf-bolts shot by witches or fairies, so that enquiries into the remote past were no less a matter of folklore as of direct observation and science.

Banks, however, never subscribed to popular myths like these, drawing instead on a body of increasingly impressive fieldwork performed by his and the preceding generation. His youthful knowledge of British antiquities derived from fieldwork undertaken before and then after the *Endeavour* voyage, and this gave him direct archaeological experience of prehistoric remains like tumuli, henges and other ancient monuments in locations ranging from Wales to Lincolnshire and the Orkney Islands. Prior to the *Endeavour* voyage, in 1767 and early 1768, Banks toured parts of Wales and the Midlands, and this enabled him to collect plants, to visit new industrial centres and also to pursue his fascination with archaeology. He had noticed barrows before, conjecturing vaguely in May 1767 on the nature of a long barrow seen near Blandford in Dorset. This had been recommended to him by the Bishop of Carlisle, Charles Lyttelton, who was President of the Society of Antiquaries and a sponsor for Banks's election both to that society and the Royal Society.[5] However, Banks's desire to inspect the barrow at Blandford was frustrated, and so he had to wait until later in the year when, on 19 October, he led a dig at a Bronze Age round barrow in the vicinity of two Welsh villages, Llansadwrn and Talley.[6] It was the first of his recorded digs, possibly the earliest recorded cairn excavation in South Wales,[7] and therefore of some significance here.

For the dig Banks employed a procedure fairly typical of such excavations up to the nineteenth century, using a trench cut through the barrow. It was a rough technique, but the work appears to have been carefully managed despite that, and Banks's account shows how he considered the mound's structure, its contents and their relative positions. Among the things he noted was that the barrow was located on a prominent part of the mountain, and he speculated that it might consequently have been raised for an important person. He measured its width and height, and established that the top layer was of earth with gravel and charcoal in it, and that underneath this was a cairn of stones. Banks took the opportunity to examine the substances of which the soil on the mound was made by allowing soil to slip into the trench as the digging progressed. Some finds were described, such as a fragment of an earthenware pot that was unglazed, of a coarse grain and not properly fired. Other finds were drawn, one being a barbed-and-tanged flint arrowhead, which led Banks to conjecture that the barrow might be more ancient than others containing metallic objects. At the centre of the mound Banks found and described a cist burial, correctly concluding from what he saw that cremation was not solely a Roman practice. In this he differed, as he wrote, with Robert Plot, a leading antiquary of the previous century. Banks measured the stone chamber, taking down its dimensions, and he described the decayed state and position of the bones of two people inside. These were lying diagonally across the chamber floor amid a layer of clay and charcoal, and Banks noted that the arrowhead was near them.

This was a reasonable start to Banks's work in archaeology, especially with regard to his assessment of the finds, their nature and situation. When he reached London late in January 1768, the dig might well have been the subject of informal discussion at the Antiquaries, including with Lyttelton. Banks's subsequent work on the Orkney Islands in 1772 was certainly discussed in London, exciting much interest there. Banks visited the Orkney Islands on his way back from the expedition he led to Iceland, and with his travelling companions examined some important sites. Work on Orcadian burials was then stirring, a local man called Graham writing about excavations he had undertaken to Robert Ramsey, the natural historian and antiquary, who passed on Graham's comments to Banks later in the year.[8] In his journal of the Iceland trip Banks refers to opening tombs near the Neolithic village of Skara Brae, and observing the Stones of Stenness.[9] The Bronze Age tombs that Banks excavated, located on the Links of Skaill, were subsequently covered by sand until early in the twentieth century when high winds exposed them again.[10] By this time Banks's visit had been all but forgotten, and in his journal mention of these digs is indeed rather brief. However, other sources exist, and they include the account of his servant, James Roberts, who wrote at greater length about Orkney.[11] There is, too, the description by George Low, a naturalist living at Stromness, who assisted Banks while he was in Orkney.[12] Despite some differences between them, these accounts show how the earliest detailed examination of the sites took place.

Banks supervised the excavations, some time around 18 October digging away the whole of two mounds in vertical cross section from one side to the other: certainly a more sweeping method than before. As with his work in Wales, the internal structure of the mounds was described, and Banks and his companions scrutinized the composition of the layers of earth and stone within. Here it should be remembered that, while acting as antiquaries, Banks's party consisted of naturalists and medical men. Banks was himself a capable botanist, and Solander and Low were also highly accomplished naturalists. With them was James Lind, a physician who took an interest in astronomy and geology. This meant that a mix of qualified professional men and experienced natural philosophers joined in interpreting the available evidence. They discovered a crouched cist inhumation in one of the mounds, and deduced the age of the male skeleton from dental evidence. At the foot of the male were laid the bones of another individual, and the group interpreted these as belonging to a younger female, whose remains might have been a secondary burial. Attempting to determine the sex and age of the occupants using their skeletons was a scientific technique, and identification of dead insects found in the burial, the *Dermestes* of Linnaeus they thought, was a no less advanced approach.

Both in its scientific aspects and as a whole the excavation was a worthy addition to antiquarian knowledge. Low sent news of it in a letter to George Paton of Edinburgh, dated 27 November 1772. Paton was an antiquary and a correspondent of Thomas Pennant and Richard Gough. He forwarded details of the Orkney finds to his friends, and in this way the network centred on London was alerted to the discoveries. On 12 and 19 March 1773, Gough read a summary of Low's letter to the Society of Antiquaries, and this was subsequently published with illustrations in *Archaeologia*.[13] The published paper described just one of the excavations at Orkney, showing a section of a mound and above this a bone and a bead close-up, but it may be considered alongside the drawings and scale plans Banks also had made of the various sites. These were completed by three draughtsmen, John Cleveley, John Frederick Miller and his brother James, as well as a Swedish surveyor, Frederick Herman Walden. The drawings and plans have survived, and are now held at the British Library.[14] Showing their place in the landscape and particulars of their construction, the visual survey of the Orkney monuments is a reliable and immediate record of the sites as seen by Banks and the others late in 1772. Taken together with the letters and journals, these materials are among the more significant archaeological works that Banks undertook, but his activities elsewhere are also revealing, his next dig being conducted on a very different kind of barrow to that encountered at Orkney.

In late July and August of 1775, the same year that Low's letter appeared in *Archaeologia,* Banks visited Mulgrave Hall, the Yorkshire home of his old friend Constantine John Phipps. Banks travelled north in his huge carriage, encumbered by his various papers and specimens, so heavy in all that the carriage was equipped with chains for braking on slopes. The company was quite as unusual as their transport. With Banks went the playwright George Colman and his son of the same name. At York Constantine's younger brother, Augustus Phipps, joined the party, which also included Omai, a native of Raiatea in the Society Islands. Omai came to England on one of the ships returning from James Cook's second voyage. Banks was given his charge, and Omai proved a popular figure in London's social circles, ably cultivating the attentions of those he met, including those of George III himself. Progress was slow on the way to Mulgrave Hall, due partly to Banks's habit of continually leaping from the carriage to collect plants, something the boys and Omai happily copied. Once at Mulgrave the group were treated to swims in the chilly North Sea with Omai leading the way, to short evening lectures from Banks on the Linnean System (illustrated by cutting up a cauliflower) and to the Polynesian method of cooking food buried in an earth oven.

By contrast with the Orkney expedition this must rank as one of the strangest parties to have entered the field of archaeology, including, as it did, an Arctic explorer in the shape of Phipps, a veteran of the South Seas in Banks, a Pacific islander, a former manager of Covent Garden Theatre and two schoolboys. Yet so it was, for from 29 to 30 August, and undoubtedly at Banks's instigation, they excavated a round barrow, locally known as a hoe.[15] Taking the operation seriously, Banks kept longer and more detailed notes than before, and so we come much closer to Banks the digger in Yorkshire than we do in Orkney. His reliance on closely observed facts is praiseworthy, as is his attention to finds, their composition and condition. The dig also introduces here the first recorded example of concerted barrow work by Banks in England. The barrow that was chosen stood just west of the village of Goldsborough. It had a commanding seaward view on a hill, many of the other hills in the area having barrows on them as well. Measuring the mound, as he always did, Banks entered by opening a large circular hole at its centre. This procedure preserved more of the external form than the other methods Banks had used previously, and was a technique preferred by later and more eminent figures in archaeology.[16] Local tradition told that the mound had been used as a beacon and not for burial, and so greater attention was paid to stratigraphy, in particular to evidence of burning. A burnt layer was found immediately under the turf, and the charred bones of animals were soon identified in other burnt layers, of which there were a number. As Banks dug deeper various finds were made, and each carefully recorded.

Pieces of an earthenware urn were revealed with fibrous roots penetrating throughout, something that led Banks to conclude the urn had been broken for some time. The urn was situated on a pavement in a collapsed stone chamber that also contained some earth and reddish grains resembling hemp seeds or even insect eggs. The grains were located to the east side of the urn fragments, but Banks did not believe the grains were eggs, and concentrated on preserving the indented pattern on the urn fragments in a drawing. Having carefully removed the fragments, he estimated the original height of the urn at about ten inches, and drew an outline of its probable shape. As always, he scrutinized the mode of manufacture, which he thought 'ill tempered', finding quartz the size of a pea in one fragment. Inside the urn were bits of bone, charcoal and 'vegetable mould', but no traces of a skull or teeth from which to ascertain the origin of this material. Thus far the barrow had proved intriguing, and with Banks providing a stew for everyone at the camp using a 'tin machine' (all Colman junior later said of this device was that it had a 'hard name' – he was only twelve when he visited Mulgrave), the party returned to work the next day.

Ash and charcoal continued to be found, and the bones of a large animal were also discovered. Three teeth were unearthed, and Banks identified these as belonging to a horse, taking note of their position in relation to the urn. Likewise, the position of a second smaller urn was recorded, this being nearly at the centre of the mound, and on a separate and larger pavement than the first. Since it was not as broken as the first urn, its shape could be discerned as 'much resembling a common Pipkin with its handle'. The manufacture of both urns was apparently the same, although the second was smaller at about five inches high, and it contained no evidence of cremation. The two pavements showed considerable evidence of burning, and Banks found that they were constructed in the same manner. Each was formed of flat stones laid level on a base of coarse gravel, all on two inches of sand. This was set on top of the clay soil of the country, which contained small stones. Having reached this last layer the dig was almost finished. However, Banks briefly described some pieces of worked flint with rounded sides, as if broken out from pebbles. These were found near the second pavement, and were evidently not from the local area. He also discovered what he thought were pieces of jet, one shaped like a button of about an inch in diameter. A piece was burned on a heated poker, its odour 'a good deal resembling the herb Tanzy'. The Yorkshire dig must have entertained Banks's host and his guests, and perhaps showed better general technique on Banks's part in the way the barrow was opened and the entire procedure recorded. On returning to London from Yorkshire, Banks, Daniel Solander and Charles Blagden burned some more of the jet, but the fragrance noticed earlier was not reproduced. With this destructive experiment the Yorkshire dig was over, if not entirely forgotten by the likes of young Colman, and Banks turned his thoughts to the conduct of the Royal Society and its dining club.

Banks's inclination to travel had started to wane, although his urge to examine barrows was still apparent in Lincolnshire, where mounds were located conveniently close to his main estates. In the last of his recorded digs, Banks followed in the footsteps of no less a figure than William Stukeley,[17] for in October 1780 he 'Employed 2 men to open the northernmost of those three Barrows in the side of the Road leading to Revesby Town, which St/o/ukely has described in his *Itineraria Curiosa*'.[18] Stukeley, renowned for his work on the ancient stone circles of Stonehenge and Avebury, also published in 1724 *Itinerarium Curiosum*.[19] This appeared in print some years before Stukeley's greatest contribution to British antiquarian studies, and contains details of tours he undertook from about 1711 onwards, including his observations on a number of barrows and other prehistoric remains. Banks was therefore drawing on the account of a travelling Lincolnshire forebear whose best work established new standards in field archaeology for antiquaries, but what Banks discovered on this occasion was that digging someone else's barrow could be a singularly unsatisfying pastime.

Using the same technique as in Yorkshire, he made an opening at the centre of the barrow, this opening being a square measuring twelve by fourteen feet. Initially, hard gravel was encountered in which coal and glass were found. One piece of coal seemed to resemble that from Newcastle, and alongside evidence like this Banks noticed marks suggesting there had been recent digging. Lumps of sandstone and granite may also have been signs of modern disturbance. A stone of one and a half inches in diameter that had been flattened and rounded by hand was uncovered, and Banks noted that this was made of granite he did not recognize. By this stage he was aware of and following closely the evidence of an earlier excavation. After digging through looser earth in what he supposed was Stukeley's original circular opening, the land surface was passed. Eleven and a half feet below the top of the mound Banks discovered a rotting switch, evidently left there by Stukeley, and had the hole filled in, adding more bits of glass and coal to show that the barrow had been opened a second time. Disappointed in his search for 'Druidical antiquities', at the very bottom he left 'a piece of freestone with the year 1780 engrav'd upon it', and there it must still lie as a hidden reminder of Banks's youthful interests.

After taking holy orders in 1729, Stukeley lapsed into fantasies about ancient Celtic priests and the monuments they supposedly left behind, but Banks's use of *Itinerarium Curiosum* was not ill-judged. Stukeley had been a leading antiquary of the previous generation, and Banks was drawing on his example and the relevant secondary literature covering British travel and prehistoric remains. Indeed, he studied other eminent forerunners, one of the most famous being William Camden. Banks used Camden's great work, *Britannia,* during his British travels, the edition he carried with him being that prepared in 1695 by Edmund Gibson. Banks used Gibson's edition to annotate the journal of his 1767 excursion to Wales and the Midlands. Camden had travelled and corresponded across Britain during the years he took to construct *Britannia*, which was first published in 1586, and in so doing he set an example in antiquarian fieldwork and scholarship for later generations to follow. Banks's reading and his own original fieldwork were combined in contributions that he made to the last of the great editions of *Britannia*, which Richard Gough issued in 1789.[20] Banks's work on Orkney is, for example, referred to in Gough's edition, which bristled with plant lists, including one for Lincolnshire. Gough corresponded with Banks about Lincolnshire when preparing this edition, and Banks responded that he thought it his duty to help elucidate the county's history.

When Gough's *Britannia* was published, Banks received a copy from the editor.[21] But whereas Gibson's *Britannia* stimulated a revival of antiquarian interest amongst English gentry at the beginning of the eighteenth century, a movement that led to the establishment of the Society of Antiquaries,[22] by Gough's time the importance of *Britannia* had waned, to be replaced by more detailed regional and county histories to which Banks also contributed. No less meticulous than these histories were the scientific land surveys conducted by the Board of Ordnance. In Banks's lifetime significant progress was made in mapping Britain and its various natural and man-made features. As President of the Royal Society, Banks helped with this work too. In 1783 he organized the British survey team that was set up in response to a French proposal for a trigonometrical operation to determine the difference in longitude between the observatories at Greenwich and Paris. The British team was led by Major-General William Roy, who also produced excellent maps and plans of Roman military sites in northern Britain, even if the historical account he gave with them was wayward.

At a local level Banks assisted with the production of maps and studies of Lincolnshire, the county he knew best. Indeed, it was in Lincolnshire that Banks drew on his strongest local connections to ensure a flow of material to the British Museum. In this way his interest in archaeology persisted, even though he was less likely to conduct excavations himself in older age. Finds were often made during the agricultural and drainage works that transformed the Lincolnshire landscape in the late eighteenth century, works in which Banks participated as an active landowner and county figure. Banks was especially strong in his knowledge of Lincolnshire's topography and architecture because his main country estates were situated around Revesby, near Horncastle. Agricultural activities, the scouring of waterways and the development of drainage throughout the county all produced coins and other artefacts that passed through Banks's hands to the British Museum and elsewhere. He eagerly watched some of these operations, knowing that important objects might be found. For example, when the River Witham was being scoured in 1788 he invited his old Welsh friend, John Lloyd, to witness the substantial harvest of Roman and Danish coins that this yielded. The Witham continued to surrender its treasures in the years that followed, and in 1815 Banks sent to the Society of Antiquaries a cup and two daggers that had been dredged up, along with his own conjectures on them using a number of footnoted sources.[23] Activities like dredging were certainly not conducted for archaeological purposes in the sense that Banks's earlier digs had been. Nevertheless, chance discoveries, construction projects and government works all impinged in various ways on early archaeology (and have had their bearing since), and Banks was quick to take advantage of any opportunities they provided.

The tradition of gentry supporting their county and publications to do with it was one to which Banks firmly adhered. As he became less mobile, and so unable to explore in the field, his interest in more recent history became increasingly apparent, and, again, this manifested itself in Lincolnshire. Banks always had an interest in buildings and documented history, and from 1789 to 1797 he employed John Claude Nattes to record over 500 Lincolnshire buildings in line and watercolour, thereby creating an extensive record of the county's architecture. Similar concerns are evident in later discussions touching generally on topics in etymology, architecture and traditional dress with Francis Douce, Keeper of Manuscripts at the British Museum, 1799–1812. No doubt these were a distraction from the infirmities of old age, and looking back over the range of Banks's pursuits he appears in many ways typical of an eighteenth-century gentleman with antiquarian tastes. However, there is evidence of some noteworthy fieldwork in Banks's early career. In particular, his British excursions followed a strong tradition of countrywide travel and observation at the head of which stood great figures like William Camden. But Banks's travels were also part of a wider movement in British tourism and taste at this time.

Through his British travels Banks increased active research in parts of Wales and in northern areas of Britain, especially the north-west of Scotland, which was being visited much more frequently by geologists, antiquaries and writers after his exploits there in 1772 on his way to Iceland.[24] Thomas Pennant was in the area at the same time as Banks, and Samuel Johnson followed in 1773, with others, like the French geologist and savant Barthélemy Faujas de St Fond, visiting in 1784. Responses to the countryside and its people were varied, and some travellers even struggled to brave the sea crossing to the Hebrides, but that was no obstacle to Banks. Unusually for an otherwise factual writer, on 11 August 1772 the coast of Morven drew from him lines of Ossianic sentiment: 'Morven the land of Heroes /once/ the seat of the Exploits of Fingal the mother of romantick scenery of Ossian I could not Even Sail past it without a touch of Enthusiasm sweet affection of the mind which can gather pleasures from the Empty Elements & realize substantial pleasure which three fourths of mankind are ignorant of … to have read ten pages of Ossian under the shades of those woods would have been a Luxury above the reach of Kings'. The translations and Gaelic poetry of Ossian, written from songs and verse collected by a Scottish schoolmaster called James Macpherson, are generally regarded as inspired forgeries (Samuel Johnson openly condemned them as such, and Macpherson challenged him to a duel for it), but tourists liked the melancholy grandeur of such works, which seemed to suit the dramatic mountainous terrain and moody Scottish weather. This new taste was itself encouraged by the fascination with Druidic mythology and ancient ruins in general, but Banks succumbed only on occasion to such reverie. More typically Augustan, he recorded the farming practices and kelp burning of the west coast of Scotland, memorably surveying Fingal's Cave on Staffa from 12 to 13 August. His survey of Staffa was subsequently published in Pennant's *Tour of Scotland and Voyage to the Hebrides*,[25] receiving much praise. At Staffa, and to show the range of responses a single Highland traveller might experience, even a veteran trained in the rigorous empirical school of the Royal Society, Banks wrote of Fingal's Cave:

> Compard to this what are the Cathedrals or the palaces built by man mere models or play things imitations as diminutive as /the/ his works /of man/ will always be when compard to those of nature where is now the boast of the Architect regularity the only part in which he fancied himself to Exceed his mistress nature is here found in her posession & here it has been for ages uncounted is not this the school where the art was originaly Studied & what had been added to this by the whole grecian school a Capital to ornament the Column /which/ of nature /had given the/ of which they could execute only a model & /that/ for that very Capital they were Obligd to a bust of Acanthus
> how amply does nature repay those who study her wonderfull works

Impressive though the natural symmetry of the island's geology certainly is, these are still remarkable words from a journalist like Banks. Having admired the basalt formations, Banks and his party rapidly set about accurately surveying them: 'Enough of the beauties of Staffa I shall now proceed to describe it & its productions more Philosophicaly'.

Banks may have eschewed the traditional Grand Tour, but he was in the vanguard of those broadening the boundaries of travel within Britain later in the eighteenth century.[26] Using his uncle's estate at Edwinsford in Carmarthenshire as a base, Banks ranged widely in Wales and the Midlands.[27] He was familiar with the landscape of Wales, its valley and mountain flora and its ancient remains. He also toured the River Wye in May 1767, a few years before William Gilpin visited there in search of the picturesque.[28] The Wye was an increasingly popular tourist attraction, and Banks considered Tintern Abbey 'a most noble Ruin by far the Lightest Peice of Gothick architecture I ever saw'. The Abbey was then festooned with plants, which was how J. M. W. Turner depicted it in 1794. Evidently, it was not the only ruin in that condition, because further down the river at Chepstow Castle Banks noted the plants growing from the outer walls. For Banks, observing nature, and especially collecting plants, was a natural accompaniment to recording antiquities. At Piercefield, the home of Valentine

Morris and a carefully managed picturesque setting, Banks thought the cliffs romantic while the cultivated land appeared highly fertile. Travelling by going nowhere, he moved in one turn from the sublime rocks rising above the river to agricultural land of exceptional fertility: '[I] Have no doubt of Pronouncing it the finest place I ever saw the transition here from very fine Lawn to naked rocks is very often Seen by turning yourself round in the very spot on which you stand the romantick in which the Cheif beauty of this Place consists is formd by a semicircle of rocks Coverd with wood the foot of which is washd by the Wye the opposite side of which is formd sometimes by Rocks over which you see the sea at other times by the Richest cultivated Land in the world Coverd with Corn & Pasture'. The Wye, it seemed, had everything a tourist could want.

From August of the same year to January 1768, Banks undertook a much more extensive tour of the Welsh countryside and the growing industrial network of the Midlands. Again using his uncle's estate as a base, from 15 September to 13 October Banks commented on twelve castles in his journal. This was as he toured Brecon and then Pembrokeshire, and some twenty-two castles appear in his complete account, of which Chepstow is the oldest stone example in Britain, the Normans starting its construction in 1067. Banks returned to Edwinsford 'well pleasd with my excursion into Pembrokeshire', and concluded the initial South Wales portion with 'general observations on the Countrey I have seen'. This was a technique he employed in his longer journals, especially during the *Endeavour* voyage, when making a final, overall judgment about an area or experience. There it is the mark of considered writing, and a rounded approach. Here, as in each of the shorter journals, accurate description is mixed with aesthetic appreciation. Many of the castles were ruins on hills affording, Banks thought, 'Prospects', their high situation 'Commanding a very Extensive & beautifull Countrey'. Such a style was suited to an essentially private journal, where personal remarks and asides have their place. Nevertheless, Banks shows in his account respect for ancient structures as relics that can be interpreted in themselves, and which require close physical inspection along with their surroundings. Even his briefer remarks include some idea of the building materials and architectural style of the remains he described, as well as reference to their situation and the configuration of features such as mounds, ramparts and ditches, some measured by being paced out.

In addition to this, the rugged hills and mountains of North Wales also attracted Banks's attention, these having been examined by other British naturalists in the middle and later seventeenth century, among them the great John Ray, and his contemporary, the naturalist and pioneering philologist, Edward Lhuyd. Banks ventured northwards for an unedifying stay with Thomas Pennant at Downing from 21 to 30 November. His route north took him from Edwinsford east through Llandovery, Brecon, Hay and Hereford, and then up through towns like Ludlow, Shrewsbury, Wrexham, Chester and thence to Downing itself. After this Banks explored the Vale of Clwyd, the banks of the Dee Estuary and next visited his estates in Staffordshire, before inspecting various mining, canal and factory works in the Midlands, including the works of Josiah Wedgwood at Burslem. Banks went on to study the canal being constructed by the Duke of Bridgewater to link his coal mine to the Manchester market. Subsequently, on 21 January 1768, Banks met Matthew Boulton for the first time and inspected Boulton's factory at Soho, Birmingham, before making his way back to London, visiting Oxford on the way. Typically on each of these excursions Banks described the scenery, settlements, various castles and other structures, including Roman remains, while collecting many plant specimens to add to his herbarium. In doing so, he covered the range of natural and artificial phenomena to be expected of a Royal Society traveller and fieldworker. Banks's 1767 tour journal for Wales and the Midlands is a considerable document of about 35,000 words, revealing much about what a British traveller might visit and describe at this time, including one soon to embark for the South Seas.

Years later, in 1773, Banks organized another tour of Wales for himself and some friends, one of whom was the naturalist John Lightfoot.[29] The water-colourist Paul Sandby was also among those accompanying Banks, and Sandby sketched the scenes encountered, building up the work necessary to produce the acclaimed aquatints of South and then North Wales that he published, the former being dedicated to Banks and Charles Francis Greville, who could not go on this tour because his father had just died.[30] Starting in June, the Banks party travelled to the estate at Edwinsford, from there visiting the Wye and, as ever, Tintern Abbey. They then ranged west to Pembrokeshire, and afterwards north through Hereford and Shropshire. John Lloyd joined the party when it reached his home at Denbigh. Together the group then travelled through Conway and Bangor to Llanberis, and on to Dolbadarn Castle, before climbing Snowdon. After this they visited Angelsey before turning back towards London, taking in Chester and finally dispersing. Banks does not appear to have kept a journal of this trip, having tired of such things by 1773, and having already covered much of this ground in 1767. He was by now a seasoned traveller in Wales. Moreover, on 3 December he was elected for the first time to the council of the Royal Society, a sign of things to come.

We see in Banks's activities that the travel and correspondence networks upon which British antiquarian studies depended still persisted in the late eighteenth century, and even that some new ground was occasionally being broken. Along with these networks, artistic endeavour and tourism in general were increasing in the parts of Britain that drew Banks's interest as a young man. In the last quarter of the eighteenth century the pattern of travel in Britain changed considerably, with improved roads and communications, and greater interest in the British landscape encouraging more people to venture to apparently remote areas of their own island. Banks was one of them. He and a number of his contemporaries explored Britain, and they steadily uncovered various British remains through the years. Among the watercolours, Gothic ruins, druids and bards of the late eighteenth century, then, there was some evidence of reasonably careful work conducted on certain archaeological sites, while detailed mapping of the country in general proceeded along scientific lines. What we might say is that where naturalists and antiquaries first travelled, there artists, writers and tourists were to follow. We might also conclude that, notwithstanding the British plant specimens that Banks gathered, as an antiquary he achieved a range in his interests that has yet to be fully appreciated. Additionally, although he published little on the subject, Banks remained a reliable source of information on Lincolnshire's history and landscape. Here, too, his reading and research are of significance, and, along with the artefacts he obtained and gave away, they may be glimpsed in the surviving works and legacy of others.

As suggested, Banks did not develop a broader framework by which to interpret the tumuli and other monuments he visited, confining himself to accounts of the digs and descriptions of sites. The type of approach to collection, comparison and classification used so effectively in the field of natural history does not seem to have been applied in a determined way by Banks to antiquities. It is understandable that Banks's early exploits as a travelling naturalist have tended to obscure those as an antiquary, but by the standards of his day Banks was a reasonably experienced barrow digger, and his geographical scope may even be considered as impressive. Additionally, by the early 1780s he had employed most of the known techniques for opening barrows, returning finds to London for further discussion or analysis as necessary. During the period of his British travels the capital provided Banks with opportunities to discuss his work with other antiquaries and natural philosophers, although he did not make public his notes, and this is probably the main reason why his digs have been neglected. As with so much else, the collections and example Banks provided encouraged others in their research, and filtered into print mainly under their names if at all.

Records of Banks's barrow digging and British travelling cease in the 1780s, by which time his movements were based around his estates and London's societies and learned organizations, including the British Museum. As with collections in natural history and ethnography, he channelled any antiquities that he obtained to particular colleagues, or to appropriate bodies like the Society of Antiquaries and the Museum. In this way he distinguished between different pursuits, and never collected antiquities on a major scale, much of what he distributed now being lost. Banks was always more prominent as a collector and distributor of plants and books, and in the 1780s these became his main concerns. With the arrival at Soho Square of Jonas Dryander in 1777, a new phase in book collecting commenced in the capital. From 1777 to 1810 Dryander was an integral part of Banks's Soho establishment, and in these years Banks increasingly concentrated attention on his library and herbarium. Educated at Uppsala and a student of Linnaeus, Dryander seems to have given Banks the support he needed to develop collections in these specific areas, and together they assembled a formidable natural history library and herbarium, each intended to be used in support of the other.

In Banks's personal library the main branches were botany, zoology and mineralogy, with a comprehensive series of learned journals, travel literature, agricultural and horticultural works, medical publications and other science-based writings. These reached back to the beginnings of print, and in natural history were unrivalled in Britain. At the British Museum Banks made particularly generous donations of Icelandic books and manuscripts, and ultimately bequeathed his entire library to the nation. The methods and routes of acquisition by which Banks's library grew, being those of purchase and exchange, with a large number of donations coming directly from authors, were ones Banks could and did employ to enrich the Museum. We now turn therefore to his work on behalf of the Museum library in order to discover how he contributed to its development through to the turn of the century.

Assisting the Museum Library: 1778–1800

One of the earliest services Banks rendered the Museum as a trustee was to assist in reviewing the collection of plays bequeathed by David Garrick. The Garrick collection consisted of many dramatic works of the great Elizabethan and Jacobean writers, along with those of numerous minor and anonymous figures. In April 1779 the decision was taken that 'Joseph Banks & Matthew Duane Esqrs. be desired with Mr Harper to meet with Mr R Wallis to view the Books and settle what should be understood to belong to the Collection bequested to the Museum'.[31] On 15 April the group met at Garrick's house, where 'they found that several Volumes containing a variety of different Plays were wanting, especially the first edition of Shakespears Plays &c ... They thought the best way would be to remove the different Volumes that they then saw ... to the Museum'.[32] This done, further investigations for the remaining material took place, but Banks's bibliographic talents had evidently been recognized.

Banks's strengths as a book collector were based on his numerous contacts and his willingness to search for and then inspect collections whenever they were on offer in the capital. His knowledge of what was available grew with his network, and consequently he was asked to search at home and abroad for library material for the Museum.[33] From the beginning he knew and used booksellers like Peter

Elmsley, who was also employed by the Museum.[34] However, Banks also developed a keen awareness of the books and collections circulating in London and further afield, and acted on his own and the Museum's behalf in monitoring the markets. In due course, he and his librarian, Jonas Dryander, became experts in what was published and sold across Europe, especially on natural history. Such extensive specialist knowledge was essential to the growth of Banks's personal library, but, importantly, it could also serve the Museum.

In addition to these activities, Banks gave generously to the Museum, starting early in his trusteeship. In February 1780 he donated manuscripts on medicine, some sermons, and also two volumes of newspapers for the years 1679 and 1680.[35] From November 1772 through to March 1781 he presented a series of valuable collections of Icelandic and Latin manuscripts and tracts. Banks had led a scientific expedition to Iceland in 1772 from which a lifelong concern with its affairs emerged, and the first of his Museum donations relating to that country comprised 31 manuscripts and 121 books.[36] This was a considerable donation, soon followed by others. In 1783 Banks presented a parcel of books, a gift he made because he had been allowed to see pages of the Museum's catalogue of printed books as they came off the press. An early sight of the catalogue undoubtedly improved Banks's own knowledge of what was in print, but it also gave him an insight into the Museum's holdings.[37] Thus, he was aware not only of what books might be worth adding to his own library, but also what the needs of the Museum were. By the beginning of the 1780s, then, the relationship between Banks and the Museum was already proving mutually beneficial to the library collections.

Armed with what he knew about the book trade and the Museum, Banks attended a standing committee regarding the Museum's library in June 1783. This committee met to monitor the purchase of books using £200 of interest on invested annuities derived from Major Arthur Edwards's Fund.[38] The Edwards Fund was a bequest of £7,000, which had been received by the trustees in 1769. Up to 1812 it was one of the main sources for spending on the library, and so a limited quantity of books was all that could be afforded until the end of Banks's career, when the acquisition of some major libraries became possible. At the June meeting it was decided that capital stock should be used to purchase manuscripts, coins and medals.[39] These were items that the Edwards Fund was occasionally used to obtain, further stretching the meagre resources available, but predominantly the bequest was spent on the library. In August 1783 Banks donated yet another volume,[40] while in November, at the request of the Principal Librarian, Charles Morton, a £100 grant was voted by the trustees for the purchase of books.[41] Since the sums available to the trustees for library purchases were so small, they came to rely no less on donations than on purchases. Banks's personal contributions to the Museum's library stock during these years were therefore always a welcome addition.[42]

There were, however, other ways in which to support the library. For example, the Museum could and did try to obtain works published by government departments or arising from public projects and missions. These were useful channels for books, maps and surveys of various kinds. Sources included the Board of Longitude, of which Banks was a member from 1778. The Board frequently sent its printed tables and observations to the Museum. In October 1784 the Board presented 'The Original Astronomical Observations Made in the Course of a Voyage to the Northern Pacific Ocean', these observations coming from James Cook's last voyage.[43] Banks had assisted greatly in the publication of Cook's voyages, and a number of other works from departments like the Admiralty were also sent to the Museum. Gifts of official maps, plans and charts were on a relatively small scale, it must be said, but, during his time as Principal Librarian, Joseph Planta tried to encourage government to send more official maps and surveys to the Museum. The arrival of George III's library in 1828 increased the number available, but thereafter it was not until 1867 that an independent department for such material was created at the Museum, and in the same decade serious consideration given to gathering more widely from government publications at home and abroad.

It was not just government and official bodies that directed their publications to the Museum. Numerous societies and academies issued journals, and Banks was a useful route for obtaining material like this. The *Philosophical Transactions* of the Royal Society, like the publications of the Board of Longitude, were regularly presented to the Museum during his tenure as President, 1778–1820. The *Philosophical Transactions* were also conveyed to other institutions in the Banks network, including Harvard University. Apart from seeing that the Society's *Transactions* went to Harvard, in 1788 Banks ensured that the British Museum's library catalogue was sent there too. This willingness to support American institutions and learning extended to the American Academy of Arts and Sciences, which received the *Philosophical Transactions* in the same year. No doubt partly as a result of such gestures, Banks was elected a member of the Academy in 1788,[44] and in 1792 Harvard University returned the compliment it had received of the Museum's library catalogue by sending back the published catalogue of its own library.[45] Exchanges like these were an effective means by which collections grew, as Banks knew only too well, and he tried to increase the circulation of material by drawing on such contacts.

In March 1786 Banks successfully proposed an exchange of one of his library books for one of the Museum's duplicate volumes.[46] This was an unusual occurrence so far as Banks and the Museum library were concerned, but duplicate books, like minerals, shells, coins and other items, were frequently exchanged or sold by the Museum in this period. Another method of acquisition was simply to allow temporary private deposits to be made in the hope that they would eventually become permanent. This was a more uncertain arrangement. For instance, Banks supported the request of the African traveller, James Bruce, to deposit his oriental manuscripts in the Museum. These were made available to the public on condition that Bruce could remove them again if he so wished, and a year after depositing them he sent Elmsley, the book dealer, to collect the papers. From 1788 to 1789, then, readers had the brief pleasure of Bruce's loan.[47]

Conversely, ten years later, the antiquary Richard Gough wanted to make a lifetime deposit of the plates illustrating his *Sepulchral Monuments* while also being permitted access to them when he wanted it. His offer was circulated to many of the trustees, including Banks, but the idea was rejected, one trustee allegedly saying that he 'would not be his [Gough's] warehouseman'.[48] It was a scruple that benefited the Bodleian Library, which was where Gough decided to send important topographical collections instead. Moreover, when in 1810 Gough's library collections were sold following his death, Joseph Planta had to purchase books for the Museum from the sale. Deposits of these kinds were not easy to negotiate, to house or, indeed, to retain, but this was an expense that might possibly have been avoided in different circumstances.[49]

Nonetheless, various contacts increased the library resources, among them Antoine Louis Henri Polier, a Swiss-born army officer and engineer formerly in the employ of the East India Company. Polier, a remarkable character, also lived as a Mughal nobleman in India, and in 1789 he gave the Museum a rare collection of oriental texts and manuscripts through Banks.[50] Gifts like Polier's show how the range of material available to museums had increased as the territories under commercial or other forms of British control had grown. This was a major trend for collecting during a period of European conflict and expansion abroad, not least in India. Just as collectors picked through the Mediterranean area for Roman, Greek and Egyptian remains, so Indian civilization attracted both the admiration and acquisitive interest of Europeans. A sign of how far collecting in the East had developed was the establishment just over ten years later of the Oriental Repository, later called the India Museum, in Leadenhall Street, London. Based at the East India Company's headquarters, this museum was intended to preserve oriental manuscripts and writings brought to Britain from the East. Later it expanded significantly to include Indian natural history, archaeology and art, finally being dispersed in 1879, with material being sent to the British Museum, Kew and South Kensington.

By the time of Polier's gift, the range of Banks's activities on behalf of the library had also grown. For example, Banks was willing to scour the London book market to retrieve rare anonymous drawings on vellum of the west coast of Australia. These had been accidentally lost from the Harleian Collection, and the search for them took Banks 'some years'.[51] In November 1790 the manuscripts were returned to their proper places, and Banks was asked to report on an auction of Persian manuscripts.[52] The following year he donated a copy of his *Icones selectae Plantarum quas in Japonia collegit et delineavit Engelbertus Kaempfer; ex archetypis in Museo Britannico asseveratis*.[53] As its title suggests, this was a suitable gift for the British Museum, since it drew on illustrations of Japanese plants located there.[54]

This gift also shows Banks's interest in the East, and generally in literature and culture related to India and the Pacific. It was an area with which he was always closely associated, so that apart from animals, plants, rocks and minerals relating to this region, books and manuscripts concerning it also arrived through Banks's intervention. On occasion he was even trusted to decide what types of library material might be needed and at what prices. In April 1795 a collection of oriental manuscripts belonging to Nathaniel Brassey Halhed was offered for sale. Halhed had returned to England from service on the subcontinent, where he had gained recognition for assisting Warren Hastings in the administration of India, notably by producing in translation *A Code of Gentoo Laws*.[55] Banks informed the trustees of the sale, and was authorized to make a purchase. By July much of the material obtained for the Museum was in its library, and subsequent purchases of Halhed papers were also made in 1796.[56] Scouring book markets and collections, and organizing purchases, were tasks that Banks undertook for the Museum alongside his committee work. He made valuable donations, and encouraged others to do the same. All this helped to maintain a tradition among some trustees of devotion both to the administration and collections of the Museum.

Such attachment was manifested in the work trustees undertook in life, but it could also be shown in death through the bequests they were willing to make. One example of someone eager to serve the Museum in these ways was Sir William Musgrave. Initially, Musgrave wrote to Banks to request help in becoming a trustee, even listing others from the Banks circle on whom he counted for support.[57] This was in January 1781, but Musgrave was not elected a trustee until 23 January 1783, for Banks did not arrange such things. Nevertheless, the general meeting at which Musgrave's election eventually took place symbolized the ties that bound such men together, and by which the Museum operated and grew during this period. Banks was present to see not only Musgrave elected, but another friend and contributor to the Museum's collections, Sir William Hamilton.[58] Each in their own ways manifested some elements of the traditional support bestowed on the Museum by gentlemen trustees and collectors.

When he died in 1800, it was Banks and Planta who were chosen to review Musgrave's collection of manuscripts and books, rich in biography.[59] One of the last acts Banks performed for his fellow trustee was therefore to pick through

Musgrave's literary remains, finding for the Museum 33 volumes of manuscripts and 1,500 volumes of printed books.[60] The library of Clayton Mordaunt Cracherode, amounting to some 4,500 volumes, also came to the Museum when he died in 1799, eclipsing somewhat Musgrave's bequest.[61] In May of this year Banks was on a standing committee regarding the Cracherode book collection, and particularly what design of cases should be used to house it.[62] Storage was a problem at the Museum, and increases in the library, desirable though they were, contributed to major difficulties with which Banks and others struggled in the first decade of the nineteenth century.

With these acquisitions a new century of change and growth was dawning, and this brought the appointment of the energetic Joseph Planta as Principal Librarian,[63] replacing the rather lax Charles Morton. At the same time, the catalogue of Banks's own library was reaching completion under the title *Catalogus Bibliothecae Historico-Naturalis Josephi Banks Baroneti*.[64] It is the best single record we have of the bibliographical riches at Soho Square up to that date. In 5 volumes, compiled by Banks's librarian, Jonas Dryander, and supervised by Banks himself, the publication's structure reflects the scope of Banks's interests, and the organization of his library. The first volume was volume 2, *Zoologi*, appearing in 1796. In succession, this was followed by: volume 3, *Botanici*, 1797; volume 1, *Scriptores Generales*, 1798; volume 4, *Mineralogi*, 1799, and finally volume 5, *Supplementum et Index Auctores*, 1800. The full work was donated to the Museum, with the last volume arriving in 1801.[65]

We can see represented in this gift Banks's sustained interest in his own library and in that of the Museum throughout the preceding twenty or so years. The interrelationship between the two is apparent from the many users who visited both, from the exchanges and publications produced, and most of all in their ultimate union in 1827. Moreover, the presentation and contents of Dryander's catalogue assisted officers at the Museum, who used it to survey publications on natural history that needed to be acquired, and who took it as an example of how to set out their own catalogues.[66] It was a landmark publication in bibliography, and indicates the extent to which Banks's library anticipated the structure of future natural history libraries, not least those now assembled at the Natural History Museum, London.[67] Although Banks's library was not transferred to the Natural History Museum, the Museum's libraries still follow the broad intellectual divisions upon which his Soho library was originally based.

Antiquities and Expansion: 1800–20

This was a time when antiquities were coming to the fore, and the collections in the Museum were to expand massively, far exceeding its ability to cope. As with the library, Banks contributed to this growth, helping London Learned

Society to organize and house the influx of antiquities. For instance, he was a senior member of the Society of Dilettanti, which led the way in bringing Greek traditions in art and architecture to the attention of scholars and travellers across Europe. Banks wrote in 1785 to communicate the Society's intention to deposit its marbles at the British Museum.[68] These had been kept in Soho Square by Banks, where they had been used as models by the sculptor John Flaxman. The pieces comprised many inscriptions, other fragments and statues that Banks must have come to know well.

On 7 January 1785 the Museum's Secretary wrote to the Dilettanti to thank them for their generosity. The donation was therefore cosily sealed by a letter addressed to Banks, the Society's Secretary, who also happened to be a trustee of the Museum.[69] Behind this polite gesture lay the realization that a private society could no longer accommodate collections on the scale that a national institution could. The donation followed by only a few years that made by the Royal Society, which gave up its own Repository to the British Museum in 1781. It is quite possible that Banks, who was himself disposing of personal collections to the Museum, suggested to the Dilettanti that Bloomsbury was a more appropriate place for antiquities than Soho Square. This would not have been inconsistent with his general approach.

In 1802, by way of another convenient contact, Banks proposed the purchase of Samuel Tyssen's collection of Saxon coins. Tyssen was a Norfolk landowner and antiquary who died in 1800, and for whom Banks was an executor. Tyssen's collection was purchased in July for £661 10s.,[70] but far greater collections arrived that year as the result of French ambition and British naval and military success in the Mediterranean. On 1 August 1798 Admiral Nelson destroyed the French Fleet at the Battle of the Nile, isolating Napoleon's ill-fated Egyptian expedition. In the summer of 1801 the French were forced to evacuate Egypt, and at Alexandria they surrendered to the British, giving up the antiquities they had intended for the Louvre, including the celebrated Rosetta Stone. These antiquities reached England in 1802, becoming the foundation of the Museum's Egyptian collections.[71] Defeating the French also assisted the British in cultivating the Ottoman Empire, against which Napoleon had directed his offensive, with the consequence that parts of the Eastern Mediterranean and of Greece became more accessible to British collectors, among them Ambassador Elgin.

With the arrival of such an important collection, lack of space became a serious problem for which a temporary cover in the courtyard was wholly inadequate.[72] Consequently, in December 1802 Banks, Charles Townley and William Hamilton formed a standing committee to consider a new building for the Egyptian antiquities.[73] By the time the committee submitted its report in 1803 Hamilton was dead. His replacement was Thomas Astle, Keeper of the Records at the Tower from 1783, and another of Banks's acquaintances.[74] The committee spent much of its meeting time at Townley's home, drawing up its plan amid Townley's magnificent collection of Graeco-Roman marbles. This, they said, provided 'abundant opportunities of studying the most approved methods of exhibiting works of Sculpture to advantage ...'.[75] The committee consulted George Saunders, the Museum's architect, and, with some adjustments, its plan was ready in May.[76]

The new gallery was to be in the restrained Palladian style, and to project from the north-west corner of Montagu House, but it was conceived as part of a much larger scheme. This involved extending the western galleries of Montagu House northwards, with a parallel extension being added to the eastern side. However, the Townley Gallery, as it became known, was the only part that was completed. The plan is interesting, and not only because of the Egyptian antiquities for which it was initially intended. Reference was made in it, presumably at Banks's instigation, to the possibility of moving in 'various matters either of Antiquity or of Natural History, such as are now deposited in the lower Apartments of the House, which may when these are filld, be kept with equal convenience in the archd Rooms, indeed it is to be hopd, as pains will be taken to effect that purpose, that these archd Rooms will be less liable to damp, than the lower Story of the present House'. The idea was to raise the room intended for the Egyptian antiquities to the level of the main floor of Montagu House, thereby forming apartments in supporting arches that might be used for storage. As we have seen, more drastic measures were taken instead, and it was not until 1823, and the commencement of Robert Smirke's new building, that overall expansion of the Museum took place, this being in the form of a quadrangle design superimposed on the plan described above.

The growth in antiquities at this time was such that the 1803 plans were themselves overtaken in 1805 by the purchase of the Townley collection.[77] Banks assisted in the negotiations for the collection belonging to his late colleague, working closely, as always, with his friends and associates. Indeed, his correspondence with Charles Abbot, Speaker of the House of Commons, shows how Banks operated as a go-between, ensuring that the delicate process of reaching an agreement with the Townley family went smoothly, and this despite painful attacks of gout. Preparation of a petition to the House of Commons for the purchase fell to Banks, as did relations with the Townley family, while the House itself was dealt with by Abbot.[78] Once the approval of William Pitt had been obtained, the details of whether the Townley bronzes should be included in the purchase, what trusteeships should be offered to the family and the drawing up of a catalogue of the collection all occupied Banks and Abbot.[79] On 5 June Abbot wrote to inform Banks: 'You will have pleasure in hearing that the Museum Petition was presented this afternoon by The Master of the Rolls and was very favourably received by The House'.[80]

Payment for the Townley collection was discussed later in June,[81] when Abbot was pleased that the simple expedient of enlarging and adapting the original plan for housing the Egyptian collection had been chosen as the best way of accommodating the Townley material. This meant that the Egyptian sculptures were placed in the principal gallery, with the Townley Marbles filling the remaining ground floor area. He wrote: 'I sincerely rejoice that our Museum Building is now likely to be finished upon a plan practically right; And that we have laid aside all visions & romances'.[82] Whether Banks shared this sentiment is not clear, but in February 1806 he was appointed to a committee to decide how the Townley Marbles were to be moved,[83] and what route through London they should take.[84] The new galleries were opened on 3 June 1808 with a royal visit,[85] and one aspect of them was the use of favourable top-lighting for the Townley Marbles. However, this technique was not used to grace the Egyptian collection, which was placed in the principal room with side-lighting only. The vases purchased from Sir William Hamilton in 1772 were displayed on the upper floor in bright light as he had requested. Demand from students and artists to visit the galleries was high following the opening. Regulations governing their admittance were drawn up, with arrangements being made for students to come from the Royal Academy, whose collections could not now rival those available at the Museum.[86]

Other routes led out of the Mediterranean for antiquities brought back to Britain. Even Banks had links to the traditional hunting ground for classical remains. These links were, of course, eclipsed by the global network he had created in his tireless search for natural history and ethnography. Nevertheless, one contact patrolling the Mediterranean Sea was Horatio Nelson, who wrote to Banks with news of a cargo of Greek antiquities seized from a French ship in 1803. Nelson wanted someone with sufficient authority to be able to deal with the British government regarding this prize. Banks was a good choice, and he replied cheerfully to the Admiral's request, promising 'I Shall undertake your Commission with Pleasure & Execute it with Zeal I Will take Care to offer the Sculpture you have Capturd to government in a Proper manner to State the Value of it with Justice & Correctness & in Case of their Chusing to Purchase for the advantage of the Arts in Britain I will see that your brave & meritorious Tars are not deprivd of any part of their Rights'.[87] Banks added a postscript to his letter, expressing the wish that more commanders might take such opportunities 'of doing Service to Literature'. Under Napoleon, the French had carried natural philosophers and scholars into Egypt, thereby initiating the modern study of Egyptology, but British military operations did not include anything on quite that scale. Instead, commanders from British voyages of discovery and of trade forwarded natural and artificial products to the British Museum, or if more appropriate to the gardens at Kew, frequently using Banks as their intermediary.

When he could, Banks sought to encourage similar activity among ambassadors, travellers and naval officers in the Mediterranean and Near East. In contrast to the Napoleonic approach, these were more modest and informal means of acquiring things like antiquities, but they seem to have been the ones generally preferred by the British.

Indeed, some prizes taken at sea were returned by the British to their former French owners. However, these tended to be those relating to natural history and not antiquities. It may therefore be worthwhile to end with the tale of just such a gesture concerning the natural history collections made by the French botanist, Jacques Julien de La Billardière. A complicated affair, the tale shows how deeply collecting could become embroiled in the rivalries and intrigue unleashed during a turbulent period of revolution and war. In 1791 La Billardière sailed under Joseph-Antoine Bruni d'Entrecasteaux in search of the navigator and explorer, Jean-François de Galaup de la Pérouse. La Pérouse had set out in 1785 on a French expedition to the South Seas, a voyage partly inspired by the example of James Cook. After La Pérouse was wrecked at Vanikoro Island, d'Entrecasteaux led a mission in the ships *La Recherche* and *L'Espérance* to discover his fate. However, the mission was dogged by bad luck, and the story of what happened to the collections made along the way has more than its fair share of twists and turns.

During the voyage La Billardière made a large botanical collection, as well as gathering mineralogical and entomological specimens, but disaster struck when d'Entrecasteaux died, and command passed to Alexandre d'Hesmivy d'Auribeau, a royalist. D'Auribeau led officers loyal to the French monarchy, and so he had little sympathy with the pro-revolutionary views of La Billardière. In 1794 he turned La Billardière over to the Dutch authorities in Java, along with his collections and colleagues. With this act ownership of the collections became a contested matter involving naturalists, politicians and even royalty, and a confrontation that started on a ship in the Far East found its way back to the heart of a politically divided Europe. La Billardière was held at Java until early in 1795, by which time his collections had been separately removed by another loyal French officer, Elisabeth-Paul-Edouard de Rossel. Rossel hoped to offer the collections to the exiled French King, Louis XVIII, however Rossel also fell victim to the unpredictable fortunes of the time.

Rossel planned to travel to Holland in a Dutch ship, but the Royal Navy caught him off the Shetland Isles. Thus, La Billardière's collections were seized yet again, this time because Holland had been annexed by France, so that both countries were now at war with Britain. Rossel was unaware of this fact, and found himself in a predicament not dissimilar to that Matthew Flinders experienced when he sailed to Mauritius in 1803 and was made captive by the French.[88] Rossel protested that he had no idea war had been declared, and since the British Government was favourably disposed towards the French Crown, it let Louis decide what should be done with the collections. Like Rossel before him, Louis saw the chance to make a gift of them, diplomatically offering everything to Queen Charlotte. It was at this point that Banks was consulted, and after an initial inspection by him in March, the Queen accepted much of the botanical material. La Billardière's property now apparently belonged to the British Queen.

There matters might have rested, except that by this time La Billardière had found his way home via Mauritius. He had no intention of relinquishing his collections, and, with the French Directory, he applied for them to be returned, arguing that they had not legitimately been in the French King's gift. Perhaps because he was also a collector and so sympathized more readily with La Billardière, and certainly wishing to cast himself in the guise of a political neutral, Banks accepted the French claim. Having received letters from La Billardière seeking his support, Banks set about the awkward task of persuading the British government and Queen that everything should be given back, something he actually managed to accomplish. This was no mean achievement in its own right, and afterwards Banks could present it as a diplomatic success for the grand eighteenth-century Republic of Letters, which in many ways it was. Of course, his own status among European, and especially French, natural philosophers was greatly enhanced by such an act. This in turn enabled him to obtain French cooperation when it came to releasing prisoners, to securing passports for voyages of discovery and circulating learned journals across the continent's troubled borders. Banks seemed a champion of disinterested knowledge over national rivalry and petty self-interest, and he duly employed his influence in areas where it was still possible to promote international collaboration and tolerance.

Yet if the unscientific tangle regarding La Billardière shows anything, it is that collecting and discovery were no less subject to political forces than any other human activity. The necessity for Banks's intervention is itself evidence of this, and his attempts to present himself as a neutral in such affairs are certainly open to question when seen in a broader context. The views being expressed by Charles Blagden in Paris in May 1802 are good evidence of why, for Blagden described Banks as desiring the return of the French collections surrendered to the British at Alexandria.[89] Here was an event where British commanders availed themselves of exactly the kind of opportunity that Banks urged to Nelson. The treaty of capitulation, specifically Article XVI, ceded to the British the best of the antiquities gathered by the French during their invasion, including the Rosetta Stone. It is probably pointless to speculate on what reception Blagden's comments might have received had they been circulated at the British Museum. They may have been some consolation to one or two French savants, but the fact is that Banks was in no position to return the entire spoils of a major French defeat. Consequently, as we have seen, in December 1802 he was on the Museum

committee set up to plan a new building to house the incoming Egyptian antiquities. Antiquities taken from a powerful enemy were, it seems, far less likely to
be seen again by their former owners than collections made from the natural
world, although it should be remembered that the French were allowed to take
away many papers, instruments, natural history specimens and other items as
part of their settlement with the British at Alexandria.

It has been argued that the sciences were never at war in this period, with
Banks's efforts on behalf of La Billardière being offered as evidence that this was
so.[90] Notwithstanding Banks's numerous gestures of help and kindness towards
French philosophers, such an interpretation is debatable. Some arrangements
could be made for natural history specimens, journals and certain individuals
to pass unmolested in times of conflict, but these were limited. So far as the arts
and antiquities were concerned there was strong pressure to retain such material
when it was taken in war. Nevertheless, it is still true to say that British willingness to release captured natural history collections back to the French was largely
due to Banks's intervention. On the occasions when this happened we see the
importance of science to diplomacy, and the ways in which Banks tried to secure
the goodwill of belligerents for favours and for the general benefit of learning.

Reviews and Reorganization: The Turn of the Century

With the turn of the century, and the enormous collections of antiquities that
started to arrive, it was time for the Museum's organization to be reviewed.
One major change was the division of antiquities from natural history in February 1807, an event partly necessitated by the influx of classical remains.
These were now becoming more prominent than the natural history collections on which the Museum was founded, and so there was a greater need to
create specialist departments to cope. Additionally, the collections in general,
their contents and condition, were being assessed. This process commenced
somewhat earlier than 1800, when the old century was coming to a close, and
was largely the result of increased pressures being placed on the Museum and
its management. In a detailed report of 1799 on the records and papers held
in the Museum, Joseph Planta, the new Principal Librarian, stated that the
building 'in which these Libraries are deposited, tho' Old & often in need of
considerable Repairs, is yet perfectly secure'.[91]

Planta's report was for a Select Committee of the House of Commons, and
his views are important here, for the costs of maintenance were growing as the
fabric of the building aged, and its capacity was exceeded. The figures for annual
average expenditure on maintaining the Museum from 1791 to 1800 show
that, exclusive of repairs, £1,892 15s. 1d. was spent each year. In addition to
this, annual average expenditure on repairs in the same period was £659 3s. 3d.

Behind the average expenditures lay a worrying pattern of escalating costs.[92] In 1800 the real figures for expenditure were £2,165 19s. 11d., with an additional £1,486 7s. 9d. going on repairs. Repairs were proving a heavy burden, and 1800 was the second year in a row that they had been at a much higher level than the average. In 1799 they amounted to £1,414 19s., and as a result, the Museum's finances, like its fabric, were deteriorating.

The figures are a good indication of the financial requirements of the Museum, which by 1811 had lapsed into a deficit of £1,272 2s. 11d., a sizeable £4,101 18s. 5d. of that year's spending being on repairs.[93] An alternative source of income was therefore considered in 1801. This was needed to supplement other forms of income, such as parliamentary grants,[94] interest on investments and the proceeds from sales of duplicates, the latter being undertaken at this time for coins.[95] It was to the vexed question of charging for admission that the trustees turned their attention, seeking to review all possibilities in an attempt to cover their spiralling expenses. There is no documentary evidence of Banks's views on this subject up to 1801, although the possibility of charging at the Museum had been examined in 1783–4 in circumstances similar to those traced here. The move was rejected on that occasion, the proceeds from any charge being deemed too low to warrant the change, and Banks participated in the committees that reached this conclusion.[96]

From the beginning of 1801 the finances of the Museum were monitored carefully at general meetings and standing committees that Banks attended. Indeed, the decision to prepare figures for average annual expenditure on maintaining the Museum from 1791 to 1800 was taken at a standing committee on 12 May 1801, with Banks present.[97] Just before this, at a general meeting on 9 May, an overall review of the Museum establishment was ordered.[98] The review, like the monitoring of the finances, took place against a background of rising costs. These further stretched the Museum's resources, with the minutes for May showing that the trustees wanted to increase salaries and staff and at the same time that they had to pay numerous incoming bills. In effect, by May 1801 a general attempt was underway to adjust the Museum to cope with the growing demands being placed on it.

Working within the committee to perform the review, it seems certain that Banks produced the unsigned draft proposal suggesting that money might be taken for tickets issued to see the Museum, dated 18 May. The proposal was entitled: 'A draught of some arguments against admitting all persons gratis who apply for permission to see the British Museum, with a Plan for receiving admission money for Tickets at the Porters Lodge'.[99] It examines in an unconvincing but not entirely unbalanced way the idea that those visitors who could pay, and who might willingly do so, should contribute to the costs of staff, repairs and the preservation of the collections. These were certainly pressing concerns, and ones this proposal was designed to address. However, it conceded that those who could not afford to pay, or who 'visit the collection from mere motives of idle curiosity', would be discouraged from seeking entrance. Admission was to be organized through the use of a system of tickets, and if charging had to be introduced it seems Banks thought that it should be used only for public tours of the Museum rooms and gallery areas. This was a duty that officers still performed, if sometimes a little wearily. There was no suggestion of charging those who wanted to use the collections to pursue their studies.

Indeed, Banks argued that facilities not dissimilar to those freely available at Soho Square should be extended to all such visitors: 'It is not however intended, by a regulation of this nature, to put those persons who use the Museum for the purpose of Study to any kind of expense, The Reading Room ought clearly to continue open without any charge to those who frequent it; and the liberality of the Officers may fairly be trusted with the charge of giving easy & gratuitous access under the regulation of the Trustees, to all who pursue the Study of Natural History, in the same manner as is now voluntarily done in all the Offices of Record, where those who pursue the Study of Antiquities constantly find access & assistance, from the liberality of those who superintend them, without fee or reward in any shape demanded or taken'. In other words, money might be made by charging the public for viewing collections exhibited in the galleries, but not from those using collections for research. This was in keeping with the way the Museum had previously acted more as a public reference collection for the books, manuscripts and natural history specimens upon which it was founded than as a showcase for things like works of art and sculptures. Such an approach gradually changed as the quantity of antiquities held by the Museum grew, growth that Banks himself helped to promote. In his proposals he referred to the use of a lottery in 1753 to raise money to pay for the original Museum collections,[100] before his paper petered out in amended rules for issuing tickets.

What was called in the minutes 'A Sketch of a Plan for a new method of Shewing the Museum' was tabled at a standing committee on 18 May 1801, with Banks and a number of his close associates present. Among these were men like Earl Spencer, Sloane, Astle, Annesley, Cavendish, Kaye and Sir William Hamilton. Banks did not lack support if he wanted to use it to press for charging, but this group ordered that Joseph Planta and the Under-Librarians should report on the plan, and a general meeting was set for 3 June.[101] On that day, at a standing committee convened before the general meeting, the report of the Librarians was received 'and being approved, it was agreed that the same should be laid before the Special General Meeting of this Day'.[102] As before, Banks was present. The staff report was dated 22 May, and was signed by Planta, Samuel Harper, Edward Whitaker Gray and Robert Nares, all of them Fellows of the Royal Society (except Nares, who was elected on 10 May 1804).[103]

The report was simple and direct. It stated that few museums of this kind charged, and that the British Museum would suffer in reputation if it started to ask for money for tickets. Even taking voluntary donations 'would soon degenerate into Abuse', it was argued. After 'much deliberation', the Librarians could devise no better system than the existing one of free entry, under which they decided they would 'strive as they can against the inconveniences that certainly attach to it'. Balancing the arguments, they added that Banks's proposals were, if implemented, 'liable to fewer Objections than any they can contrive'. They added, too, that charging might be used to fund Attendants to escort parties around the Museum 'in hopes thereby to excite their alacrity in gratifying the Curiosity of the Visitors'. This would, of course, have relieved the officers of an onerous job that many of them did not have time or inclination to perform. Thus, the advantages and disadvantages of charging were weighed by committees and officers alike.

At the ensuing general meeting spending on the Museum and its repairs was discussed first, and the average annual figures for expenditure from 1791 to 1800 were then scrutinized.[104] After this the trustees decided to appoint three Attendants to deal with visitors to the galleries, and thereby free Museum officers 'to execute the more necessary duties of their respective Offices, the first, by arranging their several departments, and making Catalogues of the Articles deposited therein, the others, by rendering the important department of the reading Room more effectually useful and more generally advantageous than it has hitherto been'. Planta and Banks would have been in complete agreement about these changes. Indeed, the recommendations to raise the salaries and the number of staff at the Museum, and to ensure greater concentration on managing the collections by freeing officers from conducting tours, appear to have been largely drafted by Banks.[105]

Thus, the salaries of the officers were all increased at the meeting, with the Under-Librarians being required to organize and to catalogue the collections in their care, and to report on progress. The Assistant Librarians (the Keeper of the Reading Room from then on being treated as an Assistant Librarian) were to attend the Reading Room and the Library in pairs, one supervising the Reading Room when it was open, and the other ensuring that books were provided for readers, that the catalogues were correct and that the books were properly marked. Moreover, at standing committee meetings this very month, with Banks present, orders were given that Reading Room regulations and supervision were to be strictly observed, and that Planta should report any failure to do so directly to the trustees.[106] The Museum administration was being generally tightened at the same time that staff were being assigned to more specific tasks.

However, one matter was not dealt with immediately. At the 3 June meeting various submissions were read on the delicate question of charging, and the spending figures and estimates that had been drawn up were also considered, but a decision was deferred. Instead, the trustees handed the financial documents and plans over 'to Mr. Sloane or Mr. Annesley, to be by them laid before the Chancellor of the Exchequer'. There was now a delay, and the *Commons Journals* reveal what was happening. They show how the Museum reserve funds, carried over from one year to the next, had shrunk. In 1799, £499 had been left over for the next year's spending, and in 1800 just £141 had been available.[107] Critically, and despite strenuous efforts to avoid it, in 1801 the Museum lapsed into a serious deficit of £1,078.[108] If they were to have any chance of coping, the trustees would need assistance. Consequently, prior to the meetings described here, they had laid their accounts and future estimates before Parliament, with an urgent petition for help: '... the said Trustees represented to Parliament, that the Sum allowed them for the Establishment and Support of the said Museum was reduced to a Capital of £.30,000, Reduced Bank Annuities, the Dividend of which, amounting to £.900, was, notwithstanding their utmost Attention to the forming their Establishment with Frugality, greatly insufficient for that Purpose; upon which Representation they have, at sundry Times, obtained from the House various Sums to Supply the Deficiency of their Income; which Sums, together with the Salary allotted to the King's Librarian, yearly amounting to about £.250, have proved insufficient to defray the necessary Expences of the said Museum, and what now remains in the Hands of the Trustees is not sufficient to carry on the Purposes of the Trust without the Aid of Parliament ...'.[109]

The trustees were making plain to Parliament their financial predicament, and that there would be an unmanageable shortfall if nothing was done about it. To be properly appreciated, the trustees' decisions to employ extra staff and to raise the salaries of the officers have to be seen against this grim financial position. The reasons why charging was an issue can barely be understood at all without some reference to it. The accounts of the Museum published in the *Commons Journals* show how the situation developed. The costs of repairs continued to vary, with some years being very high, and the accounts record a gradual increase in the total expenditure on repairs. Hitherto, Parliament had voted monies to the Museum spread over a number of payments from one year to the next. Confronted with the trustees' plea, however, a single immediate payment was made in 1802 of £2,841. It was not an increase on previous sums, but it removed the Museum's deficit, and £174 was left over for the forthcoming year.[110] The financial position was now slightly better. The Museum was surviving.

Banks was present on 8 May 1802 when the issue of charging was opened again at a general meeting.[111] As before, this followed a standing committee at which the reports of the officers were read.[112] Planta announced himself in agreement with the appointment of Attendants, wanting them to take on 'a variety of Mechanical Services' along with tours. He still felt that charging was unnecessary, and suggested that visitors might be allowed to take a number of vacant entry tickets on asking for them, the limit eventually being set at twelve. He thought that opening hours should be changed from 9 a.m until 3 p.m. to 10 a.m. until 4 p.m., while the Reading Room, then becoming overcrowded, ought to be expanded from one room to two. He also asked that the practice of opening the Museum in the afternoon on Mondays and Fridays, instead of the morning, be stopped during the summer. Planta's advice was considered and approved.

The reviews described here appear to have been undertaken by the trustees and officers in general, rather than being the initiative of any single person. This was how the Museum adapted to the new century and to the severe financial constraints that came with it, the question of charging having been fully examined and rejected for a second time. It is pleasing to note that Planta had been willing and able to voice his opinions, and also that these were fully respected. As Principal Librarian, Planta was, after all, directly responsible for the daily executive administration of the Museum, and ought to have been heeded. There is no evidence that the trustees acted against him, nor that Banks took a forceful line on charging. He drafted his proposals, no doubt as requested, and allowed them to be considered and dropped at committee. At the same time, a range of other changes went ahead to which he also set his hand. Extra staff were found, pay was raised and Museum rules were reviewed and reinforced. Banks's contribution to the broad issues raised by demands on limited Museum resources was significant and thoughtful.

Seen in the context of these developments, the reviews and restructuring that took place in 1806 and 1807 were in many ways the continuation of a process emerging at the beginning of the century. As with the preceding debates over charging and staff levels, information and opinions were gathered and, after discussion, resolutions were passed to alter the Museum's organization. This entailed dividing natural history from antiquities as part of another managed exercise. The background was again one of growing collections and the increased costs associated with them, as well as the need to have sufficient staff to cope with everything. As described above, payments were made for the Townley collection late in 1806, which would now have to be housed at the Museum.[113] The ailing Edward Whitaker Gray, Keeper of Natural History, was also given leave to go to Bath to try to regain his health.[114] Thus, at the same time as an important vacancy was opening up, a major influx of classical material had concentrated the minds of trustees and staff on how best to deal with the situation.

The result of this was that by December 1806 the trustees were 'taking into Consideration the present State of the Trust, the Establishment of Officers, their respective Duties, as at present performed, & the recent Additions made to the Collections deposited in the House'.[115] A committee was established to consider the 'most beneficial arrangement for employing the time of the Under Librarians & their Assistants'. As the trustees considered what accommodation was needed for the Townley collection, they also thought about repairs, seeking from George Saunders estimates and reports for repairs throughout the Museum.[116] In fact, another general review was taking place, and the now familiar pattern of planned development in the face of increasing demands was being followed. The report of the committee performing the review was tabled at a general meeting on Saturday 28 February 1807,[117] having been previously printed and circulated to all the trustees.[118]

This was a considerable report, which, as explained, divided the natural and artificial collections from one another, and set out what new posts and duties should be created. There were sections specifying work to be undertaken for manuscripts, printed books, natural history and for antiquities and coins. Detailed instructions were given for arranging the collections, and orders were issued as to what catalogues should be produced and how. With new streets being built around the Museum it was felt necessary to ensure that the growing collections were properly protected, and provision was therefore made for night-time security.[119] Defects in the Natural History Department were noted in the report, and it was following the events described here that the new Keeper of Natural History, George Shaw, raised the basement as a matter requiring urgent attention. As with other reports, there was mention of the hours and pay of staff, with Planta's salary being raised to £500. Overall, the meetings and this report show a concerted and reasoned attempt to be comprehensive. The final resolutions of the trustees arising from the report were printed for circulation.[120] At standing committees from 14 March onwards the report's findings were implemented, and progress was monitored.[121]

Additionally, Banks was included on a committee set up at the meeting on 28 February to see 'That Regulations be formed for the Admission of Strangers to view the Gallery of Antiquities either separately from, or together with the rest of the Museum; And also for the Admission of Artists'. The committee was also asked to consider the use that might be made by artists of drawings and manuscripts in the Museum. The arrival of the new collections greatly increased demand to see the Museum, which was what caused admissions procedures to be reformed, but the new collections also changed the Museum's character. The Museum was now a centre for art and the study of sculpture, and so another important development was the way the Museum started to make formal arrangements with the Royal Academy for students and artists to see the collections. After a delay, regulations were produced for the admission of artists and students, apparently timed for the royal opening of the Townley collection.[122] The standing committee minutes for the months of 1808 through to May detail negotiations with the Royal Academy over the regulations, which were finally approved at a general meeting of 21 May.[123] In this way, the Museum provided materials for artists to study and draw, working in conjunction with the Academy to support its efforts to promote the arts in Britain.

Planta was consulted regarding the Museum's admissions policy.[124] He produced a complex set of suggestions in response, but he was dissatisfied with these, feeling that the Museum apartments did not allow easy movement of parties from one place to another, nor 'immediate free admission'.[125] Planta did not comment much on the Royal Academy, but stated that 'Prints, Drawings Coins and Medals, should not be exhibited to the Ordinary Companies'. Planta wanted warders to help administer his system for moving visiting groups through the Museum, and suggested the use of Chelsea Pensioners for this, 'especially such as have been Non-Commission'd Officers, who are well trained to discipline & Order. Their Uniforms, added to their Veteran appearance, would give them a degree of respectability; & the loss of a limb would by no means disqualify them for this Service.' A modified version of Planta's ideas formed the basis of the regulations that were issued, with rules for the Academy also being added. These were printed for distribution throughout the Museum, and sent to the Academy.

The Museum was to be open to the public from Monday to Thursday during the hours of 10 a.m. to 4 p.m., with Friday being reserved for Academy students and special guests. Students could visit the Gallery of Antiquities from April to July. Except for Wednesdays and Saturdays, they were allowed access for every day of August and September from 12 a.m. to 4 p.m. The Academy was required to approve the students it sent to the Museum, and then to provide someone to supervise them. Museum officers and Attendants were also required to oversee the groups. The size of the groups being shown around the Museum was increased to a limit of 15 people, and the ticketing system was relaxed, with greater use being made of a book for signing in. These changes, like many introduced throughout this decade, were triggered by increases in the collections and in the demand to see them. They also reflect changing attitudes to the Museum as an institution, its structure and function, and appear to have been the result of a process of review and reorganization that followed a pattern. As a result, the numbers of visitors to the Museum gradually rose. From 1807 to 1812 a steady yearly increase occurred, with 13,046 people entering in the year at the start of the period, and 31,402 entering by the end.[126] Much credit for this improvement goes to Planta, but some is also due to the trustees who oversaw the successive reviews that made it possible.[127]

By November 1809 Planta felt that the rules involving the Academy were rather cumbersome, and that too few students were now coming through that route, so he proposed that the same system used for the Reading Room ought to be adopted for the students.[128] This meant that the Academy was no longer required to supply students, who would be allowed to apply directly for admittance. At the next general meeting, with Banks present as usual, this was discussed and changes made. Applications to use the Gallery of Antiquities were to be sent to Planta, or to a deputy if he was absent, and arrangements would be made for suitable students to have admission to the Antiquities for six months at a time.[129] With the trustees increasingly concerned to see that admission procedures were effective, at their next meeting on 10 February 1810 they asked Planta 'whether in his Opinion the Regulations will admit of any further improvements, and in what particulars'.[130] Banks was present for all of these meetings, and had been making many donations throughout these months, while also working closely with Konig to sort out plants and seeds in the Museum. When Planta responded, as usual, with a report, it was printed and circulated to the trustees, and Banks attended the meeting in March to discuss the Principal Librarian's ideas.[131]

New rules were introduced following this meeting, and these stipulated that the opening days of the Museum were to be Monday, Wednesday and Friday from 10 a.m. to 4 p.m. (with the usual exceptions of public holidays, and the months of August and September). People still had to sign in, but the ticket system was abolished, as was the use of guided tours as a means of conducting people through the Museum. Neither of these had been popular with visitors or officers, nor, it should be said, with a number of the trustees. Members of the public could now stay for as long as they liked in the upper-floor rooms and in the gallery, and extra Attendants were employed to oversee this. The Reading Rooms were, of course, not open to general visitors, and Tuesdays and Thursdays were reserved for special visitors. The procedures followed in dealing with these changes are significant for what they reveal about the approach adopted by the trustees and officers when undertaking reviews. Typically, facts were obtained and officers were asked to present reports. The trustees then acted, using committees to examine the findings and to reorganize the Museum. This shows the extent to which the trustees consulted those in charge of the collections, seeking their opinions and guidance.

Planta's reports are especially important here, because as Principal Librarian he was encouraged to make suggestions about the Museum to the trustees. In November 1814 Planta reported on amendments to Museum rules that he had been asked to draw up. Banks, the Speaker of the House of Commons and Mr Rose were appointed to a small committee that examined, refined and approved Planta's suggestions.[132] The result was improved access to coins and medals, and to prints and drawings, all evidence of steady progress in developing the Museum's collections and organization.[133] Planta argued as much when, on occasion, the Museum was criticized in the press for not making more progress. Some of these criticisms were undoubtedly warranted, but the Principal Librarian was still willing to defend the Museum when it was attacked by those who did not know, or perhaps chose to ignore, how it had struggled and was managed. In 1814 Planta was especially sensitive about admissions, and prepared a statement

Joseph Planta, Charles Picart, 1812, after Henry Edridge. Reproduced by permission
of the British Museum.
Urbane and efficient, Planta helped to develop the British Museum during the
twenty-eight years he was in charge. Like many officers, he was devoted to his work.

to the trustees on the subject when adverse letters were published in *The London Times*.[134] Some writers have subsequently agreed that criticism of the Museum needs to be seen against a background of financial and staff shortages, shortages that affected natural history in particular. Like the changes that were steadily simplifying admissions, such factors may well deserve more attention.

Banks's own views regarding the staff, many of whom he supported professionally, was that they should be paid more. Staff numbers and pay were increased as part of the various reviews and changes described above, but as always the sharp pinch of limited Museum funds was felt. In 1813 Banks wrote as a trustee about the pay and conditions provided for staff.[135] This was a chance to express his own views about their work and status, and in particular that of science in the Museum. Banks was eloquently of the opinion that extra allowances should be granted to staff for any additional duties or hours that they worked. Unable to attend the Museum due to illness, he wrote from his sick bed on 10 April. He contrasted the higher rates of pay available to various types of 'Booksellers laborers' with what was usually given to those employed in the sciences, arguing that pay in the latter should be raised to match that on offer elsewhere.

Emphasizing the point, Banks asked:

> The British Museum is the only Public Establishment where Science meets with Reward out of the public purse: will it not then be honorable to the Nation at large that there Men of Science should be better paid than elsewhere? In Short paid at a Rate which would make them happy easy & attached to their Offices? At present their extra time is not in all cases so well paid for by us as that of the Booksellers laborers, which is proved by some of them actually at present employing themselves in the service of those parsimonious Patrons of Literature.[136]

Banks thought that failure to achieve fair rates was detrimental to an institution like the British Museum, where the collections needed more and better staff in order to be properly maintained. This was important, because the alternative was to underpay staff, which would be wrong in itself, and thereby to risk failing in a primary duty to promote science. Additionally, Banks argued that greater returns would be obtained by increasing pay to staff who worked longer and harder, and that these returns would fully justify the extra expense. At the very least, collections would be better cared for by staff who felt sufficiently valued in themselves. Anything else might prove harmful to staff and collections alike.

Logically speaking this argument is hard to fault, but well into the nineteenth century officers continued to toil in conditions that caused them considerable stress and worry. The list of complaints was long. Low pay, temporary employment, no pensions, not being listened to or properly supported, a lack of understanding and respect for their work and careers were among the main difficulties encountered by staff. And this despite the fact that many laboured to make themselves experts in their fields, to publish widely and to assist others where they could. The result was that some staff worked more hours than they were paid for, while others had more than one job, all of which meant that some of them suffered poor health.[137] Banks's advice, along with that of Planta, led to the resolution 'That, in addition to the former gratuity for Extra Services, £50 per annum be given to those Officers, Employed in Extra Services, who shall dedicate an additional day in each week'.[138] This allowance was periodically increased while Banks was a trustee, and at a general meeting on 19 March 1814, with Banks in attendance, it was raised to £75 a year for an extra day of work each week.[139]

Library and Antiquities: Continued Labours, 1805–20

A survey of the final years of Banks's life shows a variety of activities still being undertaken at the British Museum, with some departments receiving major collections, including from Banks. The Museum library was steadily increased, with some large collections being acquired at the end of and after his long career. In other areas there was growth, particularly in the classical sculptures, which were impressively supplemented with the Elgin Marbles and the Phigaleian Marbles, again late in Banks's tenure. Banks encouraged research on the new sculptures, helping to have casts made for visiting French intellectuals. He also ensured that societies with which he was associated contributed material to such collections. Added to these activities were donations of coins from the Banks family, and a steady trickle of artefacts that Banks passed to the Museum from finds at British sites. Interest in such material gradually increased in these years as the study of British remains gained wider acceptance and support. However, at the British Museum significant British archaeological collections were not developed for some time, and classical remains still tended to dominate.

Turning to the first of these aspects, it became clear in the reviews described in the previous sections that a library available to so many readers needed to be more comprehensive. By 1805 many deficiencies were apparent in natural history alone when compared to Banks's library.[140] Efforts therefore needed to be made to increase the library stock. Apart from the flow of library donations and purchases already mentioned, there was the enforcement of the Copyright Act of 1709, stipulating that the Royal Library should receive a copy of every printed work registered at Stationers' Hall. The powers of this Act had been available to the Museum since the removal of the Royal Library to Bloomsbury in 1757, but many publishers failed to adhere to it, and the Museum did not pursue them. In 1806 and 1807 steps were taken at the Museum to review this situation, but these proved inconclusive.[141] It was not until the passing of a new Copyright Act in 1814 that stricter measures came into being, but publishers continued to try to evade the Act, while officers spent considerable time monitoring and policing their activities.[142]

One task to be undertaken was 'to compleat the Collection of Printed Books in the Library respecting the British Islands, & the several Possessions of the British Empire'.[143] Joseph Planta suggested this in a report of 14 December 1811 in which he argued that the library had failed to keep pace with other collections in the Museum.[144] He said that the Museum library amounted to some 70,000 volumes, containing above 140,000 articles, a large proportion of which were pamphlets, tracts and dissertations bound in single volumes. Planta thought that divinity was well represented, and that at best British history and topography were reasonably covered. Classical literature, though far from complete, was adequate. In medicine old works prevailed, while more modern publications issued since the death of Sir Hans Sloane had not been added to the holdings. All other classes were very incomplete and out of date. Even the catalogues of the library were deficient. Planta felt that the place to start was British history and topography, this 'being the most easily completed & its deficiencies in such a Library being the most open to Censure'. He estimated that some £5,000 would greatly assist in completing the most important areas, and he advocated the sale of duplicates to augment such a sum. Four hundred pounds would be needed to acquire publications as they appeared, and Planta stressed the need to enforce the Copyright Act.[145]

Planta was ordered to estimate the money required to rectify the deficiencies in the literature available on Britain and its possessions, and he thought that not less than £2,500 would suffice to start with.[146] The matter was referred to Parliament in March 1812,[147] and Planta was ordered in May 1813 to make formal applications to the Master General of the Board of Ordnance and to the Admiralty for a 'Copy of Every Article, Edited by them, to be transmitted to the Museum, in furtherance of the Plan for completing the National Library, in all that relates to the History & Topography of the Country'.[148] The Admiralty responded by directing its hydrographer and its librarian to send a copy of everything published 'by their Lordships'.[149] Thus, maps, charts and other accounts arising from British naval activity were forwarded to the Museum library. The Master General of the Board of Ordnance responded in similar fashion, instructing William Mudge to send all publications to do with the 'General Survey of the Country' that was being compiled by the Board.[150] Mudge had been made Director of the Ordnance Survey in 1798, and he was, needless to say, another contact in Banks's extensive network. Indeed, much of the early work of the Survey was published in the Royal Society's *Philosophical Transactions* due to the scientific assistance that was provided by Banks and other Fellows.

Mudge was himself a Fellow of 1798, as were many of the Admiralty and other officials exchanging letters on these subjects from 1812 to 1813. In effect, they combined to increase geographical understanding on a wide scale, and as this grew so did the collections of maps and related accounts being channelled to the Museum by them and their organizations. This was a part of the Museum library that Planta and others believed ought to be strongly represented. Indeed, we can see in the collections being made under Planta a national theme similar to that being pursued in natural history later in the same decade. In terms of the country and its empire, this showed a desire to establish more firmly the identity and character of Britain as a nation and world power, and to reflect this in collections held at its main museum. At a basic level, of course, maps showed the physical extent of the land, but, as the scientific and military minds leading the way in their design at this time knew only too well, more detailed and accurate maps also permitted greater control to be exerted over any territory. Planta had therefore chosen a theme likely to appeal to a patriotic spirit that emerged strongly in the eighteenth century, and which various forms of knowledge, including that derived from mapping and survey work, were used to reinforce.

At the very least, Planta was aiming at sufficiently comprehensive reference collections on Britain – he was, after all, Principal Librarian of the *British* Museum. Sales and purchases were organized in accordance with his requests. As a result, in December 1813 Banks was once again appointed to a standing committee regarding the library. This committee was to superintend the sale of catalogues and duplicates, and the purchase of printed books.[151] Among the works acquired by the Museum were county and topographical surveys published by antiquaries and local historians. These continued to proliferate, and, as with maps, Banks contributed to a number, particularly those for Lincolnshire and Kent. Thus, in this period there is evidence at the Museum of a library policy to address specifically British collections, but much more needed to be done if the shortcomings Planta identified were to be remedied.

Gradual progress was made up to the late years of Banks's trusteeship, during and after which a series of large libraries were acquired by the Museum, thereby considerably accelerating the growth of its collections. In 1827 Banks's own library, which had supplied the needs of naturalists for over forty years, joined some formidable contemporaries at the Museum. Banks's collections amounted to about 7,900 books and 6,100 unbound tracts, in total about 14,000 items. This compares with the collection of Baron Von Moll, the purchase of which Banks helped to organize in 1815, at approximately 20,000 mainly scientific volumes. Von Moll's library arrived with a small herbarium and a mineral collection, and on its own required Robert Smirke to prepare plans for extra space, with more staff being requested.[152] Prior to this, another collection of note to arrive was that of the solicitor and legal writer Francis Hargrave, comprising 499 manuscripts and more than 100 books, all purchased in 1813 for £8,000. The Hargrave and Von Moll collections were followed in 1817 by the classical and music library of Dr Charles Burney, consisting of some 14,000 books and manuscripts, purchased for £13,497 17s. 6d.[153] There were many duplicates in this library, which were approved for sale,[154] the relevant books having been separated for disposal by November 1818.[155]

In 1823 the Museum received a library exceeding all these in size and splendour. It had been formed by George II and George III, and comprised about 62,250 volumes, with 19,000 unbound tracts.[156] With libraries like these arriving at the Museum, and with antiquities coming from the Mediterranean and Egypt, not to mention archaeological finds being uncovered in Britain, a new building was essential. By November 1828 sufficient progress had been made with reconstruction for the Royal Library to be seen by the public in its historic Museum setting, the magnificent King's Library, designed especially for the collection by Smirke.[157] Acquisitions like these show that under Planta the Museum library stock was steadily increased. Importantly, they are also an indication of things to come, because they provided the foundations on which Anthony Panizzi (Principal Librarian from 1856 to 1866) subsequently laboured to build a national library comparable to any other in the world.

Interest was stirring in other fields, although this did not manifest itself on quite such a conspicuous scale as that seen with the King's Library. One area was material excavated in Britain, which embraced a range of prehistoric, Roman, Saxon, Danish, Norman and medieval remains. In the late eighteenth century all these were increasingly being gathered and described by antiquaries, and the pattern of Banks's donations to the Museum shows that he shared the general interest in British finds. In their own small way Banks's donations anticipated the rise at the Museum of collections of British and medieval remains as opposed to classical material from abroad. The latter certainly tended to dominate up to 1820, with a number of major collections arriving after 1800. The former did not gain any real prominence at Bloomsbury until well into the nineteenth century when, among other things, neo-classicism had given way to Romantic and Gothic tastes, and the study of British history through its physical remains had gained the general credibility it previously lacked. Banks's interest in British remains is most apparent in and around Lincolnshire, where finds were common as a result of archaeological digging, extensive navigation and drainage works, and agricultural activity.

These were the main means by which Banks obtained objects, and although it would be an exaggeration to suggest that he was prolific, the list of what Banks gave is still varied. For example, in November 1810 he gave the Museum two Roman necklaces from Lincolnshire, one of amber beads, the other a gold chain 'ornamented with Stones called Root of Emerald, with gold pendant leaves'.[158]

In November 1811 another donation from Lincolnshire was of jewellery and beads.[159] This was followed in June 1812 by 'two Celts'.[160] In February 1815 Banks presented 'an Adze of Flint found in the North of Scotland',[161] and in February 1818 he gave 'ancient bronze Celts found in Lincolnshire'.[162] Banks evidently regarded the Museum as a suitable place to send objects excavated in Britain, but not everything he obtained reached safe hands. Instead, some objects were subjected to chemical tests by colleagues at the Royal Society, such as those conducted by Dr George Pearson on an Iron Age war trumpet or *carnyx* in 1796.[163] This rarity had been discovered in 1768 at Tattershall Ferry on the River Witham, and it was illustrated, probably by Banks's artist in Lincolnshire, John Claude Nattes. Banks later passed the *carnyx* to Pearson along with a number of other artefacts dredged from the Witham, which were then sacrificed to experimental enquiry in an attempt to determine their composition. Unfortunate to note, Pearson's analysis was entirely destructive, the trumpet being melted down and cast in an ingot mould before being broken by a smart hammer stroke. This was so that Pearson could examine the freshly fractured surface of the metal. He established that the metal was bronze, made of 88 per cent copper and 12 per cent tin, but that is small consolation for the loss of such a valuable artefact. So much for early scientific analysis of British antiquities.

The distressing fate of other finds supplies more evidence of the pattern of Banks's archaeological donations both to the Museum and elsewhere. One such example is provided by a substantial collection of coins from the reign of Henry II that was dug up at Tealby in Lincolnshire in 1807. The 'Tealby Hoard' introduces Banks and his unmarried sister, Sarah Sophia, as coin collectors of note, and illustrates how Banks's interests and connections operated in a popular field of collecting, not, it must be said, without further casualties. It was Banks who ensured that the Museum had its choice of the Tealby material, a representative sample of the 6,000 or so coins being taken and listed by Taylor Combe.[164] Sarah Sophia, a great collector and a significant benefactress of the Museum, also received a selection of coins, with a few items going to other private individuals. However, the remainder, apparently numbering some 5,127 duplicates and less valuable coins, were melted at the Mint in an attempt to alleviate the bullion difficulties of the day, an expedient hardly to be appreciated by archaeologists and numismatists today. On occasion, it seems that Banks was not overly squeamish about passing on valuable material to those with uncompromising ends in mind, but the reasons for doing so here have more to do with international tensions than might at first appear to be the case.

In 1807 a new department of Antiquities and Coins was created at the British Museum with Combe as its Keeper. No doubt this was one reason why Banks looked to the Museum when considering what to do with the Tealby material. However, the dual role played by Banks in relation to the British Museum and the Mint over the Tealby coins is more fully explained by his appointment to the Privy Council in March 1797, when he became a member of its Coin Committee. This was one of the main reasons why so much of the Tealby collection went to the Mint, for Banks's interest in coins derived from a formidable knowledge not only of their history but also of the contemporary economic and monetary arrangements of the realm. Lamentable as it certainly is, the drastic action taken was more a response to serious bullion and coinage crises precipitated by the Napoleonic War than a cavalier attitude to coin collecting *per se*. Melting much of the hoard was probably seen at the time as an unfortunate necessity, and the extent to which the national emergency dictated measures like this one is therefore a delicate question for historians to judge, but for the collector today the truth is that it can only be regarded as a regrettable loss.

Be that as it may, more positive things might be said regarding Banks's subsequent contribution to the collections at Bloomsbury and his connections at the Mint. These connections were ones that the Museum could and did exploit constructively when attempting to acquire examples of all modern coinage. As with Planta's attempt to complete a British collection of topographical books to date, and similar attempts in other departments to establish comprehensive British collections, there was a plan in December 1810 to obtain a full set of Mint coinage. Accordingly, orders were given that 'the Principal Librarian be directed to apply in the name of the Trustees of the British Museum to the Right Honble the Master of the Mint ... to issue a general order for a proof Piece of every Coin till now struck at the Royal Mint ... [and for] a proof Piece on every future Coinage'.[165] At this time the Museum was preparing for a sale of coins, generally a more lucrative venture than sales from any other department, and in May a total of £809 7s. 6d. was raised.[166] Banks did not want to be involved in this sale, but he was willing to make enquiries at the Mint regarding arrangements for the proof pieces that were wanted. Authorization was subsequently given for the chief engraver at the Mint to provide what the Museum required, and thus a beneficial link was established between these two institutions.[167]

Collecting coins was, of course, a traditonal pursuit for gentlemen and antiquaries, and Banks was no exception. His involvement with the Mint and the Coin Committee, and with excavations in Lincolnshire and elsewhere, certainly helped to stimulate his interest in coins, and perhaps that of his sister. A remarkable individual, for most of her adult life Sarah Sophia was a permanent companion to her brother and sister-in-law, Dorothea. 'The Ladies', as the two Banks women became known, were significant collectors in their own rights. Dorothea was less unusual or extensive in her tastes than Sarah Sophia, but she gathered a notable porcelain collection.[168] Some of this was acquired with help from travellers and merchants from the Far East whom her husband knew, or through manufacturers like Wedgwood in Britain. Dorothea was also sometimes willing to send objects of different kinds to the British Museum.[169] As a collector she cannot, however, be compared with Sarah Sophia.

Sarah Sophia collected on an altogether greater scale than Dorothea. She was more like her brother in the scope and quantity of what she gathered, and, like those of her brother, Sarah Sophia's collections were distributed to appropriate institutions, among them the British Museum. Apart from the journals and letters of her brother that she copied, Sarah Sophia amassed a collection of coins, medals and trade tokens, and she also collected books on these subjects. Following her sudden death in 1818, Banks took steps to present his sister's collections to the British Museum. He did this in October, but Sarah Sophia had bequeathed her collections to Dorothea, and so she made the presentation instead, the Museum taking what coins it needed before passing on unwanted and duplicate items to the Mint.[170] In this way the Museum filled many gaps in its collection, and the Mint gained over 2,000 coins and medals. These were essential in forming the Mint's museum, especially that part containing British coins struck before 1800. Among the many other important aspects of Sarah Sophia's coin collection is her fine series of coins of post-Independence America, and the Mint also obtained her numismatic books, pamphlets and manuscripts. Her bequest followed the slightly earlier example of Banks himself, who had made a smaller donation of coins, medals and numismatic books in August in order to found the Mint museum.[171] Banks's gift comprised 100 or so choice coins, valuable for their exceptional workmanship. Thus, important Banks family collections went to the British Museum or were taken by the Mint.

At the British Museum the Banks family collections joined other collections made by Sarah Sophia. These comprise sixty-five volumes written in her hand on subjects like ceremonials, heraldry and the Order of the Garter. Sarah Sophia also made a list of books in Banks's library at Soho Square, one section of which is an extensive bibliography of archery. Not satisfied with these interests, she gathered together nine volumes of broadsides and caricatures, with books on chess and engravings, and a series of news cuttings. To these were added a large collection of invitation and visiting cards, amounting to some 10,000 items. Like many of her coins, these collections were lodged at the British Museum.[172] A somewhat eccentric figure, Sarah Sophia shared her brother's interests in coins and medals, and obtained various forms of ephemera and memorabilia on a scale comparable to her brother's specialist pursuits in natural history. There were obvious similarities between them, and, like Joseph, Sarah Sophia was a significant benefactor of the British Museum. She is a prominent example of an eighteenth-century female whose collections were of national worth, and her interests and personality are an important study.

On other fronts Banks continued to help with the research of scholars seeking access to Museum collections. There are many examples of him authorizing admittance to the Museum library and herbarium, as well as examples of him helping those wishing to study antiquities. Those interested in antiquities included foreign visitors to London, who sought out Banks as one way of obtaining what they wanted from the Museum. Sometimes this was more than just a sight of an object. Requests were occasionally made for casts to be taken, and, when one French visitor wished for casts of Egyptian hieroglyphs, it was Banks who arranged permission and facilities. This was the geographer, educationalist and archaeologist Edme François Jomard, who arrived in London in March 1815. Banks and Jomard had corresponded in the past, and in person Jomard impressed Banks, who wrote to his old friend Charles Blagden, then in Paris: 'Jomard is Safe here he meets Combe this morning he appears to be a Sensible man & Pleases me by his very thankfull acknowledgements of the Little Service I have & Shall Continue to do for him he talks of Casting the Egyptian Hieroglyphics in Fusible metal I See no Objection the Trustees will decide on Saturday'.[173]

Having summoned an extraordinary general meeting to discuss this, Banks and the other trustees gave their permission for casts to be made from 'the Hieroglyphics on the two great Egyptian Sarcophagi. If in Plaister £30. If in Sulphur £42.'[174] The costs of the operation were to be paid by Jomard, who, at Banks's request, was permitted to make the casts beyond the usual opening hours of the Museum, extra time being necessary for such a procedure.[175] On returning to France, Jomard wrote to thank Banks for his support. He also referred to fossil horns,[176] and to cases of material sent to Paris for its museum. A room at the Louvre was being prepared where drawings and other Egyptian objects would be exhibited.[177] Additionally, Jomard made important contacts in London, among them Dr Thomas Young, whose work interpreting hieroglyphs using the Rosetta Stone was of direct interest.[178]

These later years also saw another influx of classical antiquities, the most famous of which were the Elgin Marbles, purchased by the Museum in 1816. These had been removed from the Parthenon by Thomas Bruce, seventh Earl of Elgin, after whom they were named. The Museum committee to oversee the purchase did not include Banks, but the Earl of Aberdeen, Charles Long and Richard Payne Knight sat on it. Prior to being acquired the Marbles had been in a garden shed at Burlington House, where they were exhibited to the public and to artists for drawing and modelling. It became necessary to move them when the Duke of Devonshire wanted to build on the space they were in.[179] Communication regarding their purchase took place between Downing Street and the Museum in March 1815,[180] but disputes over the Marbles rumbled on even as a formal agreement was being reached. Richard Payne Knight, an influential connoisseur, had wrongly argued that they were Roman works of the Hadrianic period, and could not have come from Pheidias's workshop as part of the public building programme mounted under Perikles. Others questioned whether Elgin should have moved the Marbles at all, and there were disputes over whether they should be bought by the nation, and if so at what price. In the end the British Museum obtained the collection, which was soon accepted as representing some of the finest work to survive from antiquity. Indeed, for the rest of the nineteenth century it dominated thinking about how to estimate the artistic worth of most other ancient remains.

On 8 July 1816 the order was given to procure a warrant from the Prince Regent for payment of £35,000, this being the sum vested by Parliament in the trustees to buy the Elgin Marbles.[181] A further £800 and £1,700 were requested to pay for removal of the Marbles, and for the erection of a temporary building designed by Smirke to house them, this being tacked onto the west side of the Townley Gallery.[182] Combe was responsible for cataloguing and arranging the Elgin Marbles,[183] which remained in their 'temporary' accommodation until 1831 along with other classical antiquities, including the Phigaleian Marbles.[184] The Phigaleian Marbles were moved to join the Elgin Marbles from a room on the ground floor at the north-west corner of Montagu House, where they had been situated for less than a month.[185] This collection had been transported to Britain in 51 cases after being purchased at Zante for £19,000.[186] It comprised sculptures from the temple of Apollo at Bassae, including an important frieze showing two mythical battles between Lapiths and Centaurs, and Greeks and Amazons. Once in place, the collections were ready to be seen by the public. This was at the beginning of 1817, and, like all of the classical antiquities at Bloomsbury, they provided a rich source for artists to study.[187] The British Museum had become the foremost centre in London for those seeking collections of such quality, the arrival of the Elgin and Phigaleian Marbles having laid the foundation of the Museum's great sculpture collections.

In 1816 the Royal Academy contacted the Museum regarding pieces of the frieze of the Parthenon that were in its possession. The Academy wanted to give these to the Museum, and in return to obtain casts of the Elgin Marbles and certain other items. The Academy had been loaned the pieces by the Society of Dilettanti, which took a leading part in the great modern awakening of interest in the culture and remains of ancient Greece. However, neither the Dilettanti nor the Academy was now in a position to rival the Museum's collections, and the pieces were therefore donated in May.[188] As we have seen, private societies increasingly gave their collections to the British Museum, by this time in so many respects the principal repository of the country. Banks had been contacted regarding this donation in July of the previous year, when the Academy planned the transfer.[189] The Academy seemed to be under the impression that Banks had loaned the Parthenon pieces originally. He might well have held them once as Secretary of the Dilettanti, or been party to the decision to let the Academy take them. Both are likely possibilities. In any case, with Banks's help in arranging it, the Museum received yet more classical remains, and a number of casts were made for the Academy.

Not all acquisitions were dealt with quite as smoothly as this, and those coming from Egypt proved to be the source of considerable controversy in the final years of Banks's trusteeship. That controversy reveals some of the problems and limits of collecting for London Learned Society, and so we turn now to the end of Banks's career at the British Museum and to the purchase of the Egyptian collections of Henry Salt. As with other collections mentioned in previous sections, the costs of purchasing and housing larger sculptures was a significant consideration for the Museum trustees when deciding what to buy and what to refuse. Another factor was the tendency to favour Greek or Roman remains over those of other cultures, even including, as we have seen, those native to Britain. But perhaps the most important aspect highlighted by the disagreements concerning Salt is the scope for misunderstanding caused by the often informal arrangements that governed collecting through to 1820 and after.

Last Years and the Egyptian Controversy: To 1820 and After

In spring 1818, ten years after the Townley Gallery was opened, a major Egyptian sculpture came to the Museum. This was the so-called head of the Younger Memnon, today thought to be a bust of Ramesses II, which was presented by Henry Salt, Consul-General in Egypt. It arrived at Spithead in March,[190] and in June the instruction was given at a standing committee to place it on a pedestal on the east side of the Egyptian Room – an order easier to give than to execute for something of this size and weight.[191] The enormous bust had come from the ruins of Ramesses's mortuary temple at Thebes, where Salt had succeeded in shifting it with the help of Jean-Louis Burckhardt, a Swiss explorer and orientalist, and Giovanni Battista Belzoni, an Italian adventurer and strongman.[192]

Rumours had been circulating in London that the bust had been maliciously damaged by the French. On inspection Banks admired it, and commented: 'Memnons Shoulder has at Last Arrivd at the British Museum, no traces of Gunpow[d]er having been usd in separating it from the Trunk & the hole in the other Shoulder being bored in an inartificial manner very unlike to the Scientific Stile in which the French would have done all Traces of the Scandalous Report of their having mutilated the Statue is fully done away & will never again be heard we Regret having Ever Listend to it but we must admit that the hole sunk in the Right Shoulder is some Excuse for the Persons who ever they were who first Propagated the Report'.[193]

The bust of Ramesses II was duly set in its place, and became one of the great attractions in the Museum's growing Egyptian collection, but it also heralded ugly disagreements between the Museum, Salt and Belzoni. These arose from Salt's desire to recoup some £5,000 that he claimed he spent making an impressive Egyptian collection, which he also offered to the Museum. Salt had used the majority of his personal fortune, including an inheritance from his father, to assemble this collection, but the Museum trustees were unwilling to pay the price that Salt wanted. They refused to give more than £4,000 for everything, first spending £2,000 to obtain the majority of Salt's collection, and then making a final offer of £2,000 for an alabaster sarcophagus, which was rejected by Bingham Richards, Salt's agent in London.[194] By no means extravagant, such an offer might still have covered much of the money Salt had 'actually expended' during his collecting,[195] but that did not please Salt, who wrote a splendid letter to Richards in May 1824 complaining about the situation.[196] Ironically, Richards subsequently managed to sell the sarcophagus to Sir John Soane for the sum he had already refused once, that of £2,000. It was all a far cry from the small pieces of natural history and antiquities that Salt first proposed to send back to Britain when he opened correspondence with Banks on the subject in 1815.

Henry Salt, who had travelled in Abyssinia, was appointed Consul-General in Egypt in 1815, probably with Banks's help. As such, he was well placed to obtain Egyptian antiquities for dispatch to England, and did so on an extensive scale once settled in Cairo. The first gifts from Salt to Banks were sent in 1815, being four animal skins from Abyssinia.[197] Like some other officials who were sent abroad, Salt understood that he could be of service to the Museum once in post. In June 1816 he suggested that he might procure valuable antiquities for the Museum for a yearly sum of about £100–200.[198] It was one line in a long friendly letter to Banks, which received no formal mention in Museum minutes. Thus far there was no sign of the troubles to come. Referring to modest collecting activity, Salt suggested: 'If I were allowed to draw upon the Trustees of the Museum for one or two hundred pounds per annum, I think I might be able to augment with great advantage their Egyptian Collection'. However, purchasing and housing large quantities of antiquities had proved a controversial business for the nation in recent times, and one that was hard to afford. The Museum did not therefore employ collectors, and rejected many offers like Salt's because the cost of transporting objects could, on its own, prove prohibitive. Yet the sum was reasonable, and Salt's access to Egyptian antiquities was good.

When Salt departed England in 1815 he evidently carried away hopes that he could satisfy a number of patrons with collections not only of natural history, but also of increasingly fashionable Egyptian material. Consequently, in 1817 overtures were made to Joseph Planta on the subject. A letter had arrived at the Foreign Office regarding the possibility of making collections in Egypt. This was forwarded to Planta by William Richard Hamilton, a government official with a strong interest in antiquities (he retrieved the Rosetta Stone from the French when they tried to smuggle it out of Egypt). The letter came from Cairo, and it referred to Salt and Belzoni as potential collectors, explaining that they lacked the necessary finances to undertake any work.[199] The letter also included the suggestion that there were obelisks in the area of Cairo that the Museum might want. In the same month, however, government refused to transport these to Britain, £800 being thought necessary just to move them to Alexandria.[200] This was a disappointment, and, more than that, an indication of the type of difficulties that lay ahead for anyone collecting in Egypt. Nevertheless, the bust of Ramesses II showed what could be done, and Salt proceeded to spend large sums of his own money in the pursuit of Egyptian remains, expecting in due course to cover his costs by selling them in London to the British Museum and the Royal Academy.

Various ambassadors and consuls had procured artefacts to supplement their income and to enhance their standing as collectors,[201] not least Sir William Hamilton,[202] but he sold the Museum mainly Etruscan, or rather Greek, vases, whereas Salt dealt in Egyptian remains. Broadly speaking, in the hierarchy of ancient art then prevailing, Egypt was regarded as a primitive forerunner of Greece, while Rome was held to be a culture in decline by comparison with that of the Greeks. Although Banks was highly impressed by Ramesses II, he is unlikely to have differed from the accepted view of such things. In his correspondence he is largely silent regarding the artistic worth of Egyptian sculpture, occasionally repeating the comments of others on the subject but otherwise saying little. According to Banks, when he saw Ramesses II, Taylor Combe toyed with the idea 'that the Egyptians taught Sculpture to the Greeks'.[203] It was against this general background that Salt's collections were made, but while Egyptian remains were not then as highly prized as they later would be, other factors might well have had even more of a bearing on the sums that could be offered by the Museum for Salt's material.

Indeed, the government had already shown that it was cool to the idea of Salt or Belzoni being employed as collectors on business as potentially costly as this. One or two hundred pounds might be given for anything Salt came across, but beyond that funding seems to have been doubtful. Despite this Salt had embarked on an ambitious scheme, gathering together an important collection of Egyptian antiquities. He was spurred on partly by competition from his counterpart and rival, the representative of France in Egypt, Bernardino Drovetti. Both men tussled over diplomatic issues affecting the interests of Britain and France, and engaged in a race to make collections that might enhance their own fame and the prestige of the countries they represented. Salt's friend and biographer, John James Halls, eloquently described the way Salt 'engaged in the undertaking with a greater degree of zeal than possibly the dictates of selfish prudence might justify' and how 'he appears to have launched into the wide sea of speculative discovery'.

This was indeed so, and warnings were sent from London that in the prevailing economic conditions the market would probably not repay large expenditure on Egyptian remains.[204] The British Museum was not, it seems, in a position to pay for them. Nevertheless, Salt sent a list of items that he had collected to William Richard Hamilton with a price marked against each one. When seen in the capital the list was regarded by a number of people, among them Banks, as a claim the Museum simply could not afford to meet. Salt suggested a total value of £8,200 for his collection, a figure that was, he said, nothing more than a conjecture on his part. Seeking to make his case, Salt suggested that his friend, Hamilton, might advise government on the proper value of the collection. However, at the Museum a dim view was taken of Salt's actions,[205] and it was rapidly made plain that he was not likely to get the sum he had rather clumsily suggested.

By May 1819 news of this adverse reaction had reached Salt, who was alarmed at such a response. He now argued that he had never intended to charge anything more than the government might accept at their own valuation.[206] He therefore offered his collection to the British Museum unconditionally, but stated that Belzoni was entitled to a share in any payment made for it. According to Salt, a particularly fine alabaster sarcophagus had been valued by one expert at over £2,000. In his earlier annotated list he had set an even higher figure on it of £3–4,000. The sarcophagus was a discovery by Belzoni at the tomb of Seti I in the Valley of the Kings, and Salt and Belzoni drew up a contract regarding its sale. The contract, dated 20 April 1818, was subsequently seen at the British Museum. It described how much the sarcophagus might be worth, and stated that the two men had agreed Belzoni would receive half of any surplus if the price exceeded £2,000.[207] Salt and Belzoni had fallen out over the collections they were making, and the contract was probably a written attempt to rectify the situation. What it makes very clear is that a price greater than the maximum the Museum had offered was necessary for Belzoni to receive any proceeds from the find.

These complicated arrangements were hard for the Museum to resolve, and became even more difficult when Belzoni eventually arrived in London making accusations and claiming to have been offered £3,000 for the sarcophagus by a mysterious buyer. The buyer never came forward, but one of Belzoni's demands may still be read in the Museum archives.[208] It indicates that Belzoni expected payment from the Museum for the sarcophagus at a level he was never likely to receive. Another of his letters, dated 14 November 1818, reveals much about what he had been led to believe might be the terms available to him from the

Museum for assisting Salt. In it Belzoni set a considerable price on his services, suggesting to the trustees that: '... on the most economical system, they
[the costs of being employed as a collector] would amount to the sum of one
Thousand four hundred Pounds per annum, including the necessary presents to
the Beys, Kacheefs, and Kaimakans up the Country ...'. Having elaborated his
plans, Belzoni left it '... to the Trustees to decide on whatever recompense they
may think proper for my own exertions on this occasion ...'.[209] Confronted with
these charges the trustees decided in February 1819 to decline Belzoni's offer of
help.[210]

Belzoni aside, Salt's offer remained unconditional. This fact altered the
attitude of the trustees and Museum officers, who now felt that the majority
of the collection could be received, even though its price was still not settled.
The first task was to get everything back, which Banks was asked to help organize.[211] As objects arrived, he and Combe went to see them. Banks also assured
Lord Mountnorris that Salt's proposal would be laid before the Museum trustees, and that letters would be sent to the Admiralty requesting that the next
transport sent to Alexandria should take the collection to Malta.[212] But Banks
was near to death, and his health was failing. He therefore wrote to Henry Ellis
in December 1819 explaining that he would be unable to attend the Museum
for a meeting. He referred now to 'the Liberal proposal of Mr Consul Salt to
Sell His Collections of Egyptian Antiquities to them [the trustees of the British
Museum] at the Price they Chuse to Fix', and he advised that the commander
of the Mediterranean Fleet be ordered to convey everything to England in government transports.[213] Banks was happy to support the idea of acquiring Salt's
collection when the price was affordable, and he therefore worked actively for
its transferral.

He was not alone in feeling this way. A short while later a committee was
appointed to approach the Admiralty to arrange shipment, and this consisted of
Henry Bankes, the Earl of Aberdeen and Charles Long. Banks was not included,
but he was well enough to attend a general meeting on 19 February 1820 at
which a letter sent to him by Salt was tabled. This was dated 28 May 1819, and
Salt's schedule listing his collections was also read.[214] More progress seems to
have been possible once the trustees had clarified what they were able and willing
to pay Salt. From a practical point of view this was essential before any purchase
could be authorized. At the very least, Salt's collection was being moved to London. A feat in itself, this was something that the trustees were not always able
to accomplish for such bulky material. For example, at the general meeting held
on 19 February, marbles that had been waiting at Malta were refused by the
Museum because of the expense of transporting them to Britain. As suggested,
the costs and coordination involved in moving large consignments of antiquities

imposed substantial burdens on the trustees, and that was true whether or not they could agree a suitable sale price with the owner.

In the event, it was not until May 1822 that the trustees bought part of Salt's collection for £2,000. By then Banks had been dead for some time, and it may even be that his death made arrangements more difficult to expedite when at last progress was underway.[215] His drive and knowledge of how this matter had developed were perhaps wanting in the deliberations that followed. In 1824 the Museum offered Salt a further £2,000 for his sarcophagus, Salt having sought at least £3,000 for this piece.[216] The sarcophagus, as we have seen, never came to the Museum. It seems that delay, resulting from confusion and ending in recrimination, plagued the transaction to its end. This was primarily the result of conflicting claims about the market value of the collection, especially the price of the sarcophagus, and because of differences over the Museum's responsibility to pay for everything. The Museum sought to obtain and move material at affordable prices, whereas collectors sought to cover their own expenditure and to make a profit when they could. In such circumstances disagreements were inevitable, and it is perhaps surprising that they did not occur more often.

Later Salt collections went to the Louvre, but in 1835 the British Museum purchased more Egyptian antiquities gathered by Salt, this time at a Sotheby's sale for £4,800. In 1820 Salt's erstwhile colleague, Belzoni, rented the Egyptian Hall in Piccadilly. This had been built by the showman and collector William Bullock, and it provided an ideal setting for Belzoni to stage an exhibition featuring a colourful reconstruction of two rooms from the tomb of Seti I. The exhibition included many of Belzoni's own Egyptian jewels, statuettes, mummies and other antiquities, and proved very popular, but its fate was all too typical of that of many collections and displays in this period. Just two years after opening, the entire exhibition was sold off at an auction held at Christie's, the sum raised amounting to about £2,000. Ever the adventurer, Belzoni turned back to African exploration, dying in 1823 of the effects of dysentery contracted while attempting to reach the city of Timbuktu. His fate was no different than that suffered by many early African explorers, including his friend and former benefactor, Jean-Louis Burckhardt, who died exhausted at Cairo in 1817 after travelling widely on behalf of the African Association, yet another organization in the Banks network.

Salt and Belzoni both faced many problems as collectors, and made considerable sacrifices in search of information and antiquities. Together, they helped to establish the basis of the current Egyptian collections at the British Museum, a tremendous achievement on their parts. Their efforts also show that the movement of antiquities through the network operating in the Mediterranean could be a complicated affair. Perhaps ironically, then, at about this time the trustees were seeking permission from government to open up correspondence with

British officials abroad in order to obtain material.[217] This might have formalized a previously informal and sometimes muddled process, making it possible to clarify what the public duty of consuls and ambassadors was when it came to the expensive business of collecting for the nation. However, the Museum struggled to organize such an arrangement, and so what an individual like Banks was able to achieve in collecting throughout the period, across the globe, in natural history and antiquities alike, was therefore all the more remarkable. Banks's view regarding Museum acquisitions seems generally to have been that free donations were best, and he adhered to this rule in his conduct as a trustee and as a wealthy benefactor. When payments were necessary, securing the best price possible was almost certainly another priority for an institution with a limited budget. Compared to what a nation like France was willing to devote to obtaining and housing antiquities, the attitude of the British government can seem parsimonious, and this was certainly something the trustees at the British Museum always had to bear in mind.

The problems that Salt experienced arose not because any single individual was to blame, but because of wider misunderstandings. Such misunderstandings were mainly to do with the unofficial nature of relations, the different and sometimes conflicting expectations of those involved and the sheer expense of handling antiquities. All this being so, the basic lesson to be learned from such episodes seems to be that disagreements were more likely to result from a combination of these factors than from the direct actions of any individual subject to them. Another conclusion to be drawn is that London Learned Society was not a cohesive central body uniformly governing distant fields of collecting, but rather an association of individuals and institutions that could not always be expected to cooperate or act effectively. The ties that bound such associations in London and elsewhere comprised changing and sometimes competing interests, and the networks that extended from the metropolis could be tenuous and intermittent. Thus, the so-called 'centre' was itself made up of a series of networked institutions and individuals all interacting in different and sometimes loosely defined ways. Any urban centre depended very much on the talents and persistence of those seeking to maintain contacts or to mount missions beyond it, and in an uncertain and often unexplored world errors and omissions were not uncommon. Ultimately, of course, none of this prevented London Learned Society from achieving a great deal, and handing on a considerable legacy to those who followed.

In 1823 the books, bronzes and drawings of the late Richard Payne Knight were added to Henry Salt's considerable accessions. Payne Knight, with whom Banks was not especially close, was the last of the great virtuosi. These connoisseurs and collecting amateurs had made a significant contribution to the cultural life of the nation. Many of their private collections had been steadily added to the Museum's holdings through purchase or donation, joining those of various societies and academies as the British Museum became the only place where material of such importance could be ranged on quite such a scale. The growth in the Museum's collections, both of natural and artificial products, necessitated new buildings. By the time of Payne Knight's death at the age of seventy-five the plans for a new Museum building had commenced. As suggested, these were drawn up following scrutiny of plans outlined as early as 1803. Banks was consulted, as were a number of other trustees and officials, but he did not live to see the reconstruction completed.[218] Banks's main contribution was to the extensive natural history collections, and to the development of the Museum through years of turbulent change, years that saw European knowledge and influence widen on an unprecedented scale.

CONCLUSIONS

Collections 1770–1830

Banks was willing to contribute to all branches of natural history, but not necessarily to collect from them himself. Such eclecticism was more typical of Sir Ashton Lever, and should be contrasted with Banks's approach.[1] Of Lever, Charles Blagden commented to Banks: 'Mr. Lever wants anything that he happens not to have in his Museum, whether it tends to illustrate science or not: on the contrary, nothing can be an object to you, but what will conduce to the improvement of Natural History as a branch of Philosophy'.[2] In his early days Lever's collections lacked system, a point to which Blagden was certainly referring here, and the lifestyle of the showman brought Lever as much notice as his exhibits – not all of it good either.[3] Lever tried to remedy the former deficiency later on, and did so with considerable success, but he continued to mount mixed exhibitions of natural and artificial products, with a particular strength in natural history, for example in birds and seashells.[4] He has therefore been regarded as something of a rival to the British Museum, although in practice the two probably tended to eclipse many lesser private museums. At least this was the view Banks took in 1794, when he wrote to the great American museum builder Charles Willson Peale:

> Tho the Study of natural history is Certainly not upon the decline here but Continues to be prosecuted with Eagerness & Considerable success yet the business of making Private Collections of Animals is almost wholly laid aside, this Change has I beleive been principaly brought About by the Circumstance of a vast national Collection existing here to which Every subject of the Countrey has a Legal right of admission & a separate Private Collection Parkinsons Museum I mean late Levers which is also numerously Furnishd with beautifull specimens & may be seen for a payment at the Door which I beleive is always remitted to such persons as have occasion to attend frequently for the Purpose of Study
>
> It is no wonder that when two such institutions exist which vie with each other in Contriving means to advance Science that individuals possessd of any thing Curious Chuse rather to deposit it in one or the other of them than to give it to any individual Thus Private Collections which formerly usd to be

made with great ease & Little expence are now almost wholly impracticable
& in truth Scarce any one of my acquaintance attempts such a thing except
a Mr. Keate of Charlotte Street whose principal Object is the Shells of Land
Snails[5]

In any case, it seems unlikely that competition between the British Museum
and Lever could entirely explain the refusal of the Museum to buy Lever's
collections when at last he wanted to recoup his expenses.[6] More prosaic yet
significant considerations of limited space and finance may help explain many of
the purchases and refusals of the British Museum in its early years.[7] These factors
affected a number of major decisions from 1800 to 1820 in which the trustees
had to accept or refuse 'offers' of major collections at a price. Professor William
T. Stearn, the botanist and historian, thought the refusal of Lever's collections
was due to such factors, and there is much in the pattern of acquisitions and
spending at the Museum in these years to support such an interpretation.[8]

Having been rejected by the Museum, and twice by the Empress of Russia,[9]
Lever used a lottery to dispose of his collections, selling 8,000 of the 36,000
tickets he had printed. The winner in 1786 was James Parkinson, who moved the
Leverian Museum to the Rotunda, which was in a less fashionable part of London, near Blackfriars Bridge. It survived there until 1806, when, finally, it was
broken up and sold, portions being obtained by individuals such as William Bullock, but not apparently by the British Museum – a conspicuous omission. The
sale lasted from 5 May to 14 July, and annotated catalogues and notes related to
it do not appear to refer to a senior British Museum representative making purchases of natural history or ethnography.[10] This is odd as purchases from auctions
were one way of obtaining parts of a collection that could not be afforded in its
entirety. A combination of reasons might explain the lack of interest. Foremost
among these are the eventual condition of parts of the Leverian Museum, the
number of duplicates it might have contained compared to the British Museum's
collections and the lower status accorded ethnography as a science.

Changes in the staff and structure at the British Museum when the 1806 sale
took place probably also had a bearing.[11] The year 1806 was an important one
for the British Museum as a whole. Late in the year George Shaw was placed in
charge of the Natural History Department. Shaw was familiar with the Leverian
Museum, having described a selection of its specimens in two volumes published
in 1792 and 1796, both entitled *Museum Leverianum* and including engravings
commissioned by the museum's proprietor, James Parkinson.[12] Shaw had been
employed at the British Museum as an Assistant Librarian since 1791, the year
before the first of these volumes appeared, and therefore knew both museums
very well. Too late to intervene officially as Keeper in the sales themselves, it
seems likely that he would have done more to obtain some of the lots than his
predecessor, the dying Edward Whitaker Gray.

At the time of the sale Gray's health was rapidly failing, and by November it was so bad that he was given leave by the trustees to go to Bath to take the waters there. Gray did not recover, and died on 27 December. This, and the the arrival of the Townley collection, might have meant that the Leverian Museum could not be accommodated at the British Museum, even though the sale catalogues show that there was a great deal of valuable material in it. Instead, the Leverian Museum was split among a number of collectors, and some of it probably did end up at the British Museum when later sales and donations took place.[13] It might also be worth noting that James Parkinson dedicated the second volume of *Museum Leverianum* to Banks. Perhaps appropriately, this volume depicted such specimens as the 'Kanguroo', an animal by that time breeding at the Royal Gardens at Kew, and being distributed across Europe through the Banks network.

Lever's successor as a leading museum proprietor in the capital was the ambitious showman, William Bullock, who mounted innovative dramatic displays in his Egyptian Hall. This was opened in Piccadilly in April 1812. One display was entered through a mock basaltic cavern, like Fingal's Cave on the Hebridean island of Staffa, which Banks had been the first to survey in 1772. The display was situated in the 'Pantherion', and showed animals grouped in a tropical forest, although they came from more than one area and continent.[14] It seems that Banks and Bullock were on more friendly terms than Banks had enjoyed with Lever, and Bullock was undoubtedly a better businessman than Lever. Like Lever, Bullock claimed to possess substantial collections from Cook and Banks, a claim worthy of further investigation.[15]

When Bullock tired of his collections of natural history, ethnography and other objects ancient and modern,[16] the British Museum simply could not afford to buy and house everything.[17] Bullock offered his collections to more than one institution, the University of Edinburgh being his first choice, suggesting that he had decided to relinquish them partly because the public were increasingly drawn to the British Museum, where admission policies had been liberalized. With no takers, he was forced to auction everything in 1819, and he even decided to conduct the sale himself. Specimens called 'compounds' were noticed in some of the lots. These were cleverly assembled from more than one specimen, which might have adversely affected their prices.[18] Whatever he claimed to have spent on the collections, Bullock took an estimated £9,974 13*s*. at the auction, which was not too much more than the £9,000 he suggested as a sale price to the British Museum. William Elford Leach, who rather harshly thought Bullock an indifferent naturalist, bid on behalf of the Museum, and he assisted the University of Edinburgh too.

Banks thought that such large private enterprises would ultimately prove to be impermanent, however lavish the expenditure on them. He explained this in a short, cordial correspondence with Robert Ferryman,[19] and it was a view from which Ferryman did not dissent.[20] Yet if we see in the fate of Lever's and Bullock's collections a transition away from the assorted private cabinets of the past, however extensive and spectacular,[21] we also see with Banks's death the passing of a time when private members of the landed gentry exerted such a pervasive influence over the course not only of collecting but of exploration and empire. The British Museum had been greatly enriched by the generation from which Banks came, but Banks's bequest was different in kind from some of the other collections of his day. London as he knew it offered a lively array of collections and shows, and among these were specialist collections that could be freely consulted by scholars. Banks's herbarium and library were valuable examples of the latter type.

Indeed, Banks's herbarium provided the historic basis for a new specialist department in the British Museum, under his last Soho curator, Robert Brown.[22] It was the finest plant collection to arrive since that of the founder, Sir Hans Sloane,[23] and foreshadowed the formal establishment of separate scientific disciplines at the Museum. On his arrival at Bloomsbury, Brown was given the rank of Keeper or Under-Librarian in charge of the Banksian Botanical Collections, and in due course he was made responsible for the Botanical Branch, a new division of the Natural History Department. The new divisions better reflected the contents and purpose of the collections themselves. They were introduced in the 1830s when the Natural History Department was split, so that from then onwards there was a Botanical Branch, a Zoological Branch and a Mineralogical and Geological Branch. Banks's library, the herbarium's working partner, went to the Department of Printed Books under Henry Hervey Baber. Banks's library covered much published in natural history back almost to the beginnings of print. It also had a catalogue, the last part of which appeared in 1800, an updated version, interleaved and with manuscript additions, also being kept.[24] This was all made possible because, if nothing else, Banks concentrated in his collecting. In so doing, he held back the most prized of his collections until last. Up to 1820 it is therefore necessary to emphasize his work at Bloomsbury mediating between the Museum and an expanding world of exploration and empire, and his sturdy committee work year on year, work touching on almost every aspect of the Museum.[25]

We might begin to detect, too, in an institution which tended to favour antiquities in the first third of the nineteenth century, that natural history had grown and been reorganized in some if not all areas, and perhaps even that there was greater general activity and progress than has sometimes been appreciated.

Robert Brown. From a portrait of Brown, in the Botany Department, the Natural History Museum, London, artist unknown. Brown was first Keeper of the 'Banksian Department'. Reproduced by permission of the Natural History Museum, London.

Writing of Brown on 25 February 1812, Banks said: 'no doubt you have Seen Brown's Prodromus: he is now the most acute Botanist I know, & is of endless use to me, as my eyes begin to fail me & will no longer Allow me to use a Lens' (Natural History Museum, D.T.C. XVIII 146–147).

General Conclusions

Some general conclusions have been possible from this study, but it would be wrong to suppose that the history of the British Museum in this period, let alone that of London Learned Society and the extended network on which it depended, could be considered merely in terms of one man's contribution. Concentrating on Banks was useful because of his wide connections and lengthy tenure, but it has not been assumed that he is more worthy of study than any other individual or theme. Clearly, a combination of individuals and influences shaped the Museum in Banks's day. More will therefore need to be done to understand fully the Museum's historical development from 1770 to 1830. No effort has been made in this study to avoid the difficulties and controversies Banks was occasionally drawn into. These sometimes shed new light on his conduct, and more so on the problems confronted by the Museum. They have therefore been discussed whenever appropriate.

It seems that Banks was not quite the ogre that he is sometimes portrayed to be, and it may be that A. E. Gunther was a little more balanced in his assessment of Banks's trusteeship at the British Museum than others have been. Eminent writers on the British Museum and the Natural History Museum, London, have generally agreed that Banks was a remarkable benefactor and a dutiful and even 'sagacious' trustee.[26] Yet there were limits to his influence, and so he worked with Museum officers in ways that have not always been fully recognized. The cooperative efforts of Banks and different officers to improve the collections are especially good evidence of his approach, but even when certain officers did not agree with or like Banks, there is little to suggest that he acted against them for personal reasons. His occasionally cool relationship with Joseph Planta provides some support for this view, and for the idea that differences were sometimes more apparent than real. In other words, too much stress can be placed on disagreements, and not enough on the context in which they took place, thus distorting our understanding of how the Museum actually operated. There is certainly evidence that the trustees and officers could work reasonably well together, however tempting it might be to suppose otherwise. Indeed, many changes were implemented through consultation and ordinary committee work as the collections grew, especially after 1800.

Banks also strove to maintain cordial relations with the other trustees even as the number of them with scientific leanings decreased. His trusteeship coincided with periods of significant financial uncertainty at the Museum, another aspect that is perhaps worthy of additional study. Moreover, in natural history, which was overtaken by the flood of antiquities after 1800, there were particular problems of preservation that affected the collections, especially those in zoology. All collections became difficult to house as space diminished, that is if they could be afforded at all, and the interplay of developing collections and disciplines is a major theme affecting the management of the Museum in these years. Additionally, the staff available to care for the collections was insufficient compared with what followed, a situation the trustees periodically tried to improve. Banks, in particular, seems to have felt that pay for the staff ought to have been higher, and that the accommodation of natural history was not always adequate. This might have been a reason why he waited until after his death to pass on his major collections, leaving Robert Brown to decide when would be best for them to go to the Museum. Brown seems to have made the best arrangements he could for the eventual transfer, going himself to the Museum with the collections when they were moved there in 1827.

Attempts were made at the Museum to consolidate certain collections, or to use sales and exchanges to increase them. The historic use of sales and exchanges was no less, and probably more, prevalent among commercial museums in private hands. The relationship between public and private museums is therefore another important theme outlined here, and it shows what variety there was in the ways private collectors administered and disposed of their collections. Some private collectors did not use their collections for profit, but devoted them to scholarly research, freely giving away what they did not require. Others entered the market for specimens, antiquities and ethnography, but this proved an increasingly unprofitable enterprise on a large commercial scale, with a number of private collectors selling off what they could not afford to maintain. What we see, in effect, is that collections (or parts of them) were not stable entities in this period, and could deteriorate in condition or be dispersed, reforming around new interests and preoccupations, often in different places.

Such processes still operate to varying extents today, and they account for the emergence and growth of a number of major public collections into the nineteenth and twentieth centuries. The rapid increase in the number of museums outside Europe and North America during the years leading to the twentieth century shows how pervasive these processes eventually became.[27] By 1910 more than 2,000 of the museums in existence globally were scientific, and a significant number of these were under some form of government control. In order to create and extend collections, many museum directors and curators relied on private donations, sometimes of large foundation collections. They also relied on purchases, sales and exchanges similar to those conducted at the British Museum in its early years. What is more, they often encountered similar problems to those felt at Bloomsbury, not least in their finances, staffing, organization (including their relationship with government) and accommodation. Hence it may be argued that the division and reallocation of material is yet another theme linking the past to the present for a series of interrelated collections, many of which are now located not only at the British Museum but across London and the world.

We may choose to deprecate these processes, leading, as they have, to modern collections of tremendous size and complexity, and it is certainly true that such a varied history has serious implications for those who study collections today. Nevertheless, one basic point about the nature and growth of collections emerges clearly. This is that collectors drew on many sources for their collections, collections which in turn often became sources and examples for those who followed. In a number of ways the achievements of former collectors made possible what came afterwards, something of which museum builders around the world seem to have been conscious from the earliest days. Their avid use of the international networks on which expansion depended is one of the more important themes in the history of collections. Thus, while stress has been laid on such networks in this account, the tendency to construe the eighteenth-century scene in terms of our own preconceptions, whatever these may temporarily be, has been resisted.

Reference has been made to evidence of the constraints everyone laboured under, and it would be hard to overestimate their combined effects on the British Museum's management and networks, especially as the trustees and staff adjusted to the demands of the nineteenth century. In fact, these demands necessitated the creation of specialist departments to manage the collections, and a new building to house them. The problems were partly a consequence of the size and scope of the collections themselves, and attempts to concentrate were one way of remedying deficiencies in at least some areas. The long-term answer was to ensure that all collections received specialist care, and some progress was certainly made towards this end. At the Museum more than one officer chose to concentrate on particular collections, but difficulties were encountered where this meant that other collections in their charge did not receive the attention they required. The development of collections up to and including this period was not one leading inevitably from mixed 'cabinets of curiosities' to orderly and documented collections.

The specialization that took place at the Museum was similar in some respects to the way in which a private collector like Banks tended to concentrate on certain areas. For Banks this meant that his herbarium and library were carefully organized, while material that fell outside his main interests was often directed to the Museum, or to suitable friends and institutions elsewhere. Banks could not keep everything that he obtained, and, sensibly, he did not try to do so. Such specialization is an important way in which he differed from the virtuosi of preceding generations, being less willing to assemble assorted collections and more discerning in the pattern of what he kept and gave away. In these respects Banks anticipated the future development of collecting. The changes in the British Museum's structure and management also reflect a gradual move towards specialization, especially insofar as the new departments emerging in this period started to concentrate on distinct disciplines. A feature, then, of the growth and organization of collections in both the public and private spheres in Banks's day was the increased specialization that took place.

Museum officers like Konig and Leach chose to specialize. Just as Banks did, they also promoted Museum collections through friends and associates. Both Konig and Leach made trips to continental Europe in search of material, and during these trips they met other naturalists who wanted to supply specimens or to visit London. Most if not all Museum officers in this period entered into extensive correspondence with colleagues in order to obtain material and to develop networks. Sometimes, and for all manner of reasons, these networks operated inefficiently, as we have seen in the case of Henry Salt, but their exist-ence and use remain central themes in the history of the collections considered here. So are the ways in which London Learned Society was coordinated and developed by figures like Banks. Coordination was more not less necessary as the demands placed on the capital's major institutions grew, and since Banks's time it has increasingly become the responsibility of government to oversee the collections and networks built up by him and his contemporaries.

In significant ways, then, the British Museum was part of a wider network stretching out from the metropolitan centre. Sailors and their commanders, travellers of most descriptions, correspondents and scholars, numerous societies and institutions at home and abroad, all had dealings with the Museum. From his privileged position Banks sought to enhance this network through his own connections, a task he performed on a scale to match any other trustee during his tenure. He assisted a great many visitors to London, who wished to use his collections and those of the British Museum. He also drew on contacts across Britain and well beyond in his search for material. As shown, commercial and strategic contacts provided opportunities to broaden collecting in this period, and these could not be ignored. Banks became adept at shaping the courses of discovery to take advantage of such opportunities, but he also engaged in a wider quest for knowledge that led him to promote learning more or less for its own sake.

Such learning was itself a source of influence and power, enabling status to be established and control to be exercised, and, as suggested, the ways in which the collections at the British Museum were gathered and then organized tells us much about how Banks and his generation viewed themselves and the world beyond Europe.[28] The networks Banks and others maintained reflect a range of priorities, as do the collections that resulted from their use. However, these networks did not grow or operate evenly, and the means by which material and information were obtained were no less varied than the many ways in which both were interpreted and reinterpreted once received. Forms of order were not easily established, and new ideas and systems resulted from attempts to come to terms with the influx, the centre itself changing and being modified by distant encounters and the widening of contacts.

Usually a 'centre' is assumed to be all or part of a city. Such 'centres' relied on networks of various sizes and strengths. Inevitably these networks overlapped, and so it should be remembered that any particular centre always stood in complex relation to other centres and networks at home and abroad. As we look into a centre, or out from it to other centres, it can become unclear where the basic distinctions between centres and networks are actually to be drawn. Detailed concentration on how figures like Banks worked raises questions about when a centre was part of a wider network, and when a single individual might represent a centre all of his own and a group, organization or other body an extension of his aims and personal influence. Much depends on what activities were being undertaken and by whom, things which change, and do so continually. It is this pattern of change that underpins understanding of why and then how any set of contacts operated, and which extends our thinking about them well beyond the cities of Europe to the jungles, deserts and continental interiors, to the shores, islands and shipping lanes where people also met and dealt with one another in ever growing numbers.

We should therefore be careful when assigning what happened to a centralized network, convenient though this way of describing history certainly is. Contacts may occur at more or less any place in time, and result in all manner of outcomes, unplanned or otherwise. When we discuss eighteenth-century 'centres' and their 'networks', or indeed any theoretical centre or network, it is just as well to be aware that such terms may themselves be limited and limiting. Indeed, sometimes they may not be applicable at all to the myriad detail of unfolding events. What can be said is that Banks's London was a dazzling combination of internal groups and individuals that could and often did coordinate to further wider aims. In the hands of a capable enough person such systems as existed, whatever their operating boundaries were, could be made to work with effect, and it may be argued that significant advantages were offered by their sometimes indeterminate character. Not least among these was a certain amount of natural flexibility and freedom. For someone like Banks such flexibility and freedom opened a world rich with opportunity, and he was, for good or for ill, rarely slow to take advantage of this.

The movement of people and of their collections, and the changing pressures, perceptions and priorities that shaped knowledge, lie at the heart of our understanding of how collections were created, shifted, organized and then reorganized. In order to ensure the protection and use of collections, individuals like Banks sought to distribute material among the various institutions then existing. They thereby fulfilled a function that would be undertaken today by various government agencies and employees. The lack of government departments to oversee culture and heritage in this way is partly what gave individuals like Banks their niche. Later on this niche disappeared as these activities, like those in exploration and science, became increasingly institutionalized. By the end, Banks was in many ways representative of an older system of administration and patronage, and the bodies with which he was most closely involved underwent reform in the years after his death. The British Museum, the Royal Society, the gardens at Kew and the Royal Observatory are just four examples of such a pattern. Banks is no less interesting for that, and was by no means entirely backward-looking. Some of the work and changes he participated in were necessary and beneficial, and there is plenty of evidence to support the view that Banks's career spanned an important phase of development leading to subsequent changes and achievement at the British Museum.

EPITAPH

The commemoration on the statue of Joseph Banks by Francis Leggatt Chantrey, which was paid for by subscription by his colleagues at the British Museum and the Royal Society, provides an epitaph to Banks's career. At the request of the subscribers[1] it was placed in the Hall of the British Museum in 1832, and is now at the Natural History Museum, London. Translated from Latin, the inscription reads:

Joseph Banks Baronet
who
in quest of knowledge of the whole Realm of Nature
travelled by land and sea
among the remotest peoples, savage and even unknown
with daring, endurance and acceptance of danger
in the years of his youth.
Having returned to his native land
and been unanimously elected President of the Royal Society of London
he cultivated learning with the utmost diligence for the rest of his life.
He made his collections available to science
with his own unique liberality and munificence
to be fostered, extended and valued
by the patronage of others who sought to follow his example.
His friends
have contributed to dedicate this likeness
to commemorate his virtues and have presented it
to grace the British Museum.
He lived 76 years, 6 months and 6 days.
He died on the 19th of June 1820.

NOTES

In conducting research for this study I relied primarily on British Museum minutes, records of presents and reports. All citations use the relevant folio number for these papers. I am very grateful to the trustees of the British Museum, and to Christopher Date and Gary Thorn, for allowing me to make such wide use of the British Museum papers.

In longer quotations from Banks manuscripts the conventions established by H. B. Carter have been used, for which see his *Sheep and Wool Correspondence of Sir Joseph Banks 1781–1820* (London and Sydney, British Museum, 1979). Carter showed deletions in italics between obliques thus: */Deleted text/*. He showed insertions in plain text in obliques thus: /Inserted text/.

Abbreviations for manuscripts at the British Museum:

BM CE 1/-	General Meetings
BM CE 3/-	Standing Committee Minutes
BM CE 4/-	Original Papers
BM CE 5/-	Officers' Reports
BM CE 30/-	Book of Presents

Other abbreviations:

APS	American Philosophical Society, Philadelphia
BL	British Library
CKS	Centre for Kentish Studies, Maidstone
CUL	Cambridge University Library
FWM	Fitzwilliam Museum, Cambridge
HRNSW	*Historical Records of New South Wales*, 8 vols (Sydney, C. Potter, 1892–1901)
ML	Mitchell Library, Sydney
MHS	Museum of the History of Science, Oxford
NHM	Natural History Museum, London
NLW	National Library, Wales
NMM	National Maritime Museum, Greenwich
PRO	Public Record Office, Kew
RBG	Royal Botanic Gardens
RS	Royal Society, London

RSA   Royal Society of Antiquaries
SD   Society of Dilettanti
SL   Sutro Library, California
TCC   Trinity College, Cambridge
UG   Göttingen University
UW   Wisconsin University
UY   Yale University

Preface

1. G. R. de Beer, *Sir Hans Sloane and the British Museum* (London, British Museum Press, 1953). See also E. Edwards, *Lives of The Founders of the British Museum; with Notices of its Chief Augmentors and Other Benefactors, 1570–1870* (London, Trübner, 1870).

2. The conference was held at the British Museum on 4–5 April 2002, entitled 'Enlightening the British: Knowledge, Discovery and the Museum in the Eighteenth Century'. See Neil Chambers, 'Joseph Banks, the British Museum and Collections in the Age of Empire' in R. G. W. Anderson, M. L. Caygill, A. G. MacGregor and L. Syson (eds), *Enlightening the British: Knowledge, Discovery and the Museum in the Eighteenth Century* (London, British Museum Press, 2003), pp. 99–113.

Introduction

1. D. W. Wilson, *The British Museum: A History* (London, Oxford University Press, 2002), respectively pp. 10, 42.

2. J. C. Thackray, and J. R. Press, *The Natural History Museum: Nature's Treasurehouse* (London, Natural History Museum, 2001), p. 27.

3. A. E. Gunther, *The Founders of Science at the British Museum 1753–1900* (Suffolk, Halesworth Press, 1980), p. 29.

4. Banks to Lloyd, 22 January 1804, NLW 12415, f. E29.

5. According to an initial survey of the minutes, Banks attended some 112 general meetings and some 263 standing committee meetings between 1778 and 1820.

6. See note 11 to chapter 2 and notes 24–5 to chapter 3, below, pp. 147, 150–1, for references and discussion relating to this subject. Further comments regarding the Royal Society and its Repository are made in chapter 3, in the section 'From Private to Public: The Transferral of Some Major Collections, 1771–1805', pp. 21–5.

7. The Officers' Reports, BM CE 5/-, start in earnest as an archival series in July 1805.

8. For scholarly work on the Museum's early years, see K. Sloan (ed.), *Enlightenment: Discovering the World in the Eighteenth Century* (London, British Museum Press, 2003).

1 Banks as an Early Traveller and Collector, and the British Museum

1. For the 'second great age of European exploration', 1760–1805, and its various impulses, see R. MacLeod and P. F. Rehbock (eds), *Nature in its Greatest Extent* (Honolulu, University of Hawaii Press, 1988), esp. Frost, A., 'Science for Political Purposes: European Explorations of the Pacific Ocean, 1764–1806', pp. 27–44. For exploration and discovery in the seventeenth and eighteenth centuries, see D. Howse (ed.), *Background to Discovery: Pacific Exploration from Dampier to Cook* (Berkeley, University of California Press, 1990). For Banks, see J. Gascoigne, *Science in the Service of Empire: Joseph Banks,*

the British State and the Uses of Science in the Age of Revolution (Cambridge, Cambridge University Press, 1998).

2.   W. S. Shepperson, 'William Bullock – An American Failure', *Bulletin of the Historical and Philosophical Society of Ohio*, 19:2 (1961), pp. 144–52; W. H. Mullens, 'Some Museums of Old London – I The Leverian Museum', *Museum's Journal*, 15 (1915), pp. 123–9, 162–72, followed by 'Some Museums of Old London – II William Bullock's London Museum', *Museum's Journal*, 17 (1917–18), pp. 51–7, 132–7, 180–7; T. Iredale, 'Bullock's Museum', *The Australian Zoologist*, 11:3 (1948), pp. 233–7; R. W. Force and M. Force, *Art and Artifacts of the 18th Century: Objects in the Leverian Museum as Painted by Sarah Stone* (Honolulu, Bishop Museum Press, 1968).
      Although obvious similarities existed (and still do), many of the basic principles by which the British Museum was governed were unlike those of commercial museums like Lever's and Bullock's, where charges were necessarily made, and a need to advertise and to offer a degree of novelty applied. The British Museum remained free, even if gaining entry was regulated and sometimes difficult to arrange. See the Conclusions, pp. 129–39, and note 125 to chapter 6, below, p. 164.

3.   The terms 'natural and artificial curiosities' are mostly used to refer to collections that would today come under disciplines in natural history, classical and ancient studies, and archaeology or anthropology. Another term to clarify is the title 'Principal Librarian', which in Banks's day referred to the senior officer of the Museum. It was not until much later in the nineteenth century that the term 'Director' was used for this position. The 'Under-Librarians' were in charge of the Museum departments. The term 'Keeper' was also used to describe these posts from at least early as 1814, becoming in the 1830s the official designation.
      The names of collections at the British Museum have been taken from officers' reports, published guides, official histories and other similar sources. The relevant source will be found in the notes whenever a collection is discussed in detail. The term 'duplicate' needs to be clarified in reference to the natural history and other specimens that were frequently exchanged throughout the eighteenth and nineteenth centuries. Plant, animal and mineral specimens are, of course, never exactly the same, and the use made of the word 'duplicate' in this study is not intended to imply that they or any other type of material are identical. A further point is that it seems the eighteenth-century definition of 'duplicate' was broad, and might include similar objects from a range of related Museum collections. Such collections were increasingly being combined to create large central collections in this period.

4.   A. M. Lysaght (ed.), *Joseph Banks in Newfoundland and Labrador, 1766: His Diary, Manuscripts and Collections* (London, Faber and Faber, 1971).

5.   For a number of papers on the scientific aspects of this voyage, see *Notes and Records of the Royal Society*, 24:1 (1969); *Pacific Studies*, 1:2 (1978), and 2:1 (1978). See also H. B. Carter, 'The Royal Society and the Voyage of H.M.S. *Endeavour* 1768–71', *Notes and Records of the Royal Society*, 49:2 (1995), pp. 245–60.

6.   J. C. Beaglehole (ed.), *The Endeavour Journal of Joseph Banks 1768–1771*, 2 vols (Sydney, Public Library of New South Wales, 1962), vol. 2, p. 110. Banks does not dwell on this event. Cook had more to say about it: J. C. Beaglehole (ed.), *The Journals of Captain James Cook on his Voyages of Discovery*, 4 vols (Woodbridge, Boydell Press, 1999), vol. 1, pp. 386–9.

7.   E. Duyker and P. Tingbrand (eds), *Daniel Solander: Collected Correspondence 1753–1782* (Oslo, Scandinavian University Press, 1995); E. Duyker, *Nature's Argonaut: Daniel*

Solander 1733–1782. Naturalist and Voyager with Cook and Banks (Victoria, Miegunyah Press, 1998).

8.   W. Blunt, *The Compleat Naturalist: A Life of Linnaeus* (London, Collins, 1971).

9.   Sheffield, a shadowy figure, had an interest in early ethnographic collections from the Pacific, not least those given to the Ashmolean in 1776 by the Forsters: R. F. Ovenell, *The Ashmolean Museum 1683–1894* (Oxford, Clarendon Press, 1986), ch. 10: 'William Sheffield, 1772–1795'.

10. R. Holt-White (ed.), *The Life and Letters of Gilbert White of Selborne*, 2 vols (London, John Murray, 1901), vol. 1, pp. 210–12.

11. W. T. Stearn, 'The Botanical Results of the *Endeavour* Voyage', *Endeavour*, 27:100 (1968), pp. 3–10; p. 9.

12. H. B. Carter, J. A. Diment, C. J. Humphries and A. Wheeler, 'The Banksian Natural History Collections of the *Endeavour* Voyage and their Relevance to Modern Taxonomy' in *History in the Service of Systematics: Papers from the Conference to Celebrate the Centenary of the British Museum (Natural History) 13–16 April, 1981*, Society for the Bibliography of Natural History, Special Publication 1 (London, 1981), pp. 62–8.

13. Probably a reference to the 'Solander Slips' used by Solander to catalogue natural history collections. The 'Solander Slips' are at the Natural History Museum, London, bound in twenty-seven volumes in the Zoology Library, and a further twenty-four volumes in the Botany Library. See W. T. Stearn, 'Daniel Carlsson Solander (1733–1782), Pioneer Swedish Investigator of Pacific Natural History', *Archives of Natural History*, 11:3 (1984), pp. 499–503; A. Wheeler, 'Daniel Solander and the Zoology of Cook's Voyage', *Archives of Natural History*, 11:3 (1984), pp. 505–15; J. A. Diment and A. Wheeler, 'Catalogue of the Natural History Manuscripts and Letters by Daniel Solander (1733–1782), or Attributed to Him, in British Collections', *Archives of Natural History*, 11:3 (1984), pp. 457–88; E. W. Groves, 'Notes on the Botanical Specimens Collected by Banks and Solander on Cook's First Voyage, together with an Itinerary of Landing Localities', *Journal of the Society for the Bibliography of Natural History*, 4:1 (1962), pp. 57–62.

14. The engraved plates Banks had prepared have been published by Alecto Historical Editions. There is a catalogue of the relevant specimens, drawings, copper plates, related manuscripts and publications: J. A. Diment, C. J. Humphries, L. Newington, and E. Shaughnessy, 'Catalogue of the Natural History Drawings Commissioned by Joseph Banks on the *Endeavour* Voyage 1768–1771', *Bulletin of the British Museum (Natural History): Historical Series*, 11–13 (1984–7).

15. R. Desmond, *Kew: The History of the Royal Botanic Gardens* (London, Harvill with Royal Botanic Gardens, Kew, 1995).

16. Banks to Lauraguais, 6 December 1771, ML 05.01.

17. The breadfruit voyages of William Bligh were mounted under Banks's direction to ship the breadfruit and other plants of the Pacific to the West Indies to be used on the plantations. The first attempt, of 1787–9, ended in a mutiny on the HMS *Bounty*. The second, of 1791–3, involving HMS *Providence* under Bligh and HMS *Assistant* under Nathaniel Portlock, was successful. For details of the plants delivered, including those that were brought back to Kew Gardens, see D. Powell, 'The Voyage of the Plant Nursery, H.M.S. *Providence*, 1791–93', *Economic Botany*, 31 (1977), pp. 387–431. For an account of Banks's use of plant collectors, often from Kew, see D. Mackay, 'Agents of Empire: the Banksian Collectors and Evaluation of New Lands' in D. P. Miller and P. H. Reill (eds), *Visions of Empire: Voyages, Botany, and Representations of Nature* (Cambridge, Cam-

bridge University Press, 1996), pp. 38–57. See also C. Alexander, *The Bounty* (London, HarperCollins, 2003).

2 Ethnography

1. BM CE 1/3 667–8
2. BM CE 1/3 740–2.
3. BM CE 1/3 753.
4. Banks to Ingenhousz, 31 May 1782, ML 74.03. Banks went on in this letter to say that he expected to have back anything the Museum did not want, but that there had been a delay because, he suspected, the sorting of the material had been neglected. For more on ethnography at the Museum and elsewhere, see A. L. Kaeppler, 'Tracing the History of Hawaiian Cook Voyage Artefacts in the Museum of Mankind' in T. C. Mitchell (ed.), *Captain Cook and the South Pacific* (London, British Museum Press, 1979), pp. 167–98.
5. BM CE 3/6 1632, 1743–4. For more South Sea curiosities from Cleveley, the Collets – William and Joseph – Hogg, Webber and Williamson, see also BM CE 3/7 1745. Another donation from Banks, in December 1792, was 'A Boat from the Pelew Islands': BM CE 3/8 2063.
6. In August 1781 Cleveley was paid fifteen guineas for assisting in the preparation of the South Sea Room: BM CE 3/7 1771.
7. BM CE 4/1 599.
8. The Repository, as it was called, contained what we would now regard as a museum collection of objects and specimens.
9. BM CE 1/4 828; BM CE 30/2 15/6/1781.
10. W. T. Stearn, *The Natural History Museum at South Kensington: A History of the Museum 1753–1980* (London, Natural History Museum, 1998), pp. 19–20.
11. For a discussion of the Royal Society's museum, see M. Hunter, 'The Cabinet Institutionalized: The Royal Society's Repository and its Background' in O. Impey and A. MacGregor (eds), *The Origins of Museums: The Cabinet of Curiosities in Sixteenth and Seventeenth Century Europe* (Oxford, Clarendon Press, 1985), pp. 159–68. See also M. Hunter, *Establishing the New Science: The Experience of the Early Royal Society* (Woodbridge, Boydell, 1989), esp. ch. 4. For a list of objects not transferred from the Royal Society to the British Museum, see *The Record of the Royal Society of London for the Promotion of Natural Knowledge*, 4th edn (London, Royal Society, 1940), pp. 164–8. For more on the instruments possessed by the Society, and some of these that were transferred to the Natural History Museum later in the nineteenth century, see documents in RS Miscellaneous Manuscripts, vol. 13.
12. G. Dixon and N. Portlock, *A Voyage Round the World, but more particularly to the North-West Coast of America: performed in 1785, 1786, 1787, and 1788, in the King George and Queen Charlotte, Captains Portlock and Dixon*, 2 vols (London, Goulding, 1789).
13. BM CE 3/8 2005–6.
14. King to Banks, [October 1780], NHM BL D.T.C. I 304.
15. For a study of Banks's role as 'custodian' of the Cook 'model' of exploration, and of the commercial and political rivalries of the mid-1780s and early 1790s that are referred to here, see D. Mackay, *In the Wake of Cook: Exploration, Science and Empire, 1780–1801* (London, Croom Helm, 1985), esp. chs 3, 4.
16. Menzies to Banks, 7 September 1786, RBG Kew B.C. I 243; Etches to Banks, 29 September 1786, RBG Kew B.C. I 246.

17. Menzies to Banks, 21 July 1789, RBG Kew B.C. I 357.
18. Menzies to Rutherford, 19 October 1789, RBG Edinburgh.
19. Banks regarded these claims as mostly unfounded: Banks to Nepean, 15 February 1790, PRO H.O. 42/16.
20. Menzies to Banks, 8 October 1789, RBG Kew B.C. I 362.
21. Banks to Grenville, 20 January 1792, PRO H.O. 42/18 166–7 [with enclosures]; Banks to Menzies, 22 February 1791, BL Add. MS 33979, ff. 75–8.
22. Menzies to Banks, 14 September 1795, RBG Kew B.C. 2 127; Banks to Portland, 3 February 1796, NHM BL D.T.C. X(1) 15–16: '... he [Menzies] lost no opportunities of making & writing down the necessary observations respecting the produce of the soil, the manners of the Natives, & such other matters as he was instructed to remark upon'.
23. Portland to Banks, 12 February 1796, SL Banks MS P N 1:18 and 'A Catalogue of Curiosities & natural productions brought home in his Majesty's Sloop Discovery from the North West Coast of America & the South Sea Islands by Mr. Archibald Menzies'. See the Appendix, pp. 183–90.
24. BM CE 1/4 922.
25. Statement by Banks on the conduct of George Vancouver, [c. 1796]: NHM BL D.T.C. X(1) 83–6. For Banks's warning about the importance of keeping a journal on the voyage as proof of events, as well as a record of the natural history and cultures encountered, see Banks to Menzies, 10 August 1791, *HRNSW*, vol. 1, ii, pp. 521–2. For accounts of the work of Menzies on these voyages, and for an assessment of the botanical results, see D. J. Galloway and E. W. Groves, 'Archibald Menzies MD, FLS (1754–1842), Aspects of his Life, Travels and Collections', *Archives of Natural History*, 14:1 (1987), pp. 3–43; E. W. Groves, 'Archibald Menzies (1754–1842) an Early Botanist on the Northwestern Seaboard of North America, 1792–1794, with further Notes of his Life and Work', *Archives of Natural History*, 28:1 (2001), pp. 71–122.
26. A detailed inventory of the Cook material was made: TCC Add. a. 106, ff. 108–9. See also D. McKitterick (ed.), *The Making of the Wren Library, Trinity College, Cambridge* (Cambridge, Cambridge University Press, 1995), pp. 104–7.
27. For details relating to Alströmer and Fabricius respectively, see R. Stig, *The Banks Collection: An Episode in 18th Century Anglo-Swedish Relations*, Ethnographical Museum of Sweden, Monograph Series, 8 (Stockholm, Almqvist and Wiksell, 1963); J. Fabricius, *Briefe aus London vermischten Inhalts* (Dessau and Leipzig, 1784).
28. J. Coote, *Curiosities from the Endeavour: A Forgotten Collection – Pacific Artefacts Given by Joseph Banks to Christ Church, Oxford, after the First Voyage* (Whitby, Captain Cook Memorial Museum, 2004), and 'An Interim Report on a Previously Unknown Collection from Cook's First Voyage: The Christ Church Collection of the Pitt Rivers Museum', *Journal of Museum Ethnography*, 16 (2004), pp. 111–21.
29. H. B. Carter, *Sir Joseph Banks (1743–1820): A Guide to Biographical and Bibliographical Sources* (Winchester, St Paul's Bibliographies, 1987), E: 'The Collections'. Also, on ethnographic artefacts and their distribution and history, see A. L. Kaeppler, '*Artificial Curiosities*': Being an Exposition of Native Manufactures collected on the Three Pacific Voyages of Captain James Cook, R.N., at the Bernice Pauahi Bishop Museum January 18, 1978–August 31, 1978 (Honolulu, Bishop Museum Press, 1978); A. L. Kaeppler (ed.), *Cook Voyage Artifacts in Leningrad, Berne, and Florence Museums* (Honolulu, Bishop Museum Press, 1978); B. Hauser-Schäublin and G. Krüger (eds), *James Cook, Gifts and Treasures from the South Seas: The Cook/Forster Collection, Göttingen* (Munich and New York, Prestel, 1998); Wilson, *The British Museum*, pp. 42–5.

30. Banks to Jacquin, 23 August 1785, ML Banks MS.
31. For a description of 'The Otaheite & South Sea Rooms', see J. P. Malcolm, *Londinium Redivivum, or an Ancient History and Modern Description of London*, 4 vols (London, J. Nichols, 1802–7), vol. 2, pp. 520–31.
32. BM CE 5/1 57–8.
33. BM CE 5/1 106, 133.
34. BM CE 3/9 2391–2; British Museum, *Synopsis of the Contents of the British Museum* (London, 1808), pp. 4–5.
35. Some of these places had started to be colonized. From them came products made for the first time by European rather than indigenous hands, among them, from Australia, 'Cups made by the Convicts at Botany Bay ...', presented to the Museum by Banks in December 1794. These cups have not survived, and were probably never seen by the public: BM CE 3/8 2096.
36. For comments on Banks see the 1808 *Synopsis*, pp. xxiv–xxv.
37. BM CE 3/9 2606, 2610.
38. BM CE 5/3 751–2.
39. BM CE 30/2 14/11/1818, 19/12/1818; BM CE 5/5 1146, 1148, 1159; BM CE 4/4 1500, Captain Buchan to the Secretary of the British Museum, 6 November 1818, stating that he had been ordered to deposit at the Museum the specimens procured by HM ships *Dorothea* and *Trent* during the recent northern voyages, and 1501–4 is a list of the items; BM CE 3/10 2709, 2715, 2716.
40. BM CE 1/5 1143.
41. BM CE 5/5 1148.
42. 1808 *Synopsis*, pp. xxiv–xxv.
43. BM CE 3/8 2018.

3 Natural History and Zoology

1. For the progress made in natural history under these and other Museum officers, see Gunther, *The Founders of Science*, chs 3–9.
2. BM CE 1/2 444; BM CE 4/1 175, in which Solander described his method of cataloguing.
3. BM CE 1/3 682, Solander was granted leave in September 1771 to complete the arrangement and description of articles collected by Banks and himself with Cook. See also F. A. Stafleu, *Linnaeus and the Linnaeans: The Spreading of their Ideas in Systematic Botany, 1735–1789* (Utrecht, Oosthoek, 1971); J. B. Marshall, 'Daniel Carl Solander, Friend, Librarian and Assistant to Sir Joseph Banks', *Archives of Natural History*, 11:3 (1984), pp. 451–6.
4. BM CE 30/2 14/3/1779, 7/1/1780, 15/9/1780, 5/10/1781, 17/4/1783 (two birds from Lady Banks), 20/8/1784. For Pigou and Duncan, see Pigou [also signed by Duncan] to Banks, 31 May 1782, BL Add. MS 33977, f. 148; Pigou [also signed by Duncan] to Banks, 31 December 1783, RBG Kew B.C. I 155; Duncan to Banks, 18 January 1784, BL Add. MS 33977, f. 258.
5. BM CE 3/7 1825, 1829, 1859.
6. BM CE 3/7 1880–1.
7. For Banks and colonies at New South Wales, see J. M. Matra, 'A Proposal for Establishing a Settlement in New South Wales', PRO C.O. 201/1 57–61; and *HRNSW*, vol. 1, ii, pp. 1–8. Also H. B. Carter, *Sir Joseph Banks* (London, British Museum Press, 1988), pp.

212–16. For an account of the development and strategic importance of British settlements on the east coast of Australia, see A. Frost, 'The Antipodean Exchange: European Horticulture and Imperial Designs' in Miller and Reill (eds), *Visions of Empire*, pp. 58–79.

8.   BM CE 3/8 2021. The majority of the animals, plants and minerals initially sent to Banks from the colony at New South Wales came on Arthur Phillip's orders, with a consignment of animals (live and dead), ethnographic material, insects, plants and seeds also being sent by David Considen, an assistant surgeon. The Phillip correspondence relating to this is ML Banks MSS, while the Considen letter, from Port Jackson, was dated 18 November 1788, *HRNSW*, vol. 1, ii, pp. 220–1.

9.   For comment on the types of colonial contact available to a man like Banks, and their importance, see J. Browne, 'Biogeography and Empire' in N. Jardine, J. A. Secord and E. C. Spary (eds), *Cultures of Natural History* (Cambridge, Cambridge University Press, 1996), pp. 308–14, esp. the sections 'Colonial Officials' and 'Science of Empire'.

10.   Solander to Banks, 22 August 1775, RBG Kew B.C. I 51.

11.   BM CE 4/1 289–92, being Johann Reinhold Forster's gift of birds, fish and animals from his voyage with Cook, which he calls a 'compleat Set of Specimens', with an accompanying list of items.

12.   Solander to Banks, 5 September 1775, NHM BL D.T.C. I 98–9.

13.   Ibid.

14.   J. Gascoigne, *Joseph Banks and the English Enlightenment: Useful Knowledge and Polite Culture* (Cambridge, Cambridge University Press, 1994), pp. 68–9. Mullens, among others, also comments on the range of Lever's collections: 'Some Museums of Old London – I', pp. 126–8. For a description of Lever's museum in July 1778, see A. R. Ellis (ed.), *The Early Diary of Frances Burney 1768–1778*, 2 vols (London, G. Bell, 1889), vol. 2, p. 249.

15.   H. St John, 'New Species of Hawaiian Plants Collected by David Nelson in 1779', *Pacific Science*, 30:1 (1976), pp. 7–44.

16.   Clerke to Banks, 18 August 1779, NHM BL D.T.C. I 266–7.

17.   D. Medway, 'Some Ornithological Results of Cook's Third Voyage', *Journal of the Society for the Bibliography of Natural History*, 9:3 (1979), pp. 315–51; J. J. Keevil, 'William Anderson, 1748–1778: Master Surgeon, Royal Navy', *Annals of Medical History*, 5:6 (1933), pp. 511–24; J. Britten, 'William Anderson (1778) and the Plants of Cook's Third Voyage', *Journal of Botany*, 54 (1917), pp. 345–52, and 'Short Notes. William Anderson and Cook's Third Voyage', *Journal of Botany*, 55 (1917), p. 54.

18.   P. J. P. Whitehead, 'A Guide to the Dispersal of Zoological Material from Captain Cook's Voyages', *Pacific Studies*, 2:1 (1978), pp. 52–93; p. 78. Whitehead points out the competitive element in all this, and that the claim to Clerke's collections lodged by Daines Barrington on behalf of Lever was not valid (p. 64).

19.   BM CE 3/8 2049; BM CE 30/2 13/1/1792.

20.   Banks to Blumenbach, 16 August 1793, UG Blumenbach MS III 38–9.

21.   BM CE 1/4 828; BM CE 30/2 15/6/1781.

22.   BM CE 3/7 1752, 1761, 1766, 1781, 1834, 1944.

23.   BM CE 1/4 842, 844; BM CE 3/7 1801.

24.   For the famous attempt by some Royal Society Fellows to remove Banks from the presidency in the winter of 1783–4, in which Maty and the Reverend Samuel Horsley were leading figures, see C. R. Weld, *A History of The Royal Society, with Memoirs of the Presidents*, 2 vols (London, J. W. Parker, 1848), vol. 2, ch. 6. Called 'the Royal Soci-

ety Dissensions', this confrontation arose partly because some Fellows did not think a naturalist worthy to have the chair of the Society. Horsley was a mathematician, and compared Banks unfavourably with his illustrious predecessor as President, Sir Isaac Newton. Most commentators agree, however, that Horsley had designs on the chair himself, and the revolt was eventually crushed following outbursts from Horsley and his followers. The disputes do not seem to have affected the Museum directly. Maty resigned his post as Secretary at the Royal Society, but he continued to work at the Museum until 1787.

25. Most Museum officers were connected with a number of societies and organizations, including the Royal Society. They tended to have broad contacts throughout London, and studied and published on various collections. On the Royal Society and the British Museum, see Gunther, *The Founders of Science*, pp. 40–3; A. E. Gunther, 'The Royal Society and the Foundation of the British Museum', *Notes and Records of the Royal Society*, 33:2 (1979), pp. 207–16.

26. Banks to Eden, [26 January 1796], NHM BL D.T.C. X(1) 13–14.

27. P. J. P. Whitehead, 'Zoological Specimens from Captain Cook's Voyages', *Journal of the Society for the Bibliography of Natural History*, 5:3 (1969), pp. 161–201; pp. 165–7.

28. For the insects, see M. Fitton and S. Shute, 'Sir Joseph Banks's Collection of Insects' in R. E. R. Banks et al. (eds), *Sir Joseph Banks: A Global Perspective* (London, Royal Botanic Gardens, Kew, 1994), pp. 209–11. For the shells, see G. L. Wilkins, 'A Catalogue and Historical Account of the Banks Shell Collection', *The Bulletin of the British Museum (Natural History): Historical Series*, 1:3 (1955), pp. 71–119.

29. Gray had been appointed an assistant in the Museum in April 1778. See also A. E. Gunther, 'Edward Whitaker Gray (1748–1806), Keeper of the Natural Curiosities at the British Museum', *Bulletin of the British Museum (Natural History): Historical Series*, 5:2 (1976), pp. 193–210.

30. BM CE 3/7 1820.

31. BM CE 3/7 1825, 1829.

32. BM CE 3/7 1859.

33. Act 7 Geo. II. c.18. An Act to enable the Trustees of the British Museum to exchange, sell or dispose of any Duplicates, etc. (*Commons Journals*). The last sale of duplicates was held in 1832, by which time a great deal of valuable material had been sold. Exchanging duplicates went on a good deal longer (see next note).

34. BM CE 3/7 1874. On the Natural History Museum's system of exchanging plant duplicates that persisted until the 1930s, see J. Ramsbottom, 'Note: Banks's and Solander's Duplicates', *Journal of the Society for the Bibliography of Natural History*, 4:3 (1963), p. 197.

35. BM CE 3/7 1880–1.

36. BM CE 3/8 2015.

37. BM CE 3/8 2043, 2044.

38. BM CE 3/8 2048, 2118, 2122. See also, for example, the gifts made by the two navigators, Henry Waterhouse and George Bass: BM CE 3/8 2200–1.

39. BM CE 3/8 2133, 2220. See also BM CE 3/8 2271; BM CE 1/4 994–6.

40. BM CE 3/8 2221.

41. BM CE 3/8 2222; 2223. Titsingh to Banks, 26 August 1797, BL Add. MS 33980, f. 110; Titsingh to Banks, 10 December 1797, BL Add. MS 33980, ff. 124–5.

42. For the argus pheasant, see Macdonald to Banks, 18 February 1797, BL Add. MS 33980, f. 93. Additionally, fossils from Sheppey and Worcestershire were given in July, along with 'a schistus with impressions of leaves from Iceland': BM CE 3/8 2224.

43. Correspondence with governors, navigators, botanists and collectors, *c.* 1798–1805, shows the flow of material from New South Wales that reached Banks as the colony there developed. For more on Caley, see J. B. Webb, *George Caley: Nineteenth Century Naturalist* (New South Wales, S. Beatty, 1995).

44. BM CE 3/8 2231.

45. Fabbroni to Banks, [June 1794], BL Add. MS 33982, ff. 323–4; Fabbroni to Banks, 3 May 1796, BL Add. MS 8098, ff. 349–50; Banks to Fabbroni, 1 July 1796, APS; Batt to Banks, 7 February 1803, SL Banks MS. See also W. C. Smith, 'A History of the First Hundred Years of the Mineral Collection in the British Museum', *Bulletin of the British Museum (Natural History): Historical Series*, 3:8 (1969), pp. 237–59; p. 259; M. M. Grady, *Catalogue of Meteorites* (Cambridge, Cambridge University Press, 2000), p. 461. On the Republic of Letters, see J. McClellan, *Science Reorganized: Scientific Societies in the Eighteenth Century* (New York, Columbia University Press, 1985).

46. R. Cowen, 'After the Fall', *Science News*, 148:16 (1995), pp. 248–9.

47. BM CE 3/7 1978.

48. BM CE 3/8 2241; BM CE 30/2 10/12/1803

49. E. Howard, 'Experiments and Observations on certain Stony and Metalline Substances, which at different Times are said to have Fallen on the Earth; also on Various Kinds of Native Iron', *Philosophical Transactions*, 92:1 (1802), pp. 168–212, read 25 February 1802.

50. BM CE 1/4 954, 959; BM CE 3/9 2412; BM CE 5/3 792.

51. BM CE 30/2 11/11/1803; BM CE 3/8 2238. See also Banks to Novossiltzoff, 7 March 1803, RBG Kew B.C. II 275; Novossiltzoff to Banks, 7 July 1803, BL Add. MS 8099, ff. 360–1, f. 362 being the bones and horns sent, numbered in a list of items 1–11.

52. BM CE 3/8 2259, 2263, 2267, 2268, 2269; BM CE 3/9 2402. On the 'Native Minium', a recently identified substance, see BM CE 5/1 154; J. Smithson, 'Account of a Discovery of Native Minium. In a Letter from James Smithson, Esq. F.R.S. to the Right Hon. Sir Joseph Banks, K.B. P.R.S.', *Philosophical Transactions*, 96:2 (1806), pp. 267–8, read 24 April 1806.

53. See BM CE 5/3 764 [Konig] for an exchange by Banks in June 1815 using his 'account'. This concerned duplicate horns of an Irish Moose deer. Konig supported the release, referring to the fossil bones from Siberia sent to Banks by the Emperor of Russia, and presented by Banks in 1803. Konig was also able to list more donations made by Banks in 1815 of fossilized hazelnuts, for which see Stuart to Banks, 25 April 1815, NHM BL B.C. 79–80.

    Moreover, some of the early chemical experiments performed on minerals and meteorites were made possible through releases against Banks's name. On one occasion only was Banks's special arrangement extended to his wife, who was a collector of porcelain and donated items to the Museum in her own right: BM CE 30/2 17/4/1783, 22/5/1789, 13/12/1817. This occasion was when Lady Dorothea obtained a China cup and saucer in return for a feather from China in a glass tube: BM CE 3/8 2258.

54. Camper to Banks, 23 January 1786, BL Add. MS 8096, ff. 257–8.

55. BM CE 3/7 1917–18.

56. Camper to Banks, 26 March 1786, BL Add. MS 8096, ff. 259–60. Camper's list ran to fifteen numbered points, for which see letter referenced in note 54 above.

57. BM CE 3/7 1952.
58. O. Swartz, *Nova Genera et Species Plantarum, seu prodromus descriptionum Vegetabilium maximam partem incognitorum, quae sub itinere in Indiam occidentalem annis 1783–1787* (Holmiae, In Bibliopoliis Acad. M. Swederi, 1788). Swartz to Banks, 23 June 1788, BL Add. MS 8097, ff. 117–18.
59. BM CE 3/7 1973.
60. BM CE 3/7 1996.
61. BM CE 3/7 1998. For Camper's collections, see also BM CE 3/8 2098.
62. Joseph Banks (ed.), *Icones selectae Plantarum quas in Japonia collegit et delineavit Engelbertus Kaempfer; ex archetypis in Museo Britannico asseveratis* (London, W. Bulmer & Co., 1791).
63. Banks to Cotta, [July 1791], BL Add. MS 8097, f. 396 v.
64. Swartz to Banks, 9 July 1792, BM Add. MS 8098, ff. 96–8.
65. BM CE 3/8 2260. See also BM CE 1/4 972–5, and the appointment of Henry Ellis as Assistant Librarian, as well as Planta's statement that the Attendants have no guide notes for showing people round the Museum. A listing of the contents of each Museum room was ordered at this time, May 1805.
66. BM CE 1/4 977–82.
67. E. Miller, *That Noble Cabinet: A History of the British Museum* (London, A. Deutsch, 1973), pp. 99–100.
68. On Combe, see Townley to Banks, 4 February 1803, BL Add. MS 36524, f. 34. On Konig, see BM CE 1/4 994–6.
69. BM CE 1/5 1112–13.
70. BM CE 3/8 2310–6; BM CE 5/1 [Konig], n.d. [*c.* March 1807], n.f.
71. BM CE 1/5 1007–8. See also BM CE 3/9 2356–7, 2367, for Banks's supervision of Konig's early work on minerals.
72. BM CE 5/1 12–13.
73. Camper to Banks, 18 June 1786, BL Add. MS 8096, f. 408, and Camper to Banks, [October 1787], BL Add. MS 8096, ff. 413–14.
74. BM CE 5/1 27, 56.
75. BM CE 3/9 2373–4.
76. BM CE 5/1 107.
77. BM CE 1/5 1051–2.
78. BM CE 4/2 913–16.
79. BM CE 1/5 1036–7.
80. The sequence: BM CE 4/2 905–8 [Banks draft], 909 [Abbot response], 913–16 [Banks final report].
81. BM CE 5/1 130, n.d. [*c.* June 1808]
82. BM CE 3/9 2392–3, 2395–6.
83. J. Dobson, *William Clift* (London, Heinemann Medical Books, 1954), esp. pp. 31–3.
84. Gunther, *The Founders of Science*, pp. 36, 90.
85. Ibid., p. 84. These fires, lit in the Museum garden, have become the stuff of legend, with more than one Museum officer being accused by his successors of burning objects. During this period many museum owners and keepers destroyed unwanted material, and the traffic in specimens and other objects was another way of ridding a collection of unwanted material in exchange for new items.
86. BM CE 3/9 2414.
87. BM CE 1/5 1051. See also BM CE 3/9 2373–4.

88. BM CE 4/2 [Konig] 919–20, [Planta] 921–3, [Shaw] 923–4.
89. BM CE 1/5 1055–6.
90. BM CE 4/2 927. Material originally belonging to the Royal Society's Repository must have been included in the transfer to the College.
91. BM CE 5/1 234.
92. BM CE 5/1 154.
93. BM CE 5/1 200.
94. BM CE 5/1 215. See also BM CE 1/5 1059.
95. BM CE 3/9 2433.
96. BM CE 3/9 2449. See also Officers' Reports 249, 269.
97. BM CE 3/9 2464.
98. Officers' Reports 317–18.
99. W. R. Dawson, *The Banks Letters: A Calendar of the Manuscript Correspondence* (London, British Museum Press, 1958), esp. '3 The History of the Banks Papers': pp. xiii–xviii.
100. BM CE 5/1 254.
101. BM CE 5/2 353.
102. BM CE 5/2 450.
103. BM CE 5/3 507.
104. BM CE 5/3 585.
105. BM CE 1/5 1112–13.
106. BM CE 5/3 623. See also the Leach proposal in 1818 that Cuvier be allowed to select duplicates of molluscs and fishes for the French Museum, and that a system of exchange be set up between this and the British Museum, BM CE 5/5 1105–6. This was approved: BM CE 3/10 2696. Leach's suggestions followed a successful trip to Paris, when, among other things, he obtained 80 European birds, 38 molluscs, 3,700 European and exotic insects and 2,000 duplicates for exchange. He envisaged creating a considerable network.
107. BM CE 5/3 642, 692–3.
108. BM CE 5/3 782.
109. BM CE 4/3 1172–3.
110. BM CE 4/3 1174.
111. BM CE 1/5 1134.
112. BM CE 5/3 792.
113. BM CE 5/3 706, 717, 738.
114. BM CE 4/4 1403.
115. BM CE 3/9 2510–11.
116. R. J. Cleevely, 'Some Background to the Life and Publications of Colonel George Montagu (1753–1815)', *Journal of the Society for the Bibliography of Natural History*, 8:4 (1978), pp. 445–80.
117. BM CE 1/5 1141. See also BM CE 4/3 1215.
118. BM CE 3/9 2627; BM CE 4/3 1272.
119. BM CE 4/3 1176.
120. R. C. Murphy, 'Robert Ferryman, Forgotten Naturalist', *Proceedings of the American Philosophical Society*, 103:6 (1959), pp. 774–7. The correspondence between Banks and Ferryman is very small, but it appears friendly.
121. Banks to Ferryman, 5 February 1788, RBG Kew B.C. I 295 (2).
122. BM CE 4/3 1271.
123. BM CE 5/4 874.

124. BM CE 3/9 2634.
125. BM CE 5/4 874.
126. BM CE 5/4 842. Montagu's collections were at the Museum by October 1816, along with Stephens's donation, and also a donation by Charles Prideaux: BM CE 5/4 900. By July 1817 Room 11 was all but ready for Montagu's collection: BM CE 5/4 1005–6.
127. BM CE 3/10 2636.
128. For other purchases recommended by Leach this year, see that of Latham, of Compton Street, for £25, being 1,300 Indian insects, BM CE 5/4 821; that of Sims, of Norwich, for £15, being 3,187 insects: BM CE 5/4 863; BM CE 3/9 2632.
129. BM CE 3/10 2637.
130. BM CE 5/4 883–4. Leach worked hard to organize the animals to go into the room for British zoology, which was almost ready by December 1817: BM CE 4/4 1044. See also BM CE 4/4 1403.
131. BM CE 3/10 2665. One source of news and natural history for Banks at this time was: Leschenhault de la Tour to Banks, 20 March 1817, BL Add. MS 8968, f. 25.
132. Banks continued to enrich the Museum. For a small collection of minerals from Greenland, three species of tortoise from the Cape of Good Hope, and thirty-five species of insect in 'Gum Amonia', see BM CE 3/10 2711.
133. BM CE 5/4 970–1, 999. See also C. F. Cowan, 'John Francillon, F.L.S., A Few Facts', *The Entomologist's Record and Journal of Variation*, 98:7–8 (1986), pp. 139–43; C. MacKechnie Jarris, 'A History of the British Coleoptera', *Proceedings and Transactions of the British Entomological and Natural History Society*, 8:4 (1976), pp. 99–100.
134. BM CE 5/4 1014–15. For Swainson, see BM CE 5/4 970–1.
135. BM CE 4/4 1409.
136. BM CE 4/4 1404.
137. BM CE 5/5 1121–2, n.d. [*c.* June 1818].
138. BM CE 3/10 2699; BM CE 5/5 1137. See also, for further material from Leach, including some from the sale, BM CE 3/10 2703, 2707. For more payments by Leach, as authorized by Banks: £51 18*d.*, for forty species of birds and fishes and a rare turtle purchased at the sale of Edward Donovan's collections, May 1818, see BM CE 5/5 1106. Donovan's collections may have contained material purchased at the sale of Lever's collections, which Donovan attended in 1806.
139. BM CE 3/10 2709.
140. BM CE 4/4 1500–1.
141. BM CE 3/10 2711.
142. BM CE 5/5 1161. See also BM CE 5/5 1171.
143. BM CE 3/10 2716.
144. Ross to Banks, 25 July 1818, UW.
145. BM CE 5/3 BM CE 5/5 1159.
146. BM CE 4/4 1379.
147. BM CE 4/4, n.f., comprising letters between Burchell and senior trustees on this subject, October to December 1819.
148. BM CE 1/5 1172–3.
149. See Gunther, *The Founders of Science*, chs 5, 6.
150. BM CE 5/5 1240–1.
151. BM CE 5/5 1218.
152. BM CE 5/6 1326.
153. BM CE 5/6 1329. Moon to Banks, 8 May 1819, NHM BL B.C. 183–4.

154. Gray knew the collections well, since in 1824 he had been appointed an assistant (not on staff) in the Department of Natural History. This was a full two years before the Zoological Society was founded, a late addition to London Learned Society. Gray was formally appointed as an assistant in 1837.

4 Investigating Natural History: Expanding Limits after 1800

1.   Banks to King, 15 May 1798, *HRNSW*, vol. 3, pp. 382–3.
2.   G. R. de Beer, *The Sciences were Never at War* (London, Thomas Nelson, 1960), ch. 4: 'The Wars of Napoleon 1803–1815'.
3.   Banks to Spencer, [December 1800], PRO Adm. 1/4377.
4.   E. Scott, *The Life of Matthew Flinders* (Sydney, Angus and Robertson, 1914).
5.   Banks with Brown, Bauer, Westall, Good and Allen, 29 April 1801, PRO Adm. 1/4379: the collections made on the voyage were to be under Admiralty control – see condition 4.
6.   Flinders to Banks, 18 February 1801, ML Banks MS. For Banks's views on Flinders as a possible naval commander, and the need for exploration of Australia, see Banks to King, 15 May 1798, *HRNSW*, vol. 3, pp. 382–3.
7.   Flinders to Banks, 6 September 1800, ML Banks MS.
8.   Banks to Nepean, 28 April 1801, ML Banks MS; Nepean to Banks, 28 April 1801, ML Banks MS.
9.   M. Flinders, *A Voyage to Terra Australis*, 2 vols (London, G. and W. Nicol, 1814).
10. Banks to Marsden, January 1806, *HRNSW*, vol. 6, pp. 16–19. For more on the results of the voyage, especially the work of Bauer, see D. J. Mabberley, *Ferdinand Bauer: The Nature of Discovery* (London, Natural History Museum, 1999), and D. J. Mabberley and D. T. Moore, 'Catalogue of the Holdings in The Natural History Museum (London) of the Australian Botanical Drawings of Ferdinand Bauer (1760–1826) and Cognate Materials relating to the *Investigator* Voyage of 1801–1805', *Bulletin of the Natural History Museum: Botany Series*, 29:2 (1999), pp. 81–226. See also D. J. Mabberley, *Jupiter Botanicus: Robert Brown of the British Museum* (London, British Museum Press, 1985), esp. chs 3–9; T. G. Vallance, D. T. Moore and E. W. Groves (eds), *Nature's Investigator: The Diary of Robert Brown in Australia, 1801–1805* (Canberra, Australian Biological Resources Study, 2001); S. Thomas (ed.), *The Encounter, 1802: Art of the Flinders and Baudin Voyages* (Adelaide, Art Gallery of South Australia, 2002).
11. R. Brown, *Prodromus Florae Novae Hollandiae et Insulae Van-Diemen, exhibens Characteres Plantarum quas Annis 1802–1805 per oras utriusque insulae collegit et descripsit R. Brown* (London, R. Taylor, 1810).
12. F. Bauer, *Illustrationes Florae Novae Hollandiae: sive icones generum quae in Prodromo Florae Novae Hollandiae et Insulae Van-Diemen descripsit Robertus Brown / Ferdinandi Bauer* (London, Veneunt apud Auctorem, 1806–13).
13. Banks to Brown, 15 June 1801, BL Add. MS 32439, ff. 41–2. See also ff. 33–40.
14. Banks to Milnes, 20 January 1801, *HRNSW*, vol. 4, pp. 290–1.
15. Banks to Brown, 15 June 1801, BL Add. MS 32439, ff. 41–2.
16. B. Dolan, *Josiah Wedgwood: Entrepreneur to the Enlightenment* (London, HarperCollins, 2004).
17. J. Wedgwood, 'On the Analysis of a Mineral Substance from New South Wales. In a Letter from Josiah Wedgwood, Esq. F.R.S. and A.S. to Sir Joseph Banks, Bart. P.R.S.', *Philosophical Transactions*, 80:2 (1790), pp. 306–20, read 15 April 1790.

18. Blumenbach to Banks, 14 February 1791, BL Add. MS 8097, ff. 364–5.
19. C. Hatchett, 'An Analysis of the Earthy Substance from New South Wales, called Sydneia or Terra Australis', *Philosophical Transactions*, 88:1 (1798), pp. 110–29, read 8 February 1798. See also W. P. Griffith and P. J. T. Morris, 'Charles Hatchett FRS (1765–1847), Chemist and Discoverer of Niobium', *Notes and Records of the Royal Society*, 57:3 (2003), pp. 299–316.
20. Besides Phillip's remarks to Banks on this, Hunter had also commented on a subject quite familiar to Banks, see Hunter to Banks, 1 August 1797, NHM BL D.T.C. X (2) 108.
21. Banks to Navy Board, 25 March 1799, *HRNSW*, vol. 3, pp. 650–1.
22. Navy Board to Banks, 27 March 1799, *HRNSW*, vol. 3, p. 651; King to Banks, 3 April 1799, *HRNSW*, vol. 3, p. 658.
23. Kent to Banks, 1 November 1801, *HRNSW*, vol. 4, p. 608.
24. T. G. Vallance and D. T. Moore, 'Geological Aspects of H.M.S. *Investigator* in Australian Waters, 1801–5', *Bulletin of the British Museum (Natural History): Historical Series*, 10:1 (1982), pp. 1–43, esp. pp. 6, 29. See also D. T. Moore, 'An Account of those Described Rock Collections in the British Museum (Natural History) made before 1918; with a Provisional Catalogue Arranged by Continent', *Bulletin of the British Museum (Natural History): Historical Series*, 10:5 (1982), pp. 141–77. For another assessment of the natural history, see D. T. Moore and E. W. Groves, 'A Catalogue of Plants Written by Robert Brown (1773–1858) in New South Wales: First Impressions of the Flora of the Sydney Region', *Archives of Natural History*, 24:2 (1997), pp. 281–93; P. I. Edwards, 'Robert Brown (1773–1858) and the Natural History of Matthew Flinders' Voyage in H.M.S. *Investigator*, 1801–1805', *Journal of the Society for the Bibliography of Natural History*, 7:4 (1976), pp. 385–407.
25. BM CE 3/8 2207.
26. Barrow to Banks, 21 March 1811, BM CE 4/3 997; BM CE 5/2 342.
27. Banks to Admiralty, [March 1811], ML Banks MS.
28. BM CE 5/5 1148.

5 Earth Sciences

1. As one Derbyshire example, the remains of bones from a mine at Matlock, shows: BM CE 5/1 114.
2. Aall to Banks, 1 April 1812, UW Memorial Library; Banks to [Aall, *c*. April/May 1812], UW Memorial Library. For British Museum references to fossilized wood presented by Banks, wood he collected in 1772, see BM CE 30/2 9/5/1812; BM CE 5/2 452; BM CE 3/9 2525. In February 1812 Banks also gave more Icelandic MSS: BM CE 30/2 8/2/1812. An important gift of Icelandic rocks came in 1814: BM CE 5/3 511 [Konig report], 938 geological specimens from Iceland found by Dr Berger during travels in that country and presented through Banks.
3. Banks to Hamilton, 27 November 1787, BL Egerton MS 2641, ff. 141–2.
4. BM CE 5/1 241; BM CE 3/9 2438.
5. BM CE 3/9 2476, 2492, 2499, 2512, 2533; BM CE 5/2 481; BM CE 3/9 2538, 2540, 2549, 2557, 2559, 2563, 2566, 2575, 2582, 2589.
6. BM CE 5/2 348–50.
7. BM CE 5/2 372 8/3/1811.
8. BM CE 5/3 649 13/5/1814.

9.   BM CE 3/8 2164, 2165; BM CE 4/2 720–1. For an account of the Cracherode shell collection, see G. L. Wilkins, 'The Cracherode Shell Collection', *Bulletin of the British Museum (Natural History): Historical Series*, 1:4 (1957), pp. 124–84; and the Sloane shell collection, G. L. Wilkins, 'A Catalogue and Historical Account of the Sloane Shell Collection', *Bulletin of the British Museum (Natural History): Historical Series*, 1:1 (1953), pp. 1–47. See also S. P. Dance, *Shell Collecting: An Illustrated History* (London, Faber and Faber, 1966).

10. BM CE 1/4 953; BM CE 3/8 2235 [first major sale]; BM CE 5/4 815–16, 858–9, 871, 897–8 [later major sale]. See also J. M. Sweet, 'Sir Hans Sloane: Life and Mineral Collection', *The Natural History Magazine*, 5 (1935), in three parts: no. 34, pp. 49–64; no. 35, pp. 97–116 (for sales of minerals, see p. 98); and no. 36, pp. 145–64. The second of the sales followed the arrival and arrangement of Baron Von Moll's mineral collection.

11. BM CE 3/8 2155.

12. BM CE 4/2 723–5; and NHM BL D.T.C. XII 225–31.

13. Banks's own donations show how he tried to improve the collections in these areas. For example, in 1807 he gave tin ore from mines in Cornwall: BM CE 3/9 2321.

14. BM CE 4/2 723–5; and NHM BL D.T.C. XII 225–31.

15. BM CE 5/1 28.

16. Smith, 'The First Hundred Years of the Mineral Collection in the British Museum', p. 243. In 1828 Konig adopted the system of Professor Berzelius (p. 249; and BM CE 5/11 2259–62). Mervyn Herbert Nevil Story-Maskelyne, Keeper of Minerals 1857–80, reclassified the mineral collection following the crystallo-chemical system of Gustav Rose. This was prior to the move to Kensington.

17. BM CE 3/9 2404; BM CE 5/1 234.

18. BM CE 5/1 234.

19. BM CE 5/1 249.

20. BM CE 5/1 283, 295. See also Scott to Banks, [January 1796], BL Add. MS 33982, ff. 344–5; Stodart to Banks, 15 February 1800, BL Add. MS 33980, ff. 218–19.

21. BM CE 5/2 314–15.

22. Bournon departed the Museum when Gray died in 1806. In March 1807 George Shaw was appointed Keeper in Gray's place.

23. BM CE 3/9 2455.

24. The trustees were at first reluctant to consolidate the collections, but eventually agreed on condition that every specimen was marked according to the collection to which it originally belonged: BM CE 3/9 2487. The Comte de Bournon, who wished to arrange the Greville collection, put in a strong application based in part on his familiarity with it. The task was given to Konig, who had little time for Bournon's proposed schemes: BM CE 4/3 972–3, 977–8, 981. For Konig's views on Bournon's scheme, see BM CE 5/2 314–15.

25. BM CE 4/3 993; BM CE 3/9 2480, 2483, 2487; BM CE 5/2 362.

26. This was on the death of Edward Whitaker Gray on 27 December 1806. Konig had earlier asked for use of the Saloon and adjoining room in his report proposing certain specialist collections: BM CE 5/2 314–15.

27. BM CE 4/3 1167 [with enclosures]. See also BM CE 4/3 1180 [with enclosures], 1192, 1196.

28. BM CE 1/5 1134–5; BM CE 3/9 2592.

29. Banks to Blagden, 20 February 1815, RS B. 59. Another reason given for this refusal was that the Museum's collections were so extensive that the Marquis de Drée's collection did not contain enough that was new: Banks to Blagden, 11 March 1815, RS B. 102.

30. BM CE 5/4 923.

31. BM CE 4/3 995–6; BM CE 3/9 2487.

32. BM CE 5/3 724–5, 778, in which Konig reported the removal of items from Room 1 on the upper floor, except for the South Sea articles, and also the arrangements made for the reception of a 'Technical Mineralogy' in the old Mineralogy Room, Room 8. As in 1810, he argued for 'besides the Oryctognostic [i.e. mineralogical] collection and that of Technical Mineralogy, two other distinct and most necessary collections, viz. a Geological one, and one exclusively British, geographically arranged'. He hoped that the Room 1 might be used, and the South Sea Collections moved to the old Bird Room, Room 11.

33. BM CE 5/3 751, 792, 815–16.

34. BM CE 5/4 839. See also BM CE 4/4 1322.

35. BM CE 5/4 858–9.

36. The insufficient strength of the Saloon floor was a problem in 1811 and 1820 as well: BM CE 3/9 2483; BM CE 4/4 1589–90; BM CE 3/10 2750, 2751.

37. BM CE 5/4 897–8; BM CE 3/10 2640.

38. BM CE 5/4 950, and the existing contents of Room 10 to go to 8, with the nearly empty Room 1 to take any overflow.

39. BM CE 4/4 1450–1; BM CE 5/5 1135, 1118–19; BM CE 3/10 2742.

40. BM CE 3/10 2648.

41. BM CE 5/5 1118–19, 1135.

42. BM CE 5/4 966.

43. J. Farey, *General View of the Agriculture and Minerals of Derbyshire*, 2 vols (London, G. and W. Nichol, 1811–13).

44. Banks to St Fond, 11 February 1811, Bibliothèque Publique et Universitaire, Genève, Switzerland, MS suppl. 367, ff. 33r.–v.

45. W. Smith, *Delineation of the Strata of England and Wales with part of Scotland; exhibiting the Collieries and Mines; the Marshes and Fen Lands originally Overflowed by the Sea; and the Varieties of Soil according to the Variations in the Sub Strata; illustrated by the Most Descriptive Names* (London, 1815).

46. For a recent and popular account of Smith's career, see S. Winchester, *The Map that Changed the World. The Tale of William Smith and the Birth of a Science* (London, Viking, 2001). On Smith's collection and negotiations with the British Museum, see J. M. Eyles, 'William Smith: the Sale of his Geological Collection to the British Museum', *Annals of Science*, 23:3 (1967), pp. 177–212.

47. Banks to Konig, 29 August 1815, NHM Min. Lib. MS.

48. BM CE 5/4 880; BM CE 3/10 2639, 2679, 2683; BM CE 4/4 1328–9, 1413, 1423.

49. BM CE 5/4 1040.

50. BM CE 5/5 1101.

51. BM CE 5/5 1087, 1118–19.

52. BM CE 5/5 1215.

53. British Museum, *Synopsis of the Contents of the British Museum* (London, 1820), pp. 57–61.

6 Libraries and Antiquities

1. BM CE 3/9 2427.
2. RSA, Minute Book, 23 April 1765–22 December 1768, vol. X, ff. 321–3. For the later dates of Banks's council membership (1785–7 and 1813–20), see E. Smith, *The Life of Sir Joseph Banks, President of the Royal Society, with some Notices of his Friends and Contemporaries* (London, John Lane, 1911), p. 159. For the view that clashes took place in the administration of the Antiquaries due to Banks's powerful interference, see R. Sweet, *Antiquaries: The Discovery of the Past in Eighteenth-Century Britain* (London, Hambledon and London, 2004), pp. 103–5.
3. Elections: Very High Steward, SD Minute Book, 1777–93, vol. 4, 1 February 1778; Secretary, vol. 4, [no day] March 1778; Treasurer, vol. 4, [no day] April 1778. In fact, Banks had briefly held the post of Very High Steward earlier than February 1778: SD Minute Book, 1766–7, vol. 3, [no day] April 1777. Hence the use of the word 'Revived' on his reappointment. He resigned this position on becoming Secretary.
4. B. M. Marsden, *The Early Barrow Diggers* (Aylesbury, Shire Publications, 1974), p. 11. On archaeology in general, see B. G. Trigger, *A History of Archaeological Thought* (Cambridge, Cambridge University Press, 1992).
5. Banks, 'Journal of an Excursion to Eastbury & Bristol began May 15th 1767 ended June 20th 1767', CUL, Add. MS 6294 [autograph original].
6. Banks, 'Journal of an Excursion to Wales and the Midlands began August 13th 1767 ended January 29th 1768', CUL, Add. MS 6294 [autograph original].
7. C. S. Briggs, *Royal Commission on Ancient and Historical Monuments (Wales): Brecknock* (London, RCAHMW, 1997), vol. 1, part 1, p. 67.
8. Ramsey to Banks, 20 December 1772, NHM BL D.T.C. I 39, with Graham's account of Orkney finds being folio 40, dated 23 September 1772, and therefore predating Banks's digs. See also Ramsey to Banks, 9 February 1773, NHM BL D.T.C. I 46.
9. A. M. Lysaght, 'Joseph Banks at Skara Brae and Stennis, Orkney, 1772', *Notes and Records of the Royal Society*, 28:2 (1974), pp. 221–34.
10. V. G. Childe, *Skara Brae. A Pictish Village in Orkney* (London, Kegan Paul, Trench, Trübner, 1931).
11. By Banks – 'Journal of a Voyage in the Chartered Brig Sir Lawrence to the Hebrides and Iceland begun 12th July 1772 to 6th September', Blacker-Wood Library, McGill University, Montreal [autograph original, incomplete]; 'Memoranda and Notes at the Centre for Kentish Studies referring to the period 17 September to 30 September 1772, and the six days from 16 October to 22 October', CKS MS U951 Z31 [autograph original notes], ending with the remark, 'Idle tird resolve to go away fair or foul'; 'Memoranda and Notes to 21 November 1772', NHM, Banks MS [autograph original notes]. By Roberts – 'A Journal of a Voyage to the Hebrides or Western Isles of Scotland Iceland and the Orkneys undertaken by Joseph Banks Esqr. In the year 1772 By James Roberts', ML A1594.
12. G. Low, *A Tour Through the Isles of Orkney and Schetland Containing Hints Relative to their Ancient Modern and Natural History Collected in 1774*, ed. J. Anderson (Kirkwall, W. Peace and Son, 1879).
13. *Archaeologia*, 3 (1775), pp. 276–7.
14. BL Add. MSS 15509, 15511.

15. Banks, 'Mulgrave 29 August 1775 Account of the Digging up a Tumulus near this Place', MHS MS Gunther 14/5a [autograph original]. See also G. Colman, *Random Records* (London, H. Colburn and R. Bentley, 1830).

16. Marsden, *The Early Barrow Diggers*, pp. 29–30. For example, Sir Richard Coalt Hoare, the Wiltshire historian and archaeologist, invariably preferred this method.

17. S. Piggott, *William Stukeley: An Eighteenth-Century Antiquary* (London, Thames and Hudson, 1985); S. Piggott, *Ancient Britons and the Antiquarian Imagination* (London, Thames and Hudson, 1989).

18. Banks, 'Topographical Memoranda in the handwriting of Sir Joseph Banks', NHM BL D.T.C. I 304a.

19. W. Stukeley, *Itinerarium Curiosum, or, An Account of the Antiquitys and Remarkable Curiositys in Nature or Art, Observ'd in Travels thro' Great Britain, Illustrated with Copper Prints* (London, for the author, 1724).

20. W. Camden, *Camden's Britannia, Newly Translated into English: with Large Additions and Improvements*, ed. E. Gibson (London, A. Swalle and A. and J. Churchil, 1695); W. Camden, *Britannia: or, a Chorographical Description of the Flourishing Kingdoms of England, Scotland, and Ireland, and the Islands Adjacent; from the Earliest Antiquity*, ed. R. Gough (London, John Nichols, 1789).

21. Banks/Gough correspondence on *Britannia*: J. Nichols and J. B. Nichols, *Illustrations of the Literary History of the Eighteenth Century*, 8 vols (London, Nichols, Son and Bentley, 1817–58), vol. 4, pp. 693–7.

22. J. Evans, *A History of the Society of Antiquaries* (London, Society of Antiquaries, 1956), pp. 6–13, 47–51.

23. Banks to Lloyd, 23 August 1788, NLW 12415, f. 33: Banks paper, read 19 January 1815, RS Misc. MS 6, 36.

24. For comments from Banks's 1772 Iceland trip, see Banks, 'Journal of a Voyage in the Chartered Brig Sir Lawrence'.

25. T. Pennant, *A Tour in Scotland and Voyage to the Hebrides 1772* (Chester, John Monk, 1774).

26. For tours in Britain, and Banks at Staffa, see M. Andrews, *The Search for the Picturesque: Landscape, Aesthetics and Tourism in Britain, 1760–1800* (Aldershot, Scolar, 1989), p. 226. On the British on the Grand Tour, see J. Black, *The British Abroad: The Grand Tour in the Eighteenth Century* (London, Sandpiper, 1999).

27. For comments from Banks's 1767 May–June tour, see 'Journal of an Excursion to Eastbury & Bristol'.

28. W. Gilpin, *Observations on the River Wye, and Several Parts of South Wales, etc. relative chiefly to Picturesque Beauty; made in the Summer of the Year 1770* (London, R. Blamire, 1782).

29. See H. J. Riddelsdell (ed.), 'Lightfoot's Visit to Wales in 1773', *Journal of Botany*, 43 (1905), pp. 290–307; J. K. Bowden, *John Lightfooot: His Work and Travels* (London and Pittsburgh, Royal Botanic Gardens, Kew, and Hunt Institute, 1989).

30. P. Sandby, *XII Views in South Wales* (1775) and *XII Views in North Wales* (1776).

31. BM CE 3/7 1700–1.

32. BM CE 3/7 1703–5. See also BM CE 3/6 1653; BM CE 3/7 1690.

33. BM CE 3/7 1684–5.

34. BM CE 3/7 1688–9.

35. BM CE 3/7 1692.

36. See the manuscript catalogue at the British Library: 'Catalogue of books brought from Iceland and given to the British Museum by Joseph Banks, Esq.'; P. R. Harris, *A History of the British Museum Library, 1753–1973* (London, British Library, 1998), esp. pp. 19, 688. Banks made other donations of Icelandic books, manuscripts and minerals in later years, particularly from 1811 to 1814, and these appear in the standing committee minutes and officers' reports for the years concerned. For Banks and Iceland, see forthcoming publication of his Icelandic papers by Professor Anna Agnarsdóttir of the Hakluyt Society, 'Great Britain and Iceland, 1800–1820' (PhD thesis, London School of Economics and Political Science, Department of International History, 1989); R. A. Rauschenberg, 'The Journals of Joseph Banks' Voyage up Great Britain's West Coast to Iceland the Orkney Isles July to October 1772', *Proceedings of the American Philosophical Society*, 117 (1973), pp. 186–226.

37. BM CE 3/7 1833. See also BM CE 1/4 784–5.

38. BM CE 3/7 1840.

39. BM CE 1/4 852.

40. BM CE 3/7 1845. See also BM CE 3/7 1859.

41. BM CE 3/7 1851.

42. See Harris, *A History of the British Museum Library*, esp. chs 1–3.

43. BM CE 3/7 1884.

44. Willard to Banks, 29 April 1788, BM CE 4/2 663; Willard to Banks, 19 November 1788, BL Add. MS 8097, f. 253.

45. BM CE 3/8 2061.

46. BM CE 3/7 1925.

47. Banks to Bruce, 21 July 1788, NHM BL D.T.C. VI 50–1; Bruce to Banks, 6 April 1789; BM CE 3/8 2003–4; BM CE 4/2 667, 668.

48. Nichols and Nichols, *Illustrations of the Literary History*, vol. 5, p. 577. See also R. Gough, *Sepulchral Monuments in Great Britain applied to Illustrate the History of Families, Manners, Habits, and Arts, at the Different Periods from the Norman Conquest to he Seventeenth Century*, 2 vols (London, for the author, 1786–96).

49. BM CE 1/5 1079. For the sale, see also BM CE 3/9 2435, 2453. For the original offer by Gough: BM CE 4/2 729, 772; BM CE 3/8 2173. For Banks's correspondence on this matter: Gough to Banks, 17 April 1801, Nichols and Nichols, *Illustrations of the Literary History*, vol. 5, p. 572. For the other letters circulated among the Museum trustees, see ibid., pp. 571–8.

50. Polier to Banks, 20 May 1789, BL Add. MS 5346, ff. 1–4; BM CE 3/8 2005. For collecting in the East, see M. Jasanoff, *Edge of Empire: Conquest and Collecting in the East, 1750–1850* (London, Fourth Estate, 2005), with extensive reference to the career of Polier, and his Eastern manuscripts, now distributed across Europe with concentrations in Britain at Eton College and at King's College, Cambridge.

51. BM CE 4/2 673; BM CE 3/8 2019.

52. BM CE 3/8 2030.

53. BM CE 3/8 2040.

54. The volume draws on illustrations in Sloane Add. MS 2914. BM CE 1/4 861–2. See also BM CE 3/7 1820.

55. N. B. Halhed, *A Code of Gentoo Laws, or ordinations of the Pundits, from a Persian translation made from the original, written in the Shanscrit Language* (London, East India Company, 1776).

56. BM CE 3/8 2101, 2117, 2119–20.

57. Musgrave to Banks, 1 January 1781, BL Add. MS 33977, f. 127; Musgrave to Banks, 6 January 1781, BL Add. MS 33977, f. 129.
58. BM CE 1/4 848.
59. BM CE 3/8 2180, 2184–5.
60. BM CE 1/4 941, 942.
61. Musgrave's will: BM CE 4/2 720–1, immediately preceding that of Banks, 722. See also BM CE 3/8 2164.
62. BM CE 3/8 2165, 2166–7; BM CE 4/2 726.
63. BM CE 3/8 2160.
64. J. Dryander, *Catalogus Bibliothecae Historico-Naturalis Josephi Banks Baroneti*, 5 vols (London, W. Bulmer, 1796–1800).
65. BM CE 3/8 2202.
66. BM CE 1/5 1013; BM CE 5/1 1–4, being a report by Beloe on the printed book department and its deficiencies, many of which became apparent from a comparison with Banks's library catalogue.
67. F. C. Sawyer, 'A Short History of the Libraries and List of Manuscripts and Original Drawings in the British Museum (Natural History)', *Bulletin of the Natural History Museum: Historical Series*, 4:2 (1971), pp. 79–204.
68. BM CE 3/7 1892.
69. L. Cust and S. Colvin, *History of the Society of Dilettanti* (London, Macmillan, 1914), pp. 105–6.
70. BM CE 1/4 954, 959.
71. BM CE 4/2 759.
72. BM CE 3/8 2226.
73. BM CE 3/8 2228.
74. BM CE 3/8 2232.
75. BM CE 4/2 768.
76. BM CE 4/2 768–70; BM CE 1/4 963–6.
77. BM CE 1/4 977.
78. Abbot to Banks, 16 May 1805, RBG Kew B.C. 2 305–6.
79. John Townley became a trustee in April 1807: BM CE 1/5 1017.
80. Abbot to Banks, 5 June 1805, NHM BL XVI 52.
81. The price was £20,000, some of it to cover tax: BM CE 1/4 978. For the payments, see also BM CE 3/8 2295–6, 2298, 2302. For the appointment of builders, and construction work: BM CE 1/4 971–2; BM CE 3/9 2337–8.
82. Abbot to Banks, 30 June 1805, RBG Kew B.C. 2 313–14. See also BM CE 4/2 779–80.
83. BM CE 3/8 2270.
84. This was decided in July: BM CE 3/8 2293. A collection of Townley bronzes was acquired by the Museum in 1814: BM CE 4/3 1121, 1131.
85. Banks was present and appropriately dressed: Dartmouth to Banks, 3 June 1808, CUL.
86. BM CE 3/9 2317–18, 2359–60, 2382, 2386–7; BM CE 1/5 1041–6.
87. Banks to Nelson, 8 August 1803, NMM CRK/2.
88. See ch. 4 above for Matthew Flinders and the *Investigator*.
89. Blagden to Banks, 3 May 1802, BL Add. MS 33272, ff. 178–9.
90. De Beer, *The Sciences were Never at War*, ch. 5: 'La Billardière's Collections'.
91. BM CE 4/2 736–40.
92. BM CE 4/2 744.

93. Miller, *That Noble Cabinet*, p. 96.
94. Last issued on 31 October 1800 for £3,000, with £158 17s. being deducted for fees: BM CE 3/8 2196.
95. BM CE 1/4 944. £502 2s. was raised: BM CE 3/8 2211.
96. The issue of charging was raised in 1783–4 due to very bad finances: BM CE 1/4 857–64. See also BM CE 3/7 1853–9.
97. BM CE 3/8 2209.
98. BM CE 1/4 947.
99. BM CE 4/2 745–8. The draft original is at FWM.
100. Miller, *That Noble Cabinet*, pp. 46–8.
101. BM CE 3/8 2210.
102. BM CE 3/8 2211.
103. BM CE 4/2 749.
104. BM CE 1/4 948–51.
105. Compare NHM BL D.T.C. XII 221–4 and the draft original at FWM to the minutes BM CE 1/4 948–51.
106. BM CE 3/8 2212.
107. *Commons Journal*, LV, p. 296, and LVI, p. 805.
108. *Commons Journal*, LVII, p. 786.
109. *Commons Journal*, LVI, pp. 216–17.
110. *Commons Journal*, LVIII, p. 812.
111. BM CE 1/4 954–7.
112. BM CE 3/8 2222.
113. BM CE 3/8 2298, 2302.
114. BM CE 3/8 2299.
115. BM CE 1/5 1003.
116. BM CE 1/5 1004, 1006.
117. BM CE 1/5 1007–16.
118. BM CE 1/5 1007.
119. BM CE 3/8 2320.
120. BM CE 3/8 2313.
121. BM CE 3/8 2309–16.
122. BM CE 1/5 1044.
123. BM CE 1/5 1041–6.
124. BM CE 1/5 1029–30.
125. BM CE 4/2 865.
126. BM CE 4/3 1047.
127. Wilson, *The British Museum*, pp. 67–8.
128. BM CE 3/9 2425–6.
129. BM CE 1/5 1067–9.
130. BM CE 1/5 1071–2.
131. BM CE 1/5 1074–80.
132. BM CE 3/9 2578.
133. BM CE 1/5 1126–30.
134. Planta: CE 4/3 1160–1. *The London Times*, 9 September and 14 October 1814. For comment on attacks on the British Museum, see Miller, *That Noble Cabinet*, pp. 122–4, 226–33. On admission figures, see also p. 107: 1805–6, 11,989; 1808–9, 15,390; 1810–11, 29,152; 1814–15, 33,074; 1817, 40,500.

135. BM CE 1/5 1107.
136. BM CE 4/3 1068–9.
137. Miller, *That Noble Cabinet*, pp. 230–1, 248–54; Wilson, *The British Museum*, pp. 145–7.
138. BM CE 1/5 1110.
139. BM CE 1/5 1114–15.
140. BM CE 5/1 1–4.
141. BM CE 4/2 857–9; BM CE 1/4 990–1.
142. BM CE 1/5 1134–5; BM CE 5/3 710–12, when Baber noted that 200 works entered at Stationers' Hall had not been delivered to the Museum, 718, 737; BM CE 3/9 2578–80.
143. BM CE 3/9 2510–1.
144. BM CE 4/3 1014–16.
145. Harris, *A History of the British Museum Library*, pp. 34–5.
146. BM CE 4/3 1029.
147. BM CE 3/9 2515–16.
148. BM CE 1/5 1110.
149. BM CE 3/9 2550; BM CE 4/3 1081.
150. BM CE 4/3 1080.
151. BM CE 3/9 2558. See also BM CE 5/3 521. On early collections of paintings relating to English history, see Wilson, *The British Museum*, p. 48.
152. BM CE 4/3 1221; BM CE 3/9 2608–9.
153. BM CE 3/9 2578–9; BM CE 3/10 2707; BM CE 4/4 1424; BM CE 1/5 1163–4, 1165; Officers' Reports 676–7.
154. BM CE 3/10 2699.
155. BM CE 5/5 1147.
156. BM CE 1/5 1198, 1201–3.
157. BM CE 1/5 1306. The Royal Library has subsequently been moved from the British Museum to the British Library.
158. BM CE 3/9 2472.
159. BM CE 3/9 2506.
160. BM CE 3/9 2528.
161. BM CE 3/9 2591.
162. BM CE 3/10 2690.
163. G. Pearson, 'Observations on some Ancient Metallic Arms and Utensils; with Experiments to Determine their Composition', *Philosophical Transactions*, 86:2 (1796), pp. 395–451, read 9 June 1796. On Banks and the objects used in these tests, see N. Chambers, *The Letters of Sir Joseph Banks: A Selection, 1768–1820* (London, Imperial College Press, 2000), pp. 108–9. See also J. V. S. Megaw, 'Your Obedient and Humble Servant: Notes for an Antipodean Antiquary' in A. Anderson, I. Lilley and S. O'Connor (eds), *Histories of Old Ages: Essays in Honour of Rhys Jones* (Canberra, Pandanus Books, 2001), pp. 95–110.
164. BM CE 5/1 36–7. See also C. Sturman, 'Sir Joseph Banks and the Tealby Hoard', *Lincolnshire History and Archaeology*, 24 (1989), pp. 51–2.
165. BM CE 3/9 2474.
166. BM CE 3/9 2495.
167. BM CE 3/9 2478–9. For the authorization, see BM CE 4/3 992.

168. Banks, 'Collections on the Subject of Old China & Japan Wares with some Remarks on these Interesting Manufactures made in Lady Banks's Dairy at Spring Grove 1807', CKS U951 Z34 [manuscript essay by Banks].

169. See notes 4 and 53 to chapter 3, above, pp. 149, 152.

170. Banks to Trustees, 14 November 1818, BM CE 3/10 2708. Sarah Sophia donated proof dollars struck by Matthew Boulton in 1804 for circulation in England and Ireland: BM CE 30/2 30/6/1804. See also Lady Banks to Trustees, 10 December 1818, BM CE 3/10 2714 and G. Dyer, 'A Living Collection: Numismatic Holdings of the British Royal Mint', *World Coins* (September 1988), pp. 3–33.

171. Banks to Pole, 21 August 1818, R.M. Record Book 20, 122; Pole to Banks, 24 August 1818, Royal Mint Record Book, 20, 123; Pole to Banks, 22 January 1819, Royal Mint Record Book, 20, 189.

172. F. Francis, *Treasures of the British Museum* (London, Thames and Hudson, 1971), pp. 15, 29, 293; A. G. Credland, 'Sarah and Joseph Banks and Archery in the Eighteenth Century', *Journal of the Society of the Archer-Antiquaries*, 34 (1991), pp. 42–50 (including some interesting comments on Sir Ashton Lever), and 'Sarah and Joseph Banks (continued)', *Journal of the Society of the Archer-Antiquaries*, 35 (1992), pp. 54–76; A. Pincott, 'The Book Tickets of Miss Sarah Sophia Banks (1744–1818)', *The Bookplate Journal*, 2:1 (2004), pp. 3–31.

173. Banks to Blagden, 8 March 1815, RS B. 62. On casts in the British Museum: Wilson, *The British Museum*, pp. 126–8.

174. BM CE 1/5 1126–9.

175. BM CE 3/9 2594. See also BM CE 5/3 733.

176. Quite possibly duplicate Irish elk horns acquired by Banks as part of the exchange account arrangement he had at the Museum: BM CE 3/9 2606.

177. Jomard to Banks, 11 March 1816, BL Add. MS 8100, ff. 174–5.

178. For Banks's and Blagden's discussion of Young's work on the Rosetta Stone, see especially: RS B. Correspondence.

179. BM CE 4/3 1187–90.

180. BM CE 1/5 1137, 1138, 1143–4.

181. BM CE 1/5 1149–52.

182. BM CE 3/9 2633; BM CE 1/5 1149–50.

183. BM CE 1/5 1153–5.

184. I. Jenkins, *Archaeologists and Aesthetes* (London, British Museum Press, 1992), part 2: 'Arcadia in Bloomsbury: The Elgin and Phigaleian Marbles', pp. 75–101.

185. BM CE 3/9 2613–14.

186. BM CE 4/3 1199–201, 1221.

187. BM CE 3/10 2644.

188. BM CE 3/10 2662.

189. Purkis to Banks, 21 July 1816, BM CE 4/4 1334.

190. BM CE 4/4 1429.

191. BM CE 3/10 2698. See also BM CE 4/4 1564, 1565.

192. Belzoni is an interesting figure, but the trustees rejected his offer of acting as a collector for the Museum: BM CE 1/5 1169. See also Salt to Banks, 16 November 1818, NHM BL D.T.C. XX 145–6, and further discussion in the current section.

193. Banks to Blagden, 11 May 1818, UY Banks MS.

194. J. J. Halls, *The Life and Correspondence of Henry Salt, Esq., F.R.S., H.B.M. Consul General in Egypt*, 2 vols (London, R. Bentley, 1834), vol. 2, p. 372.

195. Ibid., vol. 2, pp. 385, 386.
196. Ibid., vol. 2, pp. 374–5.
197. Salt to Banks, 9 December 1815, BM CE 3/10 2617.
198. Salt to Banks, 20 June 1815, NHM BL D.T.C. XIX 289–93.
199. BM CE 4/4 1394.
200. BM CE 4/4 1410.
201. A pension was very much in Salt's mind, for example: Halls, *The Life and Correspondence of Henry Salt*, vol. 2, p. 307.
202. H. Acton, *Three Extraordinary Ambassadors* (London, Thames and Hudson, 1983); B. Fothergill, *Sir William Hamilton: Envoy Extraordinary* (London, Faber and Faber, 1969); K. Sloan and I. Jenkins (eds), *Vases and Volcanoes: Sir William Hamilton and His Collection* (London, British Museum Press, 1996).
203. Banks to Blagden, 25 April 1818, UY Banks MS.
204. Halls, *The Life and Correspondence of Henry Salt*, vol. 2, p. 381. See also a warning about this level of expenditure issued to Salt in February 1819 (p. 305).
205. Salt to Hamilton, 10 June 1818, NHM BL D.T.C. XX 83–5; and Salt to Mountnorris, 28 May 1819, NHM BL D.T.C. XX, 189–91, this last including Salt's list of Egyptian remains. For other claims about the value of this material, see Halls, *The Life and Correspondence of Henry Salt*, vol. 2, p. 308.
206. Ibid., vol. 2, pp. 305–6. See also Salt to Mountnorris, 28 May 1819, NHM BL D.T.C. XX 185–8.
207. BM CE 4/4 1490–1.
208. BM CE 4/4 1489.
209. Belzoni to Salt, 14 November 1818, NHM BL D.T.C. XX 147–8. Enclosed in a letter to Banks from Salt, all of which Banks presented to the trustees: Salt to Banks, 16 November 1818, NHM BL D.T.C. XX 145–6.
210. BM CE 1/5 1168–9.
211. Halls, *The Life and Correspondence of Henry Salt*, vol. 2, p. 319.
212. Ibid., vol. 2, p. 320.
213. Banks to Ellis, 20 December 1819, BM CE 4/4 1566–7.
214. BM CE 1/5 1173.
215. A view hinted at by John James Halls, which is probably correct.
216. BM CE 1/5 1202.
217. BM CE 4/4 1450–1.
218. J. M. Crook, *The British Museum* (London, Allen Lane, 1972), ch. 4, esp. pp. 107–10.

Conclusions

1. W. J. Smith, 'The Life and Activities of Sir Ashton Lever of Alkrington, 1729–1788', *Transactions of the Lancashire and Cheshire Antiquarian Society*, 72 (1962), pp. 61–92; p. 91, on the contrast between specialist research collections and those like Lever's that were broader in range. There are also useful remarks touching on the behaviour of Lever as a young man (pp. 64–7), on reactions to him (pp. 72–4, 80), and on the reasons why he decided to sell his collections (pp. 80–4). On the contrast between a specialist like Banks and the more generalist approach of the showmen, see T. Iredale, 'Museums of the Past', *The Australian Museum Magazine*, 2:3 (1924), p. 89. For some cutting remarks, made in 1782, about Lever's showiness and eccentricity: C. Barrett (ed.), *Diary and Letters of Madame D'Arblay*, 6 vols (London, Macmillan, 1904), vol. 2, pp. 167–8.

2.   Blagden to Banks, 28 October 1777, NHM BL D.T.C. I 148–51.
3.   R. D. Altick, *The Shows of London* (Cambridge, MA, Harvard University Press, 1978), pp. 28–33, including some interesting reactions to Lever's collections, not least from a correspondent in the *Gentleman's Magazine*, 43 (1773), pp. 219–21 (on their varied content), quoted by Altick, pp. 28–9. Altick also questions the simplistic view that both men disliked and so shunned one another, p. 32. The exchanges between Banks and the many collectors of his period indicate a far more complex set of relationships than that. A bitter remark reported by Joseph Farington is the one frequently adduced here: J. Greig (ed.), *The Farington Diary*, 8 vols (London, Hutchinson & Co., 1922–8), vol. 3, p. 273. Altick suggests that Lever disposed of his collections because he had overreached himself, p. 29, and points out too that Lever raised his prices in order to exclude troublesome 'common People' from entering his museum.
4.   In the end a number of Lever's birds went to Vienna: A. Pelzeln, 'On the Birds in the Imperial Collection at Vienna obtained from the Leverian Museum', *The Ibis, A Quarterly Journal of Ornithology*, 3:9 (1873), pp. 14–54, and 3:10 (1873), pp. 106–24. Others stayed in Britain, being purchased by Lord Stanley, with some passing to the Liverpool Museum: M. J. Largen, 'Bird Specimens Purchased by Lord Stanley at the Sale of the Leverian Museum in 1806, including those still Extant in the Collections of the Liverpool Museum', *Archives of Natural History*, 14:3 (1987), pp. 265–88.
5.   Banks to Peale, 1 December 1794, APS.
6.   For one view of the reasons why Lever disposed of his Museum, and Banks's role in that event, see W. J. Smith, 'A Museum for a Guinea', *Country Life*, 127:3288 (1960), pp. 494–5.
7.   Smith, 'Life and Activities of Sir Ashton Lever', p. 84. Limited money and space became especially prominent factors from 1815 onwards, but had always been evident to varying degrees.
8.   Stearn, *The Natural History Museum*, p. 20.
9.   Pallas to Banks, 22 October 1786 OS, BL Add. MS 8097, ff. 104–5.
10. Messrs King and Lochee, *Catalogue of the Leverian Museum* (London, 1806), parts I–VI with 'Appendix', NHM 85A o. LEV, probably annotated by William Clift, with a photocopy of a list of purchasers taken from Richard Cuming's copy of the catalogue in the Cuming Museum, Southwark.
11. A. Newton, 'Notes on Some Old Museums' in H. M. Platnauer and E. Howarth (eds), *Museums Association: Report of Proceedings with the paper read at the annual General Meeting held at Cambridge, July 7th, 8th, & 9th, 1891* (London, 1891), pp. 28–48; pp. 39–40. It may be that the large amounts being spent by the British Museum on the Townley Marbles (which also needed new accommodation) help to explain the failure of the Museum to purchase anything from the old Lever collections. Another purchase in 1807 was of the Landsdowne manuscripts for £4,925. For one view of the state of the Leverian collections at the end, see Altick, *The Shows of London*, p. 32. For more comment on Banks's role in these events, and on the ethnographic collections made during Cook's voyages that are held at the British Museum, see Kaeppler, 'Tracing the History of Hawaiian Cook Voyage Artefacts'.
12. G. Shaw and J. Parkinson, *Museum Leverianum, Containing Select Specimens from the Museum of the late Sir Ashton Lever, Kt. with descriptions in Latin and English by George Shaw, M.D., F.R.S.*, 2 vols (London, James Parkinson, 1792–6).

13. See note 10 above for details of those who made purchases at the sale of Lever's Museum, and also note 138 to chapter 3, above, p. 155. The sale of William Bullock's collections also saw some of Lever's material being redistributed.

14. E. P. Alexander, 'William Bullock: A Little-Remembered Museologist and Show-man', *Curator*, 28:2 (1985), pp. 117–47. Bullock produced catalogues to educate the public about his collections, and to promote them. A number are held at the Natural History Museum, London, and Mullens gives a list in 'Some Museums of Old London – II', p. 132. Bullock later engaged in speculative silver mining in Mexico, and utopian retirement communities in Cincinnati, and he made significant contributions to the pre-Columbian collection of the British Museum from his visits to the Americas. See also J. Edmondson, 'The Regency Exhibitionists: a Fresh Look at the Bullocks', *The Linnean: Newsletter and Proceedings of the Linnean Society of London*, 5:1 (1989), pp. 17–26; E. G. Hancock, 'One of those Dreadful Combats – a Surviving Display from William Bul-lock's London Museum, 1807–1818', *Museums Journal*, 79:4 (1980), pp. 172–5; R. D. Altick, 'Snake was Fake but Egyptian Hall Wowed London', *Smithsonian*, 9:1 (1978), pp. 68–77.

15. Whitehead, 'Zoological Specimens from Captain Cook's Voyages', pp. 167–71; Med-way, 'Some Ornithological Results of Cook's Third Voyage', pp. 339–40; A. L. Kaeppler, 'Cook Voyage Provenance of the "Artificial Curiosities" of Bullocks Museum', *Man: The Journal of the Royal Anthropological Institute*, 9:1 (1974), pp. 68–92; J. C. King, 'New Evidence for the Contents of the Leverian Museum', *Journal of the History of Collections*, 8:2 (1996), pp. 167–86.

16. Bullock to Banks, 31 March 1819, CKS Brabourne 149–50. Altick, *The Shows of Lon-don*, p. 235, where Altick refers to Egyptian Hall as a 'miscellaneous-exhibition branch of the trade for almost a century', 'William Bullock and the Egyptian Hall', ch. 18.

17. Alexander, 'William Bullock', pp. 126–7; J. M. Sweet, 'William Bullock's Collection and the University of Edinburgh, 1819', *Annals of Science*, 26:1 (1970), pp. 23–32, esp. pp. 24–5; Altick, *The Shows of London*, p. 241.

18. *The History of the Collections contained in the Natural History Departments of the British Museum*, 2 vols (London, British Museum (Natural History), 1904–12), and Appendix, esp. vol. 2, pp. 208–45. See also Sweet, 'William Bullock's Collection', pp. 27–31; Altick, 'Snake was Fake', p. 72.

19. Banks to Ferryman, 5 February 1788, RBG Kew B.C. I 295 (2).

20. Ferryman to Banks, 1 February 1788, RBG Kew B.C. I 294; Ferryman to Banks, 4 Feb-ruary 1788, RBG Kew B.C. I 295.

21. Altick, *The Shows of London*, p. 288: 'With the dispersal of the Leverian Museum in 1806 and of Bullock's collection a decade later, the era of museums modelled after the miscellaneous cabinets of old-time virtuosi ended'.

22. Stearn, *The Natural History Museum*, pp. 22–3, 279–87; *History of the Collections ... of the British Museum*, vol. 1, pp. 79–84. See also Mabberley, *Jupiter Botanicus*, esp. chs 14, 15; A. Gray, 'Notices of European Herbaria, particularly those most Interesting to the North American Botanist', *The American Journal of Science and Arts*, 40 (April 1841), pp. 1–18; J. J. Fletcher, 'On the Rise and Early Progress of our Knowledge of the Australian Fauna' in *Report of the Eighth Meeting of the Australasian Association for the Advancement of Science held at Melbourne, Victoria, 1900* (Melbourne, 1901), pp. 69–104.

23. For an assessment of Sloane's herbarium, see J. F. M. Cannon, 'Botanical Collections' in A. MacGregor (ed.), *Sir Hans Sloane: Collector, Scientist, Antiquary* (London, British Museum Press, 1994), pp. 136–49.

24. J. Dryander, *Catalogus Bibliothecae Historico-Naturalis Josephi Banks*. The annotated version is in the Botany Department at the Natural History Museum, London.

25. The year 1827 was when, after protracted negotiations, Banks's main collections were transferred, with Brown being placed in charge of what was called the Banksian Department: BM CE 4/5 1946–7, a description of Banks's library in Soho Square; *History of the Collections ... of the British Museum*, vol. 1, pp. 79–80, a description of Banks's herbarium at Bloomsbury.

26. See Stearn, *The Natural History Museum*, for a 'sagacious' Banks, p. 22, and on Banks's legacy, chs 2, 3, 16; Miller, *That Noble Cabinet*, esp. chs 3, 4, 9.

27. S. Sheets-Pyenson, 'How to Grow a Natural History Museum: the Building of Colonial Collections, 1850–1900', *Archives of Natural History*, 15:2 (1988), pp. 121–47; Sheets-Pyenson, S., *Cathedrals of Science: The Development of Colonial Natural History Museums during the Late Nineteenth Century* (Kingston, McGill-Queen's University Press, 1988); L. Pyenson and S. Sheets-Pyenson, *Servants of Nature: A History of Scientific Institutions, Enterprises, and Sensibilities* (London, HarperCollins, 1999).

28. See, for example, the work of the French geographer Bruno Latour, who speaks of 'centres of calculation' and the ways in which these operate to gather and to organize knowledge across physical space in a 'cycle of accumulation': B. Latour, *Science in Action: How to Follow Scientists and Engineers through Society* (Milton Keynes, Open University Press, 1987). These concepts have recently been discussed in terms of the exploration and literature of the Romantic period: T. Fulford, D. Lee and P. J. Kitson, *Literature, Science and Exploration in the Romantic Era: Bodies of Knowledge* (Cambridge, Cambridge University Press, 2004).

Epitaph

1.   BM CE 3/10 2792.

BIBLIOGRAPHY

Acton, H., *Three Extraordinary Ambassadors* (London, Thames and Hudson, 1983).

Agnarsdóttir, A, 'Great Britain and Iceland, 1800–1820' (PhD thesis, London School of Economics and Political Science, Department of International History, 1989).

Alexander, C., *The Bounty* (London, HarperCollins, 2003).

Alexander, E. P., 'William Bullock: A Little-Remembered Museologist and Showman', *Curator*, 28:2 (1985), pp. 117–47.

Altick, R. D., *The Shows of London* (Cambridge, MA, Harvard University Press, 1978).

—, 'Snake was Fake but Egyptian Hall Wowed London', *Smithsonian*, 9:1 (1978), pp. 68–77.

Anderson, A., I. Lilley and S. O'Connor (eds), *Histories of Old Ages: Essays in Honour of Rhys Jones* (Canberra, Pandanus Books, 2001).

Anderson, R. G. W., M. L. Caygill, A. G. MacGregor and L. Syson (eds), *Enlightening the British: Knowledge, Discovery and the Museum in the Eighteenth Century* (London, British Museum Press, 2003).

Andrews, M., *The Search for the Picturesque: Landscape, Aesthetics and Tourism in Britain, 1760–1800* (Aldershot, Scolar, 1989).

Banks, J., 'Journal of an Excursion to Eastbury & Bristol began May 15th 1767 ended June 20th 1767', Cambridge University Library, Add. MS 6294 [autograph original].

—, 'Journal of an Excursion to Wales and the Midlands began August 13th 1767 ended January 29th 1768', Cambridge University Library, Add. MS 6294 [autograph original].

—, 'Journal of a Voyage in the Chartered Brig Sir Lawrence to the Hebrides and Iceland begun 12th July 1772 to 6th September', Blacker-Wood Library, McGill University, Montreal [autograph original, incomplete].

—, 'Memoranda and Notes at the Centre for Kentish Studies referring to the period 17 September to 30 September 1772, and the six days from 16 October to 22 October', Centre for Kentish Studies, Maidstone, MS U951 Z31 [autograph original notes].

—, 'Memoranda and Notes to 21 November 1772', Natural History Museum, Banks MS [autograph original notes].

—, 'Mulgrave 29 August 1775 Account of the Digging up a Tumulus near this Place', Museum of the History of Science, Oxford, MS Gunther 14/5a [autograph original].

—, 'Collections on the Subject of Old China & Japan Wares with some Remarks on these Interesting Manufactures made in Lady Banks's Dairy at Spring Grove 1807', Centre for Kentish Studies, Maidstone, U951 Z34 [manuscript essay by Banks].

— (ed.), *Icones selectae Plantarum quas in Japonia collegit et delineavit Engelbertus Kaempfer ex archetypis in Museo Britannico asseveratis* (London, W. Bulmer & Co., 1791).

Banks, R. E. R., et al. (eds), *Sir Joseph Banks: A Global Perspective* (London, Royal Botanic Gardens, Kew, 1994).

Barrett, C. (ed.), *Diary and Letters of Madame D'Arblay*, 6 vols (London, Macmillan, 1904).

Bauer, F., *Illustrationes Florae Novae Hollandiae: sive icones generum quae in Prodromo Florae Novae Hollandiae et Insulae Van-Diemen descripsit Robertus Brown / Ferdinandi Bauer* (London, Veneunt apud Auctorem, 1806–13).

Beaglehole, J. C. (ed.), *The Endeavour Journal of Joseph Banks 1768–1771*, 2 vols (Sydney, Public Library of New South Wales, 1962).

—, *The Journals of Captain James Cook on his Voyages of Discovery*, 4 vols (Woodbridge, Boydell Press, 1999).

Black, J., *The British Abroad: The Grand Tour in the Eighteenth Century* (London, Sandpiper, 1999).

Blunt, W., *The Compleat Naturalist: A Life of Linnaeus* (London, Collins, 1971).

Bowden, J. K., *John Lightfoot: His Work and Travels* (London and Pittsburgh, Royal Botanic Gardens, Kew, and Hunt Institute, 1989).

Briggs, C. S., *Royal Commission on Ancient and Historical Monuments (Wales): Brecknock* (London, RCAHMW, 1997), vol. 1, part 1.

British Museum, *Synopsis of the Contents of the British Museum* (London, 1808).

—, *Synopsis of the Contents of the British Museum* (London, 1820).

Britten, J., 'William Anderson (1778) and the Plants of Cook's Third Voyage', *Journal of Botany*, 54 (1917), pp. 345–52.

—, 'Short Notes. William Anderson and Cook's Third Voyage', *Journal of Botany*, 55 (1917), p. 54.

Browne, J., 'Biogeography and Empire' in Jardine et al. (eds), *Cultures of Natural History*, pp. 308–14.

Brown, R., *Prodromus Florae Novae Hollandiae et Insulae Van-Diemen, exhibens Characteres Plantarum quas Annis 1802–1805 per oras utriusque insulae collegit et descripsit R. Brown* (London, R. Taylor, 1810).

Camden, W., *Camden's Britannia, Newly Translated into English: with Large Additions and Improvements*, ed. E. Gibson (London, A. Swalle and A. and J. Churchil, 1695).

—, *Britannia: or, a Chorographical Description of the Flourishing Kingdoms of England, Scotland, and Ireland, and the Islands Adjacent; from the Earliest Antiquity*, ed. R. Gough (London, John Nichols, 1789).

Cannon, J. F. M., 'Botanical Collections' in MacGregor (ed.), *Sir Hans Sloane*, pp. 136–49.

Carter, H. B., *Sheep and Wool Correspondence of Sir Joseph Banks 1781–1820* (London and Sydney, British Museum, 1979).

—, *Sir Joseph Banks (1743–1820): A Guide to Biographical and Bibliographical Sources* (Winchester, St Paul's Bibliographies, 1987).

—, *Sir Joseph Banks* (London, British Museum Press, 1988).

—, 'The Royal Society and the Voyage of H.M.S. *Endeavour* 1768–71', *Notes and Records of the Royal Society*, 49:2 (1995), pp. 245–60.

Carter, H. B., J. A. Diment, C. J. Humphries and A. Wheeler, 'The Banksian Natural History Collections of the *Endeavour* Voyage and their Relevance to Modern Taxonomy' in *History in the Service of Systematics: Papers from the Conference to Celebrate the Centenary of the British Museum (Natural History) 13–16 April, 1981*, Society for the Bibliography of Natural History, Special Publication 1 (London, 1981), pp. 62–8.

Cleevely, R. J., 'Some Background to the Life and Publications of Colonel George Montagu (1753–1815)', *Journal of the Society for the Bibliography of Natural History*, 8:4 (1978), pp. 445–80.

Chambers, N., *The Letters of Sir Joseph Banks: A Selection, 1768–1820* (London, Imperial College Press, 2000).

Childe, V. G., *Skara Brae. A Pictish Village in Orkney* (London, Kegan Paul, Trench, Trübner, 1931).

Colman, G., *Random Records* (London, H. Colburn and R. Bentley, 1830).

Coote, J., *Curiosities from the Endeavour: A Forgotten Collection – Pacific Artefacts Given by Joseph Banks to Christ Church, Oxford, after the First Voyage* (Whitby, Captain Cook Memorial Museum, 2004).

—, 'An Interim Report on a Previously Unknown Collection from Cook's First Voyage: The Christ Church Collection of the Pitt Rivers Museum', *Journal of Museum Ethnography*, 16 (2004), pp. 111–21.

Cowan, C. F., 'John Francillon, F.L.S., A Few Facts', *The Entomologist's Record and Journal of Variation*, 98:7–8 (1986), pp. 139–43.

Cowen, R., 'After the Fall', *Science News*, 148:16 (1995), pp. 248–9.

Credland, A. G., 'Sarah and Joseph Banks and Archery in the Eighteenth Century', *Journal of the Society of the Archer-Antiquaries*, 34 (1991), pp. 42–50.

—, 'Sarah and Joseph Banks (continued)', *Journal of the Society of the Archer-Antiquaries*, 35 (1992), pp. 54–76.

Crook, J. M., *The British Museum* (London, Allen Lane, 1972).

Cust, L., and S. Colvin, *History of the Society of Dilettanti* (London, Macmillan, 1914).

Dance, S. P., *Shell Collecting: An Illustrated History* (London, Faber and Faber, 1966).

Dawson, W. R., *The Banks Letters: A Calendar of the Manuscript Correspondence* (London, British Museum Press, 1958).

de Beer, G. R., *Sir Hans Sloane and the British Museum* (London, Oxford University Press, 1953).

—, *The Sciences were Never at War* (London, Thomas Nelson, 1960).

Desmond, R., *The India Museum: 1801–1879* (London, Her Majesty's Stationery Office, 1982).

—, *Kew: The History of the Royal Botanic Gardens* (London, Harvill with Royal Botanic Gardens, Kew, 1995).

Diment, J. A., and A. Wheeler, 'Catalogue of the Natural History Manuscripts and Letters by Daniel Solander (1733–1782), or Attributed to Him, in British Collections', *Archives of Natural History*, 11:3 (1984), pp. 457–88.

Diment, J. A., C. J. Humphries, L. Newington and E. Shaughnessy, 'Catalogue of the Natural History Drawings Commissioned by Joseph Banks on the *Endeavour* Voyage 1768–1771', *Bulletin of the British Museum (Natural History): Historical Series*, 11–13 (1984–7).

Dixon, G., and Portlock, N., *A Voyage Round the World, but more particularly to the North-West Coast of America: performed in 1785, 1786, 1787, and 1788, in the King George and Queen Charlotte, Captains Portlock and Dixon*, 2 vols (London, Goulding, 1789).

Dobson, J., *William Clift* (London, Heinemann Medical Books, 1954).

Dolan, B., *Josiah Wedgwood: Entrepreneur to the Enlightenment* (London, HarperCollins, 2004).

Dryander, J., *Catalogus Bibliothecae Historico-Naturalis Josephi Banks Baroneti*, 5 vols (London, W. Bulmer, 1796–1800).

Duyker, E., *Nature's Argonaut: Daniel Solander 1733–1782. Naturalist and Voyager with Cook and Banks* (Victoria, Miegunyah Press, 1998).

Duyker, E., and P. Tingbrand (eds), *Daniel Solander: Collected Correspondence 1753–1782* (Oslo, Scandinavian University Press, 1995).

Dyer, G., 'A Living Collection: Numismatic holdings of the British Royal Mint', *World Coins* (September 1988), pp. 3–33.

Edmondson, J., 'The Regency Exhibitionists: a Fresh Look at the Bullocks', *The Linnean: Newsletter and Proceedings of the Linnean Society of London*, 5:1 (1989), pp. 17–26.

Edwards, E., *Lives of the Founders of the British Museum; with Notices of its Chief Augmentors and Other Benefactors, 1570–1870* (London, Trübner, 1870).

Edwards, P. I., 'Robert Brown (1773–1858) and the Natural History of Matthew Flinders' Voyage in H.M.S. *Investigator*, 1801–1805', *Journal of the Society for the Bibliography of Natural History*, 7:4 (1976), pp. 385–407.

Ellis, A. R. (ed.), *The Early Diary of Frances Burney 1768–1778*, 2 vols (London, G. Bell, 1889).

Evans, J., *A History of the Society of Antiquaries* (London, Society of Antiquaries, 1956).

Eyles, J. M., 'William Smith: the Sale of his Geological Collection to the British Museum', *Annals of Science*, 23:3 (1967), pp. 177–212.

Fabricius, J., *Briefe aus London vermischten Inhalts* (Dessau and Leipzig, 1784).

Farey, J., *General View of the Agriculture and Minerals of Derbyshire*, 2 vols (London, G. and W. Nichol, 1811–13).

Fitton, M., and S. Shute, 'Sir Joseph Banks's Collection of Insects' in Banks et al. (eds), *Sir Joseph Banks*, pp. 209–11.

Fletcher, J. J., 'On the Rise and Early Progress of our Knowledge of the Australian Fauna' in *Report of the Eighth Meeting of the Australasian Association for the Advancement of Science held at Melbourne, Victoria, 1900* (Melbourne, 1901), pp. 69–104.

Flinders, M., *A Voyage to Terra Australis*, 2 vols (London, G. and W. Nicol, 1814).

Force, R. W., and M. Force, *Art and Artifacts of the 18th Century: Objects in the Leverian Museum as Painted by Sarah Stone* (Honolulu, Bishop Museum Press, 1968).

Fothergill, B., *Sir William Hamilton: Envoy Extraordinary* (London, Faber and Faber, 1969).

Francis, F., *Treasures of the British Museum* (London, Thames and Hudson, 1971).

Frost, A., 'Science for Political Purposes: European Explorations of the Pacific Ocean, 1764–1806' in MacLeod and Rehbock (eds), *Nature in its Greatest Extent*, pp. 27–44.

—, 'The Antipodean Exchange: European Horticulture and Imperial Designs' in Miller and Reill (eds), *Visions of Empire*, pp. 58–79.

Fulford, T., D. Lee and P. J. Kitson, *Literature, Science and Exploration in the Romantic Era: Bodies of Knowledge* (Cambridge, Cambridge University Press, 2004).

Galloway, D. J., and E. W. Groves, 'Archibald Menzies MD, FLS (1754–1842), Aspects of his Life, Travels and Collections', *Archives of Natural History*, 14:1 (1987), pp. 3–43.

Gascoigne, J., *Joseph Banks and the English Enlightenment: Useful Knowledge and Polite Culture* (Cambridge, Cambridge University Press, 1994).

—, *Science in the Service of Empire: Joseph Banks, the British State and the Uses of Science in the Age of Revolution* (Cambridge, Cambridge University Press, 1998).

Gilpin, W., *Observations on the River Wye, and Several Parts of South Wales, etc. relative chiefly to Picturesque Beauty; made in the Summer of the Year 1770* (London, R. Blamire, 1782).

Gough, R., *Sepulchral Monuments in Great Britain applied to Illustrate the History of Families, Manners, Habits, and Arts, at the Different Periods from the Norman Conquest to he Seventeenth Century*, 2 vols (London, for the author, 1786–96).

Grady, M. M., *Catalogue of Meteorites* (Cambridge, Cambridge University Press, 2000).

Gray, A., 'Notices of European Herbaria, particularly those most Interesting to the North American Botanist', *The American Journal of Science and Arts*, 40 (April 1841), pp. 1–18.

Greig, J. (ed.), *The Farington Diary*, 8 vols (London, Hutchinson & Co., 1922–8).

Griffith, W. P., and P. J. T. Morris, 'Charles Hatchett FRS (1765–1847), Chemist and Discoverer of Niobium', *Notes and Records of the Royal Society*, 57:3 (2003), pp. 299–316.

Groves, E. W., 'Notes on the Botanical Specimens Collected by Banks and Solander on Cook's First Voyage, together with an Itinerary of Landing Localities', *Journal of the Society for the Bibliography of Natural History*, 4:1 (1962), pp. 57–62.

—, 'Archibald Menzies (1754–1842) an Early Botanist on the Northwestern Seaboard of North America, 1792–1794, with further Notes of his Life and Work', *Archives of Natural History*, 28:1 (2001), pp. 71–122.

Gunther, A.E., 'Edward Whitaker Gray (1748–1806), Keeper of the Natural Curiosities at the British Museum', *Bulletin of the British Museum (Natural History): Historical Series*, 5:2 (1976), pp. 193–210.

—, 'The Royal Society and the Foundation of the British Museum', *Notes and Records of the Royal Society*, 33:2 (1979), pp. 207–16.

—, *The Founders of Science at the British Museum 1753–1900* (Suffolk, Halesworth Press, 1980).

Halhed, N. B., *A Code of Gentoo Laws, or ordinations of the Pundits, from a Persian translation made from the original, written in the Shanscrit Language* (London, East India Company, 1776).

Halls, J. J., *The Life and Correspondence of Henry Salt, Esq., F.R.S., H.B.M. Consul General in Egypt*, 2 vols (London, R. Bentley, 1834).

Hancock, E. G., 'One of those Dreadful Combats – a Surviving Display from William Bullock's London Museum, 1807–1818', *Museums Journal*, 79:4 (1980), pp. 172–5.

Harris, P. R., *A History of the British Museum Library, 1753–1973* (London, British Library, 1998).

Hatchett, C., 'An Analysis of the Earthy Substance from New South Wales, called Sydneia or Terra Australis', *Philosophical Transactions*, 88:1 (1798), pp. 110–29.

Hauser-Schäublin, B., and G. Krüger (eds), *James Cook, Gifts and Treasures from the South Seas: The Cook/Forster Collection, Göttingen* (Munich and New York, Prestel, 1998).

Historical Records of New South Wales, 8 vols (Sydney, C. Potter, 1892–1901).

History of the Collections contained in the Natural History Departments of the British Museum, The, 2 vols (London, British Museum (Natural History), 1904–12).

Holt-White, R. (ed.), *The Life and Letters of Gilbert White of Selborne*, 2 vols (London, John Murray, 1901).

Howard, E., 'Experiments and Observations on certain Stony and Metalline Substances, which at different Times are said to have Fallen on the Earth; also on Various Kinds of Native Iron', *Philosophical Transactions*, 92:1 (1802), pp. 168–212.

Howse, D. (ed.), *Background to Discovery: Pacific Exploration from Dampier to Cook* (Berkeley, University of California Press, 1990).

Hunter, M., 'The Cabinet Institutionalized: The Royal Society's Repository and its Background' in Impey and MacGregor (eds), *The Origins of Museums*, pp. 159–68.

—, *Establishing the New Science: The Experience of the Early Royal Society* (Woodbridge, Boydell, 1989).

Impey, O., and A. MacGregor (eds), *The Origins of Museums: The Cabinet of Curiosities in Sixteenth and Seventeenth Century Europe* (Oxford, Clarendon Press, 1985).

Iredale, T., 'Museums of the Past', *The Australian Museum Magazine*, 2:3 (1924), p. 89.

—, 'Bullock's Museum', *The Australian Zoologist*, 11:3 (1948), pp. 233–7.

Jasanoff, M., *Edge of Empire: Conquest and Collecting in the East, 1750–1850* (London, Fourth Estate, 2005).

Jardine, N., J. A. Secord and E. C. Spary (eds), *Cultures of Natural History* (Cambridge, Cambridge University Press, 1996).

Jenkins, I., *Archaeologists and Aesthetes* (London, British Museum Press, 1992).

Kaeppler, A. L., 'Cook Voyage Provenance of the "Artificial Curiosities" of Bullocks Museum', *Man: The Journal of the Royal Anthropological Institute*, 9:1 (1974), pp. 68–92.

—, *'Artificial Curiosities': Being an Exposition of Native Manufactures collected on the Three Pacific Voyages of Captain James Cook, R.N., at the Bernice Pauahi Bishop Museum January 18, 1978–August 31, 1978* (Honolulu, Bishop Museum Press, 1978).

—, 'Tracing the History of Hawaiian Cook Voyage Artefacts in the Museum of Mankind' in Mitchell (ed.), *Captain Cook and the South Pacific*, pp. 167–98.

— (ed.), *Cook Voyage Artifacts in Leningrad, Berne, and Florence Museums* (Honolulu, Bishop Museum Press, 1978).

Keevil, J. J., 'William Anderson, 1748–1778: Master Surgeon, Royal Navy', *Annals of Medical History*, 5:6 (1933), pp. 511–24.

King, J. C., 'New Evidence for the Contents of the Leverian Museum', *Journal of the History of Collections*, 8:2 (1996), pp. 167–86.

King and Lochee, Messrs, *Catalogue of the Leverian Museum* (London, 1806), parts I–VI with 'Appendix'.

Largen, M. J., 'Bird Specimens Purchased by Lord Stanley at the Sale of the Leverian Museum in 1806, including those still Extant in the Collections of the Liverpool Museum', *Archives of Natural History*, 14:3 (1987), pp. 265–88.

Latour, B., *Science in Action: How to Follow Scientists and Engineers through Society* (Milton Keynes, Open University Press, 1987).

Low, G., *A Tour Through the Isles of Orkney and Schetland Containing Hints Relative to their Ancient Modern and Natural History Collected in 1774*, ed. J. Anderson (Kirkwall, W. Peace & Son, 1879).

Lysaght, A. M., 'Joseph Banks at Skara Brae and Stennis, Orkney, 1772', *Notes and Records of the Royal Society*, 28:2 (1974), pp. 221–34.

— (ed.), *Joseph Banks in Newfoundland and Labrador, 1766: His Diary, Manuscripts and Collections* (London, Faber and Faber, 1971).

Mabberley, D. J., *Jupiter Botanicus: Robert Brown of the British Museum* (London, British Museum Press, 1985).

—, *Ferdinand Bauer: The Nature of Discovery* (London, Natural History Museum, 1999).

Mabberley, D. J., and D. T. Moore, 'Catalogue of the Holdings in The Natural History Museum (London) of the Australian Botanical Drawings of Ferdinand Bauer (1760–1826) and Cognate Materials relating to the *Investigator* Voyage of 1801–1805', *Bulletin of the Natural History Museum: Botany Series*, 29:2 (1999), pp. 81–226.

McClellan, J., *Science Reorganized: Scientific Societies in the Eighteenth Century* (New York, Columbia University Press, 1985).

MacGregor, A. (ed.), *Sir Hans Sloane: Collector, Scientist, Antiquary* (London, British Museum Press, 1994).

Mackay, D., *In the Wake of Cook: Exploration, Science and Empire, 1780–1801* (London, Croom Helm, 1985).

—, 'Agents of Empire: the Banksian Collectors and Evaluation of New Lands' in Miller and Reill (eds), *Visions of Empire*, pp. 38–57.

MacKechnie Jarris, C., 'A History of the British Coleoptera', *Proceedings and Transactions of the British Entomological and Natural History Society*, 8:4 (1976), pp. 99–100.

McKitterick, D. (ed.), *The Making of the Wren Library, Trinity College, Cambridge* (Cambridge, Cambridge University Press, 1995).

MacLeod, R., and P. F. Rehbock (eds), *Nature in its Greatest Extent* (Honolulu, University of Hawaii Press, 1988).

Malcolm, J. P., *Londinium Redivivum, or an Ancient History and Modern Description of London*, 4 vols (London, J. Nichols, 1802–7).

Marsden, B. M., *The Early Barrow Diggers* (Aylesbury, Shire Publications, 1974).

Marshall, J. B., 'Daniel Carl Solander, Friend, Librarian and Assistant to Sir Joseph Banks', *Archives of Natural History*, 11:3 (1984), pp. 451–6.

Medway, D., 'Some Ornithological Results of Cook's Third Voyage', *Journal of the Society for the Bibliography of Natural History*, 9:3 (1979), pp. 315–51.

Megaw, J. V. S., 'Your Obedient and Humble Servant: Notes for an Antipodean Antiquary' in Anderson et al. (eds), *Histories of Old Ages*, pp. 95–110.

Miller, D. P., and P. H. Reill (eds), *Visions of Empire: Voyages, Botany, and Representations of Nature* (Cambridge, Cambridge University Press, 1996).

Miller, E., *That Noble Cabinet: A History of the British Museum* (London, A. Deutsch, 1973).

Mitchell, T. C. (ed.), *Captain Cook and the South Pacific* (London, British Museum Press, 1979).

Moore, D. T., 'An Account of those Described Rock Collections in the British Museum (Natural History) made before 1918; with a Provisional Catalogue Arranged by Continent', *Bulletin of the British Museum (Natural History): Historical Series*, 10:5 (1982), pp. 141–77.

Moore, D. T., and E. W. Groves, 'A Catalogue of Plants Written by Robert Brown (1773–1858) in New South Wales: First Impressions of the Flora of the Sydney Region', *Archives of Natural History*, 24:2 (1997), pp. 281–93.

Mullens, W. H., 'Some Museums of Old London – I The Leverian Museum', *Museum's Journal*, 15 (1915), pp. 123–9, 162–72.

—, 'Some Museums of Old London – II William Bullock's London Museum', *Museum's Journal*, 17 (1917–18), pp. 51–7, 132–7, 180–7.

Murphy, R. C., 'Robert Ferryman, Forgotten Naturalist', *Proceedings of the American Philosophical Society*, 103:6 (1959), pp. 774–7.

Newton, A., 'Notes on Some Old Museums' in Platnauer and Howarth (eds), *Museums Association: Report of Proceedings*, pp. 28-48.

Nichols, J., and J. B. Nichols, *Illustrations of the Literary History of the Eighteenth Century*, 8 vols (London, Nichols, Son and Bentley, 1817–58).

Ovenell, R. F., *The Ashmolean Museum 1683–1894* (Oxford, Clarendon Press, 1986).

Parliament, Act 7 Geo. II. c.18. An Act to enable the Trustees of the British Museum to exchange, sell or dispose of any Duplicates, etc. *Commons Journals* [especially vols LIV–LVIII].

Pearson, G., 'Observations on some Ancient Metallic Arms and Utensils; with Experiments to Determine their Composition', *Philosophical Transactions*, 86:2 (1796), pp. 395–451.

Pelzeln, A., 'On the Birds in the Imperial Collection at Vienna obtained from the Leverian Museum', *The Ibis, A Quarterly Journal of Ornithology*, 3:9 (1873), pp. 14–54.

—, 'On the Birds in the Imperial Collection at Vienna obtained from the Leverian Museum', *The Ibis, A Quarterly Journal of Ornithology*, 3:10 (1873), pp. 106–24.

Pennant, T., *A Tour in Scotland and Voyage to the Hebrides 1772* (Chester, John Monk, 1774).

Piggott, S., *William Stukeley: An Eighteenth-Century Antiquary* (London, Thames and Hudson, 1985).

—, *Ancient Britons and the Antiquarian Imagination* (London, Thames and Hudson, 1989).

Pincott, A., 'The Book Tickets of Miss Sarah Sophia Banks (1744–1818)', *The Bookplate Journal*, 2:1 (2004), pp. 3–31.

Platnauer, H. M., and E. Howarth (eds), *Museums Association: Report of Proceedings with the paper read at the annual General Meeting held at Cambridge, July 7th, 8th, & 9th, 1891* (London, 1891).

Powell, D., 'The Voyage of the Plant Nursery, H.M.S. *Providence*, 1791–93', *Economic Botany*, 31 (1977), pp. 387–431.

Pyenson, L., and S. Sheets-Pyenson, *Servants of Nature: A History of Scientific Institutions, Enterprises, and Sensibilities* (London, HarperCollins, 1999).

Ramsbottom, J., 'Note: Banks's and Solander's Duplicates', *Journal of the Society for the Bibliography of Natural History*, 4:3 (1963), p. 197.

Rauschenberg, R. A., 'The Journals of Joseph Banks' Voyage up Great Britain's West Coast to Iceland the Orkney Isles July to October 1772', *Proceedings of the American Philosophical Society*, 117 (1973), pp. 186–226.

Riddelsdell, H. J. (ed.), 'Lightfoot's Visit to Wales in 1773', *Journal of Botany*, 43 (1905), pp. 290–307.

Roberts, J., 'A Journal of a Voyage to the Hebrides or Western Isles of Scotland Iceland and the Orkneys undertaken by Joseph Banks Esqr. In the year 1772' (Mitchell Library, Sydney, A1594).

Royal Society, *The Record of the Royal Society of London for the Promotion of Natural Knowledge*, 4th edn (London, Royal Society, 1940).

St John, H., 'New Species of Hawaiian Plants Collected by David Nelson in 1779', *Pacific Science*, 30:1 (1976), pp. 7–44.

Sandby, P., *XII Views in Aquatinta from Drawings Taken on the Spot in South Wales Dedicated to the Honourable Charles Greville and Joseph Banks Esquire By Their Ever Grateful and Much Obliged Servant Paul Sandby R.A. 1775* (London, J. Boydell, 1775).

—, *XII Views in North Wales Being Part of a Tour Through the Fertile and Romantic Country Under the Patronage of The Honourable Sir Watkin Williams Wynn Bart To Whom They Are Most Humbly Inscribed By His Most Obedient and Most Humble Servant Paul Sandby R.A* (London, P. Sandby, 1776).

Sawyer, F. C., 'A Short History of the Libraries and List of Manuscripts and Original Drawings in the British Museum (Natural History)', *Bulletin of the Natural History Museum: Historical Series*, 4:2 (1971), pp. 79–204.

Scott, E., *The Life of Matthew Flinders* (Sydney, Angus and Robertson, 1914).

Shaw, G., and J. Parkinson, *Museum Leverianum, Containing Select Specimens from the Museum of the late Sir Ashton Lever, Kt. with descriptions in Latin and English by George Shaw, M.D., F.R.S.*, 2 vols (London, James Parkinson, 1792–6).

Sheets-Pyenson, S., *Cathedrals of Science: The Development of Colonial Natural History Museums during the Late Nineteenth Century* (Kingston, McGill-Queen's University Press, 1988).

—, 'How to Grow a Natural History Museum: the Building of Colonial Collections, 1850–1900', *Archives of Natural History*, 15:2 (1988), pp. 121–47.

Shepperson, W. S., 'William Bullock – An American Failure', *Bulletin of the Historical and Philosophical Society of Ohio*, 19:2 (1961), pp. 144–52.

Sloan, K. (ed.), *Enlightenment: Discovering the World in the Eighteenth Century* (London, British Museum Press, 2003).

Sloan, K., and I. Jenkins (eds), *Vases and Volcanoes: Sir William Hamilton and His Collection* (London, British Museum Press, 1996).

Smith, E., *The Life of Sir Joseph Banks, President of the Royal Society, with some Notices of his Friends and Contemporaries* (London, John Lane, 1911).

Smith, W., *Delineation of the Strata of England and Wales with part of Scotland; exhibiting the Collieries and Mines; the Marshes and Fen Lands originally Overflowed by the Sea; and the Varieties of Soil according to the Variations in the Sub Strata; illustrated by the Most Descriptive Names* (London, 1815).

Smith, W. C., 'A History of the First Hundred Years of the Mineral Collection in the British Museum', *Bulletin of the British Museum (Natural History): Historical Series*, 3:8 (1969), pp. 237–59.

Smith, W. J., 'A Museum for a Guinea', *Country Life*, 127:3288 (1960), pp. 494–5.

—, 'The Life and Activities of Sir Ashton Lever of Alkrington, 1729–1788', *Transactions of the Lancashire and Cheshire Antiquarian Society*, 72 (1962), pp. 61–92.

Smithson, J., 'Account of a Discovery of Native Minium. In a Letter from James Smithson, Esq. F.R.S. to the Right Hon. Sir Joseph Banks, K.B. P.R.S.', *Philosophical Transactions*, 96:2 (1806), pp. 267–8.

Stafleu, F. A., *Linnaeus and the Linnaeans: The Spreading of their Ideas in Systematic Botany, 1735–1789* (Utrecht, Oosthoek, 1971).

Stearn, W. T., 'The Botanical Results of the *Endeavour* Voyage', *Endeavour*, 27:100 (1968), pp. 3–10.

—, 'Daniel Carlsson Solander (1733–1782), Pioneer Swedish Investigator of Pacific Natural History', *Archives of Natural History*, 11:3 (1984), pp. 499–503.

—, *The Natural History Museum at South Kensington: A History of the Museum 1753–1980* (London, Natural History Museum, 1998).

Stig, R., *The Banks Collection: An Episode in 18th Century Anglo-Swedish Relations*, Ethnographical Museum of Sweden, Monograph Series, 8 (Stockholm, Almqvist and Wiksell, 1963).

Stukeley, W., *Itinerarium Curiosum, or, An Account of the Antiquitys and Remarkable Curiositys in Nature or Art, Observ'd in Travels thro' Great Britain, Illustrated with Copper Prints* (London, for the author, 1724).

Sturman, C., 'Sir Joseph Banks and the Tealby Hoard', *Lincolnshire History and Archaeology*, 24 (1989), pp. 51–2.

Swartz, O., *Nova Genera et Species Plantarum, seu prodromus descriptionum Vegetabilium maximam partem incognitorum, quae sub itinere in Indiam occidentalem annis 1783–1787* (Holmiae, In Bibliopoliis Acad. M. Swederi, 1788).

Sweet, J. M., 'Sir Hans Sloane: Life and Mineral Collection I', *The Natural History Magazine*, 5:34 (1935), pp. 49–64.

—, 'Sir Hans Sloane: Life and Mineral Collection II', *The Natural History Magazine*, 5:35 (1935), pp. 97–116.

—, 'Sir Hans Sloane: Life and Mineral Collection III', *The Natural History Magazine*, 5:36 (1935), pp. 145–64.

—, 'William Bullock's Collection and the University of Edinburgh, 1819', *Annals of Science*, 26:1 (1970), pp. 23–32.

Sweet, R., *Antiquaries: The Discovery of the Past in Eighteenth-Century Britain* (London, Hambledon and London, 2004).

Thackray, J. C., and J. R. Press, *The Natural History Museum: Nature's Treasurehouse* (London, Natural History Museum, 2001).

Thomas, S. (ed.), *The Encounter, 1802: Art of the Flinders and Baudin Voyages* (Adelaide, Art Gallery of South Australia, 2002).

Trigger, B. G., *A History of Archaeological Thought* (Cambridge, Cambridge University Press, 1992).

Vallance, T. G., and D. T. Moore, 'Geological Aspects of H.M.S. *Investigator* in Australian Waters, 1801–5', *Bulletin of the British Museum (Natural History): Historical Series*, 10:1 (1982), pp. 1–43.

Vallance, T. G., D. T. Moore and E. W. Groves (eds), *Nature's Investigator: The Diary of Robert Brown in Australia, 1801–1805* (Canberra, Australian Biological Resources Study, 2001).

Webb, J. B., *George Caley: Nineteenth Century Naturalist* (New South Wales, S. Beatty, 1995).

Wedgwood, J., 'On the Analysis of a Mineral Substance from New South Wales. In a Letter from Josiah Wedgwood, Esq. F.R.S. and A.S. to Sir Joseph Banks, Bart. P.R.S.', *Philosophical Transactions*, 80:2 (1790), pp. 306–20.

Weld, C. R., *A History of the Royal Society, with Memoirs of the Presidents*, 2 vols (London, J. W. Parker, 1848).

Wheeler, A., 'Daniel Solander and the Zoology of Cook's Voyage', *Archives of Natural History*, 11:3 (1984), pp. 505–15.

Whitehead, P. J. P., 'Zoological Specimens from Captain Cook's Voyages', *Journal of the Society for the Bibliography of Natural History*, 5:3 (1969), pp. 161–201.

—, 'A Guide to the Dispersal of Zoological Material from Captain Cook's Voyages', *Pacific Studies*, 2:1 (1978), pp. 52–93.

Wilkins, G. L., 'A Catalogue and Historical Account of the Sloane Shell Collection', *Bulletin of the British Museum (Natural History): Historical Series*, 1:1 (1953), pp. 1–47.

—, 'A Catalogue and Historical Account of the Banks Shell Collection', *The Bulletin of the British Museum (Natural History): Historical Series*, 1:3 (1955), pp. 71–119.

—, 'The Cracherode Shell Collection', *Bulletin of the British Museum (Natural History): Historical Series*, 1:4 (1957), pp. 124–84.

Wilson, D. W., *The British Museum: A History* (London, British Museum Press, 2002).

Winchester, S., *The Map that Changed the World. The Tale of William Smith and the Birth of a Science* (London, Viking, 2001).

APPENDIX

Over Page: 'A Catalogue of Curiosities & natural productions brought home in his Majesty's Sloop Discovery from the North West Coast of America & the South Sea Islands by Mr. Archibald Menzies', *c*. February 1796. Reproduced by permission of the Sutro Library, California.

Reproduced in full, this list accompanied material sent to the Museum in 1796 following the voyage of Archibald Menzies in HMS Discovery, 1791–5, under George Vancouver. Note the natural history at the end of the list.

A Catalogue of Curiosities & natural productions brought home in his Majesty's Sloop Discovery from the North West Coast of America & the South Sea Islands by Mr. Archibald Menzies.

No. 1 Otai, or complete Mourning Dress
    2 Taooma or Breast Plate
    3 Feather'd Pendants of a large Canoe
    4 Stone Adzes
    5 Basket curiously wrought of Cocoa Nut fibres.
    6 Mat of the finest kind
    7 A Bag of Matting
    8 A number of Paterns of the different kind of Cloth manufactured by the Natives
    9 Bow & Arrows
    10 A collection of Shells
    11 Lines of finely platted human Hair
    12 Fish Hooks

} From Otaheite

    13 Feather'd Helmet
    14 Feather'd Tippets or small Cloaks
    15 Feather'd Necklaces
    16 A large assortment of curiously stain'd & painted Cloth shewing the different Paterns & dresses worn by the Natives.

} From the Sandwich Islands.

N.º 17 Cloth-beaters for Manufacturing the same

18 Bows & Arrows

19 Wooden War Club

20 Stone War Club

21 Spears or Javelines

22 different kinds of Fans

23 Fly Flaps the handles ornamented –
    with human bone & Tortoise Shell.

24 Wooden Bowls & a quantity of Gum –
    from the Doee Dooe Tree.

25 Variegated Wicker-work Hat

26 Bracelet of Boars Tusks

27 Anklets of Pigs Teeth

28 Hemp prepaird from a Species of Nettle

29 a quantity of Fishing lines made of the
    above Hemp.

30 Platted Rope for rigging their Canoes
    made of the same Hemp.

31 Fish Hooks

32 Necklaces of Shells

33 Necklaces of platted human Hair.

34 Shells worn on the womens Worists

35 Platted Rope for lashings to their Canoes
    from Cocoa Nut fibres

36 Two small rolling stones finely polishd

37 a large Calibash

38 Two curious wicker-work Baskets – one
    of them lind with a Calibash

39 A number of fine Mats curiously variegated
    with different figures

40 plain Mats of different kinds

From the
Sandwich
Islands

Nº 41 A Dress wrought from the inner bark
    of the American Arbor-vitæ.

  42 Bow & Arrows

  43 Fish Hooks   } From Nootka.

  44 The Head & two Skins of a New Species
    of Mustella.

  45 A curious wrought dress of woollen
    interwoven on one side with Fur.

  46 A Chiefs Leather War Dress curiously
    ornamented with Porcupine Quills.

  47 Baskets so close work'd as to contain
    Water   } From Cross Island

  48 A small carved Idol

  49 Carvd throwing Sticks for heaving
    their Darts & Harpoons.

  50 Bows & Arrows

  51 A large bone War Club inlaid &
    ornamented with Shells.

  52 Knives made of Silicious Stones

  53 An Iron Knife as made by the Natives   } From New Georgia

  54 Bone Dagger

  55 A carvd chopping Instrument

  56 Two Skins of the Brown Tyger.

Nº 57 Bone Arrows & Quiver

  58 Fish-hooks

  59 Tobacco Pipes   } From Port Trinidad

  60 A Musical Instrument

Nº 61 A Head Dress curiously wrought & variegated.

62 A feather'd fillet or head band.

63 Hemp, suppos'd to be the same as Indian Grass

64 Fishing Lines made of the above Hemp

65 Ear' Ornaments

66 Baskets of different kinds, some curiously variegated & so closely work'd as to hold water.

From Port Trinidad

67 Harpoon completely furnish'd with Lines & different kinds of Barbs.

68 Darts completely furnish'd with lines & Barbs

69 Throwing Sticks for heaving their Darts

70 Bow & Arrows

71 A model of their Hunting Canoe completely furnish'd with all the Implements for Hunting the Sea Otter.

72 Leather Bags beautifully fringd & ornamented with Needle work

73 A small bunch of split Sinews as manufactur'd for making their different lines & ropes.

74 Platted sinew lines curiously ornamented for their Harpoons

75 Platted sinew lines for their Darts

76 Sinew lines differently platted for their Canoes.

From Cook's Inlet.

Nᵒ 77 A quantity of small sinew fishing lines

78 A Basket

79 Camlico or Frocks made from the finer Membranes of the Intestines of Marine Animals & so ingeniously put together & sewd as to keep the Natives perfectly Dry in wet weather

80 A pair of Boots & Garters curiously ornamented — a present of a Chief at the head of the Inlet.

81 Tusk of the Morse or Sea Cow

82 Leather Dagger Case ornamented with Porcupine Quills

83 Ornamental fringes for the Chiefs War Dress

84 Lip Ornaments worn by the Men in their lower lip

85 Ivory Studs worn as lip ornaments by the Women

86 Two Skins & two Horns of the wild Mountain Sheep

87 Two Skin Dresses — animal unknown

} From Cook's Inlet

88 A Skin of a new species of Antilope from California.

89 Two Skins & a Horn of an Animal — suppos'd to be a wild Goat with very fine wool from Lat. 52½

90 Some of the wool of the above Animal which the Natives spin & weave with Dresses

} From the NW Coast of America!

Nº 91 Halibut Fish- hooks

92 Beaver Skin – suppos'd variety

93 Two large Sea Otters preserv'd in Spirits

94 Two young Sea Otters preserv'd in Spirits

95 Different kinds of Baskets finely work'd
      & curiously variegated from Sta Barbera
      California

96 A Netted Bag from the same place

97 Wooden Combs curiously carved –
      from the Northern parts of the
      Coast

98 Wooden War Stays from Banks's Isles

99 A set of gambling pins from the
      same place

100 A Cake of the Bread of Columbia River

101 A Cake of the Bread made of the Inner
      Bark of the Pines from the Northern
      parts of the Coast–

102 Spoons from different parts of the Coast

103 A Collection of Birds preserv'd in Spirits
      from California &c

104 A collection of Fishes & Reptiles
      preserv'd in Spirits

From the
NW Coast
of America.

105 A Box of Fossils containing 103 different
      kinds mark'd & numberd from New Georgia

106 A Box of Fossils from the Northern
      parts of the Coast of America &
      Lavas from the Owhyhee mark'd
      & numberd from 1– 80.

107 A Collection of Fossils from New Zealand
      & New Holland.

N.º 108 A Box of Shells from New Zealand

109 A small Box of Fossils from Chili —
       containing the Gold & Silver Oars
       of that Country.

110 A copious collection of dry'd Plants
       from the different places visited
       during the Voyage

111 A Collection of live Plants from the
       North West Coast of America California
       & Chili already sent to Kew.

112 A large Collection of Seeds from the same
       places as also from the Sandwich
       Islands.

INDEX